Handbook of Political Science Research on the Middle East and North Africa

EDITED BY **BERNARD REICH**

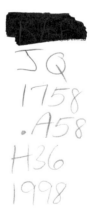

Greenwood Press
Westport, Connecticut • London

Library of Congress Cataloging-in-Publication Data

Handbook of political science research on the Middle East and North
  Africa / edited by Bernard Reich.
       p.   cm.
     Includes bibliographical references and index.
     ISBN 0–313–27372–3 (alk. paper).
     1. Middle East—Politics and government—1945– —Research.
2. Middle East—Foreign relations—Research. 3. Middle East—
Economic conditions—1945– —Research. 4. Africa, North—Politics
and government—Research. 5. Africa, North—Foreign relations—
Research. 6. Africa, North—Economic conditions—Research.
7. Middle East—Politics and government—1945– —Bibliography.
8. Middle East—Foreign relations—Bibliography. 9. Middle East—
Economic conditions—1945– —Bibliography. 10. Africa, North—
Politics and government—Bibliography. 11. Africa, North—Foreign
relations—Bibliography. 12. Africa, North—Economic conditions—
Bibliography. I. Reich, Bernard.
JQ1758.A58   1998
956'.007'2—dc21   97–37549

British Library Cataloguing in Publication Data is available.

Library of Congress Catalog Card Number: 97–37549
ISBN: 0–313–27372–3

First published in 1998

Greenwood Press, 88 Post Road West, Westport, CT 06881
An imprint of Greenwood Publishing Group, Inc.

Printed in the United States of America

The paper used in this book complies with the
Permanent Paper Standard issued by the National
Information Standards Organization (Z39.48–1984).

10 9 8 7 6 5 4 3 2 1

CONTENTS

PREFACE

The study of government and politics, including international relations, of the Middle East and North Africa is a relatively recent phenomenon, becoming significant only in the past few decades. The purpose of this reference work is to survey the extant literature on political themes in the Middle East and North Africa and to assess its coverage of those themes as well as the gaps in its content. Political research is broadly conceived to include traditional political themes, the concerns of the political economy approach, and contemporary history.

Each of the country chapters describes and assesses the trends in research in the post–World War II period, but with particular emphasis on the last several decades. What have been the main subjects and themes in the literature? How have they been treated? These might include, but are not limited to, the role of the military, the place of religion and its relationship to politics, economic issues, governmental institutions, political dynamics, legal institutions, political elites, minorities, political parties, political movements, pressure groups, elections, the significance of resources (especially oil), foreign policy, and related themes. After an evaluation of the literature and a suggestion of the most significant contributions to our knowledge and understanding of politics, the chapters conclude with an agenda for future research. To permit cross-country comparisons, each individual country study follows a common broad framework while each author, as a country expert, has been given the latitude to consider the particular circumstances of each country. Each chapter varies as a consequence of the peculiarities of the country studied and the focus of the research and publications that have appeared. There are also differences in the background and style of the authors, which account for some variations in approach. While each country chapter assesses the literature that considers the foreign policy and international relations of that state, separate chapters consider the international relations research for the region as a whole as well as the political economy school. The reader will find both a useful bibliography of the political literature on each state and topic and also an informed analysis of the contributions made and the areas still lacking substantial analyses. The appendix illustrates both the extent and range, as well as the concentration, of research resources and facilities in the region. In part, these facilities help to frame the research agenda as well as to contribute to its implementation.

A NOTE ON TRANSLITERATION FROM MIDDLE EASTERN LANGUAGES

Arabic, Turkish, Persian, and Hebrew all pose problems of transliteration and of spelling in English. Rather than following a strict linguistic approach, this volume uses the transliteration generally utilized in works on the region and in the media—that is, the most common and widely or generally accepted usage—although some variations occur even with this rule. Thus the reader will find Nasser rather than Nasir as the preferred rendering and Muammar Qaddafi rather than Mu'ammar Qadhdhafi. Diacritical marks have been omitted. With Arab names the last name is used as the family name, and the entry is in alphabetical order accordingly (that is, Nuri Said is located under Said). Kings and princes (amirs and sheikhs) are listed by their first names (for example, King Farouk under Farouk). The Arabic ''al'' or ''Al'' is disregarded in the alphabetical listing. Titles of works retain their individual usage and have not been altered to conform to a particular form.

ACKNOWLEDGMENTS

A work of this type requires the cooperation and good humor of a large number of scholars—not only those who contributed to the work, but others who have offered their sage advice. The latter group, both students and colleagues, over the years, have provided insights into the nature and state of the study of Middle East politics, and their observations have had their effect in this volume. This work is dedicated to Professor R. K. Ramazani of the University of Virginia who first enticed me to study the politics of the Middle East and has continued to serve as a model of scholarship for numerous students of the region. In addition, three individuals were very responsible for this work's final appearance. Mim Vasan originally "talked me into" producing this volume; Nita Romer has ably and cheerfully helped to move the project along; and, as usual, Suzie has put up with my preoccupation with "getting it out." To all three I owe a great debt. Mark Erickson and Craig Goldstein have produced an exceptional index. Wendi Schnaufer of Greenwood guided the production process with great skill and care.

INTRODUCTION

Bernard Reich

The Middle East has fascinated scholars and general observers for centuries, while it also has been a focal point of great-power attention and involvement. The region's strategic significance and the variety and importance of its political, social, and cultural heritage have generated this interest. Nevertheless, as we approach the twenty-first century, research on the politics of the Middle East and North Africa remains constrained by limits in both the discipline of political science and in the region known as the Middle East.

THE GEOGRAPHIC REGION AND STATE OF MIND KNOWN AS THE MIDDLE EAST

This book uses the definition, first introduced in David E. Long and Bernard Reich, editors, *The Government and Politics of the Middle East and North Africa* (Boulder, CO: Westview Press, 1980), that the Middle East includes North Africa. Thus when the term *Middle East* is employed herein, it refers to the Middle East and North Africa.[1]

The term *Middle East* was coined at the turn of the century to refer to the area situated between the Near East and the Far East, at the hub of Europe, Asia, and Africa, and serving as a crossroads and a bridge among them. Since then, it has come to incorporate the older term *Near East* and today includes North Africa as well. Political factors led to the inclusion and exclusion of various countries in the defined area over time. The core area consists of Egypt, Israel, the states of the Fertile Crescent (and the Palestinians), and the Arabian Peninsula. Because of their clear links to other Arab states, Libya, Tunisia, Morocco, and Algeria are also included. Sudan generally is grouped with the states of sub-Saharan Africa, and that approach is used here, thus excluding it from our discussions. Turkey lies in Europe, Asia, and the Middle East and is considered part of each. Similarly, while Iran is sometimes grouped with Afghanistan and Pakistan as an extension of South Asia, its location on the Persian Gulf and its linkages to the Arab states of that area suggest its inclusion in the

Middle East. Thus, although the area is subject to wide divergences in definition, this volume employs a broad approach including countries from both the Maghreb (Arab West) and Mashreq (Arab East)—from Morocco in the west to Iran in the east—as well as two non-Arab, Muslim players (Iran and Turkey) and the world's only Jewish state (Israel). Not all of the members of the Arab League are included (thus, while Djibouti may be a member of the Arab League, its politics are more appropriate to another world region). These choices are not whimsical or arbitrary; they reflect both political reality and the literature in the field. Although the area includes Turkey (owing in part to its long and substantial connections with and contributions to the Middle East and North Africa), it excludes South Asian states (e.g., Afghanistan) and those of the ''northern'' Middle East (e.g., the Islamic states of Central Asia, formerly part of the Soviet Union). This is not a book on Arab politics, for that would be artificially restrictive, and thus there are discussions of the three non-Arab states—Iran, Israel, and Turkey. Indeed, as will be clear from the individual country discussions, all three have been the focus of a very substantial literature characterized by nuanced and wide-ranging analyses of institutions and processes of politics often more detailed than comparable studies of the Arab world and similar to those often found of major Western political systems.

THE NATURE AND FOCUS OF POLITICAL RESEARCH IN THE REGION

Systematic research on the politics of the Middle East and North Africa is a relatively new phenomenon. As a consequence of this ''newness'' and restrictions imposed by many of the countries of the region on access to people (for interviews) and records (for review), scholarly research on the region is limited and uneven in amount, quality, and subject-matter coverage. For some countries and subjects even the most rudimentary work is nonexistent, while others have been the focus of substantial and detailed analytical studies on narrow and specific themes.

The Middle East in general, and Middle East politics in particular, is a relatively new area of scholarship, especially in the United States. Because the United States lacked a colonial empire in the area and had a limited political interest and involvement in the region, the study of Middle East politics tended to develop in tandem with the growing U.S. political interest and strategic and diplomatic presence in the area that began to emerge seriously and significantly only after World War II. Much of the American interest in the region before then could be linked to the area's historical association with the origins of Judaism, Christianity, and Islam. The founders of the United States were individuals who sought refuge from religious persecution and who focused on religious themes. The first American universities were church related and thus focused on the religions, religious history, languages, and culture of the region and on its ancient civilizations and their ruins. In the nineteenth and early twentieth centuries, American interests and involvements were increasingly those of missionaries and, later, businessmen, who made initial contributions to the growth of Middle East studies at American universities after they returned to the United States. Politics, however, was rarely in their purview. This began to change after World War II with the increasing involvement of the United States, politically and diplomatically as well as strategically, in the Middle East and North Africa. A growing focus on the politics of the region began with this newfound involvement by official America.

The post–World War II concern and involvement generated new academic interests. Among the earliest indicators was the founding of the Middle East Institute and the *Middle East Journal*. This reflected an interest in the politics of the region, among other subjects, that went beyond religion and linguistic studies. The Middle East Institute came into being just after World War II, and the first issue of its *Middle East Journal* appeared in January 1947.[2] Its mission, as stated in its charter, was "to increase knowledge of the Middle East among citizens of the United States" and to promote mutual understanding between the peoples of these two areas. This was in keeping with the broad notion of area studies and a need to understand a variety of areas, including the Middle East, for the formulation of an appropriate foreign policy for the United States in a new world order. The institute and the *Journal* were modeled along the lines of other area-studies organizations. They were concerned with the region as a whole, rather than any one geographical sector, and approached their study with a multidisciplinary outlook. This remains true today.

When the *Middle East Journal* published its first issue in January 1947, it argued that "no apology need be offered for adding a quarterly journal relating to the Middle East" because except for "a very few Americans . . . this area is essentially *terra incognita*."[3] This marked the beginning of a continuing approach to the understanding of the political and other forces affecting the nature of the Middle East and the countries of which it is composed. The *Journal* also undertook to define the region: "Attention will be centered on the heart of the area: Turkey, Iraq, Iran, Syria, Lebanon, Palestine, Transjordan, the Arabian Peninsula, and Egypt; but not without due reference to closely related peripheral areas, such as the Mediterranean approaches, North and Northeast Africa, Transcaucasia, Afghanistan, India and Turkestan."[4] It thus established a geographical frame of reference that has been in place until very recently, when the geographical limit was expanded to include segments of the former Soviet Union with proximity to the older Middle East and that, generally, are Muslim in character.

As postwar interest grew, so did academic programs and studies of the Middle East and North Africa in the United States, and politics was among the new areas of concern. Scholarship, whether university based or located elsewhere, began to grow. In 1966 a more academically oriented organization was founded—the Middle East Studies Association of North America (MESA)— and it grew rapidly.[5] Its membership consists primarily of scholars from the

United States and Canada, but it has a growing international membership. The fields or disciplines of the members, as they themselves designate them, suggest their focus of scholarship: political science and international relations are not the largest group, history is. In 1986 about one-fifth of the members designated their disciplines as political science and international relations; this was slightly higher in the 1996 membership roster.

Scholarship did not simply emerge, but took time to develop. The study of politics grew slowly, and the scholarship, research, and publications, as well as political interest, were not uniform in their concerns, interests, or focus. Some subjects, as will be seen in the various chapters in this volume, were more significantly covered, others less so. There is not a balance of countries covered, nor of themes, and they often vary over time. Cyclical interest and research are the norm, not the exception.

Political science research on the Middle East and North Africa has suffered from the vagaries in the discipline itself—there is not universal accord on the scope, nature, and content of political science, on its methods, or on its boundaries relative to other disciplines studying the area. Rather than engage in a long discussion of the nature of political science and its differences with other fields, we have chosen here to define political research more broadly, especially for this region, to include its overlaps with history, economics, geography, sociology, anthropology, philosophy, law, and theology and religion. We have also, more implicitly than explicitly, adopted the view that political science can be defined as much by the subjects (e.g., political phenomena) it studies as by the approaches (e.g., political economy) it utilizes. We have chosen to use a more eclectic definition to determine the content of the individual chapters and the book as a whole. Purposefully we have avoided using a narrow focus on ''scientific'' literature, for that would leave us with a very short list indeed of works on the politics of the region. Much of the extant literature is more akin not to political science literature on, say, Europe, but to work on the contemporary political history of the region, the policy issues facing regional and extraregional states. It is often more descriptive than wholly analytical.

Understanding the politics of the Middle East and North Africa requires more than an examination of the institutions of government; there is also the broader context in which politics is played. The authors have examined the literature of the political systems as well as their approach to the major problems confronting them. The machinery of government is analyzed not only in terms of what it is (institutional politics) but also in terms of why it is the way it is and how and why it works the way it does. Consideration of the legislative, executive, and judicial machinery of politics is thus complemented by study of the elements that affect the actual translation of goals and policy into action. Traditional topics such as political parties and other instruments of mobilization, political elites, and leadership are also considered.

SOME OBSERVATIONS ON MIDDLE EAST POLITICS

A series of interesting and important observations can be made about political research on the Middle East and North Africa that is described and reviewed in the chapters in this volume. Students of Middle East politics have concentrated on a wide variety of themes, but not all with equal zeal and not for each of the countries of the region. The subjects of focused investigation have changed over time, but some themes have remained constant in their centrality.

The states of the Middle East have a variety of political systems, each one reflecting its historical background, colonial experience, social and economic conditions, religious orientation, geographical setting, and population. The large and diverse region known as the Middle East is one whose heterogeneity is reflected in its governmental structures and in the processes they use to make decisions and run governments. There are nearly as many types of government as there are states in the region. The systems and the processes they employ seem to undergo constant change as they identify the need to accommodate to domestic and international pressures and demands.

The study of the system and process of Middle East politics has generally focused on each state's dominant political institution, be it the army or the political party or social groups such as the elite or religious groups. While authoritarian regimes abound, little effort has been made to compare them. Revolutions have occurred in a number of states (Egypt, Iraq, Turkey), but little effort has been made to explain or compare them. The major subjects of investigation often have concentrated on revolution and violence (now increasingly linked to terrorism). Revolutionary movements and their actions have been considered in terms of both ideology and outcome of their actions. Increasingly, clandestine groups and others, some Marxist, some secular, some Islamic (whether labeled fundamentalist or Islamist), have been attended to as new political movements. When, or if, there are political parties and interest groups, and if there are elections, genuine or not, these remain as symbols of political activity and receive their share of attention. Before the demise of the Soviet Union, Communist or Marxist parties and other local parties linked to worldwide Communist parties and groups often received disproportionate attention. In all instances governmental institutions, usually but not always at the national level, and, sometimes, legal institutions have been focal points of analysis. Leaders and leadership, whether democratically chosen or not, whether dictators, oligarchs, monarchs, generals (or colonels), or others of this ilk, have, with the political elite, been a major theme of students and scholars of Middle East politics.

Perhaps most obvious is the unevenness of coverage that reflects very different levels of scholarly interest as well as differences in the political systems themselves and in the available research opportunities (both access and materials). The wide range of political systems, the variations in institutions and their ideological underpinnings from system to system, and the significant differences in political dynamics all suggest a good deal both about the nature of politics and the ability to undertake dispassionate analysis. These are among the factors clearly identified by the authors in this volume. Nevertheless, it is perhaps particularly important to focus on an obvious conclusion based on the studies assembled here—the large amount of high-quality, academic, dispassionate analyses that already exist. While it is commonplace to equate passion and bias with perspectives on the Middle East, the authors clearly demonstrate that there is a substantial body of literature that belies that view.

Political science research has not posed a series of critical questions about the nature of Middle East politics and only recently has begun to search for theoretical explanations for the stability or instability of various regimes and for the conflicts that have characterized the region since World War II. Although instability is often the general rubric applied to the region, many of its regimes and leaders have been in place for substantial periods of time.

It is useful to recall that constitutional government is not deeply rooted in the Middle East, nor is it particularly widespread. At the same time, the monarchical principle is firmly rooted in Middle Eastern tradition and history. The systems display a wide variety of political forms and processes that often provide few points of direct contrast. This obligation applies to both executive and legislative institutions and processes. Many of the systems are dominated by executive-branch individuals who control the systems and their major decisions. Often this is a single authoritarian individual, by whatever title or name he or she may be known.

It must also be noted that while all of the political systems perform a wide and useful range of functions, the mechanisms and procedures of performing them are as diverse as the systems themselves. Each country has an executive and legislative process, but the processes and the structures are quite disparate. Whereas Israel and Turkey have multiparty parliaments that function in ways quite familiar in and similar to the Western political systems of Europe, Saudi Arabia's *majlis al-shura* is different in both form and function, and it, in turn, is unlike that found in neighboring royal systems in the Arabian Peninsula and the Gulf. Executive form and function are similarly different from state to state. Presidents in Turkey and Israel are far less crucial than those in Egypt, Syria, and Iraq, and the latter also have variations despite the commonality of a strong president. Iran's president shares powers in a unique way with that country's religious leader. Military officers continue to have disproportionate power in much of the region.

In the Middle East a few countries and themes tend to receive the bulk of attention, unlike other world regions where political scientists tend to focus their research on the larger and more accessible countries. This is not quite the case in the Middle East, where other factors tend to determine both interest and writing. Some coverage of both countries and themes falls prey to a ''herding instinct'' as scholars discover a theme that generates substantial followers to the new scholarly ''well'' for research water. Iran's revolution generated a large spate of works on that country but also energized an examination of ''political Islam.'' The Iraqi invasion of Kuwait in August 1990 and the Gulf War that followed in 1991 led to a plethora of works on Iraq. The Arab-Israeli conflict and especially Israel continue as a focal point of research and popular attention for a wide variety of reasons. The ''oil crisis'' of 1973–1974 spawned attention and research on the ''oil-rich'' Arab states of the Arabian Peninsula and the Persian Gulf that previously had been all but ignored.

Some countries seem to have attracted little attention, especially by comparison with their neighbors. Tunisia, Jordan, and Yemen seem to fall into a second tier of countries that have been less systematically studied than Israel, Iran, or Egypt. While some research is limited because of lack of interest in a country's politics, in other instances the shortage of research is a consequence of country-imposed restrictions on access to its territory, its peoples, and its archives—on the ability to conduct interviews or even to visit the country. In other cases there is a lack of documents (or access to them), or there are linguistic-cultural barriers to pursuing certain themes. Doing political research is not always, or even usually, a simple matter. Access to the country, to its officials, and to archives, libraries, and other collections of important materials is often restricted. Also, the qualities of the extant materials are of a variable nature, and sometimes sources just do not exist.

The Cold War and its bipolar world often placed the Middle East at its geo-political center as the two superpowers vied for power and mastery in the region and sought to deny it to the other. With the end of the Soviet Union and the Soviet bloc and the termination of the Cold War, attention of external powers and of scholars has focused more on the politics of Islam and of oil, the region's dominant natural resource. Increasingly, however, in recent years political analysis has begun to deal with some more specific and narrower domestic themes, including the role of women in society and in politics, issues related to education, and ofttimes student politics. Human rights have become a growing concern. In some instances media studies have complemented other political concerns. But in these areas and others noted there is a paucity of work, partly due to the difficulty in gaining access to the country, the data, or the necessary interviewees. Nevertheless, there is a growing trend toward increasing the range of both subjects and countries under examination, resulting in increased knowledge and understanding of the politics of the Middle East and North Africa.

There is a politicization of the field of Middle East studies, and this is particularly true when one examines political issues and especially the Arab-Israeli sector of the region and the conflict that bears its name. But this is also the case with such countries as Iran and Iraq. Political events have affected the content and direction of political research on the region and its components. Politics and political perspectives have been a part of the study of the contemporary Middle East from the beginning, even before the period of proliferation and growth that followed World War II. Professor Bayly Winder, a decade ago, argued that ''in recent years, especially following the 1967 and 1973 Arab-Israeli wars, politicization of Middle Eastern studies has taken a disturbing turn."[6] As he noted, and as we all understood, there was a connection to policy making. That there were personal perspectives was also to be noted. But there were also instances of connections of foreign and domestic groups to academic activity that clearly sought to influence the nature and direction of scholarly study. Such political intrusion into political research has not been limited to the Middle East, nor within this area to the Arab-Israeli sector, and there are also instances dealing with other parts of the region.

Political economy has become a new and "hot" topic on the political research agenda of Middle East specialists. It represents the latest, but certainly not the last, of the methods used by the political scientist to approach the problems, issues, and agendas of the Middle East. It utilizes the terminology (indeed, the jargon) of economics and seeks to add a different, if not wholly new, dimension to political research. To date, the literature has been uneven, due to the relative newness of the approach as well as the lack in many cases of the requisite data to ensure appropriate use of the methodology.

AGENDA FOR THE FUTURE

The Middle East and North Africa continues to be an area of great interest and importance. Because of its history and future potential, it will likely continue to be a region attractive to those interested in its politics as well as politics in general, for which it offers fascinating areas of study. Despite the plethora of works, ably noted and reviewed by the authors in this volume, there are numerous lacunae both geographic and thematic in nature.

The study of Middle East politics has undergone a substantial transformation over the past several decades in the extent of coverage both of countries and of themes. In 1976 I. William Zartman provided a very useful early systematic overview of political science scholarship on the Middle East and North Africa.[7] In some respects it offers a useful "state of the literature and field" survey to its point of publication and thus helps to "complete" the picture to be found in this volume. While useful, it suffers from two defects: it is the work of one individual whose expertise is narrower than that found here, where a number of experts and specialists concentrate on their particular countries and subjects of expertise, and it is more cursory and less detailed in its consideration of the field, partly as a consequence of space limitations. If one compares the literature as Zartman reviewed it with that contained in this volume, the evolution of the field is clear. Although some of this shift is in response to popular concern and media attention, and some tends to follow U.S. government defense, foreign policy, and commercial policy concerns, some reflects trends in political science research in general both in the United States and outside it. Of course, part of the research agenda is dictated by availability of research funds.

Some of the early critiques of "trendy" analysis that was unsystematic in nature still apply. Some studies can still be criticized as narrowly focused, some as ethnocentric, and some as atheoretical. But in some instances they may well be the only available studies or the only ones likely to be possible, given the current research atmosphere. Political history is often an essential prerequisite for analysis of subsequent political events. Institutional analysis and descriptions of required processes often must precede assessments of political dynamics and forces affecting it. At the same time there remains an interesting question about political science research as it applies to the Middle East and North Africa. Do the concepts and approaches, the methodologies and techniques, of Western political science apply to the politics of the Middle East? While some clearly do and are useful in this endeavor, others may well prove irrelevant or useless in trying to understand political processes in the Middle East.

Nevertheless, and despite the failings and problems noted here, the chapters that follow, written by some of the world's leading political experts, demonstrate that the study of the politics of the Middle East and North Africa has come a long way since its inception after World War II and that today there is a rich and variegated literature from which substantial understanding of the politics of the region can be attained and that provides much of the material for broader political questions and approaches to other systems and regions. By identifying lacunae in existing works, the chapters outline an agenda for future discourse and examination. Rather than repeat the findings of individual authors, one should note that each has identified an agenda for future work on the politics of the region. In sum, they outline a lengthy and rich series of important questions for the study of the politics of the Middle East and North Africa in the future.

NOTES

1. See also Roderic H. Davison, ''Where Is the Middle East?'' *Foreign Affairs* 38: 665–675 (July 1960), and Nikki Keddie, ''Is There a Middle East?'' *International Journal of Middle East Studies* 4:255–271 (July 1973).

2. Kathleen Manalo, ''A Short History of the Middle East Institute,'' *Middle East Journal* 41:64–73 (Winter 1987).

3. *Middle East Journal* 1, no. 1:1 (January 1947).

4. Ibid., 3.

5. Michael E. Bonine, ''MESA and Middle East Studies: An International Perspective from North America,'' *Middle East Studies Association Bulletin* 20:155–170 (December 1986).

6. R. Bayly Winder, ''Four Decades of Middle Eastern Study,'' *Middle East Journal* 41:40–63 (Winter 1987), at page 60.

7. I. William Zartman, ''Political Science,'' in Leonard Binder, ed., *The Study of the Middle East: Research and Scholarship in the Humanities and the Social Sciences* (New York: John Wiley and Sons, 1976), 265–325.

ALGERIA

Mary-Jane Deeb

It is impossible to do research on Algeria without consulting French sources. The bulk of the work on Algeria since its independence in 1962 (and certainly before that) has been done by French researchers, writers, and others who had a deep interest in that country. Algerians who have written about their country have also tended to write primarily in French.

The literature on Algeria since the mid-1960s can be divided into three major segments that follow the chronological developments in that country. The first part covers the political and historical events of French Algeria before and during the war of independence (1954–1962), the second discusses Algeria under military rule until 1992, and the more recent literature covers the ongoing armed conflict between government and Islamist forces. Some works, of course, cover more than one period.

FRENCH ALGERIA AND THE WAR OF INDEPENDENCE

Some of the earliest studies that considered the prewar and the war years were written by Algerians who were involved in the politics of the time. Ferhat Abbas, the first president of the National Assembly of the Algerian Republic, wrote *Guerre et révolution d'Algérie: La nuit coloniale* (1962) and later *Autopsie d'une guerre* (1980), where he describes the people and analyzes the events in the prewar and war periods in Algeria. Another major figure of the Algerian war of independence, Hocine Aït Ahmed, who is still a prominent Berber leader of the opposition party, the Front des Forces Socialistes (FFS), in Algeria today, has written about the war in *La guerre et l'après-guerre* (1964). Mohamed Boudiaf, one of the "chefs historiques" of the Algerian war of independence, who was called back from exile in Morocco in 1992 to become the head of the five-man High Council of State and was then assassinated in 1994, also wrote, in the aftermath of the war, *Où va l'Algérie?* (1964).

There are numerous works by French authors on the prewar and war years, among the more authoritative of which are Charles Robert Ageron's *L'Algérie algérienne de Napoléon III à de Gaulle* (1980), and his in-depth two-volume study *Histoire de l'Algérie contemporaine (1830–1964)* (1964) and *Histoire de l'Algérie contemporaine*, volume 2, *De l'insurrection de 1871 au déclenchement de la guerre de liberation 1954*. Yves Courrière wrote a four-volume study on the war of independence, *La guerre d'Algérie*, published between 1968 and 1971, while Bernard Droz and Evelyne Lever wrote a one-volume comprehensive study of that period, *Histoire de la guerre d'Algérie, 1954–1962* (1982). The work of Jean-Claude Vatin, *L'Algérie politique: Histoire et société*, originally published in 1974 and later updated in 1983, and Vatin's work with Jean Leca, *L'Algérie politique: Institutions et régime* (1975), are the definitive works on French Algeria, the war of independence, and the early years of independence. Unlike some of the other works published by French authors, Vatin analyzed various Algerian perspectives on French colonial rule, including the Islamists' movements that resisted French cultural influence, and the assimilationists' movements that accepted being part of France but argued for a fairer application of French law to Algeria.

Algerian and North African scholars made significant contributions, in French, to the literature on that period. Mohammed Harbi wrote extensively on the Front de Libération National (FLN) and its role in Algeria's war of independence. His works include *Aux origines du Front de libération nationale: La scission du PPA-MTLD* (1975); *Le FLN, mirage et réalité, des origines à la prise du pouvoir (1945–1962)* (1980); and *La guerre commence en Algérie: 1954* (1984). Ali Hardoun looked at the war from the perspective of the Algerians in France, and the conflict between the various factions there, in his study *La 7e wilaya, la guerre du FLN en France (1954–1962)* (1986). Ahmed Mahsas examined the Algerian opposition to French colonial rule from the first half of the twentieth century to the eve of the war of independence in *Le mouvement révolutionnaire en Algérie: Essai sur la formation du mouvement national de la 1re guerre mondiale à 1954* (1979).

A few works in English began to appear covering the war in Algeria even before it was over: Michael K. Clark, *Algeria in Turmoil: A History of the Rebellion* (1960); Joseph Kraft, *The Struggle for Algeria* (1961); Mohammed Bedjaoui, *Law and the Algerian Revolution* (1961); and Edward Behr, *The Algerian Problem* (1962). Later works in English included the somewhat anecdotal reportage by Arslan Humbaraci in *Algeria: A Revolution That Failed—A Political History since 1954*, published in 1966, followed by Edgar O'Ballance's *The Algerian Insurrection, 1954–62* (1967), which was a much more serious account of the war. However, it was David Gordon's work *The Passing of French Algeria* (1966), that became one of the first major works on the Algerian revolution to be used at universities throughout North America. Gordon's work was followed in swift succession by two other classical studies in English on the war of independence and its aftermath, namely, William Quandt's *Revolution and Political Leadership: Algeria, 1954–1968* (1969); and Alf Andrew Heggoy's *Insurgency and Counterinsurgency in Algeria* (1972). Three other important works covering the events of the 1954–1962 period that appeared in the late 1970s are Martha Crenshaw Hutchinson's *Revolutionary Terrorism: The FLN in Algeria, 1954–1962* (1978); Alistair Horne's *A Savage War of Peace: Algeria, 1954–1962* (1977), which is a 560-page account of the war that is more descriptive than analytical; and Tony Smith's much slimmer volume, *The French Stake in Algeria, 1945–1962* (1978) which attempts to explain why France allowed itself to be bogged down in the war for so long. Smith argues that it was in order to make up for the capitulation to the Germans in 1940 and to preserve its prestige as a major world power that France thought that it should keep control over Algeria. Some of the writings that would be the most widely read and have the most influence, however, are the translations from the French of Albert Memmi's *The Colonizer and the Colonized* (1967), recounting the experiences of a North African Jew and his treatment by the French colonizer, which became part of the anticolonial literature in the West and the Third World; and Frantz Fanon's study *The Wretched of the Earth* (1963), which first appeared in French in 1961 and became the bible of liberation movements in many of the countries of the developing world. It urged colonized people to use violence to purge themselves of the humiliation of being colonized.

THE POSTINDEPENDENCE PERIOD (1962–1992)

Beginning in the 1960s, American scholars started to pay more attention to North Africa, and their work began to cover all aspects of the field. French and Algerian scholars continued to do research on Algeria, but some Algerians began writing in English, and more works in French were translated into English. This period, therefore, is much richer in English sources than the previous one and includes biographies and autobiographical books by Algerian leaders, works on political developments, and studies on social and economic issues under three Algerian administrations.

Biographies

The new Algerian leaders fascinated many who saw them as representing a generation of Third World leaders who could serve as models for other newly independent states in Africa, the Middle East, and Asia. A number of books and articles were written about Ferhat Abbas, for instance. One of the earliest studies was published even before the end of the Algerian war of independence, *Ferhat Abbas: ou, Les chemins de la souveraineté* (1961) by Amar Naroun; and Abbas himself wrote partly autobiographical works on postindependence Algeria, including *L'indépendance confisquée* (1984), in which he criticized the policies of the military since it took power at independence.

Ahmed Ben Bella, one of the nine ''chefs historiques'' or leaders of the war of independence, who became Algeria's first president in 1962 and was ousted by his successor in 1965, was a heroic figure for many in the Third World. He wrote an autobiographical book after he was released from house arrest in 1979 that appeared in France under the title *Ben Bella revient* (1982). There had been an earlier biography in French by Robert Merle, *Ahmed Ben Bella* (1965), that appeared the year he was overthrown and focused on the first part of his life and his role in the war of independence.

Benjamin Stora wrote a biography of Messali Hadj, *Messali Hadj, 1898–1974* (1982), the most important leftist nationalist leader, who founded the Party of the Algerian People in 1937 and the Movement for the Triumph of Democratic Liberties in 1946. Hadj refused to recognize the FLN, and he and his supporters fought the FLN in France throughout the war of independence. He remained opposed to the Algerian leadership until his death in 1974. An edited biographical work of his early years by Renaud de Rochebrune, *Les mémoires de Messali Hadj, 1898–1938*, was published in 1982.

A biography was written of Houari Boumedienne, Algeria's first defense minister and later its president between 1965 and 1978, by Ania Francos and J.-P. Sereni entitled *Un Algérien nommé Boumediene* (1976). It discusses his life and work before, during, and after the war of independence and was published two years before his death. Another study, less biographical and more analytical, of Boumedienne's policies during his thirteen years in power is Juliette Minces's *L'Algérie de Boumediene* (1979).

Political Developments

The literature in English on the political developments in Algeria under Ben Bella, Boumedienne, and Chadli Benjedid is much more significant than that in the previous period. Numerous important works were prepared as North African studies began to take on the importance of a serious field of regional study in the United States.

Among the first major works in English was an edited work by L. Carl Brown entitled *State and Society in Independent North Africa* (1966), which, according to I. William Zartman, "initiated a new generation of scholars and policy analysts to a region of the world that despite its long-standing ties with the United States had lived in the shadow of colonial powers throughout most of the twentieth century" (Zartman and Habeeb, ix). The essays in Brown's volume looked at all the newly independent states of the Maghreb, including Algeria, and analyzed their political, economic, and social developments since their independence. Three years later William B. Quandt's *Revolution and Political Leadership* appeared and was one of the earliest full-length books that discussed not only the war of independence, but, most importantly, Algerian elites, thus introducing a theoretical element to the discussion of revolutionary politics in Algeria. This was followed by David and Marina Ottaway's *Algeria: The Politics of a Socialist Revolution* (1970), which discussed the politics and the policies of Ben Bella as well as those of Boumedienne during his first three years in power.

The Brown book was followed by another edited book by I. William Zartman that brought together North African, European, and American scholars to assess the progress made in the four countries of North Africa since independence. *Man, State, and Society in the Contemporary Maghrib* (1973) became a classic reference book and served as a catalyst for major research undertaken by North American scholars focusing on the Maghreb. There were a number of ground-breaking contributions on Algeria, including Raymond Vallin's "Muslim Socialism in Algeria," Pierre Bourdieu's "The Algerian Subproletariat," Mohammed Harbi's "The Party and the State," Zartman's "The Algerian Army in Politics," P. J. Vatikiotis's "Tradition and Political Leadership," and William H. Lewis's "The Decline of Algeria's FLN."

The early years of independence were also covered by French scholarly and political writings, including Gerard Chaliand's *L'Algérie est-elle socialiste?* (1965) and Daniel Guerin's more leftist analysis in *L'Algérie qui se cherche* (1964) and *L'Algérie caporalisée* (1965). Jean-Claude Douence in *La mise en place des institutions algériennes* (1964) and Hervé Bourges in *L'Algérie à l'épreuve du pouvoir* (1967) looked at the struggle for power in the early years of the republic and at the impact this struggle had on the process of institution building, as did François Buy in *La République Algérienne Démocratique et Populaire* (1965). But it would be the work by Gerard Chaliand and Juliette Minces, *L'Algérie independante: Bilan d'une révolution nationale* (1972), that would stand out as one of the best assessments of the political developments in the first decade of Algeria's postindependence era.

The next decade began to be studied by scholars on three continents writing in Arabic, French, and English. They looked at the role of the army and the FLN one-party system. They analyzed the economic and domestic policies of Boumedienne. They pondered Algeria's role in international affairs. Jean-Claude Vatin updated his 1974 book *L'Algérie politique: Histoire et société* in 1983 to include an assessment of the early years of independence. Henry Jackson wrote about the one-party system in *The FLN in Algeria: Party Development in a Revolutionary Society* (1977); Paul Balta and Claudine Rulleau evaluated the Boumedienne years from 1965 to 1978 in *La Stratégie de Boumediene* (1978); and Marnia Lazreg in *The Emergence of Classes in Algeria: Colonialism and Socio-political Change* (1976) took a Marxist approach in analyzing the impact of French colonialism on the socioeconomic and political developments in Algeria.

The best works in English covering the political and economic developments in Algeria until the mid-1980s were John Entelis's *Algeria: The Revolution Institutionalized* (1986), which analyzed the role of the army, the party (the FLN), and the state in shaping Algerian politics; and John Ruedy's *Modern Algeria: The Origins and Development of a Nation* (1992), which was a political history of Algeria from Ottoman times to the end of the 1980s and the single most comprehensive study of its kind in English to date. Two other works were published in the mid- and late 1980s, in English, by Algerians: one was by Rachid Tlemcani, who wrote *State and Revolution in Algeria* (1986) from a somewhat leftist perspective; the other, which covered part of the same historical period that Ruedy covered, was *The Making of Contemporary Algeria, 1830–1987* (1988) by Mahfoud Bennoune, whose analysis was rather polemical and sympathetic to Boumedienne.

A few studies focused on Algeria's foreign relations. Nicole Grimaud wrote the most comprehensive study on Algeria's foreign policy from independence until the early 1980s, entitled *La politique extérieure de l'Algérie (1962–1978)* (1984). She argued that the balance of power in North Africa between Morocco and Algeria was more important in shaping Algeria's foreign policy than any ideological consideration. Assassi Lassassi focused on Algeria's role in the non-aligned movement in *Nonalignment and Algerian Foreign Policy* (1988); and Salah Mouhoubi discussed French-Algerian relations since independence in his *La politique de coopération algéro-française: Bilan et perspectives* (1986).

Finally, there were a number of significant edited books in English on Algeria and the Maghreb that discussed the political, economic, and social problems Algeria faced in the 1980s. Among the earliest was I. William Zartman et al., *Political Elites in Arab North Africa* (1982), which created the theoretical framework for many later studies on leadership in Algeria and elsewhere in the Maghreb. In Halim Barakat's edited *Contemporary North Africa: Issues of Development and Integration* (1985), American and Maghrebi scholars debated various issues, including the need for industrialization and democracy to promote political and economic development in Algeria. Helen Metz, of the Federal Research Division of the Library of Congress, edited a new *Algeria: A Country Study* (1994), updating significantly the earlier 1985 edition. It covered the usual sections on the history of Algeria since prehistoric times, the French colonial experience and the war of independence, the social organization of modern Algerian society, and the economy and government and politics since independence, as well as foreign policy and security matters. Unfortunately, due to the organizational structure of the book, only four pages are devoted to the crisis in Algeria. Last but not least, John Entelis's and Phillip Naylor's edited book *State and Society in Algeria* (1992) looked at the political economy of Algeria, among other topics, as well as at the role of the Islamist opposition.

Social and Economic Issues

From the earliest days of independence, writings on Algeria included discussion of some of its economic reform programs and the impact of Algeria's policies on its people. Serge Koulytchizky wrote a major study, *L'autogestion, l'homme, et l'état: L'expérience algérienne* (1974), about the experiment of self-management in Algeria, which, he argued, was indigenous, with no precedent elsewhere in the world, but was eventually taken over by the state. A number of other studies covered self-management in Algeria, some of which linked this essentially economic and managerial process to the creation of political bases of power. These include Monique Laks's *Autogestion ouvrière et pouvoir pol-*

itique en Algérie (1962–1965) (1970); Ian Clegg's *Workers' Self-Management in Algeria* (1972); and Thomas Blair's book entitled *The Land to Those Who Work It: Algeria's Experiment in Workers' Management* (1970). Two later works that were more comprehensive and that essentially covered the Boumedienne era were prepared by Tahar Benhouria, *L'économie de l'Algérie* (1980), and M. E. Benissad, *L'économie algérienne contemporaine* (1980), and published in France.

There were also a number of important studies that were undertaken during the 1980s to analyze the impact of the socialist policies of Boumedienne on the Algerian economy. Karen Pfeifer prepared a major economic study on *Agrarian Reform under State Capitalism in Algeria* (1985); and François Burgat and Michel Nancy wrote about that same issue in *Les villages socialistes de la révolution agraire algérienne* (1984). Important edited volumes included that of François Perroux, *Problèmes de l'Algérie indépendante* (1963) and that of François d'Arcy, Annie Krieger, and Alan Marill, *Essais sur l'économie de l'Algérie nouvelle* (1965), which looked at the political, economic, and social problems faced by the newly independent state.

There were also studies by Algerians published in Algeria that covered not only the economic changes taking place during that first decade but the social and cultural developments as well. One such study was by the Algerian Ahmed Taleb Ibrahimi, who wrote *De la décolonisation à la révolution culturelle (1962–1972)* (1976); another was by Mostefa Lacheraf, who wrote *La culture algérienne contemporaine: Essai de définitions et perspectives* (1968); and a third, published by UNESCO in 1977, was by Sid-Ahmed Baghli, entitled *Aspects of Cultural Policy in Algeria*.

THE STATE AND THE ISLAMIST OPPOSITION

A number of works have appeared in the 1990s that have tried to explain the reasons behind the civil strife in Algeria since the annulment of the 1991–1992 elections by the military. Some of the studies mentioned earlier, such as Ruedy's *Modern Algeria* and Entelis's and Naylor's *State and Society in Algeria*, began analyzing the reasons behind the armed confrontations, as did Remy Leveau in his excellent study of Islamic movements in North Africa, *Le sabre et le turban* (1993). Andrew J. Pierre and William B. Quandt produced a slim volume entitled *The Algerian Crisis: Policy Options for the West* (1996), published by the Carnegie Endowment for International Peace. It looks at the roots of the conflict, its impact on France and French policy toward Algeria, and Europe's potential role in solving the problem and concludes with policy suggestions for U.S. policymakers, including support for economic reforms and democratization.

One of the best in-depth analyses of the Islamist opposition in Algeria is Severine Labat's *Les islamistes algériens: Entre les urnes et le maquis* (1995). It focuses on the major Islamist group, the Islamic Salvation Front (FIS), and relies on extensive interviews. Labat also identifies factions of the FIS that use force and violence to achieve their ends and others that prefer more political means to create an Islamic state. Another major study that addresses the causes of the conflict is Omar Carlier's *Entre nation et jihad: Histoire sociale des radicalismes algériens* (1995). The author, a well-known social and cultural anthropologist, links the present events in Algeria to parallel political developments during the nationalist period between 1930 and 1954, just before the war of independence. He argues that the present-day youth were socialized by their elders into a culture that accepted violence as a means of overthrowing a hated government. François Burgat and William Dowell published in English a comparative work on *The Islamic Movement in North Africa* (1993). The latest work on Algeria is a Rand report by Graham E. Fuller, *Algeria: The Next Fundamentalist State?* (1996), in which the author argues that despite its rhetoric, the Islamic Salvation Front does not represent a serious challenge to Western interests in the region, and if such a movement were to take over power in Algeria, the West might not find it too difficult to deal with.

A number of Algerians have covered the events from their own perspectives. Aissa Kheladi has written about the historical confrontation between Islamist leaders and the state in *Algérie: Les islamistes face au pouvoir* (1992). Ahmad Rouadjia discussed the role of the mosque in building Islamist networks in *Les frères et la mosquée: Enquête sur le mouvement islamiste en Algérie* (1990). Marnia Lazreg in *The Eloquence of Silence: Algerian Women in Question* argues that the conflict between the state and the Islamists is, in part, about control over women. Khalida Messaoudi in *Une Algérienne debout* (1995) discusses with a French journalist, Elisabeth Schemla of the *Nouvel Observateur*, the conditions in Algeria that have led to the crisis. She is an Algerian woman journalist on the run from the Islamic Salvation Front, which has sworn to have her killed.

Politicians have also written about the conditions in Algeria, criticizing the state or the Islamists or both. Said Sadi, the leader of the Berber-based Rally for Culture and Democracy (RCD) and one of the four presidential candidates in the 1995 presidential election, wrote an autobiographical account of the war, *Algérie: Heure de vérité* (1996), in which he analyzed the events, the leaders, and their programs from an insider's perspective. He does not claim to be objective and is very critical of both the men in power and the Islamist opposition. The account, however, is fascinating and gives the reader an insight into the political developments at the highest level of power in Algeria.

A number of edited works have also appeared in English and French focusing either exclusively or in part on the Algerian crisis. One such book is *Le drame algérien: Un peuple en otage*, prepared by a group of twenty-seven reporters and academicians, Algerians and French, under the name of Reporters sans Frontières (Reporters Without Borders). The real editor is José Garcson, a correspondent for the Paris-based *Libération*. The book is critical of the military regime in power and of its policies: it discusses the violence and repression, the problems of corruption and mismanagement, and the myths that have been fabricated around the Islamic Salvation Front and other Islamic organizations to demonize them. Although it is not an objective study of the events, it provides excellent insights into the political developments in Algeria since 1991. John Ruedy edited *Islamism and Secularism in North Africa* (1994), in which Severine Labat wrote about "Islamism and Islamists: The Emergence of New Types of Politico-Religious Militants" in Algeria; Hugh Roberts discussed "Doctrinaire Economics and Political Opportunism in the Strategy of Algerian Islamism"; John Entelis looked at the relationship of the state and Islamic movements in "Islam, Democracy, and the State: The Reemergence of Authoritarian Politics in Algeria"; and Mary-Jane Deeb compared Islamist movements in "Islam and the State in Algeria and Morocco: A Dialectical Model." *Polity and Society in Contemporary North Africa* (1993) was edited by I. William Zartman and William Mark Habeeb and covered Islamist opposition in Algeria in various chapters, including one by Mohammed Tozy entitled "Islam and the State."

FUTURE RESEARCH

The contribution of the scholarship on Algeria in the 1960s was very important: it enabled us to understand the impact of colonialism on the development of postcolonial government and society; it provided a detailed description of the process of institution building in the wake of a devastating war of independence; and it gave us an insight into the attempt at creating a "new society" and the reasons why this succeeded at the outset. Later writings, covering the 1970s and 1980s, uncovered the strains in Algerian society due to mismanagement and inept policies. In-depth analysis of political decision making, economic planning, and social strategies revealed major problems that allowed us to better understand the crisis that unfolded at the end of the 1980s. The scholarship of the 1990s has focused primarily on the rise of Islamist movements and has tried to explain the reasons behind the spiraling violence. These works, however, do not as yet possess the wisdom of hindsight, and although they have provided us with some insights into the conflict that is wrecking Algeria today, much remains unclear, and more research needs to be done to explain the crisis.

The extant literature on French colonialism and the Algerian war of independence is extensive, and little more needs to be said about the actual events. The impact, however, of those 132 years of colonialism and warfare on the Algerian psyche, on the concept of resistance and opposition to "unjust government," on issues of national and religious identity, on authoritarianism, on the use of force, and on civilian involvement needs to be better understood. Omar Carlier's book *Entre nation et jihad*, mentioned earlier, may be one of the very few works that have begun to make the connection between Algeria's past and its present state of upheaval.

Studies of the socioeconomic, regional, tribal, and ethnic distribution of political and economic power in Algeria have yet to be undertaken seriously. Traditional political science approaches have relegated such studies to anthropologists and sociologists and have consequently missed the link that exists between the various socioeconomic and regional groups and religion, politics, wealth, and power. Research has focused on the externalities of political power (the state apparatus, parties, the military) rather than on the internal manifestations of that power along regional, ethnic, and tribal lines. More interdisciplinary work needs to be done in order to better understand and be able to predict the course of events in Algeria.

Finally, the conceptual tools that Western political scientists use to classify, categorize, analyze, and compare political systems may not always be useful to understand the breakdown of a system such as that in Algeria. Simply put, we may be asking the wrong questions and looking at the wrong phenomena because our methodological tools are not attuned to the specificities of Algerian culture. More field research is needed, and existing conceptual frameworks need to be expanded and revised to help rather than hinder our understanding of societies such as Algeria.

REFERENCES

Abbas, Ferhat. 1962. *Guerre et révolution d'Algérie: La nuit coloniale.* Paris: Julliard.
———. 1980. *Autopsie d'une guerre.* Paris: Garnier.
———. 1984. *L'indépendance confisquée.* Paris: Flammarion.
Ageron, Charles Robert. 1979. *Histoire de l'Algérie contemporaine.* Vol. 2, *De l'insurrection de 1871 au déclenchement de la guerre de libération, 1954.* Paris: Presses Universitaires de France.
———. 1980. *L'Algérie algérienne de Napoléon III à de Gaulle.* Paris: Sindbad.
Ahmed, Hocine Aït. 1964. *La guerre et l'après-guerre.* Paris: Minuit.
d'Arcy, François, et al. 1965. *Essais sur l'économie de l'Algérie nouvelle.* Paris: Presses Universitaires de France.
Baghli, Sid-Ahmed. 1977. *Aspects of Cultural Policy in Algeria.* Paris: UNESCO.
Balta, Paul, and Claudine Rulleau. 1978. *La stratégie de Boumediene.* Paris: Sindbad.
Barakat, Halim, ed. 1985. *Contemporary North Africa: Issues of Development and Integration.* London: Croom Helm.
Bedjaoui, Mohammed. 1961. *Law and the Algerian Revolution.* Brussels: International Lawyers' Committee.
Behr, Edward. 1962. *The Algerian Problem.* New York: W. W. Norton.
Ben Bella, Ahmed. 1982. *Ben Bella revient.* Paris: Jean Picollec.
Benhouria, Tahar. 1980. *L'économie de l'Algérie.* Paris: Maspero.
Benissad, M. E. 1980. *L'économie algérienne contemporaine.* Paris: Presses Universitaires de France.
Bennoune, Mahfoud. 1988. *The Making of Contemporary Algeria, 1830–1987.* Cambridge: Cambridge University Press.
Blair, Thomas. 1970. *The Land to Those Who Work It: Algeria's Experiment in Workers' Management.* Garden City, NY: Anchor Books–Doubleday.
Boudiaf, Mohamed. 1964. *Où va l'Algérie?* Paris: Librairie de l'Etoile.
Bourges, Hervé. 1967. *L'Algérie à l'épreuve du pouvoir.* Paris: Grasset.

Brown, L. Carl, ed. 1966. *State and Society in Independent North Africa*. Washington, DC: Middle East Institute.

Burgat, François, and William Dowell. 1993. *The Islamic Movement in North Africa*. Austin: University of Texas Press.

Burgat, François, and Michel Nancy. 1984. *Les villages socialistes de la révolution agraire algérienne*. Paris: CNRS.

Buy, François. 1965. *La Republique Algérienne Démocratique et Populaire*. Paris: La Librairie Française.

Carlier, Omar. 1995. *Entre nation et jihad: Histoire sociale des radicalismes algériens*. Paris: Presses de la Fondation nationale des sciences politiques.

Chaliand, Gerard. 1965. *L'Algérie est-elle socialiste?* Paris: Maspero.

Chaliand, Gerard, and Juliette Minces. 1972. *L'Algérie indépendante: Bilan d'une révolution nationale*. Paris: Maspero.

Clark, Michael K. 1960. *Algeria in Turmoil: A History of the Rebellion*. New York: Praeger.

Clegg, Ian. 1972. *Workers' Self-Management in Algeria*. New York: Monthly Review Press.

Courrière, Yves. 1968–1971. *La guerre d'Algérie*. 4 vols. Paris: Fayard.

Douence, Jean-Claude. 1964. *La mise en place des institutions algériennes*. Paris: Fondation nationale des sciences politiques.

Droz, Bernard, and Evelyne Lever. 1982. *Histoire de la guerre d'Algérie, 1954–1962*. Paris: Seuil.

Entelis, John P. 1986. *Algeria: The Revolution Institutionalized*. Boulder, CO: Westview Press.

Entelis, John P., and Phillip C. Naylor, eds. 1992. *State and Society in Algeria*. Boulder, CO: Westview Press.

Fanon, Frantz. 1963. *The Wretched of the Earth*. New York: Grove Press.

Francos, Ania, and Jean-Pierre Sereni. 1976. *Un Algérien nommé Boumediene*. Paris: Stock

Fuller, Graham E. 1996. *Algeria: The Next Fundamentalist State?* Santa Monica, CA: Rand.

Gordon, David. 1966. *The Passing of French Algeria*. London: Oxford University Press.

Grimaud, Nicole. 1984. *La politique extérieure de l'Algérie (1962–1978)*. Paris: Karthala.

Guerin, Daniel. 1964. *L'Algérie qui se cherche*. Paris: Présence Africaine.

———. 1965. *L'Algérie caporalisée*. Paris: Centre d'Etudes Socialistes.

Harbi, Mohammed. 1975. *Aux origines du F.L.N.: La scission du PPA-MTLD*. Paris: Christian Bourgeois.

———. 1980. *Le FLN, mirage et réalité, des origines à la prise du pouvoir (1945–1962)*. Paris: Editions Jeune Afrique.

———. 1984. *La guerre commence en Algérie: 1954*. Brussels: Editions Complexe.

Hardoun, Ali. 1986. *La 7e wilaya, la guerre du FLN en France (1954–1962)*. Paris: Seuil.

Heggoy, Alf Andrew. 1972. *Insurgency and Counterinsurgency in Algeria*. Bloomington: Indiana University Press.

Horne, Alistair. 1985. *A Savage War of Peace: Algeria, 1954–1962*. New York: Viking.

Humbaraci, Arslan. 1966. *Algeria: A Revolution That Failed—A Political History since 1954*. New York: Praeger.

Hutchinson, Martha Crenshaw. 1978. *Revolutionary Terrorism: The FLN in Algeria, 1954–1962*. Stanford, CA: Hoover Institution Press.

Ibrahimi, Ahmed Taleb. 1976. *De la décolonisation à la révolution culturelle (1962–1972)*. 2d ed. Algiers: SNED.

Jackson, Henry F. 1977. *The FLN in Algeria: Party Development in a Revolutionary Society*. Westport, CT: Greenwood Press.

Kheladi, Aissa. 1992. *Algérie: Les islamistes face au pouvoir*. Algiers: ALFA.

Koulytchizky, Serge. 1974. *L'autogestion, l'homme, et l'état: L'expérience algérienne*. Paris: Mouton.

Kraft, Joseph. 1961. *The Struggle for Algeria*. Garden City, NY: Doubleday.

Labat, Severine. 1995. *Les islamistes algériens: Entre les urnes et le maquis*. Paris: Editions du Seuil.

Lacheraf, Mostefa. 1968. *La culture algérienne contemporaine: Essai de définitions et perspectives*. Algiers: Services Culturels du Parti.

Laks, Monique. 1970. *Autogestion ouvrière et pouvoir politique en Algérie (1962–1965)*. Paris: Etudes et Documentation Internationales.

Lassassi, Assassi. 1988. *Nonalignment and Algerian Foreign Policy*. Brookfield, VT: Avebury.

Lazreg, Marnia. 1976. *The Emergence of Classes in Algeria: Colonialism and Sociopolitical Change*. Boulder, CO: Westview Press.

———. 1994. *The Eloquence of Silence: Algerian Women in Question*. London: Routledge.

Leca, Jean, and Jean-Claude Vatin. 1975. *L'Algérie politique: Institutions et régime*. Paris: Colin.

Leveau, Remy. 1993. *Le sabre et le turban: L'avenir du Maghreb*. Paris: Editions François Bourin.

Mahsas, Ahmed. 1979. *Le mouvement révolutionnaire en Algérie: Essai sur la formation du mouvement national de la 1re guerre mondiale à 1954*. Paris: L'Harmattan.

Memmi, Albert. 1967. *The Colonizer and the Colonized*. Boston: Beacon Press.

Merle, Robert. 1965. *Ahmed Ben Bella*. Paris: Gallimard.

Messaoudi, Khalida, and Elisabeth Schemla. 1995. *Khalida Messaoudi Entretiens avec Elisabeth Schemla: Une Algerienne debout*. Paris: Flammarion.

Metz, Helen, ed. 1994. *Algeria: A Country Study*. Washington, DC: Library of Congress.

Minces, Juliette. 1979. *L'Algérie de Boumediene*. Paris: Presses de la Cité.

Mouhoubi, Salah. 1986. *La politique de coopération algéro-française: Bilan et perspectives*. Algiers: Office des publications universitaires.

Naroun, Amar. 1961. *Ferhat Abbas: ou, Les chemins de la souveraineté*. Paris: Denoël.

O'Ballance, Edgar. 1967. *The Algerian Insurrection, 1954–62*. London: Faber.

Ottaway, David, and Marina Ottaway. 1970. *Algeria: The Politics of a Socialist Revolution*. Berkeley: University of California Press.

Perroux, François. 1963. *Problèmes de l'Algérie indépendante*. Paris: Presses Universitaires de France.

Pfeifer, Karen. 1985. *Agrarian Reform under State Capitalism in Algeria*. Boulder, CO: Westview Press.

Pierre, Andrew J., and William B. Quandt. 1996. *The Algerian Crisis: Policy Options for the West*. Washington, DC: Carnegie Endowment for International Peace.

Quandt, William. 1969. *Revolution and Political Leadership: Algeria, 1954–1968*. Cambridge, MA: MIT Press.

Reporters sans Frontières. 1994. *Le drame algérien: Un peuple en otage*. Paris: Editions La Decouverte.

Rochebrune, Renaud de, ed. 1982. *Les mémoires de Messali Hadj, 1898–1938*.

Rouadjia, Ahmad. 1990. *Les frères et la mosquée: Enquête sur le mouvement islamiste en Algérie*. Paris: Karthala.

Ruedy, John. 1992. *Modern Algeria: The Origins and Development of a Nation*. Bloomington: Indiana University Press.

———, ed. 1994. *Islamism and Secularism in North Africa*. New York: St. Martin's Press.

Sadi, Said. 1996. *Algérie: l'heure de verité*. Paris: Flammarion.

Smith, Tony. 1978. *The French Stake in Algeria, 1945–1962*. Ithaca: Cornell University Press.

Stora, Benjamin. 1982. *Messali Hadj 1898–1974*. Paris: Sycomore.

Tlemcani, Rachid. 1986. *State and Revolution in Algeria*. Boulder, CO: Westview Press.

Vatin, Jean-Claude. 1983. *L'Algérie politique: Histoire et société*. Paris: Presses de la Fondation nationale des sciences politiques.

Zartman, I. William, ed. 1973. *Man, State, and Society in the Contemporary Maghrib*. New York: Praeger.

Zartman, I. William, et al., eds. 1982. *Political Elites in Arab North Africa*. New York: Longman.

Zartman, I. William, and William Mark Habeeb, eds. 1993. *Polity and Society in Contemporary North Africa*. Boulder, CO: Westview Press.

EGYPT

Robert Springborg and Pamela Day Pelletreau

Political scientists have devoted more attention to Egypt than to any other Arab country. The political trendsetter in the Arab world, Egypt has been the focus of innovative political science research that has introduced methods and concepts into the study of Arab political systems more generally. The library of political science works on Egypt thus provides an accurate barometer of changing trends and generational shifts in approaches to understanding Middle Eastern politics. These approaches typically have been informed by, if not borrowed outright from, scholarship on other regions of the world. So, for example, the behavioral revolution that swept political science in the late 1950s and early 1960s, and whose first manifestations were in studies of American politics, inspired Morroe Berger's pioneering *Bureaucracy and Society in Modern Egypt* (1957), which investigated the performance of this venerable institution through the innovative use of an attitudinal survey. Similar behaviorally oriented studies of other Egyptian institutions, including the army (e.g., P. J. Vatikiotis, *The Egyptian Army in Politics*, 1961), local politics (e.g., James B. Mayfield, *Rural Politics in Nasser's Egypt*, 1971, and Iliya Harik, *The Political Mobilization of Peasants*, 1974), and the political elite (e.g., R. Hrair Dekmejian, *Egypt under Nasir*, 1971), followed.

Just as behavioralist-oriented studies of Egyptian political institutions introduced that approach to the study of Arab politics more generally, so were other pioneering works of successive generations of scholarship focused on Egypt. Marxist and neo-Marxist studies, which were in many cases self-conscious antitheses to the behavioral thesis, and which were also inspired by political radicalism that obtained in Egypt and elsewhere in the world in the 1960s, made their Arab debut in Egypt. Hassan Riad's *L'Egypte nasserienne* (1964), Anouar Abdel-Malek's *Egypt: Military Society* (1968), and Mahmoud Hussein's *Class Conflict in Egypt, 1945–1970* (1973) set the tone for similar studies conducted elsewhere in the Arab world.

Marxist and neo-Marxist scholarship evolved after the 1960s into separate approaches. One emphasized dependency of the Third World periphery on the capitalist core. Another, labeled "political economy," while retaining social classes and conflict between them as important concepts, added other considerations, the most important of which is the composition and role of the state.

Both dependency and political economy approaches had comparatively early impacts on scholarship on Egypt. The volume edited by Malcolm H. Kerr and El Sayed Yassin, *Rich and Poor States in the Middle East* (1982), contains articles that investigate how global and regional structures of political and economic power impact upon Egypt. Eric Davis's *Challenging Colonialism* (1983) utilizes the historical case study of Bank Misr to investigate the impact of the inegalitarian world order on national capital formation. John Waterbury's *The Egypt of Nasser and Sadat* (1983) was the first macro political economy analysis of an Arab country. The initial second-generation political economy analysis in the region, drawing upon the notion of "rent-seeking" as explicated by Anne O. Krueger and Mancur Olson, was similarly focused on Egypt, Yahya Sadowski's *Political Vegetables?* (1991). Also inspired at least in part by Marxism is that scholarship that seeks to investigate power and authority in relationships other than just the economic and that utilizes "discourse," broadly defined, as the material evidence of those relationships. Timothy Mitchell's *Colonising Egypt* (1988) draws on a wide array of historical evidence to demonstrate the impact of the inegalitarian imperial order on the perceptual worlds of colonizer and colonized.

Egypt has also served as the initial and primary case study in the Arab world for approaches that have conceptualized political systems as dyadic, consisting of state and society. In the 1970s, as the reaction against Nasserism set in, and as the autonomous role of the state appeared more evident and to have been overlooked by both Marxist analysis (which focuses on classes) and institutional analysis (which disaggregates the state into its components), the state as political actor became a focal point for analysis. More specifically, the authoritarian state, its variants, its degree of autonomy from the class base, and its strengths and weaknesses were investigated. Mark N. Cooper's *The Transformation of Egypt* (1982), Raymond Hinnebusch's *Egyptian Politics under Sadat* (1988), and Hamied Ansari's *Egypt: The Stalled Society* (1986) are examples of state-centered analyses.

By the early 1990s, the pendulum of research had begun to swing away from the state and toward civil society. This change resulted in part from rapid and dramatic democratizations, especially in Eastern Europe, where civil society was credited with having risen up and overwhelmed entrenched state power. The new focus on civil society also resulted from the manifest weakening of states in the Middle East and elsewhere as a result of declining governmental revenues and shrinking ideological legitimacy. Egypt's civil society, accordingly, attracted new interest among political scientists. Robert Bianchi, for example, in his *Unruly Corporatism* (1989), conceptualizes Egyptian civil society as consisting of corporatized (i.e., government-controlled) and pluralized (i.e., independent) interest groups, with the latter gradually becoming more important as political liberalization proceeds. Raymond Baker's *Sadat and After* (1990) seeks to demonstrate the significant contribution of Egypt's civil society to political thought and action by chronicling the activities of various groups and organizations. Joel Beinin and Zachary Lockman's *Workers on the Nile* (1987) concentrates on labor organization as a manifestation of the dynamism of civil society. The periodical *Civil Society* (the subtitle of which is *Democratic Transformation in the Arab World*), published since 1991 by the Ibn Khaldun Center in Cairo, chronicles and analyzes developments in civil society in the Arab world, especially Egypt. It is the only such publication in the Arab world.

The rise of religious fundamentalism around the globe and in the Middle East in particular has spawned a veritable library, the earliest works of which are focused on Egypt. Richard P. Mitchell's *The Society of the Muslim Brothers* (1969) remains the definitive study of this organization. Saad Eddin Ibrahim's seminal "Anatomy of Egypt's Militant Groups" (1980), on the social background characteristics of Islamic radicals, was one of the first empirically based investigations of Islamic radicalism. Muhammad H. Heikal's *Autumn of Fury* (1983) investigates the relationship between the government of Anwar al-Sadat and the rise of militant Islamic groups. Gilles Kepel's *Muslim Extremism in Egypt* (1986) combined an analysis of the doctrine and the practice of Egypt's Muslim radicals in order to explain their political behavior.

MACROPOLITICAL STUDIES AND CONTEMPORARY HISTORIES

Macropolitical studies include accounts of contemporary politics approached within a modern history framework, many of which have been written by English scholars or by journalists, as well as general overviews of the political system that are more descriptive than analytical. More such works have been devoted to the Nasser and Sadat eras than to the Mubarak period. Most have focused on the person of the leader and his impact on the political system. Examples of such books (in chronological order) include Keith Wheelock, *Nasser's New Egypt* (1960); Robert St. John, *The Boss* (1960); Peter Mansfield, *Nasser's Egypt* (1965); P. J. Vatikiotis, *Egypt since the Revolution* (1968); Jean Lacouture, *Nasser* (1971); Robert Stephens, *Nasser* (1971); Anthony Nutting, *Nasser* (1972); Robert Burrill and Abbas Kelidar, *Egypt* (1977); Raymond Baker, *Egypt's Uncertain Revolution under Nasser and Sadat* (1978); David Hirst and Irene Beeson, *Sadat* (1981); Raphael Israeli, *Man of Defiance* (1985); Anthony McDermott, *Egypt from Nasser to Mubarak* (1988); Thomas W. Lippman, *Egypt after Nasser* (1989); Joel Gordon, *Nasser's Blessed Movement* (1991); P. J. Vatikiotis, *The History of Modern Egypt* (1991); Peter Woodward, *Nasser* (1992); and Abdel Majid Farid, *Nasser* (1994). President Nasser's confidant and the former editor of *al-Ahram*, Muhammad Hassanein Heikal, has produced a steady stream of books that combine personal reminiscences and descriptions and analyses of various events during and after the Nasser era, including *Nasser: The Cairo Documents* (1972), *The Road to Ramadan* (1975), *The Sphinx and the Commissar* (1978), *Autumn of Fury* (1983), *Cutting the Lion's Tail* (1987), and *1967—Al-Infijar (The Explosion)* (in Arabic, 1990).

GOVERNMENT INSTITUTIONS AND POLITICAL ORGANIZATIONS

The Military

The 1952 coup d'état that brought Gamal Abdel Nasser and the Free Officers to power initiated a political role for the military that it continues to play. Despite its persisting political power and its increasing involvement in economic production and distribution, the popularity of the military as a subject for political science analysis has declined steadily since the 1950s. The wave of coups that swept through newly independent states in the 1950s and 1960s stimulated great interest among political scientists, whereas more subtle, ongoing military influence within the political economy has received scant attention.

The first major study of the Egyptian military in the Nasser era was that by P. J. Vatikiotis, *The Egyptian Army in Politics* (1961). Eliezer Beeri's *Army Officers in Arab Politics and Society* (1970) and George Haddad's *Revolutions and Military Rule in the Middle East* (1965–1973) devoted chapters to Egypt in which they described the intervention of the Egyptian military in politics and examined the political character of the military in terms of the social background characteristics of its officers. The Egyptian army and its relations with other political institutions and social forces provided much of the empirical basis for Manfred Halpern's influential work, *The Politics of Social Change in the Middle East and North Africa* (1963). Amos Perlmutter investigated the continuing influence of the military in the Egyptian political system in his *Egypt* (1974). Saad El-Shazli provides insights into civilian-military relations at the highest levels in *The Crossing of the Suez* (1980), as does Mohamed Abdel Ghani El-Gamasy in *The October War* (1993). R. Hrair Dekmejian compared the political role of the Egyptian and Turkish militaries in "Egypt and Turkey" (1982). Ahmad Abdalla's *The Army and Democracy in Egypt* (1990, in Arabic) is a collection of analytical essays on the historical and contemporary role of the military within the political economy.

Various works contain some material on political aspects of the Egyptian military. Nazih Ayubi analyzes recruitment into the civilian bureaucracy from the military in *Bureaucracy and Politics in Contemporary Egypt* (1980). Kirk J. Beattie's *Egypt during the Nasser Years* (1994) examines conflicting political ideologies within the Nasserist military and the manner in which the military consolidated its power. Raymond Hinnebusch's *Egyptian Politics under Sadat* (1988) documents the declining influence in the political elite of the army in the Sadat period. Robert Springborg's *Mubarak's Egypt* (1989) analyzes the army's expanding influence in the polity and economy under Mubarak. Michael

N. Barnett's *Confronting the Costs of War* (1992) investigates the relationship between militarization and state power.

Political Elite

Because of the high visibility of Egyptian political leadership, both domestically and internationally, and because power has been concentrated at the elite level, political scientists have been attracted to elite analyses. R. Hrair Dekmejian's *Egypt under Nasir* (1971) and *Patterns of Political Leadership* (1975) utilized the concept of charisma, as well as the social background characteristics of the elite, to account for politics under Nasser. P. J. Vatikiotis sought to explain the formative influences on the Nasserist elite in his *Nasser and His Generation* (1978). Miles Copeland in *The Game of Nations* (1969) and Wilbur Crane Eveland in *Ropes of Sand* (1980) both looked to the machinations of intelligence agencies to account for political outcomes. Robert Springborg's *Family, Power, and Politics in Egypt* (1982) utilized the vehicle of a prominent politician and his family to analyze elite dynamics in the Nasser and Sadat periods. Leonard Binder's *In a Moment of Enthusiasm* (1978) presented data on the social background characteristics of members of the elite that he interpreted as demonstrating the continuing presence within it of a second stratum of landowners.

Local Government and Rural Politics

Local government organization, as distinct from rural politics, has not been extensively studied, although several works that deal primarily with the latter also illuminate institutional aspects of rural government. James B. Mayfield's *Local Government in Egypt* (1996) updates and expands his earlier study mentioned previously. Hanan Hamdy Radwan's ''Democratization in Rural Egypt'' (1994) assesses village local popular councils and the impact on them of the USAID local development project. Richard H. Adams, Jr.,'s *Development and Social Change in Rural Egypt* (1986) argues that local landowners exercise considerably greater power in rural Egypt than do administrators who represent the national government. Nicholas S. Hopkins's *Agrarian Transformation in Egypt* (1987) demonstrates that in rural areas patron-client relations are ubiquitous in both formal and informal political organizations. Louis J. Cantori and Iliya Harik's edited volume *Local Politics and Development in the Middle East* (1984) analyzes Egyptian rural politics in comparative perspective. The politics of Cairo are compared to those of Beirut and Tehran in Guilain Denoeux's *Urban Unrest in the Middle East* (1993). Understanding of the historical development of local government and politics can be gained from Gabriel Baer, *Fellah and Townsman in the Middle East* (1982).

Several studies evaluate local politics within the broader context of agricultural modernization and rural development more generally. Alan Richards's *Egypt's Agricultural Development, 1800–1980* (1982) shows how the modernization of agriculture has impacted rural class structure, which has in turn affected local political processes. Samir Radwan and Eddy Lee's *Agrarian Change in Egypt* (1986) reveals through analysis of survey data the degree of poverty in rural Egypt and its implications for politics. Simon Commander's *The State and Agricultural Development in Egypt since 1973* (1987) reviews changing state policies toward agriculture and their impact on production, distribution, and rural political relations. Nathan J. Brown's *Peasant Politics in Modern Egypt* (1990) dispels the myth of a politically quiescent peasantry.

Bureaucracy, Universities, and the Legal System

The two most thorough and recent analyses of the Egyptian bureaucracy are Nazih Ayubi's *Bureaucracy and Politics in Contemporary Egypt* (1980) and Monte Palmer, Ali Leila, and El Sayed Yassin's *The Egyptian Bureaucracy* (1988). Cairo University has played a key role for more than half a century in educating and shaping the political elite, and it has been a battleground for various political forces. These struggles and the university's role in twentieth-century political history are described and analyzed in Donald M. Reid, *Cairo University and the Making of Modern Egypt* (1990). The development of law and the court system are analyzed within a political context by Byron Cannon, *Politics of Law and the Courts in Nineteenth-Century Egypt* (1988). Enid Hill assesses the impact of Egypt's most famous modern jurist in *Al-Sanhuri and Islamic Law* (1987), provides a case-study-based analysis of the legal system in *Mahkama!* (1979), and analyzes the growing importance of Islamic law in "Law and Courts in Egypt" (1990).

Interest Groups, Political Parties, and the Media

Labor unions and professional associations are the interest groups that have received the most attention by political scientists. Ellis Goldberg investigates unionization of the textile industry in *Tinker, Tailor, and Textile Worker* (1986). The influence of unions over economic policy making in the Nasser and Mubarak eras is analyzed in Robert Bianchi, "The Corporatization of the Egyptian Labor Movement" (1986), Marsha Pripstein Posusney, "Labor as an Obstacle to Privatization" (1992), and Ellis Goldberg, "The Foundations of State-Labor Relations in Contemporary Egypt" (1992). Joel E. Beinin compares the shift from internationalist, leftist perspectives to nationalist ones among Egyptian and Israeli unionists and leftists more generally in *Was the Red Flag Flying There?* (1990).

Professionals, their associations, and their role in the political process have been reasonably well studied. Farhat J. Ziadeh's *Lawyers, the Rule of Law, and Liberalism in Egypt* (1968) and Donald M. Reid's *Lawyers and Politics in the Arab World, 1880–1960* (1981) focus on the legal profession. Clement H.

Moore's *Images of Development* (1980) reveals the limitations of engineers' influence in the political process.

The most comprehensive overviews of interest groups within Egyptian politics are provided by Mustafa Kamil al-Sayyid, *Society and Politics in Egypt* (1983) (in Arabic), and Amani Kandil, *Civil Society in the Arab World* (1995). Private voluntary associations, also known as nongovernmental organizations (NGOs), are the focus of Denis J. Sullivan's *Private Voluntary Organizations in Egypt* (1994).

Leftist movements and political organizations have attracted more scholarly interest than mainstream political parties. In addition to the works referred to earlier on labor unions, Selma Botman's *The Rise of Egyptian Communism, 1939–1970* (1988), Tareq Y. Ismael and Rifaat El-Said's *The Communist Movement in Egypt, 1920–1988* (1988), and Gilles Perrault's *A Man Apart* (1987) all deal with Egyptian communism. Marius Deeb's *Party Politics in Egypt* (1979) is a study of the Wafd party, as is Zaheer M. Quraishi's *Liberal Nationalism in Egypt* (1967). The Muslim Brotherhood is analyzed as a political party by Christina P. Harris, *Nationalism and Revolution in Egypt* (1964).

The role of the press under Nasser, in particular *al-Ahram* and its editor, Muhammad Hassanein Heikal, is the subject of Munir K. Nasser's *Press, Politics, and Power* (1979). The same author provides a structural analysis of the government's relations with the media in *Egyptian Mass Media under Nasser and Sadat* (1990).

POLITICAL ECONOMY

Political economy in its broadest sense describes studies that investigate linkages between the economy and polity. Several such studies on Egypt focus primarily on the economy, with the authors drawing conclusions about the polity on the basis of their understanding of economic policies. Such works include Bent Hansen and Girgis A. Marzouk, *Development and Economic Policy in the UAR* (1965), Patrick K. O'Brien, *The Revolution in Egypt's Economic System* (1966), Charles Issawi, *Egypt in Revolution* (1963), Robert Mabro, *The Egyptian Economy, 1952–1972* (1974), Bent Hansen and Karim Nashashibi, *Foreign Trade Regimes and Economic Development* (1975), Khalid Ikram, *Egypt* (1980), Mahmoud Abdel-Fadil, *The Political Economy of Nasserism* (1980), and Bent Hansen, *The Political Economy of Poverty, Equity, and Growth: Egypt and Turkey* (1991).

Studies that have focused primarily on political factors that facilitate or impede economic stabilization measures and structural adjustment include sections of Alan Richards and John Waterbury, *A Political Economy of the Middle East* (1990), John Waterbury, *Exposed to Innumerable Delusions* (1993), Iliya Harik and Denis Sullivan, editors, *Privatization and Liberalization in the Middle East* (1992), Tim Niblock and Emma Murphy, editors, *Economic and Political Liberalization in the Middle East* (1993), and Ibrahim Oweiss, editor, *The Political*

Economy of Contemporary Egypt (1990). Nazih N. Ayubi provides an overall critique of liberalization policies and their political origins in *The State and Public Policies in Egypt since Sadat* (1991b).

Accounts that emphasize economic as opposed to political dimensions of stabilization and structural adjustment include Said El-Naggar's *Adjustment Policies and Development Strategies in the Arab World* (1987), *Privatization and Structural Adjustment in the Arab Countries* (1989), and *Investment Policies in the Arab Countries* (1990). The work of Heba Handoussa and Gillian Potter, editors, *Employment and Structural Adjustment* (1991), includes data relevant to and analyses of the performance of the public and private sectors.

Gouda Abdel-Khalek and Robert Tignor, editors, and the contributors to their volume examine the nature and political causes and consequences of income distribution in *The Political Economy of Income Distribution in Egypt* (1982). Robert Tignor explores state-business relations in *State, Private Enterprise, and Economic Change in Egypt, 1918–1952* (1984) and *Egyptian Textiles and British Capital, 1930–1956* (1989). Malak Zaalouk, *Power, Class, and Foreign Capital in Egypt* (1989), traces the rise of the new bourgeoisie in Sadat's Egypt and seeks to analyze its impact on state policies. John Waterbury analyzes various public policies in Sadat's Egypt in *Egypt* (1978) and Nile water policies specifically in *Hydropolitics of the Nile Valley* (1979). Fawzy Mansour argues in *The Arab World* (1992) that the inability of classes and their political manifestations to win autonomy from the state has been the primary cause of Egypt's historic inability to engender sustainable development. Ghali Shoukri's *Egypt* (1981) is a critique of the Sadat era from a leftist perspective.

Since the early 1980s, several works have appeared on international aspects of Egypt's political economy. David William Carr's *Foreign Investment and Development in Egypt* (1979) was an early investigation of the impact of external investment. Kate Gillespie's *The Tripartite Relationship* (1984) is an account of the relationship between the state and domestic and foreign investors during the economic opening under Sadat. Marvin G. Weinbaum provides an assessment of U.S. assistance to Egypt in *Egypt and the Politics of U.S. Economic Aid* (1986). A study that situates that aid more in the context of U.S. foreign policy objectives is William J. Burns, *Economic Aid and American Policy toward Egypt, 1955–1981* (1985).

POLITICAL IDEOLOGIES, POLITICAL MOVEMENTS, AND SOCIAL FORCES

The vast majority of works devoted to political ideologies and political movements in Egypt are focused on either Nasserism or political Islam. Books wholly or partially committed to the former include Leonard Binder, *The Ideological Revolution in the Middle East* (1964), Nissim Rejwan, *Nasserist Ideology* (1974), Malcolm Kerr, *The Arab Cold War* (1965), and Sylvia G. Haim, editor, *Arab Nationalism* (1962), as well as many of the works on the Nasser era cited earlier. Malcolm Kerr's "The Emergence of a Socialist Ideology in Egypt" (1962) is a seminal article on the incorporation into Nasserism of socialist concepts and practices. Afaf Lutfi al-Sayyid-Marsot provides an account of political ideologies and their organizational manifestations prior to the rise of Nasser in *Egypt's Liberal Experiment, 1922–1936* (1977).

Malcolm Kerr's *Islamic Reform* (1966) is a comparative study of the political thought of Muhammad Abduh and Rashid Rida. Morroe Berger describes social and political aspects of popular Islam in *Islam in Egypt Today* (1970). The sociopolitical role of Cairo's venerable Islamic institution, al-Azhar, is examined by A. Chris Eccel in *Egypt, Islam, and Social Change* (1984). Michael Gilsenan argues that contemporary Sufi orders are basically apolitical in *Saint and Sufi in Modern Egypt* (1973).

With the rise of Islamic activism in the Middle East, articles, collected volumes, and monographs on the phenomenon began to appear, with most including at least some material on Egypt. Such works include Nazih N. Ayubi, *Political Islam* (1991a), Barry Rubin, *Islamic Fundamentalism in Egyptian Politics* (1990), A. Cudsi and Ali E. Hillal Dessouki, editors, *Islam and Power* (1981), Ali E. Hillal Dessouki, *Islamic Resurgence in the Arab World* (1982), R. Hrair Dekmejian, *Islam in Revolution* (1985), and Edmund Burke and Ira M. Lapidus, *Islam, Politics, and Social Movements* (1988). The first in-depth study of one of Egypt's radical Islamist organizations is Nemat Guenena's "The Jihad" (1986). Patrick D. Gaffney has studied the role of Muslim preaching against the backdrop of Islamism, especially in Minya, in *The Prophet's Pulpit* (1994).

Two principal social forces that have played important political roles in this century are students and religious minorities. Ahmad Abdalla, a student activist in the 1970s and an accomplished political scientist, has described the student movement under Sadat in *The Student Movement and National Politics in Egypt* (1985). Religious minorities, including Jews and Copts, the former of which supplied much of the leadership of pre-1952 leftist organizations, and the latter of which were disproportionately represented among the elite of the Wafd party, have received some attention in the literature. Gudrun Kramer's *The Jews in Modern Egypt, 1914–1952* (1989) and Michael Laskier's *The Jews of Egypt, 1920–1970* (1992) analyze the social, economic, and political roles of that community. Barbara Lynn Carter investigates the political role of the Coptic minority in *The Copts in Egyptian Politics* (1986).

HUMAN RIGHTS, WOMEN, AND FAMILY

The relationship between women and the political system has been examined from several approaches: history, anthropology, and political economy. Biographical and autobiographical studies have also contributed to the available material. The outstanding early Egyptian feminist was Huda Sharawi, whose *Harem Years: The Memoirs of an Egyptian Feminist, 1879–1924* (1987), translated, edited, and introduced by Margot Badran, opens the study of Egyptian feminism. Beth Baron in *The Women's Awakening in Egypt* (1994) discusses women's journals published from the late nineteenth century to 1919 and relates social transformation to the literary culture. Soha Abdel Kader in *Egyptian Women in a Changing Society, 1899–1987* (1987) studies the impact of social change on the status and roles of Egyptian women over three-quarters of a century. Earl L. Sullivan, in *Women in Egyptian Public Life* (1986), argues that the participation of women in public life has steadily increased since the Nasser era. Jihan Sadat, widow of Anwar al-Sadat, provides insights to their relationship and their political thought and behavior in her autobiography, *A Woman of Egypt* (1987). Recent translations of two books of Amin Qasim (1863–1908) by Samiha Sidhom Peterson expand the accessibility of late-nineteenth-century writing on Egyptian feminism.

Several books address the relationship between Egyptian women and the political economy. Judith Tucker's *Women in Nineteenth-Century Egypt* (1985) draws on court and government records to explore four interlocking dimensions of women's position and power: access to property, position in the family unit, participation in the social unit of production, and the prevailing ideological definitions of women's roles. Diane Singerman's *Avenues of Participation* (1995) examines the tactics and strategies used by the popular classes in Cairo to achieve their goals. Arlene Elowe Macleod's *Accommodating Protest* (1993) concludes that if veiling is conceptualized as accommodating protest, the role women play in renegotiations of power in a time of change is better understood. Ghada Talhami in *The Mobilization of Muslim Women in Egypt* (1996) analyzes current changes in women's role. A precursor of these books is Andrea Rugh's *Family in Contemporary Egypt* (1984), which marshals a range of evidence in support of the proposition that the family plays an unusually important role in Egypt's social, economic, and political systems. Margot Badran in *Feminists, Islam, and Nation* (1995) discusses how the Egyptian feminist movement in the first half of the twentieth century advanced the nationalist cause while working within the parameters of Islam. Nawal Sadawi's several volumes highlight and condemn human rights abuses, particularly those committed against Egyptian women. Some of her works include *Hidden Face of Eve* (1980), *Women at Point Zero* (1983), *God Dies by the Nile* (1985), *Memoirs from the Women's Prison* (1986), and *Searching* (1991).

Human rights in Egypt are described annually in the Department of State's *Human Rights Report* and from time to time in special studies by Amnesty International and Human Rights Watch. A comprehensive overview of human rights by the Egyptian Organization for Human Rights is *The Condition of Human Rights in Egypt* (1993). Kevin Dwyer's *Arab Voices* (1991) includes Egyptians among those whose discussions of human rights he reports and analyzes.

FOREIGN POLICY

Bahgat Korany and Ali Eddin Hillal Dessouki in *The Foreign Policies of Arab States* (1991) characterize Egypt's foreign policy process as an activity whose main objective is the mobilization of external resources for the sake of internal development. Adeed Dawisha's *Egypt in the Arab World* (1976) sees classic balance-of-power calculations underlying Egyptian foreign policy behavior. Egypt's involvement in the Arab-Israeli conflict has spawned several studies, including an analysis of Nasser's fateful decisions in the spring of 1967 by Richard Parker, *The Politics of Miscalculation in the Middle East* (1993). Ann Mosely Lesch and Mark Tessler in *Israel, Egypt, and the Palestinians* (1989) discuss Egyptian-Israeli relations since Camp David. Shibley Telhami's *Power and Leadership in International Bargaining* (1990) concludes that the Camp David Accords resulted from the distribution of military and economic power between the competing states. Salwa Gomaa's *Egyptian Diplomacy in the 1970s* (1985) and Gamal Zahran's *Egypt's Foreign Policy, 1970–1981* (1987), both in Arabic, provide overviews of Egyptian foreign policy during this critical decade. An alternate perspective is presented in Shimon Shamir's edited volume *Egypt from Monarchy to Republic: A Reassessment of Revolution and Change* (1995).

Egyptian-U.S. relations have been the subject of several works, including several referred to earlier in the political economy section. Gail E. Meyer's *Egypt and the United States* (1980) analyzes that relationship during the early Nasser years. William Quandt's *The United States and Egypt* (1990) signaled that a shift from the primacy of political and strategic issues to the dominance of economic concerns would occur in U.S.-Egyptian relations. In *The Middle East* (1988), edited by William Quandt, various aspects of Egyptian foreign policy, including the relationship with the United States, are discussed.

FUTURE RESEARCH

Over the past three decades, political science scholarship on Egypt has broadened and deepened. Whereas the political elite and the central role of the president were the focus of most early work, since then other components of the state, as well as many aspects of civil society, have been studied in varying degrees of detail. In some cases, such as the investigation of Islamic activism, scholarship on Egypt far surpasses that available on other Arab countries. It is worth noting, however, that one of the barriers that confronts the further expansion of political science research on Egypt is reticence on the part of the government to permit field research. Despite the political liberalization that has occurred since the Nasser era, it remains difficult to obtain the approval necessary to conduct research in Egypt. Partly as a result of such restrictions, various topics, including those of regional and local politics, the conduct of campaigns and elections, and the formation of most aspects of public policy, remain little studied and poorly understood. Nevertheless, by comparison to other Arab countries, the political science library on Egypt is reasonably large and diverse.

Writings on politics in Egypt are more voluminous than on any other Arab country, and in virtually all sectors of the discipline, studies of Egypt have preceded those that have been done on other Arab countries. Yet despite this comparative abundance, significant gaps in our knowledge persist. The manner in which governmental and political institutions operate is not well described or understood. Courts, the parliament, local government bodies, and political parties have been the subject of only intermittent research efforts, at best. The process by which public policy is made has yet to be systematically investigated. These deficiencies are due in part to the widespread belief that despite the highly bureaucratic nature of the Egyptian government, politics remains poorly institutionalized, dependent more upon executive initiative and personal connections than on formal, institutionalized practices and organizations. While this may be the case, organizations and institutions of the state and civil society, as well as the linkages between them, do perform political functions and are, therefore, worthy of sustained investigation.

Another major lacuna in research on Egypt is that of contemporary political thought. In the 1960s, numerous works on Arab political thought were produced, of which Nadav Safran's *Egypt in Search of Political Community* (1961) is an example. Since that time, virtually the only studies of Egyptian political thought in European languages have focused exclusively on Islamist formulations and thinkers, such as Leonard Binder's *Islamic Liberalism* (1988) or Emmanuel Sivan's *Radical Islam* (1985), although Fouad Ajami's *The Arab Predicament* (1981) and Derek Hopwood's *Egypt: Politics and Society 1945–1990* (1991) do contain relevant material. But a wide-ranging, in-depth study of contemporary Egyptian political thought is not available.

As the review of political analyses of Egypt will suggest, coverage of several other topics in European languages is also sketchy, as it is in the available Arabic-language materials, which tend to overlap subjects and methods of studies in European languages. The comparatively small amount of indigenous political science writing in Arabic (as distinct from journalistic analyses of contemporary political events) and its overlap with studies in European languages are caused by several factors. First among them may be that Egyptian political scientists operate in a quasi-authoritarian political environment. What they say and write can, and sometimes is, held against them. Not only does this discourage intellectual activity as a whole, but it influences the choice of topic and the manner in which that topic is analyzed.

Second, although the readership for Arabic journalistic accounts and analyses of Egyptian politics is sizeable, the audience for academic, political science analyses is limited. Although Egypt has more university departments of political science than any other Arab country, the discipline is still of insufficient size to support a flourishing academic publishing industry. Moreover, many of the country's leading social scientists resident in Egypt, including Mahmoud Abdel-Fadil, Ahmed Abdalla, Galal Amin, Ali E. Hillal Dessouki, Saad Eddin Ibrahim, Amani Kandil, and Fawzy Mansour, frequently write in English and by so doing reach a broader audience and encounter fewer restrictions on expression. The Strategic Studies Center of al-Ahram, which is the oldest and most prestigious think tank in Egypt and which employs a large number of political scientists, began in 1992 to publish its annual *Arab Strategic Report*, which contains valuable information and analyses of Egyptian politics, in English as well as Arabic. Many of that center's staff, including Usama al-Ghazali Harb, Muhammad El-Sayed Said, Mustafa Kamil al-Sayyid, El Sayed Yassin, and others, publish in Arabic and English, as does the newer Ibn Khaldun Center.

Third, Arabic- and European-language studies of Egyptian politics overlap because Egypt's political scientists are part of the global academic community. A large number have taken graduate degrees from Western institutions. The curricula taught in Egyptian political science courses are heavily influenced by Western, especially American, political science, and an increasing number of studies written in European languages are available in Arabic translations. Egyptian political scientists regularly interact with their European and North American colleagues. These interrelationships in turn lead to shared professional outlooks, research agendas, and methodologies.

This is not to suggest that there are no political science writings in Arabic on Egypt, or that such writings are not valuable. Indeed, signal contributions to our understanding of the relationships between social classes—especially large landowners—and Egyptian politics are Abd al-Azim Ramadan's *Class Conflict in Egypt, 1837–1952* (1978) (in Arabic) and *Social Conflict and Politics in Egypt* (1989) (in Arabic), and Asim Disuqi's *Large Landowners and Their Role in Egyptian Society, 1914–1952* (1975) (in Arabic). Other topics are also well covered in the Arabic literature. Nevertheless, the point here is that a review of political science writings on Egypt that by and large excludes Arabic materials does not misrepresent the general coverage of subjects or the approaches taken to them.

REFERENCES

Abdalla, Ahmed. 1985. *The Student Movement and National Politics in Egypt*. London: Al Saqi Books.

———. 1990. *The Army and Democracy in Egypt* (in Arabic). Cairo: Dar al Sina.

Abdel-Fadil, Mahmoud. 1975. *Development, Income Distribution, and Social Change in Rural Egypt (1952–1970): A Study in the Political Economy of Agrarian Transition*. Cambridge: Cambridge University Press.

———. 1980. *The Political Economy of Nasserism*. Cambridge: Cambridge University Press.

Abdel Kader, Soha. 1987. *Egyptian Women in a Changing Society, 1899–1987*. Boulder, CO: Lynne Rienner.

Abdel-Khalek, Gouda, and Robert Tignor, eds. 1982. *The Political Economy of Income Distribution in Egypt*. New York: Holmes and Meier.

Abdel-Malek, Anouar. 1968. *Egypt: Military Society*. New York: Vintage.

Adams, Richard H., Jr. 1986. *Development and Social Change in Rural Egypt*. Syracuse: Syracuse University Press.

Ahmed, Jamal Mohammed. 1960. *The Intellectual Origins of Egyptian Nationalism*. London: Oxford University Press.

Ajami, Fouad. 1981. *The Arab Predicament: Arab Political Thought and Practice since 1967*. Cambridge: Cambridge University Press.

Ansari, Hamied. 1986. *Egypt: The Stalled Society*. Albany: State University of New York Press.

Ayubi, Nazih N. 1980. *Bureaucracy and Politics in Contemporary Egypt*. London: Ithaca Press.

———. 1991a. *Political Islam: Religion and Politics in the Arab World*. New York: Routledge.

———. 1991b. *The State and Public Policies in Egypt since Sadat*. Reading, UK: Ithaca Press.

Ayubi, Shaheen. 1992. *Nasser and Sadat: Decision Making and Foreign Policy, 1970–1972*. Lanham, MD: University Press of America.

Badran, Margot. 1995. *Feminists, Islam, and Nation: Gender and the Making of Modern Egypt*. Princeton: Princeton University Press.

Baer, Gabriel. 1982. *Fellah and Townsman in the Middle East: Studies in Social History*. London: Frank Cass.

Baker, Raymond William. 1978. *Egypt's Uncertain Revolution under Nasser and Sadat*. Cambridge, MA: Harvard University Press.

———. 1990. *Sadat and After: Struggles for Egypt's Political Soul*. Cambridge, MA: Harvard University Press.

Barnett, Michael N. 1992. *Confronting the Costs of War: Military Power, State, and Society in Egypt and Israel*. Princeton: Princeton University Press.

Baron, Beth. 1994. *The Women's Awakening in Egypt: Culture, Society, and the Press*. New Haven: Yale University Press.

Beattie, Kirk J. 1994. *Egypt during the Nasser Years: Ideology, Politics, and Civil Society*. Boulder, CO: Westview Press.

Beeri, Eliezer. 1970. *Army Officers in Arab Politics and Society*. London: Praeger–Pall Mall.

Beinin, Joel. 1990. *Was the Red Flag Flying There? Marxist Politics and the Arab-Israeli Conflict in Egypt and Israel, 1948–1965*. Berkeley: University of California Press.

Beinin, Joel, and Zachary Lockman. 1987. *Workers on the Nile: Nationalism, Communism, Islam, and the Egyptian Working Class, 1882–1954*. Princeton: Princeton University Press.

Berger, Morroe. 1957. *Bureaucracy and Society in Modern Egypt: A Study of the Higher Civil Service*. Princeton: Princeton University Press.

———. 1970. *Islam in Egypt Today: Social and Political Aspects of Popular Religion*. Cambridge: Cambridge University Press.

Bianchi, Robert. 1986. "The Corporatization of the Egyptian Labor Movement." *Middle East Journal* 40:429–444.

———. 1989. *Unruly Corporatism: Associational Life in Twentieth-Century Egypt*. New York: Oxford University Press.

Binder, Leonard. 1964. *The Ideological Revolution in the Middle East*. New York: Wiley.

———. 1978. *In a Moment of Enthusiasm: Political Power and the Second Stratum in Egypt*. Chicago: University of Chicago Press.

———. 1988. *Islamic Liberalism*. Chicago: University of Chicago Press.

Botman, Selma. 1988. *The Rise of Egyptian Communism, 1939–1970*. Syracuse: Syracuse University Press.

Brown, Nathan J. 1990. *Peasant Politics in Modern Egypt: The Struggle against the State*. New Haven: Yale University Press.

Burke, Edmund, III, and Ira M. Lapidus, eds. 1988. *Islam, Politics, and Social Movements*. Berkeley: University of California Press.

Burns, William J. 1985. *Economic Aid and American Policy toward Egypt, 1955–1981*. Albany: State University of New York Press.

Burrill, Robert, and Abbas Kelidar. 1977. *Egypt: The Dilemmas of a Nation, 1970–1977*. Beverly Hills, CA: Sage Publications.

Cannon, Byron. 1988. *Politics of Law and the Courts in Nineteenth-Century Egypt*. Salt Lake City: University of Utah Press.

Cantori, Louis J., and Iliya Harik, eds. 1984. *Local Politics and Development in the Middle East*. Boulder, CO: Westview Press.

Carr, David William. 1979. *Foreign Investment and Development in Egypt*. New York: Praeger.

Carter, B.L. (Barbara Lynn). 1986. *The Copts in Egyptian Politics*. Dover, NH: Croom Helm.

Commander, Simon. 1987. *The State and Agricultural Development in Egypt since 1973*. London: Ithaca Press.

Cooper, Mark N. 1982. *The Transformation of Egypt*. Baltimore: Johns Hopkins University Press.

Copeland, Miles. 1969. *The Game of Nations: The Amorality of Power Politics*. New York: Simon and Schuster.

Cudsi, A., and Ali E. Hillal Dessouki, eds. 1981. *Islam and Power*. Baltimore: Johns Hopkins University Press.

Davis, Eric. 1983. *Challenging Colonialism: Bank Misr and Egyptian Industrialization, 1920–1941*. Princeton: Princeton University Press.

Dawisha, Adeed. 1976. *Egypt in the Arab World: The Elements of Foreign Policy*. London: Macmillan.

Deeb, Marius. 1979. *Party Politics in Egypt: The Wafd and Its Rivals, 1919–1939*. London: Ithaca Press.

Dekmejian, R. Hrair. 1971. *Egypt under Nasir: A Study in Political Dynamics*. Albany: State University of New York Press.

———. 1975. *Patterns of Political Leadership: Egypt, Israel, Lebanon*. Albany: State University of New York Press.

———. 1982. "Egypt and Turkey: The Military in the Background," In Roman Kolkowicz and Andrzej Korbonski, eds., *Soldiers, Peasants, and Bureaucrats*. New York: Routledge.

———. 1985. *Islam in Revolution*. Syracuse: Syracuse University Press.

Denoeux, Guilain. 1993. *Urban Unrest in the Middle East: A Comparative Study of Informal Networks in Egypt, Iran, and Lebanon*. Albany: State University of New York Press.

Dessouki, Ali E. Hillal, ed. 1978. "Democracy in Egypt: Problems and Prospects." *Cairo Papers in Social Science* 1, no. 2. Cairo: American University in Cairo Press.

———, ed. 1982. *Islamic Resurgence in the Arab World*. New York: Praeger.

Disuqi, Asim. 1975. *Large Landowners and Their Role in Egyptian Society, 1914–1952* (in Arabic). Cairo: Dar al-Thiqafa al Gadida.

Dwyer, Kevin. 1991. *Arab Voices: The Human Rights Debate in the Middle East*. London: Routledge.

Eccel, A. Chris. 1984. *Egypt, Islam, and Social Change: Al-Azhar in Conflict and Accommodation.* Berlin: Klaus Schwarz.

Egyptian Organization for Human Rights. 1993. *The Condition of Human Rights in Egypt.* Cairo: Egyptian Organization for Human Rights.

Eveland, Wilbur Crane. 1980. *Ropes of Sand.* New York: W. W. Norton.

Fahmy, Ismail. 1983. *Negotiating for Peace in the Middle East.* Baltimore: Johns Hopkins University Press.

Farid, Abdel Majid. 1994. *Nasser: The Final Years.* Reading, UK: Ithaca Press.

Gaffney, Patrick D. 1994. *The Prophet's Pulpit: Islamic Preaching in Contemporary Egypt.* Berkeley: University of California Press.

El-Gamasy, Mohamed Abdel Ghani. 1993. *The October War: Memoirs of Field Marshal El-Gamasy of Egypt.* Cairo: American University in Cairo Press.

Gillespie, Kate. 1984. *The Tripartite Relationship: Government, Foreign Investors, and Local Investors during Egypt's Economic Opening.* New York: Praeger.

Gilsenan, Michael D. 1973. *Saint and Sufi in Modern Egypt.* London: Oxford University Press.

Goldberg, Ellis. 1986. *Tinker, Tailor, and Textile Worker.* Berkeley: University of California Press.

———. 1992. ''The Foundations of State-Labor Relations in Contemporary Egypt.'' *Comparative Politics* 24, no. 2 (January): 147–161.

Gomaa, Salwa. 1985. *Egyptian Diplomacy in the 1970s: A Study in a Leadership Issue* (in Arabic). Beirut: Center for Arab Unity Studies.

Gordon, Joel. 1991. *Nasser's Blessed Movement: Egypt's Free Officers and the July Revolution.* New York: Oxford University Press.

Guenena, Nemat. 1986. ''The Jihad: An Islamic Alternative in Egypt.'' *Cairo Papers in Social Science* 9, no. 2. Cairo: American University in Cairo Press.

Haddad, George Meri. 1965–1973. *Revolutions and Military Rule in the Middle East.* New York: R. Speller.

Haim, Sylvia G., ed. 1962. *Arab Nationalism.* Berkeley: University of California Press.

Halpern, Manfred. 1963. *The Politics of Social Change in the Middle East and North Africa.* Princeton: Princeton University Press.

Handoussa, Heba, and Gillian Potter, eds. 1991. *Employment and Structural Adjustment: Egypt in the 1990s.* Cairo: American University in Cairo Press.

Hansen, Bent. 1991. *The Political Economy of Poverty, Equity, and Growth: Egypt and Turkey.* New York: Oxford University Press.

Hansen, Bent, and Girgis A. Marzouk. 1965. *Development and Economic Policy in the UAR.* Amsterdam: North-Holland.

Hansen, Bent, and Karim Nashashibi. 1975. *Foreign Trade Regimes and Economic Development.* New York: Columbia University Press.

Harik, Iliya. 1974. *The Political Mobilization of Peasants.* Bloomington: Indiana University Press.

Harik, Iliya, and Denis J. Sullivan, eds. 1992. *Privatization and Liberalization in the Middle East.* Bloomington: Indiana University Press.

Harris, Christina Phelps. 1964. *Nationalism and Revolution in Egypt: The Role of the Muslim Brotherhood.* The Hague: Mouton.

Harris, Lillian Craig, eds. 1988. *Egypt: Internal Challenges and Regional Stability.* London: Routledge and Kegan Paul.

Heikal, Muhammad Hassanein. 1972. *Nasser: The Cairo Documents*. London: New English Library.

————. 1975. *The Road to Ramadan*. New York: Ballantine Books.

————. 1978. *The Sphinx and the Commissar*. London: Collins.

————. 1983. *Autumn of Fury: The Assassination of Sadat*. New York: Random House.

————. 1987. *Cutting the Lion's Tail: Suez through Egyptian Eyes*. New York: Arbor House.

————. 1990. *1967: Al-Infijar* (in Arabic). Cairo: Markaz al-Ahram li-l-Targama wa-l-Nashr.

Hill, Enid. 1979. *Mahkama! Studies in the Egyptian Legal System*. London: Ithaca Press.

————. 1987. *Al-Sanhuri and Islamic Law*. Cairo Papers in Social Science. Cairo: American University in Cairo Press.

————. 1990. "Law and Courts in Egypt: Recent Issues and Events Concerning Islamic Law." In Ibrahim M. Oweiss, ed. *The Political Economy of Contemporary Egypt*. Washington, DC: Center for Contemporary Arab Studies, Georgetown University.

Hinnebusch, Raymond A. 1988. *Egyptian Politics under Sadat: The Post-populist Development of an Authoritarian-modernizing State*. Boulder, CO: Lynne Rienner.

Hirst, David, and Irene Beeson. 1981. *Sadat*. London: Faber and Faber.

Hopkins, Nicholas S. 1987. *Agrarian Transformation in Egypt*. Boulder, CO: Westview Press.

Hopwood, Derek. 1991. *Egypt: Politics and Society, 1945–1990*. London: Allen and Unwin.

Human Rights Report. Annual. Washington, DC: U.S. Department of State, Bureau of Public Affairs.

Hussein, Mahmoud. 1973. *Class Conflict in Egypt, 1945–1970*. New York: Monthly Review Press.

Ibrahim, Saad Eddin. 1980. "Anatomy of Egypt's Militant Groups." *International Journal of Middle East Studies*, 12 (December): 423–453.

Ikram, Khalid. 1980. *Egypt: Economic Management in a Period of Transition*. Baltimore: Johns Hopkins University Press.

Ismael, Tareq Y., and Rifaat El-Said. 1988. *The Communist Movement in Egypt, 1920–1988*. Syracuse: Syracuse University Press.

Israeli, Raphael. 1985. *Man of Defiance: A Political Biography of Anwar al Sadat*. London: Weidenfeld and Nicolson.

Issawi, Charles. 1963. *Egypt in Revolution: An Economic Analysis*. London: Oxford University Press.

Kandil, Amani. 1995. *Civil Society in the Arab World*. Washington, DC: Civicus.

Kepel, Gilles. 1985. *The Prophet and Pharoah: Muslim Extremism in Egypt*. London: Al Saqi Books.

Kerr, Malcolm. 1962. "The Emergence of a Socialist Ideology in Egypt." *Middle East Journal* 16: 127–144.

————. 1965. *The Arab Cold War, 1958–1964: A Study of Ideology in Politics*. London: Oxford University Press.

————. 1966. *Islamic Reform: The Political and Legal Theories of Muhammad Abduh and Rashid Rida*. Berkeley: University of California Press.

Kerr, Malcolm, and El Sayed Yassin, eds. 1982. *Rich and Poor States in the Middle East*. Boulder, CO: Westview Press.

Korany, Bahgat, and Ali E. Hillal Dessouki. 1991. *The Foreign Policies of Arab States: The Challenge of Change*. 2d ed. Boulder, CO: Westview Press.

Kramer, Gudrun. 1989. *The Jews in Modern Egypt, 1914–1952*. Seattle: University of Washington Press.

Lacouture, Jean. 1971. *Nasser*. Paris: Seuil.

Laskier, Michael M. 1992. *The Jews of Egypt, 1920–1970: In the Midst of Zionism, Anti-Semitism, and the Middle East Conflict*. New York: New York University Press.

Lesch, Ann Mosely, and Mark Tessler. 1989. *Israel, Egypt, and the Palestinians: From Camp David to the Intifada*. Bloomington: Indiana University Press.

Lippman, Thomas W. 1989. *Egypt after Nasser: Sadat, Peace, and the Mirage of Prosperity*. New York: Paragon House.

Lorenz, Joseph P. 1990. *Egypt and the Arabs: Foreign Policy and the Search for National Identity*. Boulder, CO: Westview Press.

Mabro, Robert. 1974. *The Egyptian Economy, 1952–1972*. Oxford: Clarendon Press.

Macleod, Arlene Elowe. 1993. *Accommodating Protest: Working Women, the New Veiling, and Change in Cairo*. New York: Columbia University Press.

Mansfield, Peter. 1965. *Nasser's Egypt*. Baltimore: Penguin Books.

Mansour, Fawzy. 1992. *The Arab World: Nation, State, and Democracy*. London: Zed Books.

Mayfield, James B. 1971. *Rural Politics in Nasser's Egypt: A Quest for Legitimacy*. Austin: University of Texas Press.

———. 1996. *Local Government in Egypt: Structure, Process, and the Challenges of Reform*. Cairo: American University in Cairo Press.

McDermott, Anthony. 1988. *Egypt from Nasser to Mubarak: A Flawed Revolution*. London: Croom Helm.

Meyer, Gail E. 1980. *Egypt and the United States: The Formative Years*. Rutherford, NJ: Fairleigh Dickinson University Press.

Mitchell, Richard P. 1969. *The Society of the Muslim Brothers*. London: Oxford University Press.

Mitchell, Timothy. 1988. *Colonising Egypt*. Cambridge, MA: Cambridge University Press.

Moore, Clement H. 1980. *Images of Development: Egyptian Engineers in Search of Industry*. Cambridge, MA: MIT Press.

El-Naggar, Said, ed. 1987. *Adjustment Policies and Development Strategies in the Arab World*. Washington, DC: International Monetary Fund.

———, ed. 1989. *Privatization and Structural Adjustment in the Arab Countries*. Washington, DC: International Monetary Fund.

———, ed. 1990. *Investment Policies in the Arab Countries*. Washington, D.C.: International Monetary Fund.

Nasser, Munir K. 1979. *Press, Politics, and Power: Egypt's Heikal and Al-Ahram*. Ames: Iowa State University Press.

———. 1990. *Egyptian Mass Media under Nasser and Sadat: Two Models of Press Management and Control*. Columbia, SC: Association for Education in Journalism and Mass Communication.

Nelson, Cynthia. 1996. *Doria Shafik, Egyptian Feminist: A Woman Apart*. Gainesville: University Press of Florida.

Niblock, Tim, and Emma Murphy, eds. 1993. *Economic and Political Liberalization in the Middle East*. London: British Academic Press.

Nutting, Anthony. 1972. *Nasser*. London: Constable.

O'Brien, Patrick. 1966. *The Revolution in Egypt's Economic System: From Private Enterprise to Socialism, 1952–1965*. London: Oxford University Press.

Oweiss, Ibrahim, ed. 1990. *The Political Economy of Contemporary Egypt*. Washington, DC: Center for Contemporary Arab Studies, Georgetown University.

Palmer, Monte, Ali Leila, and El Sayed Yassin. 1988. *The Egyptian Bureaucracy*. Syracuse: Syracuse University Press.

Parker, Richard. 1993. *The Politics of Miscalculation in the Middle East*. Bloomington: Indiana University Press.

Perlmutter, Amos. 1974. *Egypt: The Praetorian State*. New Brunswick, NJ: Transaction Books.

Perrault, Gilles. 1987. *A Man Apart: The Life of Henri Curiel*. London: Zed Books.

Posusney, Marsha Pripstein. 1992. ''Labor as an Obstacle to Privatization: The Case of Egypt.'' In Iliya Harik and Denis J. Sullivan, eds., *Privatization and Liberalization in the Middle East*. Bloomington: Indiana University Press.

Qasim, Amin (1863–1908). 1992. *The Liberation of Women: A Document in the History of Egyptian Feminism*. Trans. Samiha Sidhom Peterson. Cairo: American University in Cairo Press.

———. 1995. *The New Woman: A Document in the Early Debate on Egyptian Feminism*. Trans. Samiha Sidhom Peterson. Cairo: American University in Cairo Press.

Quandt, William B., ed. 1988. *The Middle East: Ten Years after Camp David*. Washington, DC: Brookings Institution.

———. 1990. *The United States and Egypt*. Washington, DC: Brookings Institution.

Quraishi, Zaheer M. 1967. *Liberal Nationalism in Egypt: Rise and Fall of the Wafd Party*. Allahabad: Kitab Mahal.

Radwan, Hanan Hamdy. 1994. ''Democratization in Rural Egypt: A Study of the Village Local Popular Council.'' *Cairo Papers in Social Science* 17, no. 1 (Spring).

Radwan, Samir, and Eddy Lee. 1986. *Agrarian Change in Egypt: An Anatomy of Rural Poverty*. London: Croom Helm.

Ramadan, Abd al-Azim. 1978. *Class Conflict in Egypt, 1837–1952* (in Arabic). Cairo: al-Muassassat al-Arabiyya li-l-Dirasat wa-l-Nashr.

———. 1989. *Social Conflict and Politics in Egypt* (in Arabic). Cairo: al-Muassassat al-Arabiyya li-l-Dirasat wa-l-Nashr.

Reid, Donald M. 1981. *Lawyers and Politics in the Arab World, 1880–1960*. Minneapolis: Bibliotheca Islamica.

———. 1990. *Cairo University and the Making of Modern Egypt*. Cambridge: Cambridge University Press.

Rejwan, Nissim. 1974. *Nasserist Ideology: Its Exponents and Critics*. New York: John Wiley and Sons.

Riad, Hassan. 1964. *L'Egypte nasserienne*. Paris: Editions de Minuit.

Richards, Alan. 1982. *Egypt's Agricultural Development, 1800–1980: Technical and Social Change*. Boulder, CO: Westview Press.

Richards, Alan, and John Waterbury. 1990. *A Political Economy of the Middle East*. Boulder, CO: Westview Press.

Rivlin, Paul. 1985. *The Dynamics of Economic Policy Making in Egypt*. New York: Praeger.

Rubin, Barry. 1990. *Islamic Fundamentalism in Egyptian Politics*. New York: St. Martin's Press.

Rugh, Andrea. 1984. *Family in Contemporary Egypt*. Syracuse: Syracuse University Press.

Sadat, Jihan. 1987. *A Woman of Egypt*. New York: Simon and Schuster.

Sadawi, Nawal. 1980. *The Hidden Face of Eve: Women in the Arab World*. London: Zed Books.

————. 1983. *Woman at Point Zero*. London: Zed Books.

————. 1985. *God Dies by the Nile*. London: Zed Books.

————. 1986. *Memoirs from the Women's Prison*. London: Women's Press.

————. 1991. *Searching*. London: Zed Books.

Sadowski, Yahya M. 1991. *Political Vegetables? Businessman and Bureaucrat in the Development of Egyptian Agriculture*. Washington, DC: Brookings Institution.

Safran, Nadav. 1961. *Egypt in Search of Political Community*. Cambridge, MA: Harvard University Press.

St. John, Robert. 1960. *The Boss*. London: Arthur Barber.

al-Sayyid, Mustafa Kamil. 1983. *Society and Politics in Egypt: The Role of Interest Groups in the Egyptian Political System* (in Arabic). Cairo: Dar al-Mustaqbal al-Arabi.

al-Sayyid-Marsot, Afaf Lutfi. 1977. *Egypt's Liberal Experiment, 1922–1936*. Berkeley: University of California Press.

Shaked, Haim, and Itamar Rabinovich, eds. 1980. *The Middle East and the United States: Perceptions and Policies*. New Brunswick, NJ: Transaction Books.

Shamir, Shimon, ed. 1995. *Egypt from Monarchy to Republic: A Reassessment of Revolution and Change*. Boulder, CO: Westview Press.

Sharawi, Huda. 1987. *Harem Years: The Memoirs of an Egyptian Feminist, 1879–1924*. Translated, edited, and introduced by Margot Badran. New York: Feminist Press at the City University of New York.

El-Shazli, Saad. 1980. *The Crossing of the Suez*. San Francisco: American Mideast Research.

Shoukri, Ghali. 1981. *Egypt: Portrait of a President, 1971–1981*. London: Zed Press.

Singerman, Diane. 1995. *Avenues of Participation: Families, Politics, and Networks in Urban Quarters of Cairo*. Princeton: Princeton University Press.

Singerman, Diane, and Hoodfor Homa. 1996. *Development, Change, and Gender in Cairo: A View from the Household*. Bloomington: Indiana University Press.

Sivan, Emmanuel. 1985. *Radical Islam: Medieval Theology and Modern Politics*. New Haven: Yale University Press.

Springborg, Robert. 1982. *Family, Power, and Politics in Egypt: Sayed Bey Marei—His Clan, Clients, and Cohorts*. Philadelphia: University of Pennsylvania Press.

————. 1989. *Mubarak's Egypt: Fragmentation of the Political Order*. Boulder, CO: Westview Press.

Stephens, Robert. 1971. *Nasser: A Political Biography*. London: Allen Lane.

Sullivan, Denis J. 1994. *Private Voluntary Organizations in Egypt: Islamic Development, Private Initiative, and State Control*. Gainesville: University Press of Florida.

Sullivan, Earl L. 1986. *Women in Egyptian Public Life*. Syracuse: Syracuse University Press.

Talhami, Ghada Hashem. 1992. *Palestine and Egyptian National Identity*. New York: Praeger.

————. 1996. *The Mobilization of Muslim Women in Egypt*. Gainesville: University Press of Florida.

Telhami, Shibley. 1990. *Power and Leadership in International Bargaining: The Path to the Camp David Accords*. New York: Columbia University Press.

Tignor, Robert. 1984. *State, Private Enterprise, and Economic Change in Egypt, 1918–1952*. Princeton: Princeton University Press.

———. 1989. *Egyptian Textiles and British Capital, 1930–1956*. Cairo: American University in Cairo Press.

Tripp, Charles, ed. 1993. *Contemporary Egypt: Through Egyptian Eyes*. London: Routledge.

Tripp, Charles, and Roger Owen, eds. 1989. *Egypt under Mubarak*. London: Routledge.

Tucker, Judith. 1985. *Women in Nineteenth-Century Egypt*. Cambridge: Cambridge University Press.

Vatikiotis, P. J. 1961. *The Egyptian Army in Politics*. Bloomington: Indiana University Press.

———, ed. 1968. *Egypt since the Revolution*. New York: Praeger.

———. 1978. *Nasser and His Generation*. London: Croom Helm.

———. 1991. *The History of Modern Egypt*. Baltimore: Johns Hopkins University Press.

Waterbury, John. 1978. *Egypt: Burdens of the Past, Options for the Future*. Bloomington: Indiana University Press.

———. 1979. *Hydropolitics of the Nile Valley*. Syracuse: Syracuse University Press.

———. 1983. *The Egypt of Nasser and Sadat: The Political Economy of Two Regimes*. Princeton: Princeton University Press.

———. 1993. *Exposed to Innumerable Delusions: Public Enterprise and State Power in Egypt, India, Mexico, and Turkey*. New York: Cambridge University Press.

Weinbaum, Marvin G. 1986. *Egypt and the Politics of U.S. Economic Aid*. Boulder, CO: Westview Press.

Wheelock, Keith. 1960. *Nasser's New Egypt*. New York: Praeger.

Woodward, Peter. 1992. *Nasser*. London: Longman.

Zaalouk, Malak. 1989. *Power, Class, and Foreign Capital in Egypt: The Rise of the New Bourgeoisie*. London: Zed Books.

Zahran, Gamal. 1987. *Egypt's Foreign Policy, 1970–1981* (in Arabic). Cairo: Madbouli Bookshop.

Ziadeh, Farhat J. 1968. *Lawyers, the Rule of Law, and Liberalism in Egypt*. Stanford, CA: Hoover Institution.

Zuhur, Sherifa. 1992. *Revealing Reveiling: Islamist Gender Ideology in Contemporary Egypt*. Albany: State University of New York Press.

THE GULF ARAB STATES: BAHRAIN, KUWAIT, OMAN, QATAR, AND THE UNITED ARAB EMIRATES

Malcolm C. Peck

Significant numbers of scholarly published works on the Gulf Arab states, Bahrain, Kuwait, Oman, Qatar, and the United Arab Emirates, have begun to appear only in the past few years. Indeed, it was not until recently that this area emerged as a field of serious academic study, well after scholars in considerable numbers had undertaken research and writing on the other countries of the Middle East. Since the ending of the United Kingdom's protector status in the Gulf states (1961 in Kuwait, 1971 in the other states), the conduct of scholarly research there has become somewhat easier than previously. The growth of universities and the development of national documentation and research centers in these countries have created a more receptive atmosphere for visiting scholars. There are, moreover, growing contacts between indigenous scholars and colleagues elsewhere who share interests in the same Gulf subjects. Nevertheless, conservative social and political sensitivities still pose obstacles to the pursuit of research in the Gulf states, and this continues to constrain serious scholarship on this part of the Middle East.

Dramatic events in the Persian/Arab Gulf area, beginning with the oil-price rises of the 1970s, have generated a considerable quantity of journalistic writing, much if not most of it of dubious quality. Nevertheless, some of the better early sources on the Gulf states were journalists' books, together with the writing of former diplomats and oilmen. A great deal of this was and continues to be of significant value as a source of information and insight on the societies, political systems, and economies of these states. However, the general quality of writing on this area has been significantly enhanced by two developments in the field of Middle East studies, particularly in the United States. First, scholars who had established their credentials through work on other parts of the Middle East turned their attention to the Gulf area when it became more feasible to do so.

Second, a new generation has emerged of young scholars who have conducted significant doctoral and postdoctoral studies in the area. The work of the last group figures prominently in the survey of scholarship falling broadly under the heading "political science" that follows.

COUNTRY AND COMPARATIVE STUDIES

Much of what has been written on the Gulf Arab states falls under the rubric of country and comparative studies, and the bulk of it dates from the past decade. The most systematic coverage is provided in the volumes published as part of the Westview Press series Nations of the Contemporary Middle East, edited by Bernard Reich and David E. Long. The volumes covering Bahrain, Kuwait, Oman, and the United Arab Emirates (UAE) have appeared. Each study adheres to a general format whereby the geographic setting, historical background, society, culture, economy, political institutions, and external relations are treated concisely. The studies of Bahrain and Oman, *Bahrain: The Modernization of Autocracy* (1989) by Fred H. Lawson and *Oman: The Modernization of the Sultanate* (1987) by Calvin H. Allen, Jr., emphasize the history and modern evolution of these two states. Jill Crystal's *Kuwait: The Transformation of an Oil State* (1992) offers probing insights into the structure and dynamics of that country's society and politics. The final chapter examines the aftermath of the Iraqi invasion of August 1990. Malcolm C. Peck's *The United Arab Emirates: A Venture in Unity* (1986) carries UAE developments to the mid-1980s. *Perspectives of the United Arab Emirates*, edited by Ibrahim Al Abed and Edmund Ghareeb, provides a broad update on UAE developments over the country's first quarter-century. Though somewhat dated, Rosemarie Said Zahlan's *The Creation of Qatar* (1979) serves to fill the gap in the Westview series. Other country studies that may usefully be consulted are Donald Hawley, *Oman and Its Renaissance*, 4th revised edition (1987); Peter Mansfield, *Kuwait: Vanguard of the Gulf* (1990); Jeffrey B. Nugent and Theodore Thomas, editors, *Bahrain and the Gulf: Past Perspectives and Alternative Futures* (1985); and Ian Skeet, *Oman: Politics and Development* (1992), which provides a broader survey than the title might suggest. The March 1996 issue of *Middle East Policy* published an edited transcript of an October 12, 1995, symposium on Oman, "Contemporary Oman and U.S.-Oman Relations," reflecting the insights of a senior U.S. government official, a leading journalist, and several scholars. Joseph A. Kechichian's *Oman and the World: The Emergence of an Independent Foreign Policy* (1995) is an extended treatment of Oman's relations with its neighbors and the wider world.

Several single-volume works survey the Gulf Arab states in briefer compass. A solid, fact-filled treatment that devotes a lengthy chapter to each state is *Persian Gulf States: Country Studies* (1994), edited by Helen Chapin Metz. The extended introductory chapter by Laraine Newhouse Carter to the earlier (1984) edition of this work remains an excellent, informative overview. More succinct treatments of the Gulf Arab states are found in Rosemarie Said Zahlan's *The*

Making of the Modern Gulf States (1989) and in *The Turbulent Gulf: People, Politics, and Power* (1992) by Liesl Graz, a well-informed journalistic observer. A general reference work that includes brief chapters on each of the Gulf Arab states is the *Historical Dictionary of the Gulf Arab States* (1997) by Malcolm Peck.

A number of earlier works remain useful sources of information and insight. John Duke Anthony's *Arab States of the Lower Gulf: People, Politics, Petroleum* (1975) provides an in-depth analysis of the internal political dynamics of Bahrain, Qatar, and the seven member states of the UAE that retains much of its validity. Frauke Heard-Bey's revised edition of *From Trucial States to United Arab Emirates* (1996) is a compendious work that is especially strong in its delineation of traditional, tribal society, the preoil economy, and the events that preceded the UAE's postoil transformation. The second volume of *La Péninsule Arabique d'aujourd'hui* (1982), edited by Paul Bonnenfant, brings together contributions mostly by French scholars and covers the five Gulf Arab states as well as Yemen and Saudi Arabia. For each state the geographical and historical background is sketched; contemporary economic, social, and political developments are analyzed; and useful chronologies are included. *The Persian Gulf: A General Survey* (1980), Alvin J. Cottrell, general editor, is a large, ambitious, and rather eclectic collection of essays with much useful material on the geography, history, society, and culture of the Gulf states.

Two significant recent comparative studies are Jill Crystal's *Oil and Politics in the Gulf: Rulers and Merchants in Kuwait and Qatar* (1990b) and F. Gregory Gause III's *Oil Monarchies: Domestic and Security Challenges in the Arab Gulf States* (1994). These books by leading younger scholars probe the phenomenon of the rentier state. Crystal's study contrasts the ways in which two Gulf states developed with oil wealth, looking especially at the interaction of powerful new economic forces and traditional political structures. Gause reexamines traditional politics in the Gulf states (his survey includes Saudi Arabia, the only one of the six states ruled by a king), offering a subtle analysis of the interaction of Islam, tribalism, oil wealth, domestic impulses for greater political participation, and external threats.

DEMOGRAPHIC ISSUES

Colbert C. Held's enormously informative work, *Middle East Patterns: Places, Peoples, and Politics*, 2d edition (1994), provides superb overviews of the Gulf Arab states from the perspective of physical and cultural geography. The *Gazetteer of Arabia: A Geographical and Tribal History of the Arabian Peninsula*, volume 1, *A–E* (1979), consists mostly of reproduced material written early in the century, supplemented by more recent information provided by the editor, Sheila Scoville.

Rapid urbanization is a leading demographic feature of all the Gulf Arab states and a profoundly important element of their modernization process with major current and future implications for society and government. It has received scant scholarly attention, however, as most scholarship in the field has been devoted to the development of Arab cities of premodern origin. A good starting point among extant sources is Michael E. Bonine, "The Urbanization of the Persian Gulf Nations," in Cottrell et al., *The Persian Gulf States*. This chapter covers Iran and Iraq as well as the five smaller Gulf Arab states. Another study that covers these states is N. C. Grill, *Urbanisation in the Arabian Peninsula* (1984). A classic study of Gulf urbanization is Saba George Shiber, *The Kuwait Urbanization* (1964). The author, a distinguished city planner, examines the challenge of preserving a traditional Gulf settlement's aesthetic and cultural heritage while accommodating rapid, oil-fuelled, urban growth. An interesting study on the way that development of Gulf oil resources has affected urbanization is *Work Camps and Company Towns: Settlement Patterns and the Gulf Oil Industry* (1987) by Ian Seccombe and Richard Lawless.

The amassing of sudden recent wealth in the Gulf Arab states has led to the immigration of great numbers of workers from other countries, primarily Middle Eastern and South and East Asian, to perform tasks for which adequate numbers of trained or willing natives are lacking. As much as 90 percent of the labor force in Kuwait, Qatar, and the UAE, nearly half in Bahrain, and a considerable minority in Oman is of foreign origin. Thus the phenomenon of immigrant labor is a very major demographic consideration in these states, as well as a significant economic, cultural, and political issue for the countries from which the expatriate workers come. An important book on the subject is Ismail Serageldin et al., *Manpower and International Migration in the Middle East and North Africa* (1983), which devotes considerable attention to the Gulf Arab states. Serageldin and others contributed articles to a special issue of the *Middle East Journal* (1984) on the same subject. Economic, political, security, and cultural aspects of the expatriate labor situation are thoughtfully examined in Roger Webster, "Human Resources in the Gulf" (1986). Several works deal with the conditions, attitudes, and expectations of the expatriates and their families. Among them are two studies of the Palestinians in Kuwait, the largest Arab expatriate community in the smaller Gulf Arab states, Shafeeq N. Ghabra, *Palestinians in Kuwait: The Family and the Politics of Survival* (1987), and Ann Lesch, "Palestinians in Kuwait" (1991). The latter looks at the plight of the Palestinians after the invasion by Iraq. Two articles dealing with shifting patterns in immigrant labor in Kuwait, reflected elsewhere in the Gulf as well, are N. Shah et al, "Asian Women Workers in Kuwait" (1991), and N. Shaw and S. al-Qudsi, "The Changing Characteristics of Migrant Workers in Kuwait" (1989). The Gulf states have increased their reliance on Asian workers while decreasing the numbers of Palestinian and other Arab workers, a development with important repercussions for the labor-exporting countries. This subject is treated in Rashid Amjad, editor, *To the Gulf and Back: Studies on the Economic Impact of Asian Labour Migration* (1989), and Jonathan S. Addleton, *Undermining the Centre: The Gulf Migration and Pakistan* (1992). Georges Sabah examines the expatriate worker phenomenon broadly in "Immigrants in the Gulf Arab Countries: Sojourners or Settlers?" (1990). The case of significant labor migration from a single Asian country to the Gulf is examined at length in *Labour Migration to the Middle East: From Sri Lanka to the Gulf*, edited by F. Eelens, T. Schampers, and J. D. Speckmann.

Although most of the borders of the Gulf Arab states have been determined and demarcated, at least provisionally, the matter of interstate boundaries remains a sensitive and important issue. Its potential for causing interstate violence was evident when Iraq invaded Kuwait at least in part because of the latter's refusal to consider adjustments in their common border, which restricts Iraqi access to the Gulf. Recent works by Richard N. Schofield on national borders in this area are the leading sources, particularly two edited volumes, *Arabian Boundary Disputes* (1992) and *Territorial Foundations of the Gulf States* (1994a). The second book examines in considerable depth the role of the British in establishing state boundaries in the region and includes a masterful overview essay by the editor. Schofield has also provided an excellent treatment of the Iraq-Kuwait boundary issue in a monograph, *Kuwait and Iraq: Historical Claims and Territorial Disputes* (1993), as has David H. Finnie in his *Shifting Lines in the Sand: Kuwait's Elusive Frontier with Iraq* (1992). On the UAE-Iran dispute over the islands in the southern Gulf, Schofield's *Unfinished Business: Iran, the UAE, Abu Musa, and the Tunbs* (1994b) provides the leading source.

LEADERS AND LEADERSHIP

All of the rulers of the Gulf Arab states are profiled in Bernard Reich, editor, *Political Leaders of the Contemporary Middle East and North Africa* (1990). Jill Crystal contributed the chapter on Kuwait's ruler, Jabir Al-Ahmad Al-Sabah; Steven R. Dorr wrote the piece on Khalifa ibn Hamad Al-Thani, ruler of Qatar; Fred Lawson is the author of the chapter on Isa bin Sulman Al-Khalifah, ruler of Bahrain; Malcolm C. Peck provided the biography of Zayed bin Sultan Al-Nuhayyan, ruler of Abu Dhabi and president of the UAE; and John E. Peterson wrote the chapter on Sultan Qabus bin Said Al-Bu Said of Oman. In *Arab Personalities in Politics* (1981) Majid Khadduri provides a substantial chapter on Zayed bin Sultan Al-Nuhayyan. A semiofficial, full-length biography of the same subject is *The Leader and the March* by Hamdi Tammam, a journalist who served as director of press affairs for Khalifa bin Zayed Al-Nuhayyan, crown prince of Abu Dhabi, and who was for many years close to Shaikh Zayed. Useful for background information on Kuwait is Alan Rush's monograph *Al-Sabah: History and Genealogy of Kuwait's Ruling Family, 1752–1987*. In addition to biographical and genealogical literature, the works cited in this chapter under "Country and Comparative Studies" and "Government Institutions and Political Development" should be consulted for descriptions and analyses of leaders and the nature of leadership in the Gulf Arab states.

GOVERNMENT INSTITUTIONS AND POLITICAL DEVELOPMENT

Government institutions and political development in the Gulf Arab states have not received extensive treatment largely because of official sensitivities that limit serious scholarly inquiry. Moreover, the absence of political parties, at least in the formal sense, and the continued existence of traditional forms of government have tended to exclude political developments in the Gulf Arab states from consideration in the general scholarly literature on comparative government. Nevertheless, the structure and dynamics of these states' governments and politics are undergoing interesting and consequential changes that have been surveyed in a number of thoughtful and informative studies.

A good general starting point is the sections devoted to domestic political matters in the books previously cited under "Country and Comparative Studies." Jacqueline and Tareq Ismael provide a helpful overview of the Gulf governments in the chapter "Comparative Governments: The Arabian Peninsula," in Tareq Y. Ismael and Jacqueline Ismael, eds., *Politics and Government in the Middle East* (1991). *Society and State in the Gulf and Arab Peninsula: A Different Perspective* (1990) by Khaldoun Hasan al-Naqeeb, translated by L. M. Kenny, provides a useful analysis of the process whereby oil wealth has led to the development of authoritarian political structures in the Gulf Arab states and engendered new opposition groups. John E. Peterson writes with keen insight of significant adaptations that the Gulf Arab state governments have made to attempt to maintain their legitimacy and effectiveness in evolving from traditional to modern societies in *The Arab Gulf States: Steps toward Political Participation* (1988).

Several books and articles explore the development of representative or protorepresentative political institutions in the Gulf Arab states. Abdo Baaklini discusses the first phase of Kuwait's experience with its National Assembly in "Legislatures in the Gulf Area: The Experience of Kuwait, 1961–1976" (1982), while Dale Eickelman surveys Oman's first step toward representative government in "Kings and People: Oman's State Consultative Council," (1984). In this area there are several examples of indigenous Gulf scholarship. One is A. al-Baz, "Forms of Parliamentary Systems between Traditionalism and Modernization: An Applied Contrastive Study of the Constitutions of Kuwait, the GCC States, and Egypt" (in Arabic) (1989). Another is Shafeeq Ghabra's "Voluntary Associations in Kuwait: The Foundation of a New System" (1991), which offers a penetrating look at the way in which the Iraqi occupation and subsequent liberation of Kuwait politicized the population, enhancing the role of Islamic and secular opposition forces in parliament and that of democratizing associational groups. In "Democratization in a Middle Eastern State: Kuwait, 1993" (1994), Ghabra presents a thoughtful analysis of the October 1992 election in Kuwait and the way in which its aftermath reflects the positions of the opposition forces that won the majority of seats. His article maintains that the situation in Kuwait represents a "transition from semi-authoritarian rule to semi-democratic rule." In "The Politics of Participation in the Gulf Cooperation Council States: The Omani Consultative Council" (1996), Abdullah Juma al-Haj examines the council established in 1991 as an attempt to introduce political participation to Omanis. Finally, Jamal al-Suwaidi makes a thoughtful contribution to the discussion of prospects for democratic forms of government in the Gulf Arab states (and the wider Arab world) in "Arab and Western Conceptions of Democracy: Evidence from a UAE Opinion Survey," in *Democracy, War, and Peace in the Middle East* (1995), edited by David Garnham and Mark Tessler.

Interesting recent work has been done on important changes in the political culture of the Gulf Arab states and the impact of these changes on the prevailing structure and dynamics of Gulf governments. Chapter 4 of Gause's previously cited *Oil Monarchies*, "Representation and Participation," looks at newly emerged opposition groups and seeks to counter the conventional wisdom that the reasonably equitable distribution of great oil wealth among the populations of the Gulf Arab states effectively blunts serious demands for more representative government. Jill Crystal carries further her revision of the rentier-state model in the Gulf in her discussion of "Civil Society in the Arabian Gulf," in *Civil Society in the Middle East* (1996), edited by Augustus Richard Norton. In *Women in Kuwait: The Politics of Gender* (1993), Haya al-Mughni adds to the discussion of civil society in the Gulf by examining four voluntary women's organizations, historically and as they are related to current political issues and personalities. She and Mary Ann Tétreault address the possible social and political consequences of the continued subordination of women in "Modernization and Its Discontents: State and Gender in Kuwait" (1995). In Eric Davis and Nicolas Gavrieledes, *Statecraft in the Middle East: Oil, Historical Memory, and Popular Culture* (1991), the uses of the past as expressed in political ideology are examined. The chapter by Davis, "Theorizing Statecraft and Social Change in Arab Oil-producing Countries," explores the importance for a newly formed state of defining the past in a period of rapid social change and alien cultural challenge. The chapter on "Statecraft, Historical Memory, and Popular Culture in Iraq and Kuwait," by Davis and Gavrieledes, compares the ways in which these two states have tried to manipulate historical memory to reinforce political authority. The impact of resurgent Islam has been felt in the Gulf Arab states as elsewhere in the Arab world, though its impact has been mitigated by the conservative Islam embraced by rulers and their subjects. Two studies that look at this phenomenon are Joseph Kostiner, "Kuwait and Bahrain," in Shireen Hunter, editor, *The Politics of Islamic Revivalism: Diversity and Unity* (1988), and David E. Long, "The Impact of the Iranian Revolution on the Arab Gulf States," in John L. Esposito, editor, *The Iranian Revolution: Its Global Impact* (1990).

ECONOMIC ISSUES

The Gulf region's vast hydrocarbon deposits confer commanding importance upon an area that otherwise would have remained a relatively quiet backwater. A good introduction to the development of the Gulf's oil and its ramifications is found in Daniel Yergin, *The Prize: The Epic Quest for Oil, Money, and Power*, revised edition (1993). The perspective of a major player in the Gulf and international oil arenas is reflected in *Essays on Petroleum* (1982) by Mani Said Utaybah (Mana Said al-Oteibah), longtime petroleum minister for the UAE. Several works survey recent changes in marketing and other aspects of the Gulf oil industry and assess its future. An informed survey of these changes and the way they affect the structure and dynamics of oil, primarily in the Gulf, is found in three studies edited by Dorothea El Mallakh, *Energy Watchers I: Shadow OPEC: New Element for Stability and A Reintegrated Oil Industry: Implications for Supply, Marketing, Pricing, and Investment* (1990); and *Energy Watchers II: Phoenix-like OPEC: Changing Structures, Markets, and Future Stability and the Oil-Gas Relationship* (1991). In "The Coming Oil Revolution" (1990/1991), Edward L. Morse observes that Gulf Arab state producers, with others, have been part of a trend away from resource nationalism toward internationalism, with state oil-company investments beyond their own borders becoming a common phenomenon. This theme is further developed in Joseph Stanislaw and Daniel Yergin, "Oil: Reopening the Door" (1993), which emphasizes the new complex net of security concerns linking oil-exporting nations and oil companies. An abiding fear of the Gulf Arab state oil producers (including, of course, Saudi Arabia) is replacement of oil by various energy substitutes, an issue explored in Naiem A. Sherbiny, *Trends in Alternative Energies: Their Implications for Arab Members of OPEC* (1989). The possible scope of the dangers of depressed oil revenues is examined by Philip Robins in "Can Gulf Oil Monarchies Survive the Oil Bust?" (1994). Efforts to create a cooperative relationship with Europe, including resolution of the thorny issue of Gulf petrochemical exports to Europe, are considered in Bichara Khader's *L'Europe et les pays arabes du Golfe: Des partenaires distants* (1994).

Aspects of the political economy of the Gulf Arab states have received fairly extensive treatment, much of it dealing with governmental efforts to promote economic modernization, diversification, and restructuring. Among the few broad overviews is Hazem Beblawi, *The Arab Gulf Economy in a Turbulent Age* (1984). The same writer has surveyed the peculiar characteristics of single-resource oil states with great surplus wealth in "The Rentier State in the Arab World," in *The Arab State* (1990), edited by Giacomo Luciani. A lengthier study of the same phenomenon, focused on its clearest representative in the Gulf, is Jacqueline Ismael, *Kuwait: Dependency and Class in a Rentier State*, second ed. (1993), which analyzes the interaction of economic, social, and political factors. In *Manpower Policies and Development in the Persian Gulf Re-*

gion (1994), Robert E. Looney offers a penetrating analysis of the continuing manpower dilemma in the Gulf Arab states.

The great wealth of Kuwait and the other oil-rich states has been used not only to promote rapid domestic economic development but also as an effective foreign policy tool. Until the Iraqi invasion of 1990, Kuwait's security was largely purchased through an ambitious foreign assistance program, which served as a model for Abu Dhabi's similar program. An overview of these and other Arab foreign aid strategies is provided in M. Imady, "Arab Aid to Developing Countries" (1984). Two useful studies of Kuwait's foreign aid are Walid E. Moubarak, "The Kuwait Fund in the Context of Arab and Third World Politics" (1987), and A. Assiri, "Kuwait's Dinar Diplomacy: The Role of Donor-Mediator" (1991). Well before the Iraqi invasion, declining oil prices had severely reduced the Gulf Arab states' income, leading to cutbacks in the funding of various programs, including foreign aid. For Kuwait this is analyzed in Ala'a al-Yousuf, *Kuwait and Saudi Arabia: From Prosperity to Retrenchment* (1990).

In the past decade the Gulf Arab states have increasingly stressed diversification in their economies. A good general survey is Robert Looney, "Structural and Economic Changes in the Arab Gulf after 1973" (1990). The role of the Gulf Cooperation Council (GCC) in helping to diversify is assessed in M. Cain and K. al-Badri, "An Assessment of the Trade and Restructuring Effects of the Gulf Co-operation Council" (1989). The potential result of the GCC's efforts to integrate the Gulf Arab economies is dealt with in Robert Looney, "An Assessment of the Benefits of Economic Integration for the Arabian Gulf States: The Effects of Increased Size" (1989). The case of Bahrain, the Gulf's pioneer in industrial diversification, is analyzed by that country's minister of industry, Yousuf A. Shirawi, in "GCC Diversification and Industrialization: The Bahrain Example" (1990). The services sector has grown significantly in several of the Gulf Arab state economies, a phenomenon surveyed in M. Sami Kassem et al, *Strategic Management of Services in the Arab Gulf States: Company and Industry Cases* (1989). The Gulf's most successful effort to capture the area's rich entrepôt trade is that of Dubai in the UAE, described in R. Meyer-Reumann, "The Jebel Ali Free Trade Zone in the Emirate of Dubai: A Commercial Alternative after the Gulf Crisis" (1991). In recent years the financial sector has assumed greater significance. A helpful introduction is Andrew Cunningham, *Gulf Banking and Finance: Facing up to Change* (1989). Bahrain's and Kuwait's rather problematic experiments with stock markets are assessed in Ayman S. Abdul-Hadi, *Stock Markets of the Arab World: Trends, Problems, and Prospects for Integration* (1988). Offsets programs, aimed at promoting industrial cooperation mechanisms between industrialized and developing countries, are analyzed by Amin Badr El-Din in "The Offsets Program in the United Arab Emirates" (1997).

Michael Field's *The Merchants: The Big Business Families of Saudi Arabia and the Gulf States* (1985) deals with a part of the economic picture that is less prominent than in the past, though some of the big merchant families remain significant. Two studies that seek to discern the economic future after the Gulf War are Mehran Nakhjavani, *After the Persian Gulf War: The Potential for Economic Reconstruction and Development in the Persian Gulf Region* (1991) and Yahya Sadowski, ''Power, Poverty, and Petrodollars: Arab Economies after the Gulf War'' (1991), which looks at the war's economic impact in a wider setting.

MILITARY AND SECURITY ISSUES

All the states covered in this chapter are militarily extremely weak, vulnerable to threats from both their immediate neighbors and powers outside the Gulf region. The demise of the Soviet Union removed a source of potential security threat that had long concerned U.S. strategic planners, and the 1990 Iraqi invasion of Kuwait underscored the regional source of threat. Thus much of the literature on security threats is decidedly dated, and a considerable literature has been produced analyzing the 1991 Gulf War and its implications for the security situation.

A very useful background for helping to understand contemporary security issues is J. E. Peterson, *Defending Arabia* (1986), which traces the evolution of British security concerns, the introduction of air power to the region, and the American assumption of the principal role in providing external protection to the states of the area. David Lee, *Flight from the Middle East: A History of the Royal Air Force in the Arabian Peninsula and Adjacent Territories, 1945–1972* (1980), provides an account of the role of British air power. Direct American military intervention in the Gulf to protect Kuwaiti oil tankers from Iranian attack in the last phase of the Iran-Iraq War and the collapse of the Soviet Union profoundly affected the realities and perceptions of Gulf security. In ''Through the Gulf Labyrinth: Naval Escort and U.S. Policy'' (1989), James Noyes examines what was, in a sense, the prelude to the much more ambitious intervention of Desert Shield/Desert Storm. In *The Gulf and the West: Strategic Relations and Military Realities* (1988), Anthony Cordesman examines in lengthy detail the nature of the Gulf Arab states' security ties with the United States and other Western states when Soviet as well as regional threats were envisioned. Mark N. Katz, *Russia and Arabia: Soviet Foreign Policy toward the Arabian Peninsula* (1986), considers Soviet aims and ambitions in the Gulf area, with a chapter devoted to Oman and another to the remaining small Gulf Arab states.

Though dated, Thomas L. McNaugher, *Arms and Oil: U.S. Military Strategy and the Persian Gulf* (1985) remains a very thoughtful inquiry into the problems of the interaction between American and Gulf Arab security concerns and policies related to the region's vast oil resources. A set of excellent essays carries further the investigation of these problems in Charles F. Doran and Stephen W. Buck, editors, *The Gulf, Energy, and Global Security: Political and Economic*

Issues (1991). Through the Gulf Cooperation Council, the small Gulf Arab states and Saudi Arabia have tried to increase their own capacity to provide for their security, whether alone or in concert with U.S. and other outside forces. These efforts are considered in Talat Wizarat, "The Role of the Gulf Cooperation Council in Regional Security" (1987), and D. Sullivan, "The Gulf Cooperation Council: Regional Security or Collective Defense?" (1989). In the article "From Alliance to Collective Security: Rethinking the Gulf Cooperation Council" (1996), Rolin G. Mainuddin, Joseph R. Aicher, Jr., and Jeffrey M. Elliot, writing from a perspective of five years after Desert Storm, review the GCC's efforts to promote Gulf security and conclude that the council should be broadened to become a Middle Eastern, not just a Gulf, institution.

The events that followed the August 1990 Iraqi invasion of Kuwait, culminating in operations Desert Shield and Desert Storm, formed a dramatic watershed in the evolution of security issues and concerns in the Gulf. Some of the more thoughtful studies on the Gulf crisis and its implications for present and future Gulf security are noted here. *Persian Gulf War Almanac* by Harry Summers, Jr. (1995), provides a convenient reference guide to the 1991 conflict, including historical background, a chronology of events, and a bibliography. Among the best of the studies appearing on the political impact of the Gulf crisis is Joseph Kechichian, *Political Dynamics and Security in the Arabian Peninsula through the 1990s* (1993), which analyzes the challenge posed by that crisis to the legitimacy of the Gulf Arab states' governments as well as its divisive impact on the wider Arab world. Another significant analysis of the subject is Tareq Ismael and Janet Ismael's article "Arab Politics and the Gulf War: Political Opinion and Political Culture" (1993). Roger Hardy, in *Arabia after the Storm: Internal Stability of the Gulf Arab States* (1992), has examined the Gulf War's exacerbation of pressures for political change. Graham Fuller, a distinguished specialist on Soviet and Middle East affairs, indicates in "Moscow and the Gulf War" (1991), that Russia had been moving toward pursuit of its interests in the Gulf in a way congruous with U.N. and American positions before the war and the breakup of the Soviet Union. In *Aftermath of the Gulf War: An Assessment of UN Action* (1994) Ian Johnstone examines the role of the United Nations in the Gulf War and the postwar period, covering border demarcation among other topics. Anthony Cordesman's *After the Storm: The Changing Military Balance in the Middle East* (1993) devotes a lengthy chapter to the five small Gulf Arab states, analyzing in depth their security threats and strategic needs and vulnerabilities and offering a negative assessment of their efforts to promote regional military security. Cordesman's *Iran and Iraq: The Threat from the Northern Gulf* (1994) expands on some of the descriptions and analysis of Gulf security issues presented in *After the Storm* and provides significant additional material. The same indefatigable author has produced six monographs, all published in 1997, on aspects of Gulf security, two of which focus on countries considered here: *Bahrain, Oman, Qatar, and the UAE: Challenges of Security* and *Kuwait: Recovery and Security after the Gulf War.* Two articles that offer cogent analyses of the prospects for renewed military conflict in the Gulf are David Isenberg, "Desert Storm Redux?" (1993), and David E. Long, "Prospects for Armed Conflict in the Gulf in the 1990s: The Impact of the Gulf War" (1993). *Powder Keg in the Middle East: The Struggle for Gulf Security* (1995), edited by Geoffrey Kemp and Janice Gross Stein, presents analyses that generally foresee a possible explosion in the Gulf.

Much post–Gulf War rhetoric was devoted to the desirability and possibility of imposing a meaningful arms-control regime in the Gulf region. Kenneth Watman, Marcy Agmon, and Charles Wolf, Jr., discuss the prospects for doing so in *Controlling Conventional Arms Transfers: A New Approach with Application to the Persian Gulf* (1994). In a thoughtful study, *Scuds or Butter? The Political Economy of Arms Control in the Middle East* (1993), Yahya M. Sadowski argues that oil revenues are the real foundation of the arms race in the Middle East and examines the Gulf War and its ramifications in conjunction with the "Arab economic crisis."

Among useful commentaries on Gulf security from the American perspective are *Future Gulf Dynamics and U.S. Security: Documented Briefing* (1994) by Bruce Nardulli et al. and "U.S. Perception of Persian/Arabian Gulf Security" (1994) by the distinguished diplomat and scholar Hermann F. Eilts. In "Five Years after Desert Storm: Gulf Security, Stability, and the U.S. Presence" (1996), Michael Collins Dunn reviews the developments that have confirmed the U.S. presence in the Gulf and changed regional relationships, while Alon Ben-Meier voices criticism (which has continued to grow) of the U.S. strategy to protect the Gulf against Iraq in "The Dual Containment Strategy Is No Longer Viable" (1996).

Two books look at the Gulf crisis from vantage points not represented in much of the literature. In *Islamic Fundamentalisms and the Gulf Crisis* (1991), edited by James Piscatori, several scholars analyze the responses of Islamic movements to the Gulf War. *The Gulf Crisis: An Attempt to Understand* (1993) offers the perspective of a perceptive Saudi Arab technocrat, diplomat, and scholar, Ghazi A. Algosaibi.

REGIONAL RELATIONS

The central factor in the Gulf Arab states' regional relations is the Gulf Cooperation Council, which includes their large neighbor, Saudi Arabia. At its founding in 1981, the GCC was meant to foster both economic cooperation and eventual unity as well as a collective approach to military security. Emile Nakhleh, *The Gulf Cooperation Council: Policies, Problems, and Prospects* (1986), remains a good overview and starting point. *The Gulf Cooperation Council: Search for Unity in a Dynamic Region* (1988) by Erik R. Peterson is a solid description and analysis of the GCC with a lengthy, useful compilation of council documents. A thoughtful and judicious presentation of key GCC documents and analysis of them are presented in R. K. Ramazani, *The Gulf Cooperation*

Council: Record and Analysis (1988), and an excellent set of essays on economic, political, legal, military, and other aspects of the GCC is to be found in John A. Sandwick, ed., *The Gulf Cooperation Council: Moderation and Stability in an Interdependent World* (1987). *The Gulf, Cooperation, and the Council: An American Perspective* (1992) by Joseph W. Twinam offers the reflections of a scholar and diplomat with long practical experience in the Gulf, including service as the first U.S. ambassador to Bahrain. The perspective of the council's first secretary-general is reflected in Abdulla Y. Bishara, *Gulf Cooperation: Its Nature and Outlook* (1986).

The Gulf crisis of 1990–1991 led to considerable rethinking of the Gulf Arab states' relations among themselves and, still more, to a reconsideration of their relations with the wider Arab world. Useful background from a precrisis perspective is found in B. R. Pridham, editor, *The Arab Gulf and the Arab World* (1988). The reaction of the Gulf states to the Iraqi invasion of Kuwait and its aftermath is considered in A. Nufal, "The Arab States and the Crisis over Kuwait" (1991). In "Arab Nationalism and the Persian Gulf War" (1994), E. Evans examines the impact of the Iraqi invasion and the intervention of the U.S.-led coalition on the wider Arab world. R. Brynen and P. Noble, in "The Gulf Conflict and the Arab State System: A New Regional Order?" (1991), look at the prospects for overcoming the lines of division created or exacerbated by the Gulf crisis. John Duke Anthony's "Iran in GCC Dynamics" (1993) examines the areas of tension that remain between the small Gulf Arab states and their large neighbor in the wake of the Gulf crisis.

THE FUTURE OF ACADEMIC RESEARCH ON THE GULF

The inherent difficulties of conducting serious scholarly inquiry in the Gulf Arab states on subjects in the field of political science, broadly defined, are significant and will not soon dramatically diminish. Nevertheless, the liberalization of political authority, notably apparent in Kuwait and arguably under way all along the Arab littoral of the Gulf, will have a beneficent impact. Although Gulf universities do not enjoy the same measure of academic freedom nor meet the academic standards of Western universities, or indeed those of some other developing countries, a number of their scholars are doing excellent work in Gulf studies. They and the scholars working at research and documentation centers will continue to be valuable points of contact for American and other foreign scholars pursuing research in the Gulf area. Further, for the past several years, the Society for Gulf Arab Studies, a recently established affiliate of the Middle East Studies Association, has helped to promote communication internationally among scholars working on Gulf issues.

What is most encouraging about scholarship on the Gulf Arab states is that whatever the challenges to carrying out research there, increasing numbers of serious scholars have been doing valuable work even in areas that could be deemed politically sensitive. While the ideal freedom of inquiry that scholars seek is not likely to be achieved at any time soon, many have shown that serious research can be conducted without compromising academic integrity if sufficient care and patience are exercised and relations of trust are established with one's hosts. As noted at the opening of this chapter, optimism for the future of Gulf Arab studies rests largely with the growing corps of able younger scholars in the United States, the Gulf region itself, and elsewhere who have made this their field of study and are beginning to produce important work.

REFERENCES

Abdul-Hadi, Ayman S. 1988. *Stock Markets of the Arab World: Trends, Problems, and Prospects for Integration.* New York: Routledge.

Addleton, Jonathan S. 1992. *Undermining the Centre: The Gulf Migration and Pakistan.* Karachi: Oxford University Press.

Algosaibi, Ghazi A. 1993. *The Gulf Crisis: An Attempt to Understand.* New York: Kegan Paul International.

Allen, Calvin H., Jr. 1987. *Oman: The Modernization of the Sultanate.* Boulder, CO: Westview Press.

Anthony, John Duke. 1975. *Arab States of the Lower Gulf: People, Politics, Petroleum.* Washington, DC: Middle East Institute.

———. 1993. "Iran in GCC Dynamics." *Middle East Policy* 2, no. 3:107–120.

Assiri, A. 1991. "Kuwait's Dinar Diplomacy: The Role of Donor-Mediator." *Journal of South Asian and Middle Eastern Studies* 14, no. 3:24–32.

Baaklini, A. 1982. "Legislatures in the Gulf Area: The Experience of Kuwait, 1961–1976." *International Journal of Middle East Studies* 14, no. 3:359–379.

al-Baz, A. 1989. "Forms of Parliamentary Systems between Traditionalism and Modernization: An Applied Contrastive Study of the Constitutions of Kuwait, the GCC States, and Egypt" (in Arabic). *Majall al-Dirasat al-Khalij wa'l-Jazira al-Arabiyya (Journal of Gulf and Arabian Peninsula Studies)* no. 58:77–145.

Beblawi, Hazem. 1984. *The Arab Gulf Economy in a Turbulent Age.* New York: St. Martin's Press.

———. 1990. "The Rentier State in the Arab World." In Giacomo Luciani, ed., *The Arab State.* Berkeley: University of California Press.

Ben-Meier, Alon. 1996. "The Dual Containment Strategy Is No Longer Viable." *Middle East Policy* 4, no. 3 (March):58–71.

Bishara, Abdulla Y. 1986. *Gulf Cooperation: Its Nature and Outlook.* Gulf Cooperation Council Reports Series no. 1. Washington, DC: National Council on US-Arab Relations.

Bonine, Michael E. 1980. "The Urbanization of the Persian Gulf Nations." In Alvin J. Cottrell, gen. ed. *The Persian Gulf: A General Survey.* Baltimore: Johns Hopkins University Press.

Bonnenfant, Paul, ed. 1982. *La Péninsule Arabique d'aujourd'hui.* Vols. 1–2. Paris: Editions du Centre National de la Recherche Scientifique.

Brynen, R., and P. Noble. 1991. "The Gulf Conflict and the Arab State System: A New Regional Order?" *Arab Studies Quarterly* 13, nos. 1–2:117–140.

Cain, M., and K. al-Badri. 1989. "An Assessment of the Trade and Restructuring Effects of the Gulf Co-operation Council." *International Journal of Middle East Studies* 21, no. 1:57–69.

Carter, Laraine Newhouse. 1984. "Historical Setting." In Richard F. Nyrop, ed., *Persian Gulf States: Country Studies*. Washington, DC: U. S. Government Printing Office.

"Contemporary Oman and U.S.-Oman Relations." 1996. Edited transcript of the proceedings of a symposium recognizing the 25th anniversary of the accession of H. M. Qabus bin Said, Sultan of Oman, held in the Dirksen Senate Office Building on October 12, 1995. Participants: Robert H. Pelletreau, Jr., John Page, Jr., Michael Collins Dunn, Joseph A. Kechichian, Georgie Anne Geyer, and Christine Eickelman. *Middle East Policy* 4, no. 3 (March):12–123.

Cordesman, Anthony H. 1988. *The Gulf and the West: Strategic Relations and Military Realities*. Boulder, CO: Westview Press.

————. 1993. *After the Storm: The Changing Military Balance in the Middle East*. Boulder, CO: Westview Press.

————. 1994. *Iran and Iraq: The Threat from the Northern Gulf*. Boulder, CO: Westview Press.

————. 1997a. *Bahrain, Oman, Qatar, and the UAE: Challenges of Security*. Boulder, CO: Westview Press. Published in cooperation with the Center for Strategic and International Studies, Washington, DC.

————. 1997b. *Kuwait: Recovery and Security after the Gulf War*. Boulder, CO: Westview Press. Published in cooperation with the Center for Strategic and International Studies, Washington, DC.

Cottrell, Alvin J., et al., eds. 1980. *The Persian Gulf States: A General Survey*. Baltimore: Johns Hopkins University Press.

Crystal, Jill. 1990a. "Jabir Al-Ahmad Al Sabah." In Bernard Reich, ed., *Political Leaders of the Contemporary Middle East and North Africa*. Westport, CT: Greenwood Press.

————. 1990b. *Oil and Politics in the Gulf: Rulers and Merchants in Kuwait and Qatar*. New York: Cambridge University Press.

————. 1992. *Kuwait: The Transformation of an Oil State*. Boulder, CO: Westview Press.

————. 1996. "Civil Society in the Arabian Gulf." In Augustus Richard Norton, ed., *Civil Society in the Middle East*, Vol. 2. Leiden: E. J. Brill.

Cunningham, Andrew. 1989. *Gulf Banking and Finance: Facing up to Change*. MEED Industry Perspective no. 1. London: Middle East Economic Digest.

Davis, Eric. 1991. "Theorizing Statecraft and Social Change in Arab Oil-producing Countries." In Eric Davis and Nicolas Gavrieledes, eds., *Statecraft in the Middle East: Oil, Historical Memory, and Popular Culture*. Miami: Florida International University Press.

Davis, Eric, and Nicolas Gavrieledes. 1991. "Statecraft, Historical Memory, and Popular Culture in Iraq and Kuwait." In Eric Davis and Nicolas Gavrieledes, eds., *Statecraft in the Middle East: Oil, Historical Memory, and Popular Culture*. Miami: Florida International University Press.

El-Din, Amin Badr. 1997. "The Offsets Program in the United Arab Republics." *Middle East Policy* 5, no. 1 (January):100–123.

Doran, Charles F., and Stephen W. Buck, eds. 1991. *The Gulf, Energy, and Global Security: Political and Economic Issues*. Boulder, CO: Lynne Rienner.

Dorr, Steven R. "Khalifah ibn Hamad Al Thani." In Bernard Reich, ed., *Political Lead-*

ers of the Contemporary Middle East and North Africa. Westport, CT: Greenwood Press.

Dunn, Michael Collins. 1996. "Five Years after Desert Storm: Security, Stability, and the U.S. Presence." *Middle East Policy* 4, no. 3:30–38.

Eelens, F., T. Schampers, and J. D. Speckmann, eds. 1992. *Labour Migration to the Middle East: From Sri Lanka to the Gulf*. London: Kegan Paul International.

Ehteshami, Anoushiravan, and Gerd Nonneman, with a contribution by Charles Tripp. 1991. *War and Peace in the Gulf: Domestic Politics and Regional Relations into the 1990s*. Reading, UK: Ithaca Press.

Eickelman, Dale. 1984. "Kings and People: Oman's State Consultative Council." *Middle East Journal* 38, no. 1.

Eilts, Hermann Frederick. 1994. "U.S. Perception of Persian/Arab Gulf Security." *Asian Affairs* 25, no. 3 (Summer):270–280.

Evans, E. 1994. "Arab Nationalism and the Persian Gulf War." *Harvard Middle Eastern and Islamic Review* 1, no. 1:27–51.

Field, Michael. 1985. *The Merchants: The Big Business Families of Saudi Arabia and the Gulf States*. Woodstock, NY: Overlook Press.

Finnie, David H. 1992. *Shifting Lines in the Sand: Kuwait's Elusive Frontier with Iraq*. Cambridge, MA: Harvard University Press.

Fuller, Graham E. 1991. "Moscow and the Gulf War." *Foreign Affairs* 70, no. 3:55–76.

Gause, F. Gregory, III. 1994. *Oil Monarchies: Domestic and Security Challenges in the Arab Gulf States*. New York: Council on Foreign Relations Press.

Ghabra, Shafeeq N. 1987. *Palestinians in Kuwait: The Family and Politics of Survival*. Boulder, CO: Westview Press.

———. 1991. "Voluntary Associations in Kuwait: The Foundation of a New System." *Middle East Journal* 45, no. 2:199–215.

———. 1994. "Democratization in a Middle Eastern State: Kuwait, 1993." *Middle East Policy* 3, no. 1:102–119.

Graz, Liesl. 1992. *The Turbulent Gulf: People, Politics, and Power*. New York: I. B. Tauris.

Grill, N. C. 1984. *Urbanisation in the Arabian Peninsula*. Durham, UK: Centre for Middle Eastern and Islamic Studies, University of Durham.

al-Haj, Abdullah Juma. 1996. "The Politics of Participation in the Gulf Cooperation Council States: The Omani Consultative Council." *Middle East Journal* 50, no. 4 (Autumn): 559–571.

Hardy, Roger. 1992. *Arabia after the Storm: Internal Stability of the Gulf Arab States*. London: Royal Institute of International Affairs.

Hawley, Donald. 1987. *Oman and Its Renaissance*. 4th rev. ed. Atlantic Heights, NJ: Humanities Press.

Heard-Bey, Frauke. 1996. *From Trucial States to United Arab Emirates: A Society in Transition*. New York: Longman.

Held, Colbert C. 1994. *Middle East Patterns: Places, Peoples, and Politics*. 2d ed. Boulder, CO: Westview Press.

Imady, M. 1984. "Arab Aid to Developing Countries." *Arab Gulf Journal* 4, supp. 2: 43–51.

Isenberg, David. 1993. "Desert Storm Redux?" *Middle East Journal* 47, no. 3: 429–443.

Ismael, Jacqueline S. 1993. *Kuwait: Dependency and Class in a Rentier State*. 2d ed. Gainesville: University Press of Florida.

Ismael, Jacqueline S., and Tareq Y. Ismael. 1991. "Comparative Governments: The Arabian Peninsula." In Jacqueline S. Ismael and Tareq Y. Ismael, eds., *Politics and Government in the Middle East*. Miami: Florida International University Press.

———. 1993. "Arab Politics and the Gulf War: Political Opinion and Political Culture." *Arab Studies Quarterly* 15, no. 1:1–11.

Johnstone, Ian. 1994. *Aftermath of the Gulf War: An Assessment of UN Action*. International Peace Academy, Occasional Paper Series. Boulder, CO: Lynne Rienner.

Kassem, M. Sami, et al. 1989. *Strategic Management of Services in the Arab Gulf States: Company and Industry Cases*. New York: Walter de Gruyter.

Katz, Mark N. 1986. *Russia and Arabia: Soviet Foreign Policy toward the Arabian Peninsula*. Baltimore: Johns Hopkins University Press.

Kechichian, Joseph A. 1993. *Political Dynamics and Security in the Arabian Peninsula through the 1990s*. Santa Monica, CA: Rand Corporation.

———. 1995. *Oman and the World: The Emergence of an Independent Foreign Policy*. Santa Monica, CA.: Rand Corporation.

Kemp, Geoffrey, and Janice Gross Stein, eds. 1995. *Powder Keg in the Middle East: The Struggle for Gulf Security*. London: Rowman and Littlefield.

Khadduri, Majid. 1981. *Arab Personalities in Politics*. Washington, DC: Middle East Institute.

Khader, Bichara. 1994. *L'Europe et les pays arabes du Golfe: Des partenaires distants*. Paris: Quorum-Cermac.

Khaled bin Sultan, with Patrick Seale. 1995. *Desert Warrior: A Personal View of the Gulf War by the Joint Forces Commander*. New York: HarperCollins.

Kostiner, Joseph. 1988. "Kuwait and Bahrain." In Shireen Hunter, ed., *The Politics of Islamic Revivalism: Diversity and Unity*. Bloomington: Indiana University Press.

Lawson, Fred. 1989. *Bahrain: The Modernization of Autocracy*. Boulder, CO: Westview Press.

———. 1990. "Isa bin Sulman Al Khalifah." In Bernard Reich, ed., *Political Leaders of the Contemporary Middle East and North Africa*. Westport, CT.: Greenwood Press.

Lee, David. 1980. *Flight from the Middle East: A History of the Royal Air Force in the Arabian Peninsula and Adjacent Territories, 1945–1972*. London: Her Majesty's Stationery Office.

Lesch, Ann. 1991. "Palestinians in Kuwait." *Journal of Palestine Studies* 20, no. 4: 42–54.

Long, David E. 1990. "The Impact of the Iranian Revolution on the Arabian Peninsula and the Gulf States." In John Esposito, ed., *The Iranian Revolution: Its Global Impact*. Miami: Florida International University Press.

———. 1993. "Prospects for Armed Conflict in the Gulf in the 1990s: The Impact of the Gulf War." *Middle East Policy* 2, no. 1:113–125.

Looney, Robert. 1989. "An Assessment of the Benefits of Economic Integration for the Arabian Gulf States: The Effects of Increased Size." *Journal of Economic Cooperation among Islamic Countries* 10, no. 2:81–101.

———. 1990. "Structural and Economic Changes in the Arab Gulf after 1973." *Middle East Studies* 26, no. 4.

————. 1994. *Manpower Policies and Development in the Persian Gulf Region.* West-
    port, CT: Praeger.
Mainuddin, Rolin G., Joseph R. Aicher, Jr., and Jeffrey M. Elliot. 1996. ''From Alliance
    to Collective Security: Rethinking the Gulf Cooperation Council.'' *Middle East
    Policy* 4, no. 3 (March):39–49.
El Mallakh, Dorothea H., ed. 1990. *Energy Watchers I: Shadow OPEC: New Element
    for Stability? and A Reintegrated Oil Industry: Implications for Supply, Market-
    ing, Pricing, and Investment.* Boulder, CO: International Research Center for En-
    ergy and Economic Development.
————, ed. 1991. *Energy Watchers II: Phoenix-like OPEC: Changing Structures, Mar-
    kets, and Future Stability and the Oil-Gas Relationship.* Boulder, CO: Interna-
    tional Research Center for Energy and Economic Development.
Mansfield, Peter. 1990. *Kuwait: Vanguard of the Gulf.* London: Hutchinson.
McNaugher, Thomas L. 1985. *Arms and Oil: U.S. Military Strategy and the Persian
    Gulf.* Washington, DC: Brookings Institution.
Metz, Helen Chapin, ed. 1994. *Persian Gulf States: Country Studies.* Rev. ed. Washing-
    ton, DC: U.S. Government Printing Office.
Meyer-Reumann, R. 1991. ''The Jebel Ali Free Trade Zone in the Emirate of Dubai: A
    Commercial Alternative after the Gulf Crisis.'' *Arab Law Quarterly* 6, no. 1:68–
    78.
Morse, Edward L. 1990/1991. ''The Coming Oil Revolution.'' *Foreign Affairs* 69,
    no. 5.
Moubarak, Walid E. 1987. ''The Kuwait Fund in the Context of Arab and Third World
    Politics.'' *Middle East Journal* 41, no. 4.
al-Mughni, Haya. 1993. *Women in Kuwait: The Politics of Gender.* London: Saqi Books.
Nakhjavani, Mehran. 1991. *After the Persian Gulf War: The Potential for Economic
    Reconstruction and Development in the Persian Gulf Region.* Working Papers no.
    34. Ottawa: Canadian Institute for International Peace and Security.
Nakhleh, Emile A. 1986. *The Gulf Cooperation Council: Policies, Problems, and Pros-
    pects.* Westport, CT: Praeger.
al-Naqeeb, Khaldoun Hasan. 1990. *Society and State in the Gulf and Arab Peninsula: A
    Different Perspective.* Trans. L. M. Kenny. New York: Routledge.
Nardulli, Bruce, et al. 1994. *Future Gulf Dynamics and U.S. Security: Documented Brief-
    ing.* Santa Monica, CA: Rand Corporation.
Noyes, James H. 1989. ''Through the Gulf Labyrinth: Naval Escort and U.S. Policy.''
    American-Arab Affairs, no. 29:1–19.
Nufal, A. 1991. ''The Gulf States and the Crisis over Kuwait.'' *Arab Studies Quarterly*
    13, nos. 1–2.
Nugent, Jeffrey B., and Theodore Thomas, eds. 1985. *Bahrain and the Gulf: Past Per-
    spectives and Alternative Futures.* New York: St. Martin's Press.
Peck, Malcolm C. 1986. *The United Arab Emirates: A Venture in Unity.* Boulder, CO:
    Westview Press.
————. 1990. ''Zayed bin Sultan Al Nuhayyan.'' In Bernard Reich, ed., *Political Lead-
    ers of the Contemporary Middle East and North Africa.* Westport, CT: Green-
    wood Press.
————. 1997. *Historical Dictionary of the Gulf Arab States.* Lanham, MD: Scarecrow
    Press.

Peterson, Erik R. 1988. *The Gulf Cooperation Council: Search for Unity in a Dynamic Region*. Boulder, CO: Westview Press.

Peterson, John E. 1986. *Defending Arabia*. New York: St. Martin's Press.

———. 1988. *The Arab Gulf States: Steps toward Political Participation*. The Washington Papers, Center for Strategic and International Studies, Washington, DC, no. 131. New York: Praeger.

———. 1990. "Qabus bin Said." In Bernard Reich, ed., *Political Leaders of the Contemporary Middle East and North Africa*. Westport, CT: Greenwood Press.

Piscatori, James, ed. 1991. *Islamic Fundamentalisms and the Gulf Crisis*. Chicago: Fundamentalism Project, American Academy of Arts and Sciences.

Pridham, B. R., ed. 1988. *The Arab Gulf and the Arab World*. London: Croom Helm.

Ramazani, R. K. 1988. *The Gulf Cooperation Council: Record and Analysis*. Charlottesville, VA: University Press of Virginia.

Rashid, Amjad, ed. 1989. *To the Gulf and Back: Studies on the Economic Impact of Asian Labour Migration*. New Delhi: International Labour Organisation.

Robins, Philip. 1994. "Can Gulf Oil Monarchies Survive the Oil Bust?" *Middle East Quarterly* 1, no. 4:13–21.

Rush, Alan. 1987. *Al-Sabah: History and Genealogy of Kuwait's Ruling Family, 1752–1987*. London: Ithaca Press.

Sabah, Georges. 1990. "Immigrants in the Gulf Arab Countries: Sojourners or Settlers?" In Giacomo Luciani, ed., *The Arab State*. Berkeley: University of California Press.

Sadowski, Yahya M. 1991. "Arab Economies after the Gulf War." *Middle East Report: Power, Poverty and Petrodollars*, no. 170:4–10.

———. 1993. *Scuds or Butter? The Political Economy of Arms Control in the Middle East*. Washington, DC: Brookings Institution.

Sandwick, John A., ed. 1987. *The Gulf Cooperation Council: Moderation and Stability in an Interdependent World*. Boulder, CO: Westview Press.

Schofield, Richard N., ed. 1992. *Arabian Boundary Disputes*, 20 vols. Farnham Common, UK: Archive Editions.

———. 1993. *Kuwait and Iraq: Historical Claims and Territorial Disputes*. Rev. ed. London: Royal Institute of International Affairs.

———, ed. 1994a. *Territorial Foundations of the Gulf States*. New York: St. Martin's Press.

———. 1994b. *Unfinished Business: Iran, the UAE, Abu Musa, and the Tunbs*. London: Royal Institute of International Affairs.

Scoville, Sheila A., ed. 1979. *Gazetteer of Arabia: A Geographical and Tribal History of the Arabian Peninsula*. Vol. 1, A–E. Graz, Austria: Akademische Druck- u. Verlagsanstalt.

Seccombe, Ian, and David Lawless. 1987. *Work Camps and Company Towns: Settlement Patterns and the Gulf Oil Industry*. Durham, UK: Centre for Middle Eastern and Islamic Studies, University of Durham.

Serageldin, Ismail, et al. 1983. *Manpower and International Labor Migration in the Middle East and North Africa*. New York: Oxford University Press.

———. 1984. "Some Issues Related to Labor Migration in the Middle East and North Africa." *Middle East Journal* 38, no. 4:615–642.

Shah, N., et al. 1991. "Asian Women Workers in Kuwait." *International Migration Review* 25, no. 3:464–486.

Shaw, N., and S. al-Qudsi. 1989. "The Changing Characteristics of Migrant Workers in Kuwait." *International Journal of Middle East Studies* 21, no. 1.

Sherbiny, Naiem A. 1989. *Trends in Alternative Energies: Their Implications for Arab Members of OPEC*. Safat, Kuwait: Industrial Bank of Kuwait.

Shiber, Saba George. 1964. *The Kuwait Urbanization*. Kuwait: Government Printing Press.

Shirawi, Yousuf A. 1990. "GCC Diversification and Industrialization: The Bahrain Example." *American-Arab Affairs*, no. 32.

Skeet, Ian. 1992. *Oman: Politics and Development*. New York: St. Martin's Press.

Stanislaw, Joseph, and Daniel Yergin. 1993. "Oil: Reopening the Door." *Foreign Affairs* 72, no. 4:81–93.

Sullivan, D. 1989. "The Gulf Cooperation Council: Regional Security or Collective Defense?" *Journal of South Asian and Middle Eastern Studies* 7, no. 4.

Summers, Harry G., Jr. 1995. *Persian Gulf War Almanac*. New York: Facts on File.

al-Suwaidi, Jamal. 1995. "Arab and Western Conceptions of Democracy: Evidence from a UAE Opinion Survey." In David Garnham and Mark Tessler, eds., *Democracy, War, and Peace in the Middle East*. Bloomington: Indiana University Press.

Tammam, Hamdi. 1981. *Zayed bin Sultan Al Nahayyan: The Leader and the March*. Abu Dhabi/Tokyo: Dai Nippon Printing Co.

Tétreault, Mary Ann, and Haya al-Mughni. 1995. "Modernization and Its Discontents: State and Gender in Kuwait." *Middle East Journal* 49, no. 3 (Summer).

Twinam, Joseph W. 1992. *The Gulf, Cooperation, and the Council*. Washington, DC: Middle East Policy Council.

Utaybah, Mani Said. 1982. *Essays on Petroleum*. London: Croom Helm.

Vinc, Peter, ed. 1997. *Perspectives of the United Arab Emirates*. London: Trident Press.

Watman, Kenneth, Marcy Agmon, and Charles Wolf, Jr. 1994. *Controlling Conventional Arms Transfers: A New Approach with Application to the Persian Gulf*. Santa Monica, Calif.: Rand Corporation.

Webster, Roger. 1986. "Human Resources in the Gulf." In Ian R. Netton, ed., *Arabia and the Gulf: From Traditional Society to Modern States*. Totowa, NJ: Barnes and Noble.

Wizarat, Talat. 1987. "The Role of the Gulf Cooperation Council in Regional Security." *Strategic Studies* 10, no. 1.

Yergin, Daniel. 1993. *The Prize: The Epic Quest for Oil, Money, and Power*. Rev. ed. New York: Simon and Schuster.

al-Yousuf, Ala'a. 1990. *Kuwait and Saudi Arabia: From Prosperity to Retrenchment*. Oxford, UK: Oxford Institute for Energy Studies.

Zahlan, Rosemarie Said. 1979. *The Creation of Qatar*. New York: Barnes and Noble.

IRAN

Mohsen M. Milani

During the past four decades, a great deal has been published about Iranian politics. This scholarly attention is well deserved, as Iran is at the heart of a geostrategically vital region. Historically a bridge between the West and the East, it controls the Strait of Hormuz, the gate to the Persian Gulf and its vast oil reserves. Iran itself is well endowed with natural resources, including oil and natural gas. It is the largest market in the Middle East and North Africa and is a major player in the Islamic world.

Iran has also been an important country for the United States since World War II. Sharing some 1,400 miles of borders with the USSR, Iran played a crucial strategic role in Washington's global policy of containing the Soviet Union until the Islamic Revolution in 1979. By 1975, Iran had emerged as the leading buyer of American military hardware, America's largest trading partner in the Middle East, and the main pillar of Washington's "twin pillar" policy in the Persian Gulf. At the time, some 40,000 Americans were living in Iran, more than in any other country in the Middle East except Israel. Since the Tehran hostage crisis that began in 1979, the two countries have been on a collision course, but they continue to influence each other's politics. Iran's care-fully timed release of the American hostages helped defeat U.S. President Jimmy Carter in 1980, and the revelation of the secret Iran-Contra affair created an embarrassing scandal for President Ronald Reagan. Of course, the U.S. impact on Iran has been more consequential. The U.S. tilt toward Iraq during the Iran-Iraq War and the current policy of "containing Iran" have profoundly affected Iran's political landscape. In short, Washington and Tehran may each detest the other, but they cannot ignore each other.

REFLECTIONS ON THE POLITICAL LITERATURE ON IRAN

It was only after World War II, when the United States emerged as a super-power with global interests and commitments, that studying developing countries became a national security imperative generating study grants and the establishment of research centers. Iranian studies followed this general trend. Until World War II, American contacts with Iran were minimal, as was American scholarship on Iran. U.S. involvement in Iran increased with the introduction of U.S. troops into Iran during World War II and the inauguration of the Cold War. Subsequent events that brought Iran to the attention of the U.S. public and academia included Mohammad Mossadeq's nationalization of the Iranian oil industry and the CIA/MI6-engineered coup that overthrew his government in 1953. In subsequent years, as the United States expanded its involvement in Iran, the literature on Iran grew as well, but the qualitative and quantitative jump in the literature on Iran took place after 1979 when Ayatollah Ruhollah Khomeini toppled Mohammad Reza Shah's regime in a popular revolution.

In its formative phase in the 1940s and 1950s, the field of Iranian studies was profoundly influenced by a rich reservoir of writings by British Iranologists, some of whom were unashamed apologists for British colonialism. In fact, much of the "public knowledge" about Iran, particularly about its culture and history, was derived from British scholarship and occasionally from French scholarship. By the 1960s, as American scholars began to dominate Iranian studies, British influence waned and the "Americanization" of Iranian studies began, a process that continues today. As a result, Iranian studies have become more systematic and more sensitive to theory building and to methodological vigor. Gradually, but especially since the Islamic Revolution, a new breed of Iranian and Iranian-American scholars, who are often sensitive to Iran's cultural nuances, has penetrated Iranian studies. Consequently, the field of Iranian studies is no longer completely Eurocentric, American-centric, or "orientalist" in nature.

These major changes in Iranian studies become obvious by comparing the bibliographies of two works on Iran. In his 1957 *Iran: Country Survey Series*, Herbert H. Vreeland cited some 72 sources. Of those, 28 were by British scholars, 7 of them full-length books; 26, mostly journal articles, were by American scholars. Only 3, all journal articles, were by Iranian scholars (M. A. Djamalzadeh, S. F. Shadman, and S. R. Shafaq), and 2 of them were published in England. The contrast with *Iran*, edited by Helen Chapin Metz (1989), is striking. Metz's bibliography contains 256 references. Some 45 are by British scholars, compared to 116 from American and 95 from Iranian and Iranian-American writers. A large portion of the output of the latter two groups consists of books.

Political science has had a substantial impact on the political literature on Iran. Every significant theory that had some pertinence to the developing world and every paradigmal shift had a noticeable impact on political research on Iran. For example, many books and articles published in the 1960s and 1970s were either applications of the theories of development and modernization or were implicitly based on the fundamental assumptions of such theories. Notable examples were Leonard Binder's *Iran: Political Development in a Changing Society* (1962) and James Bill's *The Politics of Iran: Groups, Classes, and Modernization* (1972). The dependency theories also permeated political studies of Iran, but to a lesser extent. Thomas Ricks (1976), for example, applied that framework to explain Iran's recent history. Many doctoral dissertations examined Iran's "dependent development" and its "dependency on the West." When the behavioral revolution changed the face of political science, there were attempts to render research on Iran more empirical and methodologically sophisticated. For example, in *The Political Elite of Iran* (1971), Marvin Zonis used survey research techniques to study the elite.

Political science research on Iran, in fact, political studies of Iran, have relied too heavily on Western theories, which have been formulated based on Western experience. Popular as they were, many assumptions of such theories have little relevance to Iran. For example, before the Islamic Revolution, it was misleadingly assumed that the Western model of development was universally applicable. Scholars ignored the differing circumstances of Europe's, and Iran's, entries into the modern age. Simply put, what worked for the West may not work for Iran.

Equally erroneous was the presumption that religion had become an irrelevant political force. Modernization in Iran, as in the West, was thought to go hand in hand with secularization. The establishment of the Islamic Republic, managed directly by the ulama, is testimony to the bankruptcy of such a view.

Political studies on Iran have also been excessively state-centric. A sizeable portion of the literature on Iran has been directly or indirectly related to the state. Because it has been the most powerful agent of change, the Iranian state must surely be studied, but not at the cost of ignoring other variables such as the civil society, the bazaar, and the political culture. Although some progress has recently been made studying such variables, much more research is needed.

Finally, political expediency rather than objectivity has occasionally influenced political research on Iran (Ricks, 1980). Under the Pahlavis, much of the literature was friendly or neutral toward the shah. There were, however, a few exceptions, like Richard Cottam's *Nationalism in Iran* (1979) or the polemical *Iran: The New Imperialism in Action* (which was translated into English in 1969) by B. Nirumand, an Iranian political activist in Germany. Hoping not to antagonize the shah, official Washington discouraged critical reports about Iran. The Pahlavis' close contact with some influential members of the U.S. government, business community, media, and academia helped create an image of Iran that was often misleading. George Lenczowski's *Iran under the Pahlavis* (1978) and Jane W. Jacqz's *Iran: Past, Present and Future* (1976) were examples of such work. A review of the literature published before the Islamic Revolution will not lead to the impression that Iran was about to experience a popular revolution.

After the intense emotions the Islamic Revolution generated, the literature on Iran has become even more partisan and polarized, either demonizing the Islamic Republic or, occasionally, glorifying it. Urgently needed is more independent research on Iran, uninfluenced by the agendas of either the Iranian or the U.S. governments.

STUDIES OF ISLAM DURING THE PAHLAVI ERA

Little was written about Islam in Iran before the revolution in 1979. That historians and anthropologists, and not political scientists, were interested in studying Islam says much about the way Islam was perceived. The mainstream view was that Islam had become a peripheral force in the politics of Iran. Leonard Binder, a gifted theorist and one of the very few political scientists who wrote a few short pieces about Islam in Iran before its revolution, echoed the dominant paradigm about Islam. In 1972 he wrote that the "Shah has striven to weaken the religious institution as an autonomous force without alienating traditional religious support. . . . By successfully putting down religious opposition in 1963 . . . the Shah has strengthened the relative position of his supporters among the clergy" (1972, 378).

The perception of Islam as a traditional and dying force was well entrenched among experts and policymakers. As late as 1979, when the Islamic Revolution had already taken place, James Bill, one of the most perceptive scholars with a solid understanding of Iran's politics and culture, argued that "the ulama would never participate directly in the formal governmental structures" (1979, 333). Ervand Abrahamian, a prolific historian who has contributed immensely to Iranian studies, indicated that "religious reactionaries will soon begin to lose their hold over the labor movement and the left will have an easy entry into an arena that includes more than two and a half million wage earners" (1979, 55). Even those few who studied Islam did not fully appreciate its revolutionary potential. When it was not fashionable to do so, Nikki Keddie, a prolific historian, wrote about Shiism. But even Keddie maintained that because of the growth of the state power and secular education, "the political power of the ulama will continue to decline as it has in the past half century," and that the ulama would not be able to influence the "basic thrust and direction of the state" (1972, 229).

No expert predicted Islam's ascendance in Iran before the Islamic Revolution. Among the few who did understand the power of Islam was Hamid Algar, a productive historian and a pioneer of Islamic studies in the United States. Discussing the oppositional role of the ulama in Iran's popular protest movements, Algar wrote that "protests in religious terms will continue to be voiced and the appeals of men such as Ayatollah Khomeini to be widely heeded" (1972, 255). Perceptive as Algar's assertion was, it should not be confused with predicting an Islamic revolution in Iran.

Leonard Binder also wrote a small piece about the Iranian ulama (1965b). He did not, however, recognize the real or potential power of the ulama establishment. With Fuzlur Rahman, Binder directed the Islam and Social Change Project at the University of Chicago in the mid-1970s. Among the most valuable contributions of that project were two fine books by Shahrough Akhavi, a political scientist, and Michael Fischer, an anthropologist. While both writers completed their research earlier, they published their volumes after the revolution. Akhavi dealt with the impact of secularization on the *madrasas*, or the traditional Islamic schools, and on the nature of the state-ulama relationship under the Pahlavis. The most valuable part of Akhavi's book is his detailed discussion of the areas of cooperation and friction between the ulama and the state. He showed that there is an inverse relationship "between clergy authority and influence and state power" (1980, 184) and concluded that under the Pahlavis the ulama's power had substantially diminished. Fischer (1980) focused on religious education in Qom, the site of Iran's main seminaries. He provided excellent information on the internal structures of Qom's competing *madrases*, their curricula, the socioeconomic backgrounds of their teachers and students, and even their budgets. Together the books by Akhavi and Fischer were the best scholarship produced about Islam in the prerevolutionary period.

THE ISLAMIC REVOLUTION

Much more has been written about the Islamic Revolution than about any other issue related to Iran. In fact, there has been a fascination, bordering on intellectual obsession, to explain how and why an Islamic theocracy could replace a pro-American regime that was for decades so passionately dedicated to Iran's modernization. To assist appreciation of the general orientation of this enormous literature, I have divided it into three interrelated categories: causes and phases of the revolution, the U.S. role in the revolution, and documents of and memoirs about the revolution.

Causes and Phases of the Islamic Revolution

Many scholars have sought to explain the Islamic Revolution within the framework of one or more of the many existing theories of revolution. One of the most popular kinds of explanation draws a causal connection between the revolution and the type, tempo, or consequences of the shah's modernization policies. Jerrold Green (1982), for example, maintains that modernization politicized many segments of the population: denying these people a chance at political participation eventually led to a revolution. Ervand Abrahamian argues that Iran's was a bourgeois revolution, and that it "came because the Shah modernized on the socioeconomic level . . . but failed to modernize on another level—the political level" (1982, 427). I have modified and somewhat expanded this theory by arguing that the gap between economic and political development ruptured because Iran's economic difficulties immediately preceding the revolution coincided with the shah's policy of liberalizing his autocratic system after many years of repression (1994b). I argued that the revolution was not inevitable: The shah lost it because he was reluctant to put to work all the repressive resources at his disposal, because he acted belatedly to prevent the formation of the alliance of convenience between the secular and Islamic forces, and because the United States, the shah's main bastion of support, was unable to define precisely the objectives of its human rights policy and oscillated in its policies toward the beleaguered monarchy.

Tim McDaniel maintains that the shah's "autocratic modernization" and his desire to create "an urban industrial society as a prerequisite for present or future great-power status" (1991, 7) sapped the effectiveness and legitimacy of the state, retarded the development of the corporate organizations that an industrial society needed to function, and deprived the regime of any significant social base of support. Nikkie Keddie identifies the rise of the new classes, itself a product of modernization, and the shah's autocracy as the critical preconditions of the revolution (1981), and Homa Katouzian argues that the shah's absolute autocracy and pseudomodernization initiatives led to the outbreak of the revolution (1981).

Explaining the revolution within the Marxist and structuralist frameworks is equally popular. Hossein Bashiriyeh (1984) focuses on the state and class conflict, using Nicos Poulantza's concept of class. He argues that the fundamental conflict of interests between the state and the upper bourgeois, the disintegration of the regime's foreign support, and the mobilization of the lower classes led to the Islamic Revolution. Mansoor Moaddel (1993) concentrates on the interaction between class, politics, and ideology to show how Shiism was first used as a popular ideology to overthrow the shah and then was misused to establish a "fascist" regime. He believes that the combined forces of the bazaaries, the landed upper class, and the ulama consolidated the rule of the counterrevolutionary forces and kept a "progressive social revolution" from occurring. Mohammed Amjad (1989) explains the role of the state in, and the drastic consequences of, Iran's transformation to capitalism. Relying on such concepts as hegemony and the relative autonomy of the state, he discusses how class struggle mixed with Shiism destroyed the old dictatorship and created a new theocratic order. Misagh Parsa (1989) relies on a structural theory of revolution to show how economic development changed the social structures and generated intractable social conflict. Concentrating on the behavior of different classes, he then demonstrates how and why social conflict was eventually transformed into a revolution. His book is arguably the most persuasive and logical in this category.

In a 1982 article, Theda Skocpol uses Iran to rescue the structural theory of revolution she had developed in her *States and Social Revolutions* (1979). In that book, she had argued that revolutions are not made; rather, "they come." Thus she emphasized the nonvoluntaristic aspects of revolutions. She paid no attention to the role of ideology and insisted that the peasantry must play a pivotal role in all revolutions. But for Iran, she came to admit that the revolution was actually "made" and was "urban" in origin (1982). She argues that Shiism and the alliance between the bazaaries and the ulama proved effective in mobilizing the masses against the shah. Despite these major revisions of her original theory, she emphasizes, without much justification, that her structural theory can still be applied to Iran, and Farideh Farhi (1990) does precisely that. Based on an interesting comparative study of the Iranian and Nicaraguan revolutions, she regards both revolutions as "state-centered crises" and shows how "the specific interaction of class and class structures as situated within the global states and economic systems" led to these two popular revolutions.

Operating within a somewhat different conceptual framework, Mark Gasiorowski (1991) makes an explicit and plausible connection among the Iranian state, U.S. policy toward Iran, and the revolution. For Gasiorowski, the rentier nature of the state—its reliance on oil revenues—and the unconditional support it received from the United States made Iran's "client state" highly autonomous. This autonomy, in turn, allowed the state to sponsor policies that alienated many groups that were eventually unified to overthrow the shah. Gasiorowski's book is not only an intelligent analysis of the revolution but also a provocative indictment of the U.S. policy toward Iran.

Another group of theorists looks to the Iranian economy for the root causes of the Islamic Revolution. Robert Looney (1982) identifies the economic origins of the Iranian upheaval, and M. H. Pesaran (1985) shows the correlation between political instability and economic recession following a period of economic growth. Norriss S. Hetherington (1982) maintains that Iran's rapid industrialization generated too many unmet expectations that, in turn, contributed to the shah's fall.

Much less popular are the psychological explanations of the revolution. Farrokh Moshiri (1985) applies to Iran a modified and expanded version of Ted Gurr's theory of relative deprivation. Marvin Zonis (1991) focuses on the shah's psychological orientation to explain why he was overthrown. Zonis concludes that the shah's "grandiosity and his fall are linked" (61) and that "the people of Iran . . . did not so much win the revolution as the Shah lost it" (2). According to Zonis, once the revolutionary movement began, the shah lost his appetite to suppress it. Zonis attributes this paralysis of will to the shah's deadly battle with cancer, to the confusing signals he was receiving from Washington, and to the fact that most of the monarch's trusted confidants, people like Ernest Peron and Asadollah Alam, who provided him with "psychic strength," had died before the revolution. Zonis believes that "the United States will forever bear significant responsibility for his fall" (261). His is one of the most perceptive books written about Mohammad Reza Shah Pahlavi and the Islamic Revolution.

Another group of scholars has focused on ideology as the most critical variable and has developed four distinct approaches to the question of ideology in the Islamic Revolution. First is the sociological approach. Said Amir Arjomand (1988) applies Weberian concepts to explain the nature and consequences of the struggle between hierocracy and the state during the past five centuries. He points out that several factors tipped the balance of power in favor of the hierocracy in the 1960s and 1970s, including the rapid increase in the number of Islamic associations, migration from the rural areas to the urban centers, and the ulama's ability to mobilize the lower classes. He blames the middle class for giving up too quickly and the shah for acting indecisively against his opponents.

In the second approach, Islam is viewed as the primary cause of the revolution. Here, Islam is treated as a unique and revolutionary religion that mobilized the masses and gave direction and cohesion to the revolutionary movement. Works by Hamid Algar (1983) and Asaf Hussein (1985) fall into this category.

In the third category, the major works by the ideologues of the revolution are translated. Hamid Algar (1979, 1981) has translated some of the works of Ayatollah Khomeini and Ali Shariati; R. Campbell (1982, 1985) those of Ayatollah Mutahari and Taleqani; and M. R. Ghanoonparvar (1981) those of Abolhassan Bani Sadr.

In the fourth category, the nature and characteristics of the ideas of the Shii thinkers are analyzed. Farhang Rejaee (1983) discusses Khomeini's views on a variety of issues, from politics to international relations; Michael Fischer (1983) explains four levels of understanding Khomeini's thought; Hamid Enayat (1983) deals with Khomeini's Velayte-e Faqih doctrine, the foundation of the new order in Iran; Shahrough Akhavi (1988) analyzes the political thought of Khomeini, Shariati, and Taleqani; and Abdulaziz Sachedina (1983) describes the works of Ali Shariati.

It is Hamid Dabashi (1993) who has written the most comprehensive account of the ideological orientations of the leading ideologues of the Islamic Revolution. Using primary Persian-language sources, he discusses the ideas of eight influential Islamic ideologues, including Khomeini, Taleqani, Bazargan, Ale-Ahmad, and Bani Sadr. He discusses the ideological evolution of the influential thinkers and their contributions to creating a revolutionary situation in Iran. Dabashi's is arguably the best book written about the ideological dimensions of the revolution.

A number of scholars have focused less on the etiology of the Islamic Revolution and more on its evolution or one of its specific aspects. Manochehr Dorraj (1990) describes the populist features of the Islamic Revolution; Farhad Kazemi (1980) discusses the role of the migrant poor in the revolution, and Assef Bayat (1986) concentrates on workers' contributions to the coming of the revolution. Shaul Bakhash (1984) provides a detailed and solid account of how the revolution was won by the ulama, how the Bazargan government was forced to resign, how the Islamic Constitution was drafted, and how Bani Sadr was forced into exile. Bakhash's book is one of the best accounts of the Islamic Revolution.

The distinct phases of the revolution have also been studied. Bashiriyeh (1984) applies Crane Brinton's famous theory of stages of revolution to the Iranian case. In my book (1994b), I describe in detail the activities of the shah, Khomeini, and the United States in eight different phases of the revolution. Ahmad Ashraf and Ali Banuazizi (1985) have written an excellent article about the characteristics of the different phases of the revolutionary movement and the role played by the shah and the anti-shah coalition in every phase. Their original research contains a wealth of valuable information and data on the revolutionary movement and its different phases.

The U.S. Role in the Islamic Revolution

Since the "loss of Iran," much has been written about the role and impact of U.S. policy toward the Islamic Revolution. This body of literature can be divided into four groups. Focusing on President Carter's policy toward the revolution, the first group blames Carter for the fall of the shah, while the second group defends him. Analyzing Carter's policy in the context of what it considers an essentially flawed U.S. policy toward Iran after World War II, the third group sees little that Carter could have done to save the shah, while the last group insists that an enlightened policy could have placed the United States on the victorious side of the revolution.

Michael Ledeen and William Lewis (1982), neither an Iran expert, consider Carter's policies a major factor in the fall of the Peacock Throne. They maintain that Carter's policy was based on some ambiguous notion of human rights and not, as it should have been, on national security concerns. It was formulated mainly by people from the "Vietnam generation" who had no love for the shah, and who failed to grasp the importance of Iran "in a geopolitical context" (237). For them, there was nothing inevitable about the revolution: It succeeded only because the United States failed to pressure the shah to resort to an iron-fist approach. The shah, Ledeen and Lewis argue tautologically, "was not a great oppressor. Had he been such, the revolution in all probability could not have triumphed" (34). Although they are critical of the U.S. intelligence community for misreading and misunderstanding the revolution, they credit, without any documentation, Israel and France for having predicted the shah's downfall.

Ironically, a much more realistic and rational criticism of Carter's policies comes from one of President Carter's appointees, William Sullivan, the last American ambassador to Iran. Sullivan (1981) presents the most comprehensive account of the U.S. embassy's role during the revolutionary movement. He complains that Washington was consistently falling a step or two behind the pace of the revolution and rejected his proposals that could have placed the United States on the victorious side of the revolution. But Sullivan appreciated the power of Islam belatedly; as late as mid-October, he was insisting that "our destiny is to work with the Shah." By mid-November 1987, however, he became one of the first officials to question the stability of the shah's regime. In a cable to Washington, "Thinking the Unthinkable," he posited a situation in which, after the army failed to restore order, not only the shah but the most senior Iranian military officers would leave the country. In fact, Sullivan was proposing an alliance between the religious forces and the younger military officers. Not only were Sullivan's proposals ignored, Carter seriously contemplated firing him. John Stempel (1981), who worked for the embassy in Tehran during the revolutionary movement, has written a good book that complements Sullivan's.

The second group of experts defends Carter's policy, viewing it as not a determining factor in the revolution. The most persuasive defense of Carter's policy, and a very balanced approach to the Islamic Revolution, is that of Gary Sick (1985), the principal White House aide for Iran on the National Security Council during the Revolution. Sick believes that the U.S. government was ill equipped to deal with revolutionary societies, and that when religion was added to revolution, "we became paralyzed." He argues that the errors of perception and judgment were distributed almost equally among the various actors. The British, French, and Israelis were as surprised by the revolution as were the Americans, he writes (37). While the majority of policymakers were consistently wrong about the shah's invincibility and Khomeini's intentions, the few policymakers who understood the nature of the revolution chose silence to protect their jobs, we are told. Sick recalls that in a meeting of the top policymakers on January 11, 1979, when the shah had been forced into exile and Khomeini had emerged as Iran's new strongman, there was an agreement that "Khomeini was no great threat . . . and was uninterested in foreign affairs" (131). He concludes that even if we had had a better understanding of the revolution, there was little we could have done to change the outcome of a revolution that was indigenous and highly popular. Sick's is the best and fairest book on Carter's policy toward Iran.

The third group analyzes Carter's policy in the larger context of U.S. policy toward Iran after World War II and maintains that there was little Carter could have done to save the shah. For Richard Cottam (1988), a brilliant expert on Iran and one of the few Americans who knows what makes the Iranians tick, the coup of 1953 was a "historical mistake" that pushed Iran toward autocracy, deprived the shah of political "legitimacy," and sowed the seeds of the Islamic Revolution. While recognizing that Carter's human rights policy "was a major, if inadvertent, factor in determining the form and rhythm of the Revolution" (187), Cottam shows that Carter did not abandon the shah "until the disintegration of his regime was almost complete" (187). Once the revolutionary movement began, Carter, who like his predecessors had accepted the shah's invincibility, was slow to deal with it. This slow reaction, Cottam believes, was the inevitable outcome of an essentially flawed policy toward, and a conceptual crisis about, Iran. Cottam reminds us that American policymakers looked at Iran through their "century-old Eurocentric lenses" and failed to recognize that Iran had entered the age of mass politics. He concludes that "a return to the era of prolonged U.S. dominance in Iran is no longer feasible" (271). Cottam's is one of the most perceptive books written about U.S. policy toward Iran.

Finally, the last group, accepting the flawed nature of U.S. policy toward imperial Iran, insists that Carter could have placed the United States on the winning side of the revolution. James Bill (1988) is the most eloquent defender of this thesis. By befriending the moderate elements of the anti-shah coalition, as William Sullivan had suggested, the United States could have secured its interests in the postrevolutionary period. More than any other source, Bill attacks the National Security Council and its director, Zbigniew Brzezinski, for having a sophomoric understanding of Iran, for neutralizing the attempts to build bridges with the moderate elements of the revolutionary coalition, and for contributing to the "extremism of the post-revolutionary period" (252). For Bill, the embarrassingly high level of ignorance about Iran in the United States is the core cause of the many problems the two countries have faced. Most interesting is his analysis of the U.S. embassy in Tehran. Because most Americans lived in "splendid isolation" in Iran, they "crippled the capacity of official Americans to understand Iran" (389). No American ambassador ever "posted to Iran spoke the Persian language" (392), and only 10 percent of the American diplomatic personnel spoke and read Persian in 1979, wheras the comparable figures were much higher for the British and Soviet embassies.

R. K. Ramazani (1982), the most authoritative source on Iranian foreign policy, is also critical of Washington for having failed to develop a farsighted policy toward the shah and the Islamic Revolution. He maintains that the U.S. involvement in the shah's military buildup, the obsession with containing the USSR, and the misleading assumptions about the direct correlation between economic growth in Iran and the shah's stability prevented Washington from pressuring the shah to open up his autocratic system. Moreover, Ramazani maintains that America's failure to appreciate the subtleties of Iran's culture prevented the Carter administration from pursuing an enlightened policy toward the revolutionary movement.

Documents and Memoirs

In November 1979, five hundred or so angry individuals, who came to be known as Students Following the Line of the Imam, attacked and occupied the American embassy in Tehran. After they took embassy personnel hostage, they confiscated hundreds of documents not shredded by the embassy officers and painstakingly pieced together thousands of shredded documents. They then released some of these documents to prove the depth of U.S. involvement in Iran's internal affairs and to defame as U.S. spies hundreds of nationalists and intellectuals who had been in contact with the embassy. Systematically organized, the documents eventually filled some sixty-five volumes, called the *Asnad-e Lane-ye Jasusi* (Documents of the spy nest) (1979).

It has been suggested that not all the captured documents are accurate (Limbert 1992). While it is unlikely that the released documents have been doctored in any major way, it is possible that not all the captured documents have been released. These documents are an excellent supplemental source of information for the scholar. They cover a host of issues, from the personality profiles of Iranian leaders and dissidents to the workings of Bazargan's Provisional Revolutionary Government. They also show that a number of capable analysts in the U.S. embassy in fact understood Iran quite well, certainly much better than those who formulated the U.S. policy toward Iran.

The Iranian Oral History Collection at Harvard University is another useful source of information on the revolution. It contains about eight hundred hours of taped interviews with some of the most powerful figures of the former regime.

Finally, there are the published memoirs of Iranian and American officials involved in the revolution. Few memoirs by Iranians have been translated into English. Of those published in English or translated into English, the most fascinating is the shah's (1980). It is what we expect from a man who lost his throne: bitter and highly conspiratorial. The shah blames everyone but himself and accuses the United States and England of undermining him and facilitating a "holy alliance between the forces of Red and Black," the latter referring to the ulama. Also revealing are other memoirs. Those by the shah's twin sister, Ashraf Pahlavi (1980), are much like her brother's; Asadollah Alam (1992) does not deal with the revolution but provides exceptional insights into the shah's mind-set; Abolhassan Bani Sadr (1991) writes a conspiracy-ridden interpretation of how everyone had betrayed him; Ehsan Naraghi (1994) discusses his eight audiences with Mohammad Reza Shah in 1978 and his experience as a prisoner in the Islamic Republic. Two more interesting books are by Fereydoun Hoveyda (1979), the brother of Prime Minister Abbas Hoveyda who was executed by the Islamic Republic, and Parviz Radji (1983), the shah's last ambassador to Great Britain.

Most of the top officials of the Carter administration have also written about their experience with Iran. President Carter (1982) accepts no responsibility for what happened to the shah and criticizes some of his subordinates for giving him misleading information. Zbigniew Brzezinski (1983) insists that had the Carter administration followed his strategy, the shah could have been saved. Secretary of State Cyrus Vance (1983), one of the architects of the U.S. human rights policy toward Iran, offers a picture of the Carter administration very different from those drawn by Carter and Brzezinski. Also informative are books by General Robert Huyser (1986), whose mission to Iran during the last month of the Pahlavi rule continues to be controversial; Hamilton Jordan (1982), press secretary for the Carter White House; and Jody Powell (1984), State Department spokesman.

POLITICAL CONDITIONS IN IMPERIAL AND ISLAMIC IRAN

Despite easy accessibility to Iran during Mohammad Reza Shah's rule, and despite Iran's growing strategic importance as a close U.S. ally, remarkably little was written about imperial Iran's domestic politics. Of the few topics researched, the land reform of 1963 received more attention than any other. In the early 1960s, Mohammad Reza Shah launched his "White Revolution," the most ambitious and consequential reform of his thirty-seven-year-long rule. The linchpin of the "White Revolution" was land reform. Ann Lambton (1969), an erudite British scholar whose academic contributions to Iranian studies are immense and solid, wrote the first comprehensive account of the land reform in English. Her book will remain a classic. She provides a wealth of information about the land-tenure system before and after the land reform, meticulously describes the politics of the land-distribution policies, and carefully documents the vehement opposition orchestrated by landlords against the land reform. She shows how the land reform changed the nature of the land-tenure system, distributed much land to the landless peasants, improved their morale, broke the social and political power of the landlords, and liberated the peasant from archaic institutions and unfair customs. She renders no judgments, however, about the economic impact of the Persian land reform.

Eric Hooglund (1982) has also written a good analysis of the Persian land reform, providing conclusions much gloomier than Lambton's. According to Hooglund, the land reform made agricultural production stagnant, increased Iran's dependence on the exporting of agricultural products, caused millions of landless peasants to migrate to the urban centers, and allowed the state to replace landlords as the ultimate source of authority in the rural areas. Having visited a number of Iranian villages, Hooglund offered an interesting discussion of how the state "utilized the village elites and political institutions and its own agents to consolidate its authority" (123).

A few other good works are also available. Afsaneh Najmabadi (1987) intelligently analyzes the impact of the land reform on the rural areas; Homa Katouzian (1974) discusses the event as an example of the shah's "crass and devastating social engineering"; and D. Denman (1978) portrays it as a progressive reform that accelerated the country's drive toward modernization.

The Pahlavis were determined to modernize Iran, and to some extent they succeeded. The impact of modernization on Iran's political system has been investigated by Leonard Binder (1962b) and James Bill (1972). Binder's book is theoretically sophisticated, but jargon loaded and often hard to follow. Basing his work on a field trip to Iran, and relying heavily on the theories of political development so popular in the mid-1960s, Binder analyzed the potential sources of instability as Iran's traditional political system was undergoing "political development." He looked at the way each component of the system, like the Majles, was dealing with the pressures of modernization, and identified the potentially destabilizing frictions within the system. Binder concluded that the system was quite stable and capable of coping with the challenges of modernization.

Bill focused on the impact of modernization on politics and the social classes. Like Binder's book, Bill's was based on a field trip to Iran. His book contains a good analysis of the country's class structure, with an interesting section on the emergence of the professional-bureaucratic intelligentsia and their ongoing struggle with the state. Although Bill, like Binder, concluded that the political system was based on a solid foundation, he suggested that the modern middle class posed a potential threat to the Pahlavis.

Various institutions of the Pahlavi state have also been studied, but never in great detail. Binder (1962a) focused on the limited policy-making power of the cabinet, and George Lenczowski (1978) discussed the major amendments to the 1906 Constitution and the role of the Majles and political parties in the political process. Bill (1971) wrote a small chapter on the Majles, and Hossein Mahdavi (1970), an economist, studied the rentier nature of the state, a popular concept among political scientists who have studied the Iranian Revolution.

Since the shah was the ultimate source of power, the institution of monarchy received considerable attention, more than other organs. For example, Pio Fillippani-Ronconi (1978) focused on the tradition of "sacred kingship" and concluded that the shah had successfully revived that traditional doctrine, and E. A. Bayne (1968) described his many interviews with the shah. For obvious reasons, the best biographical scholarship on the shah was published after his death. Besides Zonis's *Majestic Failure*, noted earlier, William Shawcross (1988) and Ryszard Kapuscinski (1985) have written two revealing books. Particularly fascinating is Shawcross's sorry tale of the shah's last two years as the once-powerful monarch became a political exile, wanted by no one and traveling from one country to another in search of the safe sanctuary he never did find. The picture that emerges from Shawcross's beautifully written book is that the shah was not, contrary to the public perception, a weak and timid man. He stood tall until his last breath. A few other small works have been written about the shah and the monarchy. Gholam Reza Afghami (1988) describes the nature of the Pahlavi dynasty, and Khosrow Fatemi's (1982) excellent article details the shah's modus operandi, the hierarchy of power, and the intricate relationship between different layers of the power structure in Iran. Fatemi shows how the shah made all the critical decisions, trusted no one, and deliberately perpetuated mistrust among his subordinates.

Some of Fatemi's conclusions had been confirmed earlier by Marvin Zonis (1971), who provided the most comprehensive account of the attitudinal characteristics of the political elite under the shah. The political elite, which Zonis called the "second stratum," was the intermediary between the shah and the people. Based on personal interviews with some 170 powerful figures and the responses to his Persian-language questionnaire, Zonis identified political cynicism, personal mistrust, manifest insecurity, and interpersonal exploitation as the most salient characteristics of the political elite. He analyzed the political costs of such attitudes for modernization and for the regime's long-term stability. While he argued that the political elite was incapable of serving as an effective player in the transition to modernity, Zonis, like Binder and Bill, considered imperial Iran an "island of stability."

The Islamic Revolution fundamentally changed Iran's political system. By and large, the way the new system operates remains a mystery. Although a few institutions of the new system have been studied, there is no comprehensive analysis of the entire political system and the relationships among its components. We know much more about the causes of the revolution and about Iran's foreign policy than we do about the dynamics of Iran's internal politics. While most books reviewed in the section on "Causes and Phases of the Islamic Revolution" contain valuable information about the evolving political system, a few additional sources deserve mention here.

The closest thing to a discussion of the Islamic Republic's complicated political system is a small but insightful piece by Akhavi (1985). Akhavi discusses the institutionalization of the Islamic Republic, the role of the various institutions, and the intricate connection between the state and the revolutionary organizations. Hunter (1992) focuses more on the nature of the Islamic Constitution, observing that the framers of the Islamic Constitution underestimated the strength of the people's attachment to their Persian cultural identity.

The presidency and the Velayat-e Faqih are the two entirely new institutions of the Islamic Republic; the first symbolizes the republican component of the system and the second its Islamic orientation. As a jurisprudential and theoretical concept, the Velayat-e Faqih has been thoroughly studied by Enayat (1983) and others. Abrahamian's *Khomeinism: Essays on the Islamic Republic* (1993), a collection of a few good but unrelated articles, addresses the Velayat-e Faqih as an essential component of Iran's new populist ideology and discusses how the Islamic Republic has manipulated it to institutionalize its popular support. I have also written about the reasons for creating an Islamic republic based on the Velayat-e Faqih doctrine by discussing the deliberations of the Assembly of Experts that drafted the Islamic Constitution (1992). But no one has done solid research about the internal structure and the political role of this powerful institution. Nor has there been a thorough analysis of the presidency, although I have studied the evolution of the Iranian presidency (1993). In 1979, the framers of the Islamic Constitution designed a weak presidency and a divided executive headed by a president with more ceremonial than actual power. A decade later, the constitution was revised. In the new system, the executive branch is no longer divided and has at its helm a powerful president. I have explained the reasons for these major changes.

The Iranian Majles is one of the most powerful institutions of the Islamic Republic. Bahman Baktiari (1996) has produced the definitive scholarship on the Iranian Majles, its internal structures, its activities, and its role in the political system. Basing his work on Persian-language sources and hundreds of interviews, Baktiari discusses how the competing factions have attempted to dominate the Majles in the past seventeen years. Most interesting is Baktiari's discussion of the tension between the Majles and the Rafsanjani administration. The Islamic Majles, he concludes, is not a rubber-stamp institution, as it was under the shah's rule, and it will continue to play a critical role in Iranian politics for years to come.

The clerical establishment is the core of the governing elite in Islamic Iran. Nikola Schahgaldian (1989) provides valuable information about the organization of the ulama, the hierarchical system within the ulama establishment, factional rivalry within the ulama's ranks, and the ulama's connection to the state. This is one of the best books on the topic. Akhavi (1987) has written an informative article about clerical politics and factionalism in the Islamic Republic. Although he focuses on economics and planning in Islamic Iran, Hooshang Amirahmadi (1990) provides a wealth of information about factionalism and politics of revolutionary Iran. Based on his many interviews with Iranian officials, Amirahmadi gives us many interesting insights that are rare in other books about Islamic Iran.

The socioeconomic backgrounds of the new elites are studied by Ahmad Ashraf (1990), an exceptionally brilliant analyst of modern Iran, and by Hooglund (1982). Neither study is detailed, but they are the only ones available. Although it is not directly related to the "elite studies," Roy Mottahedeh's *The Mantle of the Prophet* (1985) is a fascinating and well-written book about Islamic education. One cannot begin to comprehend the outlook and the mind-set of Iran's new governing elites without consulting this classic work.

POLITICAL PARTIES IN IMPERIAL AND ISLAMIC IRAN

The political system under Mohammad Reza Shah was truly autocratic. The political parties or organizations critical of the shah were banned or silenced, and the pro-shah parties were devoid of autonomy and integrity and were exploited as convenient vehicles to perpetuate the prevalent despotism. Both the Pahlavi regime and the Islamic Republic have resorted to a variety of methods, including torture, to silence dissidents and to create an atmosphere of fear and intimidation. Obviously, political parties cannot operate under such an inhospitable environment. Abbas Samii has written an excellent doctoral dissertation (1994) about the role and organization of SAVAK, the notorious secret organization that the shah used to suppress his opponents. Darius Rejali's theoretically sophisticated and exceptional *Torture and Modernity* (1994) offers the most solid and comprehensive research on the history and evolution of torture in twentieth-century Iran. It is one of the best books written about Iran in the past few years.

A few short works were written about the pro-shah political parties. Rezi (1961) and Cottam (1968) discussed the genesis and evolution of political parties in Iran from the early 1940s until the early 1960s. Miller (1969) analyzed the importance of the *dowreh*, an informal but regular gathering of people with similar interests, in the evolution of political parties. Weinbaum (1973) described the Iran Novin party, which he saw as having been institutionalized. Afghami and Elahi (1976) discussed political participation in the context of the role of the Rastakhiz party, created by a royal decree in 1975.

For obvious reasons related to the Cold War, the Communist movement in Iran was studied carefully. As early as 1947, Lenczowski wrote a short article about the creation and the internal structure of the Tudeh party and its connection to the Soviet Union. L. P. Elwell-Sutton (1949) studied the Tudeh's activities in the 1940s. In the mid-1960s, Sepehr Zabih produced a detailed study of the Communist movement in general and the Tudeh party in particular. At the time, Zabih's was the first and most comprehensive book on the Tudeh and included some primary Persian-language sources. However, the most authoritative work on the Tudeh party, its role in Iranian politics, its ideology, and its internal structure was written by Ervand Abrahamian (1982). The Tudeh party was the last non-Islamic political party to be banned in Iran. It operated rather freely until 1983, when the Islamic authorities crushed it. I have discussed the activities of the Tudeh and the reasons it collaborated with the Islamic Republic (1993).

The National Front, correctly identified as the most important force representing Iranian nationalism, was studied by Elwell-Sutton (1958) and Binder (1965a). Richard Cottam (1979), however, has written the definitive work on nationalism and the National Front. He discussed the evolution of Iranian nationalism, offering an excellent account of the birth of liberal nationalism under Mohammad Mossadeq in the 1940s, its confrontation with the West, and the reasons for its eventual eclipse. Cottam argued that the West pushed Iran toward autocracy by not supporting liberal nationalism and by siding with the shah, who enjoyed very little popular support. After the monarchy collapsed in 1979, the National Front continued to play a role in Iranian politics, but only briefly. Sussan Siavoshi (1990) has discussed the role of the National Front in the postrevolutionary period and the reasons it failed.

Splitting from the National Front, Mehdi Bazargan created Iran's Liberation Movement. H. E. Chehabi (1990) has written the most authoritative book on the evolution, role, significance, and ideology of the Freedom Movement in both the pre- and postrevolutionary periods. An Islamic/nationalist group, the Freedom Movement was among the more important forces opposing the shah; it played a critical role in the Islamic Revolution, as Bazargan formed the first revolutionary government after the monarchy collapsed in 1979. Chehabi's discussion of the Shiia modernist thought, which the Liberation Movement continues to espouse, is enlightening.

Two small organizations, the People's Mojahedin-e Khaleq and the People's Fadeyoun-e Khaleq, were chiefly responsible for starting the urban guerrilla war against the Pahlavis in the early 1970s. Both organizations succeeded in assassinating several of the shah's top officials and a few Americans, and both enjoyed considerable popularity among the youth. They were checkmated, however, by the SAVAK before the revolution started. Ervand Abrahamian's discussion (1985) of the guerrilla movement is comprehensive and provides, among other things, the socioeconomic backgrounds of the members of both organizations. In recent years, the Mojahedin has been involved in bloody clashes with the Islamic Republic. In fact, the Mojahedin, stationed in Iraq, is the most organized and the best-armed opposition group against the Islamic Republic. Abrahamian's history and evolution of the Mojahedin (1989) is the definitive and most detailed work on that organization, including its activities against the Islamic Republic from Iraq. He maintains that the once-popular organization has now lost much of its appeal and has evolved into a political cult.

NATIONAL SECURITY

Surprisingly, no solid study of the imperial armed forces has ever been published. Various aspects and components of the imperial armed forces were studied, but often in a journalistic fashion. In eleven short pages, for example, Victor Croizat (1975) and Thomas Green (1978) discussed Iran's gendarmerie and navy, respectively. An exception was Alvin Cottrel's informative work (1978) about Iran's armed forces under the Pahlavis. Cottrel described the status and organization of the armed forces and the profound impact that Iran's alliance with the United States had on the development of the imperial armed forces.

The shah's obsession with buying sophisticated weapons received more attention than the nature or role of the Iranian armed forces. The most critical exposés of the arms transfers were by Leslie Pryor (1978), who argued against unrestrained arms transfers to Iran, and M. Parvin (1968), who maintained that money spent on economic and social development would better guarantee internal security and stability than money spent on arms purchases.

The conditions and capabilities of the Iranian military under the Islamic Republic have received more attention than the imperial armed forces or any other aspects of revolutionary Iran, perhaps with the exception of Islam itself. Generally, writers on this topic have been highly suspicious of Iran's "real" intentions. At times, they tend to exaggerate Iran's "military threat" or its capabilities.

William Hickman (1982) produced the first comprehensive account of the Iranian armed forces in the postrevolutionary period. He shows how the Islamic authorities first weakened the armed forces, which they thought posed a real threat to the very survival of the infant regime; then, after the war with Iraq, Khomeini began to strengthen the army. Nikola Schahgaldian (1987) provides a comprehensive and intelligent account of the military under the Islamic Republic, with much useful background information about the nature and role of the military and the Revolutionary Guards, which Ayatollah Khomeini created in 1979. From Mark Roberts (1996) comes an excellent and perhaps the only theoretical work on the role of the armed forces during the transition of power from the old regime to the Islamic revolutionaries. He shows how the armed forces were actually incorporated into the new system of the Islamic Republic. Kenneth Katzman (1993) has written a fine book about the Revolutionary Guards. His is the only available and detailed source in English about the Revolutionary Guards. Anthony Cordesman (1994) has done a superb job of analyzing Iran's military capability and its weapon systems and arms purchases. Finally, Patrick Clawson's edited book (1994) and Shahram Chubin's monograph (1994) provide valuable information about Iran's overall strategic planning, its political and military intentions, and its capabilities.

FOREIGN RELATIONS

Only two comprehensive books have been written about the shah's foreign policy. Both were published in the mid-1970s, and both reached somewhat similar conclusions. R. K. Ramazani (1975) provided the most detailed account and the best analysis of Iran's foreign policy under the shah. Focusing on Iran's foreign policy since 1950, he established the link between Iran's domestic politics and its international behavior. For him, the "twofold quest for autonomy in the international system and authority in domestic policies" was the driving force of the shah's foreign policy. He discussed the reasons the shah adopted an "independent national policy" as the cornerstone of Iranian foreign policy, and elaborated the characteristics and consequences of this posture. He credited Iran for taking advantage of the changes in international politics to emerge as the hegemon of the Persian Gulf.

The second book was written by Shahram Chubin and Sephr Zabih (1974). They too maintained that in the early 1960s the shah began to pursue a "non-aligned policy" (7). They credited Iran with accurately assessing trends in international politics and maneuvering accordingly. For example, they pointed out, the shah in the early 1960s had concluded that the USSR was no longer a real threat to Iran; therefore, he developed better relations with Moscow. They also considered the shah's diplomacy vis-à-vis the United States a success because it enabled him to build up his armed forces and "gain U.S. diplomatic support— and most important, bought time for himself and the country" (269–270).

The Islamic Revolution has radically changed the direction of Iranian foreign policy. Most important, Iran left the Western camp and pursued a policy Khomeini called "neither East nor West." The question most analysts have sought to answer in the past seventeen years is whether Islamic Iran's foreign policy has been moving toward moderation, toward pragmatism, or toward adventurism and export of the Islamic Revolution.

R. K. Ramazani was the first to argue that Iran was actually moving toward moderation (1986). He has identified the elements of change and continuity in revolutionary Iran's foreign policy and maintains that with the consolidation of the Islamic Revolution, the more moderate elements of the governing elites have been pushing Iran toward pragmatism. Thus, as in his previous works, Ramazani has shown the intricate relationship between Iran's domestic politics and its international posture. Following Ramazani's pioneering work, I argued that Iran's foreign policy in the Persian Gulf has become more pragmatic and less confrontational (1994a).

Hunter (1990), agreeing with Ramazani's general assessment, has emphasized the nonideological dimensions of Iran's foreign policy. She too has shown that Islamic Iran's foreign policy continues much of the prerevolutionary policy. Ehteshami and Varasteh (1991) and Keddie and Gasiorowski (1990) have edited two useful books that cover many aspects of Iran's foreign policy. Geoffrey Kemp's book (1994) is a good analysis of America's relations with the Islamic

Republic since the dawn of the Islamic Revolution. Mohiaddin Mesbahi (1994) has offered a perceptive analysis of Russia's policy toward Iran. Kaveh Afrasiabi (1994) has discussed the new direction in Iran's foreign policy in the post-Khomeini era. Graham Fuller (1991) has successfully combined elements of Iran's geopolitics, history, political culture, and psychological tendencies to produce a perceptive and well-written book that says as much about elements of continuity and change in revolutionary Iran's foreign policy as about Iran's internal politics. Daniel Pipes and Patrick Clawson (1992–1993) have provided the best critical analysis of Iranian foreign policy. Portraying Iran as a dangerous state with expansionist goals, they reject the thesis that Iranian foreign policy has become more pragmatic and moderate.

SUGGESTIONS FOR FURTHER RESEARCH ON ISLAMIC IRAN

Thanks to the pioneering scholarship of a small but growing circle of Iran experts, and to the institutional and governmental support they have received over the past four decades, we now know more about Iran than we ever did before. Quantitatively, more literature about Iranian politics has been published in the United States in the past four decades than anywhere in the world, with the exception of Iran itself. Qualitatively, this rich literature is arguably the best produced anywhere in the West, including England, which has a long and prestigious tradition of solid scholarship on Iran.

Welcome as this progress is, our knowledge about Islamic Iran remains insufficient and sometimes superficial. We need more research about Iran, a country with vital geostrategic significance that has one of the world's oldest surviving civilizations. In many ways, Iran is geostrategically more important today than it was during the Cold War. Iran is an economic and strategic bridge between the two most energy-rich regions of the world: To its south is the Persian Gulf and to its north the Caspian Sea.

Research on some specific aspects of Islamic Iran, such as its foreign policy and its military capabilities, has been rather extensive. One neglected area of research is the process or the mechanism through which foreign policy is formulated in Iran. What groups and governmental agencies play the decisive role in formulating foreign policy? What role does the National Security Council play in determining Iran's foreign policy?

Research on the dynamics of Iran's domestic politics has been quite primitive and often politicized. Many important topics have received no scholarly attention. No one has done solid research about the internal structures of the Velayat-e Faqih institution, its relationship with the state and with the ulama community, and its role in governmental decision making.

There has not been any research about the role and impact of the private foundations in revolutionary Iran and their connection to the ulama. About half a dozen foundations are quite influential, including the Mostazefan Foundation, the Fifteenth of Khordad Foundation, and the Martyrs Foundation. They are neither controlled by the government nor accountable to it. The office of the Velayat-e Faqih exercises some degree of control over them, although the extent of that control is not fully known. They perform a variety of functions, including supporting Islamic movements in other countries and organizing philanthropic activities inside and outside Iran. In addition to employing thousands of people, they provide many kinds of social services.

Nor has there ever been any solid research about the role of the Committees, which were formed as vigilante organizations in the early days of the revolution, or about the hundreds of small Islamic Associations (*anjomnahay-e Islami*) that operate in every factory, university, and government agency. We know very little about the Revolutionary Courts, the judicial branch, the powerful Council of Guardians, and the Council of Experts.

The way powerful groups and factions have operated in Islamic Iran is largely unknown. Consider the cases of the United Islamic Societies and the Islamic Republican party. The Islamic Republican party, formed in 1979 by the pro-Khomeini ulama, became the largest and most powerful political party of the postrevolutionary period. It opened branches in every major city and published its own newspaper. Because he could no longer control the ongoing factionalism within the Islamic Republican party, Ayatollah Khomeini dissolved it in 1987. Our knowledge about this party and its role in Iranian politics is simply insufficient.

Before Ayatollah Khomeini was forced from Iran in 1964, he blessed the formation of the United Islamic Societies (UIS), which was a merger of three small groups, including the Fadaeyun-e Islam, a small Islamic organization that assassinated some officials of the Pahlavi regime. Less than two months after Khomeini's exile, Prime Minister Hassan Ali Mansur was assassinated by Mohammad Bokharai, whom the government identified as a member of the Fadaeyun-e Islam. But in fact, the UIS had orchestrated the assassination. Although Amir H. Ferdows (1983) has written about the Fadaeyun-e Islam, we know little of how the UIS operated during the shah's rule and how it worked with other organizations or about the vital role it now plays in Iran.

Part of the problem, of course, is Iran's inaccessibility to many American scholars. Some of the best scholarship on Iran has come from academics who made successful research trips to Iran. Since the Islamic Revolution, however, few scholars have been able or willing to travel to Iran to conduct such field research. Washington's policy of "dual containment" has made accessibility to Iran even more difficult. We must not turn Washington's policy of containing Iran into an academic policy of containing or limiting research about Iran. There is certainly a desperate need to increase governmental and private funds for Iranian studies in the United States. Equally critical is our commitment to scholarly objectivity and fairness. Because bilateral relations between Iran and the United States have become hostile, political scientists have a special responsibility to conduct neutral research about Iran, uninfluenced by the agendas of the two national governments. Such a commitment to the pursuit of knowledge and objectivity will increase our understanding of one of the least understood countries in the Middle East and, eventually, will help policymakers formulate a more enlightened policy toward Iran.

REFERENCES

Abrahamian, Ervand. 1979. "Political Forces in the Iranian Revolution." *Radical America* 13, no. 3 (June):45–55.

———. 1982. *Iran between Two Revolutions.* Princeton: Princeton University Press.

———. 1985. "The Guerrilla Movement in Iran, 1963–1977." In H. Afshar, ed., *Iran: A Revolution in Turmoil.* Albany: State University of New York Press.

———. 1989. *The Iranian Mojahedin.* New Haven: Yale University Press.

———. 1993. *Khomeinism: Essays on the Islamic Republic.* Berkeley: University of California Press.

Afghami, G. R. 1988. "The Nature of the Pahlavi Monarchy." In P. Chelkowski and R. Pranger, eds., *Ideology and Power in the Middle East: Studies in Honor of George Lenczowski.* Durham, NC: Duke University Press.

Afghami, G., and C. Elahi, 1976. "Social Mobilization and Participation in Iran." In J. Jacqz, ed., *Iran: Past, Present, and Future.* Aspen, CO: Aspen Institute for Humanistic Studies.

Afrasiabi, Kaveh. 1994. *After Khomeini: New Directions in Iran's Foreign Policy.* Boulder, CO: Westview Press.

Akhavi, Shahrough. 1980. *Religion and Politics in Contemporary Iran: Clergy-State Relations in the Pahlavi Period.* Albany: State University of New York Press.

———. 1987. "Elite Factionalism in the Islamic Republic of Iran." *Middle East Journal* 41, no. 2 (Spring): 181–202.

———. 1988. "Islam, Politics, and Society in the Thought of Ayatollah Khomeini, Ayatollah Taleqani, and Ali Shari'ati." *Middle Eastern Studies* 24 (October): 404–431.

Alam, Asadollah. 1992. *The Shah and I: 'Confidential Diary of Iran's Royal Court, 1969-1977.* Ed. A. Alikhani. New York: St. Martin's Press.

Algar, Hamid. 1972. "The Oppositional Role of the Ulama in Twentieth-Century Iran." In N. Keddie, ed., *Scholars, Saints, and Sufis: Muslim Religious Institutions in the Middle East since 1500.* Berkeley: University of California Press.

———, trans. 1979. *On the Sociology of Islam: Lectures*, by Ali Shari'ati. Berkeley, CA: Mizan Press.

———, trans. 1981. *Islam and Revolution: Writings and Declarations of Imam Khomeini.* Berkeley, CA: Mizan Press.

———. 1983. *The Roots of the Islamic Revolution.* London: Muslim Institute.

Amirahmadi, Hooshang. 1990. *Revolution and Economic Transition: The Iranian Experience.* Albany: State University of New York Press.

Amirahmadi, H., and M. Parvin, eds. 1988. *Post-revolutionary Iran.* Boulder, CO: Westview Press.

Amjad, Mohammed. 1989. *Iran: From Royal Dictatorship to Theocracy.* New York: Greenwood Press.

Arjomand, Said Amir. *1988. The Turban for the Crown: The Islamic Revolution in Iran*. New York: Oxford University Press.

Ashraf, Ahmad. 1990. "Theocracy and Charisma: New Men of Power in Iran." *International Journal of Politics, Culture, and Society* 4, no. 1:43–52.

Ashraf, Ahmad, and Ali Banuazizi. 1985. "The State, Classes, and Modes of Mobilization in the Iranian Revolution." *State, Culture, and Society* 1, no. 3 (Spring): 3–39.

Asnad-e Lane-ye Jasusi [Documents of the spy nest]. Various volumes. Teheran, 1979.

Bakhash, Shaul. 1984. *The Reign of the Ayatollahs: Iran and the Islamic Revolution*. New York: Basic Books.

Baktiari, Bahman. 1996. *Parliamentary Politics in Revolutionary Iran: The Institutionalization of Factional Politics*. Gainesville: University Press of Florida.

Bani Sadr, Abolhassan. 1991. *My Turn to Speak: Iran, the Revolution and Secret Deals with the U.S.* Washington, DC: Brassey's.

Banuazizi, Ali. 1995. "Faltering Legitimacy: The Ruling Clerics and Civil Society in Contemporary Iran." *International Journal of Politics, Culture, and Society* 8, no. 4:563–577.

Bashiriyeh, Hossein. 1984. *The State and Revolution in Iran, 1962–1982*. New York: St. Martin's Press.

Bayat, Assef. 1986. *Workers and Revolution in Iran: A Third World Experience of Workers' Control*. London: Zed Books.

Bayne, E. A. 1968. *Persian Kingship in Transition: Conversations with a Monarch Whose Office Is Traditional and Whose Goal Is Modernization*. New York: American Universities Field Staff.

Bill, James. 1971. "The Politics of Legislative Monarchy: The Iranian Majles." In H. Hirsch and M. D. Hancock, eds., *Comparative Legislative Systems: A Reader in Theory and Research*. New York: Free Press.

———. 1972. *The Politics of Iran: Groups, Classes and Modernization*. Columbus, OH: Charles E. Merrill.

———. 1979. "Iran and the Crisis of '78." *Foreign Affairs* 57, no. 2 (January): 323–342.

———. 1988. *The Eagle and the Lion: The Tragedy of American-Iranian Relations*. New Haven: Yale University Press.

Binder, Leonard. 1962a. "The Cabinet of Iran." *Middle East Journal* 16, no.1: 29–47.

———. 1962b. *Iran: Political Development in a Changing Society*. Berkeley: University of California Press.

———. 1965a. "Iranian Nationalism." In R. Benjamin and J. Szyliowicz, eds., *The Contemporary Middle East: Tradition and Innovation*. New York: Random House.

———. 1965b. "The Proofs of Islam." In G. Makdisi, ed., *Arabic and Islamic Studies in Honor of Hamilton A. R. Gibb*. Leiden: E. J. Brill.

———. 1972. "Iran's Potential as a Regional Power." In Paul Y. Hammond and S. Alexander, eds., *Political Dynamics in the Middle East*. New York: American Elsevier.

Brzezinski, Zbigniew K. 1983. *Power and Principle: Memoirs of the National Security Advisor, 1977–1981*. New York: Farrar, Straus, Giroux.

Campbell, R. trans. 1982. *Society and Economics in Islam: Writings and Declarations of Ayatullah Sayyid Mahmud Taleghani.* Berkeley, CA: Mizan Press.

———. trans. 1985. *Fundamentals of Islamic Thought: God, Man, and the Universe,* by Murteza Mutahhari. Berkeley, CA: Mizan Press.

Carter, Jimmy. 1982. *Keeping Faith: Memoirs of a President.* New York: Bantam Books.

Chehabi, H. E. 1990. *Iranian Politics and Religious Modernism.* Ithaca: Cornell University Press.

Chubin, Shahram. 1994. *Iran's National Security Policy: Capabilities, Intentions and Impact.* Washington, DC: Carnegie Endowment for International Peace.

Chubin, S., and S. Zabih. 1974. *The Foreign Relations of Iran: A Developing State in a Zone of Great-Power Conflict.* Berkeley: University of California Press.

Clawson, Patrick, ed. 1994. *Iran's Strategic Intentions and Capabilities.* Washington, DC: Institute for National Strategic Studies, National Defense University.

Cordesman, Anthony. 1994. *Iran and Iraq: The Threat from the Northern Gulf.* Boulder, CO: Westview Press.

Cottam, Richard. 1968. "Political Party Development in Iran." *Iranian Studies* 1, no. 3: 82–95.

———. 1979. *Nationalism in Iran: Updated through 1978.* Pittsburgh: University of Pittsburgh Press.

———. 1988. *Iran and the United States: A Cold War Case Study.* Pittsburgh: University of Pittsburgh Press.

Cottrel, Alvin. 1978. "Iran's Armed Forces under the Pahlavi Dynasty." In G. Lenczowski, ed., *Iran under the Pahlavis.* Stanford, CA: Hoover Institution Press.

Croizat, Victor. 1975. "Imperial Iranian Gendarmerie." *Marine Corps Gazette* 59, no. 10:28–31.

Dabashi, Hamid. 1993. *Theology of Discontent: The Ideological Foundations of the Islamic Revolution in Iran.* New York: New York University Press.

Denman, D. 1978. "Land Reforms of Shah and People." In George Lenczowski, ed., *Iran under the Pahlavis.* Stanford, CA: Hoover Institution Press.

Dorraj, Manochehr. 1990. *From Zarathustra to Khomeini.* Boulder, CO: Lynne Rienner.

Ehteshami, Anoushiravan. 1995. *After Khomeini: The Iranian Second Republic.* New York: Routledge.

Ehteshami, A., and M. Varasteh, eds. 1991. *Iran and the International Community.* New York: Routledge.

Elwell-Sutton, L. P. 1949. "Political Parties in Iran, 1941–1948." *Middle East Journal* 3, no. 1:45–62.

———. 1958. "Nationalism and Neutralism in Iran." *Middle East Journal* 12, no. 1: 20–32.

Enayat, Hamid. 1983. "Iran: Khumayni's Concept of the 'Guardianship of the Jurisconsult.' " In J. Piscatori, ed., *Islam in the Political Process.* Cambridge: Cambridge University Press.

Farhi, Farideh. 1990. *States and Urban-based Revolutions: Iran and Nicaragua.* Urbana.: University of Illinois Press.

Fatemi, Khosrow. 1982. "Leadership by Distrust: The Shah's *Modus Operandi.*" *Middle East Journal* 36, no. 1:48–61.

Ferdows, Amir. 1983. "Khomeini and Fadayan's Society." *International Journal of Middle East Studies* 15:241–257.

Fillippani-Ronconi, Pio. 1978. "The Tradition of Sacred Kingship in Iran." In G. Len-
    czowski, ed., *Iran under the Pahlavis.* Stanford, CA: Hoover Institution Press.
Fischer, Michael. 1980. *Iran: From Religious Dispute to Revolution.* Cambridge, MA:
    Harvard University Press.
———. 1983. "Imam Khomeini: Four Levels of Understanding." In J. Esposito, ed.,
    Voices of Resurgent Islam. New York: Oxford University Press.
Floor, William. 1980. "The Revolutionary Character of the Iranian Ulama: Wishful
    Thinking or Reality?" *International Journal of Middle East Studies* 12, no. 4:
    501–524.
Fuller, Graham. 1991. *The Center of the Universe: The Geopolitics of Iran.* Boulder,
    CO: Westview Press.
Gasiorowski, Mark. 1991. *U.S. Foreign Policy and the Shah: Building a Client State in
    Iran.* Ithaca: Cornell University Press.
Ghanoonparvar, M. R., trans. 1981. *The Fundamental Principles and Precepts of Islamic
    Government,* by Abolhassan Bani Sadr. Lexington, KY: Mazda Publishers.
Green, Jerrold. 1982. *Revolution in Iran.* New York: Praeger.
Green, Thomas. 1978. "Building a Navy in a Hurry." *U.S. Naval Institute Proceedings*
    104, no. 1:41–49.
Hashim, Ahmed. 1995. *The Crisis of the Iranian State.* New York: Oxford University
    Press for the International Institute for Strategic Studies.
Hetherington, Norriss S. 1982. "Industrialization and Revolution in Iran: Forced Progress
    or Unmet Expectation?" *Middle East Journal* 36, no. 3:362–373.
Hickman, William. 1982. *Ravaged and Reborn: The Iranian Army, 1982.* Washington,
    DC: Brookings Institution.
Hooglund, Eric. 1982. *Land and Revolution in Iran, 1960–1980.* Austin: University of
    Texas Press.
Hoveyda, Fereydoun. 1979. *The Fall of the Shah.* New York: Wyndam Books.
Hunter, Shireen, ed. 1985. *Internal Developments in Iran.* Washington, DC: Center for
    Strategic and International Studies.
———. 1990. *Iran and the World: Continuity in a Revolutionary Decade.* Bloomington:
    Indiana University Press.
———. 1992. *Iran after Khomeini.* Westport, CT: Praeger.
Hussain, Asaf. 1985. *Islamic Iran: Revolution and Counter Revolution.* New York: St.
    Martin's Press.
Huyser, Robert. 1986. *Mission to Iran.* New York: Harper and Row.
Jacqz, Jane. W. *Iran: Past, Present and Future.* New York: Aspen Institute for Human-
    istic Studies, 1976.
Jordan, Hamilton. 1982. *Crisis: The Last Year of the Carter Presidency.* New York: G.
    Putnam's Sons.
Kapuscinski, Ryszard. 1985. *Shah of Shahs.* San Diego, CA: Harcourt Brace Jovanovich.
Katouzian, Homa. 1974. "Land Reform in Iran." *Journal of Peasant Studies* 2 (January):
    220–239.
———. 1981. *The Political Economy of Modern Iran: Despotism and Pseudo-
    Modernism, 1926–1979.* New York: New York University Press.
Katzman, Kenneth. 1993. *The Warriors of Islam: Iran's Revolutionary Guard.* Boulder,
    CO: Westview Press.
Kazemi, Farhad. 1980. *Poverty and Revolution in Iran: The Migrant Poor, Urban Mar-
    ginality and Politics.* New York: New York University Press.

Keddie, Nikki. 1972. ''The Roots of the Ulama's Power in Modern Iran.'' In N. Keddie, ed., *Scholars, Saints, and Sufis: Muslim Religious Institutions in the Middle East since 1500*. Berkeley: University of California Press.

Keddie, Nikki, and Mark Gasiorowski, eds. 1990. *Neither East nor West: Iran, the Soviet Union, and the United States*. New Haven: Yale University Press.

Keddie, Nikki, and Eric Hooglund, eds. 1986. *The Iranian Revolution and the Islamic Republic*. Syracuse: Syracuse University Press.

Keddie, Nikki, with a section by Yann Richard. 1981. *Roots of Revolution: An Interpretive History of Modern Iran*. New Haven: Yale University Press.

Kemp, Geoffrey. 1994. *Forever Enemies? American Policy and the Islamic Republic of Iran*. Washington, DC: Carnegie Endowment for International Peace.

Lambton, A.K.S. 1969. *The Persian Land Reform, 1962–1966*. Oxford: Clarendon Press.

Ledeen, Michael, and William Lewis. 1982. *Debacle: The American Failure in Iran*. New York: Vintage Books.

Lenczowski, George. 1947. ''The Communist Movement in Iran.'' *Middle East Journal* 1, no. 1:29–45.

———. 1978. ''Political Process and Institutions in Iran.'' In G. Lenczowski, ed., *Iran under the Pahlavis*. Stanford, CA: Hoover Institution Press.

Limbert, John. 1992. ''Nest of Spies: Pack of Lies.'' *Washington Quarterly* (Spring): 75–82.

Looney, Robert. 1982. *Economic Origins of the Iranian Revolution*. New York: Pergamon Press.

Mahdavi, Hossein. 1970. ''The Patterns and Problems of Economic Development in Rentier States: The Case of Iran.'' In M. A. Cook, ed., *Studies in the Economic History of the Middle East: From the Rise of Islam to the Present Day*. New York: Oxford University Press.

McDaniel, Tim. 1991. *Autocracy, Modernization, and Revolution in Russia and Iran*. Princeton: Princeton University Press.

Mesbahi, Mohiaddin, ed. 1994. *Russia and the Third World in the Post-Soviet Era*. Gainesville: University Press of Florida.

Metz, Helen Chapin, ed. 1989. *Iran: A Country Study*. Washington, DC: Federal Research Division.

Milani, Mohsen. 1992. ''The Transformation of the *Velayat-e Faqih* Institution.'' *Moslem World* 72, nos. 3–4, (July–October): 175–190.

———. 1993. ''The Evolution of the Iranian Presidency.'' *British Journal of Middle Eastern Studies* 20, no.1:83–97.

———. 1994a. ''Iran's Post–Cold War Policy in the Persian Gulf.'' *International Journal* 49 (Spring): 326–354.

———. 1994b. *The Making of Iran's Islamic Revolution: From Monarchy to Islamic Republic*. 2nd ed. Boulder, CO: Westview Press.

Miller, William. 1969. ''Political Organization in Iran: From Dowreh to Political Party.'' *Middle East Journal* 23:159–167, 343–350.

Moaddel, Mansoor. 1993. *Class, Politics, and Ideology in the Iranian Revolution*. New York: Columbia University Press.

Moshiri, Farrokh. 1985. *The State and Social Revolution in Iran: A Theoretical Perspective*. New York: Peter Lang.

Mottahedeh, Roy. 1985. *The Mantle of the Prophet: Religion and Politics in Iran*. New York: Pantheon Books.

Najmabadi, Afsaneh. 1987. *Land Reform and Social Change in Iran*. Salt Lake City: University of Utah Press.

Naraghi, Ehsan. 1994. *From Palace to Prison: Inside the Iranian Revolution*. Chicago: Ivan R. Dee.

Nirumand, Bahman. 1969. *Iran: The New Imperialism in Action*. New York: Monthly Review Press.

Pahlavi, Ashraf. 1980. *Faces in a Mirror*. Englewood Cliffs, NJ: Prentice-Hall.

Pahlavi, Mohammad Reza. 1980. *Answer to History*. New York: Stein and Day.

Parsa, Misagh. 1989. *Social Origins of the Iranian Revolution*. New Brunswick, NJ: Rutgers University Press.

Parvin, Manoucher. 1968. "Military Expenditures in Iran." *Iranian Studies* 1, no. 4:149–154.

Pesaran, M. H. 1985. "Economic Development and Revolutionary Upheaval in Iran." In H. Afshar, ed., *Iran: A Revolution in Turmoil*. Albany: State University of New York Press.

Pipes, Daniel, and Patrick Clawson. 1992–1993. "Ambitious Iran, Troubled Neighbors." *Foreign Affairs* 72, no. 1:124–141.

Powell, Jody. 1984. *The Other Side of the Story*. New York: William Morrow.

Pryor, Leslie. 1978. "Arms and the Shah." *Foreign Policy* 31:56–71.

Radji, Parviz. 1983. *In the Service of the Peacock Throne*. London: Hamish Hamilton.

Ramazani, R. K. 1975. *Iran's Foreign Policy, 1941–1973*. Charlottesville: University Press of Virginia.

———. 1982. *The United States and Iran*. New York: Praeger.

———. 1986. *Revolutionary Iran*. Baltimore: Johns Hopkins University Press.

Reference Guide to the Iranian Oral History Collection. 1993. 2d ed. Habib Ladjevardi, Project Director. Cambridge, MA: Center for Middle Eastern Studies, Harvard University.

Rejaee, Farhang. 1983. *Islamic Values and World View: Khomeyni on Man, the State, and International Politics*. Washington, DC: University Press of America.

Rejali, Darius M. 1994. *Torture and Modernity: Self, Society, and State in Modern Iran*. Boulder, CO: Westview Press.

Rezi, G. H. 1961. "Genesis of Party in Iran: A Case Study of the Interaction between the Political System and Political Parties." *Iranian Studies* 3, no. 2:58–90.

Ricks, Thomas. 1976. "Contemporary Iranian Economy and History: An Overview." *Review of Iranian Political Economy and History* 1, no. 1:24–58.

———. 1980. "Iran and Imperialism: Academics in the Service of the People or the Shah?" *Arab Studies Quarterly* 2 (Summer): 265–277.

Roberts, Mark. 1996. *Khomeini's Incorporation of the Iranian Military*. Washington, DC: National Defense University.

Rosen, Barry, ed. 1985. *Iran since the Revolution: Internal Dynamics, Regional Conflicts and the Superpowers*. New York: Columbia University Press.

Rubin, Barry. 1980. *Paved with Good Intentions: The American Experience in Iran*. New York: Oxford University Press.

Sachedina, Abdulaziz. 1983. "Ali Shari'ati: Ideologue of the Iranian Revolution." In J. Esposito, ed., *Voices of Resurgent Islam*. New York: Oxford University Press.

Samii, Abbas. 1994. "The Role of SAVAK in the 1978–80 Iranian Revolution." Doctoral dissertation, Cambridge University.

Schahgaldian, Nikola. 1987. *The Iranian Military under the Islamic Republic*. Santa
    Monica: CA: Rand Corporation.

———. 1989. *The Clerical Establishment in Iran*. Santa Monica, CA: Rand Corporation.

Shawcross, William. 1988. *The Shah's Last Ride: The Fate of an Ally*. New York: Simon
    and Schuster.

Siavoshi, Sussan. 1990. *Liberal Nationalism in Iran: The Failure of a Movement*. Boul-
    der, CO: Westview Press.

Sick, Gary. 1985. *All Fall Down*. New York: Random House.

Skocpol, Theda. 1982. ''Rentier State and Shi'a Islam in the Iranian Revolution.'' *Theory
    and Society* 11 (May): 265–283.

Stempel, John. 1981. *Inside the Iranian Revolution*. Bloomington: Indiana University
    Press.

Sullivan, William. 1981. *Mission to Iran*. New York: W. W. Norton.

Vance, Cyrus. 1983. *Hard Choices: Four Critical Years in Managing America's Foreign
    Policy*. New York: Simon and Schuster.

Vreeland, Herbert. 1957. *Iran: Country Survey Series*. New Haven: Human Relations
    Area Files.

Weinbaum, M. G. 1973. ''Iran Finds a Party System: The Institutionalization of Iran
    Novin.'' *Middle East Journal* 27, no. 4:439–455.

Zabih, Sepher. 1966. *The Communist Movement in Iran*. Berkeley: University of Cali-
    fornia Press.

———. 1988. *The Iranian Military in Revolution and War*. New York: Routledge.

Zonis, Marvin. 1971. *The Political Elite of Iran*. Princeton: Princeton University Press.

———. 1991. *Majestic Failure*. Chicago: University of Chicago Press.

IRAQ

Amatzia Baram and Michael Eppel

The main issues with which scholars have dealt when studying the Iraqi nation-state apply to the survival and consolidation of the united Iraqi state since it was established following World War I. From its inception, the state, under Sunni Arab hegemony, was challenged by various ethnic, tribal, and denominational centrifugal forces within Iraq, often enhanced from across the borders, mainly from Iran, but also from Arab neighbors, as well as from Turkey. The fact that at least during the first decades of the state's existence, its heterogeneous population was devoid of a unifying national credo made the processes of developing a modern political system and the modernization of Iraqi society particularly complex. These processes constitute one of the more important foci of research. However, most research examines the political and social development of Iraq from the perspective of the Iraqi state, or the Sunni Arab center, and the way in which it strove to preserve the country's unity while maintaining the status quo of Sunni Arab dominance. This does not mean that this research is in any way unimportant. On the contrary, much of it is of great value, indispensable for any student of Iraq. Yet it is also important to note that relatively little research has been done so far from the equally important Kurdish and Shiite perspectives.

Scholars studying Iraq recognized a few phenomena in its development that, on the face of it, seem incongruous: (1) In Iraq as a region, up to World War I, and as a state thereafter, the processes of modernization and Westernization lagged behind those in other central Middle Eastern states like Egypt, Syria, and Turkey. (2) All the same, Iraq preceded the other Arab states in the development of certain political trends. The first modern military coup d'état occurred in Baghdad. The weakness of the center and the intercommunal tensions resulted in the first incidents of vicious center-periphery (as opposed to anticolonial) violence in the post–World War I era: it started with the violent suppression of Kurdish and Shii revolts and continued with the massacre of the Assyrians in 1933. Iraq was the first to transform pan-Arab nationalism into its dominant political ideology and to use it as a powerful tool in its foreign policy. Iraq was also deeply involved in the Palestine question since the late 1920s, earlier than most, if not all, other Arab states. On the economic level, too, Iraq was the first Arab state where oil became of great importance in the national economy. (3) Though its political community never reached a high degree of national consolidation, in 1932 Iraq became the first Arab state to gain formal independence. Since then, in repeated attempts to solidify the Iraqi political community, the various regimes have launched their country into hectic activity in the regional arena. Despite intervals of relative inactivity, between 1932 and 1990–1991 Iraq was a hyperactive state in regional and international arenas: from 1932 on it conducted wide-scale diplomatic activity to unite the Fertile Crescent under Hashemite dominance; it led the Arab intervention in the 1936–1939 Arab revolt in Palestine; it pushed the Arabs to the invasion of Palestine in May 1948 and sent a large force from Baghdad to participate in the war; it participated actively also in the 1967 and 1973 Arab-Israeli wars; it launched the first full-scale war by an Arab state against an Islamic non-Arab neighbor when it attacked Iran in September 1980; it was the first Arab state ever to have conquered and annexed an Arab state (Kuwait); and finally, Iraq is the first Arab state to have developed medium-range missiles and to have come close to the establishment of a nuclear arsenal.

The usual periodization of the history of the Iraqi state divides it into two main eras. The first one is the Hashemite monarchy (1921–1958), which is lumped together with the British military occupation (1914–1920) and largely overlaps with the British mandatory period (1920–1932). The second is the period since July 14, 1958, labeled by the new rulers as the "revolutionary" or the "republican" era. Research on nineteenth-century Iraq and the beginning of the modernization process is still scanty, and only the period immediately prior to World War I and the British policy in that period have been the subject of more significant research.

There may be no doubt that the establishment of the Iraqi state by the British at the end of World War I is a starting point after which researchers could relate to Iraq as a well-defined political entity, rather than a purely geographical region. The fall of the monarchy in 1958 and the establishment of the regime of General Abd al-Karim Qasim constitute an important turning point that marks the end of a political era, the ripening of social processes, and a rather revolutionary change in both the society and the political system of Iraq. No less important, from the standpoint of research, is the subdivision of the main periods. A considerable part of the historical and political science research centers on these subperiods.

Research on the monarchical-Hashemite period focuses on three subperiods: (1) from the establishment of the Iraqi state (1920–1921) under the British mandate until the latter's conclusion in 1932; (2) the period of independence, from 1932 to the pro-German revolt headed by Rashid Ali al-Gaylani and the war against Britain in 1941; and (3) from the conclusion of the Rashid Ali revolt until the fall of the monarchy. Research on the period of the "republican" or "revolutionary" regimes since 1958 is divided into subperiods according to the changing regimes: (1) the regime of Abd al-Karim Qasim (July 1958–February 1963); (2) the Baath regime, with Abd el-Salam Arif as titular president (February–November 1963); (3) the rule of the Arif brothers (November 1963–July 1968); and (4) the second Baath regime (July 1968–   ) and, as part of it but also as a period in its own right, Saddam Hussein's regime, starting when Hussein became president in July 1979.

GENERAL AND HISTORICAL OVERVIEW MONOGRAPHS

Most of the books dealing with modern Iraq focus on one specific period, or even subperiod, of its history. Only a few books provide an overview of modern Iraqi history. In the last twenty years, three important books have been published that give readers an overview beyond the scope of any one historical period, those by Hanna Batatu (1978), Edith and E. F. Penrose (1978), and Phebe Marr (1985). Phebe Marr's book focuses mainly on political history, though it also studies, if more briefly, the socioeconomic conditions and how they affect the political arena, as well as important cultural aspects. The Penroses' book combines political history with important sections dedicated to the development of the Iraqi economy, including the development of the petroleum industry. Both books are very informative and contain much helpful analysis. Marr's book is particularly suitable for guiding the reader through the complex and often perplexing political events and developments. Both books are written mainly from the viewpoint of the central governments in Baghdad. Another book that discusses the immediately premonarchical and monarchical periods, as well as the years following the revolution in 1958, is the monumental work by Hanna Batatu (see the next section).

THE SOCIAL STRUCTURE, PROCESSES OF SOCIAL CHANGE, AND THEIR EFFECT ON THE POLITICAL SYSTEM IN MONARCHICAL IRAQ

The complexity of Iraqi society and the internal tensions that characterized it (Sunni Arabs, Shii Arabs, Kurds, Turkomans, Christians, Jews, and other communities; the ruling elite vis-à-vis the tribes and the modern middle and lower-middle strata, the tribes vis-à-vis the urban administration, and the Shii holy cities vis-à-vis Baghdad and Basra), as well as its regional geopolitical status, were the factors that affected the nature of the political conditions within Iraq and its foreign policy. Most sociological research on monarchical Iraq centers on the development of the elite, or ruling classes, and the relations between it and the Shii, Kurdish, and tribal centrifugal forces. The social developments among the Shiis and the Kurds have not been properly covered in research to date. In addition, the social processes among the Westernized modern middle strata—which, throughout the entire monarchical period, suffered from inadequate political representation, but exerted a powerful influence over the growth of pan-Arab nationalism as well as over the conditions under which the Baghdadi politicians operated—have not yet been thoroughly examined.

The most thorough and comprehensive study written on the sociopolitical conditions and political developments in Iraq is that of Hanna Batatu (1978). This is a study of Iraq's old landed and commercial class and its Baathists and Free Officers, but it centers mainly on Iraq's Communist party. The book is based on twenty years of research, using a vast quantity of primary and secondary Iraqi, British, and other sources. Batatu had access to Iraqi sources that were not open to other scholars. The book includes a wealth of information on personalities, tribes, and political movements, parties, and developments from the end of the nineteenth century to 1974. Batatu's book is composed of three parts, two of which are actually independent books in their own right. His contribution to the history of Iraq and the modern Middle East relates principally to the first two parts. The first part comprises an analysis of the social structure of the ruling elite in Iraq at the end of the Ottoman period; the second part provides a detailed and enlightening description and analysis of the Communist movement in Iraq. The third part discusses the period from the late 1950s to the mid-1970s and provides a great deal of historical data; however, by contrast to the two previous parts, the author did not have access to the same scope of sources as those of the previous periods. The result is a far less impressive account and occasional conceptual mistakes (like the definition of the Baath regime in the mid-1970s as essentially an army officers' regime). Despite the fact that Batatu's own ideological outlook is Marxist, he is not dogmatic and does not attempt to bend reality to conform to his social theory. Batatu makes skillful use of his method as a tool for historical and social analysis and is aware of its limitations, in view of the difference between the conditions prevailing in Iraq and non-European Middle Eastern countries and those of the Western European countries where this method originated.

Despite this book's unmatched impact on the study of Iraq's socioeconomic history, it also has a number of weak points. The Westernized modern middle class is not sufficiently addressed or exhaustively discussed with regard to the political consequences of its rise in Iraq in the 1930s and 1940s. Accordingly, the discussion of the role of nationalism and pan-Arab ideology is marginal in comparison to the effect it had on the political climate during the monarchical period. The focus on the development of the Communist party is somewhat disproportionate to the actual political (as different from the intellectual) impact of this party on Iraq's history. Also, as Batatu concentrated on the social conditions and the internal political arena, the book does not sufficiently consider the reciprocal relationship between the social structure, the internal political system, and the geopolitical status of modern Iraq and its foreign policy. Finally, Batatu pays too little attention to the state and its role. Despite these limitations, however, Batatu's book is a major milestone in the study of modern Iraq.

Thirteen years after the publication of *The Old Social Classes*, an anthology of articles in honor of Hanna Batatu edited by Robert Fernea and William Roger Louis (1991) appeared, dealing with the background of the 1958 revolution in light of his book and providing a critical examination of its arguments. This anthology includes a number of important articles that discuss the social conditions and political developments that led to the fall of the monarchy in 1958. Unlike Batatu's book, most of the articles place more emphasis on the external effects exerted by the conditions prevailing in the Middle Eastern arena and by Britain and the United States, noting the various trends in their policy and discussing the modern middle class and the minorities. Of particular importance are the articles by Marion Farouk-Sluglett and Peter Sluglett, "The Social Classes and the Origins of the Revolution"; Robert Fernea, "State and Tribe in Southern Iraq; The Struggle for Hegemony before the 1958 Revolution"; Sami Zubaida, "Community, Class, and Minorities in Iraqi Politics"; and Roger Owen, "Class and Class Politics in Iraq before 1958: The 'Colonial and Postcolonial State.' "

The development of the elite in monarchical Iraq and its acquisition of ruling status are discussed in an article by David Pool (1980). This article also appeared in an anthology edited by Abbas Kelidar (1979). The development of the agrarian regime and its social consequences are analyzed in an important article by Marion Farouk Sluglett and Peter Sluglett, "The Transformation of Land Tenure and Rural Social Structures in Central and Southern Iraq, 1870–1958" (1983).

THE SHIIS AND THE TRIBES IN IRAQ

The Shiis constitute more than 50 percent of the population of Iraq, which has been ruled by the Sunni minority and its constituent ruling elites since the establishment of the state. During the monarchical period, the Sunni Arab urban ruling elite succeeded in co-opting individual Shiis into the political establishment, and Shii tribal dignitaries-turned-landowners became a part of the social elite. In this way, to a certain extent, the ruling elite disarmed the Shii threat to the status quo, which ensured Sunni Arab dominance.

The Shii tribes of southern and central Iraq have been discussed in several works, generally from an anthropological angle: G. Maxwell (1957); W. Thesiger (1964); Elizabeth Fernea (1969); and Robert Fernea (1970). These studies are extremely important in describing the influence of modernization on the rural tribal social structure in southern Iraq and in the Middle East in general; however, they make nearly no reference to the Shii nature of the tribes. This way of life is now dying as a result of the regime's draining of the marshes. It is quite possible that these are the last studies of the Iraqi marsh Arabs that will ever be written.

The Shiis as a denominational and political community in Iraq have been almost entirely ignored by research. The one full-length book on their history during the nineteenth century, but more so during the first half of the twentieth century, is that of Yitzhak Nakash (1994). Although it has its weaknesses, this book is an important contribution to the field. In part 1, Nakash discusses the rise of the Shii holy cities Najaf and Karbala, the conversion in the Iraqi south of Sunni Arab tribes to Shiism, and relations between the Shiis and the Ottoman authorities leading to the British occupation. This part represents a good overview of the issues under discussion, but it is based mainly on secondary sources and makes no independent use of the crucial and rich Ottoman archives. Likewise, the epilogue, which is dedicated to the 1990–1991 Gulf crisis, seems to be based entirely on secondary sources (there is no mention of any specific source, and thus the reader is left with learned guesses), and it leaves much to be desired. The actual idea of investigating the connection between social and political developments that occurred during the first half of the twentieth century and the Shii intifada of March 1991 is a very promising one. However, because the connection with the rest of the book is very tenuous, the epilogue adds little. More important, the larger part of the book, describing the various struggles within the Shii community and between it and the British and Iraqi authorities during 1919–1958, as well as the evolution of the Shii rituals, is based on solid independent research and brings much new information and analysis.

ECONOMY AND PETROLEUM IN IRAQ DURING THE MONARCHICAL PERIOD

The economy of Iraq under the monarchy has been discussed in several books, which investigate it from several different standpoints. At the same time, there is still no systematic comprehensive work that provides both an overview and a detailed picture of the Iraqi economy in this period. Also missing is the link between the economic and political spheres.

A significant contribution to the economic history of Iraq is the book by Joseph Sassoon (1987). The book focuses on economic policy and does not examine its broader political and social contexts. Two books dealing with the industrialization of Iraq that cover a period extending beyond the fall of the monarchical regime are those of Ferhang Jalal (1972) and Kathleen Langley (1961). An extensive chapter on the economy of monarchical Iraq is included in the general book on Iraq by Edith and E. F. Penrose (1978).

The subject of petroleum and the Iraqi economy is discussed in several books on petroleum and the Middle East in general. Most useful are those by Benjamin Shwadran (1959) and Stephen H. Longrigg (1961). Iraqi petroleum as a consideration in British policy in the early years of the twentieth century is discussed in two books based on British documents: those by Marian Kent (1976) and Helmut Mejcher (1976).

THE BEGINNING OF MODERNIZATION IN THE NINETEENTH CENTURY

The beginning of modernization in Iraq has been given only minimal consideration in research. The political developments of Iraq in the nineteenth and early twentieth centuries have been neglected, as has Iraq of that period, whose Ottoman vilayets (districts) were only marginal from the standpoint of the Ottoman center. Tom Nieuewenhuis (1982) deals with the end of the Mamluk period in the early nineteenth century. This was when the first stirrings of modernization began to be felt in what is today Iraq; the collapse of Mamluk rule opened the way to the integration of the three Ottoman vilayets that later became Iraq into the modernization process of the Ottoman Empire. The book deals with relations between the tribes and the Mamluk rulers and, to a more limited degree, between them and the central Ottoman administration. The paucity of sociopolitical research to date on Iraq during the nineteenth century and the beginning of the modern era is especially striking in view of the lack of even a single monograph or comprehensive article on the role of Midhat Pasha, the Ottoman ruler who pushed the three vilayets into the modern era (1869–1872). The only noteworthy study on this topic was published in the 1960s, that by Albertine Jwaidah (1963). The political developments at the end of the Ottoman period are discussed in a comprehensive, detailed study by Ghassan Atiyah (1973).

THE ESTABLISHMENT AND CONSOLIDATION OF THE IRAQI STATE AND BRITISH POLICY

The Iraqi state was established by Britain following World War I and the defeat and dismemberment of the Ottoman Empire. The establishment of Iraq from three former Ottoman vilayets, Baghdad, Basra, and Mosul, was the result of imperial calculations and struggles within the British administration of Mesopotamia (Iraq) and in London. After a few years of British military rule in the area, starting with the occupation of Basra in 1914, Britain received a mandate from the League of Nations in 1920 to govern Iraq and prepare it for political independence. Having decided against direct rule, the British established an Arab government in 1920, and in 1921 they made King Feisal, of the Hashemite house, king of Iraq. The mandate years (1920–1932) were also the formative years of the Iraqi state. In the 1920s, a long, wearisome, and crisis-laden series of negotiations took place between Britain and Iraq with regard to a treaty intended to define the relations between the two countries and to transform Iraq into an independent state while guaranteeing the vital British interests. The 1930 Anglo-Iraqi treaty, by which Iraq received its formal independence in 1932, did not put an end to the complex, bitter, and distrustful nature of British-Iraqi relations. The result was an anti-British revolt in 1941, led by Rashid Ali al-Gaylani, and eventually war between Iraq and Britain.

The establishment and consolidation of Iraq have been reviewed in three books, all published in the 1930s, by P. W. Ireland (1937), E. Main (1935), and H. A. Foster (1935). This topic is also discussed in S. H. Longrigg's book on the political and administrative history of Iraq throughout the first half of the twentieth century (1953). All were based mainly on British sources and present the British perspective, paying little attention to Iraqi sources and points of view. Some primary British sources were available to the authors, but during the period when the works were written, the main body of British documents was not yet available. Of the four, that by Ireland is both best written and most solidly based.

A breakthrough in research on the last years of the Ottoman Empire and the establishment of the Iraqi state was achieved with the publication of two studies during the 1970s, those by Peter Sluglett (1976) and Ghassan Atiyah (1973). One article by Amal Vinogradov (1972) is useful in some respects.

In the first part of his book, Batatu (1978) provides a comprehensive picture of Iraqi society during the last decades of Ottoman rule and under the monarchy. The first part of Atiyah's book deals with the advent of organized political activity in Iraq since the turn of the century and discusses the first steps in the organizational process of the nationalist political movement in Iraq. The second part discusses British policy in Iraq during World War I and immediately thereafter. The third part covers the anti-British revolt of 1920 and the establishment of the Iraqi state by Britain. One interpretation, and a highly controversial one at that, of the nature and circumstances of the 1920 revolt is provided by Vinogradov (1972). Rather than a tribal and a Shii religious revolt with some early Iraqi-national characteristics, as widely seen by most scholars, Vinogradov presents it as a straightforward secular-nationalist revolt.

Peter Sluglett's pioneering work centers on the establishment and political development of Iraq during the British mandate and on Britain's policy toward Mesopotamia and Iraq from the outbreak of World War I in 1914 to Iraqi formal independence in 1932. Sluglett's study is based primarily on British sources of which he was the first to make systematic use. Despite its author's lack of access to Iraqi archival sources, its contribution to the study of Iraq is considerable. Britain's policy in Mesopotamia on the eve of World War I is covered extensively in a book by Stuart Cohen (1976). The political process that led to the inclusion of Mosul and a part of Kurdistan in the Iraqi state is described very ably by Robert Olson (1992) in an article based on British documents. Changes in British policy toward Iraq and British status in Iraq from the end of the mandate until the crisis of the Rashid Ali revolt in 1941 are discussed by Daniel Silverfarb (1986). Based on British sources, the book examines the developments in Iraqi-British relations up to the 1941 crisis, and the weakening of Britain's position in Iraq in the face of anti-British nationalism.

THE INTERNAL POLITICS AND THE REGIONAL AND FOREIGN POLICIES OF MONARCHICAL IRAQ

As pointed out previously, the Hashemite monarchical period in Iraq may be divided into three subperiods: 1920–1932 (the creation of the state, the crowning of Feisal I, and Feisal's rule under the mandate); 1932–1941 (from formal independence to the Rashid Ali revolt); and 1941–1958 (from the revolt to the downfall of the monarchy). The first two subperiods have been extensively researched, and a number of monographs and articles have been written on them. The third period (1941–1958) has not yet been sufficiently explored, yet two good books have been devoted to it, those by Silverfarb (1994) and Matthew Elliot (1996). Silverfarb's book is based mainly on recently released British documents and discusses in a methodical and comprehensive way the beginning of the decline of British status in Iraq following the suppression of the 1941 revolt, despite the British military victory. Elliot examines the British influence on Iraq and British-Iraqi relations until 1958. His book is based on British and American documents as well as on secondary Iraqi sources.

Iraq between independence and the 1958 revolution is the subject of an extensive and very helpful book by Majid Khadduri (1960). An important critical-interpretative article on monarchical Iraq written by Elie Kedourie, ''Iraqi Kingdom: A Retrospect'' (1970), provides a rare insight by a great historian and a native of Iraq into the essence of Iraqi history. One book that reviews Iraq's political development and international policy and status in the 1920s and 1930s is that by Ahmad Shikara (1987). This book is based on British and Iraqi sources and gives a general picture of Iraq's political history in the period between the two world wars and of the reciprocal relationship between foreign policy and internal politics.

Iraq was the first Arab state in which pan-Arab nationalist ideology became a dominant force in domestic politics and a central factor in regional foreign policy, which was directed at dominance throughout the Fertile Crescent and leadership status in the entire Arab world. Pan-Arab foreign policy during the period of Feisal I (1921–1933) is the subject of an article by Nur al-Din Masalha (1991). Another article on the subject was written by Ahmad Shikara, which appears in an anthology edited by Abbas Kelidar (1979). (This anthology includes several articles that deal with post-1958 Iraq.) The growth of pan-Arab nationalism in Iraq and the transformation of pan-Arab ideology into a dominant force in Iraq are discussed in a book by Reeva Simon (1986). Simon focused her discussion on the development and formation of the educational system and the indoctrination of the army and its officer class.

Iraq was also the first modern Arab state to undergo coups d'état, and the first in which the army became the central political force (between 1936 and 1941). The development of the Iraqi army and its transformation into the central political force in the second half of the 1930s are the subject of a book by Mohammad A. Tarbush (1982). This study, which reviews and analyzes the military coups in Iraq between 1936 and 1941, is well based on British, Iraqi, and German sources. An additional article dealing with the development of the Iraqi army in the 1920s is that by Paul P. J. Hemphill in Kelidar (1979), and an overview of the history of the Iraqi army is to be found in Mark A. Heller, ''Iraq's Army: Military Weakness, Political Utility,'' in A. Baram and B. Rubin (1994).

Since the 1930s, Iraq has played a unique and central role in the Palestine question. Iraq was the first Arab state for which the Palestine conflict became a domestic political issue: whenever a political opposition group within the oligarchy wanted to hurt the government-of-the-day in the most painful way, it attacked it by claiming that it was betraying the Palestinian cause. As soon as this group came to power, it, in its own turn, became the target of similar accusations. Likewise, when the educated, but politically disempowered, city middle social strata rebelled against the ruling oligarchy, more often than not they, too, used the Palestinian issue as a battering ram. The Palestine issue also served as a tool with which monarchical Iraq sought to advance its ambitions in all-Arab and foreign policy: most Iraqi governments tried to assume Arab leadership through radical positions in this particular realm.

A book that deals with the growth of Iraq's involvement and commitment in the Palestine question is that by Michael Eppel (1994). It analyzes how the Palestine question became an issue in domestic politics in Iraq and why Iraq became the flagship of extremism in the Palestine question during the 1930s and 1940s. Eppel shows how Iraq's weakness as a political community, along with the complex relationships between its conservative ruling elite, whose politicians carried the standard of pan-Arabism, and the modern middle and lower-middle class recruited by means of pan-Arab ideology, constituted the internal background for the growth of Iraq's involvement in the Palestine question. By examining the role played by the Palestine conflict in Iraqi politics, Eppel clarifies the function of pan-Arab ideology and sheds light on the convoluted relationship between the conservative ruling elite and the new social forces in Iraq of the 1930s and 1940s.

The pro-German, anti-British Rashid Ali movement in 1941 constitutes a watershed in the history of monarchical Iraq. The revolt and the subsequent war between Iraq and Britain became especially symbolic for the adherents of nationalist ideology in Iraq. All the books that deal with Iraq during the 1930s and 1940s devote important sections to this subject. There is also an extensive body of descriptive literature that reviews the events of 1941. From the standpoint of historical and political science research, it is important to note the chapters in a book by Lukasz Hirszowicz on the Third Reich and the Arab East (1966). Hirszowicz's study is based on British and German sources, as well as some Iraqi sources. A book based on the study of British and Iraqi sources, with a distinct pro-Iraqi slant, is that by Walid M. S. Hamdi (1987). In an effort to present the Rashid Ali movement as a national revolution, the author downplays (but does not ignore) the effects of the Fascist and pro-Nazi trends in Iraq. The advantage of this book lies in the combination of a social and political analysis of the conditions in Iraq with a discussion of those that prevailed in the international arena in the 1930s and up to 1941.

After the end of World War II and the establishment of the Arab League, the Arab world underwent a process of polarization between the Egyptian-Saudi bloc and the Hashemite bloc, in which Iraq was the dominant partner. A dis-

cussion of postwar Iraqi foreign policy is provided in an article by Michael
Eppel (1992) and by Silverfarb (1994).

THE 1958 REVOLUTION AND THE POSTREVOLUTIONARY ERA

The fall of the monarchy, the murder of the king, and the expulsion of the
Hashemite dynasty and the old ruling elite in 1958 opened the door to a new
era in the history of modern Iraq. The regime established in July 1958 under
Brigadier General Abd al-Karim Qasim was based on populism, vaguely related
to communism, with an emphasis on Iraqi territorial nationalism, and yet paid
some lip service to pan-Arab nationalism; accordingly, it was characterized by
a struggle between pan-Arab and Iraqi-territorial orientations, as well as by an
attempt to involve Shiis and, although less so, Kurds, in addition to Sunni Arabs,
in the building of a new Iraq.

General Books

Two thorough monographs have been written on the Qasim regime. The one
by Uriel Dann (1969), despite the fact that it is based principally on articles and
items from the press, is an excellent historical work. The other, which includes
also a number of illuminating interviews, is that by Majid Khadduri (1969).
Both books, however, do not extend beyond political history. They deal only in
passing with socioeconomic issues and ignore culture and the culturally carried
ideology. As a result, both missed a critical ideological component, central to
the understanding of the regime, namely, Qasim's fascination with the ancient,
pre-Islamic history of Mesopotamia (see Baram 1991).

An important study of postmonarchical Iraq from 1958 through the mid-1980s
is that by Marion Farouk-Sluglett and Peter Sluglett (1987). It sums up the
information that was available and adds much new information and analysis. A
meaningful contribution of the book is that it extends beyond the field of pure
political history, as it includes sections devoted to Iraqi economy and society.
Batatu's book (1978) includes several chapters with much information on
Qasim's regime. Batatu's treatment of the Arif brothers' period is scant, but he
provides more information about the Baath period up to 1974–1975.

Majid Khadduri (1969) deals very ably with Qasim's rule and with part of
the Arif period, but the period beyond 1966 is not adequately researched. His
Socialist Iraq (1978), however, is a shallow and biased account of the political
history of the Baath regime until 1977. Christine Moss Helms's *Iraq* (1984)
should be consulted for valuable information regarding the ruling Baath party.
It includes useful information and interesting interviews with Baathi luminaries.
A major shortcoming, however, is the author's uncritical approach to the regime.

Samir al-Khalil's *Republic of Fear* (1989) is a passionate manifesto against
terror and its use by the Baath regime to repress and dominate the Iraqi people.

Khalil (a pen name chosen by the Iraqi architect Kanan Makiya) gives a very convincing description of life in a terror-stricken and controlled society. Rather than dispassionate historical analysis, this is a philosophical treatise and a study of the nature of modern dictatorship and the routinization of evil. Khalil's booklet *The Monument* (1991) is an essay on the political use of architecture and public monuments in Baathist Iraq. Makiya's third book (1993), this time under his own name, is a powerful indictment of Arab intellectuals who, as a result of their Arab nationalist convictions, were ready to turn a blind eye to the massacre of the Kurds and the oppression of the Arab Shiis by the Sunni Arab–controlled Baath regime. These intellectuals, both in the Arab lands and in the West, even went so far as to accuse the United States and its Western allies of intentionally sucking Saddam Hussein into the Kuwaiti ''trap'' between 1988 and the summer of 1990. Makiya asserts that these conspiracy theories, which could never be substantiated, are designed to present Saddam Hussein as a victim, rather than as what he is: a whimsical and cruel tyrant.

Helen Chapin Metz's edited volume (1990) is very helpful, giving most of the basic facts needed by those who have never studied modern Iraq. From borders and geography, through society and the economy, to the military and political history, the volume offers a wealth of information in a concise and clear fashion.

By far the best history to date of the Baath party, not only in Iraq but in the Arab East as a whole, up to 1966, is Devlin (1976). The study is both detailed and comprehensive and gives an excellent picture of the formative years of a party that, since the 1960s, has been ruling the two most important Arab states east of the Mediterranean.

Studies of the Ruling Elites

Phebe Marr's articles (1970, 1975) paved the way for elite studies in modern Iraq. They cover a long period, from 1948 to the early 1970s, and are a must in this area. Batatu (1978) provides much useful information regarding the Iraqi ruling elites since the 1920s. While the Arif period is only sparsely covered, Batatu provides much information on Qasim's elite and the Baathi leadership and is the first to discuss, albeit very briefly, the tribal background and connections of the Arifs and central Baathi figures like President Ahmad Hasan al-Bakr and his deputy, Saddam Hussein. His analysis, however, is not systematic, and the information is updated only to the early 1970s. More analysis is provided by Batatu (1985).

Detailed information, updated to 1986, and a systematic analysis of the Baathi power elite and its transformation since 1966 are provided by Amatzia Baram (1989). The article demonstrates that by 1986 the new rulers of Baghdad hailed from the lower (though not the lowest) social strata of the Iraqi countryside. They are civilian party apparatchicks with little formal education. They were born mainly between 1938 and 1942 and are mainly Sunni Arabs, with a sprinkle of Shiis. Finally, within the ruling elite, Saddam's own extended family is very prominent. Baram's main findings still hold true in 1997, but in view of new information there is need to expand substantially the tribal component, a very central one under Saddam Hussein.

The Islamic Fundamentalist Movements

A phenomenon unique to postmonarchical Iraq is the predominance of the Shii fundamentalist movements among the Iraqi movements of political Islam. Under the monarchy, particularly since the late 1940s, one could observe the low-level activities of two small Sunni-Arab political parties, the Muslim Brothers and Hizb al-Tahrir (the Liberation party). A few religious Shii young men, looking for active political work along modern lines, which they could not find in the Shii centers, joined these parties, but they were an exception. Because these parties were essentially a part of the establishment and refrained from any radical action against the ruling regimes, their limited activities were tolerated at least until the early 1970s. Because they made no attempt to oppose the regimes, and because their activities were diffused and small-scale and their organization almost nonexistent, the Sunni religious movements were almost invisible to the researcher's eye, and very little is known about them. By contrast, much more is known about the Shii opposition movements.

There are only three authors who have dealt more or less extensively with the radical Shii movements of Iraq and their credo. The contribution to the renewal of important aspects of Islamic law by Ayatollah Muhammad Baqir al-Sadr (1933–1980), the most charismatic Iraqi Shii jurist in the postmonarchical era, is analyzed very ably by Chibli Mallat (1993). Sadr's main contributions were to open a new debate in the areas of Islamic banking and economics and to chart the first map for an Islamic constitution. In view of his young age, his influence on the Iranian constitution was almost unbelievable. Sadr's influence on the Iraqi Shii movements' political thought and practice, as well as the social and political history of these movements, is analyzed by Joyce N. Wiley (1992), Chibli Mallat (1988), and Amatzia Baram (1990a, 1994). Wiley's main contribution is her analysis of the social origins of the revolutionary Shiis, but she also deals well with the birth and activities mainly of the Najaf-born (1957) Dawa (''Call'') Islamic party. Both her primary and secondary sources regarding the ideology of the movements, however, are insufficient, with the result that her analysis does not reach its full potential. Baram's main contributions are an account of the Dawa's inception and its organization and recruiting techniques and an analysis of its discourse, as well as that of the Tehran-born (1981) and -based Supreme Assembly of the Islamic Revolution of Iraq and the Karbala-born (1960s) Hizb al-Amal al-Islami (Islamic Action party), and the cultural activities of the movements and the political messages they convey. Baram (1990a) and Mallat (1988) reach very different conclusions as to the degree and limits of ecumenical (Shii-Sunni) discourse in Sadr's writings. The comparison between these two interpretations of Sadr's theory is fascinating.

IRAQ'S FOREIGN RELATIONS AND THE IRAN-IRAQ WAR

To date, there are only two comprehensive (and valuable) studies that analyze Iraq's foreign relations, those of Haim Shemesh (1992) and Eberhard Kienle (1990). Shemesh deals almost exclusively with only one aspect, that of Soviet-Iraqi relations under the Baath during 1968–1988, and Kienle with Iraqi-Syrian relations during 1968–1989. Shemesh's work is an excellent example of how one may study a subject from afar, basing oneself almost exclusively on open, nonarchival sources (all Soviet and Iraqi archives were still unavailable), and yet come up with an impressive work (Kienle's work will be discussed later).

Khadduri (1988) is an attempt to explain the historical setting and the diplomatic, legal, and ideological background of the Iran-Iraq war. Even though the book is strongly inclined towards the Iraqi viewpoint, when read critically, it offers useful information. Cordesman and Wagner (1990) is a highly professional and, to date, by far the best military analysis of this long and complex war, so replete with tactical and strategic surprises. Starting with an overview of the conditions that shaped the war, the authors describe the war in detail, phase by phase, in a clear and well-informed fashion, and in the end they draw important conclusions. The main emphasis is on the military aspects, but the political dimension is also discussed when necessary. The professional soldier and the military historian could have further benefitted from additional maps describing the main battles. Bergquist (1988) and Pelletiere (1992) are recommended as additional, more narrowly focused reading. An excellent comprehensive study mainly of the political (local, regional, and international) aspects of the war, but dealing also with its diplomatic and socioeconomic aspects, is Chubin and Tripp (1988). Relatively little is dedicated to the military aspects, but the appendixes include the military balance throughout most of the war. This book complements Cordesman and Wagner well. Despite some too-sweeping generalizations, Dilip Hiro (1989) provides a clear description and analysis of the political aspects of the war, with due attention both to the warring sides and the forces on the sideline: the superpowers and the Arabs. Hiro's account of the military aspects of the war is rudimentary. A very promising book-in-the-making is Kenneth Pollack's analysis of Arab armies, which includes an excellent chapter on the Iraqi army.

The Kuwait Crisis and the Gulf War: The Political, Social, and Economic Aspects

Baram and Rubin (1994) and Danchev and Keohane (1994) are both edited volumes containing contributions by Middle East historians and political scientists, many of whom are country specialists. Both volumes deal methodically and in depth with the socioeconomic and political processes in Baghdad and in the regional and international capitals that led to the Kuwait crisis, but more so with the unfolding crisis following the invasion, the Gulf War and its immediate aftermath. The main contributions of Baram and Rubin's volume are its discussion of decision making in Baghdad and the way in which the regional capitals and forces reacted, the Shii and Kurdish revolts in the wake of the war, a discussion of the historical weaknesses of the Iraqi army, and the economic ramifications of the crisis for Iraq and the oil market. Danchev and Keohane provide a particularly instructive analysis of the European angles, as well as some military, theoretical, and legal aspects of the war. The two volumes offer somewhat different viewpoints and complement each other. The book of Freedman and Karsh (1993) provides a good analysis of the international (non–Middle Eastern) aspects of the Kuwait crisis. By contrast, its treatment of the Middle Eastern arena and, in particular, Iraq, leaves a great deal to be desired.

The American angle of the road to war is the subject of numerous journal articles and a few books, noteworthy among which is Woodward (1991). However, the first (and, so far, only) studies to be based not only on interviews with American officials but also on a systematic examination of numerous U.S. government documents, declassified since 1992, are Karabell (1995) and Baram (1996a). Karabell's study analyzes carefully, and very ably, American policies from the end of the Iran-Iraq War to the invasion (1988–August 2, 1990). The study is well documented and very convincing. Baram starts at the dawn of the new Iraqi-American relationship (1979–1980), but he too focuses on the crucial years of 1988–1990. The main difference between the two articles is that while Karabell deals almost exclusively with the decision-making circles in Washington, D.C., Baram places his emphasis on the interaction between Washington and Baghdad.

The Gulf War and Its Aftermath: The Military and American Political Dimensions

Numerous authors have attempted an analysis of this swift and decisive military victory, which resulted in a political stalemate. Schwarzkopf and Petre (1992) is an account of the war as it looked from the command post, fascinating, yet very personal and delineating only the broadest contours. Atkinson (1993) and U.S. News and World Report Staff (1992) are more detailed studies. A very good overview of the military aspects of the war is Gordon and Trainor (1995). By far the most exhaustive analysis of the air war, written for the benefit of professional military analysts, is Eliot A. Cohen, editor (1993), a five-volume study done in cooperation with the U.S. Air Force. Scales (1993), for his part, provides the most detailed study to date of the role of the U.S. Army in the war, accompanied by many useful battle maps. The combination of Scales, on the one hand, and Gordon and Trainor, on the other, which reveals some differences, may be very beneficial for the reader. Cordesman and Wagner (1996) is a superb and most comprehensive study of the war, using all these sources and adding much original analysis and new information.

The military balance in the Gulf area following the Gulf War and how the threats from Iraq and Iran may be dealt with are the subjects of Cordesman (1994). In his usual systematic approach, Cordesman analyzes the developments in both armies between 1991 and 1993 and assesses their regional and international implications. Cordesman's political observations are also of great value to anyone who wishes to probe the uncertainties of the postwar situation in the Gulf. Eisenstadt (1993) is an in-depth but more narrowly focused study, dealing with the efforts at reconstructing the Iraqi army after the defeat and heavy losses of January–February 1991. The study is thorough and very well informed. Between Cordesman and Eisenstadt the reader is well informed of the military consequences of the war.

An interesting and challenging attempt to look toward the year 2000 in terms of Gulf security, Iraqi domestic affairs and foreign policies, energy, and U.S. and European attitudes toward the Gulf countries is Doran and Buck (1991). Most relevant to our subject is Phebe Marr's contribution. Most of the article's information and assessments remain relevant due to the fact that to date, almost as if trapped in a time capsule, Iraq remains under the rule of Saddam Hussein, uncooperative with the United Nations, relatively isolated, and unable to sell much of its oil on the world markets. As a result, it still faces essentially the same dilemmas as it did in 1991. The same may be said about Baram (1993) and Mylroie (1991), which discuss the power structure in Iraq in the wake of the Gulf War. Even though some very central members of Saddam Hussein's family have been murdered by him or demoted since Baram's article was published, and power has been shifted from his elder son, Udayy, his cousins, and his half-brothers mainly to Saddam Hussein's younger son, Qusayy, as well as to party old-timers, the same structure is still essentially there. A new dimension of the Iraqi Baathi regime's power structure, the tribal one, is exposed and analyzed in Baram (1997).

Political Biographies of Saddam Hussein

An academic, well-informed, and comprehensive political biography of Saddam Hussein has still to be written. The first biography ever to appear in English was a short article (Baram 1980, updated in Baram 1990b). A few months later two biographies appeared in English, Iskandar (1980) and Matar (1981). Even though semiofficial, these biographies, and particularly Iskandar's, are rich with important details and useful inferences that may be found nowhere else. Curiously, even though they started some of the myths of Saddam Hussein's heroism, at an early stage of his presidency (1979) he still allowed many embarrassing facts to permeate. Thus, for example, there was no attempt to hide the important role that many of his comrades whom he murdered in the 1970s had played in the 1950s and 1960s during the underground struggle. When read critically, these are valuable sources. For hitherto-unknown episodes in Saddam Hussein's prenatal and very early childhood history, one should turn to the article of Peter Waldman (1991).

Karsh and Rautsi (1991) is based in large part on secondary sources, summing them up well. When the authors come up with something original, however, they are often confused or simply wrong. To give only one example: on the one hand, the authors define Saddam Hussein as a typical product of the Iraqi political culture: "[His] ruthlessness," they argue, "has not so much to do with personal whims as with the nature of the Iraqi state. . . . He did not set the rules of the game in this cruel system." On the other hand, however, a few lines later the authors' thesis collapses by itself when they correctly point out that the secret of his success was "forging . . . alliances only to break them . . . betraying friends and foes alike" (4). In the first place, it is not very clear how one can "betray" one's foes. More significantly, the conclusion from this account must be that only Saddam Hussein understood what the authors consider to be "the rules of the [Iraqi] game." Apparently, the hundreds of his own Iraqi party old-timers, some of them people who recruited Saddam Hussein himself, who died at his hand in total bewilderment and disbelief, were ignorant of these rules. The truth, of course, is that Saddam is indeed unique, even in the violent political ambiance of Iraq. No other ruler or ruling elite in Iraq since 1920 ever slew their own associates only because they had a hunch that they might oppose them later, or executed a very senior Shii clergyman as he did. No other head of the Iraqi state—king, dictator, or "president"—ordered the mass murder of many scores of thousands of Iraqi citizens as Saddam Hussein has done. Saddam set his own rules, and they were very different from those of his predecessors. This book is particularly disappointing in view of the good advice the authors received from a number of solid scholars specializing in Iraq.

The Kurds of Iraq and Human Rights

Ghareeb (1981) and Jawad (1981) are very informative studies. Jawad goes as far as the March 1970 agreement between the Baath regime and Mulla Mustafa al-Barazani, and Ghareeb continues to the collapse of the Kurdish revolt in 1975. O'Ballance (1973) is a detailed study of the relations between the central governments in Baghdad and their Kurds during the tense years of 1961–1970. A more general book, an edited volume dealing with Kurdish history all over the Middle East since the Ottoman period, is Chaliand (1980). Only a small part (Vanly 1980) on Iraq may be found there, however. The same applies to Mac-Donald (1988). An outstanding historical and social study of the Kurds in the Middle East is Bruinessen (1978). Another valuable study, dealing, however, only in passing with the Kurds of Iraq, is Olson (1989). It focuses mainly on the 1925 Kurdish revolt of Shaykh Said in Kemalist Turkey and its background. McDowall (1996) is yet another example of worthwhile research dedicated to the Kurds of the Middle East since the nineteenth century. It provides a particularly good account of the Kurdish revolt of 1991 and its aftermath. Gunter (1992) is an overview of events from the Kurdish revolt of March–April 1991 to the establishment of a de facto Kurdish state in Iraqi Kurdistan. Its treatment of the political and diplomatic (regional and international) aspects is very professional and fills a large gap. However, the military side, as well as the inter-Kurdish tensions (which, admittedly, were fully exposed only after the book came out), is discussed only in passing.

The 1987–1988 massacre of the Kurds by the Baath regime in Operation Anfal is the subject of two volumes issued by Middle East Watch (1993a, 1993b). *The Destruction of Koreme* describes the end of a Kurdish village: the murder of its men and boys and the relocation of the women and children, based on oral testimonies and forensic evidence. *Genocide in Iraq* brings home the full horror of the operation, starting on a large scale in March and ending in September 1988. The operation resulted in the murder of at least 100,000 and possibly around 180,000 Kurdish men, women, and children. A comprehensive study of the state of human rights in Iraq is Middle East Watch (1990). It deals with the legal system and the institutions of repression, as well as the Kurds, the Iranian prisoners of war, and efforts to cover up violations of human rights.

Iraq and Its Neighbors

The only book on the convoluted relations between the twin Baath regimes in Baghdad and Damascus is Kienle (1990). This is a rich, well-researched, and well-written study. The Syrian side is analyzed in greater detail and with more intimate knowledge than the Iraqi one. The reason seems to be that the author was not allowed into Iraq, whereas he could spend much time in Syria, which also is a more open society than its Iraqi Baathi counterpart. Interestingly, Kienle's conclusions as to who is the more "guilty" party in sabotaging bilateral relations is in some cases very different from Baram's (1986).

Relations with all neighbors toward and during the Gulf War are discussed in Baram and Rubin (1994) and Danchev and Keohane (1994). Ottoman-Kuwaiti, Ottoman-British, Iraqi-Kuwaiti, and Iraqi-British relations in connection with the border issue and, occasionally, the Iraqi claim to Kuwait as a whole are the subject of two fine studies. Schofield (1991) and Finnie (1992) discuss the historical background of this conflict very ably, basing themselves on a wealth of archival documents. A very detailed compilation of U.N. documents connected with the Kuwait crisis and its aftermath (August 1990–early 1996) is U.N. Department of Public Information (1996). The book includes a very large number of U.N. documents, indispensable for any researcher who is interested in this unique experience in the history of relations between the United Nations and a member state. It includes an introduction by U.N. Secretary General Boutros Boutros-Ghali. Schofield (1994) is a seven-volume collection of mainly British documents from the Public Record Office (PRO) and the Oriental and India offices and the British Military Survey, and some from the U.S. National Archives and the U.N. archives. The documents deal with the period 1830–1994, including relations between the Ottoman Empire and the autonomous sheikhdom of Kuwait, Kuwaiti-British relations during the Ottoman and post-Ottoman periods, and Kuwaiti-Iraqi relations since 1920, when Great Britain created the first Iraqi government and decided to unite three disparate Ottoman provinces (Basrah, mainly Shii-Arab; Baghdad, mainly Sunni Arab; and Mosul-Kurdistan, combining mainly Sunni Kurds, Sunni Arabs, Sunni Turkomans, and Chaldean and Assyrian Christians) into one nation-state that they decided to call "Iraq," thus resurrecting a historical name of a geographical district covering part of the contemporary state. The seventh volume consists entirely of maps. Schofield (1989) consists of eleven volumes of documents, including two volumes of maps, covering the period in Iranian-Ottoman relations over the provinces of Basrah, Baghdad, and Mosul between 1840 and 1914, Iranian relations involving the same three provinces with Great Britain and the Ottomans, 1914–1920, and Iranian-Iraqi relations, 1920–1958. The main focus is on the borders issue, and the documents come from the PRO, the India office, some American correspondence with the British authorities regarding Iraq, and the private papers of C. J. Edmonds at St. Antony's College, Oxford. Schofield (1992) contains documents from the PRO and the Oriental and India offices. The last volume contains the Special Reports by the British Government to the League of Nations on the Progress of Iraq, 1920–1932. The organization of the documents in the three collections is sometimes confusing, and not all the relevant material has been gathered, but these are minor flaws: the collections are rich and extremely helpful for graduate students and researchers who would like to engage in independent research, but who cannot spend a few months in London.

Nationalism in Baathi Iraq

The only full-length book discussing the development of an Iraqi national myth under the Baath party is Baram (1991). Articles are Baram (1983b, 1983a, 1996b). The book and the earlier articles try to explain how and why the Baath regime, mainly under the influence of Saddam Hussein, endeavored during the 1970s and early 1980s to create for Iraqi Arabs a composite identity, combining Arabism, pre-Islamic Mesopotamian themes, and a whiff of Islam, with aspirations of Arab leadership and militarism. Baram's articles (1996b and 1997) analyze the new ingredients, added since the mid-1980s: neotribalism and a heavy Islamic aroma. A very different identity, democratic and liberal, is offered by the Iraqi National Congress (1993). This is an important document that is to be followed by further manifestos. The book discusses human rights violations by the regime and suggests a way to deal with the offenders once the regime is toppled. The book contains many accusations (to be verified in trial) against the regime's luminaries.

General Studies

Since 1960 the Dayan Center (previously the Shiloah Institute) of Tel Aviv University has issued annual volumes analyzing mainly political, but also economic and demographic developments in the various Middle Eastern countries. Not every year saw a volume (volumes exist only for 1960–1961, 1967, 1968, and 1969–1970), but the gaps were in most part covered when the next volume came out. The first contributions on Iraq were made by Uriel Dann and Dina Kehat, but the majority of these studies were written by Ofra Bengio. Both produced solid research and wrote cogently, turning the publication (at first *Middle East Record* and since 1976–1977 *Middle East Contemporary Survey*) into a must for any student of history and politics who needs to follow events year by year. The volumes' shortcoming, in terms of Iraqi history and politics, is their lack of a longer perspective, but this can easily be offset by consulting books that discuss the postmonarchical and Baathi periods as wholes. The combination of these annual studies and such books is highly recommended.

FUTURE RESEARCH

There are a few areas in the political and social history of Iraq that deserve much more academic attention than they have received so far. In the first place, nineteenth-century Mesopotamia-Iraq has been studied only in the most rudimentary way. To date, there is no study based on Ottoman archives dealing with the rule of the Mamluks, with the Shiis, with Midhat Pasha's government in Baghdad, and many other crucial issues. As for twentieth-century Iraq, no systematic and comprehensive study of the role and status of women in Iraq exists. Likewise, very little has been written so far about the tribes and the interaction between them and the monarchy. The period of the "old regime" of the 1940s and 1950s deserves much more attention as well, and archival and other sources are rich and available. Especially intriguing is the whole complex of the downfall of the old ruling elite and the upper social classes associated with it, which paved the way for the rise of the city lower-middle class and later the lower classes of the countryside to power. The Arifs era (1963–1968) has not been studied yet. Under the Baath regime certain key issues remained a near mystery. The regime's tribal power structure and the interaction between the center and the tribal countryside won far less attention than it deserves. Likewise, the study of the composition of the ruling and administrative elite is only at its earliest stage. The gradual opening of the Soviet archives and the opening of the Stassi archives of East Germany can provide rich source material for the study of Soviet-Iraqi and East German–Iraqi relations. The study of the Shii Islamic fundamentalist movements can still be greatly expanded. More broadly, the survival of the Baath regime despite the horrendous blows dealt to Iraq under it, starting with the Iran-Iraq War and ending with the Gulf War and the international embargo, deserves a thorough study. Such a study is closely connected with another one, long overdue, an original and analytical biography of Saddam Hussein, based mainly on the Iraqi press, books, and media records, but also on other available sources. Finally, there is much room for historical and contemporary study of the centrifugal forces that have been at work: the poor-rich, Shii-Sunni, Arab-Kurdish, and tribe-state tensions, as well as the reasons behind the survival of the Iraqi nation-state.

REFERENCES

Atiyah, Ghassan R. 1973. *Iraq, 1908–1921: A Socio-political Study.* Beirut: Arab Institute for Research and Publications.

Atkinson, Rick. 1993. *Crusade: The Untold Story of the Persian Gulf War.* Boston: Houghton Mifflin.

Baram, Amatzia. 1980. "Saddam Hussein: A Political Biography." *Jerusalem Quarterly,* no. 17 (Fall): 115–144.

———. 1983a. "Culture in the Service of Wataniyya: The Treatment of Mesopotamian-inspired Art in Baathi Iraq." *Asian and African Studies* 17:265–313.

———. 1983b. "Mesopotamian Identity in Baathi Iraq." *Middle Eastern Studies* 19, no. 4 (October): 426–455.

———. 1986. "Ideology and Power Politics in Syrian–Iraqi Relations, 1968–1984." In Moshe Maoz and Avner Yaniv, eds., *Syria under Assad.* London: Croom Helm.

———. 1989. "The Ruling Political Elite in Baathi Iraq, 1968–1986: The Changing Features of a Collective Profile." *International Journal of Middle East Studies* 21:447–493.

———. 1990a. "The Radical Shiite Opposition Movements in Iraq." In Emmanuel Sivan and Menachem Friedman, eds., *Religious Radicalism and Politics in the Middle East.* New York: State University of New York Press.

———. 1990b. "Saddam Hussein." In Bernard Reich, ed. *Political Leaders of the Contemporary Middle East and North Africa: A Biographical Dictionary.* Westport, CT: Greenwood Press.

———. 1991. *Culture, History, and Ideology in the Formation of Ba'thi Iraq, 1968–1989.* London: Macmillan.

———. 1993. "The Future of Ba'thist Iraq: Power Structure, Challenges, and Prospects." In Robert Satloff, ed., *The Politics of Change in the Middle East.* Boulder, CO: Westview Press.

———. 1994. "Two Roads to Revolutionary Shi'ite Fundamentalism in Iraq." In Martin E. Marty and R. Scott Appleby, eds., *Accounting for Fundamentalisms: The Dynamic Character of Movements.* Chicago: Chicago University Press and American Academy of Arts and Sciences.

———. 1996a. "The American Input into the Iraqi Decision Making, 1988–1990." In David Lesch, ed., *The Middle East and the United States: A Historical and Political Reassessment.* Boulder, CO: Westview Press.

———. 1996b. "Re-Inventing Nationalism in Ba'thi Iraq, 1968–1994." *Princeton Papers* no. 5, (Autumn).

———. 1997. "Neo-Tribalism in Iraq: Saddam Hussein's Tribal Policies, 1991–1996." *International Journal of Middle Eastern Studies* 29.

————. 1998. *Wither Iraq? Saddam Husayn Between His Power Base and Foreign Relations 1995–1997.* Washington, DC: Washington Institute for Near East Policy.

Baram, Amatzia, and Barry Rubin, eds. 1994. *Iraq's Road to War.* New York: St.
Martin's Press.

Batatu, Hanna. 1978. *The Old Social Classes and the Revolutionary Movements of Iraq.*
Princeton: Princeton University Press.

————. 1985. "Political Power and Social Structure in Syria and Iraq." In Samih K.
Farsoun, ed., *Arab Society.* Dover, NH: Croom Helm.

Bengio, Ofra. 1968, 1976–. Annual reports in *Middle East Record* and *Middle East
Contemporary Survey*, Tel Aviv University.

————. 1992. *Saddam Speaks on the Gulf Crisis.* Tel Aviv: Tel Aviv University.

Bergquist, Ronald E. 1988. *The Role of Airpower in the Iraq-Iran War.* Maxwell Air
Force Base, AL: Air University Press.

Bruinessen, Maarten M. Van. 1992. *Agha, Shaikh, and State: On the Social and Political
Organization of Kurdistan.* London: Zed Books.

CARDRI. 1986. *Saddam's Iraq: Revolution or Reaction?* London: Zed Books.

Chaliand, Gerard, ed. 1980. *People without a Country: The Kurds and Kurdistan.* London: Zed Books.

Chubin, Shahram, and Charles Tripp. 1988. *Iran and Iraq at War.* London: I. B. Tauris.

Cohen, Eliot, ed. 1993. *Gulf War Air Power Survey.* Vols. 1–5. Washington, DC: Office
of the Secretary of the Air Force.

Cohen, Stuart A. 1976. *British Policy in Mesopotamia, 1903–1914.* Oxford: St. Antony's
College.

Cordesman, Anthony H. 1994. *Iran and Iraq: The Threat from the Northern Gulf.* Boulder, CO: Westview Press.

Cordesman, Anthony H., and Abraham R. Wagner. 1990. *The Lessons of Modern War.*
Vol. 2, *The Iran-Iraq War.* Boulder, CO: Westview Press.

————. 1996. *The Lessons of Modern War.* Vol. 4, *The Gulf War.* Boulder, CO: Westview Press.

Danchev, Alex, and Dan Keohane, eds. 1994. *International Perspectives on the Gulf
Conflict, 1990–91.* London: Macmillan.

Dann, Uriel. 1969. *Iraq under Qassem: A Political History, 1958–1963.* Jerusalem: Israel
Universities Press.

Devlin, John F. 1976. *The Bath Party: A History from Its Origins to 1966.* Stanford,
CA: Hoover Institution Press.

Doran, Charles, and Stephen W. Buck, eds. 1991. *The Gulf, Energy and Global Security:
Political and Economic Issues.* Boulder, CO: Lynne Rienner.

Eisenstadt, Michael. 1993. *Like a Phoenix from the Ashes? The Future of Iraqi Military
Power.* Washington, DC: Washington Institute for Near East Policy.

Elliot, Matthew. 1996. *"Independent Iraq": The Monarchy and British Influence, 1941–
58.* London: Tauris Academic Studies.

Eppel, Michael. 1992. "Iraqi Politics and Regional Policies, 1945–1949." *Middle Eastern Studies* 28.

————. 1994. *The Palestine Conflict in the History of Modern Iraq: The Dynamics of
Involvement, 1928–1948.* London: Frank Cass.

Farouk-Sluglett, Marion, and Peter Sluglett. 1983. "The Transformation of Land Tenure
and Rural Social Structures in Central and Southern Iraq, 1870–1958." *International Journal of Middle Eastern Studies* 15:491–505.

——. 1987. *Iraq since 1958: From Revolution to Dictatorship.* London: KPI. 2d ed.: London: I. B. Tauris, 1990.

——. 1992. "Sunnis and Shiis Revisited: Sectarianism and Ethnicity in Authoritarian Iraq." In John P. Spagnolo, ed., *Problems in the Modern Middle East in Historical Perspective: Essays in Honor of Albert Hourani.* Reading, UK: Ithaca Press.

Fernea, Elizabeth Warnock. 1969. *Guests of the Sheik.* Garden City, NY: Doubleday.

Fernea, Robert A. 1970. *Shaykh and Effendi: Changing Patterns of Authority among the Shabana of Southern Iraq.* Cambridge, MA: Harvard University Press.

Fernea, Robert, and William Roger Louis, eds., 1991. *The Iraqi Revolution of 1958: The Old Social Classes Revisited.* London: I. B. Tauris.

Finnie, David H. 1992. *Shifting Lines in the Sand: Kuwait's Elusive Frontier with Iraq.* Cambridge, MA: Harvard University Press.

Foster, H. A. 1935. *The Making of Modern Iraq.* Norman: University of Oklahoma Press.

Freedman, Lawrence, and Efraim Karsh. 1993. *The Gulf Conflict, 1990–1991: Diplomacy and War in the New World Order.* Princeton: Princeton University Press.

Ghareeb, Edmund. 1981. *The Kurdish Question in Iraq.* Syracuse: Syracuse University Press.

Gordon, Michael R., and Bernard E. Trainor. 1995. *The Generals' War: The Inside Story of the Conflict in the Gulf.* Boston: Little, Brown.

Gunter, Michael M. 1992. *The Kurds of Iraq: Tragedy and Hope.* New York: St. Martin's Press.

Haj, Samira. 1997. *The Making of Iraq, 1900–1963: Capital, Power, and Ideology.* Ithaca, NY: State University of New York Press.

Hamdi, Walid M. S. 1987. *Rashid Ali al-Gailani and the Nationalist Movement in Iraq, 1939– 1941: A Political and Military Study of the British Campaign in Iraq and the National Revolution of May 1941.* London: Darf.

Heller, Mark A. 1994. "Iraq's Army: Military Weakness, Political Unity." In A. Baram and B. Rubin, eds., *Iraq's Road to War.* New York: St. Martin's Press.

Helms, Christine Moss. 1984. *Iraq: Eastern Flank of the Arab World.* Washington, DC: Brookings Institution.

Hemphill, Paul P. J. 1979. "The Formation of the Iraqi Army, 1921–33." In Abbas Kelidar, ed., *The Integration of Modern Iraq.* New York: St. Martin's Press.

Henderson, Simon. 1991. *Instant Empire: Saddam Hussein's Ambition for Iraq.* San Francisco: Mercury House.

Hiro, Dilip. 1989. *The Longest War: The Iran-Iraq Military Conflict.* London: Grafton Books.

——. 1992. *Desert Shield to Desert Storm: The Second Gulf War.* London: HarperCollins.

Hirszowicz, Lukasz. 1966. *The Third Reich and the Arab East.* Toronto: Toronto University Press.

Iraqi National Congress. 1993. *Crimes against Humanity and the Transition from Dictatorship to Democracy.* Salahudin, Iraq: Iraqi National Congress.

Ireland, Philip W. 1937. *Iraq: A Study in Political Development.* London: J. Cape.

Iskandar, Amir. 1980. *Saddam Hussein: The Fighter, the Thinker, and the Man.* Paris: Hachette.

Jalal, Ferhang. 1972. *The Role of Government in the Industrialization of Iraq, 1950– 1965.* London: Frank Cass.

Jawad, Saad. 1981. *Iraq and the Kurdish Question, 1958–1970*. London: Ithaca Press.

Jwaidah, Albertine. 1963. "Midhat Pasha and the Land System in Lower Iraq." *St. Antony's Papers: Middle Eastern Affairs* 3:106–136.

Karabell, Zachary. 1995. "Backfire: US Policy toward Iraq, 1988–2 August 1990." *Middle East Journal* 49, no. 1 (Winter): 28–47.

Karsh, Efraim, and Inari Rautsi [Karsh]. 1991. *Saddam Hussein, a Political Biography*. New York: Free Press.

Kedourie, Elie. 1970. "Iraqi Kingdom: A Retrospect." In Elie Kedourie, ed., *The Chatham House Version and Other Middle Eastern Studies*. London: Weidenfeld Nicholson.

Kehat, Dina. 1969. Annual report in *Middle East Record*, Shibah Center, Tel Aviv University.

Kelidar, Abbas, ed. 1979. *The Integration of Modern Iraq*. London: Croom Helm.

Kent, Marian. 1976. *Oil and Empire: British Policy and Mesopotamian Oil, 1900–1920*. New York: Harper and Row.

Khadduri, Majid. 1960. *Independent Iraq, 1932–1958: A Study in Iraqi Politics*. London: Oxford University Press.

———. 1969. *Republican Iraq: A Study in Iraqi Politics since the Revolution of 1958*. London: Oxford University Press.

———. 1978. *Socialist Iraq: A Study in Iraqi Politics since 1968*. Washington, DC: Middle East Institute.

———. 1988. *The Gulf War: The Origins and Implications of the Iraq-Iran Conflict*. New York: Oxford University Press.

al-Khalil, Samir. 1989. *Republic of Fear*. London: Hutchinson Radius.

———. 1991. *The Monument: Art, Vulgarity, and Responsibility in Iraq*. Berkeley: University of California Press.

Kienle, Eberhard. 1990. *Ba'th v. Ba'th: The Conflict between Syria and Iraq, 1968–1989*. London: I. B. Tauris.

Langley, Kathleen M. 1961. *The Industrialization of Iraq*. Cambridge, MA: Harvard University Press.

Longrigg, Stephen Himsley. 1950. *Iraq, 1900 to 1950*. New York: Oxford University Press.

———. 1961. *Oil in the Middle East, Its Discovery and Development*. New York: Oxford University Press.

Lukitz, Liora. 1995. *Iraq: The Search for National Identity*. London: Frank Cass.

MacDonald, Charles G. 1988. "The Kurdish Question in the 1980s." In Milton J. Esman and Itamar Rabinovich, eds., *Ethnicity, Pluralism, and the State in the Middle East*. Ithaca: Cornell University Press.

Main, Ernest. 1935. *Iraq from Mandate to Independence*. London: G. Allen and Unwin.

Makiya, Kanan. 1993. *Cruelty and Silence: War, Tyranny, Uprising, and the Arab World*. New York: W. W. Norton.

Mallat, Chibli. 1988. "Religious Militancy in Contemporary Iraq: Muhammad Baqir al-Sadr and the Sunni-Shi'i Paradigm." *Third World Quarterly* 10:699–729.

———. 1993. *The Renewal of Islamic Law: Muhammad Baqer as-Sadr, Najaf, and the Shi'i International*. Cambridge: Cambridge University Press.

Marr, Phebe. 1970. "Iraq's Leadership Dilemma: A Study in Leadership Trends, 1948–1968." *Middle East Journal* 24:283–301.

———. 1975. "The Political Elite in Iraq." In George Lenczowski, ed., *Political Elites in the Middle East.* Washington, DC: American Enterprise Institute for Public Policy Research.

―――. 1985. *The Modern History of Iraq.* Boulder, CO: Westview Press; London: Longmans.

―――. 1991. "Iraq in the Year 2000." In Charles F. Doran and Stephen W. Buck, eds., *The Gulf, Energy, and Global Security: Political and Economic Issues.* Boulder, CO: Lynne Rienner.

Masalha, Nur al-Din. 1991. "Faisal's Pan-Arabism." *Middle Eastern Studies* 27:679– 691.

Matar, Fuad. 1981. *Saddam Hussein: The Man, the Cause, and the Future.* London: Third World Centre.

Maxwell, Gavin. 1957. *A Reed Shaken by the Wind.* London: Longmans, Green.

McDowall, David. 1996. *A Modern History of the Kurds.* London: I. B. Tauris.

Mejcher, Helmut. 1976. *Imperial Quest for Oil: Iraq, 1910–1928.* London: Ithaca Press.

Metz, Helen Chapin, ed. 1990. *Iraq: A Country Study.* Washington, DC: Federal Research Division of the Library of Congress.

Middle East Watch. 1990. *Human Rights in Iraq.* New Haven: Yale University Press and Human Rights Watch.

―――. 1993a. *The Anfal Campaign in Iraqi Kurdistan: The Destruction of Koreme.* New York: Physicians For Human Rights.

―――. 1993b. *Genocide in Iraq: The Anfal Campaign Against the Kurds.* New York: Human Rights Watch.

Miller, Judith, and Laurie Mylroie. 1990. *Saddam Hussein and the Crisis in the Gulf.* New York: Times Books.

Mylroie, Laurie. 1991. *The Future of Iraq.* Washington Institute for Near East Policy Papers, no. 24.

Nakash, Yitzhak. 1994. *The Shi'is of Iraq.* Princeton: Princeton University Press.

Niblock, Tim, ed. 1982. *Iraq: The Contemporary State.* London: Croom Helm.

Nieuewenhuis, Tom. 1982. *Politics and Society in Early Modern Iraq: Mamluk Pashas, Tribal Shaykhs, and Local Rule between 1802 and 1831.* The Hague: Martinus Nijhoff.

O'Ballance, Edgar. 1973. *The Kurdish Revolt, 1961–1970.* Hamden, CT: Archon Books.

Olson, Robert. 1989. *The Emergence of Kurdish Nationalism and the Sheikh Said Rebellion, 1880–1925.* Austin: University of Texas Press.

―――. 1992. "Battle for Kurdistan: The Churchill-Cox Correspondence Regarding the Creation of the State of Iraq." *Kurdish Studies* 5:29–44.

Pelletiere, Stephen C. 1992. *The Iran-Iraq War: Chaos in a Vacuum.* New York: Praeger.

Penrose, Edith, and E. F. Penrose. 1978. *Iraq: International Relations and National Development.* Boulder, CO: Westview Press.

Pollack, Kenneth. *The Arabs at War: Arab Military Effectiveness from 1945–1991.* Manuscript.

Pool, David. 1980. "From Elite to Class: The Transformation of Iraqi Leadership." *International Journal of Middle Eastern Studies* 12:331–349.

Sassoon, Joseph. 1987. *Economic Policy in Iraq, 1932–1950.* London: Frank Cass.

Satloff, Robert B., ed. 1993. *The Politics of Change in the Middle East.* Boulder, CO: Westview Press.

Scales, Robert H., Jr. 1993. *Certain Victory.* Washington, DC: Office of the Chief of Staff, U.S. Army.

Schofield, Richard, ed. 1989. *The Iran-Iraq Border, 1840–1958*. Oxford: Archives Editions, the International Boundaries Research Unit, University of Durham, UK.

———. 1991. *Kuwait and Iraq: Historical Claims and Territorial Disputes*. London: Royal Institute of International Affairs.

———, ed. 1992. *Iraq Administration Reports, 1914–1932*. Oxford: Redwood Press.

———, ed. 1994. *The Iraq-Kuwait Dispute*. Arabian Geo-Politics 3, Regional Documentary Studies. Oxford: Archive Editions.

Schwarzkopf, H. Norman, and Peter Petre. 1992. *It Doesn't Take a Hero: General H. Norman Schwarzkopf, the Autobiography*. New York: Bantam Books.

Sciolino, Elaine. 1991. *The Outlaw State: Saddam Hussein's Quest for Power and the Gulf Crisis*. New York: John Wiley and Sons.

Shemesh, Haim. 1992. *Soviet-Iraqi Relations, 1968–1988*. Boulder, CO: Lynne Rienner.

Shikara, Ahmad. 1979. "Faisal's Ambitions of Leadership in the Fertile Crescent: Aspirations and Constraints." In Abbas Kelidar, ed., *The Integration of Modern Iraq*. London: Croom Helm.

———. 1987. *Iraqi Politics, 1921–41: Interaction between Domestic Politics and Foreign Policy*. London: Laam.

Sharadran, Benjamin. 1959. *The Middle East, Oil and the Great Powers*. New York: Council for Middle Eastern Affairs Press.

Silverfarb, Daniel. 1986. *Britain's Informal Empire in the Middle East*. New York: Oxford University Press.

———. 1994. *The Twilight of British Ascendancy in the Middle East: A Case Study of Iraq, 1941–1950*. New York: St. Martin's Press.

Simon, Reeva. 1986. *Iraq between the Two World Wars: The Creation and Implementation of a Nationalist Ideology*. New York: Columbia University Press.

Sluglett, Peter. 1976. *Britain in Iraq, 1914–1932*. London: Ithaca Press.

Tarbush, Mohammad A. 1982. *The Role of the Military in Politics: A Case Study of Iraq to 1941*. London: Kegan Paul.

Thesiger, Wilfred. 1964. *The Marsh Arabs*. London: Longman.

U.N. Department of Public Information, ed. 1996. *The United Nations and the Iraq-Kuwait Conflict, 1990–1996*. With Introduction by Boutros Boutros-Ghali, Secretary General of the United Nations. New York: Department of Public Information, United Nations.

U.S. News and World Report Staff. 1992. *Triumph without Victory*. New York: Times Books.

Vanly, Ismet Sherif. 1980. "Kurdistan in Iraq." In Gerard Chaliand, ed., *People without a Country: The Kurds and Kurdistan*. London: Zed Books.

Vinogradov, Amal. 1972. "The 1920 Revolt in Iraq Reconsidered: The Role of Tribes in National Politics." *International Journal of Middle Eastern Studies* 3:123–139.

Waldman, Peter. 1991. "A Tale Emerges of Saddam's Origins That Even He May Not Have Known." *Wall Street Journal*, February 7.

Wiley, Joyce N. 1992. *The Islamic Movement of Iraqi Shi'as*. Boulder, CO: Lynne Rienner.

Woodward, Bob. 1991. *The Commanders*. New York: Simon and Schuster.

ISRAEL

Gershon R. Kieval

Scholarly interest in Israel mirrors the general international interest in Israel as a consequence of its unique situation as the world's only Jewish state, its linkage to Jews everywhere, and the role Israel plays in international affairs far out of proportion to its small size and population. As a result, political science research on Israel has generated a vast and somewhat bewildering amount of material on topics that are similar to those studied by political scientists with regard to many countries as well as topics that are unique to the study of Israel. In the former category are such issues as the constitutional and legal parameters of the political system, elections and patterns of voting behavior, and political leadership and parties. Other topics are more specific to political research on Israel owing to factors unique to Israel. One such topic is the study of Zionism. Israel is a product of, and has adopted as its ideology, modern political Zionism, which had its origins in the historical-traditional pledges recorded in the Bible, linking the Jewish people to the land of Israel. An understanding of Zionism is critical to understanding the creation of the state of Israel, and the issue remains a major dimension of political research on the contemporary state.

Not unique to political research on Israel is the study of the military and national security, particularly the role that the armed forces play in the country's national defense and the military's relationship to civilian political authority and institutions. In the case of Israel, however, the study of the military is more significant than in the study of many other countries. Israel's history is often recounted in terms of the wars it has fought with its Arab neighbors who have challenged its right to exist since before independence. These wars have been important turning points in Israel's domestic development and foreign policy and have marked watersheds in its history. As a result, Israel's national security policies, armed forces, and military history, among other topics, have been of continuing importance to Israel since even before independence, although some issues, such as the role of the military in Israeli politics, have been neglected by researchers in recent years.

Related to the study of Israel's military is the Arab-Israeli conflict. Included in this research is an examination of the events leading up to and following the six major wars and countless skirmishes that Israel has fought with its Arab neighbors in its nearly five decades of independence. It also includes research on such topics as Israel's relationship with the Palestinians, its policy toward the territories occupied as a result of the Six-Day War of 1967, the question of Jerusalem, and Israel's borders.

Significant research has been carried out on Israel's salient domestic political and social issues, many of which have been of continuing importance to Israel throughout its history as an independent state. Political research in this area focuses on such issues as religion and its relationship to the state, including the key question of "Who is a Jew?" The unique role of immigration in Israel's creation and subsequent development makes it an important topic of analysis, as are the related matters of immigrant settlement and absorption and ethnic relations. Not surprisingly, the "ethnic" question has focused for the most part on relations between Israeli Ashkenazim, Jews primarily from Eastern and Central Europe who were the main components of the first waves of Zionist immigration to Palestine, and Sephardim or Orientals, Jews of Afro-Asian origin, most of whom immigrated to Israel after its independence. In the aftermath of the influx of new immigrants from the countries of the former Soviet Union beginning in 1989, the "ethnic" question has gained a new analytic dimension.

Another important ethnic question, but one that has not received the attention that it merits, is that of Israel's non-Jewish Arab minority. This will grow in importance as Palestinian autonomy and perhaps statehood become more firmly established in the Gaza Strip and parts of the West Bank, thereby changing the nature of relations between Arabs living in Israel and those in Palestinian-controlled areas and, by extension, relations between Israel's Jewish and Arab communities.

Given the foregoing, what follows is only a selective discussion of the vast literature. Two general works are worth noting at the outset insofar as they provide convenient reference material on all aspects of Israel: *Israel: Land of Tradition and Conflict*, second edition (1993), by Bernard Reich and Gershon R. Kieval, and *Historical Dictionary of Israel* (1992) by Bernard Reich.

HISTORY OF ZIONISM AND ISRAEL

In a real sense, Jewish history forms the prehistory of the modern state of Israel. Although Israel is a young country, having achieved its modern independence in 1948, it has an intimate connection to the ancient Jewish state and to Jewish history. The land of Israel was the ancient birthplace of the Jewish people, and it is in this area that the religious and national identity of that people was formed and developed. Later, the ancient Jewish state, the Holy Land, and Jerusalem became the spiritual focal points of the Jewish religion, a part of its hopes, rituals, and goals, in addition to providing the historical link for the Jews. Thus understanding Israel requires inquiry into Jewish history as well as into the prestate period of the British mandate and the Zionist efforts at state creation. For an introduction to the subject, see David Ben-Gurion, *The Jews in Their Land* (1966); Louis Finkelstein, editor, *The Jews: Their History, Culture, and Religion* (1960); Heinrich Graetz, *History of the Jews* (1891–1898); and Abba Eban, *My People: The Story of the Jews* (1969).

Howard M. Sachar, *A History of Israel: From the Rise of Zionism to Our Time* (1976); Noah Lucas, *The Modern History of Israel* (1975); and Connor Cruise O'Brien, *The Siege: The Saga of Israel and Zionism* (1986), provide histories of Israel that antedate independence. Howard M. Sachar, *A History of Israel, II: From the Aftermath of the Yom Kippur War* (1987) updates the history. The period of the British mandate is discussed in J. C. Hurewitz's *The Struggle for Palestine* (1950) and Christopher Sykes's *Crossroads to Israel* (1965). Itzhak Galnoor's *The Partition of Palestine: Decision Crossroads in the Zionist Movement* (1995) looks at the Zionist movement's struggle over the question of how to respond to the British (Peel) Royal Commission's recommendation to partition Palestine.

Zionism had a long history before its conversion at the end of the nineteenth century into its modern political form as the Jewish national movement that saw the establishment of a Jewish state as a logical consequence of its actions. Since biblical days the Jews of the Diaspora longed for the time when they would return to Zion, the Promised Land. Much of this hope was religious in nature and orientation and viewed a return to the Promised Land as an achievement that would result from some form of divine action. At the same time, Jewish writers developed spiritual, religious, cultural, social, and historical concepts linking Jews to the land of the historical Jewish state in Israel. Shlomo Avineri's *The Making of Modern Zionism: The Intellectual Origins of the Jewish State* (1981) and Walter Laqueur's *A History of Zionism* (1972) provide a comprehensive history and examination of the Zionist movement, its origins, and diverse ideological trends, as does the trilogy by David Vital, *The Origins of Zionism* (1975), *Zionism: The Formative Years* (1982), and *Zionism: The Crucial Phase* (1987). Ben Halpern's *The Idea of the Jewish State*, second edition (1970), is a sympathetic study of the origins and development of the Zionist idea.

The evolution of Zionism into its modern political form was facilitated by the political currents and fertile conditions presented by nineteenth-century European nationalism and anti-Semitism. It was in this environment that such Jewish intellectuals as Moses Hess and Leo Pinsker began to write about the Jews and the conditions in which they lived, thereby providing the underpinnings for the Jewish nationalist movement and its founder, Theodor Herzl, who wrote *Der Judenstaat* (The Jewish State) (1896), the tract providing the best-known operational basis for modern political Zionism. The classic biography of the Zionist movement's founder is Alex Bein, *Theodore Herzl: A Biography* (1940), but see also Amos Elon's *Herzl* (1975).

Zionism was never a monolithic movement. It experienced a fundamental split in the 1920s as a result of the British decision to separate the territory east of the Jordan River from the western portion of Palestine, thereby creating the Amirate of Transjordan and leaving the Palestine mandate with only the territory west of the river. This action led to the creation of Vladimir Zeev Jabotinsky's World Union of Zionist Revisionists (ultimately the New Zionist Organization) that has provided the ideological basis for Herut and Likud, under the leadership of Menachem Begin and, later, Yitzhak Shamir. Jabotinsky rejected the partition of Palestine into a Jewish and an Arab state; his goal was the establishment of a Jewish state, with a Jewish majority, on both sides of the Jordan River. The Revisionist party, established by Jabotinsky in 1925, and his New Zionist Organization supported the principle of Shlemut Hamoledet, the right of the Jewish people to all of Eretz Yisrael, the historic Land of Israel. On Jabotinsky, see Joseph B. Schechtman, *The Vladimir Jabotinsky Story*, volume 1, *Rebel and Statesman: The Early Years* (1956), and *The Vladimir Jabotinsky Story*, volume 2, *Fighter and Prophet: The Last Years* (1961).

GOVERNMENT AND POLITICAL SYSTEM

Israel's system of government is based on an unwritten constitution. The first legislative act of the Constituent Assembly, which first convened in February 1949 and declared itself Israel's first Knesset or parliament, was to enact a Transition Law, often referred to as the Small Constitution, that became the basis of constitutional life in the new state. Administrative and executive procedures were based on a combination of prestate experience in self-government, elements adapted from the former mandatory structure, and new legislation. According to the Small Constitution, Israel was established as a republic with a weak president and a strong cabinet and parliament. It was anticipated that this document would be replaced in due course by a more extensive and permanent one, although that has never been realized. The constitutional and legal parameters of Israel's political system are considered in Emanuel Rackman, *Israel's Emerging Constitution, 1948–51* (1955), which deals with the problems involved in the development of a constitution; in Henry E. Baker, *The Legal System of Israel* (1968); and in *Fundamental Laws of the State of Israel* (1961), edited by Joseph Badi.

The Knesset is the supreme authority in the state, and its laws are theoretically the source of all power and authority, although in reality decisions are made by the prime minister and the government and then ratified by the legislators. The Knesset is based, to a large extent, on the British model, adapted to Israel's needs and special requirements. It is a unicameral body of 120 members elected to four-year terms by general, national, direct, equal, secret, and proportional suffrage in accordance with the Knesset Elections Law. The entire country elects all members; there are no separate constituencies. This system derives from that used by the World Zionist Organization (WZO) and the Histadrut labor federation and other elements in the Yishuv, the Jewish community in Palestine, prior to Israel's independence. An important study of the parliament is Asher Zidon, *Knesset: The Parliament of Israel* (1967), which is complemented by Eliahu S. Likhovski, *Israel's Parliament: The Law of the Knesset* (1971). Gregory S. Mahler's *The Knesset: Parliament in the Israeli Political System* (1981) and Samuel Sager's *The Parliamentary System of Israel* (1985) provide assessments of the Knesset's activities and performance in more recent years.

General descriptions and analyses of the basic features and issues of the political system are contained in Joseph Badi, *The Government of the State of Israel: A Critical Account of Its Parliament, Executive, and Judiciary* (1963); Marver H. Bernstein, *The Politics of Israel: The First Decade of Statehood* (1957); Leonard J. Fein, *Israel: Politics and People* (1968); Yehoshua Freudenheim, *Government in Israel* (1967); Oscar Kraines, *Government and Politics in Israel* (1961); Asher Arian, *Politics in Israel: The Second Generation*, revised edition (1989); and Gregory S. Mahler, *Israel: Government and Politics in a Maturing State* (1989). Gad Yaacobi's *The Government of Israel* (1982) provides unique insight into the political process by a leader of the Labor party who has served as a member of the Knesset, as a cabinet minister, and as Israel's ambassador to the United Nations.

Israeli Democracy under Stress (1993), edited by Ehud Sprinzak and Larry Diamond, is a collection of essays that look at Israel's polity and society from the perspective of the evolution of its democratic system. The contributors highlight the numerous problems facing Israel's democracy in the early 1990s, including its fragmented party system, deeply divided society, bloated public sector, inequitable electoral system, ineffective government, and uneasy political culture. An earlier work, *Israeli Democracy: The Middle of the Journey* (1982) by Daniel Shimshoni, examines the ways in which public policies were formed in Israel until 1977. Ira Sharkansky's *What Makes Israel Tick? How Domestic Policy-Makers Cope with Constraints* (1985) is another valuable study of public policy making in Israel.

POLITICS, POLITICAL PARTIES, AND ELECTIONS

Politics in Israel is characterized by a wide range of intensely held political and social viewpoints that are given expression not only in political parties but also in newspapers and a host of social, religious, cultural, and other organizations. Numerous minority and splinter factions freely criticize the government. This diversity has been most apparent in the existence of multiple parties contesting parliamentary elections, in the factions within most of the major parties, and in the various coalition governments that have been characteristic of Israel since its inception. Aspects of Israeli politics and policy have been the subject of specialized studies, including Myron J. Aronoff, *Israeli Visions and Divi-*

sions: Cultural Change and Political Conflict (1989); Marcia Drezon-Tepler, *Interest Groups and Political Change in Israel* (1990); Eva Etzioni-Halevy, *Political Culture in Israel: Cleavage and Integration among Israeli Jews* (1977); Lester G. Seligman, *Leadership in a New Nation: Political Development in Israel* (1964); David Hall-Cathala, *The Peace Movement in Israel, 1967–1987* (1990); Dan Horowitz and Moshe Lissak, *Trouble in Utopia: The Overburdened Polity of Israel* (1989); Baruch Kimmerling, editor, *The Israeli State and Society: Boundaries and Frontiers* (1989); Bernard Reich and Gershon R. Kieval, editors, *Israel Faces the Future* (1986) and *Israeli Politics in the 1990s: Key Domestic and Foreign Policy Factors* (1991); Ehud Sprinzak, *The Ascendance of Israel's Radical Right* (1991); Yossi Beilin, *Israel: A Concise Political History* (1993); and Raphael Cohen-Almagor, *The Boundaries of Liberty and Tolerance: The Struggle against Kahanism in Israel* (1994). Amnon Rubinstein, the former dean of Tel Aviv University Law School and leader of the Shinui faction of the MERETZ bloc, traces the evolution of Zionist thinking in the wake of the Six-Day War of 1967 and the development of the Gush Emunim settlement movement in *The Zionist Dream Revisited: From Herzl to Gush Emunim and Back* (1984).

Political parties play a central role in the social and economic, as well as political, life of Israel. Many of Israel's parties had their origins in the mandate period when the political parties and movements competed with each other for control of the institutions and political life of the Zionist organizations and of the Yishuv. After independence they continued their activity with little change.

Israel's complex party structure demonstrates various dimensions of cleavage, but areas of socioeconomic, religious-secular, and foreign policy and national security issues tend to be the most significant. Israel's parties have economic views ranging from Marxism through liberal socialism to free enterprise. There are also different views concerning the role of government in economic—and consequently social—policy. The role of religion has differentiated those who seek to make Jewish religious law a central factor in state activity from others who have sought to enhance the secular nature of the system and those who have worked to eliminate virtually all vestiges of religious influence. Some have opposed Zionism and the authority of the state. Views of the ultimate extent of the state and the role of Zionism have divided groups (for example, the Communists) that oppose the concept of a Zionist state from others that have supported the notion of a binational entity or a truncated Jewish state, and from others that favor an exclusively Jewish-Zionist state in the whole of Palestine, both east and west of the Jordan River. Foreign policy issues have been somewhat less divisive than in the early days of the state. When the Soviet Union was an ardent suitor of the new Jewish state, it facilitated the adoption of pro-Soviet foreign policy stances by political groups with a Marxist orientation, such as MAPAM. At the same time parties of the right, such as the General Zionists and Herut, advocated a Western orientation. Soon, however, the choice was unrealistic, and since the early 1950s a pro-Western orientation has dominated Israeli thinking.

Israel's political parties may be categorized on foreign policy issues into three groupings: parties of the left, parties of the right, and the religious parties. There are also various particularistic parties that tend on the whole to be small and short-lived. Research on Israel's political parties has tended to focus on the dominant parties of the left and right, the Labor party and Likud (and its core Herut party), respectively. Myron J. Aronoff, *Power and Ritual in the Israel Labor Party*, revised edition (1993), and Peter Y. Medding, *Mapai in Israel: Political Organization and Government in a New Society* (1972) and *The Founding of Israeli Democracy, 1948–1988* (1989) look at the Labor party, particularly its organization, its recruitment, and the views of the party elite. Yonathan Shapiro's *The Road to Power: Herut Party in Israel* (1991) provides an in-depth analysis of the factors leading up to Likud's accession to power in 1977. Colin Shindler's study of Likud, *Israel, Likud, and the Zionist Dream: Power, Politics, and Ideology from Begin to Netanyahu* (1995), carries the story of Likud forward to include the leadership transition from Begin's successor, Yitzhak Shamir, to Benjamin Netanyahu. A growing gap in the research on Israel's political parties is analysis of the smaller, newer parties, particularly the religious parties (such as the Sephardi Torah Guardians or SHAS) and ultranationalist parties of the political right (such as Rafael Eitan's TZOMET movement and Rehavam Zeevi's Moledet). The center-left bloc MERETZ deserves analytical attention as well.

Israel's elections have been studied from two perspectives. Most research has focused on specific elections, assessing the performance of the significant political parties and leaders and the issues believed to have affected the outcome of the voting. Most of this literature is characterized by collections of essays written by noted scholars in Israel and the United States. Examples of this type of research are Alan Arian, editor, *The Elections in Israel—1969* (1972); Howard R. Penniman, editor, *Israel at the Polls: The Knesset Elections of 1977* (1979); Dan Caspi, Abraham Diskin, and Emanuel Gutmann, editors, *The Roots of Begin's Success: The 1981 Israeli Elections* (1984); Asher Arian, editor, *The Elections in Israel, 1981* (1984); Asher Arian and Michal Shamir, editors, *The Elections in Israel: 1984* (1986), *The Elections in Israel, 1988* (1990), and *The Elections in Israel, 1992* (1995); and Daniel J. Elazar and Shmuel Sandler, editors, *Israel's Odd Couple: The Nineteen Eighty-Four Knesset Elections and the National Unity Government* (1990), *Who's the Boss in Israel: Israel at the Polls, 1988–89* (1992), and *Israel at the Polls, 1992* (1995). Other research on Israel's elections looks at issues across several elections in an attempt to generate theories of Israeli electoral behavior. Alan Arian's *The Choosing People: Voting Behavior in Israel* (1973) takes this approach.

POLITICAL, ECONOMIC, AND SOCIAL ISSUES

The Israel that gained independence in 1948 was significantly different from the state that continues to celebrate its independence each spring. Israel is a dynamic country and is constantly undergoing change in all sectors. Israeli society is characterized by extensive debate over virtually all aspects of state activity, from the nature of governmental process to political leadership, to the substance of foreign and security policy, to the role that religion might play, and to the questions of demographic change and their implications. These issues are examined in a number of studies. Among the more reliable are S. N. Eisenstadt's *Israeli Society* (1967) and *The Transformation of Israeli Society* (1985); Judith T. Shuval's *Immigrants on the Threshold* (1963); Alex Weingrod's *Israel: Group Relations in a New Society* (1965); and Calvin Goldscheider's *Israel's Changing Society: Population, Ethnicity, and Development* (1996) and *Population and Social Change in Israel* (1992).

Israel's economy has undergone substantial change since independence, and the economic well-being of its people has improved significantly, belying the preindependence prophecies that its troubled economy could not long endure. Instead, a country virtually bereft of natural resources and faced with substantial burdens imposed by massive immigration and by Arab hostility had achieved a relatively prosperous economic level by the 1990s. Despite Israel's impressive economic achievements since independence, only a few scholars have examined the economy in any depth. The best works include David Horowitz, *The Economics of Israel* (1967); Yair Aharoni, *The Israeli Economy: Dreams and Realities* (1991); Yoram Ben-Porath, editor, *The Israeli Economy: Maturing through Crises* (1986); Haim Barkai, *The Lessons of Israel's Great Inflation* (1995); and Assaf Razin and Efraim Sadka, *The Economy of Modern Israel: Malaise and Promise* (1993).

Since independence, Israel has had to come to terms with the concept of its "Jewishness" and the definition of "who is a Jew," and thus it has had to address the meaning of a "Jewish state" and the roles to be played by religious forces and movements within the state. The conflict between secular and religious perspectives on these and related matters, as the research shows, has been a continuing characteristic of Israel; indeed, it was foreshadowed in the drafting of the Declaration of Independence, which recalls the religious and spiritual connection of the Jewish people to the land of Israel, but also guarantees Israel's citizens "freedom of religion and conscience." The conflict also was the cause of hot debate during consideration of the proposed constitution. One faction insisted on the primacy and enshrinement of Jewish religious values, while the other sought to focus on more secular themes, thus limiting the role of religion in the state.

The role of religion in Israel and the relationship between religious institutions and the state continues to be an intensely emotional issue that deeply divides the population and affects many and diverse aspects of Israeli life. This issue is considered in the following: Joseph Badi, *Religion in Israel Today: The Relationship between State and Religion* (1959); Oscar Kraines, *The Impossible Dilemma: Who Is a Jew in the State of Israel?* (1976); Gary S. Schiff, *Tradition and Politics: The Religious Parties of Israel* (1977); and Charles S. Liebman and Eliezer Don-Yehiya, *Civil Religion in Israel: Traditional Judaism and Political Culture in the Jewish State* (1983) and *Religion and Politics in Israel* (1984). Zvi Sobel, in *A Small Place in Galilee: Religion and Social Conflict in an Israeli Village* (1993), examines relations between the Orthodox Jewish minority and the secular majority in the small farming community of Yavne'el in Galilee. The study shows how even secular Israelis incorporate some level of religious observance into their lives and concludes that Israelis are much less polarized in the way in which they practice their religion than is generally presumed.

Geographically and demographically, Israel is an Oriental country; culturally, socially, and politically, it is Western in nature and orientation. The early Zionists laid the foundations for an essentially European culture in Palestine, with attendant concepts, ideals, and ideologies, and subsequent immigration accelerated the trend. The Western immigrants created and developed the Yishuv structure of land settlement, institutions, trade unions, and political parties, as well as an educational system, all in preparation for a Western-oriented Jewish national state. Later immigrants had to adapt to a society that had formed these institutions. Massive Oriental immigration has created a country in which a large portion of the population has societal and cultural traditions, customs, practices, and attitudes akin to the populations among whom they had lived for generations and different from those of their Western coreligionists.

Israel's communal differences have existed since the Oriental and occidental communities came into contact during the mandate period. At the outset, the communities had limited contact, in part because social groups with similar ethnic, cultural, and religious backgrounds tended to reside in specific neighborhoods with others of similar perspectives, separated or isolated from those with different backgrounds. The majority of the Oriental community held a larger portion of more menial jobs as the Ashkenazim moved out of those sectors of employment. The Oriental community was also undereducated compared to its Ashkenazi counterpart and included larger numbers of uneducated and illiterate individuals. The communities were also separate in terms of their involvement in politics and public affairs, as the Oriental communities were not involved in public activity within the framework of Yishuv political life.

The Jewish communal problem did not change much once Israel gained independence; indeed, the major distinction today between Israel's two major Jewish communities remains that of socioeconomic status. The "social gap" has been the focus of several researchers. Two recent works that analyze relations between Israel's Sephardi and Ashkenazi communities are Daniel J. Elazar's *The Other Jews: The Sephardim Today* (1989) and Shlomo Swirski's *Israel: The Oriental Majority* (1989).

The "ethnic" question in Israel has gained a new analytic dimension in recent years with the influx of new immigrants from Ethiopia and from the countries of the former Soviet Union. Teshome Wagaw's *For Our Soul: Ethiopian Jews in Israel* (1993) examines the immigration and assimilation of Ethiopian Jews into Israel during the period 1977–1992. *Uprooted in Old Age: Soviet Jews and Their Social Networks in Israel* (1995), by Howard Litwin, studies the immigration experience of elderly Jews from the former Soviet Union, particularly the émigrés' networks in Israel and their impact on social support, well-being, family life, and service utilization.

Another critical dimension to the "ethnic" question in Israel is the issue of Israel's non-Jewish Arab minority. There is significant separation between Israel's Arab and Jewish communities, and those few areas of contact that exist are not intimate. The Arabs tend to live in separate villages and in separate sections of the major cities. As research shows, the Jews and Arabs are separate societies who generally continue to hold stereotypical images of each other, often reinforced by the schools, the press, social distance, and, more significantly, the tensions and problems created by the larger Arab-Israeli conflict in its numerous dimensions. There is mutual suspicion and antagonism, and there is still a Jewish fear of Arabs—a result of wars and terrorism. The Jewish educational system displays a lack of knowledge of and information about Israeli Arabs, even while there is considerable expertise about the Arabs of the surrounding countries. The lack of knowledge and contact is reinforced by the separateness of the two communities, and this is apparently a result of a mutual desire to maintain the individual cultures and societies.

For the Arabs of Israel, both Muslim and Christian, there is a major dilemma: they are torn between their country (they are citizens of Israel) and their people (the Arabs). As an Arab minority in a country threatened by much of the Arab world, they are objects of suspicion, surveillance, and discrimination; are denied certain jobs; and are subjected to extra scrutiny because of the security factor. Yet they possess virtually all the rights and privileges (and most of the obligations) of Israel's Jewish citizens. They have a right to vote, secure seats in the Knesset, participate in local government, serve in government offices, enjoy equality before the law, receive economic and social welfare benefits, have their own schools and courts, and prosper materially. Yet because most Arabs do not serve in the military, they do not receive the additional generous social welfare support that is provided to Israelis who do serve in the army. There also is discrimination in the allocation of government funds to Arab towns as compared with Jewish villages, although the precise reasons for this remain obscure and appear to be a result of actions at both the national and local levels.

The relationship between Israel's Jewish and Arab communities is examined in a number of works. Jacob M. Landau, in *The Arab Minority in Israel, 1967– 1991: Political Aspects* (1993), presents a carefully balanced look at the Israeli Arab community, particularly its social and economic status and political activity. He calls for the complete integration of Israel's Arab citizens lest the continued denial of full equality lead to their increasing radicalization. This study follows up on an earlier work by Landau, *The Arabs in Israel: A Political Study* (1969), which presents a comprehensive survey and analysis of the role of the Arabs during the first twenty years of Israel's statehood. An alternative perspective is provided by Sabri Jiryis, *The Arabs in Israel* (1976). See also David Kretzmer, *The Legal Status of the Arabs in Israel* (1990); Michael Romann and Alex Weingrod, *Living Together Separately: Arabs and Jews in Contemporary Jerusalem* (1991); and Noah Lewin-Epstein, *The Arab Minority in Israel's Economy: Patterns of Ethnic Inequality* (1993).

Other more specialized discussions of the political and social issues facing Israel today include Yehoshafat Harkabi, *Israel's Fateful Decisions* (1988), which looks at the political and demographic dilemmas facing Israel from the occupation of the West Bank and Gaza Strip; Moshe Schwartz, Susan Lees, and Gideon Kressel, editors, *Rural Cooperatives in Socialist Utopia: Thirty Years of Moshav Development in Israel* (1995); Amir Ben-Porat, *Divided We Stand: Class Structure in Israel from 1948 to the 1980s* (1989); Eliezer Ben-Rafael, *Status, Power, and Conflict in the Kibbutz* (1988); Eliezer Ben-Rafael and Stephen Sharot, *Ethnicity, Religion, and Class in Israeli Society* (1991); Elisha Efrat, editor, *Geography and Politics in Israel since 1967* (1988); Sam N. Lehman-Wilzig, *Stiff-necked People, Bottle-necked System: The Evolution and Roots of Israeli Public Protest, 1949–1986* (1991); Moshe Sanbar, editor, *Economic and Social Policy in Israel: The First Generation* (1990); Avraham Schweitzer, *Israel: The Changing National Agenda* (1986); Keith Kyle and Joel Peters, editors, *Whither Israel? The Domestic Challenges* (1993); Michael Shalev, *Labour and the Political Economy in Israel* (1989); and Vered Kraus, *Promises in the Promised Land: Mobility and Inequality in Israel* (1990).

FOREIGN POLICY AND INTERNATIONAL RELATIONS

Israel's approach to foreign policy began to take shape once it became clear that peace would not follow the armistice accords that marked the end of its War of Independence. Israel directed its attention beyond the circle of neighboring Arab states to the broader international community in an effort to establish friendly relations with the states of Europe and the developing world, as well as with the superpowers. These relationships were seen as having a positive effect on the Arab-Israeli conflict and as having bilateral political and economic advantages that would help to ensure Israel's deterrent strength through national armed power and through increased international support for its position. Israel has seen Europe and the developing world, especially Africa and Latin America, as important components of its overall policy. It has sought to maintain positive relations with Europe based on the commonality of the Judeo-Christian heritage and democratic tradition and the memories of the Holocaust; its approach to the developing world, which began in earnest in the late 1950s, has focused on Israel's ability to provide technical assistance in the development process. Despite substantial effort in these sectors, the centrality of the Arab-Israeli conflict enlarged and enhanced the role of the superpowers, particularly the United States, in Israeli eyes.

Aaron S. Klieman, in *Israel and the World after 40 Years* (1989), and Gideon Rafael, in *Destination Peace: Three Decades of Israeli Foreign Policy* (1981), provide excellent overviews of Israel's foreign policy. Ernest Stock's *Israel on the Road to Sinai, 1949–1956* (1967) is an incisive study of Israel's foreign policy from 1948 to the Sinai campaign, with a sequel on the June 1967 war. Walter Eytan, a ranking Israeli diplomat, has written *The First Ten Years: A Diplomatic History of Israel* (1958). Israel's international relations are discussed in Theodore Draper, *Israel and World Politics: Roots of the Third Arab-Israeli War* (1968); Aaron S. Klieman, *Statecraft in the Dark: Israel's Practice of Quiet Diplomacy* (1988); Ilan Peleg, *Begin's Foreign Policy, 1977–1983: Israel's Move to the Right* (1987); Bernard Reich and Gershon R. Kieval, editors, *Israeli National Security Policy: Political Actors and Perspectives* (1988); Ofira Seliktar, *New Zionism and the Foreign Policy System of Israel* (1986); and Avner Yaniv, *Dilemmas of Security: Politics, Strategy, and the Israeli Experience in Lebanon* (1987).

Throughout most of Israel's history, its relationship with the United Nations has been ambivalent. On the one hand, that organization was instrumental in the creation of the state and was generally supportive during the first two decades. After 1967, however, and especially after the 1973 war, Israel regarded the United Nations as an essentially negative factor inimical to its interests. See *Israel and the United Nations* (1956), the report of a study group set up by the Hebrew University of Jerusalem, and Avi Beker, *The United Nations and Israel: From Recognition to Reprehension* (1988). With the election of a Labor party government under Yitzhak Rabin in 1992 and the accompanying shift in Israel's peace-process policy stressing greater flexibility, Israel's relationship with the United Nations became more positive. There are, however, no studies of this turnaround in the Israeli-U.N. relationship.

Beginning in the late 1950s, Israel's relations with Asia and Africa grew significantly. Israel sought to develop friendly relations with Third World states that would help to counter growing Arab-sponsored anti-Israel pressure in various international forums. Israel embarked on an intensive and extensive program of economic aid and technical assistance to developing countries, which is discussed in Leopold Laufer, *Israel and the Developing Countries: New Approaches to Cooperation* (1967); Shimeon Amir, *Israel's Development Cooperation with Africa, Asia, and Latin America* (1974); Michael Curtis and Susan Aurelia Gitelson, editors, *Israel in the Third World* (1974); and Olusola Ojo, *Africa and Israel: Relations in Perspective* (1988).

Michael Brecher's *Decisions in Israel's Foreign Policy* (1975) and *The Foreign Policy System of Israel: Setting, Images, Processes* (1972) provide a comprehensive approach to Israel's foreign policy process and examine some major decisions. Meron Medzini, in *Israel's Foreign Relations: Selected Documents,*

1947–1994, 14 volumes (1976–1995), provides the major documents of Israel's foreign policy from its inception through 1994. This is an official publication of Israel's Ministry for Foreign Affairs.

Nadav Safran, in *Israel: The Embattled Ally* (1981), provides coverage of Israel's domestic scene as it affects foreign policy. Asher Arian, *Security Threatened: Surveying Israeli Opinion on Peace and War* (1995), and Asher Arian, Ilan Talmud, and Tamar Hermann, *National Security and Public Opinion in Israel* (1988), examine Israeli public opinion on key issues related to war and peace. Yehoshafat Harkabi, in *Arab Strategies and Israel's Response* (1977), and Gabriel Sheffer, editor, in *Dynamics of a Conflict: A Re-examination of the Arab-Israeli Conflict* (1975), deal with aspects of the Arab-Israeli conflict and Israel's position and perspective. Bernard Reich's *Israel and the Occupied Territories* (1973) focuses on the problem of the territories occupied by Israel in the 1967 war, and Gershon R. Kieval's *Party Politics in Israel and the Occupied Territories* (1983) provides a more detailed analysis of Israel's policy and the impact of factionalism in the Labor party and Likud on the decision-making process. Bernard Reich, in *Quest for Peace: United States–Israel Relations and the Arab-Israeli Conflict* (1977), deals with Israel's relations with the United States in the context of the efforts to resolve the Arab-Israeli conflict. Reich's *The United States and Israel: Influence in the Special Relationship* (1984) and Abraham Ben-Zvi's *The United States and Israel: The Limits of the Special Relationship* (1993) provide a broader examination of Israel's crucial links with the United States. Reich's *Securing the Covenant: United States–Israel Relations after the Cold War* (1995) assesses the impact of the disintegration of the Soviet Union and the end of the Cold War on U.S.-Israeli ties.

THE ISRAELI ARMY AND DEFENSE POLICIES

The failure to achieve peace with all of its Arab neighbors and the continuation of Arab hostility has fostered Israel's focus on security. Israel's response to the Arab military threat has taken the form of an effective military capability based on the Israel Defense Forces (IDF) and a carefully constructed military doctrine designed to take account of the "asymmetry" of Israel's situation as compared with the Arabs—its numerical inferiority and territory and resource disparity. Shimon Peres, in *David's Sling: The Arming of Israel* (1970), Yigal Allon, in *The Making of Israel's Army* (1971), Edward Luttwak and Dan Horowitz, in *The Israeli Army* (1975), and Zeev Schiff, in *A History of the Israeli Army (1870–1974)* (1974) provide general overviews of the IDF, its background, and its development. Amos Perlmutter's *Military and Politics in Israel: Nationbuilding and Role Expansion* (1969) considers the role of the military in Israeli society and politics during Israel's formative years. Yoram Peri, in *Between Battles and Ballots: Israeli Military in Politics* (1983), argues that state control over the military in Israel has been weak and that a pattern of civil-military partnership has consequently developed. With the signing of the Israel-PLO

Declaration of Principles in September 1993 and the Israel-Jordan peace treaty in October 1994, and the inevitable self-examination that the Israeli army will need to undergo as its mission changes, the question of civil-military relations in Israel will need a fresh look. Yehuda Ben-Meir's *Civil-Military Relations in Israel* (1995) successfully provides this look. Ben-Meir, a former member of the National Religious party in the Knesset and former deputy foreign minister, analyzes the key role the Israeli army plays in shaping Israel's national security policy, not just in decisions to go to war, but increasingly in critical decisions related to peace, as demonstrated by the army's involvement in peace negotiations with the Palestinians and Jordanians. Ben-Meir's conclusions have important implications for the future of civil-military relations in Israel, for Israeli national security policy, and for the ability of the army to fight the potential wars in the next century.

In building its military power, Israel has had to exploit fully its national resources—personnel, equipment, and vehicles—in time of war, and there has been a constant need for readiness and alert. Because of its small population, Israel has relied on a relatively small standing force of approximately 150,000 and a large number of reserves (some 500,000) that can be mobilized quickly and yet fight with a high level of efficiency. But this creates an additional burden. In personal terms the contribution is virtually universal; young men and women (with some exceptions for religious and other reasons) serve in the IDF upon reaching the required age, and former male soldiers (and some females in special areas) are called to fulfill reserve obligations each year. Baruch Kimmerling, in *The Interrupted System: Israeli Civilians in War and Routine Times* (1985), and Moshe Lissak, editor, in *Israeli Society and Its Defense Establishment* (1984), examine the social and political impact of maintaining Israel's military power.

An indigenous military industry has been an element of Israel's security planning since independence, and considerable resources have been invested in it, with uneven results. Its basic shortcoming has been natural and financial resources, and there also is the problem of economies of scale and the difficulties posed by the enormous start-up costs involved in the development and production of a sophisticated weapons system. Many of the technological problems that plagued the industry in earlier years appear to have been overcome, and the military-industrial infrastructure has been relatively well suited to the advanced technology of a sophisticated armaments industry. Israel's military industry, particularly the foreign policy aspects, is examined in Stewart Reiser, *The Israeli Arms Industry: Foreign Policy, Arms Transfers, and Military Doctrine of a Small State* (1989), and Aaron S. Klieman, *Israel's Global Reach: Arms Sales as Diplomacy* (1985).

Other specialized studies of the Israeli military and defense policies include Shai Feldman, *Israeli Nuclear Deterrence: A Strategy for the 1980s* (1982); Yair Evron, *Israel's Nuclear Dilemma* (1994); Aharon Klieman and Reuven Pedatzur, *Rearming Israel: Defense Procurement through the 1990s* (1991); and

Efraim Karsh, editor, *Between War and Peace: Dilemmas of Israeli Security* (1996). For further research on the Israeli military, see Jehuda L. Wallach, *Israeli Military History: A Guide to the Sources* (1984). An indispensable source in Hebrew for Israel's security and defense problems and policies is Zeev Schiff and Eitan Haber, editors, Arie Hashavia, associate editor, *A Lexicon of Israel's Defense* (1976).

THE ARAB-ISRAELI CONFLICT

The conflict side of the Arab-Israeli conflict has been the subject of much research. For an overview of the conflicts, see Chaim Herzog, *The Arab-Israeli Wars: War and Peace in the Middle East* (1982). On the War of Independence, see, for example, Netanel Lorch, *The Edge of the Sword: Israel's War of Independence, 1947–1949* (1961); Lynne Reid Banks, *Torn Country: An Oral History of the Israeli War of Independence* (1982); and Jon Kimche and David Kimche, *A Clash of Destinies: The Arab-Jewish War and the Founding of the State of Israel* (1960). Aryeh Shalev, in *The Israel-Syria Armistice Regime, 1949–1955* (1993), looks at the record of negotiations between Syria and Israel in the period between the War of Independence and the Sinai Campaign of 1956. The author was an Israeli member of the Mixed Armistice Commission with Syria that was set up to help administer the armistice agreement signed in 1949, and his study makes excellent use of Israeli and U.N. sources.

On the 1956 Sinai campaign, see Robert Henriques, *A Hundred Hours to Suez: An Account of Israel's Campaign in the Sinai Peninsula* (1957), and Moshe Dayan, *Diary of the Sinai Campaign* (1966). Benny Morris, a controversial Israeli historian because of his penchant for revisionism, looks at the cycle of Arab infiltration and Israeli retaliation in the period leading up to the Suez War in *Israel's Border Wars, 1949–1956: Arab Infiltration, Israeli Retaliation, and the Countdown to the Suez War* (1993). Based extensively on documents from official Israeli archives and Western diplomatic reports, Morris's study challenges the conventional story that the 1949–1956 period was characterized by constant waves of Arab terrorism that prompted the new state of Israel to strike back in legitimate acts of self-defense. A contrasting view is offered by Jonathan Shimshoni in *Israel and Conventional Deterrence* (1988), which takes a broader look at Israel's strategy of reprisals during three protracted periods of low-level violence—1953 to 1954, when Israel experienced violence along the Jordanian frontier; from 1953 to 1956, when Israel and Egypt were involved in border disputes; and from 1967 to 1970, during the Israeli-Egyptian war of attrition.

On the 1967 Arab-Israeli war, see David Kimche and Dan Bawly, *The Six-Day War: Prologue and Aftermath* (1971), originally published as *The Sandstorm* (1968); Edgar O'Ballance, *The Third Arab-Israeli War* (1972); and Randolph S. Churchill and Winston S. Churchill, *The Six Day War* (1967). Yaacov Bar-Siman-Tov in *The Israeli-Egyptian War of Attrition, 1969–1970: A*

Case-Study of Limited Local War (1980) analyzes the 1969–1970 war of attrition.

On the Yom Kippur War of 1973, see Chaim Herzog, *The War of Atonement: October, 1973* (1975); Edgar O'Ballance, *No Victor, No Vanquished: The Yom Kippur War* (1978); and *The Sunday Times, Insight on the Middle East War* (1974). Itamar Rabinovich in *The War for Lebanon, 1970–1983* (1984) and Zeev Schiff and Ehud Yaari in *Israel's Lebanon War* (1984) examine the 1982 war in Lebanon.

The dramatic progress in the peace process beginning with the 1993 breakthrough in negotiations between Israel and the Palestine Liberation Organization has yet to yield much fruitful material for researchers. That said, *Jerusalem Post* reporter David Makovsky, in *Making Peace with the PLO: The Rabin Government's Road to the Oslo Accord* (1995), has produced a well-written and informative study of Israel's negotiations with the PLO leading up to the Oslo Accord.

ISRAEL'S POLICYMAKERS AND DECISION MAKERS

Very little has been written about who controls the sources of political power in Israel and how they came to occupy positions of leadership. Two veteran Israeli journalists, Yuval Elizur and Eliahu Salpeter, made an early attempt to identify Israel's "power elite" in their study, *Who Rules Israel?* (1973). Although their approach is far from scientific, their findings nonetheless provide an insightful look at the leaders of the Labor party establishment during Israel's first two and one-half decades of independence. More scientific examinations of the paths to political power in both the Labor party and the Likud bloc are needed.

Books about senior Israeli policy and decision makers offer valuable insights into the past and present of Israel. Jacob Abadi, in *Israel's Leadership: From Utopia to Crisis* (1993), provides brief sketches of the backgrounds of ten of Israel's leaders, from Chaim Weizmann to Yitzhak Shamir. The following works deal with Israel's first prime minister: Michael Bar-Zohar, *Ben-Gurion: The Armed Prophet* (1968) and *Ben Gurion: A Biography*, translated by Peretz Kidron, (1979); Shabtai Teveth, *Ben-Gurion: The Burning Ground, 1886–1948* (1987) and *Ben-Gurion and the Palestinian Arabs: From Peace to War* (1985); Dan Kurzman, *Ben-Gurion: Prophet of Fire* (1983); and Barnet Litvinoff, *Ben-Gurion of Israel* (1954).

On Israel's first president, Chaim Weizmann, see Jehuda Reinharz, *Chaim Weizmann: The Making of a Zionist Leader* (1985); Samuel Shihor, *Hollow Glory: The Last Days of Chaim Weizmann, First President of Israel* (1960); Meyer W. Weisgal and Joel Carmichael, editors, *Chaim Weizmann: A Biography by Several Hands* (1963); and Isaiah Berlin, *Chaim Weizmann* (1958).

Several modern-day Israeli leaders have received a disproportionate share of the attention of contemporary Israeli and Western researchers. Menachem Begin, the founder of the right-wing Herut party and its successor Likud bloc, is the subject of a number of studies, including Eitan Haber, *Menachem Begin: The Legend and the Man* (1978); Eric Silver, *Begin: The Haunted Prophet* (1984); Ned Temko, *To Win or to Die: A Personal Portrait of Menachem Begin* (1987); Amos Perlmutter, *The Life and Times of Menachem Begin* (1987); and Sasson Sofer, *Begin: An Anatomy of Leadership* (1988). Among the leaders of the Labor party, Moshe Dayan has been studied by several researchers, including Shabtai Teveth, *Moshe Dayan: The Soldier, the Man, the Legend* (1973); and Naftali Lau-Lavie, *Moshe Dayan: A Biography* (1969). Insights into the lives and viewpoints of other past and present Labor party and Likud leaders can be found in Terence Prittie, *Eshkol: The Man and the Nation* (1969); Marie Syrkin, *Golda Meir: Woman with a Cause* (1963); Matti Golan, *Shimon Peres: A Biography* (1982); Robert Slater, *Rabin of Israel* (1993); Uzi Benziman, *Sharon: An Israeli Caesar* (1985); and Merrill Simon, *Moshe Arens, Statesman and Scientist, Speaks Out* (1988).

Autobiographical works and memoirs by Israeli leaders are indispensable sources for scholars. Some of the best works of this type include Yitzhak Shamir, *Summing Up: An Autobiography* (1994); Moshe Arens, *Broken Covenant: American Foreign Policy and the Crisis between the U.S. and Israel* (1995); Shimon Peres, *Battling for Peace* (1995) and (with Arye Naor) *The New Middle East* (1993); Yitzhak Rabin, *The Rabin Memoirs* (1979); Moshe Dayan, *Breakthrough: A Personal Account of the Egypt-Israel Peace Negotiations* (1981) and *Moshe Dayan: Story of My Life* (1976); Ezer Weizman, *The Battle for Peace* (1981); Abba Eban, *An Autobiography* (1977); and Golda Meir, *My Life* (1975).

Researchers have paid little attention to the younger generation of Israeli leaders, including such key Likud personalities as Prime Minister Benjamin Netanyahu and David Levy. To gain insight into Netanyahu's thinking, for example, researchers have had to rely on his own writing (*A Place among the Nations: Israel and the World* [1993]). Our knowledge of the second generation of Labor party leaders, such as Ehud Barak, Ephraim Sneh, and Yossi Beilin, is similarly deficient.

FUTURE RESEARCH

Scholarly interest in Israel has clearly generated a vast literature that covers the gamut of issues familiar to all political scientists. Such topics as the political system, elections and voting behavior, political parties and leadership, history, the armed forces, decision making, and national security policy have been dealt with extensively by researchers. Some topics, such as Zionism, that are unique to the study of Israel also have a substantial literature devoted to them.

There are, however, important gaps in the extant work, some of which have been discussed earlier. The ethnic question in Israel, which heretofore almost exclusively has referred to relations between Israel's politically dominant Ashkenazi and numerically dominant Sephardi populations, has taken on new dimensions in recent years that demand greater scholarly attention. The new aspects include the absorption and assimilation of new immigrants from Ethiopia and from the former Soviet Union, as well as changing relations between Israel's Jewish majority and Arab minority in light of recent progress in the peace process and the growing specter of Palestinian statehood in the Gaza Strip and parts of the West Bank evacuated by Israel. Other issues requiring attention by researchers include the changing role of the army in Israeli politics and the key question of who are Israel's up-and-coming leaders.

REFERENCES

Abadi, Jacob. 1993. *Israel's Leadership: From Utopia to Crisis*. Westport, CT: Greenwood Press.

Aharoni, Yair. 1991. *The Israeli Economy: Dreams and Realities*. London: Routledge.

Allon, Yigal. 1971. *The Making of Israel's Army*. New York: Bantam Books.

Amir, Shimeon. 1974. *Israel's Development Cooperation with Africa, Asia, and Latin America*. New York: Praeger.

Arens, Moshe. 1995. *Broken Covenant: American Foreign Policy and the Crisis between the U.S. and Israel*. New York: Simon and Schuster.

Arian, Alan, ed. 1972. *The Elections in Israel—1969*. Jerusalem: Jerusalem Academic Press.

———. 1973. *The Choosing People: Voting Behavior in Israel*. Cleveland, OH: Press of Case Western Reserve University.

Arian, Asher, ed. 1984. *The Elections in Israel, 1981*. New Brunswick, NJ: Transaction Books.

———. 1989. *Politics in Israel: The Second Generation*. Rev. ed. Chatham, NJ: Chatham House.

———. 1995. *Security Threatened: Surveying Israeli Opinion on Peace and War*. New York: Cambridge University Press.

Arian, Asher, Ilan Talmud, and Tamar Hermann. 1988. *National Security and Public Opinion in Israel*. Tel Aviv: Jaffee Center for Strategic Studies, Tel Aviv University; Boulder, CO: Westview Press.

Arian, Asher, and Michal Shamir, eds. 1986. *The Elections in Israel, 1984*. New Brunswick, NJ: Transaction Books.

———, eds. 1990. *The Elections in Israel, 1988*. Boulder, CO: Westview Press.

———, eds. 1995. *The Elections in Israel, 1992*. Albany, NY: State University of New York Press.

Aronoff, Myron J. 1989. *Israeli Visions and Divisions: Cultural Change and Political Conflict*. New Brunswick, NJ: Transaction Books.

———. 1993. *Power and Ritual in the Israel Labor Party*. Rev. ed. Armonk, NY: M. E. Sharpe.

Avineri, Shlomo. 1981. *The Making of Modern Zionism: The Intellectual Origins of the Jewish State*. New York: Basic Books.

Badi, Joseph. 1959. *Religion in Israel Today: The Relationship between State and Religion*. New York: Bookman Associates.

————, ed. 1961. *Fundamental Laws of the State of Israel*. New York: Twayne.

————. 1963. *The Government of the State of Israel: A Critical Account of Its Parliament, Executive, and Judiciary*. New York: Twayne.

Baker, Henry E. 1968. *The Legal System of Israel*. Jerusalem: Israel Universities Press.

Banks, Lynne Reid. 1982. *Torn Country: An Oral History of the Israeli War of Independence*. New York: Watts.

Barkai, Haim. 1995. *The Lessons of Israel's Great Inflation*. Westport, CT: Praeger.

Bar-Siman-Tov, Yaacov. 1980. *The Israeli-Egyptian War of Attrition, 1969–1970: A Case-Study of Limited Local War*. New York: Columbia University Press.

Bar-Zohar, Michael. 1968. *Ben-Gurion: The Armed Prophet*. Englewood Cliffs, NJ: Prentice-Hall.

————. 1979. *Ben-Gurion: A Biography*. Trans. Peretz Kidron. New York: Delacorte Press.

Beilin, Yossi. 1993. *Israel: A Concise Political History*. New York: St. Martin's Press.

Bein, Alex. 1940. *Theodore Herzl: A Biography*. Philadelphia: Jewish Publication Society of America.

Beker, Avi. 1988. *The United Nations and Israel: From Recognition to Reprehension*. Lexington, MA: Lexington Books.

Ben-Gurion, David. 1966. *The Jews in Their Land*. Garden City, NY: Doubleday.

Ben-Meir, Yehuda. 1995. *Civil-Military Relations in Israel*. New York: Columbia University Press.

Ben-Porat, Amir. 1989. *Divided We Stand: Class Structure in Israel from 1948 to the 1980s*. Westport, CT: Greenwood Press.

Ben-Porath, Yoram, ed. 1986. *The Israeli Economy: Maturing through Crises*. Cambridge, MA: Harvard University Press.

Ben-Rafael, Eliezer. 1988. *Status, Power, and Conflict in the Kibbutz*. Brookfield, VT: Gower.

Ben-Rafael, Eliezer, and Stephen Sharot. 1991. *Ethnicity, Religion, and Class in Israeli Society*. New York: Cambridge University Press.

Benziman, Uzi. 1985. *Sharon: An Israeli Caesar*. New York: Adama Books.

Ben-Zvi, Abraham. 1993. *The United States and Israel: The Limits of the Special Relationship*. New York: Columbia University Press.

Berlin, Isaiah. 1958. *Chaim Weizmann*. New York: Farrar, Straus and Cudahy.

Bernstein, Marver H. 1957. *The Politics of Israel: The First Decade of Statehood*. Princeton: Princeton University Press.

Brecher, Michael. 1972. *The Foreign Policy System of Israel: Setting, Images, Processes*. New Haven: Yale University Press.

————. 1975. *Decisions in Israel's Foreign Policy*. New Haven: Yale University Press.

Caspi, Dan, Abraham Diskin, and Emanuel Gutmann, eds. 1984. *The Roots of Begin's Success: The 1981 Israeli Elections*. London: Croom Helm; New York: St. Martin's Press.

Churchill, Randolph S., and Winston S. Churchill. 1967. *The Six Day War*. Boston: Houghton Mifflin.

Cohen-Almagor, Raphael. 1994. *The Boundaries of Liberty and Tolerance: The Struggle against Kahanism in Israel*. Gainesville: University Press of Florida.

Curtis, Michael, and Susan Aurelia Gitelson, eds. 1974. *Israel in the Third World*. New Brunswick, NJ: Transaction Books.

Dayan, Moshe. 1966. *Diary of the Sinai Campaign*. New York: Schocken.

———. 1976. *Moshe Dayan: Story of My Life*. New York: Warner Books.

———. 1981. *Breakthrough: A Personal Account of the Egypt-Israel Peace Negotiations*. New York: Alfred A. Knopf.

Diskin, Abraham. 1991. *Elections and Voters in Israel*. Westport, CT: Praeger Publishers.

Draper, Theodore. 1968. *Israel and World Politics: Roots of the Third Arab-Israeli War*. New York: Viking Press.

Drezon-Tepler, Marcia. 1990. *Interest Groups and Political Change in Israel*. Albany: State University of New York Press.

Eban, Abba. 1969. *My People: The Story of the Jews*. New York: Random House.

———. 1977. *An Autobiography*. New York: Random House.

Efrat, Elisha, ed. 1988. *Geography and Politics in Israel since 1967*. London: Frank Cass.

Eisenstadt, S. N. 1967. *Israeli Society*. New York: Basic Books.

———. 1985. *The Transformation of Israeli Society*. Boulder, CO: Westview Press.

Elazar, Daniel J. 1989. *The Other Jews: The Sephardim Today*. New York: Basic Books.

Elazar, Daniel J., and Shmuel Sandler, eds. 1990. *Israel's Odd Couple: The Nineteen Eighty-Four Knesset Elections and the National Unity Government*. Detroit, MI: Wayne State University Press.

———, eds. 1992. *Who's the Boss in Israel: Israel at the Polls, 1988–89*. Detroit, MI: Wayne State University Press.

———, eds. 1995. *Israel at the Polls, 1992*. Lanham, MD: Rowman and Littlefield.

Elizur, Yuval, and Eliahu Salpeter. 1973. *Who Rules Israel?* New York: Harper and Row.

Elon, Amos. 1975. *Herzl*. New York: Holt, Rinehart and Winston.

Etzioni-Halevy, Eva. 1977. *Political Culture in Israel: Cleavage and Integration among Israeli Jews*. New York: Praeger.

Evron, Yair. 1994. *Israel's Nuclear Dilemma*. Ithaca: Cornell University Press.

Eytan, Walter. 1958. *The First Ten Years: A Diplomatic History of Israel*. New York: Simon and Schuster.

Fein, Leonard J. 1968. *Israel: Politics and People*. Boston: Little, Brown.

Feldman, Shai. 1982. *Israeli Nuclear Deterrence: A Strategy for the 1980s*. New York: Columbia University Press.

Finkelstein, Louis, ed. 1960. *The Jews: Their History, Culture, and Religion*. New York: Harper.

Frenkel, Erwin. 1994. *The Press and Politics in Israel: The Jerusalem Post from 1932 to the Present*. Westport, CT: Greenwood Press.

Freudenheim, Yehoshua. 1967. *Government in Israel*. Dobbs Ferry, NY: Oceana Publications.

Galnoor, Itzhak. 1995. *The Partition of Palestine: Decision Crossroads in the Zionist Movement*. Albany: State University of New York Press.

Golan, Matti. 1982. *Shimon Peres: A Biography*. New York: St. Martin's Press.

Goldscheider, Calvin. 1992. *Population and Social Change in Israel*. Boulder, CO: Westview Press.

———. 1996. *Israel's Changing Society: Population, Ethnicity, and Development*. Boulder, CO: Westview Press.

Graetz, Heinrich. 1891–1898. *History of the Jews*, 6 vols. Philadelphia: Jewish Publication Society of America.

Grossman, David. 1988. *The Yellow Wind.* Trans. Haim Watzman. New York: Farrar, Straus and Giroux.

Haber, Eitan. 1978. *Menachem Begin: The Legend and the Man.* Trans. Louis Williams. New York: Delacorte Press.

Hall-Cathala, David. 1990. *The Peace Movement in Israel, 1967–1987.* New York: St. Martin's Press.

Halpern, Ben. 1970. *The Idea of the Jewish State.* 2d ed. Cambridge, MA: Harvard University Press.

Harkabi, Yehoshafat. 1977. *Arab Strategies and Israel's Response.* New York: Free Press.

———. 1988. *Israel's Fateful Decisions.* Trans. Lenn Schramm. London: I. B. Tauris.

Henriques, Robert. 1957. *A Hundred Hours to Suez: An Account of Israel's Campaign in the Sinai Peninsula.* New York: Viking Press.

Herzl, Theodor. 1970. *The Jewish State.* (Der Judenstaat). Trans. Harry Zohn. New York: Herzl Press.

Herzog, Chaim. 1975. *The War of Atonement: October, 1973.* Boston: Little, Brown.

———. 1982. *The Arab-Israeli Wars: War and Peace in the Middle East.* New York: Random House.

Horowitz, Dan, and Moshe Lissak. 1989. *Trouble in Utopia: The Overburdened Polity of Israel.* Albany: State University of New York Press.

Horowitz, David. 1967. *The Economics of Israel.* Oxford: Pergamon Press.

Hurewitz, J. C. 1950. *The Struggle for Palestine.* New York: W. W. Norton.

Jacobsohn, Gary Jeffrey. 1993. *Apple of Gold: Constitutionalism in Israel and the United States.* Princeton: Princeton University Press.

Jiryis, Sabri. 1976. *The Arabs in Israel.* New York and London: Monthly Review Press.

Karsh, Efraim, ed. 1996. *Between War and Peace: Dilemmas of Israeli Security.* London: Frank Cass.

Kieval, Gershon R. 1983. *Party Politics in Israel and the Occupied Territories.* Westport, CT: Greenwood Press.

Kimche, David, and Dan Bawly. 1971. *The Six-Day War: Prologue and Aftermath.* New York: Stein and Day.

Kimche, Jon, and David Kimche. 1960. *A Clash of Destinies: The Arab-Jewish War and the Founding of the State of Israel.* New York: Praeger.

Kimmerling, Baruch. 1985. *The Interrupted System: Israeli Civilians in War and Routine Times.* New Brunswick, NJ: Transaction Books.

———, ed. 1989. *The Israeli State and Society: Boundaries and Frontiers.* Albany: State University of New York Press.

Klieman, Aaron S. 1985. *Israel's Global Reach: Arms Sales as Diplomacy.* Washington, DC: Pergamon-Brassey's.

———. 1988. *Statecraft in the Dark: Israel's Practice of Quiet Diplomacy.* Boulder, CO: Westview Press.

———. 1989. *Israel and the World after 40 Years.* Elmsford, NY: Pergamon.

Klieman, Aharon, and Reuven Pedatzur. 1991. *Rearming Israel: Defense Procurement through the 1990s.* Tel Aviv: Jaffee Center for Strategic Studies, Tel Aviv University; Boulder, CO: Westview Press.

Kraines, Oscar. 1961. *Government and Politics in Israel.* Boston: Houghton Mifflin.

———. 1976. *The Impossible Dilemma: Who Is a Jew in the State of Israel?* New York: Bloch.

Kraus, Vered. 1990. *Promises in the Promised Land: Mobility and Inequality in Israel*. Westport, CT: Greenwood Press.

Kretzmer, David. 1990. *The Legal Status of the Arabs in Israel*. Boulder, CO: Westview Press.

Kurzman, Dan. 1983. *Ben-Gurion: Prophet of Fire*. New York: Simon and Schuster.

Kyle, Keith, and Joel Peters, eds. 1993. *Whither Israel? The Domestic Challenges*. New York: I. B. Tauris.

Landau, Jacob M. 1969. *The Arabs in Israel: A Political Study*. London: Oxford University Press.

———. 1993. *The Arab Minority in Israel, 1967–1991: Political Aspects*. Oxford: Clarendon Press.

Laqueur, Walter. 1972. *A History of Zionism*. New York: Holt, Rinehart and Winston.

Laufer, Leopold. 1967. *Israel and the Developing Countries: New Approaches to Co-operation*. New York: Twentieth Century Fund.

Lau-Lavie, Naftali. 1969. *Moshe Dayan: A Biography*. London: Vallentine, Mitchell.

Lehman-Wilzig, Sam N. 1991. *Stiff-necked People, Bottle-necked System: The Evolution and Roots of Israeli Public Protest, 1949–1986*. Bloomington: Indiana University Press.

Lewin-Epstein, Noah. 1993. *The Arab Minority in Israel's Economy: Patterns of Ethnic Inequality*. Boulder, CO: Westview Press.

Liebman, Charles S., and Eliezer Don-Yehiya. 1983. *Civil Religion in Israel: Traditional Judaism and Political Culture in the Jewish State*. Berkeley: University of California Press.

———. 1984. *Religion and Politics in Israel*. Bloomington: Indiana University Press.

Likhovski, Eliahu S. 1971. *Israel's Parliament: The Law of the Knesset*. Oxford: Clarendon Press.

Lissak, Moshe, ed. 1984. *Israeli Society and Its Defense Establishment: The Social and Political Impact of a Protracted Violent Conflict*. London: Frank Cass.

Litvinoff, Barnet. 1954. *Ben-Gurion of Israel*. New York: Praeger.

Litwin, Howard. 1995. *Uprooted in Old Age: Soviet Jews and Their Social Networks in Israel*. Westport, CT: Greenwood Press.

Lorch, Netanel. 1961. *The Edge of the Sword: Israel's War of Independence, 1947–1949*. New York: Putnam.

Lucas, Noah. 1975. *The Modern History of Israel*. New York: Praeger.

Luttwak, Edward, and Dan Horowitz. 1975. *The Israeli Army*. New York: Harper and Row.

Mahler, Gregory S. 1981. *The Knesset: Parliament in the Israeli Political System*. Rutherford, NJ: Fairleigh Dickinson University Press.

———. 1989. *Israel: Government and Politics in a Maturing State*. New York: Harcourt Brace Jovanovich.

Makovsky, David. 1995. *Making Peace with the PLO: The Rabin Government's Road to the Oslo Accord*. Boulder, CO: Westview Press.

Medding, Peter Y. 1972. *Mapai in Israel: Political Organization and Government in a New Society*. Cambridge: Cambridge University Press.

———. 1989. *The Founding of Israeli Democracy, 1948–1988*. London: Oxford University Press.

Medzini, Meron, ed. 1976–1995. *Israel's Foreign Relations: Selected Documents, 1947–1994*. 14 vols. Jerusalem: Ministry for Foreign Affairs.

Meir, Golda. 1975. *My Life*. New York: Dell.

Morris, Benny. 1993. *Israel's Border Wars, 1949–1956: Arab Infiltration, Israeli Retaliation, and the Countdown to the Suez War*. New York: Oxford University Press.

Netanyahu, Benjamin. 1993. *A Place among the Nations: Israel and the World*. New York: Bantam Books.

O'Ballance, Edgar. 1972. *The Third Arab-Israeli War*. London: Faber.

———. 1978. *No Victor, No Vanquished: The Yom Kippur War*. San Rafael, CA: Presidio Press.

O'Brien, Connor Cruise. 1986. *The Siege: The Saga of Israel and Zionism*. New York: Simon and Schuster.

Ojo, Olusola. 1988. *Africa and Israel: Relations in Perspective*. Boulder, CO: Westview Press.

Orni, Efraim, and Elisha Efrat. 1971. *Geography of Israel*. Jerusalem: Israel Universities Press.

Peleg, Ilan. 1987. *Begin's Foreign Policy, 1977–1983: Israel's Move to the Right*. Westport, CT: Greenwood Press.

Penniman, Howard R., ed. 1979. *Israel at the Polls: The Knesset Elections of 1977*. Washington, DC: American Enterprise Institute for Public Policy Research.

Peres, Shimon. 1970. *David's Sling: The Arming of Israel*. London: Weidenfeld and Nicolson.

———. 1995. *Battling for Peace*. New York: Random House.

Peres, Shimon, with Arye Naor. 1993. *The New Middle East*. New York: Henry Holt.

Peri, Yoram. 1983. *Between Battles and Ballots: Israeli Military in Politics*. Cambridge: Cambridge University Press.

Perlmutter, Amos. 1969. *Military and Politics in Israel: Nation-building and Role Expansion*. London: Frank Cass.

———. 1987. *The Life and Times of Menachem Begin*. Garden City, NY: Doubleday.

Prittie, Terence. 1969. *Eshkol: The Man and the Nation*. New York: Putnam.

Rabin, Yitzhak. 1979. *The Rabin Memoirs*. Boston: Little, Brown.

Rabinovich, Itamar. 1984. *The War for Lebanon, 1970–1983*. Ithaca: Cornell University Press.

Rackman, Emanuel. 1955. *Israel's Emerging Constitution, 1948–51*. New York: Columbia University Press.

Rafael, Gideon. 1981. *Destination Peace: Three Decades of Israeli Foreign Policy*. New York: Stein and Day.

Razin, Assaf, and Efraim Sadka. 1993. *The Economy of Modern Israel: Malaise and Promise*. Chicago: University of Chicago Press.

Reich, Bernard. 1973. *Israel and the Occupied Territories*. Washington, DC: U.S. Department of State.

———. 1977. *Quest for Peace: United States–Israel Relations and the Arab-Israeli Conflict*. New Brunswick, NJ: Transaction Books.

———. 1984. *The United States and Israel: Influence in the Special Relationship*. New York: Praeger.

———. 1992. *Historical Dictionary of Israel*. Metuchen, NJ: Scarecrow Press.

———. 1995. *Securing the Covenant: United States–Israel Relations after the Cold War*. Westport, CT: Praeger.

Reich, Bernard, and Gershon R. Kieval, eds. 1986. *Israel Faces the Future*. New York: Praeger.

————, eds. 1988. *Israeli National Security Policy: Political Actors and Perspectives.* Westport, CT: Greenwood Press.

————, eds. 1991. *Israeli Politics in the 1990s: Key Domestic and Foreign Policy Factors.* Westport, CT: Greenwood Press.

————. 1993. *Israel: Land of Tradition and Conflict.* 2d ed. Boulder, CO: Westview Press.

Reinharz, Jehuda. 1985. *Chaim Weizmann: The Making of a Zionist Leader.* New York: Oxford University Press.

Reiser, Stewart. 1989. *The Israeli Arms Industry: Foreign Policy, Arms Transfers, and Military Doctrine of a Small State.* New York: Holmes and Meier.

Romann, Michael, and Alex Weingrod. 1991. *Living Together Separately: Arabs and Jews in Contemporary Jerusalem.* Princeton: Princeton University Press.

Rubinstein, Amnon. 1984. *The Zionist Dream Revisited: From Herzl to Gush Emunim and Back.* New York: Schocken.

Sachar, Howard M. 1976. *A History of Israel: From the Rise of Zionism to Our Time.* New York: Alfred A. Knopf.

————. 1987. *A History of Israel, II: From the Aftermath of the Yom Kippur War.* Oxford: Oxford University Press.

Safran, Nadav. 1981. *Israel: The Embattled Ally.* Cambridge, MA: Belknap Press of Harvard University Press.

Sager, Samuel. 1985. *The Parliamentary System of Israel.* Syracuse: Syracuse University Press.

Sanbar, Moshe, ed. 1990. *Economic and Social Policy in Israel: The First Generation.* Lanham, MD: University Press of America.

Schechtman, Joseph B. 1956. *The Vladimir Jabotinsky Story.* Vol. 1, *Rebel and Statesman: The Early Years.* New York: Thomas Yoseloff.

————. 1961. *The Vladimir Jabotinsky Story.* Vol. 2, *Fighter and Prophet: The Last Years.* New York: Thomas Yoseloff.

Schiff, Gary S. 1977. *Tradition and Politics: The Religious Parties of Israel.* Detroit, MI: Wayne State University Press.

Schiff, Zeev. 1974. *A History of the Israeli Army (1870–1974).* New York: Simon and Schuster.

Schiff, Zeev, and Eitan Haber, eds., and Arie Hashavia, assoc. ed. 1976. *Lehsikon levitahon yisrael* (A Lexicon of Israel's Defense). Tel Aviv: Zmora, Bitan, Modan.

Schiff, Zeev, and Ehud Yaari. 1984. *Israel's Lebanon War.* New York: Simon and Schuster.

Schwartz, Moshe, Susan Lees, and Gideon M. Kressel, eds. 1995. *Rural Cooperatives in Socialist Utopia: Thirty Years of Moshav Development in Israel.* Westport, CT: Praeger.

Schweitzer, Avraham. 1986. *Israel: The Changing National Agenda.* London: Croom Helm.

Segev, Tom. 1986. *1949: The First Israelis.* New York: Free Press.

Seligman, Lester G. 1964. *Leadership in a New Nation: Political Development in Israel.* New York: Atherton Press.

Seliktar, Ofira. 1986. *New Zionism and the Foreign Policy System of Israel.* London: Croom Helm.

Shalev, Aryeh. 1993. *The Israel-Syria Armistice Regime, 1949–1955.* Boulder, CO: Westview Press.

Shalev, Michael. 1989. *Labour and the Political Economy in Israel*. London: Oxford University Press.

Shamir, Yitzhak. 1994. *Summing Up: An Autobiography*. Boston: Little, Brown.

Shapiro, Yonathan. 1991. *The Road to Power: Herut Party in Israel*. Albany, NY: State University of New York Press.

Sharkansky, Ira. 1985. *What Makes Israel Tick? How Domestic Policy-Makers Cope with Constraints*. Chicago: Nelson-Hall.

Sheffer, Gabriel, ed. 1975. *Dynamics of a Conflict: A Re-examination of the Arab-Israeli Conflict*. Atlantic Highlands, NJ: Humanities Press.

Shihor, Samuel. 1960. *Hollow Glory: The Last Days of Chaim Weizmann, First President of Israel*. New York: Thomas Yoseloff.

Shimshoni, Daniel. 1982. *Israeli Democracy: The Middle of the Journey*. New York: Free Press; London: Collier Macmillan.

Shimshoni, Jonathan. 1988. *Israel and Conventional Deterrence: Border Warfare from 1953 to 1970*. Ithaca: Cornell University Press.

Shindler, Colin. 1995. *Israel, Likud, and the Zionist Dream: Power, Politics, and Ideology from Begin to Netanyahu*. New York: St. Martin's Press.

Shuval, Judith T. 1963. *Immigrants on the Threshold*. New York: Atherton Press.

Silver, Eric. 1984. *Begin: The Haunted Prophet*. New York: Random House.

Simon, Merrill. 1988. *Moshe Arens, Statesman and Scientist, Speaks Out*. Middle Island, NY: Dean Books.

Slater, Robert. 1993. *Rabin of Israel*. New York: St. Martin's Press.

Sobel, Zvi. 1993. *A Small Place in Galilee: Religion and Social Conflict in an Israeli Village*. New York: Holmes and Meier.

Sofer, Sasson. 1988. *Begin: An Anatomy of Leadership*. Oxford: Basil Blackwell.

Sprinzak, Ehud. 1991. *The Ascendance of Israel's Radical Right*. New York: Oxford University Press.

Sprinzak, Ehud, and Larry Diamond, eds. 1993. *Israeli Democracy under Stress*. Boulder, CO: Lynne Rienner.

Stock, Ernest. 1967. *Israel on the Road to Sinai, 1949–1956*. Ithaca: Cornell University Press.

The Sunday Times. Insight on the Middle East War. 1974. London: The Sunday Times.

Swirski, Shlomo. 1989. *Israel: The Oriental Majority*. London: Zed Books.

Sykes, Christopher. 1965. *Crossroads to Israel*. Cleveland, OH: World Publishing.

Syrkin, Marie. 1963. *Golda Meir: Woman with a Cause*. New York: Putnam.

Temko, Ned. 1987. *To Win or to Die: A Personal Portrait of Menachem Begin*. New York: William Morrow.

Teveth, Shabtai. 1973. *Moshe Dayan: The Soldier, the Man, the Legend*. Boston: Houghton Mifflin.

———. 1985. *Ben-Gurion and the Palestinian Arabs: From Peace to War*. New York: Oxford University Press.

———. 1987. *Ben-Gurion: The Burning Ground, 1886–1948*. Boston: Houghton Mifflin.

Vital, David. 1975. *The Origins of Zionism*. London: Oxford University Press.

———. 1982. *Zionism: The Formative Years*. New York: Oxford University Press.

———. 1987. *Zionism: The Crucial Phase*. New York: Oxford University Press.

Wagaw, Teshome G. 1993. *For Our Soul: Ethiopian Jews in Israel*. Detroit, MI: Wayne State University Press.

Wallach, Jehuda L. 1984. *Israeli Military History: A Guide to the Sources*. New York: Garland.

Weingrod, Alex. 1965. *Israel: Group Relations in a New Society*. New York: Frederick A. Praeger for the Institute of Race Relations.

Weisgal, Meyer W., and Joel Carmichael, eds. 1963. *Chaim Weizmann: A Biography by Several Hands*. New York: Atheneum.

Weizman, Ezer. 1981. *The Battle for Peace*. New York: Bantam Books.

Yaacobi, Gad. 1982. *The Government of Israel*. New York: Praeger.

Yaniv, Avner. 1987. *Dilemmas of Security: Politics, Strategy, and the Israeli Experience in Lebanon*. New York: Oxford University Press.

———, ed. 1993. *National Security and Democracy in Israel*. Boulder, CO: Lynne Rienner.

Zidon, Asher. 1967. *Knesset: The Parliament of Israel*. New York: Herzl Press.

Zohar, David. 1974. *Political Parties in Israel: The Evolution of Israeli Democracy*. New York: Praeger.

JORDAN

Robert B. Satloff and Becky Diamond

Jordan makes a great story. In the beginning, there was a stroke of Churchill's pen and a wandering Arabian prince stopping at a dusty way station along the road to Damascus, and a principality was born. When the native population took none too kindly to the creation of this new state, the Arabians and their British officer corps called upon Syrians, Circassians, and Palestinians to impose their rule; with the outcome certain, the recalcitrant bedouin tribesmen threw their lot in with the new rulers and became the backbone of the state. Surrounded by larger, more powerful, and more populous neighbors, Jordan was the only Arab state to emerge from the 1948 war against Israel with more territory, but it came with more people, too. For years, Jordan lived on the edge of extinction, threatened variously by the mesmerizing attraction of Arab nationalism, the suffocating embrace of the wealthier Baghdad-based wing of the Hashemite family, the heavy hand of Israel's policy of retaliation for border raids by Palestinians who cared little for the survival of an independent Jordan, and the explosive mix of interference and indifference from the kingdom's external patrons, Britain and then America. Yet Jordan survived, with an economy woefully inadequate for the demographic burden of a refugee population that today is about one million, with a country that has virtually no natural resources except the labor and ingenuity of its people, and with a feisty but beleaguered ruling family that is astonishingly small in number. Indeed, of the Arab principals who fought in Palestine in 1948, Jordan's is the only regime that remained intact (though shaky) a decade later and the only one to have avoided assassination or radical change in government since.

Until recently, however, little of this fascinating story was told or explained in the scholarly literature. While some has been written on various aspects of Jordanian political life, little has focused on the central questions of how and

A number of prominent books on Jordan were published since this chapter was written.

why the Hashemite regime survived. Instead, taking their cue from a regime that for three decades sought to portray an image of Jordan that focused almost exclusively on its resilient, long-serving monarch, King Hussein bin Talal, scholarly studies have generally tended to be limited to biographical sketches of the king, to sociological and anthropological studies on a local (i.e., village or tribal) level, or to Palestinian-centric examinations of Jordan's political, social, and economic life. Politics—the process of decision making and the distribution of power throughout the kingdom—has only recently been the fare of Western scholars.

Two preliminary observations are in order. First, almost all the works discussed here are written by Westerners; Jordanians do not, on the whole, write Jordanian history. Other than biographical and autobiographical works and official, commissioned histories, there are very few works of consequence by Jordanians that touch on the political history of the kingdom, whether in English or Arabic. This reticence is slowly fading, as a number of the works cited herein attest, and will surely fade more quickly should Jordan's liberal experiment of the late 1980s and early 1990s survive. But this reticence is deeply entrenched in the national psyche: Too much of Jordan's sensitive past is bound up in the no-less-sensitive present for Jordanians (and the kingdom's rulers) to feel comfortable examining their history and politics with a critical eye.

Second, it is important to note the vital role played by the gradual opening of foreign archives in transforming writing on Jordan from personalized, journalistic accounts into scholarly treatises. Indeed, it is useful to divide the literature into pre- and postarchival, indicating whether the works relied on newspapers and interviews or had the benefit of foreign archives. British, American, and Israeli archives are essential for understanding politics inside the kingdom; Soviet archives (which are partially available) and French papers (which are not) should be helpful, too. It should be noted that for nearly two decades after the 1967 war, researchers could examine a slice of domestic Jordanian politics via the hefty cache of internal security files captured by Israel from various West Bank offices of Jordanian government ministries. That archive, however, was closed by Israel for security reasons early in the Palestinian uprising (intifada) because it was thought that some reprisal attacks by Palestinians against collaborators with the Hashemites were based on information gleaned from these records. All this compensates for the paucity of official Jordanian government archives. The archives of the Hashemite Royal Court are closed; many government records have been open for several years, though a rudimentary classification system impedes systematic research; some of the most sensitive material from the 1940s and 1950s, however, was lost in the bomb blast that killed Prime Minister Hazza al-Majali and destroyed the prime ministry building in 1960. Of central government documents, researchers are left largely with parliamentary records and the Official Gazette. While foreign archives go far toward compensating for this lacuna, some imaginative scholars are beginning to turn to alternative sources like Sharia court records and Chamber of Commerce files.

COUNTRY STUDIES

There is no good, single volume examining the history and politics of the Hashemite Kingdom of Jordan since its founding. One book in Arabic that has played a considerable role in shaping scholarship on Jordan is Munib al-Madi and Sulayman Musa's *Tarikh al-urdunn fi al-qarn al-'ashrin* (The history of Jordan in the twentieth century) (1959), a chronicler's history replete with lists of ministries, parliamentary candidates, and gazetted laws but little critical analysis. A number of early works attempted analysis and were valuable for the period in which they appeared, but have since become obsolete. Several other works are general overviews that are useful as an introduction to the kingdom but do not take the reader much further. In the late 1980s, the opening of foreign archives gave rise to a boom in Jordanian studies that is now bearing fruit. This boom has produced a number of high-quality studies of limited periods of Jordanian history but so far no integrated account that either explains the kingdom's political development over seven decades or its evolving role in regional politics over that time.

The least rigorous country study was the first to appear, Ann Dearden's *Jordan* (1958). Sometime correspondent for the *Manchester Guardian* and wife of the British intelligence liaison in Amman, Dearden offers a sympathetic, pro-Hashemite, pro-British account of the manichean descent from British-managed order into Arab nationalist chaos that marked Jordan in the 1940s and 1950s. In a striking repetition of official British views at the time, for example, Dearden writes that political opposition in Jordan was virtually "born" with Egypt's Czech arms deal (113). Indeed, she presents a simplistic image of Jordan throughout: "Broadly speaking, the towns are modern, the villages medieval, and the tents of the desert, Biblical" (163). A more detailed and less upbeat assessment is found in Benjamin Shwadran's *Jordan: A State of Tension* (1959), which incorporated much of the information Shwadran had published over the years on Jordan in the journal *Middle Eastern Affairs*. Shwadran underscores the uncertainty of Hashemite rule, especially its tenuous popular support and dependence on foreign economic and military assistance. For Shwadran, the survival or extinction of the Hashemite regime was largely the function of Cold War decisions taken in Washington or London; politics in Amman was petty and almost immaterial. As he noted on prime-ministerial rotations, "The alignments and re-alignments were so frequent that it was almost impossible to keep up with the real reasons behind the many changes" (390). In fact, the reasons were real and important, but fell outside Shwadran's main focus.

By a large margin, the most lucid, insightful, and comprehensive of these early attempts at Jordanian political history is A. H. H. Abidi's *Jordan: A Political Study, 1948–1957* (1965). Abidi offers a detailed, critical, and largely dispassionate analysis relying heavily on the documentary sources then available, spiced with numerous interviews of significant players on the Jordanian political scene. Unlike his predecessors, Abidi includes accurate citations, appendixes, and bibliographical entries. In addition to this professionalism of style, Abidi was the first to examine the complexity of domestic Jordanian politics, taking Jordanian political history in directions not previously traveled. Jordan is not, as some have contended, simply a clash between East Bankers and West Bankers, between Transjordanians and Palestinians, between monarchical reactionaries and forward-thinking nationalists. "The changing social phenomena and values have given vent to a complex situation," he writes. "There exist tendencies of regional, religious and racial conflict among the Jordanians" (174). Abidi takes the sound middle ground, neither papering over the deep divisions that scar Jordanian society nor letting them devolve into stereotypes. For example, he states insightfully that despite the West Bank's reputation for more advanced political awareness than the East Bank, Palestinian politics was still governed by a "prevalence of the family cult and loyalty" (169). Moreover, he offers the first sophisticated assessment of the development of political blocs and institutions in the country as well as the first examination of the Talal interlude, highlighting the role of an oligarchy that ruled in Talal's name. While sometimes tantalizing without offering full explanations, Abidi's work remains a valuable reference for the tumultuous decade it examines.

In contrast, Naseer Aruri's *Jordan: A Study in Political Development* (1972), the first significant Palestinian-centric study of the kingdom's political history, is neither sober nor detached. Aruri's central theme is that the essence of Jordanian politics is the use of coercion by the central government against its largely Palestinian population. While there may be much to justify this characterization in the late 1960s and early 1970s, when Aruri prepared this text as a doctoral dissertation, it is less defensible as a description of Jordanian politics in earlier decades. Aruri, however, covers Jordanian history from 1921 to 1965, and throughout most of that period it is difficult to speak of an identifiable political corporate identity for Jordan's Palestinians, especially outside the refugee camps. Viewed in its totality, Aruri's work is not so much a dispassionate critical analysis of Jordanian political development as it is a sophisticated attempt to deconstruct the historical bases of the Hashemite regime. Although it does have its strong points, including a useful discussion of the role of the proregime "palace group," even that seems only to complement Abidi's earlier discussion of the "oligarchy." Indeed, compared to Abidi's, Aruri's book does not pass muster.

In addition to these period-specific country studies, a number of general accounts of Jordanian history, politics, society, and culture have appeared over the years that have served as useful introductions to Jordan but not as thoroughgoing analyses of political development within the kingdom. These include Raphael Patai's *The Kingdom of Jordan* (1958); George L. Harris's *Jordan: Its People, Its Society, Its Culture* (1958); Peter Gubser's *Jordan: Crossroads of Middle Eastern Events* (1983); and Kamal S. Salibi's *The Modern History of Jordan* (1993). Of these, Gubser's work retains relevance and utility today. Salibi's work is most disappointing; despite all the new material that has become available in the last fifteen years, he presents a composite review of well-known themes and vignettes that relies almost exclusively on the secondary literature of the pre-1980s. The promise of its grandiose title remains unfulfilled.

For more than a decade following the publication of Aruri's study, the scholarly literature on Jordan remained static. Then, as closure periods for British and American archives ended and tens of thousands of documents became available for scholarly research, interest in the origin and political development of the kingdom picked up pace. This led to the preparation of a number of works examining both the pre- and post-1948 periods. Those dealing with the period from the founding of the state through the 1948 war included Maan Abu Nuwar's *The History of the Hashemite Kingdom of Jordan*, volume 1, *The Creation and Development of Transjordan, 1920–1929* (1989); Philip Robins's "The Consolidation of Hashimite Power in Jordan, 1921–1946" (University of Exeter dissertation, 1988); Mary C. Wilson's *King Abdullah, Britain, and the Making of Jordan* (1987); and Avi Shlaim's *Collusion across the Jordan: King Abdullah, the Zionist Movement, and the Partition of Palestine* (1988). Those examining the turbulent 1950s and 1960s included Uriel Dann's *King Hussein and the Challenge of Arab Radicalism: Jordan, 1955–1967* (1989); Robert B. Satloff's *From Abdullah to Hussein: Jordan in Transition* (1994); and Asher Susser's *On Both Banks of the Jordan: A Political Biography of Wasfi al-Tall* (1994). Except for the first named, all are studies by professional historians or political scientists that collectively serve to elevate the historiography of Jordan.

Concerning the pre-1948 period, Abu Nuwar's book should be dismissed as apologia masquerading as scholarship. A former general acquitted on charges of conspiring to overthrow Hussein in the 1957 Zerqa plot, Abu Nuwar was rehabilitated by the regime, was elevated to senior military and diplomatic positions (including ambassador to London), and served as deputy prime minister in a government headed by Abdul Salam al-Majali. During an interlude at Oxford, Abu Nuwar compiled a defense of Abdullah's early years in Transjordan and especially of his intriguing dealings with Zionist land agents.

On the other end of the political spectrum, though far more scholarly, analytical, and comprehensive in their treatment, are the works of Wilson and Shlaim, both of which tend to view the preunion phase almost singularly through the Hashemite-Palestinian-Zionist prism—the former even more than the latter, despite the title of Shlaim's book. (The inflammatory notion of "collusion" was deleted from the paperback version of Shlaim's book, which appeared under the title *The Politics of Partition: King Abdullah, the Zionists, and Palestine.*) Shlaim's introduction and Wilson's conclusion attest to the two authors' political agendas: Shlaim criticizes from the start a Zionist propensity to violence, whereas Wilson laments the early death of a Palestinian national political consciousness that had not yet really been born. In another episode that underscores their predilection for focusing on the treachery inflicted upon the Palestinians, both (along with Barry Rubin in *The Arab States and the Palestine Conflict,* though for different reasons) choose to depict Abdullah's assassination as an act of retribution by Palestinian nationalists, perhaps even acting on behalf of Hajj Amin al-Husayni, overlooking any reference to archival suggestions (by Alec Seath Kirkbride, among others) that the Mufti was not connected to the murder, an opinion also accepted in London. Read with these sorts of caveats, Wilson and Shlaim present substantial and important works of scholarship, not likely the last word on Abdullah's state- and nation-building efforts but surely works to be reckoned with by any future historian.

Into this mix one should add Robins's dissertation, a solid, apolitical piece of scholarship that makes contributions on the critical theme of Hashemite reliance on non-Transjordanians, that is, Circassians, Syrians, and Palestinians. Also, one should note the important tonic to the Shlaim-Wilson themes provided in Itamar Rabinovich's *The Road Not Taken: Early Arab-Israeli Negotiations* (1991), which highlights the complexity of reasons for the failure of Israel-Jordan negotiations, not just Israeli reluctance.

Interestingly, as one moves from the pre-1948 to the post-1948 period, historical scholarship becomes a bit more sympathetic to the Hashemite enterprise. Ron Pundik's fine *The Struggle for Sovereignty* straddles the two eras, examining Jordan's relations with Britain from 1946 to 1951; he emphasizes (a bit too heavily) Abdullah's pragmatism in his complex relationship with his superpower patron. Robert Satloff's *From Abdullah to Hussein* reviews the volatile years from Abdullah's assassination in 1951 to the reassertion of royal prerogative and the imposition of martial law in 1957; its objective is to explain how the Jordanian monarchy survived domestic tempests without the hand of a strong monarch (rather, with the ill-starred Talal and the novice Hussein) on the rudder. Dann's book, a delightful volume that is the distillation of a lifetime's observation of the Hashemites, similarly explains Jordan's survival, though on a wider stage (the inter-Arab system) over a longer period of time (from the Baghdad Pact through the debacle of 1967). Dann's conclusion (which Satloff draws upon) is that will, chance, and the exertions of loyal ''king's men'' each had a role in ensuring the survival of Hussein's reign. Susser's excellent study of Jordanian statesman, regime stalwart, and national martyr Wasfi al-Tall highlights the contribution of the third leg of that mutually dependent triad. In an extended essay published posthumously, Dann (1992) expanded on his explication of King Hussein's survival strategy that to this day remains the most coherent and incisive explanation of what makes Hussein and his kingdom work.

Looking toward the future of conventional, top-down histories, the process appears certain—as archives open, new groups of doctoral students and other scholars will investigate eras and episodes of Jordanian history. However, with the passage of time, the utility of British and American source material will decrease, as Jordan's patrons held less and less sway over the kingdom's political life and, by extension, were privy to less and less of its secret (and even not-so-secret) goings-on. Three topics of interest upon which archives will shed some light are Jordan's role in the Arab cold war of the late 1950s and early

1960s; the impact of Iraq's revolution on the Hashemites inside Jordan; and a domestic political explanation for Hussein's decision to do in 1967 what he wanted to but did not in 1956: attack Israel. Samir A. Mutawi, former public relations advisor in the royal palace, attempted this in *Jordan in the 1967 War* (1987). While Mutawi presented an interesting schema of the process of national security decision making in Jordan, based largely on a series of interviews with principals, his analysis of decisions before, during, and after the war itself is unfulfilling, bordering on the apologetic. Some scholars have already wagered on the expected limitations of British and American archives in revisiting more recent episodes, such as Jordan's 1970–1971 civil strife, by proceeding apace with dissertation research based on alternative sources. This, for example, is the theme of an Oxford dissertation by Paul Lalor (1992), based largely on Palestinian and other Arab sources. An earlier study on the topic is Paul Jureidini's dissertation, "The Relationship of the Palestinian Guerilla Movement with the Government of Jordan, 1967–1970" (1975).

A discussion of the significance and value of autobiographical and other English-language, firsthand accounts of events in Jordan since the 1940s falls outside the scope of this chapter. The most notable include memoirs by Kings Abdullah and Hussein; British diplomats Alec Kirkbride and Charles Johnston; American diplomats Joseph Coy Green (unpublished) and Richard Sanger; and British soldiers John Bagot Glubb (Glubb Pasha), and Peter Young. Though Glubb wrote a number of works on Jordan, his autobiographical ones are the most valuable, though not altogether accurate.

FOREIGN RELATIONS AND NATIONAL SECURITY

In addition to historical studies focusing generally on the political core (the king, the palace, and so on), a number of works are dedicated to aspects of central government decision making, especially foreign and defense policy. Given Jordan's novel position as a weak, impoverished, and overburdened state surrounded on all sides by stronger neighbors, all of whom at various times have at least considered territorial aggrandizement at Amman's expense, one would expect significant academic attention to foreign and defense themes. This, however, is not the case, largely because Jordan is viewed as a bit player on the larger regional stage. Indeed, that is a theme developed by Dann to help explain how Jordan avoided Gamal Abdel Nasser's grasp: the Egyptian leader, Dann argued, simply had bigger fish to fry. In fact, except for a single work, Mohammad Ibrahim Faddah's *The Middle East in Transition: A Study of Jordan's Foreign Policy* (1974), all studies on Jordan's foreign relations have been viewed through the lens of the Arab-Israeli conflict.

Faddah's book did for foreign relations what Abidi's did for domestic politics: it provided a sober, methodical, and well-documented overview of the subject. No singular theme emerges from Faddah's chronicle, however, other than the image of the kingdom continually seeking to balance its relations among competing parties. While providing valuable source material, Faddah does not also offer an interpretive model for understanding Jordan's relationships with its neighbors.

Several books make strong cases for a functional understanding of Jordan's relations with Israel, the belligerent with whom the kingdom maintained an on-again, off-again covert relationship for decades. These include Uri Bar-Joseph's *The Best of Enemies: Israel and Transjordan in the War of 1948* (1987) and Adam Garfinkle's *Israel and Jordan in the Shadow of War* (1992). Bar-Joseph argues that the two parties maintained a carefully scripted relationship even following the invasion of Israel by Jordan's Arab Legion the day Israel declared its independence, a relationship based on a tacit understanding that Jordan would not fight the creation of Israel within its U.N.-mandated borders so long as Jordan was the beneficiary of the remainder of Palestine. This theme is a small part of the larger saga described less sympathetically by Shlaim and Wilson. Garfinkle's book is broader, examining the sweep of the often-but-not-always-secret ties that evolved between the two countries through the early 1990s. From the mundane (e.g., mosquito eradication) to the truly important (e.g., water management, counterterrorism), he describes them all and places them within the context of the functional approach to peacemaking. While recognizing that nothing can substitute for the real thing—public, transparent political commitments—Garfinkle's work sheds light on how states technically at war find ways around that predicament. The functionalist theme also plays a starring role in *Behind the Uprising: Israelis, Jordanians, and Palestinians* by Yossi Melman and Dan Raviv (1989), which is a journalistic account of this triangular relationship that attempts to provide context to the onset of the Palestinian intifada.

The scholarship on Jordanian foreign relations is especially thin, and the subject deserves greater attention. In terms of Jordan's relations with the great powers, only Mary Wilson's *King Abdullah, Britain, and the Making of Jordan* sustains the theme throughout; Jordan would make a useful study of patron-client relations and the limits of patronage. Madiha Rashid al-Madfai brings together valuable material in her *Jordan, the United States, and the Middle East Peace Process, 1974–1991* (1993), but the book reads as special pleading, with Jordan bearing virtually none of the responsibility for the lack of favorable movement in the peace process over the years. On regional issues, Jordan deserves study as a classic example of the buffer state that is weaker than its neighbors, all of whom in turn share some interest in the kingdom's survival. Of specific topics in Jordan's foreign relations, two that would make especially interesting reading would be a history of the Hashemite-Saudi feud, pitting conservative monarchies against each other, as well as a more limited examination of the rise and fall of Jordan's special relationship with Saddam Hussein's Iraq.

While Jordan's foreign relations have not captured the attention of scholars, military issues have fared marginally better. The two most important studies are P. J. Vatikiotis's *Politics and the Military in Jordan* (1967) and Sayed Ali el-Edroos's *The Hashemite Arab Army, 1908–1979: An Appreciation and Analysis of Military Operations* (1980). Both these books are critical contributions to the literature; at the same time, though they both deal with the Jordanian armed forces, they could not be more different.

Vatikiotis presents a political history viewed through the lens of the army because his central argument is that the army was the key actor in the kingdom's politics. In fact, his contention, the most widely quoted passage of this classic study, is that the army not only preceded the establishment of Jordan as an independent state, but that it actually created the state. He turns traditional political history on its head by tracing the politics of the kingdom as it revolved around the evolution of the armed forces, rather than vice versa. Events such as the expulsion of Glubb and the Zerqa conspiracy are evaluated from the inside out, extrapolating their political significance from their more immediate military impact. Throughout, Vatikiotis, who makes no effort to hide his sympathies with the Hashemites, suggests several important reasons to explain key aspects of Jordanian politics, such as why military rebelliousness never translated into successful coups d'état. In contrast to the analytical rigor of Vatikiotis, Ali el-Edroos's book is valuable for the sheer amount of information compiled on the organization and operations of the Jordanian army. A Pakistani officer, Ali el-Edroos was given special access to army general staff records to chart the development of the army from its British-officered beginnings to its contributions to the various Arab-Israeli wars. (For his book, Vatikiotis was also given special access.) His product is a massive volume that is long on fact and short on analysis, but not so short that a careful reading fails to shed significant light on the political themes raised earlier by Vatikiotis. Given his access, it is unlikely that an independent scholar will be able to replicate his work, not that there is much to dispute in Ali el-Edroos's chronicle, though there is certainly more to the story than even this thousand-page book describes.

ASPECTS OF DOMESTIC POLITICS

Below the high politics that is the primary focus of the works previously discussed lies a number of themes that have been the subject of scholarly attention. These include the Palestinian dimension of Jordanian politics, the role of bedouin, and politics on a local level.

From 1950 to 1967, the West Bank was an integral part of the Hashemite Kingdom of Jordan, linked to the East Bank by law, economics, demography, and, at times, common urban-based, popular opposition to rule by Amman. Under the umbrella of Jordanian political history, there is a special subset of works that focus singularly on West Bank/Palestinian politics. It is special for several reasons, including the fact that there is no comparable subset of works that focuses on East Bank politics (indeed, virtually none exist) and the fact that it is almost solely the province of Israeli scholars. There are a number of explanations for the Israeli connection. Sometimes this is the result of special access, as in the case of Amnon Cohen's *Political Parties in the West Bank under the Jordanian Regime, 1949–1967* (1982). This book, the only English-language study of party life inside the kingdom, is a condensed and edited version of a six-hundred-page review of a cache of Jordanian internal security documents captured by Israeli forces in 1967 undertaken by a team of Hebrew University graduate students under Cohen's direction. This is a unique contribution to the literature, not only because the source material, the captured archive, has been closed to researchers since the early days of the Palestinian intifada, but also because of the high quality of the research and analysis. But it should not be read as a history of party politics in general during this period, only the West Bank part of it; for example, Sulayman al-Nabulsi's National Socialist party does not appear even in Cohen's index, let alone his table of contents.

Another reason Israelis look at these issues is because they often address questions that are important to the Israeli national psyche. This is true of works by Benny Morris, including *The Birth of the Palestinian Refugee Problem, 1947–1949* (1987) and *Israel's Border Wars, 1949–1956* (1993). Morris, like Shlaim, is a revisionist who attempts to separate out truth from the myths that have developed over the decades about seminal episodes; on both the origins of the Palestinian refugees in the 1940s and the border violence of the 1950s, his general conclusion is that the truth is much grayer than the commonly held black-and-white versions. As self-styled revisionist studies, these works are colored (or, perhaps, discolored) by a political hue, and given the volatile subject matter, they are sure not to be the final word on these subjects, especially should Jordanian documents become more accessible.

Whatever the reason, the Israeli connection is key to understanding Jordanian-Palestinian relations. Avi Plascov's *The Palestinian Refugees in Jordan, 1948–1957* (1981) is a classic and an excellent piece of scholarship. Plascov provides in subdued, detached language a well-researched study of how the Jordanian regime dealt with the hundreds of thousands of refugees that came under its rule in 1948–1949 and how various trends within the refugee community responded. It is one of those rare works that is unlikely to be rendered obsolete by future research. Whereas Plascov examined the lowest rung on the Palestinian political ladder, Moshe Maoz focused on the highest, the notables, in his *Palestinian Leadership on the West Bank: The Changing Role of the Arab Mayors under Jordan and Israel* (1984). This too is a valuable study, though less for what it says about Amman's relationship to Palestinian notables than for how the notables' own relationship to central government authority changed with the advent of Israeli rule and the differing approaches that Israel and Jordan adopted toward Palestinian local government. In addition, a number of works address in a more general manner the demographic/political divide between Jordan and its large Palestinian population. These include *West Bank/East Bank: The Palestinians in Jordan, 1949–1967* by Shaul Mishal (1978) and *Jordan's Palestinian Challenge, 1948–1983: A Political History* (1984) by Clinton Bailey. Mishal's work is more theoretical than informative; Bailey's suffers from overreliance on his doctoral dissertation on the subject, which was completed in 1966.

In contrast to the high-profile studies on the Jordanian-Palestinian relationship, the literature on the role of tribes and on local politics, especially on the East Bank, is more modest. Both facts illustrate the skewed nature of the historiography of Jordan—these are the sort of topics that are essential to any understanding of Jordanian political dynamics, yet they are largely overlooked. Though there is a universal reverence for the role that the tribes play in Jordanian politics, it has never been dissected and examined in a scholarly way; if that were done, scholars would most likely find a web of overlapping interests far more complex than originally anticipated. So far, the literature can claim a number of valuable introductions on the subject but nothing that can compare with the achievements in understanding the Palestinian angle of Jordan. The two most informative studies focus on individual communities, from which one could draw useful generalizations about local politics throughout the East Bank. These are Peter Gubser's *Politics and Change in al-Karak, Jordan: A Study of a Small Arab Town and Its District* (1973) and Richard Antoun's *Low-Key Politics: Local-Level Leadership and Change in the Middle East* (1979), a study of grassroots politics in Kufr al-Ma. Norman Lewis's *Nomads and Settlers in Syria and Jordan, 1800–1980* (1987) provides an unsatisfying prefatory discussion of some of the key actors in the Jordanian story, the Bani Sakhr tribe and the Circassian and Chechen minorities. While Lewis does not pretend to provide a political assessment, he does not even present an adequate historical or sociological assessment of these two groups: there is no mention, for example, of the arrival in Jordan of hundreds of Circassian refugees in the aftermath of World War II, a remarkable feat given that Jordan had just taken in hundreds of thousands of Palestinian refugees, nor is there in the Bani Sakhr chapter more than cursory reference to internal tribal hierarchies.

Though no single volume examines the historic role of the tribes in Jordanian political development, two have addressed the effect that social and economic change has had on that role. These include the collaborative works of Kamal Abu Jaber, Fawzi Gharaibeh, Saleh Khasawneh, and Allen Hill, *Bedouins in Jordan: A People in Transition* (1978), and Paul Jureidini and Ronald D. McLaurin, *Jordan: The Impact of Social Change on the Role of the Tribes* (1984). Both make interesting reading—the former, because it is a rare statement on the topic emanating from the University of Jordan; the latter, because it discusses the political implications of modernity—but the absence of a seminal work on the role of tribes to serve as a point of reference for these studies leaves them as spokes without a hub.

While they are less scholarly works than policy analysis, a small number of books and monographs have appeared in recent years attempting to address the question of domestic stability in Jordan by analyzing at rapid pace a series of key factors: the role of the tribes, the Palestinian conundrum, the emergence of Islamic political activism, the impact of economic decline, the fate of the post-

Hussein monarchy, and prospects for the peace process. They span the range from hedged optimism to hedged skepticism about the kingdom's political fortunes. These include Arthur Day's *East Bank/West Bank: Jordan and the Prospects for Peace* (1986); Valerie Yorke's *Domestic Politics and Regional Security—Jordan, Syria, and Israel: The End of an Era?* (1988); and Robert B. Satloff's *Troubles on the East Bank: Challenges to the Domestic Stability of Jordan* (1986). A more detailed monograph on the Islamist phenomenon, *"They Cannot Stop Our Tongues": Islamic Activism in Jordan* (1987) grew out of a chapter in Satloff's book.

FUTURE RESEARCH

As noted earlier, students and scholars should not consider as settled the debates engaged in the works discussed here. Moreover, many important themes remain untouched in the literature. The following include five of the most fruitful areas of future research.

Biographies

Except for Susser's work on Wasfi al-Tall, the historiography of Jordan is bereft of critical biographies, both of royals and nonroyals who were essential to the survival of the state. While a number of books view Jordan through the highly personalistic lens of the king, only one—Peter Snow's *Hussein: A Biography* (1972)—even resembles a detached, critical account of the king and his rule, and already more years have passed since its publication than are covered of Hussein's reign. Gerald Sparrow's *Hussein of Jordan* (1960) is irrelevant, and James Lunt's *Hussein of Jordan: Searching for a Just and Lasting Peace* (1989) is both apologia (it was written with "the King's agreement" and dedicated to him "by gracious permission") and full of errors, an unsatisfying combination. There is, therefore, no definitive biography of Hussein, nor even one on the horizon. In that light, it is no surprise that other fascinating and important actors like Tawfiq Abul Huda, Hazza al-Majali, Samir al-Rifai, and Alec Kirkbride have not yet been the subject of a biographer's inquiry. However, Abd al-Hamid Sharaf merited a chapter in Patrick Seale, editor, *The Shaping of an Arab Statesman: Abd al-Hamid Sharaf and the Modern Arab World* (1983). While biographies are scant, there are a number of valuable memoirs and autobiographies of significant (and not-so-significant) personages in Jordanian history. These include works by Kings Abdullah (1978) and Hussein (1962); Prime Minister Hazza al-Majali (1960); Communist leader Yacoub Ziyadin (1981); Free Officer leader Shahir Yusuf Abu Shahut (1985); anti-Abdullah conspirator Abdullah al-Tall (1959); Christian politician Jamal al-Shair (1987); one-time general Salih al-Shara (1988); British envoys Kirkbride and Charles Johnston (1972); U.S. diplomat Richard Sanger; and as-yet-unpublished diaries by one-

time Defense Minister Farhan Shubalyat; Communist leader Abdul Rahman
Shuqayr; and U.S. ambassador Joseph C. Green.

Political Economy

There are no thorough examinations of Jordan's political economy. The World
Bank's forty-year-old study *The Economic Development of Jordan* (1957) remains the standard work, with more recent contributions by Michael P. Mazur,
Economic Growth and Development in Jordan (1979) and Eliyahu Kanovsky,
The Economic Development of Jordan (1976) and *Jordan's Economy: From
Prosperity to Crisis* (1989). None of them, however, are complete treatments of
the subject. In addition, a number of edited volumes are useful, though not
normally cohesive. One of the better collections is Rodney Wilson's *Politics
and Economy in Jordan* (1991). Bassam Saket, who went on to a successful
ministerial career in Amman, plowed important ground in his doctoral dissertation "Foreign Aid to Jordan, 1924/25–1972/73: Its Magnitude, Composition,
and Effect" (1976). But given the centrality of economic issues to national
decision making—with virtually no natural resources, Jordan's diplomatic relationships and economic relationships go hand in hand—the general issue
deserves far greater attention. Also, economic-based studies on Jordanian-
Palestinian relations inside the kingdom, intra-Palestinian politics (e.g., the
schism between Jordan's Palestinian commercial class and its more radical Palestinian refugee population), and the economic component of Jordan's inter-
Arab relations would be especially enlightening.

Conventional Politics

Though Jordan enjoyed one of the Arab world's freest elections and most
vibrant political environments—that is, in 1956—there is virtually no scholarly
examination of party life, political institutions, or other themes related to political science. Indeed, except for Cohen's book on the West Bank, the literature
is totally empty of any discussion of conventional politics inside Jordan, and
even Cohen's book ends in 1967. This is a glaring lacuna that needs to be filled
with basic research on political parties, party affiliations, organizations, elections, and related matters. An interesting doctoral dissertation by Epiphan Sabella, "External Events and Circulation of Political Elites: Cabinet Turnover in
Jordan, 1946–1980" (1980) addresses this issue, though at its margins.

Palestinian Integration

Though the Palestinian angle of Jordanian politics is well-plowed ground,
much of the story has focused on the clash between the regime and its most
violent opponents and not on the bulk of the story, which is how so many
Palestinians have integrated into Jordanian society. After all, Jordan is a success

story in that regard, underscored by the relatively peaceful integration of another 350,000 Palestinians expelled from Kuwait and other Persian Gulf states during the Gulf War. The politics of that integration is a fascinating area of research. A study of municipal politics in Amman (home to the world's largest concentration of Palestinians), Zarqa, or Irbid would be particularly useful.

Decision Making

For all the writing on King Hussein and Jordanian high politics, there is little written on the actual process of political decision making inside the kingdom. Though Jordan is a monarchy, not all decisions are made by the king, and even that process of defining what is and is not the king's preserve has changed over time. Mutawi's *Jordan in the 1967 War* has a chapter on the topic, and there are passing discussions in Dann and in Satloff's *From Abdullah to Hussein*. An integrated look at this issue, as well as the relative significance of key institutions, families, and interest groups, would mark a major contribution.

In short, scholarship on Jordan has progressed considerably in recent years, given Jordan's small size and the relative openness of Jordanian society. Much more, however, can and needs to be done to provide a full picture of Jordanian political development over the past half-century. A focus away from two powerful attractions, the magnetic personalities of Jordan's kings and the pull of the Arab-Israeli peace process, and toward the men and women who have built the modern country of Jordan in all its aspects would be the most important shift in helping to answer the questions that surround the remarkable survival of a country whose raison d'être is still in formation.

REFERENCES

Abdullah bin Hussein. 1978. *My Memoirs Completed: "Al-Takmilah."* London: Longman.

Abidi, Aqil Hyder Hasan. 1965. *Jordan: A Political Study, 1948–1957.* London: Asia Publishing House.

Abu Jaber, Kamal, Fawzi Gharaibeh, Saleh Khasawneh, and Allan Hill. 1978. *Bedouins of Jordan: A People in Transition.* Amman: Royal Scientific Society.

Abu Jaber, Raouf Sad. 1989. *Pioneers over Jordan: The Frontier of Settlement in Transjordan, 1860–1914.* London: I. B. Tauris.

Abu Nuwar, Maan. 1989. *The History of the Hashemite Kingdom of Jordan.* Vol. 1, *The Creation and Development of Transjordan, 1920–1929.* Oxford: St. Antony's College.

Abu Shahut, Shahir Yusif. 1985. *Al-Jaysh wa'l-siyasa fi al-urdunn: dhikriyat 'an harakat al-dhubat al-urdunniyeen al-ahrar* (Army and politics in Jordan: Memories of the Jordanian Free Officers movement). n.p.: al-Qabas.

Ali el-Edroos, Sayed. 1980. *The Hashemite Arab Army, 1908–1979: An Appreciation and Analysis of Military Operations.* Amman: Publishing Committee.

Antoun, Richard. 1979. *Low-Key Politics: Local-Level Leadership and Change in the Middle East*. Albany: State University of New York Press.

———. 1989. *Muslim Preacher in the Modern World: A Jordanian Case Study in Comparative Perspective*. Princeton: Princeton University Press.

Aruri, Naseer. 1972. *Jordan: A Study in Political Development, 1921–1965*. The Hague: Nijhoff.

Bailey, Clinton. 1984. *Jordan's Palestinian Challenge, 1948–1983: A Political History*. Boulder, CO: Westview Press.

Bar-Joseph, Uri. 1987. *The Best of Enemies: Israel and Transjordan in the War of 1948*. London: Frank Cass.

Clawson, Patrick, and Howard Rosen. 1991. *The Economic Consequences of Peace for Israel, the Palestinians, and Jordan*. Policy Paper no. 25. Washington, DC: Washington Institute for Near East Policy.

Cohen, Amnon. 1982. *Political Parties in the West Bank under the Jordanian Regime, 1949–1967*. Ithaca: Cornell University Press.

Cooley, John K. 1973. *Green March, Black September: The Story of the Palestinian Arabs*. London: Frank Cass.

Cordesman, Anthony. 1983. *Jordanian Arms and the Middle East Balance*. Washington, DC: Middle East Institute.

Dann, Uriel. 1984. *Studies in the History of Transjordan, 1920–1949: The Making of a State*. Boulder, CO: Westview Press.

———. 1989. *King Hussein and the Challenge of Arab Radicalism: Jordan, 1955–1967*. New York: Oxford University Press.

———. 1992. *King Hussein's Strategy of Survival*. Policy Paper no. 29. Washington, DC: Washington Institute for Near East Policy.

Day, Arthur. 1986. *East Bank/West Bank: Jordan and the Prospects for Peace*. New York: Council on Foreign Relations.

Dearden, Ann. 1958. *Jordan*. London: Robert Hale.

Faddah, Mohammad Ibrahim. 1974. *The Middle East in Transition: A Study of Jordan's Foreign Policy*. New York: Asia Publishing House.

Garfinkle, Adam. 1992. *Israel and Jordan in the Shadow of War*. New York: St. Martin's Press.

Glubb, John Bagot. 1957. *A Soldier with the Arabs*. London: Hodder and Stoughton.

Goichon, A. M. 1967. *Jordanie réelle*. Paris: G. P. Maisonneuve et Larose.

Graves, Philip R., ed. 1950. *Memoirs of King Abdullah*. London: Jonathan Cape.

Green, Joseph Coy. "Jordan Journal, 1952–1953." Unpublished memoirs. John Foster Dulles Library, Princeton University, Princeton, NJ.

Gubser, Peter. 1973. *Politics and Change in al-Karak, Jordan: A Study of a Small Arab Town and Its District*. London: Oxford University Press.

———. 1983. *Jordan: Crossroads of Middle Eastern Events*. London: Croom Helm.

———. 1991. *Historical Dictionary of the Hashemite Kingdom of Jordan*. Asian Historical Dictionaries, no. 4. Metuchen, NJ: Scarecrow Press.

Hacker, Jane. 1960. *Modern Amman: A Social Survey*. Durham, UK: University of Durham Press.

Harris, George. 1958. *Jordan: Its People, Its Society, Its Culture*. New York: Grove Press.

Hussein bin Talal. 1962. *Uneasy Lies the Head*. London: Heinemann.

Israeli, Raphael. 1991. *Palestinians between Israel and Jordan: Squaring the Triangle.* New York: Praeger.

Johnston, Charles. 1972. *The Brink of Jordan.* London: Hamish Hamilton.

Jureidini, Paul. 1975. ''The Relationship of the Palestinian Guerilla Movement with the Government of Jordan, 1967–1970.'' Ph.D. dissertation, American University.

Jureidini, Paul, and R. D. McLaurin. 1984. *Jordan: The Impact of Social Change on the Role of the Tribes.* New York: Praeger.

Kanovsky, Eliyahu. 1970. *The Economic Impact of the Six-Day War.* New York: Praeger.

———. 1976. *The Economic Development of Jordan.* Tel Aviv: University Publishing Projects.

———. 1989. *Jordan's Economy: From Prosperity to Crisis.* Tel Aviv: Tel Aviv University Press.

Kirkbride, Alec Seath. 1956. *A Crackle of Thorns.* London: Murray.

———. 1976. *From the Wings: Amman Memoirs, 1947–1951.* London: Frank Cass.

Lewis, Norman N. 1987. *Nomads and Settlers in Syria and Jordan, 1800–1980.* New York: Cambridge University Press.

Lalor, Paul. 1992. ''Black September 1970: The Palestinian Resistance Movement in Jordan, 1967–1971.'' Ph.D. dissertation, Oxford University.

Lunt, James. 1984. *Glubb Pasha, A Biography: Lieutenant-General Sir John Bagot Glubb, Commander of the Arab Legion, 1939–1956.* London: Harville Press.

———. 1989. *Hussein of Jordan: Searching for a Just and Lasting Peace.* London: Macmillan.

al-Madfai, Madiha. 1993. *Jordan, the United States, and the Middle East Peace Process, 1974–1991.* New York: Cambridge University Press.

al-Madi, Munib, and Sulayman Musa. 1959. *Tarikh al-urdunn fi al-qarn al-'ashrin* (The history of Jordan in the twentieth century). Amman: n.p.

al-Majali, Hazza. 1960. *Mudhakkarati* (My memoirs). Beirut: Dar al-ilm lil-malayeen.

Maoz, Moshe. 1984. *Palestinian Leadership on the West Bank: The Changing Role of the Arab Mayors under Jordan and Israel.* London: Frank Cass.

Mazur, Michael P. 1979. *Economic Growth and Development in Jordan.* Boulder, CO: Westview Press.

Melman, Yossi, and Dan Raviv. 1989. *Behind the Uprising: Israelis, Jordanians, and Palestinians.* New York: Greenwood Press.

Miller, Aaron David. 1986. *The Arab States and the Palestine Question: Between Ideology and Self-Interest.* New York: Praeger.

Mishal, Shaul. 1978. *West Bank/East Bank: The Palestinians in Jordan, 1949–1967.* New Haven: Yale University Press.

Morris, Benny. 1987. *The Birth of the Palestinian Refugee Problem, 1947–1949.* Cambridge: Cambridge University Press.

———. 1993. *Israel's Border Wars, 1949–1956: Arab Infiltration, Israeli Retaliation, and the Countdown to the Suez War.* Oxford: Clarendon Press.

Morris, James. 1959. *The Hashemite Kings.* London: Faber and Faber.

Mutawi, Samir A. 1987. *Jordan in the 1967 War.* Cambridge: Cambridge University Press.

O'Ballance, Edgar. 1974. *Arab Guerilla Power, 1967–1972.* London: Faber and Faber.

Patai, Raphael. 1958. *The Kingdom of Jordan.* Princeton: Princeton University Press.

Peake, Frederick P. (Peake Pasha). 1958. *History and Tribes of Jordan.* Miami: University of Miami Press.

Plascov, Avi. 1981. *The Palestinian Refugees in Jordan, 1948–1957*. London: Cass.

Pundik, Ron. 1994. *The Struggle for Sovereignty: Relations between Great Britain and Jordan, 1946–1951*. Oxford: Blackwell.

Rabinovich, Itamar. 1991. *The Road Not Taken: Early Arab-Israeli Negotiations*. New York: Oxford University Press.

Robins, Philip. 1988. "The Consolidation of Hashimite Power in Jordan, 1921–1946." Ph.D. dissertation, University of Exeter.

Rubin, Barry. 1981. *The Arab States and the Palestine Conflict*. Syracuse: Syracuse University Press.

Sabella, Epiphan. 1980. "External Events and Circulation of Political Elites: Cabinet Turnover in Jordan, 1946–1980." Ph.D. dissertation, University of Virginia.

Saket, Bassem. 1976. "Foreign Aid to Jordan, 1924/25–1972/73: Its Magnitude, Composition, and Effect." Ph.D. dissertation, University of Keele.

Salibi, Kamal S. 1993. *The Modern History of Jordan*. New York: St. Martin's Press.

Sanger, Richard. 1963. *Where the Jordan Flows*. Washington, DC: Middle East Institute.

Satloff, Robert B. 1987. *They Cannot Stop Our Tongues: Islamic Activism in Jordan*. Policy Paper no. 5. Washington, DC: Washington Institute for Near East Policy.

———. 1986. *Troubles on the East Bank: Challenges to the Domestic Stability of Jordan*. Washington Papers no. 123. New York: Praeger.

———. 1994. *From Abdullah to Hussein: Jordan in Transition*. New York: Oxford University Press.

Seale, Patrick, ed. 1983. *The Shaping of an Arab Statesman: Abd al-Hamid Sharaf and the Modern Arab World*. London: Quartet Books.

al-Shair, Jamal. 1987. *Siyasi yatadhakkir* (A politician remembers). London: Riyad al-Rayyes.

al-Shara, Salih. 1988. *Mudhakkarat jundi* (Memoirs of a soldier). Amman: n.p.

Shemesh, Moshe. 1988. The Palestinian Entity, 1959–1974. London: Frank Cass.

Shlaim, Avi. 1988. *Collusion across the Jordan: King Abdullah, the Zionist Movement, and the Partition of Palestine*. New York: Columbia University Press.

al-Shubaylat, Farhan. Unpublished Arabic memoirs.

Shuqayr, Abdul Rahman. Unpublished Arabic memoirs.

Shwadran, Benjamin. 1959. *Jordan: A State of Tension*. New York: Council for Middle Eastern Affairs Press.

Sinai, A., and A. Pollack, eds. 1971. *The Hashemite Kingdom of Jordan and the West Bank: A Handbook*. New York: American Academic Association for Peace in the Middle East.

Snow, Peter. 1972. *Hussein: A Biography*. London: Barrie and Jenkins.

Sparrow, Gerald. 1960. *Hussein of Jordan*. London: Harrap of London.

Susser, Asher. 1990. *In through the Out Door: Jordan's Disengagement and the Peace Process*. Policy Paper no. 19. Washington, DC: Washington Institute for Near East Policy.

———. 1994. *On Both Banks of the Jordan: A Political Biography of Wasfi al-Tall*. London: Frank Cass.

al-Tall, Abdullah. 1959. *Karithat Filastin: Mudhakkarat Abdullah al-Tall* (The Palestine disaster: Memoirs of Abdullah al-Tall). Cairo: Dar al-Qalm Press.

Vatikiotis, P. J. 1967. *Politics and the Military in Jordan*. New York: Praeger.

Wilson, Mary C. 1987. *King Abdullah, Britain, and the Making of Jordan*. New York: Cambridge University Press.

Wilson, Rodney. 1991. *Politics and Economy in Jordan*. New York: Routledge.

World Bank. 1957. *The Economic Development of Jordan*. Baltimore: Johns Hopkins University Press.

Yorke, Valerie. 1988. *Domestic Politics and Regional Security—Jordan, Syria, and Israel: The End of an Era?* Brookfield, VT: Ashgate.

Young, Peter. 1956. *Bedouin Command: With the Arab Legion, 1953–1956*. London: William Kimber.

Ziyadin, Yacoub. 1981. *Al-Bidayat* (Beginnings). N.p.: Salah al-Din.

LEBANON

Marius Deeb

Lebanon was famous in its heyday as a model of what Arend Lijphart (1977) called a consociational democracy and, as such, was in the company of advanced European countries such as Switzerland and Austria. Since the eruption of the civil war in 1975 Lebanon has become everything the Lebanese establishment had hitherto tried to avoid, namely, the playground of the armed and unruly Palestine Liberation Organization (PLO), at first in conjunction with the Alawi-controlled Syrian regime that has always sponsored terrorism. Since 1979, the obscurantist Khomeinist Iran has joined in by sponsoring terrorist organizations such as Hezbollah. All these destructive trends have continued to manifest themselves in the artificially contrived conflict in southern Lebanon where Hezbollah wages a senseless war supported ideologically and financially by Iran and orchestrated by Syria. One book that captures this change that took place in Lebanon is *Beirut: City of Regrets* (1988), which consists of 128 color photographs by Eli Reed and a moving essay of 47 pages by Fouad Ajami depicting in an elegant poetic prose, in which he draws upon his personal memories, the many Beiruts of the past and the one ravaged by the war as illustrated by the photographs.

Published books and articles on Lebanon fall into two major categories: the publications that cover the 1960s and the early 1970s and analyze the heyday of Lebanon, that is, the period prior to the 1975 civil war, and, second, books and articles that examine the period since 1975. In the second category there are three kinds of publications: scholarly works; somewhat less scholarly publications intended for the general reader, but from which one can gain some insights, especially when they are written by well-informed journalists; and memoirs and diaries, especially of politicians or journalists or other observers of the conflict.

THE LEBANESE POLITY PRIOR TO 1975

Major works on the politics of Lebanon are *Politics in Lebanon* (1966), edited by Leonard Binder, and *The Precarious Republic: Political Modernization in*

Lebanon (1968), authored by Michael C. Hudson. Both were written when Lebanon's experiment in consociational democracy was functioning. A third major study is that of Elie Salem, entitled *Modernization without Revolution: Lebanon's Experience* (1973). The author, who after an academic career at the American University of Beirut was the minister of foreign affairs from 1982 to 1984, continued to have a prominent political role until 1988. Salem has always regretted the title chosen for this book, but the study shows a deep understanding of the Lebanese polity, whether in its achievements or its fragility when faced with a major Middle East crisis. The study by David and Audrey Smock, *The Politics of Pluralism: A Comparative Study of Lebanon and Ghana* (1975), is outstanding in its analysis of the religious communities and the various segments of civil society, based on the local press and interviews with leading political and religious figures. *Politics in Lebanon* is a collection of seventeen chapters ranging from the development of Lebanon as a political society by Albert Hourani to the relationship between economic development and political liberalism by Charles Issawi. Most chapters examine different dimensions of the political system, such as political parties by Labib Zuwiyya-Yamak, the political role of the Maronite church by Iliya Harik, the impact of confessionalism on public administration by Ralph Crow, and political decision making in a confessional context by Malcolm Kerr. Hudson's *The Precarious Republic* is divided into three parts. The first deals with the parochial and the external historical influences that made Lebanon a separate polity in 1943 (independence), as well as with the problems of modernization in conjunction with the sectarian legacy that impeded the process of national integration. The second part examines the politics of the members of the establishment and those who were more or less outsiders, whether on the left or the right. The third part analyzes both parliament and the presidency as functioning institutions. Hudson was somewhat pessimistic when he concluded that ''the Republic's political future will be stormy.'' Charles Issawi was even more pessimistic in his prophetic article in *Politics in Lebanon* when he stated that ''Lebanon is too conspicuous and successful an example of political democracy and political liberalism to be tolerated in a region that has turned its back on both systems'' (80). This explains in a fundamental way the civil war and external intervention that have bedevilled Lebanon since 1975.

Lebanon prior to 1975 had managed wisely to avoid both the 1967 and 1973 Arab-Israeli wars. By doing so, the Lebanese rulers had fulfilled the terms of the National Pact of 1943, which stipulated that it would neither invite a Western power to protect it nor be dominated by its Arab hinterland and plagued by its problems. The way the PLO operated from Lebanon since the late 1960s, protected by the Cairo Agreement signed in November 1969 between the PLO and the Lebanese government, rendered the National Pact ineffective and destroyed the balance that was inherent in the consociational democracy that was ingeniously devised by the founding fathers of Lebanon, Riyad al-Sulh and Bishara al-Khuri. When Syria intervened militarily in June 1976 and refused to leave Lebanon when asked repeatedly in 1978, 1982, and 1989 to do so, a basic principle of the National Pact had been negated, as clearly shown in the state of affairs of Syrian-occupied and dominated Lebanon. The peaceful transition of power (the miniature civil war of 1958 notwithstanding) that characterized the period prior to 1975, that is, when presidents were not killed in office and were allowed to retire peacefully, is a distant memory.

LEBANON SINCE 1975

One of the earliest books on the Lebanese civil war was Kamal Salibi's *Crossroads to Civil War: Lebanon, 1958–1976* (1976). It covers the historical background from the 1958 civil war to that of 1975–1976, but Salibi's narrative stops at the end of January 1976. It is basically a rendition of the unfolding of events with limited analysis, but despite that it remains a useful source. *Essays on the Crisis in Lebanon* (1976), edited by Roger Owen in 1976, suffers from its publication in the midst of the early phases of the conflict and from the uneven character of the chapters. The best chapters are by Roger Owen on the Lebanese economy and Albert Hourani on the ideologies of the Mountain and the City. *Lebanon in Crisis: Participants and Issues* (1979), edited by P. Edward Haley and Lewis S. Snider, is a useful collection of fourteen articles. All except two are on the role of external powers in the Lebanese conflict ranging from the PLO and Syria to the United States, the Soviet Union, the United Nations, and the Arab League. A more interesting collection is *The Emergence of a New Lebanon: Fantasy or Reality?* (1984), edited by Edward E. Azar, especially the articles on political culture by Azar, on the Lebanese army by R. D. McLaurin, and on Lebanon's regional policy by Paul A. Jureidini. A work with some insights into the complex politics of the Lebanese conflict and its regional dimensions is Walid Khalidi's *Conflict and Violence in Lebanon: Confrontation in the Middle East* (1979). The author is a Palestinian academic who taught political science from the early 1960s at the American University of Beirut and from the early 1980s at Harvard University. He also played a political role in the early stages of the Lebanese conflict by trying to bridge the gap between the Lebanese government and the Christian conservative politicians, on the one hand, and the PLO and the traditional Muslim politicians, on the other hand. The author of this book has analyzed the conflict in Lebanon with a remarkable objectivity, not hesitating to criticize the PLO itself. Nevertheless, Khalidi's analysis of the Syrian role in Lebanon and the Middle East leaves much to be desired, perhaps because the narrative of the conflict ends with the Israeli Litani Operation of March 1978. The best general book on Lebanon is David C. Gordon's *The Republic of Lebanon: Nation in Jeopardy* (1983). The author, who resided in Lebanon and taught history at the American University of Beirut, successfully discerns the major features of the Lebanese society and the polity and the causes of the civil war. A comprehensive and detailed study of Lebanon is *Lebanon: A Country Study* (1989), edited by Thomas Collelo. The various chapters are basically sound, especially those on history, society, economy, and national security.

In the classic work *The Lebanese Civil War* (1980), Marius Deeb divides the civil war into seven phases clearly demarcated by significant landmarks. The author looks at the civil war from the viewpoints of the five major parties to the conflict, namely, the Christian Lebanese Front, the leftist National Movement, the traditional Muslim leaders, the PLO, and Syria, with a detailed objective analysis of their positions as events unfold. The lasting nature of this study lies in the thorough utilization of primary sources, including the remarkably free local Lebanese press as well as memoirs and diaries of leading political figures such as Camille Chamoun. In his "Lebanon: Prospects for National Reconciliation in the Mid-1980s" (1984), Marius Deeb outlines the changes in the positions of the various effective political leaders in the major religious communities from 1977 until early 1984. He writes prophetically of the paramount importance of the events of February 1984 when Syrian proxy militias took over West Beirut and the Lebanese army had splintered again: "An independent, sovereign, and democratic Lebanon will not see the light as long as . . . the Asad regime [in Syria] is in power." Developments in the stands and viewpoints of the various Lebanese sects from March 1984 until the end of the decade were analyzed in a detailed manner in the chapter on Lebanon by Marius Deeb in Robert O. Freedman's *The Middle East from the Iran-Contra Affair to the Intifada* (1991), based on primary sources and interviews with major political and religious figures. *Militant Islamic Movements in Lebanon: Origins, Social Basis, and Ideology* (1986), by Marius Deeb, delves into the causes that led to the rise of militant Islamic movements, such as Hezbollah, which evolved from AMAL through Islamic AMAL. The author examines in depth Hezbollah as well as the Islamic Tawhid Movement and the Islamic Group. *Militant Islamic Movements* is based on a large number of primary sources from the Lebanese press and the original publications of these movements, making it unique whether in its perceptive analysis or comprehensiveness. The best study on AMAL and its leader, Imam Musa al-Sadr, is Fouad Ajami's *The Vanished Imam: Musa al-Sadr and the Shia of Lebanon* (1986). The figure of Musa al-Sadr comes to life as the author with his deep insights and profound knowledge of Lebanese society and polity sheds new light on this heroic and charismatic personality. *The Vanished Imam* is a definitive work based on interviews with the closest associates of Musa al-Sadr and a vast number of original primary sources in Arabic, as well as U.S. archival material.

A major scholarly work is Itamar Rabinovich's *The War for Lebanon, 1970–1985* (1985), which deals with both the Lebanese domestic situation and the external dimensions, including the Israeli invasion of 1982 and its aftermath. The entire spring 1984 issue of the *Middle East Journal* was devoted to the conflict in Lebanon. Articles by Zeev Schiff on Israel's policy in Lebanon and William B. Quandt on Reagan's Lebanon policy are particularly outstanding. *Toward a Viable Lebanon* (1987), edited by Halim Barakat, is a collection of twenty papers of uneven quality. The best are Albert Hourani's chapter on visions of Lebanon, Roger Owen's chapter on the economic history of Lebanon from 1943 to 1974, Marius Deeb's chapter on Saudi Arabian policy toward Lebanon, Michael C. Hudson's chapter on the involvement of the United States in Lebanon, and Robert O. Freedman's chapter on Soviet policy toward the Lebanese crisis. *Amal and the Shi'a: Struggle for the Soul of Lebanon* (1987), by Augustus Richard Norton, is basically a straightforward study of AMAL and its relationships with other political players in Lebanon. Wade R. Goria's *Sovereignty and Leadership in Lebanon, 1943–1976* (1985), is a scholarly work that covers the background to the 1975–1976 civil war, but it seems to lack a clear focus. Samir Khalaf's *Lebanon's Predicament* (1987) is a superb collection of articles by a leading sociologist who discerns the themes that constitute the dialectics of modernity and tradition in the Lebanese context. Elizabeth Picard's *Lebanon, a Shattered Country: Myths and Realities of the Wars in Lebanon* (1996) is an insightful study of the conflict in Lebanon until the 1990s that could be of use to both students of Lebanese politics and the general reader. For a more scholarly perspective within the context of theories of conflict resolution and mediation, see the article by Mary-Jane Deeb and Marius Deeb, "Internal Negotiations in a Centralist Conflict: Lebanon," in I. William Zartman, *Elusive Peace: Negotiating an End to Civil Wars* (1995).

One of the best books written by journalists who covered the conflict in Lebanon is Robert Fisk's *Pity the Nation: The Abduction of Lebanon* (1990), which is an objective and comprehensive analysis of the various phases of the conflict up until 1990. An equally sound study of the civil war is Dilip Hiro's *Lebanon: Fire and Embers: A History of the Lebanese Civil War* (1993). Both Fisk's and Hiro's books are well documented. This is in stark contrast to that by Jonathan Randal, who worked as a correspondent in Beirut during the conflict. Randal, in his undocumented (there are no footnotes nor a bibliography), gossipy *Going All the Way: Christian Warlords, Israeli Adventurers, and the War in Lebanon* (1983), boasted in the preface of the book that he predicted the civil war six months in advance. Randal had tried with his strong passions and prejudices to make up for his abysmal ignorance of Lebanese society and polity, which resulted in a product that leaves much to be desired. Helena Cobban's *The Making of Modern Lebanon* (1985) is equally divided between a historical section and the part that narrates the civil-war period. It is remarkable that the book's bibliography has only two sources in Arabic. In the part on the civil war the author has drawn from her experience as a correspondent in Beirut of leading Western newspapers. The best journalistic coverage of the Israeli invasion of Lebanon in 1982 is *Israel's Lebanon War* (1984), by Zeev Schiff and Ehud Yaari.

There is a dearth of memoirs by major figures in Lebanon. The Syrian domination of Lebanon has made it difficult for officials to write freely about their role in the civil war. Kamal Joumblatt conducted a series of interviews with a French journalist published in English under the title *I Speak for Lebanon*

(1982), a quasi-memoir in which he was critical, inter alia, of Syria. The latter's agents assassinated Joumblatt in March 1977. The memoirs of Elie Salem, entitled *Violence and Diplomacy in Lebanon: The Troubled Years 1982–1988* (1995), has many insights into the characters of the various actors, but it suffers from self-censorship because the author resides in Lebanon. One of the best memoirs available was published in French by a close advisor of the late Lebanese president Elias Sarkis, Karim Pakradouni, in his *La paix manquée: Le mandat d'Elias Sarkis (1976–1982)* (1983). The author provides good insights into the character and actions of the leading personalities during that period of the conflict. A superb and perceptive memoir by an astute student and participant in Middle Eastern politics is Cecil Hourani's *An Unfinished Odyssey: Lebanon and Beyond* (1984). The author's analysis of the role of the PLO in the conflict in southern Lebanon is both original and outstanding.

There is a spate of writing by former hostages in Lebanon that sheds light on the conflict. One of the best is *Hostage Bound, Hostage Free* (1987), written by Ben and Carol Weir, who had lived and worked for many years in Lebanon. David Jacobsen's *My Life as a Hostage* (1993) is a good account of his ordeal and also enlightens us on his captors.

FUTURE RESEARCH

For the period prior to 1975 there is a need for more research despite the books by Binder and Hudson. The free and open political system during that period makes research easier than in other countries in the Middle East. The role of the presidency and the relationship between the executive and legislative branches of government have not been studied. The influence of the bankers, merchants, and industrialists on the political system has not been documented. The ideological orientations of the various religious communities, especially the Shii, have not been researched. There is a need for a new look at political parties and movements during that period despite the work of Michael Suleiman, *Political Parties in Lebanon* (1967). The study of the role of the political press would be of utmost importance, as the free press had influence within and beyond Lebanon.

The period since 1975 has been dominated by the civil war. There are a few outstanding works on the earlier phases of the civil war by Fouad Ajami, Marius Deeb, Itamar Rabinovich, and Walid Khalidi, but the later phases of the civil war and the ongoing conflict in southern Lebanon have not been researched. The fields of conflict resolution and mediation are still basically untouched in terms of works published in English. Other topics for research are the pervasive corruption in Syrian-dominated Lebanon and how the Syrian army in Lebanon and its intelligence services control Lebanon. The different roles of the various political movements and organizations, especially the Party of God (Hezbollah), since the late 1980s have not been studied. Various opposition movements such as the followers of General Michel Awn have not been examined in scholarly works. Except for a few general books that are solid, like those of Gordon and Picard, there is also a gap in this literature.

REFERENCES

Ajami, Fouad. 1986. *The Vanished Imam: Musa al-Sadr and the Shia of Lebanon*. Ithaca: Cornell University Press.

———. 1988. *Beirut: City of Regrets*. New York: W. W. Norton.

Anderson, Terry. 1993. *Den of Lions: Memoirs of Seven Years*. New York: Crown.

Azar, Edward E., ed. 1984. *The Emergence of a New Lebanon: Fantasy or Reality?* New York: Praeger.

Barakat, Halim, ed. 1987. *Toward a Viable Lebanon*. London: Croom Helm.

Binder, Leonard, ed. 1966. *Politics in Lebanon*. New York: John Wiley and Sons.

Cobban, Helena. 1985. *The Making of Modern Lebanon*. Boulder, CO: Westview Press.

Collelo, Thomas, ed. 1989. *Lebanon: A Country Study*. Washington, DC: U.S. Government Printing Office.

Deeb, Marius. 1980. *The Lebanese Civil War*. New York: Praeger.

———. 1984. "Lebanon: Prospects for National Reconciliation in the Mid-1980s." *Middle East Journal* 38, no. 2 (Spring): 267–283.

———. 1986. *Militant Islamic Movements in Lebanon: Origins, Social Basis, and Ideology*. Washington, DC: Center for Contemporary Arab Studies, Georgetown University.

———. 1991. "Lebanon in the Aftermath of the Abrogation of the Israeli-Lebanese Accord: The Dominant Role of Syria." In Robert O. Freedman, ed., *The Middle East from the Iran-Contra Affair to the Intifada*. Syracuse, NY: Syracuse University Press.

Deeb, Mary-Jane, and Marius Deeb. 1995. "Internal Negotiations in a Centralist Conflict: Lebanon." In I. William Zartman, ed., *Elusive Peace: Negotiating an End to Civil Wars*. Washington, DC: Brookings Institution.

Fisk, Robert. 1990. *Pity the Nation: The Abduction of Lebanon*. New York: Atheneum.

Gordon, David C. 1980. *Lebanon: The Fragmented Nation*. London: Croom Helm.

———. 1983. *The Republic of Lebanon: Nation in Jeopardy*. Boulder, CO: Westview Press.

Goria, Wade R. 1985. *Sovereignty and Leadership in Lebanon, 1943–1976*. London: Ithaca Press.

Haddad, Wadi D. 1985. *Lebanon: The Politics of Revolving Doors*. New York: Praeger.

Haley, P. Edward, and Lewis W. Snider, eds. 1979. *Lebanon in Crisis: Participants and Issues*. Syracuse: Syracuse University Press.

Hiro, Dilip. 1993. *Lebanon: Fire and Embers: A History of the Lebanese Civil War*. New York: St. Martin's Press.

Hourani, Albert. 1976. "Ideologies of the Mountain and the City." In Roger Owen, ed., *Essays on the Crisis in Lebanon*. London: Ithaca Press.

Hourani, Cecil. 1984. *An Unfinished Odyssey: Lebanon and Beyond*. London: Weidenfeld and Nicolson.

Hudson, Michael C. 1968. *The Precarious Republic: Political Modernization in Lebanon*. New York: Random House.

Issawi, Charles. 1966. "Economic Development and Political Liberalism in Lebanon." In Leonard Binder, ed., *Politics in Lebanon*. New York: John Wiley.

Jacobsen, David, with Gerald Astor. 1993. *My Life as a Hostage: The Nightmare in Beirut*. New York: Shapolsky.

Jansen, Michael. 1982. *The Battle of Beirut: Why Israel Invaded Lebanon*. London: Zed Books.

Joumblatt, Kamal. 1982. *I Speak for Lebanon*. London: Zed Books.

Jureidini, Paul. 1984. ''Lebanon Regional Policy.'' In Edward E. Azar, ed., *The Emergence of a New Lebanon: Fantasy or Reality?* New York: Praeger.

Kashan, Hilal. 1992. *Inside the Lebanese Confessional Mind*. Lanham, MD: University Press of America.

Khalaf, Samir. 1987. *Lebanon's Predicament*. New York: Columbia University Press.

Khalidi, Walid. 1979. *Conflict and Violence in Lebanon: Confrontation in the Middle East*. Cambridge, MA: Harvard University Press.

Lijphart, Arend. 1977. *Democracy in Plural Societies: A Comparative Exploration*. New Haven: Yale University Press.

Mackey, Sandra. 1989. *Lebanon: Death of a Nation*. New York: Congdon and Weed.

McLaurin, R. D. 1984. ''Lebanon and Its Army: Past, Present and Future.'' In Edward E. Azar, ed., *The Emergence of a New Lebanon: Fantasy or Reality?* New York: Praeger.

Mikdadi, Lina. 1983. *Surviving the Siege of Beirut: A Personal Account*. London: Onyx Press.

Newman, Barbara, with Barbara Rogan. 1989. *The Covenant: Love and Death in Beirut*. New York: Crown.

Norton, Augustus Richard. 1987. *Amal and the Shi'a: Struggle for the Soul of Lebanon*. Austin: University of Texas Press.

Owen, Roger, ed. 1976. *Essays on the Crisis in Lebanon*. London: Ithaca Press.

Pakradouni, Karim. 1983. *La paix manquée: Le mandat d'Elias Sarkis (1976–1982)*. Beirut: Fiche du Monde Arabe.

Picard, Elizabeth. 1996. *Lebanon, a Shattered Country: Myths and Realities of the Wars in Lebanon*. New York: Holmes and Meier.

Quandt, William B. 1984. ''Reagan's Lebanon Policy: Trial and Error.'' *Middle East Journal* 38, no. 2 (Spring): 237–254.

Rabinovich, Itamar. 1985. *The War for Lebanon, 1970–1985*. Ithaca: Cornell University Press.

Randal, Jonathan C. 1983. *Going All the Way: Christian Warlords, Israeli Adventurers, and the War in Lebanon*. New York: Viking Press.

Salem, Elie A. 1973. *Modernization without Revolution: Lebanon's Experience*. Bloomington: Indiana University Press.

———. 1995. *Violence and Diplomacy in Lebanon: The Troubled Years 1982–1988*. London: I. B. Tauris.

Salibi, Kamal S. 1976. *Crossroads to Civil War: Lebanon, 1958–1976*. Delmar, NY: Caravan Books.

Schiff, Zeev. 1984. ''Lebanon: Motivations and Interests in Israel's Policy.'' *Middle East Journal* 38, no. 2 (Spring): 220–227.

Schiff, Zeev, and Ehud Yaari. 1984. *Israel's Lebanon War*. New York: Simon and Schuster.

Scruton, Roger. 1987. *A Land Held Hostage: Lebanon and the West*. London: Claridge Press.

Smock, David R., and Audrey C. Smock. 1975. *The Politics of Pluralism: A Comparative Study of Lebanon and Ghana*. New York: Elsevier.

Suleiman, Michael W. 1967. *Political Parties in Lebanon.* Ithaca: Cornell University Press.

Testrake, John. 1987. *Triumph over Terror on Flight 847.* Old Tappan, NJ: Fleming H. Revell.

Timerman, Jacobo. 1982. *The Longest War: Israel in Lebanon.* New York: Vintage Books.

Weir, Ben, and Carol Weir. 1987. *Hostage Bound, Hostage Free.* Philadelphia: Westminster Press.

LIBYA

Mary-Jane Deeb

The literature in English on Libya since independence in 1951 can be divided into three categories. The first deals with the historical developments under King Idris, the Libyan leader of the Sanusiyya brotherhood and Libya's first postindependence head of state; the second examines social and economic developments under the Qaddafi regime; and the last examines the foreign and domestic policies of Muammar Qaddafi since the overthrow of the monarchy in 1969.

A few works that do not technically cover the monarchical period should be noted here because of their relevance to Libya's postindependence period. The classical study on the political and tribal social structure of Libyan society is E. E. Evans-Pritchard's *The Sanusi of Cyrenaica* (1949). Written by an Oxford anthropologist who was also working for the British government, it examines in great depth the tribal base of the Sanusiyya brotherhood in Cyrenaica and its relations to the tribes in the region. A somewhat comparable study was carried out by Nicola Ziadeh, *Sanusiyah: A Study of a Revivalist Movement in Islam* (1968), which focused on the beliefs and social organization of the Sanusiyya in the nineteenth and first part of the twentieth centuries.

Another valuable study that appeared more recently is by Ali Abdullatif Ahmida, *The Making of Modern Libya: State Formation, Colonization, and Resistance, 1830–1932* (1994). The author examines the political economy of Cyrenaica over a century and discusses the role of tribes and tribal leaders and their relation to the Italian colonizers. He analyzes the role of Islam and nationalism and describes the way they were interpreted differently by various tribes, factions, and urban classes in different parts of the country. Finally, he demonstrates how both King Idris and Qaddafi reinterpreted and distorted the history of that period for their own political motives.

In *The State and Social Transformation in Tunisia and Libya, 1830–1980* (1986), Lisa Anderson covers that same period and brings the political analysis to the present period. She argues that the differences that exist between the political and social structures in Tunisia and Libya today are due to "each country's experience of modern state formation and bureaucratic development"

(3) over a period of 150 years. John Wright in *Libya: A Modern History* (1982) does the same: he focuses half his book on prerevolutionary Libya, with a brief overview of the nineteenth century, then links the political events of that period to the more recent political developments in Libya under Qaddafi. He is, however, much less theoretically inclined than Anderson. Mansour O. El-Kikhia's study *Libya's Qaddafi: The Politics of Contradiction* (1997) is the most recent work on Libya to cover both the history and politics of that country. He covers briefly the Greek, Roman, Ottoman, and colonial periods, as well as the monarchy, but focuses primarily on the post-1969 period. He argues that Qaddafi has deliberately chosen to destabilize the country in order to control it and to remain in power.

The best political history of twentieth-century Libya until 1961 is Majid Khadduri's *Modern Libya: A Study in Political Development* (1963). The author not only discusses the period of Italian colonialism and the Libyan resistance, but covers the British military administration of Libya until 1949, the achievement of independence, the constitutional evolution of the state under King Idris, and the relations of that little kingdom with the major Western powers.

The best study on Libya's accession to independence is by Adrian Pelt, who was assistant secretary general of the United Nations and was appointed U.N. commissioner in Libya in 1949. His book *Libyan Independence and the United Nations: A Case of Planned Decolonization* (1970) is a firsthand account of the manner in which Libya became the first state to achieve independence via the United Nations. Another firsthand account is by Henry Villard, who was the first U.S. representative in postindependence Libya and held the position of minister in the U.S. legation in Benghazi. His book is one of the earliest written about U.S.-Libyan relations since independence.

SOCIAL AND ECONOMIC DEVELOPMENTS

Among the earliest works that focused on the economic and social developments in postindependence Libya was that carried out by the International Bank for Reconstruction and Development entitled *The Economic Development of Libya* (1960). Not only did it survey the agricultural, industrial, and financial sectors of the economy, but it also examined the education system, the health and community services, the tourist trade, and the transport and communications system. It also chronicled some of the earliest oil discoveries. Finally, it suggested that the government should play a more significant role in planning and implementing economic development programs, although since the 1980s it has advocated the pullout of the government from economic affairs. Abdul Amir Q. Kubbah's *Libya: Its Oil Industry and Economic System* (1964) was another landmark study that was used as the standard work on the Libyan oil industry for almost a decade. John Norman's *Labor and Politics in Libya and Arab Africa* (1965) was one of the first studies to examine Libya's work force and its impact on Libyan domestic and foreign policy. Finally, there were two general surveys with very similar titles that appeared in the late 1960s in English: one by Paul Copeland, *The Land and People of Libya* (1967), and the other by Terence Blunsum, *Libya: The Country and its People* (1968), neither of which was particularly noteworthy.

A study on agriculture prepared by J. A. Allan, K. S. McLachlan, and Edith Penrose in 1973 as a joint project between the Libyan University and the School of Oriental and African Studies of London University (SOAS) entitled *Libya: Agriculture and Economic Development* was one of the earliest made in Libya after Qaddafi came to power. It assessed the situation of the agricultural sector and made policy recommendations.

The early 1980s saw a plethora of books in English on Libya. Marius and Mary-Jane Deeb wrote *Libya since the Revolution: Aspects of Social and Political Development* (1982), based on primary sources they had collected during their yearlong stay in Libya in the late 1970s. They wrote about topics that had not previously received much attention: demography, women in Libya, the education system, Qaddafi's rejection of the Sanusi tradition and his interpretation of Islamic jurisprudence, popular committees and revolutionary committees, and Qaddafi's economic and Arab policies. The study looked at Libyan society as a whole, from within, in the decade that followed the 1969 revolution.

That same year two other books on socioeconomic and political developments in Libya appeared in England, the product of a conference held in 1981 at SOAS. Both were edited by veteran North Africa specialists. E.G.H. Joffe and K. S. McLachlan prepared *Social and Economic Development of Libya* (1982), while J. A. Allan edited *Libya since Independence: Economic and Political Development* (1982). Each was a collection of articles by Arab, primarily Libyan, scholars and Western experts on the region. The first was more historical, covered the preindependence period, and examined Libya's tribal structure and organization since the nineteenth century, the Italian colonization of Libya, and the Tripolitanian Republic of 1918–1922. The second focused on the independence period and the role of King Idris in developing a Libyan national identity, Qaddafi's *Green Book*, changes in the Libyan political elite after 1971, and Libya's economic, social, and urban problems.

A number of other works covered social and economic issues in post-1969 Libya, including one edited by M. M. Buru, Shukri M. Ghanem, and K. S. McLachlan, entitled *Planning and Development in Modern Libya* (1985); and another edited by Bichara Khader and Bashir el-Wifati, *The Economic Development of Libya* (1987). Frank Waddams's study *The Libyan Oil Industry* (1980) discussed Libya's role in nationalizing that industry in the 1970s and starting a trend that would revolutionize the relationship between oil producers and Western oil companies in the Middle East. Finally, Maja Naur's study *Political Mobilization and Industry in Libya* (1986) would have been an original contribution to the political economy of Libya had the author not plagiarized the work of others.

FOREIGN AND DOMESTIC POLICIES UNDER QADDAFI

One of the earliest and most significant studies of the Qaddafi regime was Ruth First's *Libya: The Elusive Revolution* (1974). After examining Libya's geography, history, and politics under King Idris, First focused on a four-year period from the end of 1969 to the early months of 1974. She discussed Qaddafi's ideology, economic policies, and the changes introduced in Libya's relations with the Western oil companies that set the stage for a change in the relations between those companies and oil-producing countries in the Middle East and elsewhere. What makes this book particularly valuable is the fact that it was based on interviews with Qaddafi and a number of people in and out of government, official archives, and other primary sources. Another, much less significant book, written by Mirella Bianco, *Gadafi: Voice from the Desert* (1975), was also based on extensive interviews with Qaddafi and some of his close associates. It focused on the man and his worldview, making a hero, almost a prophet, of the Libyan leader. The book was published originally in French as *Kadhafi: Messager du desert*, although the author is Italian and the wife of an Arab diplomat, and was translated into English and Arabic a year later.

A systematic study of the impact of the socioeconomic and political changes introduced by Qaddafi was carried out by a Libyan scholar and some of his professors at Florida State University. The product of that study was two books. The first was prepared by Omar El Fathaly, Monte Palmer, and Richard Chackerian and entitled *Political Development and Bureaucracy in Libya* (1977), and the second, by El Fathaly and Palmer, was called *Political Development and Social Change in Libya* (1980). Both books are especially important because they are based on extensive surveys of Libyans in the Zawya province, interviews with local tribal chiefs and government administrators, and interviews with national government officials who served before or after the revolution. A somewhat similar study was carried out by John Davis and entitled *Libyan Politics: Tribe and Revolution* (1988). Its focus was narrower, as it analyzed the impact of Libya's colonial history, its Islamic traditions, the revolution, oil wealth, and statelessness on a single tribe, the Zuwaya. The study was carried out between 1975 and 1979.

Libyan Sandstorm: The Complete Account of Qaddafi's Revolution by John Cooley (1982) is another important work on the Libyan revolution. Cooley argues that "the story of modern Libya is the story of oil" (42) and maintains that because of the importance of Libya's high-quality oil for European economies, and to a much lesser extent for that of the United States, the West supported Qaddafi's regime, directly or indirectly, throughout the first decade of the revolution. However, when Qaddafi's regional and international policies began to annoy Western nations and their allies in the Middle East and Africa, the West changed its attitude, and the United States broke its relations with Libya in 1981.

Lillian C. Harris, at the time a political analyst for North Africa in the U.S.

Department of State's Bureau of Intelligence and Research, wrote a good overall study of Libya entitled *Libya: Qadhafi's Revolution and the Modern State* (1986). She covered both domestic and foreign policy issues, discussed the Libyan opposition domestically and abroad, and analyzed the state of the economy. Her assessment of the ability of Qaddafi to remain in power despite significant domestic and foreign opposition to his regime has proven correct. Other works that examined the overall developments in Libya include Henri Habib's descriptive study of Libya's governmental political organization in the early years of the revolution, entitled *Politics and Government of Revolutionary Libya* (1975); Helen Metz's edited *Libya: A Country Study* (1989), an area handbook publication by the Federal Research Division of the Library of Congress that surveyed the history, politics, economy, and military developments in Libya; and, more recently, Dirk Vandewalle's *Qadhafi's Libya, 1969–1994* (1995), also an edited work, which focused primarily on internal economic and political developments but also addressed issues of oil and foreign policy.

A number of books written by journalists also attempted to give an overall picture of Libya in the first two decades of the revolution. Jonathan Bearman's *Qadhafi's Libya* (1986), for instance, discussed Qaddafi's rise to power, his Arab nationalist and socialist ideology, his interpretation of Islam, his economic and foreign policies, and the U.S. relation with Libya. Although the work is based primarily on secondary sources in English, the author also used Libyan government publications and BBC summaries of world broadcasts. David Blundy and Andrew Lycett, one a correspondent, the other a freelance journalist for the London *Sunday Times*, wrote a more sensationalist book, *Qaddafi and the Libyan Revolution* (1987). Although they discussed briefly issues such as Qaddafi's *Green Book*, they focused primarily on his support for terrorism, with chapters entitled "Terror Inc.," "Stray Dogs," and "Murder in London."

A number of scholars on Libya focused their work on U.S.-Libyan relations: P. Edward Haley wrote a rather long study, *Qaddafi and the United States since 1969* (1984), that relied heavily on the U.S. press and the Keesings archives. He did little more, however, than chronicle the ups and downs of that relationship. He also discussed Libya's relations with the Soviet Union and the PLO and retold, at great length, the story of Qaddafi's involvement in international terrorism. Mahmoud El Warfally's book *Imagery and Ideology in U.S. Policy toward Libya, 1969–1982* (1988) analyzed U.S. policy toward Libya utilizing Richard Cottam's ideal patterns of images in a foreign policy theoretical framework. The author examined U.S. foreign policy actions toward Libya to see whether they were the consequence of the prevailing images the United States held of Libya, or the result of Libya's foreign policy behavior. Finally, Geoff Simons argued in his book *Libya: The Struggle for Survival* (1993) that "the bitter U.S. hostility to Libya over the years has nothing to do with terrorism . . . ; the hostility stems from the simple fact that Libya was able to rock the international oil industry and, in so doing, embarrass and inconvenience the global corporations" (189).

Books on Libya's foreign policy include Ronald Bruce St. John's *Qaddafi's World Design: Libyan Foreign Policy, 1969–1987* (1987). It examines factors the author believes have shaped Libya's foreign policy, including Arab nationalism, Islam, and what Qaddafi called the Third Universal Theory. St. John then proceeds to explain Libya's attitude toward the Palestine issue, its attempts at unity with various Arab countries, and its position of "active neutrality" between East and West blocs in terms of those factors.

Martin Sicker's *The Making of a Pariah State* (1987) appeared the same year as St. John's study. In the introduction, Sicker states his view of Libya, which he then proceeds to develop in the rest of the work: "The Qaddafi regime attempted to impose national cohesion by force and intimidation, but has succeeded primarily in creating social and economic chaos while pursuing fantastic foreign policy goals" (5). These goals, according to Sicker, include pan-Arabist attempts at unity with a variety of states in the region, the creation of a wedge between those states and the West, the building of a large Islamic state in sub-Saharan Africa, the improvement of relations with the Soviet Union, and fighting the United States by means of terrorism.

Four books have focused on Libya's relations with countries on the African continent. In *Libya's Foreign Policy in North Africa* (1991), I used a neorealist approach to explain and analyze Qaddafi's policies in North Africa. I first created a pyramidal model of regions of interests, at the apex of which I placed North Africa, the region of Libya's core interests. I then argued that the "farther a situation is from Libya's area of core interest (namely, North Africa), the more Libya's foreign policy becomes ideologically motivated; and . . . the closer a situation is to Libya's area of core interests, the more policy is motivated by pragmatic, geopolitical considerations" (9). This book is one of a handful of studies that have attempted to use a theoretical framework to analyze, rather than merely describe, Libya's foreign policy.

The first part of *The Green and the Black: Qadhafi's Policies in Africa* (1988), edited by René Lemarchand, examines the determinants of Libya's foreign policy. Chapters by Mary-Jane Deeb on "The Primacy of Libya's National Interest," E.G.H. Joffe on "The Role of Islam," and William J. Foltz on "Libya's Military Power" analyze some of the factors that have shaped Libya's policy in Africa. The second part of the book focuses on case studies of that policy in Morocco, Chad, and sub-Saharan Africa and on Libya's role within the Organization of African Unity (OAU).

Finally, two other studies have focused more narrowly on Libya's relations with Chad. The first is a monograph prepared by Benyamin Neuberger of the Shiloah Center for Middle Eastern and African Studies, entitled *Involvement, Invasion, and Withdrawal: Qadhdhāfi's Libya and Chad, 1969–1981* (1982), which is a first-rate analysis of the complex relations between Chad and Libya and the causes of the war and conflict that started long before Qaddafi appeared on the political scene. The second is by John Wright, *Libya, Chad, and the Central Sahara* (1989), and gives a historical perspective on Libyan-Chadian relations going back to the first part of the nineteenth century and bringing the discussion to the end of the 1980s.

FUTURE RESEARCH

Despite some important studies on Libya, the country is still a terra incognita for most scholars of North Africa and the Middle East. By comparison to the work done on the other countries of the Maghreb, serious scholarship on Libya is scant. A significant number of books, relatively speaking, have been written by journalists and have tended to be sensationalist accounts of Libya's role in international terrorism. United States–Libyan relations have also been the focus of a number of studies that have told us more about U.S. foreign policy than about Libya. Little has been done to analyze the socioeconomic and political base of power of the monarchy or of Qaddafi. It may be difficult to do fieldwork in Libya today, but the Italian, British, and French archives do provide materials for research at least until the 1969 revolution. There are also numerous Libyans living abroad, not necessarily in the opposition, who know a great deal about what is going on in Libya today and could be interviewed about the domestic situation in that country. Also, Libya's neighbors, especially Tunisia and Egypt, keep extensive files on the Qaddafi regime and should be consulted by anyone planning to write a serious study on Libya. There is no aspect of the Libyan society, economy, or political system that has received serious attention. The field is wide open for future scholars to carry out research on that country.

REFERENCES

Ahmida, Ali Abdullatif. 1994. *The Making of Modern Libya: State Formation, Colonization, and Resistance, 1830–1932*. Albany: State University of New York Press.

Allan, J. A., ed. 1982. *Libya since Independence: Economic and Political Development*. New York: St. Martin's Press.

Allan, J. A., K. S. McLachlan, and Edith T. Penrose, eds. 1973. *Libya: Agriculture and Economic Development*. London: Frank Cass.

Anderson, Lisa. 1986. *The State and Social Transformation in Tunisia and Libya, 1830–1980*. Princeton: Princeton University Press.

Ansell, M. O., and T. M. Arif, eds. 1972. *The Libyan Revolution: A Sourcebook of Legal and Historical Documents*. Harrow, UK: Oleander Press.

Bearman, Jonathan. 1986. *Qadhafi's Libya*. London: Zed Books.

Bianco, Mirella. 1975. *Gadafi: Voice from the Desert*. London: Longman.

Blundy, David, and Andrew Lycett. 1987. *Qaddafi and the Libyan Revolution*. Boston: Little, Brown.

Blunsum, Terence. 1968. *Libya: The Country and Its People*. London: Queen Ann Press.

Buru, M. M., Shukri M. Ghanem, and K. S. McLachlan, eds. 1985. *Planning and Development in Modern Libya*. Wisbech, UK: MENAS Press.

Chambour, Raafat. 1977. *Power and Concept of the Libyan Revolution*. Lausanne: Editions Méditeranéenes.

Cooley, John K. 1982. *Libyan Sandstorm: The Complete Account of Qaddafi's Revolution.* New York: Holt, Rinehart and Winston.

Copeland, Paul W. 1967. *The Land and People of Libya.* Philadelphia: Lippincott.

Davis, John. 1988. *Libyan Politics: Tribe and Revolution.* Berkeley: University of California Press.

Deeb, Marius K., and Mary-Jane Deeb. 1982. *Libya since the Revolution: Aspects of Social and Political Development.* New York: Praeger.

Deeb, Mary-Jane. 1991. *Libya's Foreign Policy in North Africa.* Boulder, CO: Westview Press.

Evans-Pritchard, E. E. 1949. *The Sanusi of Cyrenaica.* Oxford: Clarendon Press.

El Fathaly, Omar I., and Monte Palmer. 1980. *Political Development and Social Change in Libya.* Lexington, MA: D. C. Heath.

El Fathaly, Omar I., Monte Palmer, and Richard Chackerian. 1977. *Political Development and Bureaucracy in Libya.* Lexington, MA: D. C. Heath.

First, Ruth. 1974. *Libya: The Elusive Revolution.* Middlesex, UK: Penguin Books.

Habib, Henri. 1975. *Politics and Government of Revolutionary Libya.* Ottawa: Le Cercle du Livre.

Haley, P. Edward. 1984. *Qaddafi and the United States since 1969.* New York: Praeger.

Harris, Lillian C. 1986. *Libya: Qadhafi's Revolution and the Modern State.* Boulder, CO: Westview Press; London: Croom Helm.

International Bank for Reconstruction and Development. 1960. *The Economic Development of Libya.* Baltimore: Johns Hopkins University Press.

Joffe, E.G.H., and K. S. McLachlan, eds. 1982. *Social and Economic Development of Libya.* Wisbech, Cambridgeshire, UK: MENAS Press.

Khadduri, Majid. 1963. *Modern Libya: A Study in Political Development.* Baltimore: Johns Hopkins University Press.

Khader, Bichara, and Bashir el-Wifati, eds. 1987. *The Economic Development of Libya.* London: Croom Helm.

El-Khawas, M. A. 1986. *Qaddafi: His Ideology in Theory and Practice.* Brattleboro, VT: Amana Books.

El-Kikhia, Mansour O. 1997. *Libya's Qaddafi: The Politics of Contradiction.* Gainesville: University Press of Florida.

Kubbah, Abdul Amir Q. 1964. *Libya: Its Oil Industry and Economic System.* Baghdad: Arab Petro-Economic Research Center.

Lemarchand, René, ed. 1988. *The Green and the Black: Qadhafi's Policies in Africa.* Bloomington: Indiana University Press.

Metz, Helen C., ed. 1989. *Libya: A Country Study.* Washington, DC: Federal Research Division, Library of Congress.

National Front for the Salvation of Libya. 1992. *Libya under Gaddafi and the NFSL Challenge.* Chicago: NFSL.

Naur, Maja. 1986. *Political Mobilization and Industry in Libya.* Copenhagen: Akademisk Forlag.

Neuberger, Benyamin. 1982. *Involvement, Invasion, and Withdrawal: Qadhdhāfi's Libya and Chad, 1969–1981.* Tel Aviv: Shiloah Center for Middle Eastern and African Studies, Tel Aviv University.

Norman, John. 1965. *Labor and Politics in Libya and Arab Africa.* New York: Bookman.

Pelt, Adrian. 1970. *Libyan Independence and the United Nations: A Case of Planned Decolonization.* New Haven: Yale University Press.

Peters, Emrys L. 1990. *The Bedouin of Cyrenaica: Studies in Personal and Corporate Power*. New York: Cambridge University Press.

St. John, Ronald Bruce. 1987. *Qaddafi's World Design: Libyan Foreign Policy, 1969–1987*. London: Saqi Books.

Seale, Patrick, and Maureen McConville. 1973. *The Hilton Assignment*. New York: Praeger.

Sicker, Martin. 1987. *The Making of a Pariah State: The Adventurist Politics of Muammar Qaddafi*. New York: Praeger.

Simons, Geoff. 1993. *Libya: The Struggle for Survival*. New York: St. Martin's Press.

Sterling, Claire. 1981. *The Terror Network*. New York: Holt, Rinehart and Winston.

Vandewalle, Dirk, ed. 1995. *Qadhafi's Libya, 1969–1994*. New York: St. Martin's Press.

Villard, Henry S. 1956. *Libya: The New Arab Kingdom of North Africa*. Ithaca: Cornell University Press.

Waddams, Frank C. 1980. *The Libyan Oil Industry*. Baltimore: Johns Hopkins University Press; London: Croom Helm.

El Warfally, Mahmoud G. 1988. *Imagery and Ideology in U.S. Policy toward Libya, 1969–1982*. Pittsburgh: University of Pittsburgh Press.

Wright, John. 1982. *Libya: A Modern History*. Baltimore: Johns Hopkins University Press.

———. 1989. *Libya, Chad, and the Central Sahara*. Savage, MD: Barnes and Noble Books.

Ziadeh, Nicola A. 1968. *Sanusiyah: A Study of a Revivalist Movement in Islam*. Leiden: E. J. Brill.

MOROCCO

Gregory White

Postcolonial political science research on Morocco has focused on King Hassan II. This preoccupation may be entirely appropriate, given the monarch's domination of the political, economic, and social landscape, but may have distracted attention from other significant aspects of Moroccan politics since the 1950s. Moreover, one must wonder to what extent an intellectual focus on the monarchy and Moroccan paternalism has served to reify and support it. Often, American political science's concentration on the personal rule of postcolonial leaders—for example, Kenya's Jomo Kenyatta, Ivory Coast's Félix Houphouët-Boigny, or Tunisia's Habib Bourguiba—has served to explain and, perhaps, even excuse the leaders' demand for unquestioning obedience as part of a modernization imperative. In addition, an exclusive focus on Hassan may reinforce the view that he is a skillful and omniscient manipulator able to survey the wide sweep of the political landscape from the high position of the palace. However, Hassan is just a man; even with the extraordinary resources at his disposal, he may ultimately be as puzzled and uncertain about the disorderly complexity of Moroccan politics as any other government official, citizen, or observer.

Perhaps the dominant theme in recent decades has been the recurrent observation that the Moroccan political system was fragile and would not survive much longer. Waterbury (1970) seemed to launch such observations more than twenty-five years ago, with others (Tessler 1982; Leveau 1985; Swearingen 1986; Entelis 1989) suggesting similar views. Given the persistence of Hassan's regime, one is tempted to criticize such predictions as incorrect. The value of the studies, however, is that they have illuminated an underlying instability beneath the seeming certainty of the 1980s and 1990s.

COLONIAL LEGACY

While it is easy to argue that colonialism stopped forty years ago and, therefore, should not receive blame for Morocco's problems in the 1990s, several influential studies illuminate the lasting impact of French colonialism. Early works by Ashford (1961) and Zartman (1964) provide analyses of the change from the French protectorate (1912–1956) to the early years of Moroccan independence with explicit reference to the impact of French administrative structures. Ashford (1961) wrote about the usefulness of the charismatic leadership of Hassan's father, Mohammed V, and leaders of the nationalist movement, the Istiqlal. Hassan replaced his father as king in 1961. The challenge for new nations, according to Ashford, was to deepen popular participation and democratic institutions, a difficult task given the power of those already skilled in politics. For his part, Zartman (1964) posited that the nature of Moroccan government and politics between 1956 and 1961 could be revealed through an analysis of decision making. The government's efforts to solve several problems concerning decolonization—diplomatic, military, economic, social, and political—would shape long-term prospects for the new country.

Bidwell (1973) studied the attempts by French administrator General Hubert Lyautey to control rural and nomadic populations in the *Bled es-Siba* (realm of dissidence). Lyautey's efforts contributed to the construction and support of the *Bled el-Makhzen* (realm of the sultan). Many analysts—for example, Anderson (1991) and Munson (1993)—have pointed to the pivotal French role in the construction and maintenance of the Moroccan monarchy. Bidwell's treatment displays the importance of the subjugation of rural populations in that effort.

The legacy of French efforts to, in Anderson's words, "install, retain, and refurbish" the Moroccan monarchy is evident in the postindependence era. Alain Claisse wrote, for example: "In the 1970s, it was added to the constitution that the king is the 'supreme representative of the nation.' This concept has nothing to do with either the Islamic tradition or Western constitutional law. It stems rather from European monarchical theories of the eighteenth century, which saw the king as the incarnation of the whole nation" (quoted in Anderson 1991, 9). The ongoing legacy of European colonialism in Africa continues to receive attention by American social scientists (Young 1994; Anderson 1986) and merits further study.

Gellner's (1969) historical and anthropological study of the Berbers of the central High Atlas of Morocco focuses on the tribes themselves. It also treats the French effort to pacify dissident areas between the world wars. In 1930, French authorities promulgated the famous Dahir Berbère (the Berber decree), a policy of permitting Berber tribes to remain outside the national Moroccan Muslim (Arab) legal system, but under supervision of the French. From the nationalist movement's perspective, this was a "divide-and-rule" policy; religious authorities viewed it as an attempt to undercut their influence.

Gellner also coedited two useful volumes. Gellner and Micaud (1972) brings together a collection of chapters that consider Berbers and Arabs in Morocco and Algeria. The overarching argument is that there are no deeply felt, self-conscious enclaves in North Africa, as one finds in the Middle East. To be sure, Arabs and Berbers are different linguistic categories, but "internal ethnic nationalism or irredentism is not a major force in the Maghreb" (21). Gellner and

Waterbury (1977) is valuable as well, with Brown's (1977) study of patron-client relations in the city of Salé of particular use for the student of Moroccan politics.

Abu-Lughod's (1980) superb treatment of French urban policy concentrates on the development of Rabat-Salé. Using the loaded and highly charged term "apartheid" outside its South African context may have been ill advised. Nevertheless, *Rabat: Urban Apartheid in Morocco* provides a historical case study of the development of Rabat as a French administrative center, with the Moroccan population relegated to Salé across the Bou Regreg River.

Perhaps the finest treatment of the colonial legacy is Laroui's (1993) study of Moroccan nationalism. Originally published in 1977 by the Paris-based Maspéro, *Les origines sociales et culturelles du nationalisme marocain (1830–1912)* is one of Laroui's several "landmark works," a "painstaking submersion" into the phenomenon (Saaf 1991, 33, 44). Laroui identified Moroccan nationalism as a synergistic response to colonial domination by the French, Spanish, and, to a lesser extent, British. This required, first, an analysis of the historical background before the onslaught of late-nineteenth-century colonialism and, second, the "dialectical reaction" (239) of Moroccan nationalism. When Laroui's work is combined with Burke's (1976) treatment of preprotectorate resistance, one becomes aware that Moroccan nationalism did not emerge of its own accord but instead is, quite literally, artificial, a dynamic reaction to external pressure(s).

MONARCHY AND POLITICS

King Hassan has received the greatest part of scholarly attention, entirely justified because of his centrality in the Moroccan political landscape since coming to power in 1961. The *amir al-Muminin* or "commander of the faithful" has skillfully maintained power as a head of state while carefully retaining his status as a traditional leader. Moreover, in contrast to other contemporary monarchs, Hassan remains at the apex of the political system. His decisions and actions carry far greater weight than those of parliament, ministers, or ministerial technocrats. Hassan has argued that it would be an irresponsible rejection of his historical role as monarch to eschew such participation.

It appears that a more stable political system exists in the 1980s and 1990s than was found in the 1960s and 1970s. Whether the pivot point was the coup attempts against Hassan in 1971 and 1972, the Green March into the Western Sahara in 1975, or the adoption of structural adjustment policies in 1983, the political system appears to be less fluid and more stable in recent years. On the one hand, some differences in the trajectory of scholarly analyses are due to this change. On the other hand, striking continuities are evident.

The preeminent study of the monarchy is Waterbury's *The Commander of the Faithful* (1970), a superb treatment of the Moroccan state that is officially banned in Morocco. To be sure, Waterbury unfortunately employed the Western-centric dichotomy between tradition and modernity that characterizes so many studies. Instead of taking "modernity" as a temporal category—that is, a view of a social phenomenon as modern because it is contemporary—Waterbury perceived "tradition" as irrational and Middle Eastern, "modernity" as Western, rational, and industrial. Nonetheless, his scathing indictment of the Moroccan elite and, in particular, the throne, written before the coup attempts of the early 1970s, remains provocative more than twenty-five years later. By controlling both the political elite and the security forces, Waterbury argued, the monarchy had succeeded (for the time being) in maintaining an immobilism and, thereby, control. Waterbury wrote: "The essential dilemma of such a monarch is to promote economic development without upsetting the delicate political stalemate that he has helped maintain . . . under highly favorable economic circumstances, a monarch can encourage, at least on a short-term basis, economic development while maintaining the political status quo. . . . King Hassan has no financial cushion with which to meet the country's economic crisis" (1970, 318). Hassan remains in power. Thus Waterbury's prediction in 1970 of the monarchy's ultimate demise has not proven true, at least not yet. Nevertheless, he offered at least two crucial insights into the character of the Moroccan state. First, there has been a "territorial inversion" of the *Bled es-Siba* and the *Bled el-Makhzen* so that the urban centers are now the source of dissidence. Second, Hassan's reliance on the Ministry of Interior illustrates the fundamental insecurity of the throne.

Leveau's (1985) study of the skillful manner in which the monarchy has maintained the support of local, rural elites also demonstrates the reasons for the stability of the regime. Like the works of Waterbury and many others, Leveau's study is well within the "modernization" framework. Although independence and the nationalist movement compromised the power that rural elites had accrued under the protectorate, support from the monarchy proved crucial to maintain the rural bourgeoisie's economic power. Leveau argued that rural elites—in his view, "tradition"—had become "defenders of the throne" against the burgeoning power of urban centers; as such, rural notables have diminished the country's ability to pursue industrialization (modernization). Leveau also noted the central role that the monarchy plays in the private sector, particularly through the development of the Omnium Nord-africain (ONA). This holding company has tentacles in various sectors: auto imports, agro-industry, dairies, public works, supermarkets, publishing houses, mines, and utilities. Leveau asserted that in contrast to his father, Mohammed V, Hassan had become head of a financial empire and is, therefore, the *premier entrepreneur privé marocain* (257).

Also highly noteworthy is Basri's (1988) study of territorial administration. He is the long-standing and extremely powerful minister of interior and a close confidant of Hassan. His doctoral thesis at the Université des Sciences de Grenoble is most revealing. In it, he argued that the primary mission of the state is to penetrate the entire country and, most of all, to maintain order. Without order, "development" and "progress" are impossible. How does the state maintain order? Through *autonomie locale*—that is, by staying in touch with the people at the local level, providing services and supporting economic activity. Since September 1976, the state has supported the creation of *collectivités territoriales*, local authorities responsible for development. In so doing, the state is best able to maintain *tutelle*, or guardianship, of the country. Finally, Basri argued that the one word to describe the method of state is *l'adaptation*—an ongoing adaptation to changes in society and the economy and to challenges to power. Sluglett and Sluglett's (1984) study of the monarchy's role in the country argued that *l'adaptation* characterizes the monarch himself.

Tessler offered useful analyses in the 1980s. A focus on elites (1982) provides insight into the continuity of Hassan's hold on power and the structure of party politics. Tessler (1982) stressed that dominant institutions are controlled by a privileged few, with concentric circles emanating from Hassan at the center. The dominant group of bourgeois elite families originated in Fes and the Suss area of southern Morocco. Fassis and Sussis, therefore, have dominated commerce and have become very influential. Benamour (1993) and Mednicoff (1994), discussed later, also offered treatments of the party system.

Tessler's (1985) study of Hassan's use of populist strategies for co-opting and containing domestic (and international) opposition focuses, in particular, on the August 1984 Arab-African Union with Libya's Muammar Qaddafi. Pointing to Hassan's need to contend with domestic and international pressures simultaneously, Tessler highlighted the paradox of pursuing a populist strategy in an authoritarian context.

Entelis's (1989) analysis of "countercultural" politics is an elegant meditation on the challenge posed to the monarchy by, above all, Islamist opposition. Because of the monarchy's religious legitimacy, the use of prebends, and tactics of co-optation, Hassan has counteracted Islamist opposition. Nonetheless, Entelis argued, the monarchy would have to contend with antigovernment behavior from students, workers, leftists, party leaders, and politicized religious authorities. Like Waterbury, Leveau, and others before him, Entelis did not see Hassan's ability to co-opt (and suppress) opposition as a viable method for the long term.

Finally, Santucci's *Le Maroc actuel* (1992) is an invaluable resource that includes contributions from leading French and Moroccan social scientists. Most notable is an awesome piece of empirical research on domestic capital formation by Saadi and Berrada (1992), in which the authors analyzed the historical formation and activity of domestic capitalists.

ISLAM

Students of politics have much to learn from anthropologists, and vice versa. One compelling reason for engaging the anthropological literature on Morocco is that Clifford Geertz, one of the most widely read anthropologists of the post–World War II generation, conducted a significant amount of fieldwork in northern Morocco. *Islam Observed* (1968), a comparison of Indonesia and Morocco, has provided the touchstone for subsequent fieldwork and criticism. Geertz not only offered an analysis of Indonesian and Moroccan cultures and their experiences of Islam, he also displayed the value of cross-national, comparative inquiry. At bottom, Geertz strove to understand the "systems of significance," or socially observable rituals and belief systems that manifest subjective life (95).

Geertz, along with Hildred Geertz and Lawrence Rosen, also released a magnificent volume in 1979 that analyzed the town of Sefrou in the Middle Atlas Mountains. The authors attempted to elucidate the "systems of meaning" and social structures of Morocco. Rosen studied social structure, Hildred Geertz focused on kinship and family, and photographer Paul Hyman provided beautiful photographs of the region. Clifford Geertz's own essay on the *suq* in Sefrou is magisterial in its in-depth empirical analysis of the bazaar economy. He does, however, move away from the observed realm toward a high degree of hyperbole at the essay's end: "In the details of a bazaar life something of the spirit that animates that society—an odd mixture of restlessness, practicality, contentiousness, eloquence, inclemency and moralism—can be seen with a particular and revelatory vividness" (235). The predilection to project societal traits based on the observation of one facet of an economy may ultimately say more about the anthropologist than about the society under study.

Following Geertz, Rabinow (1975) published a study of Sidi Lahcen in the areas surrounding Sefrou. Indeed, Rabinow was a student of Geertz's at Chicago and worked in Morocco under Geertz's guidance. Employing an actor-oriented methodology that "attempts to understand the actor's view of his own social world" (3), Rabinow traced the evolution of the *wlad siyyed*—the followers of the seventeenth-century saint Sidi Lahcen Lyussi—and their gradual loss of power during the French protectorate. Colonial administrators allied with more secular urban officials, while *wlad siyyed* resisted the colonial presence, preferring to follow religious tradition as a source of authority. In the end, however, this left the *wlad* at a disadvantage: their saint possessed great power as their own power diminished.

Unfortunately, a more popular companion piece is Rabinow's (1977) meditation on fieldwork—"unfortunate" because it has been used in U.S. universities for years. Rabinow's *Reflections on Fieldwork in Morocco* is a self-absorbed autoethnography about his experience in the Middle Atlas. The work regards "informants" as "quick-learning" and presumes to make broad generalizations about "Moroccan culture" based on several conversations with townspeople, most notably a seedy character named Ali. Many of Rabinow's proclamations about "Moroccan" culture might be applicable to other cultures, and his characterizations of Moroccans are condescending as well (97–98). Rabinow was somehow appalled that Moroccans would take advantage of him; yet any American researcher must acknowledge that in a certain sense, she or he is using the people of a country to build a career. Finally, women are virtually absent in the memoir; they are present only as whores (59), mistresses, an unnamed "Berber girl'' with whom he had a sexual encounter (69), or ''the chatter of women as they wash their clothes in the river'' (32).

For his part, Eickelman has provided useful studies of Morocco. The very title of *Moroccan Islam* (1976) suggests Eickelman's approach. He posited that there are uniquely Moroccan forms of popular Islam, something that may run counter to the ideological and theological pronouncements of Hassan as a descendant of the Prophet. Through his study of Boujad, Eickelman argued that Islam has been incorporated and practiced at a decidedly local level. In synergistic tandem with a *Marabout*, such as the Sidi Mhammed Sherqi in Boujad, Islam in a pilgrimage center becomes a religious code very different from the official Islam of the government and the educated intelligentsia. *Marabouts* are venerated individuals who, because of God's grace (*baraka*), are able to serve as intermediaries with the supernatural.

In *Knowledge and Power in Morocco* (1985), Eickelman created a ''social biography,'' a dialogue with the rural judge Qadi Hajj Abd ar-Rahman Mansuri, and provided an alternative to the view that Islamic scholars are necessarily radical and militant. Using Abd ar-Rahman's life, Eickelman emphasized the important role of religious leaders during the colonial era; during the Berber Decree in 1930 religious leaders were just as active in the protests as more secular nationalists. By the end of the colonial period, however, the French had effectively gutted religious education. Eickelman (1986) also studied the elections of 1976–1977 and 1983–1984, arguing that Hassan has adapted more readily than political parties and social movements, thereby ensuring his long-term survival.

Combs-Schilling's (1989) controversial defense of Hassan offers a view of the Moroccan monarchy as concurrently Islamic and Moroccan. In other words, for example, the rituals associated with *Aïd el Kebir* bring people into contact with the monarchy and its Islamic foundations, yet set the monarch apart as the prince of the faithful, the descendant of Muhammed. For Combs-Schilling, the ''nation-state'' (297) is central, as is the ''body politic'' (299), in contrast to Ossman's (1994) willingness to interrogate such unitary and corporatistic conceptions. According to Combs-Schilling, Hassan is at the pinnacle of the nation and possesses legitimacy because he is ''the last caliph the world knows, the last ruling Prince of the Faithful, the center of Moroccan political identity for over a millennium, the definer of the nation, the definer of man, the great sacrificer who each year slays a ram on the population's behalf, the ruler in whose veins Muhammad's blood still flows, the ruler who is surrounded by truth's light and Quranic words'' (1989, 309).

Munson (1993) offered a highly charged criticism of Hassan, as well as scholarly treatments of Moroccan politics and society. Fellow anthropologists Geertz and Combs-Schilling received particular criticism for their facile view that the Moroccan monarchy, in the words of Geertz, is the ''key institution in the Moroccan religious system.'' Similar to Eickelman's (1976) study of *maraboutism*, Munson argued that the Moroccan monarchy is, in fact, ''a tangential aspect'' of everyday religious activity. Moreover, Munson claimed that most anthropological work and conventional journalistic accounts of Morocco (for example, Peretz 1996) ignore the politics of terror that emanates from the monarchy. ''In a society where everyone is forced to manifest reverential loyalty to a ruler, it is hard to know if any of it is real'' (Munson 1993, 147). Munson finished several consecutive paragraphs treating the full details of human rights horrors with exclamations like ''None of this is mentioned in [Geertz's] *Islam Observed*'' (1993). The book also provided an insightful treatment of political Islamism—that is, opposition to Hassan's rule (and religious legitimacy) by religious leaders.

One final note about the contribution of anthropology is a new and intriguing work by Ossman (1994). It is interesting to note that Ossman studied with Rabinow at Berkeley. A study of urban culture, Ossman's *Picturing Casablanca* also incorporates insights from women's studies, film studies, art history, development studies, and political science. She argued, for example, that the introduction of visual media (films, television, and photography, in particular) began during the protectorate, and mass images have been crucial to change in contemporary Morocco. To cite a common example, the mandatory photographs of Hassan in public places render his image ubiquitous. Ossman's work is most provocative regarding one's conceptions of ''Moroccan'' culture, asking, ''How can [one] distinguish between 'European' and 'Moroccan' discourses about sight and society in a place where such talk had developed in a context of constant interrelation?'' (1994, 12). Anthropological work on the multifaceted character of popular perceptions of state authority, including Bennani-Chraïbi's (1994) study of urban youth, provides an essential complement to political science.

FOREIGN POLICY

The dominant issue in Moroccan foreign policy in the 1990s continues to be the country's relationship with the European Union (EU). To be sure, there are other principal concerns such as relations (or lack thereof) with war-torn Algeria, the U.N.-sponsored referendum on the Western Sahara, official acknowledgment of deepening ties with Israel, and relations with North America. In addition, official media discourse gets a considerable amount of ideological and moral mileage over issues such as the war in Bosnia or Palestinian rights. At bottom, however, the Moroccan-EU relationship will remain the central concern for the Moroccan state. The basis for this centrality is Morocco's location in a larger economic space dominated by European economies.

Crown Prince Mohamed Ben El-Hassan Alaoui (1994), Hassan's son and the likely successor to the throne, published his doctoral dissertation on relations between the EU and the Maghreb. Although one might conclude that having one's father as the king of Morocco is a surefire way to get one's dissertation published, the important thing is the topic Sidi Mohamed chose. In fact, he wrote that he chose the topic of EU-Maghrebi relations at the urging of his father. The bulk of the analysis treats Morocco, and Sidi Mohamed argued that the EU should not lose sight of the importance of its southern frontier.

Pomfret (1987) also approached Morocco in this regard, noting the devastating impact of the EU's Common Agricultural Policy (CAP) and Spain and Portugal's adhesion to the EU in 1986. Since its inception in 1957, the EU has slowly become self-sufficient in the agricultural goods that had been the core of Morocco's economy since the protectorate. More than one Moroccan has commented ruefully that the country enjoyed greater access to European markets during the protectorate than in the postindependence era. By the late 1980s and 1990s, Morocco's political economy was sharply constrained by its position in the international arena. In the same vein, White (1996) examined Morocco's recent efforts to obtain a "Partnership Accord" with the EU.

The early 1980s saw the appearance of several studies of the conflict in the Western Sahara. Hodges (1983) stressed that Morocco's designs on the Western Sahara had to be situated within the context of a territorial integrity and the re-creation of what Benedict Anderson called "an imagined community." In the end, he was very critical of Morocco's efforts to obtain the Western Sahara, arguing that it was an attempt by Hassan to divert attention from domestic problems.

For his part, Damis (1983) noted the conflicting claims between international observers supporting Sahraoui self-determination and Morocco's conviction that it was an issue of national integrity. Despite the costs of waging the war, popular support for the Moroccan regime remained intact as Hassan skillfully manipulated a national consensus. Damis analyzed the war in light of a larger, regional struggle between Morocco and Algeria, emphasizing, in turn, that there was only minimal superpower involvement. A resolution to the conflict, he argued, would come only when Algeria and Morocco reached a broader agreement.

Maddy-Weitzman's (1991) treatment of the Western Sahara conflict posed several questions regarding the eventual resolution. Zartman (1987b) also offered a study of the conflict in the Western Sahara. While Algeria's internal problems have prompted Algiers to be less interventionist on behalf of Polisario, expectations that the conflict would be solved by 1992 have not proven true. Still, both Maddy-Weitzman and Zartman stressed that an eventual resolution will ultimately require Hassan and the Moroccan leadership to come to grips with real issues—issues that have been conveniently set aside by the conflict—and contend with pressures prompted by the army's demobilization. Morocco's eastern border is in dispute with Algeria; its southern border is in question because of the Western Sahara conflict; and it is in constant negotiation with the EU over access to the fishing grounds off its coast. The observation made by Laroui (1993) and others that Moroccan nationalism is formed in constant interaction with external actors remains pertinent.

Tessler's (1990) analysis of Morocco's increasingly publicized relationship with Israel also deserves mention. In recent years, the government has increasingly pursued deeper ties with Israel, holding, for example, an unprecedented

regional economic summit in Casablanca in 1995 with significant Israeli participation. Tessler viewed the 1986 meeting between Hassan and the then Israeli
foreign minister Shimon Peres as a pivotal event, displaying Hassan's calculation that the meeting would improve both relations with the United States and
prospects for peace in the region. Hassan also consulted with other Arab leaders,
thereby helping to encourage a shift in attitudes about Israel.

ECONOMIC POLICY

Economic development is the subject of several outstanding studies. A recent
French-language book popular in Morocco claims that the country is positioned
to be the "next dragon" (Leymarie and Tripier 1992). Whether Morocco is a
newly industrializing country on the order of the East Asian dragons is highly
debatable, and the work employs an astonishingly archaic conception of neo-
liberal comparative advantage. Nevertheless, it serves to identify Morocco as a
new, emerging market.

A more conventional, and outstanding, study of Morocco's political economy
is Swearingen's (1986) analysis of Moroccan agricultural policy, another example of the value of assessing the impact of protectorate rule on Morocco.
Swearingen's approach as a geographer helped to illuminate the development
of Morocco's agro-alimentary insecurity. The "California Policy" implemented
by protectorate officials conditioned the country's reliance on a few commodi-
ties; Swearingen emphasized the "striking continuity" between colonial and
postcolonial policies. The country's contemporary crisis is a function of the
underdevelopment by colonial authorities and the continuation of such policies
after independence. Again, as in the analyses offered by Waterbury and others,
Swearingen pointed to the fundamentally conservative political views of the
rural elite. The transfer of French-owned land to affluent Moroccan elites pre-
served a class structure in the rural sector and the perpetuation of a postcolonial
agricultural policy à la Californie.

By contrast, Brejon de Lavergnée's (1991) revealing study of government
efforts to manage the rural economy is strikingly compatible with the political
agenda of Interior Minister Basri's (1988) book. Indeed, Brejon de Lavergnée
worked at the Institut National d'Aménagement et d'Urbanisme (INAU), a research center of the Ministry of Interior. Brejon de Lavergnée argued that the
collectivités territoriales—social services provided to rural populations—serve
as a "brake" on urban migration. His approach is explicitly Catholic and European, arguing that Morocco needed an entrepreneurial spirit like the Europeans
and that the country should heed the urgings of the message delivered by Pope
John Paul II in Casablanca in 1985 to assume individual responsibility.

Sutton (1987) also provided an extensive overview of the Moroccan economy.
Although it is promarket and also offered from the perspective of Europe, it is
done with a proficiency typical of the Economist Intelligence Unit. Benamour's
(1993) meditation on the character of the Moroccan political economy is also

of note and is refreshing because of its social democratic orientation. Benamour traced the antisocial implications of the structural adjustment package implemented in 1983 and called for a more humane economic liberalism.

Finally, although Zartman's (1987a) compendium is increasingly out of date, it is immensely useful as a uniformly excellent collection of chapters on various aspects of Moroccan political economy. Particularly useful to political scientists are the chapters by Tessler, Swearingen, Pomfret, Suleiman, and Eickelman. Zartman's own introductory chapter points to the relative stability that Morocco was enjoying in the 1980s, in comparison to the confrontational politics of the 1960s and 1970s. Like many others, however, he pointed to the tenuousness of this stability.

HUMAN RIGHTS

The Moroccan government has been embroiled in several human rights controversies stemming from the Western Sahara and incarceration of political opposition. In January 1992, the European Parliament canceled a lucrative aid package from the EU because of Morocco's perceived intransigence on the Western Sahara. The catalyst was, in part, the publication of Perrault's *Notre ami le roi* (1991), a book that has since been translated into English and Spanish but is not available in Morocco. It was Perrault's book that prompted the criticism from the European Parliament, plus reproach from Danielle Mitterand. As Munson noted (1993, 142), Perrault's work is more that of a muckraking journalist than a scholar. Nonetheless, Perrault amplifies the use of terror in Moroccan political culture and implicates European governments (and the United States) for their long-standing support of the Moroccan monarchy.

Recognizing the controversy as an issue of public relations and perception, Hassan countered with several appearances on French television and the release of his own memoirs (1993). The product of interviews conducted with French journalist Eric Laurent, who apparently refrained from asking pointed questions, *La mémoire d'un roi* is nonetheless an invaluable resource, especially for Hassan's recollections of the coups in the 1970s.

Michel Laurent (1994) compiled a fascinating volume in close collaboration with the Moroccan government and ruling family. Indeed, its release in 1994 was accompanied by a lavish July reception presided over by members of the Alaoui family at the Hotel al-Mansour in Casablanca. The book was designed to present Morocco in a favorable light to French readers, emphasizing Morocco's purported movement toward democracy and stability. Despite the ideological agenda of the book, it is rewarding because of its compendium of interviews and data.

Waltz's (1991) study of the Moroccan Human Rights Organization (OMDH, Organisation marocaine des droits de l'homme) is a valuable examination of the state's toleration of a politically independent organization. Given the much-publicized efforts by the Moroccan government to release political prisoners and participate in dialogue with organizations such as the OMDH, human rights issues will surely remain on the agenda for years to come.

COMPARATIVE REGIONAL STUDIES

Finally, several regional and comparative works deserve mention for the student of Moroccan politics. Spencer (1993), like Sutton (1987), provides a Eurocentric, but practical treatment of Maghrebi politics and the prospects for regional cooperation. Tessler, Entelis, and White (1995) offer a synoptic chapter on the history of Moroccan politics. Mednicoff's (1994) study of political parties is notable for its analysis of the infrequent and irregular parliamentary elections held since independence—1963, 1977, 1984, and 1993. Parker's (1984) superb study of the Maghreb also provides a chapter on Morocco. Although Parker was the U.S. ambassador to Morocco in the late 1970s, he was a staunch critic of Hassan. Zartman (1982) and Gellner and Waterbury (1977) offer collections of essays on the region.

Earlier comparative works by Hermassi (1972), Moore (1970), and Entelis (1980) remain valuable to the student as well. Hermassi's study of the different impact of French colonialism on the three Maghrebi countries is an intriguing companion to Anderson's (1986) comparison of French and Italian colonialisms in Tunisia and Libya. A more recent comparative work is Burgat's (1993) study of political Islam in North Africa. Although giving very short shrift to issues associated with gender in Islamism, the book contains extensive excerpts of interviews with Islamist leaders like Morocco's Abd as-Slam Yasin and Tunisia's Rachid Ghannouchi. Yasin is currently under house arrest in Salé. The interviews alone make this a helpful volume, especially if read in tandem with Munson's (1993) chapter on "Islamic Fundamentalism."

Despite its absurdly essentialist title, Luciani's (1990) *The Arab State* contains an analysis by Zartman of Morocco's official opposition, principally the Istiqlal party and the Socialist Union of Popular Forces (USFP). Zartman's chapter is insightful regarding the official opposition's experience with co-optation by (and cooperation with) Hassan. Luciani's volume is excellent, despite the shortcomings of the overall framework. In the introductory essay, Luciani offered seven generalizations about the "Arab" state. Yet such observations could be made about non-Arab states in the Middle East and North Africa, as well as countries throughout the former Third World. One is left wondering, then, how useful the descriptive category of "Arab" really is.

Zartman and Habeeb's (1993) edited volume yields truly comparative work in that its contributors pursued thematic concerns, rather than country-by-country analyses. Themes treated include Islam, relations with Europe, domestic politics, and economic crises. Layachi's (1990) study of U.S. foreign policy toward the Maghreb also treats Morocco, especially regarding U.S. perceptions of the country and the high level of arms sales. Finally, a survey of the literature on Morocco would not be complete without mentioning the *Annuaire de l'Afrique du*

Nord, an indispensable source of analysis and information. It includes analytic articles, chronologies, indexes, and bibliographic summaries.

FUTURE RESEARCH

In the future, scholars will be absorbed with several concerns. In addition to the ongoing attention to issues of Hassan's succession and the challenges of an Islamist opposition, other tests of political authority need to be examined. For example, public and civic associations—nongovernmental organizations—have emerged in recent years and represent the slow, grudging political liberalization that may be taking place in the 1990s. In addition, language and education policy, particularly with respect to the Berber-speaking portions of the population, remains an undertilled field of inquiry. Issues pertaining to women's status in Moroccan political life have not received the attention they have received in the literature on Tunisia. Finally, the economic straits of the country are enormous as the country confronts a European Union, with which it signed a Partnership Agreement in 1995, and a liberalizing international economy. With half of its economy devoted to agricultural production, the ability of all of the country to "compete" in the global economy is questionable.

REFERENCES

Abu-Lughod, Janet. 1980. *Rabat: Urban Apartheid in Morocco*. Princeton: Princeton University Press.

Alaoui, Mohamed Ben El-Hassan, Crown Prince of Morocco. 1994. *La coopération entre l'Union Européenne et les pays du Maghreb*. Paris: Éditions Nathan.

Anderson, Lisa. 1986. *The State and Social Transformation in Tunisia and Libya, 1830–1980*. Princeton: Princeton University Press.

———. 1991. "Absolutism and the Resilience of Monarchy in the Middle East." *Political Science Quarterly* 106, no. 1: 1–15.

Annuaire de l'Afrique du Nord. Annual volumes. Paris: CNRS.

Ashford, Douglas. 1961. *Political Change in Morocco*. Princeton: Princeton University Press.

Basri, Driss. 1988. *L'administration territoriale: L'expérience marocaine*. Paris: Dunod.

Benamour, Abdelali. 1993. *Le Maroc interpellé*. Casablanca: Eddif.

Bennani-Chraïbi, Mounia. 1994. *Soumis et rebelles: Les jeunes au Maroc*. Paris: CNRS.

Bidwell, Robin. 1973. *Morocco under Colonial Rule: French Administration of Tribal Areas, 1912–1956*. London: Frank Cass.

Brejon de Lavergnée, Nicolas. 1991. *Politiques d'aménagement du territoire au Maroc*. Paris: Harmattan.

Brown, Kenneth. 1977. "Changing Forms of Patronage in a Moroccan City." In Ernest Gellner and John Waterbury, eds., *Patrons and Clients in Mediterranean Societies* London: Duckworth.

Burgat, François. 1993. *The Islamic Movement in North Africa*. Trans. William Dowell. Austin: University of Texas Press.

Burke, Edmund III. 1976. *Prelude to Protectorate in Morocco: Precolonial Protest and Resistance (1860–1912)*. Chicago: University of Chicago Press.

Combs-Schilling, M. E. 1989. *Sacred Performances: Islam, Sexuality, and Sacrifice.* New York: Columbia University Press.

Damis, John. 1983. *Conflict in Northwest Africa: The Western Sahara Dispute.* Stanford, CA: Hoover Institution Press.

Eickelman, Dale. 1976. *Moroccan Islam: Tradition and Society in a Pilgrimage Center.* Austin: University of Texas Press.

———. 1985. *Knowledge and Power in Morocco: The Education of a Twentieth-Century Notable.* Princeton: Princeton University Press.

———. 1986. ''Royal Authority and Religious Legitimacy: Morocco's Elections, 1960–1984.'' In M. J. Aronoff, ed., *The Frailty of Authority.* New Brunswick, NJ: Transaction Books.

———. 1987. ''Religion in Polity and Society.'' In I. William Zartman, ed., *The Political Economy of Morocco.* New York: Praeger.

Entelis, John. 1980. *Comparative Politics of North Africa.* Syracuse: Syracuse University Press.

———. 1989. *Culture and Counterculture in Moroccan Politics.* Boulder, CO: Westview Press.

Geertz, Clifford. 1968. *Islam Observed: Religious Development in Morocco and Indonesia.* New Haven: Yale University Press.

Geertz, Clifford, Hildred Geertz, and Lawrence Rosen. 1979. *Meaning and Order in Moroccan Society: Three Essays in Cultural Analysis.* New York: Cambridge University Press.

Gellner, Ernest. 1969. *Saints of the Atlas.* Chicago: University of Chicago Press.

Gellner, Ernest, and Charles Micaud, eds. 1972. *Arabs and Berbers: From Tribe to Nation in North Africa.* Lexington, MA: Lexington Books.

Gellner, Ernest, and John Waterbury, eds. 1977. *Patrons and Clients in Mediterranean Societies.* London: Duckworth.

Hassan II, King of Morocco. 1993. *La mémoire d'un roi: Entretiens avec Eric Laurent.* Paris: Plon.

Hermassi, Elbaki. 1972. *Leadership and National Development in North Africa.* Berkeley: University of California Press.

Hodges, Tony. 1983. *Western Sahara: The Roots of a Desert War.* Westport, CT: Lawrence Hill.

Laroui, Abdallah. 1993. *Les origines sociales et culturelles du nationalisme marocain (1830–1912).* Casablanca: Centre Culturel Arabe.

Laurent, Michel. 1994. *Le Maroc de l'espoir.* Paris: SEPEG International—Editions La Porte.

Layachi, Azzedine. 1990. *The United States and North Africa: A Cognitive Approach to Foreign Policy.* New York: Praeger.

Leveau, Remy. 1985. *Le fellah marocain: Défenseur du trône.* 2d ed. Paris: Presses de la Fondation nationale des sciences politiques.

Leymarie, Serge, and Jean Tripier. 1992. *Maroc: Le prochain dragon?* Casablanca: Eddif.

Luciani, Giacomo, ed. 1990. *The Arab State.* Berkeley: University of California Press.

Maddy-Weitzman, Bruce. 1991. ''Conflict and Conflict Management in the Western Sahara: Is the Endgame Near?'' *Middle East Journal* 45, no. 4: 594–607.

Mednicoff, David M. 1994. "Morocco." In Frank Tachau, ed., *Political Parties of the Middle East and North Africa*. Westport, CT: Greenwood Press.

Moore, Clement Henry. 1970. *Politics in North Africa: Algeria, Morocco, and Tunisia*. Boston: Little, Brown.

Munson, Henry. 1993. *Religion and Power in Morocco*. New Haven: Yale University Press.

Ossman, Susan. 1994. *Picturing Casablanca: Portraits of Power in a Modern City*. Berkeley: University of California Press.

Parker, Richard. 1984. *North Africa: Regional Tensions and Strategic Concerns*. New York: Praeger.

Peretz, Martin. 1996. "Morocco Diarist: Hide and Souk." *New Republic* (April 22): 42.

Perrault, Gilles. 1991. *Notre ami le roi*. Paris: Gallimard.

Pomfret, Richard. 1987. "Morocco's International Economic Relations." In I. William Zartman, ed., *The Political Economy of Morocco*. New York: Praeger.

Rabinow, Paul. 1975. *Symbolic Domination: Cultural Form and Historical Change in Morocco*. Chicago: University of Chicago Press.

———. 1977. *Reflections on Fieldwork in Morocco*. Berkeley: University of California Press.

Saadi, Saïd, and A. Berrada. 1992. "Le capital privé marocain dominant." In Jean-Claude Santucci, ed., *Le Maroc actuel: Une modernisation au miroir de la tradition?* Paris: CNRS.

Saaf, Abdallah. 1991. *Politique et savoir au maroc*. Rabat: SMER.

Santucci, Jean-Claude, ed. 1992. *Le Maroc actuel: Une modernisation au miroir de la tradition?* Paris: CNRS.

Sluglett, Peter, and Marion Sluglett. 1984. "Modern Morocco: Political Immobilism, Economic Dependence." In Richard Lawless and Allan Findlay, eds., *North Africa*. London: Croom Helm.

Spencer, Claire. 1993. *The Maghreb in the 1990s: Political and Economic Developments in Algeria, Morocco, and Tunisia*. London: International Institute for Strategic Studies.

Suleiman, Michael W. 1987. "Attitudes, Values, and the Political Process in Morocco." In I. William Zartman, ed., *The Political Economy of Morocco*. New York: Praeger.

Sutton, Michael. 1987. *Morocco to 1992 (Growth against the Odds)*. London: Economist Intelligence Unit.

Swearingen, Will D. 1986. *Moroccan Mirages: Agrarian Dreams and Deceptions, 1912–1986*. Princeton: Princeton University Press.

———. 1987. "Morocco's Agricultural Crisis." In I. William Zartman, ed., *The Political Economy of Morocco*. New York: Praeger.

Tessler, Mark. 1982. "Morocco: Institutional Pluralism and Monarchical Dominance." In I. William Zartman, ed., *Political Elites in Arab North Africa: Morocco, Algeria, Tunisia, Libya, Egypt*. New York: Longman.

———. 1985. "The Uses and Limits of Populism: The Political Strategy of King Hassan II of Morocco." *Middle East Review* (Spring): 44–51.

———. 1987. "Image and Reality in Moroccan Political Economy." In I. William Zartman, ed., *The Political Economy of Morocco*. New York: Praeger.

———. 1990. "Israel and Morocco: The Political Calculus of a 'Moderate' Arab State." In G. Mahler, ed., *Israel after Begin*. Albany: State University of New York Press.

Tessler, Mark, John Entelis, and Gregory White. 1995. "Kingdom of Morocco." In David Long and Bernard Reich, eds., *Government and Politics of the Middle East and North Africa*. Boulder, CO: Westview Press.

Waltz, Susan. 1991. "Making Waves: The Political Impact of Human Rights Groups in North Africa." *Journal of Modern African Studies* 29: 481–504.

Waterbury, John. 1970. *The Commander of the Faithful: The Moroccan Political Elite*. New York: Columbia University Press.

White, Gregory. 1996. "The Mexico of Europe: Morocco's Pursuit of Partnership with the European Union." In Dirk Vandewalle, ed., *The New Global Economy: North African Responses*. New York: St. Martin's Press.

Young, Crawford. 1994. *The African Colonial State in Comparative Perspective*. New Haven: Yale University Press.

Zartman, I. William. 1964. *Morocco: Problems of New Power*. New York: Atherton Press.

———, ed. 1987a. *The Political Economy of Morocco*. New York: Praeger.

———. 1987b. *Ripe for Resolution: Conflict and Intervention in Africa*. 2nd ed. New York: Oxford University Press.

———. 1990. "Opposition as Support of the State." In Giacomo Luciani, ed., *The Arab State*. Berkeley: University of California Press.

Zartman, I. William, and William Mark Habeeb, eds. 1993. *Polity and Society in Contemporary North Africa*. Boulder, CO: Westview Press.

SAUDI ARABIA

David E. Long

Political science research on Saudi Arabia in the last thirty years roughly co-incides with the transformation of Saudi Arabia from a traditional desert principality into a modern oil kingdom. The transformation process was actually begun by King Abd al-Aziz (d. 1953), who created the Kingdom of Saudi Arabia in 1932, and was continued under his son, King Saud (ruled 1952–1964); but it came to fruition during the reigns of King Faysal ibn Abd al-Aziz Al Saud (ruled 1964–1975) and his successors Kings Khalid (ruled 1975–1982) and Fahd (1982—   ), all sons of Abd al-Aziz.

The last thirty years have also been a period of unprecedented contact with the West by what had previously been one of the most inaccessible and isolated countries in the world, particularly to non-Muslims. Extensive contact with the West is almost entirely attributable to oil, discovered in the 1930s but not produced in commercial quantities until after World War II. The economic and strategic importance of oil and the purchasing power of oil revenues have placed Saudi Arabia on center stage as the world's single greatest source of energy and as a major market for goods and services.

Despite the increasing economic and strategic importance of Saudi oil, the kingdom was largely ignored as an object of social science research until the energy crisis of 1973–1974 made Saudi Arabia a household word. Interest was rekindled by the Iraqi invasion of Kuwait of 1990 and Desert Storm in 1991. Thus in the past twenty years, the number of political studies of Saudi Arabia has risen from almost negligible to copious.

The quality of research has been very uneven, however. This is in great measure because of the Saudis themselves. The government has discouraged social science research, and only a handful of trained political scientists have been granted access to the country to do research (many of them through Aramco, particularly when it was still American owned). Even they, however, found Saudi society to be closed to outsiders and difficult to penetrate. Moreover, its traditional culture is highly resistant to many accepted Western statistical research techniques such as random sampling, polling, and questionnaires, making the results of such research unreliable.

The mixed quality of political research on Saudi Arabia is also in large part the result of an extraordinary penchant for negative stereotyping by Western scholars. The traditionalist, Islamic nature of Saudi society is generally both antisecularist and antidemocratic, factors that are anathema to many Western academics who tend to evaluate political systems by their degree of secularism and democratization. In addition, an uncomfortable Western dependence on Saudi oil and long-standing Saudi opposition to the creation of the State of Israel have also stimulated a tendency among some scholars to impugn the motives underlying Saudi political and petroleum policies. These difficulties have tended to leave the field of political research in the kingdom largely to journalistic and anecdotal historical treatments in the trade press. Although the descriptive narrative of many of these books is excellent, the level of analytical rigor and objectivity is often questionable.

One resource just beginning to be tapped is the growing number of doctoral dissertations in English being produced by Saudi scholars in Western universities. Even here there are pitfalls, however. Most university dissertation committees, particularly in the United States, require strict adherence to Western research methodologies that are often inappropriate for research on Saudi Arabia. For example, Saudi society is still largely tribal in nature, revolving around the extended family, and while it has upper-, middle-, and lower-income groups and even a technocratic professional class, it does not have an upper-, middle-, and lower-social-class system in the Western sense. Yet references by Saudi doctoral students to ''the new Saudi middle class'' abound. Moreover, Saudi society is so rooted in Islam that the political behavior of even the most modernized Saudis cannot be assessed by the secular standards used in most Western universities.

In sum, while there is growing scholarly attention to politics of the kingdom, and the amount of research on Saudi Arabia by Saudi students in Western universities is increasing, the gaps in understanding of Saudi political behavior are still large. Nevertheless, the quality and understanding of politics are on the rise, and with the increasing volume of studies on the kingdom, the problem of distinguishing between the good, the bad, and the excellent is ever more difficult. The works cited here are a representative sample of what is being produced.

COUNTRY STUDIES

There are few comprehensive country studies of Saudi Arabia. The Aramco Handbook series comprised excellent, though now dated, surveys. The first, *American Employees Handbook*, originally appeared in 1950 in five spiral-bound booklets. New editions appeared in 1960 and 1968. The final edition, entitled

Aramco and Its World (1980), was edited by Ismail I. Nawwab, Peter C. Spears, and Paul F. Hoye.

Many of the more recent surveys are histories rather than political analyses, and of those, most are popularly written rather than scholarly, such as Robert Lacey, *The Kingdom* (1981), and David Holden and Richard Johns, *The House of Saud* (1981). The best country handbook series on Saudi Arabia was prepared by American University for the U.S. Department of the Army. The most recent edition is Richard Nyrop, editor, *Saudi Arabia: A Country Study*, 4th edition (1984). Though comprehensive, it is nevertheless primarily a compendium of information rather than a social science research analysis. Another survey is Tim Niblock, editor, *State, Society, and Economy in Saudi Arabia* (1982). One of the best resource books in recent years is J. E. Peterson's *Historical Dictionary of Saudi Arabia* (1993). Its bibliography is particularly good and quite extensive. The analytical gap in general works on Saudi Arabia is addressed in David E. Long, *The Kingdom of Saudi Arabia*, (1997), which seeks to combine scholarly research with an informal style for readability. It introduces some seldom-studied concepts such as the traditional Arab system of consultation and consensus that underlies virtually all collective political decision making in the kingdom.

OIL POLITICS

As might be expected, there have been numerous studies of the politics of Saudi oil, many of them excellent. In general, works addressing oil economics are less emotionally charged than those discussing the politics of oil, but not always. Two articles written on the eve of the energy crisis by two highly respected oil experts provide a case in point. James E. Akins, a U.S. Foreign Service officer and an ambassador to Saudi Arabia, argued in "The Oil Crisis: This Time the Wolf Is Here" (1973) that oil was underpriced and that the price would soon rise; M. A. Adelman, an economist at MIT, presented an opposing view in "Is the Oil Shortage Real? Oil Companies as OPEC Tax Collectors," (1972–1973).

One of the better small studies on the energy crisis is Richard Chadbourn Weisberg's *The Politics of Crude Oil Pricing in the Middle East, 1970–1975* (1977). A Saudi perspective of the role of Saudi Arabia in OPEC is found in Ali D. Johany's *The Myth of the OPEC Cartel: The Role of Saudi Arabia* (1982). Another work published in the 1970s is Sheikh Rustum Ali, *Saudi Arabia and Oil Diplomacy* (1976). Some of the most comprehensive studies of Middle East oil are actually histories: George W. Stocking's *Middle East Oil: A Study in Political and Economic Controversy* (1970), Aaron David Miller's *Search for Security: Saudi Arabian Oil and American Foreign Policy, 1939–1949* (1980), David Sydney Painter's *Oil and the American Century* (1986), and Daniel Yergin's more popularly written but exhaustively researched *The Prize: The Epic Quest for Oil, Money, and Power* (1991).

POLITICAL ECONOMY

Saudi Arabia's great oil wealth has led to numerous studies of its political economy and economic development, ranging from technical to journalistic and from rigorously analytical to polemic. An example of a relatively technical study is Edmond Y. Asfour, *Saudi Arabia: Long-Term Projections of a Demand for Agricultural Products* (1965), which is particularly interesting as a baseline to evaluate the tremendous subsequent expenditures in agricultural development in a largely desert environment in the last third of a century. Ramon Knauerhase's *The Saudi Arabian Economy* (1975) was written early in the energy boom period of the 1970s. Robert E. Looney has written a number of studies on Saudi economic development, including *Saudi Arabia's Economic Development Strategy* (1980), *Saudi Arabia's Development Potential: Application of an Islamic Growth Model* (1982), and *Economic Development in Saudi Arabia* (1990).

There are also some interesting historical accounts of the development of Saudi banking institutions. One such study is a historical account of the Saudi central bank, Mohammad Said AlHaj Ali, *Saudi Arabian Monetary Agency: A Review of Its Accomplishments, 1372–1411 AH/1952–1991 AD* (1991). A more personal account is Arthur N. Young, *Saudi Arabia: The Making of a Financial Giant* (1983). Ragaei and Dorothea El Mallakh edited a comprehensive survey on Saudi development, *Saudi Arabia: Energy, Development, and Industrialization* (1982). Fouad al-Farsy's *Saudi Arabia: A Case Study in Development* (1978) and *Modernity and Tradition: The Saudi Equation* (1990) also survey Saudi economic development. The impact of development on society and politics is the subject of John A. Shaw and David E. Long, *Saudi Arabian Modernization: The Impact of Change on Stability* (1982). On the polemic side is Eliyahu Kanovsky, *The Economy of Saudi Arabia: Troubled Present, Grim Future* (1994), which explores real problems but with unwarranted animosity and sensationalism.

POLITICAL DYNAMICS

Saudi Arabia's closed society and secretive style of governance has made the study of its political dynamics particularly difficult. An early monograph seeking to explore Saudi political dynamics was David E. Long, *Saudi Arabia* (1976). A well-written survey looking back at the reign of King Faisal is Willard A. Beling, editor, *King Faisal and the Modernisation of Saudi Arabia* (1980).

Mordechai Abir has written extensively on Middle East oil and Saudi politics, focusing on crises. His works include *Oil Power and Politics: Conflict in Arabia, the Persian Gulf, and the Red Sea* (1974), *Saudi Arabia in the Oil Era: Regime and Elites—Conflict and Collaboration* (1988), and *Saudi Arabia: Government, Society, and the Gulf Crisis* (1993). Well researched, but lacking the same insight, is Mark Heller and Nadav Safran, *The New Middle Class and Regime Stability in Saudi Arabia* (1985). An interesting study on Saudi government is

Summer Scott Huyette, *Political Adaptation in Sa'udi Arabia: A Study of the Council of Ministers* (1985).

One area of Saudi political dynamics that has fascinated Western scholars for years is the role of the royal family, probably because so little is known about it. Long's *Saudi Arabia* (1976) presents some material on the royal family. A more comprehensive volume is Bryan Lees, *A Handbook of the Al Sa'ud Ruling Family of Sa'udi Arabia* (1980). Much of the curiosity about the family centers on royal succession, and every decade or so, someone writes a book about the implications of the succession on stability. The problems of succession usually raised in these books, however, are usually greatly overstated. Alexander Bligh wrote such a book, *From Prince to King: Royal Succession in the House of Saud in the Twentieth Century* (1984). Ten years later, Simon Henderson wrote *After King Fahd: Succession in Saudi Arabia* (1994).

As the field of women's studies has grown, particularly in the United States, a number of works on women in Saudi Arabia have appeared. Some of them are frankly sensationalist, full of anecdotal material claiming to portray a thoroughly downtrodden gender. There are also some serious scholarly studies, however. Three representative published works (there are many more in dissertation form) are Soraya Altorki, *Women in Saudi Arabia: Ideology and Behavior among the Elite* (1986), and Eleanor A. Duomoto's "Women and the Stability of Saudi Arabia" (1991) and "Gender, Monarchy, and National Identity in Saudi Arabia" (1992).

RELIGION

The role of religion in Saudi Arabia is as great as or greater than in nearly any other country on earth. The kingdom is the cradle of Islam and the site of Islam's two holiest sites, Mecca and Medina, to which millions make the Hajj, or Great Pilgrimage, each year. The Sharia, or Islamic law, comprises the Saudi constitution, and the 250-year-old Islamic revival movement known as Wahhabism (adherents prefer to be called Unitarians, not Wahhabis, and their doctrine, Tawhid rather than Wahhabism, connoting strict monotheism) serves as the state's political ideology.

Despite the centrality of Islam in Saudi society, culture, politics, and even economics, relatively little scholarly research has been conducted on the role of Islam in the Saudi state. The origins and nature of the Hanbali school of Sunni Islam, which most Saudis practice, are well known to Islamic scholars in the discipline of comparative religion, as are the intellectual bases of the Wahhabi revival. Western political science research, however, has generally taken a position (usually negative) on the impact of Islam on Saudi Arabia without thoroughly inquiring into the unique role Islam plays in the kingdom. There are some notable exceptions. John L. Esposito has written extensively on Islam in contemporary Middle East politics, including *Islam: The Straight Path* (1988) and *Voices of Resurgent Islam* (1983). He also edited *Islam and Development:*

Religion and Sociopolitical Change (1980), to which James Piscatori contributed a chapter, ''The Roles of Islam in Saudi Political Development.'' Joseph A. Kechichian has written ''Islamic Revivalism and Change in Saudi Arabia: Juhayman al-'Utaybi's 'Letters' to the Saudi People'' (1979), about the man who led a brief uprising in the Haram Mosque in Makkah, and ''The Role of the Ulama in the Politics of an Islamic State: The Case Study of Saudi Arabia'' (1990). One of the few broader studies of religion and politics in the kingdom is Ayman al-Yassini, *Religion and State in the Kingdom of Saudi Arabia* (1985).

Although there are many works on the historical and religious aspects of the Hajj, there is very little on the contemporary pilgrimage. Probably the most comprehensive in English is David E. Long's *The Hajj Today: A Survey of the Contemporary Pilgrimage to Makkah* (1979). Other books on the contemporary hajj in English include Ziauddin Sardar and M. A. Badawi, editors, *Hajj Studies* (1981), and Ghazy Abdul Wahed Makky, *Mecca, The Pilgrim City: A Study of Pilgrim Accommodation* (1978).

NATIONAL SECURITY AND FOREIGN POLICY

Because Saudi oil reserves are so crucial to the economic health of the world, Western scholars have long been intensely interested in national security issues relating to the kingdom. Some, of course, have been more concerned with as well as anxious about how Saudi Arabia affects the national security of their own countries, but for the same reasons, Saudi national security itself has been a frequent topic of study, particularly since the energy-crisis years of the 1970s made Saudi Arabia a household word in the West.

One of the most prolific scholars in the field is Anthony H. Cordesman, whose works are invaluable in looking at the military dimension. They include *The Gulf and the Search for Strategic Stability: Saudi Arabia, the Military Balance in the Gulf, and Trends in the Arab-Israeli Military Balance* (1984) and *The Gulf and the West* (1988). Cordesman's latest book is a political and national security assessment of the kingdom, *Saudi Arabia: Guarding the Desert Kingdom* (1997). It has a broader focus than just military affairs, also looking at political, economic, and demographic factors affecting security. An extremely well researched, if somewhat formalistic, treatment of the political-military dimension is found in Nadav Safran, *Saudi Arabia: The Ceaseless Quest for Security* (1985). For a different point of view, see Adeed I. Dawisha, *Saudi Arabia's Search for Security* (1979–1980).

Saudi foreign policy has generally been treated in a similar fashion to national security policy. There is universal acknowledgment of a close diplomatic as well as security relationship between the kingdom and the United States and the West, and much has been written on which party or parties have gotten the better part of the bargain. Many of these sentiments have been expressed in works already cited on oil, economics, politics, and national security. A survey of U.S.-Saudi relations in all these areas is David E. Long, *The United States and Saudi Arabia: Ambivalent Allies* (1985). The book, though short, is authoritative to the degree that the author had access to U.S. State Department archives. The earlier period of U.S.-Saudi relations is covered in Rex J. Cassilas, *Oil and Diplomacy: The Evolution of American Foreign Policy in Saudi Arabia, 1933–1945* (1988). A topical and therefore dated but well-designed book looking at Saudi foreign policy itself is William B. Quandt, *Saudi Arabia in the 1980s: Foreign Policy, Security, and Oil* (1981). Regional foreign policy studies include F. Gregory Gause III, *Saudi-Yemeni Relations: Domestic Structures and Foreign Influence* (1990), and Saeed M. Badeeb's two studies, *The Saudi-Egyptian Conflict over North Yemen, 1962–1970* (1986) and *Saudi-Iranian Relations, 1932–1982* (1993).

REFERENCES

Abir, Mordechai. 1974. *Oil Power and Politics: Conflict in Arabia, the Persian Gulf, and the Red Sea.* London: Frank Cass.

———. 1988. *Saudi Arabia in the Oil Era: Regime and Elites—Conflict and Collaboration.* Boulder, CO: Westview Press.

———. 1993. *Saudi Arabia: Government, Society, and the Gulf Crisis.* London: Routledge.

Adelman, M. A. 1972–1973. "Is the Oil Shortage Real? Oil Companies as OPEC Tax Collectors." *Foreign Policy* 9 (Winter): 69–107.

Akins, James E. 1973. "The Oil Crisis: This Time the Wolf Is Here," *Foreign Affairs* 51, no. 3: 462–490.

Ali, Mohammad Said AlHaj. 1991. *Saudi Arabian Monetary Agency: A Review of Its Accomplishments, 1372–1411 AH/1952–1991 AD.* Riyadh: Saudi Arabian Ministry of Information.

Ali, Sheikh Rustum. 1976. *Saudi Arabia and Oil Diplomacy.* New York: Praeger.

Altorki, Soraya. 1986. *Women in Saudi Arabia: Ideology and Behavior among the Elite.* New York: Columbia University Press.

Asfour, Edmond Y. 1965. *Saudi Arabia: Long-Term Projections of Supply and Demand for Agricultural Products.* Beirut: Economic Research Institute, American University of Beirut.

Badeeb, Saeed M. 1986. *The Saudi-Egyptian Conflict over North Yemen, 1962–1970.* Boulder, CO: Westview Press.

———. 1993. *Saudi-Iranian Relations, 1932–1982.* London: Centre for Arab and Iranian Studies, and Echoes.

Beling, Willard A., ed. 1980. *King Faisal and the Modernisation of Saudi Arabia.* London: Croom Helm; Boulder, CO: Westview Press.

Bligh, Alexander. 1984. *From Prince to King: Royal Succession in the House of Saud in the Twentieth Century.* New York: New York University Press.

Cassilas, Rex J. 1988. *Oil and Diplomacy: The Evolution of American Foreign Policy in Saudi Arabia, 1933–1945.* New York: Garland.

Cordesman, Anthony. 1984. *The Gulf and the Search for Strategic Stability: Saudi Arabia, the Military Balance in the Gulf, and Trends in the Arab-Israeli Military Balance.* Boulder, CO: Westview Press; London: Mansell.

————. 1988. *The Gulf and the West*. Boulder, CO: Westview Press.

————. 1997. *Saudi Arabia: Guarding the Desert Kingdom*. CSIS Middle East Dynamic Net Assessment. Boulder, CO: Westview Press.

Dawisha, Adeed I. 1979–1980. *Saudi Arabia's Search for Security*. Adelphi Paper no. 158. London: International Institute for Strategic Studies.

De Gaury, Gerald. 1967. *Faysal: King of Saudi Arabia*. New York: Praeger.

Duomoto, Eleanor A. 1991. ''Women and the Stability of Saudi Arabia.'' *MERIP Middle East Report* 27, no. 4:34–37.

————. 1992. ''Gender, Monarchy, and National Identity in Saudi Arabia.'' *British Journal of Middle Eastern Studies* 19, no. 1:31–47.

Esposito, John L., ed. 1980. *Islam and Development: Religion and Sociopolitical Change*. Syracuse: Syracuse University Press.

————, ed. 1983. *Voices of Resurgent Islam*. New York: Oxford University Press.

————. 1988. *Islam: The Straight Path*. New York: Oxford University Press.

Al-Farsy, Fouad. 1978. *Saudi Arabia: A Case Study in Development*. London: Stacey International.

————. 1990. *Modernity and Tradition: The Saudi Equation*. London: Kegan Paul International.

Gause, F. Gregory, III. 1990. *Saudi-Yemeni Relations: Domestic Structures and Foreign Influence*. New York: Columbia University Press.

Habib, John S. 1978. *Ibn Saud's Warriors of Islam: The Ikhwan and Their Role in the Creation of the Sa'udi Kingdom, 1910–1930*. Leiden: E. J. Brill.

Hamza, Fuad. 1968. *Al-Bilad al-'Arabiyya al-Su'udiyya* (The country of Saudi Arabia). Riyadh: Maktabah al-Nasr al-Haditha.

Heller, Mark, and Nadav Safran. 1985. *The New Middle Class and Regime Stability in Saudi Arabia*. Harvard Middle East Papers, Modern Series, no. 3. Cambridge, MA: Harvard Center for Middle Eastern Studies.

Helms, Christine Moss. 1981. *The Cohesion of Saudi Arabia*. London: Croom Helm; Baltimore: Johns Hopkins University Press.

Henderson, Simon. 1994. *After King Fahd: Succession in Saudi Arabia*. Washington Institute Policy Papers, no. 37. Washington, DC: Washington Institute for Near East Policy.

Holden, David. 1966. *Farewell to Arabia*. London: Faber.

Holden, David, and Richard Johns. 1981. *The House of Saud*. London: Sidgwick and Jackson.

Howarth, David. 1964. *The Desert King: Ibn Saud and His Arabia*. New York: McGraw-Hill.

Huyette, Summer Scott. 1985. *Political Adaptation in Sa'udi Arabia*. Boulder, CO: Westview Press.

Ibn Taymiyyah, Taqi al-Din Ahmad. 1966. *Al-Siyasa al-Shari'iyyah* (Islamic politics). Beirut: Dar al-Kutub al-'Arabiyyah.

Johany, Ali D. 1982. *The Myth of the OPEC Cartel: The Role of Saudi Arabia*. New York: John Wiley.

Kanovsky, Eliyahu, 1994. *The Economy of Saudi Arabia: Troubled Present, Grim Future*. Washington Institute Policy Papers, no. 38. Washington, DC: Washington Institute for Near East Policy.

Kechichian, Joseph A. 1979. ''Islamic Revivalism and Change in Saudi Arabia: Juhayman al-'Utaybi's 'Letters' to the Saudi People.'' *Muslim World* 80, no. 1:1–16.

————. 1990. "The Role of the Ulama in the Politics of an Islamic State: The Case Study of Saudi Arabia." *International Journal of Middle East Studies* 18, no. 1: 53–71.

Knauerhase, Ramon. 1975. *The Saudi Arabian Economy.* New York: Praeger.

Kostiner, Joseph. 1994. *The Making of Saudi Arabia, 1916–1936: From Chieftaincy to Monarchical State.* New York: Oxford University Press.

Lacey, Robert. 1981. *The Kingdom.* London: Hutchinson.

Lees, Bryan. 1980. *A Handbook of the Al Sa'ud Ruling Family of Sa'udi Arabia.* London: Royal Genealogies.

Long, David E. 1976. *Saudi Arabia.* The Washington Papers 4, no. 39. Beverly Hills, CA: Sage Publications.

————. 1979. *The Hajj Today: A Survey of the Contemporary Pilgrimage to Makkah.* Albany: State University of New York Press.

————. 1985. *The United States and Saudi Arabia: Ambivalent Allies.* Boulder, CO: Westview Press.

————. 1997. *The Kingdom of Saudi Arabia.* Gainesville: University Press of Florida.

Looney, Robert E. 1980. *Saudi Arabia's Economic Development Strategy.* Oslo: Norwegian Institute of International Affairs.

————. 1982. *Saudi Arabia's Development Potential: Application of an Islamic Growth Model.* Lexington, MA: Lexington Books.

————. 1990. *Economic Development in Saudi Arabia.* Greenwich, CT: JAI Press.

El Mallakh, Ragaei, Dorothea H. El Mallakh, eds. 1982. *Saudi Arabia: Developmental Planning and Industrialization.* Lexington, MA: Lexington Books.

Makky, Ghazy Abdul Wahed. 1978. *Mecca, The Pilgrim City: A Study of Pilgrim Accommodation.* Hajj Research Centre Studies. London: Croom Helm.

Miller, Aaron David. 1980. *Search for Security: Saudi Arabian Oil and American Foreign Policy, 1939–1949.* Chapel Hill: University of North Carolina Press.

Nawwab, Ismail I., Peter C. Spears, and Paul F. Hoye. 1980. *Aramco and Its World.* Dhahran, Saudi Arabia: Aramco.

Niblock, Tim ed., 1982. *State, Society, and Economy in Saudi Arabia.* London: Croom Helm, for the University of Exeter Centre for Arab Gulf Studies.

Nyrop, Richard F., ed. 1984. *Saudi Arabia: A Country Study.* 4th ed. Washington, DC: U. S. Government Printing Office.

Painter, David S. 1986. *Oil and the American Century.* Baltimore: Johns Hopkins University Press.

Peterson, J. E. 1993. *Historical Dictionary of Saudi Arabia.* Asian History Dictionaries, no. 14. Metuchen, NJ: Scarecrow Press.

Quandt, William B. 1981. *Saudi Arabia in the 1980s: Foreign Policy, Security, and Oil.* Washington, DC: Brookings Institution.

Safran, Nadav. 1985. *Saudi Arabia: The Ceaseless Quest for Security.* Cambridge, MA: Belknap Press of Harvard University Press.

Sardar, Ziauddin, and M. A. Badawi, eds. 1981. *Hajj Studies.* Hajj Research Centre Study, King Abdul Aziz University. London: Croom Helm.

Shaw, John A., and David E. Long. 1982. *Saudi Arabian Modernization: The Impact of Change on Stability.* The Washington Papers, no. 89. New York: Praeger.

Stocking, George W. 1970. *Middle East Oil: A Study in Political and Economic Controversy.* Nashville, TN: Vanderbilt University Press.

Twitchell, Karl S. 1958. *Saudi Arabia: With an Account of the Development of Its Natural Resources*. Princeton: Princeton University Press.

Weisberg, Richard Chadbourn. 1977. *The Politics of Crude Oil Pricing in the Middle East, 1970–1975: A Study in International Bargaining*. Research Series no. 31. Berkeley: Institute of International Studies, University of California.

al-Yassini, Ayman. 1985. *Religion and State in the Kingdom of Saudi Arabia*. Boulder, CO: Westview Press.

Yergin, Daniel. 1991. *The Prize: The Epic Quest for Oil, Money, and Power*. New York: Simon and Schuster.

Young, Arthur N. 1983. *Saudi Arabia: The Making of a Financial Giant*. New York: New York University Press.

SYRIA

Marius Deeb

The June War of 1967 was a watershed of paramount importance in the Middle East, especially with respect to countries bordering Israel like Syria and Lebanon. Syria has had a turbulent history since 1949, when the first military coup d'état occurred. When the 1967 war broke out, the Syrian neo-Baathist regime that came to power by ousting the old guard Baathists in February 1966 had contributed significantly to an escalating series of events that precipitated the 1967 war. Hafez Asad was the minister of defense in June 1967 and was one of the two leaders (the other being Salah Jadid) who controlled Syria. In November 1970 Asad became the undisputed leader of Syria by staging a coup, predictably called "the Corrective Movement" (*Al-Harakah al-Tashihiya*) against Salah Jadid and his mostly civilian followers. Since then the key to understanding Syrian domestic politics and foreign policy has been to unravel the intentions, objectives, and modus operandi of the Syrian president, Hafez Asad.

Scholarly works on Syria since World War II and prior to the 1967 war are not numerous. Albert Hourani's work *Syria and Lebanon: A Political Essay* (1946) is an excellent study of the mandate period in terms of both political developments and the impact of Westernization. On the political economy of Syria, there is the report of the mission organized by the World Bank published as *The Economic Development of Syria* (1955). To the same period belongs Patrick Seale's *The Struggle for Syria: A Study of Post-war Arab Politics, 1945–1958*, originally published in 1965, with a new edition in 1986. This book is a classic based on a large number of primary sources, mostly in Arabic. The politics of that period was so ideological or seemingly so that there is no single mention in the whole book of the Alawi community that dominates Syria now. Andrew Rathmell's *Secret War in the Middle East: The Covert Struggle for Syria, 1949–1961* (1995) appears to be more interested in the cloak-and-dagger dimension of the struggle for Syria. Despite the impressive British and American archival sources that were consulted, the author comes out with trite conclusions such as that the role of the CIA was insignificant with respect to Husni al-Zaim's coup of 1949.

Works on Syria since the 1967 war can be divided into four categories. First is the category of general books that serve as an introduction to Syria but are still insightful. To this category belongs Tabitha Petran's *Syria* (1972), which is an informative general survey of Syrian society and politics. It is based on a good number of primary sources in Arabic as well as some interviews with former Syrian politicians. Derek Hopwood's *Syria, 1945–1986* (1988) is another perceptive general survey written by a leading Arabist historian. John Devlin's *Syria: Modern State in an Ancient Land* (1983) is a general and useful study by an intelligence analyst who had previously written a solid book on the Baath party, *The Ba'th Party: A History from Its Origins to 1966* (1976). Martha Neff Kessler, a U.S. government intelligence officer, wrote a succinct and precise overview of Syria covering both domestic and regional politics entitled *Syria: Fragile Mosaic of Power* (1987). Itamar Rabinovich has also written a classic on the Baath and the military, entitled *Syria under the Ba'th, 1963–66* (1972), which was based on primary documentary sources captured by the Israelis in the 1967 war.

ASAD AND THE MILITARY

The second category is that of Asad and the Syrian military. Nikolaos Van Dam's *The Struggle for Power in Syria: Sectarianism, Regionalism, and Trib- alism, 1961–1980* (1981) is one of the earliest studies in this category. It is basically a study of the religious and regional background of the various military officers who rose to prominence at different phases of the rule of the military, culminating in the dominance of the Alawis since 1966. Van Dam utilizes a variety of primary sources in Arabic, including periodicals and memoirs. In the latest edition of this book, Van Dam changed the title to *The Struggle for Power in Syria: Politics and Society under Asad and the Ba'th Party* (1996) and up- dated it to include the grooming as a successor of Asad's second son Bashshar after the death of Asad's eldest son Basil in a car accident in January 1994. Hanna Batatu's seminal article in the *Middle East Journal*, published in 1981, is entitled "Some Observations on the Social Roots of Syria's Ruling Military Group and the Causes for Its Dominance." Batatu based his article on a large number of primary sources and interviews documenting how Hafez Asad's Alawi faction became willy-nilly the absolute rulers of Syria. Batatu emphasized in his article that all real political power in Syria is derived from Asad himself. Batatu's work on Syria culminates in his book *Syria's Peasantry: Descendants of Its Lesser Rural Notables and Their Politics* (to be published in 1998), in which he traces the revolutionary changes that took place in rural Syria with a lengthy analysis of the Hafez Asad regime.

Two major works on Asad are those of Patrick Seale and Moshe Maoz. Seale's book, *Asad of Syria: The Struggle for the Middle East* (1988), is a treasure of information gathered from his interviews with Syrians and his pro- found knowledge of Syrian politics. Seale's book is essential for understanding the nature of the state under Asad, which has been imposed on Syrian society rather than derived from it. Maoz in his book entitled *Asad: The Sphinx of Damascus* (1988) shows an excellent understanding of Syrian history and the complex relationships between the Sunni majority and the various minorities. In *Syria under Asad* (1986), edited by Moshe Maoz and Avner Yaniv, articles by Moshe Maoz and Zeev Maoz deal respectively with the historical process of state formation and state power. Another study that sheds light on how the Asad regime functions is the report published by Middle East Watch in November 1990, *Human Rights in Syria* (1990). This report documents how the Asad regime routinely arrests, for political reasons, citizens without charge, tortures them, and imprisons them without trial.

POLITICAL ECONOMY

The third category of works deals with either the political economy of Syria or with domestic institutions such as the Baath party itself and other Baath-controlled organizations as well as leading opposition groups and parties. The works of Raymond A. Hinnebusch belong to this genre, in particular his *Authoritarian Power and State Formation in Ba'thist Syria: Army, Party, and Peasant* (1990). The basic thrust of this book is that the Asad regime is rooted in rural grievances, and consequently one can see the land reform under the Baath, as well as the expansion of education and social services in the country-side, as an attempt by Asad to provide patronage to the Baath's rural constituency, thus enabling Asad to stay in power. Hinnebusch is right (like Batatu) in pointing out that the social origins of those in power in Syria are rural and that the Asad regime has favored the countryside in its policies. Hinnebusch is off the mark when he tries to link the longevity of the Asad regime to these policies. Asad has been able to stay in power because he has crushed ruthlessly all those who have tried to oppose him, using his Alawi cronies who command the Syrian military and the intelligence agencies (*Mukhabarat*), thus enabling him to control the country. Asad has failed since the mid-1970s to become popular, let alone acquire legitimacy. Another subject that constitutes an essential ingredient of the Asad regime is corruption, which has been studied in a seminal article by Yahya Sadowski entitled "Patronage and the Ba'th: Corruption and Control in Contemporary Syria" (1987).

Among the works on political economy, one can mention *Contemporary Syria: Liberalization between Cold War and Cold Peace* (1994), edited by Eberhard Kienle, which is a collection of papers, the most interesting of which deal with the private sector, the economic crisis of 1986, the Syrian business community, and the various phases of economic liberalization from the 1970s until the 1990s. Volker Perthes in his *The Political Economy of Syria under Asad* (1995) is an example of how difficult it is to understand a *Mukhabarat* Alawi regime, that is, the intelligence-services–controlled sectarian regime like that of Asad in Syria, even when or perhaps because the researcher has lived in the country. Perthes is taken in by the propaganda of the Asad regime when he contends that Asad's popularity is quite broad, or that the importance of sectarianism and the political influence of the military are both declining. A more recent publication, *Why Syria Goes To War: Thirty Years of Confrontation* (1996), by Fred H. Lawson, which tries to connect the Syrian political economy and whether there are domestic economic crises or not with Asad's willingness or unwillingness to intervene militarily in regional conflicts, is basically flawed. The lack of legitimacy and the Alawi-minority base of the Asad regime shed greater light on Asad's actions or inactions in the region than the author's quasi-Marxist deterministic thesis of the link between political economy and specific foreign policies.

Books and articles on the political opposition in Syria are not numerous. Two outstanding articles on the Syrian opposition appeared in the same issue of *MERIP (Middle East Research and Information Project) Reports* (November–December 1982) Hanna Batatu's "Syria's Muslim Brethren" and Gerard Michaud's "The Importance of Bodyguards." Batatu's article traces the origins of the Muslim Brethren movement, its ideology and program, and its opposition to the Baath regime particularly in its last manifestation, namely, the Asad Alawi regime. Gerard Michaud is the pseudonym of Michel Seurat, and his article brilliantly dissects the Asad regime whether in its corruption, its sectarianism, or the numerous private bodyguards who protect the Alawi cronies of the Asad regime. Seurat eventually paid with his life for his scholarly work on Syria. He was kidnapped in Lebanon and eventually murdered by Syrian intelligence officers in 1985. Seurat's masterpiece, which was published posthumously in French, entitled *L'état de barbarie* (1989), focuses on Syria's domestic politics with an emphasis on the nature of the Asad regime and the Islamic opposition. This book could be regarded as the best study on Syria ever written in any language. *The Islamic Struggle in Syria* (1983), by Umar F. Abd-Allah, examines the Islamic opposition in Syria with a somewhat clear bias against the Asad regime. This study tends to be more objective when the author deals with the detailed history of the Syrian Muslim Brethren than in the analysis of the political program of the Muslim Brethren in 1980, which is reproduced in full in the appendix of the book.

FOREIGN POLICY

The fourth category focuses on studies of Syrian foreign policy and the military intervention in Lebanon since 1976. The mystery that shrouds the foreign policies of Syrian president Asad toward his neighbors, the Arab-Israeli conflict, and the West continues despite the attempts by scholars to unravel it. *Syria and the Lebanese Crisis* (1980), by Adeed Dawisha, examines the decision-making process by the Syrian officials at various levels leading to Syrian military intervention in Lebanon in 1976. Naomi Weinberger's *Syrian Intervention in Lebanon: The 1975–76 Civil War* (1986) is a study of a similar genre with a variety of primary and secondary sources as well as interviews with Syrian officials. Both Dawisha and Weinberger regard the Syrian intervention in Lebanon as a bottomless pit or a quagmire, a thesis that is moot at best. These studies are very much in the same vein as Seale's chapter on Lebanon in his *Asad of Syria: The Struggle for the Middle East*, revealingly called "The Lebanese Trap." The theory that Asad's military intervention in Lebanon since 1976 has been a quagmire, a bottomless pit, or a trap has been refuted by Marius Deeb in "The External Dimension of the Conflict in Lebanon: The Role of Syria" (1989). The article deals with Asad's modus operandi as well as his ultimate objectives in Lebanon, thus enabling us to predict Asad's future behavior in Lebanon and the region. Another article that sheds light on the Syrian military intervention in Lebanon is Marius Deeb's "Lebanon in the Aftermath of the Abrogation of the Israeli-Lebanese Accord: The Dominant Role of Syria," in *The Middle East from the Iran-Contra Affair to the Intifada* (1991), edited by Robert O. Freedman. The author explains the Syrian role in the conflicts that engulfed Lebanon between 1984 and 1990.

Writings on the Syrian role in the Arab-Israeli conflict have been numerous. Helena Cobban's *The Superpowers and the Syrian-Israeli Conflict: Beyond Crisis Management?* (1991b) is an example of how a journalist who managed to interview a large number of Syrian, Israeli, Soviet, and American officials was still unable to come up with any original analysis and only rehashed what other writers have already said about the subject. Cobban, like many others, has accepted fully the Syrian doctrine of "strategic parity" with Israel that Asad invented in the wake of Sadat's visit to Jerusalem, with the purpose, inter alia, of undermining the peace process by postponing it until the envisaged parity is achieved. Another illustration of writers, in this case scholars, who have tried unsuccessfully to unravel the enigma of Asad's policy toward the Arab-Israeli conflict is the study by Alasdair Drysdale and Raymond Hinnebusch, *Syria and the Middle East Peace Process* (1991). The major thrust of the book is that Syria is moving slowly toward peace, and that Asad can sign a peace treaty and honor it, especially after the Gulf War and the demise of the Soviet Union. Needless to say, nothing of the sort has taken place since the publication of the book in 1991. Moshe Maoz's more recent study *Syria and Israel: From War to Peacemaking* (1995) is very well documented, as the author has tapped a variety of archival material and primary sources. The historical part of the study is excellent, while the contemporary analysis suffers from a basic misunderstanding of Asad's motives and goals, which gives the author's optimistic prospect for peace between Syria and Israel an unrealistic character.

FUTURE RESEARCH

Syria in the pre–1967 war period is still a virgin land in terms of research done despite the works of Hourani and Seale. There is no work in English covering the period of the United Arab Republic when Syria merged with Egypt, that is, from February 1958 to September 1961. This is equally true of the fascinating period of the Separation (*Al-Infisal*), that is, from September 1961 to March 1963. There is some good work on the period of Baath rule leading to the undisputed leadership of Hafez Asad, especially the work of Batatu.

On the whole, Syria under Hafez Asad has not been thoroughly researched (except for the works of Batatu, Seale, and Seurat) as have other countries of the Middle East, primarily because of the secretive nature of the Alawi regime and the *Mukhabarat* state that has been imposed on a relatively open political and social system. It is reasonable to maintain that Syria has not been studied, especially in the field of foreign policy. Save for some exceptional articles on the role of Syria in Lebanon by Deeb, the enigma that surrounds President Asad and the sphinx nature of his character remain the order of the day. The paucity of analysis and the lack of major scholarly works on foreign policy have contributed in considerable measure to the failure of the U.S. policy toward Syria since the late 1970s. Other fields of potential research are the study of the Syrian military, the political role of the Alawi community (a taboo subject in Asad's Syria), the role of the old notable families of the major urban cities, and the political role and social status of the Druze community. Concerning the military, a major research project could be how the Asad regime recruits its officer corps. How does Asad control the military, rendering Syria a coup-proof regime? Except for a few outstanding articles, the subject of corruption in the government and in the civil society as a whole has not been studied, especially as a means of providing favors and controlling both the ruling elite and the populace. Political economy studies have to become more rigorous as well as more relevant by studying the specificity of the Syrian case.

REFERENCES

Abd-Allah, Umar F. 1983. *The Islamic Struggle in Syria*. Berkeley, CA: Mizan Press.

Antoun, Richard T., and Donald Quataert, eds., 1991. *Syria: Society, Culture, and Polity*. Albany: State University of New York Press.

Batatu, Hanna. 1981. ''Some Observations on the Social Roots of Syria's Ruling Military Group and the Causes for Its Dominance.'' *Middle East Journal* 35, no. 3 (Summer).

———. 1982. ''Syria's Muslim Brethren.'' *Middle East Research and Information Project (MERIP) Reports*, no. 110, vol. 12, no. 9 (November–December): 12–20.

———. Forthcoming. *Syria's Peasantry: Descendants of Its Lesser Rural Notables and Their Politics*. Princeton: Princeton University Press.

Cobban, Helena. 1991a. ''The Nature of the Soviet-Syrian Link under Asad and Gorbachev.'' In Richard T. Antoun and Donald Quataert, eds., *Syria: Society, Culture, and Polity*. Albany: State University of New York Press.

———. 1991b. *The Superpowers and the Syrian-Israeli Conflict: Beyond Crisis Management?* New York: Praeger; Washington, DC: Center for Strategic and International Studies.

Dawisha, Adeed. 1980. *Syria and the Lebanese Crisis*. New York: St. Martin's Press.

Deeb, Marius. 1989. "The External Dimension of the Conflict in Lebanon: The Role of Syria." *Journal of South Asian and Middle Eastern Studies* 12, no. 3 (Spring): 37–51.

———. 1991. "Lebanon in the Aftermath of the Abrogation of the Israeli-Lebanese Accord: The Dominant Role of Syria." In Robert O. Freedman, ed., *The Middle East from the Iran-Contra Affair to the Intifada*. Syracuse: Syracuse University Press.

Devlin, John F. 1976. *The Ba'th Party: A History from Its Origins to 1966*. Stanford, CA: Hoover Institution Press.

———. 1983. *Syria: Modern State in an Ancient Land*. Boulder, CO: Westview Press.

Drysdale, Alasdair. 1981. "The Syrian Political Elite, 1966–1976: A Spatial and Social Analysis." *Middle Eastern Studies* 17, no. 1:3–30.

———. 1982. "The Asad Regime and Its Troubles." *Middle East Research and Information Project (MERIP) Reports*, no. 110, vol. 12, no. 9 (November–December): 3–11.

———. 1985. "The Succession Question in Syria." *Middle East Journal* 39, no. 2 (Spring): 246–257.

Drysdale, Alasdair, and Raymond A. Hinnebusch. 1991. *Syria and the Middle East Peace Process*. New York: Council on Foreign Relations Press.

Faksh, Mahmud A. 1984. "The Alawi Community of Syria: A New Dominant Political Force." *Middle Eastern Studies* 20, no. 2:133–153.

Hinnebusch, Raymond A. 1989. *Peasant and Bureaucracy in Ba'thist Syria: The Political Economy of Rural Development*. Boulder, CO: Westview Press.

———. 1990. *Authoritarian Power and State Formation in Ba'thist Syria: Army, Party, and Peasant*. Boulder, CO: Westview Press.

———. 1993. "State and Civil Society in Syria." *Middle East Journal* 47, no. 2 (Spring): 243–257.

Hopwood, Derek. 1988. *Syria, 1945–1986: Politics and Society*. London: Unwin Hyman.

Hourani, Albert H. 1946. *Syria and Lebanon: A Political Essay*. London: Oxford University Press.

Kerr, Malcolm H. 1971. *The Arab Cold War: Gamal 'Abd Al-Nasir and His Rivals, 1958–1970*. London: Oxford University Press.

———. 1973. "Hafiz Asad and the Changing Patterns of Syrian Politics." *International Journal* 28, no. 4 (Autumn): 689–706.

Kessler, Martha Neff. 1987. *Syria: Fragile Mosaic of Power*. Washington, DC: National Defense University Press.

Khuri, Fuad I. 1991. "The Alawis of Syria: Religious Ideology and Organization." In Richard T. Antoun and Donald Quataert, eds., *Syria: Society, Culture, and Polity*. Albany: State University of New York Press.

Kienle, Eberhard, ed. 1994. *Contemporary Syria: Liberalization between Cold War and Cold Peace*. London: British Academic Press.

Lawson, Fred H. 1996. *Why Syria Goes to War: Thirty Years of Confrontation*. Ithaca: Cornell University Press.

Maoz, Moshe. 1988. *Asad: The Sphinx of Damascus*. London: Weidenfeld and Nicolson.

———. 1995. *Syria and Israel: From War to Peacemaking*. Oxford: Oxford University Press.

Maoz, Moshe, and Avner Yaniv, eds. 1986. *Syria under Assad: Domestic Constraints and Regional Risks*. New York: St. Martin's Press.

Middle East Watch. 1990. *Human Rights in Syria: A Middle East Watch Report.* New
    York: Human Rights Watch.

Perthes, Volker. 1995. *The Political Economy of Syria under Asad.* London: I. B. Tauris.

Petran, Tabitha. 1972. *Syria.* New York: Praeger.

Rabinovich, Itamar. 1972. *Syria under the Ba'th, 1963–66.* Jerusalem: Israel Universities
    Press.

Rathmell, Andrew. 1995. *Secret War in the Middle East: The Covert Struggle for Syria,
    1949–1961.* London: I. B. Tauris.

Sadowski, Yahya M. 1985. ''Cadres, Guns, and Money: The Eighth Regional Congress
    of the Syrian Ba'th.'' *Middle East Research and Information Project (MERIP)
    Reports*, no. 134, vol. 15, no. 6 (July–August): 3–8.

———. 1987. ''Patronage and the Ba'th: Corruption and Control in Contemporary Syr-
    ia.'' *Arab Studies Quarterly* 9, no. 4:442–461.

Seale, Patrick. 1986. *The Struggle for Syria : A Study of Post-war Arab Politics, 1945–
    1958.* New Haven: Yale University Press.

———. 1988. *Asad of Syria : The Struggle for the Middle East.* London: I. B. Tauris.

Seurat, Michel (pseudonym, Gerard Michaud). 1982. ''The Importance of Bodyguards.''
    Middle East Research and Information Project (MERIP) Reports, no. 110, vol.
    12, no. 9 (November–December): 29–31.

———. 1989. *L'état de barbarie.* Paris: Seuil.

Van Dam, Nikolaos. 1996. *The Struggle for Power in Syria: Politics and Society under
    Asad and the Ba'th Party.* London: I. B. Tauris.

Van Dusen, Michael H. 1972. ''Political Integration and Regionalism in Syria.'' *Middle
    East Journal* 26, no. 2 (Spring): 123–148.

Weinberger, Naomi Joy. 1986. *Syrian Intervention in Lebanon: The 1975–76 Civil War.*
    New York: Oxford University Press.

World Bank. 1955. *The Economic Development of Syria.* Baltimore: Johns Hopkins Uni-
    versity Press.

TUNISIA

Gregory White

Ibn Khaldun wrote six hundred years ago in *The Muqaddimah*, "The knowledge that has not come down to us is larger than the knowledge that has" (1967, 39). Born in Tunis in 1332, the student of Avicenna, Averroës, and Aristotle also held the view that "human beings have to dwell in common and settle together in cities and hamlets for the comforts of companionship and for the satisfaction of human needs, as a result of the natural disposition of human beings toward co-operation in order to be able to make a living" (43). Although postcolonial political science scholarship has not improved markedly on the wisdom of Tunis's native son, it has furnished valuable insight into the character of Tunisian politics.

The point of departure for most scholarship on Tunisia during the early years of independence emphasized its exceptional character and its uniqueness in the context of Arab politics: stable, moderate, secular, Western, peaceful, modern, and liberal. Hudson (1977, 377), for example, averred that Tunisia was "perhaps the most politically modern . . . in terms of secularism, rationality, and institutionalized participation." On the one hand, the thesis of exceptionalism may have been somewhat accurate in the 1950s, 1960s, and 1970s. On the other hand, one wonders if the favorable comparison to other countries in the region was "damning with faint praise." Moreover, scholars during the Cold War may have been excessively enamored with the anticommunism and "modernization-from-above" efforts of Tunisia's *suprême combattant*, President Habib Bourguiba. Leader of the nationalist movement, Bourguiba was president until his removal from office on November 7, 1987, by Prime Minister General Zine al-Abidine Ben Ali. Now, hindsight gives us the understanding that the profound problems Tunisia has experienced in the 1980s and 1990s were presaged in its earlier years.

COLONIAL LEGACY

Tunisia has had a long history of foreign invasion and occupation, ranging from the Phoenicians to the Romans to the Ottomans to the French. Carthage's glory gave way to Tunisia's role as the "granary of Rome" during the Roman Empire before the Ottoman invasion of the late seventeenth century. Since the late eighteenth century, European powers expanded their presence in North Africa for strategic, economic, and ideological reasons. For example, Marsden (1971) detailed British interests in Tunisia and in the Mediterranean during the nineteenth century. Valensi (1977) detailed the French effort to import olive oil in the late eighteenth century to supply Marseilles's soap industry.

Long before the French occupation of Tunis in 1881 and the formal establishment of the French protectorate in 1883 with the Convention of al-Marsa, the French vied with Britain and Italy for control of the narrow straits separating Tunisia from Sicily. The French had occupied Algeria in 1830 and were concerned about the stability of their possession. Brown's (1974) study detailed the rule of Ahmad Bey between 1837 and 1855, specifically focusing on Ahmad's efforts to reform the military in a European-inspired fashion. Ahmad's rule succeeded in destroying some of the old political culture without setting up a successful new culture in its place.

In his majestic study of the Maghreb's history, Abun-Nasr (1987) treated the events surrounding the decision to create an International Financial Commission in 1869. The IFC was created by the Europeans after the Tunisian government defaulted on loans to European creditors, an experience in which "Tunisia lost its economic independence" (Abun-Nasr 1987, 282). Comprised of British, Italian, and French administrators, the IFC attempted to rectify Tunisia's financial straits, but to little avail. Another useful historical overview is provided by Perkins (1986).

Findlay noted that during the protectorate, which lasted from 1881 until Tunisian independence in 1956, the French occupation was to "provide the most favorable environment for French economic activity at the least cost to France" (1984, 220). For his part, Hermassi (1972) demonstrated that although the colonization was not as extensive or "total" as Algeria's colonial experience, the French protectorate was thorough in its domination. Memmi wrote of the dialectics of oppression in his classic memoir on colonialism, *The Colonizer and the Colonized* (1967):

There undoubtedly exists—at some point in its evolution—a certain adherence of the colonized to colonization. However, this adherence is the result of colonization not its cause. It arises after and not before colonial occupation. In order for the colonizer to be complete master, it is not enough for him to be so in actual fact, but he must believe in its legitimacy. In order for the legitimacy to be complete, it is not enough for the colonized to be a slave, he must also accept this role. (1967, 88–89)

By far the most impressive treatment of Tunisia's experience under French colonialism is Anderson's (1986) superb study of state formation in Tunisia and Libya. In the tradition of Barrington Moore and Theda Skocpol, Anderson's comparative historical sociology contrasts the French colonialism in Tunisia to Italian colonialism in Libya. The value of Anderson's book lies in its attention to the development of state-society relations in Tunisia and the impact of European colonialism well into the postindependence era. The volume offers the insight that the interaction of indigenous structures with French colonialism provided the institutional legacy that marked the postindependence period. Tunisia's possession of a reasonably well developed state is one of the attributes that set it apart from its neighbors in the Middle East and North Africa. As Anderson wrote elsewhere, Tunisia is one of the few states in the region, along with Turkey and Egypt, endowed with the "conventional attributes of statehood: stable civilian administrations, well-organized military establishments, and adequate revenue extraction" (1987, 3). This endowment is a function of the interaction of local society with the colonial invasion and has proved significant in postindependence politics.

DOMESTIC POLITICS

Perhaps the most significant pivot point in Tunisia's postindependence history was 1969, and it is around this pivot point that much scholarship turns. In September 1969, President Bourguiba dismissed the prominent minister of the economy, Ahmed Ben Salah. Ben Salah's dismissal marked the end of an eight-year period of central, state economic planning, marked by a pronounced socialist rhetoric and the celebrated effort to establish agricultural cooperatives. Official state policy established the cooperatives on the land expropriated in 1964 from former French and Italian colonials. Besides the agricultural efforts, Ben Salah and state economic policy strove to diversify trade partners beyond France and to develop economic self-sufficiency. Useful treatments of the Ben Salah era and the cooperative experiment can be found in Zussman (1986), Anderson (1986), Moore (1970), and Kamelgarn (1980). In particular, Rudebeck's (1970) consideration of developmental pressures on the Tunisian state has proven especially useful. Rudebeck highlighted the limits of Ben Salah's radical reform efforts in the context of a "small and economically vulnerable Third-World country." Simmons's (1970 and 1971) two-part article in the *Middle East Journal* is also an indispensable study of the cooperative experiment.

A noteworthy sociological treatment of Tunisia in the 1960s is Duvignaud's *Change at Shebika* (1970), an analysis of a small town situated near the Algerian border in southern Tunisia. Outside the ambit of Bourguiban "modernization" efforts, Shebikans found themselves watching the processes of urbanization and industrialization with a very skeptical eye. Jean-Louis Bertuccelli based the film *Ramparts of Clay* on Duvignaud's book, and Geertz (1971) pronounced both works as worthy efforts to transcend the limitations of social science.

After Ben Salah's removal, Tunisia turned to a policy of *al-infitah* (economic openness). Similar to the more celebrated effort of Egypt's Sadat, Tunisia's *infitah* was oriented to the French and European market and was characterized by economic liberalization and export-oriented industrialization. As Richards and Waterbury (1990) wrote, "If Egypt provides the prototype of *infitah*, Tunisia was the pioneer'' (244). Nicholas Hopkins (1981) conducted a comparison between Tunisia and Egypt.

The *infitah* to European investors and state efforts to promote trade with Europe prompted political problems, however, as opposition emerged from labor and religious quarters to the secular, procapitalist orientation of the ruling party, the Socialist Destourian party (Parti Socialiste Destourien, or PSD). Tunisia's nationalist movement, the Neo-Destour, was led by Bourguiba during the latter years of the protectorate. At the height of the Ben Salah era, the Neo-Destour changed its name to the PSD, and throughout the 1960s and into the 1970s it served as a valuable coalition of Tunisian society (Micaud, Brown, and Moore 1964; Moore 1965). Moore (1965) noted that since the elimination of a challenge from the more traditional Ben Youssef in the late 1950s, the PSD had become the center of Tunisian politics. In the early 1970s, however, challenges to Bourguiba's preeminence and his change of heart toward a more economically liberal orientation threatened party stability. Moore (1977) analyzed the tensions and conflict within the PSD, especially between Bourguiba and political liberals such as Ahmed Mestiri, who called for more debate and dialogue. For his part, Camau offered several valuable treatments of Tunisian politics in the "Chronique Politique Tunisie" of *L'Annuaire de l'Afrique du Nord* (1973–1975), and Deeb's (1994) treatment of Tunisia's party politics is superb.

Critical analyses of the direction of Tunisia's politics during the pivotal 1970s can be found from various quarters. Ben Salah (1977) himself offered a scathing critique of his dismissal and Tunisia's turn to extroverted development.

The national economy is open to investment by foreign, private capital aiming to create enclaves that help to uphold the establishment and thus ensure its "protection." . . . With the neo-colonial model chosen, our economy tends to function, not according to the imperatives of our development, but according to the needs of the economy of the rich world. This model . . . is responsible . . . for the freezing of institutional structures, for the reinforcement of authoritarianism and for absolutism . . . since the end of 1969.

Ben Salah also accorded an intriguing series of interviews with Nerfin (1974). Kamelgarn (1978) provided a sharp critique of Tunisia's dependent relationship with advanced capitalist countries. Maschino and Mrabet's (1975) controversial article in *Le Monde Diplomatique* prompted Tunisian authorities to ban the paper from the country. Maschino and Mrabet concluded: "Economic regression, political repression: the myth of liberalism has not kept its promise, and the country sinks into dependence." Bourguiba, one assumes, did not like it. Stone (1982) examined the relatively well unified Tunisian elite, small, somewhat heterogeneous, "mildly socialistic." Stone noted that by the late 1970s real schisms were evident, albeit not well understood.

Analyses of Tunisian politics in the 1980s and 1990s have focused on the connections between economic performance and political pressures and the growing Islamist opposition. For now, Seddon's (1986) study of "politics and the price of bread'' seeks to explain the food riots of January 1984, popular protests that erupted after Bourguiba approved government measures to remove food subsidies. Bourguiba had to back off from the effort. But by 1986, Tunisia had adopted an IMF-sponsored Structural Adjustment Program.

For her part, Larif-Beatrix (1987) complemented Stone's study and focused on the increasing ossification of the PSD and "l'état bourguibien" led by the aging Bourguiba. According to Larif-Beatrix, the patrimonialism of the Tunisian polity was reinforced by Bourguiba's fixation on remaining in power without ensuring a viable succession. Camau (1984) analyzed the state's relationship with "civil society," noting that "liberalization" measures would require a disengagement from a society that had been formed in a dialectic fashion with the state.

On November 7, 1987, Prime Minister Ben Ali replaced Bourguiba, ostensibly because the ailing Bourguiba was unable to conduct his office at the age of eighty-four. The first military officer to hold high political office in postindependence Tunisia, Ben Ali had served as secretary of state for national security before becoming interior minister and, in the summer of 1987, prime minister. In July 1988, Ben Ali and the Central Committee of the PSD changed the party's name to the Democratic Constitutional Rally. Vandewalle (1988), Ware (1988), Leveau (1989), and Tessler (1990) offered early discussions of the "new beginning" in Tunisia's politics.

WOMEN AND POLITICS

The status of women in Tunisia has been the subject of several studies attempting to put into perspective "modernization-from-above" efforts to improve the position of women. Bourguiba led legislative efforts at independence to reform juridical and social strictures, most notably with the Code du Statut Personnel of 1956. The Personnel Status Code prohibited polygamy, introduced judicial divorce for women, set a minimum age for marriage, gave women the right to vote, and provided for equal education. Durrani (1976) examined the opportunities for women in education after independence and noted that the advances made affected primarily affluent households, not the poorer classes, where "the traditional norms [that] discourage women from working remain unchanged and the practice is admitted only out of economic hardship" (69).

Marshall and Stokes (1981) provided a comparison of the status of women in Algeria and Tunisia. Marshall and Stokes noted the stark contrast between the commitment to gender equality in Tunisia and the lack of a similar undertaking in Algeria and argued that it was a function of the differing colonial experiences. In contrast to Tunisia's commitment to female emancipation from traditional Muslim customs—which Bourguiba denounced as a state of "servility, decadence, and bondage," postindependence Algerian patriarchal elites sought to reaffirm (reinvent?) Islamic tradition after the "legitimation crisis" prompted by French colonialism. "The Algerian élite . . . experienced a much stronger need for traditional legitimation than did the Tunisian élite'' (Marshall and Stokes 1981, 645).

In her study of a Tunisian village, Larson (1984) challenged the view that Tunisian women had somehow become liberated. In the face of state efforts to improve women's status, villagers had accepted laws and policies to varying degrees, reflecting an ambivalence that depended on the impact of a given policy on everyday life. People generally liked the idea of progress except where it altered prevailing patterns. In fact, women themselves were sometimes less than receptive of change since it altered facets of their lives in which they held power. ''Modernization'' prompted changes in everyday life that damaged women's traditional sources of power and influence without replacing them. Waltz's (1986) study of Islamist politics, discussed later, also treats the proclivity of young women to wear the ''traditional'' *hijab* (head scarf) as a means of protecting themselves from the uncertainties of rapid change.

Finally, Ferchiou's (1985) study of women in agricultural activity also notes the profound challenges facing women well into the 1980s. Men controlled the property and agricultural activity, enjoying the benefits of automation and mechanization. Men drove the machines and turned the valves on irrigation projects, but, as in so many societies, women did the bulk of the agricultural labor. Moreover, the division between ''agricultural'' labor and ''household'' labor was muddy. Women shucked, cleaned, processed, and prepared the harvest for market as part of their day-to-day ''domestic'' labor.

ISLAMISM

The appeal of Islamist political opposition has grown rapidly in recent decades throughout the region, and Tunisia is no exception. The Harakat al-ittijah al-Islami—translated into French as the Mouvement de la Tendance Islamique (MTI) and into English as the Movement of the Islamic Way—emerged in the 1970s and was renamed Ennahda (Renaissance) in 1989. As many have noted, Islamism paradoxically enjoyed early support from the state, which was seeking to counterbalance leftist opposition. Entelis (1974) discovered the emergence of a ''counter-culture'' in the 1970s in interviews with university students that expressed itself as pan-Arab and anti-Western; he did not detect Islamism per se in the early 1970s, but the political orientation of Islamism seems consistent with the antiestablishment orientation of students. By the end of the 1970s, MTI had strengthened under the leadership of Rachid Ghannouchi and Abd al-Fatih Mourou.

Waltz's (1986) treatment of the bases and origins of the ''Islamist appeal'' is very valuable. Like Entelis (1974), she points to the younger strata, noting the complementarity of economic, political, and psychosocial explanations of Islam's appeal. Contrary to many analyses, she argues that an upturn in the economy is not likely to reduce the Islamist appeal. The young cohort's cry for *asala* (authenticity) is bound to a quest for identity. Coupled with Munson's

(1986) study of the social bases of Islamism in Morocco, Waltz's work sheds light on the complex social, political, and economic bases of Islamist activity. Hermassi (1991), Zghal (1991), and Magnuson (1991) all offer valuable analyses of the diversity and origins of the Islamist movement. Burgat's (1993) work is a Maghrebi-wide study and, therefore, also valuable; it contains extensive excerpts of interviews with Ghannouchi.

HUMAN RIGHTS

Tunisia's experience with human rights has been the subject of increasing attention. As Waltz (1991b) noted, the Tunisian League of Human Rights (Ligue tunisienne des droits de l'homme, LTDH) was founded in 1977 and received support from the Ben Ali regime, at least in the early years. While her study focuses on the Moroccan Organization of Human Rights (Organisation marocaine des droits de l'homme, OMDH), it stresses that the indigenous nature of domestic human rights organizations was a force with which North African regimes would have to continue to contend. In another article, Waltz (1991a) treated early efforts by Ben Ali to contend with human rights pressures.

Manaï's *Supplice tunisien* (1995) serves as a companion to Perrault's (1991) scathing critique of Morocco's King Hassan II and French support for the monarch, *Notre ami le roi*. Indeed, Perrault proffered a preface to Manaï's book in which he denounced Ben Ali as ''le dictateur de Carthage.'' Directed to a French and European audience, *Supplice tunisien* is a first-hand exposé of the human rights abuses within Ben Ali's Tunisia by a man who was seized and brutally tortured by security officials. In the aftermath of the military coup and the cancellation of Algeria's election in 1992, European officials (and the United States) are keenly interested in maintaining stability in Tunisia and may ignore the severe repression of opposition movements.

ECONOMIC POLICY

Since Tunisia is a small country on the periphery of a bloc of advanced industrialized countries, the European Union (EU), it is difficult to separate domestic economic policy from foreign economic policy. Tunisia's small size, as Rudebeck (1970) stressed, constrained its ability to pursue autarkic policies of import-substitution industrialization (ISI) during the 1960s under Ben Salah. Nellis (1983) conducted a paired comparison of Tunisia and Algeria's development performance, noting also the difference in resource endowment between the massive Algeria and the relatively small Tunisia. As noted earlier, Marshall and Stokes (1981) used the same paired comparison for their study of the status of women in Tunisia and Algeria. Nellis argued that Tunisia's capitalism since the *infitah* had led to a higher rate of growth of GNP per capita in Tunisia. Algeria's economy is five times larger and had derived tremendous rents since independence from oil exports. But Tunisia had become more diversified economically.

The structure of Tunisia's agricultural sector has also received attention because of its central role in the Tunisian economy and, of course, the cooperativization experience under Ben Salah. Simmons (1970 and 1971) detailed the Ben Salah era, Poncet (1975) offered a study of the economic structures of the sector, and Gachet (1987) provided an analysis of official discourse toward the sector. By the 1970s, the agricultural sector had become perceived as a brake on industrialization and development by state officials, leading to an "ideology of scorn" toward the backward ways of farmers (Gachet 1987, 192). Zussman (1986) pointed to the cynicism and skepticism with which farmers met repeated efforts by external sources to modernize them. Attia's (1985) study of the Jerid Oasis near the southern town of Tozeur details efforts by officials to promote the monocultural development of *deglet nur* dates, a commodity prized in European markets. Larson (1991) focused on the impact of state policy in central Tunisia and efforts by the local population to contend with changes.

Ben Romdhane's (1990) highly critical study of Tunisia's development trajectory pointed to the underdevelopment of the agricultural sector to benefit domestic and foreign capital. The *infitah*, coupled with the strength of the EU's Common Agricultural Policy (CAP), had turned Tunisia away from the historic role of the agricultural sector as the backbone of the economy and toward an export industrialization oriented toward the European market. Tourism and light manufactures now received the bulk of supports. Pomfret (1986) detailed the discrimination of the EU's Mediterranean Policy and CAP, noting that although Tunisia had done well in terms of GDP growth, its agricultural sector had suffered since independence. A country once able to feed itself, Tunisia had developed a severe agro-alimentary deficit by the late 1970s. Michael Hopkins (1989) also positioned Tunisia within the broader international political economy, and White and Cason (forthcoming) compared Tunisia and Brazil's development strategies.

Bellin offered two superb studies. She noted the influence industrialists enjoyed in state policy since the early 1970s, but also argued that the state had provided a favorable climate for business classes since the *infitah* (1991). Similarly, in "The Politics of Profit in Tunisia" (1994), she examined the influence of "parasitic cronyism" and determined that it need not undermine industrial policy. In her view, Tunisia's industrial class has not restricted the autonomy or capacity of the state.

FOREIGN POLICY

Tunisia has long been viewed by Western observers as moderate and pro-Western. Especially since the *infitah* in the early 1970s, Tunisian foreign policy has been devoted to maintaining close ties with the West; this orientation has persisted under Ben Ali. At the same time, Tunisia maintained close ties during the Cold War with Third World groupings such as the Non-Aligned Movement and the Organization of African Unity. It was also a key participant in the founding of the Arab Maghrebi Union (UMA) in 1989. Analyses of the historical development of Maghrebi cooperation (or lack thereof) were conducted by Slim (1980) and Deeb (1989). Aghrout and Sutton (1990) provided a valuable early study of the UMA, with a rather skeptical assessment of the grouping's potential given the economic problems of regional cooperation between developing countries.

Because of Tunisia's small size, much of Tunisia's domestic economic policy has foreign economic policy implications. Both Perkins (1986) and Deeb and Laipson (1991) highlighted this connection in their respective chapters on Tunisia's foreign policy. Works cited earlier on domestic politics and economic policy have a bearing on foreign policy, for example, Kamelgarn (1978). Simon (1979) offered a study of Tunisian immigration to Europe, also drawing attention to Tunisia's position within an economic space dominated by Europe.

COMPARATIVE REGIONAL STUDIES

Finally, one is able to gain insight into Tunisia with the help of several regional and comparative works. Spencer's (1993) study of Maghrebi politics highlights Tunisia's role in the UMA. Tessler, Entelis, and White (1995) offer a chapter on Tunisian politics. Moore's (1970) and Entelis's (1980) comparative treatments of Maghrebi politics contain extensive analyses of Tunisian politics. Parker's (1984) study of the Maghreb treats Bourguiba's Tunisia as a firm ally of the United States. Zartman and Habeeb's (1993) edited volume pursued thematic concerns, rather than country-by-country analyses. Hermassi and Vandewalle's article on state-society relations in that volume is of particular note. Finally, the *Annuaire de l'Afrique du Nord* is an indispensable source of analysis and information.

FUTURE RESEARCH CONCERNS

Future scholarship may find it valuable to engage Tunisian politics on two perhaps related levels. At the level of domestic politics, the Tunisian political system continues to close. The promise of the early years of the change of regime on November 7, 1987, has given way to disappointment ten years later as the Ben Ali regime continues to eradicate all opposition in the name of stopping Islamists. While the government is supported by the European Union and the United States because the country is "not Algeria," Tunisia risks losing entirely a loyal opposition. The implications of Tunisia's closure need to be examined more directly.

At the international level, Tunisia continues to place its stock in an economic space dominated by Europe. The government signed a Partnership Agreement with the European Union in July 1995. The agreement will create a free-trade zone with Europe—for industrial products—by 2009. The transformations and dislocations prompted by such developments are sure to be profound, but as yet are not well understood.

REFERENCES

Abun-Nasr, Jamil M. 1987. *A History of the Maghrib in the Islamic Period.* New York: Cambridge University Press.

Aghrout, Ahmed, and Keith Sutton. 1990. ''Regional Economic Union in the Maghreb.'' *Journal of Modern African Studies* 28, no. 1:115–139.

Anderson, Lisa. 1986. *The State and Social Transformation in Tunisia and Libya, 1830–1980.* Princeton: Princeton University Press.

———. 1987. ''The State in the Middle East and North Africa.'' *Comparative Politics* 20, no. 1:1–20.

Annuaire de l'Afrique du Nord. Annual volumes. Paris: CNRS.

Attia, Habib. 1985. ''Water-sharing Rights in the Jerid Oasis of Tunisia.'' In Ann E. Mayer, ed., *Property, Social Structure, and Law in the Modern Middle East.* Albany: State University of New York Press.

Bellin, Eva. 1991. ''Tunisian Industrialists and the State.'' In I. William Zartman, ed., *Tunisia: The Political Economy of Reform.* Boulder, CO: Lynne Rienner.

———. 1994. ''The Politics of Profit in Tunisia: Utility of the Rentier Paradigm?'' *World Development* 22, no. 3:427–436.

Ben Romdhane, Mahmoud. 1990. ''Tunisia: The State, the Peasantry, and Food Independence.'' In Hamid Aït Amara and Bernard Founou-Tchuigoua, eds., *African Agriculture: The Critical Choices.* London: Zed Books.

Ben Salah, Ahmed, 1977. ''Tunisia: Endogenous Development and Structural Transformations.'' *Another Development: Approaches and Strategies.* Uppsala, Sweden: Dag Hammarskjöld Foundation.

Brown, L. Carl. 1974. *The Tunisia of Ahmad Bey, 1837–1855.* Princeton: Princeton University Press.

Burgat, François. 1993. *The Islamic Movement in North Africa.* Trans. William Dowell. Austin: University of Texas Press.

Camau, Michel. 1973. ''Chronique politique: Tunisie.'' *Annuaire de l'Afrique du Nord* 12:411–436.

———. 1974. ''Chronique politique: Tunisie.'' *Annuaire de l'Afrique du Nord* 13:345–372.

———. 1975. ''Chronique politique: Tunisie.'' *Annuaire de l'Afrique du Nord* 14:477–496.

———. 1984. ''L'état tunisien: De la tutelle au désengagement.'' *Maghreb-Machrek* 103:8–38.

———, ed. 1987. *Tunisie: au présent: une modernité au-dessous de tout soupçon?* Paris: CNRS.

Deeb, Mary-Jane. 1989. ''Inter-Maghribi Relations since 1969: A Study of the Modalities of Unions and Mergers.'' *Middle East Journal* 43, no. 1:20–33.

———. 1994. ''Tunisia.'' In Frank Tachau, ed., *Political Parties of the Middle East and North Africa.* Westport, CT: Greenwood Press.

Deeb, Mary-Jane, and Ellen Laipson. 1991. ''Tunisian Foreign Policy: Continuity and

Change under Bourguiba and Ben Ali.'' In I. William Zartman, ed., *Tunisia: The Political Economy of Reform*. Boulder, CO: Lynne Rienner.

Durrani, Lorna Hawker. 1976. ''Employment of Women and Social Change.'' In Russell Stone and John L. Simmons, eds., *Change in Tunisia: Studies in the Social Sciences*. Albany: State University of New York Press.

Duvignaud, Jean. 1970. *Change at Shebika: Report from a North African Village*. Trans. Frances Frenaye. New York: Pantheon.

Entelis, John. 1974. ''Ideological Change and an Emerging Counter-Culture in Tunisian Politics.'' *Journal of Modern African Studies* 12, no. 4:543–568.

———. 1980. *Comparative Politics of North Africa*. Syracuse: Syracuse University Press.

Ferchiou, Sophie. 1985. *Les femmes dans l'agriculture tunisienne*. Marseilles: Edisud.

Findlay, Allan. 1984. ''Tunisia: The Vicissitudes of Economic Development.'' In Richard Lawless and Allan Findlay, eds., *North Africa: Contemporary Politics and Economic Development*. London: Croom Helm.

Gachet, Jean Paul. 1987. ''L'agriculture: Discours et strategies.'' In Michel Camau, ed., *Tunisie au Présent: une Modernité au-dessous de tout soupcon?* Paris: CNRS.

Geertz, Clifford. 1971. ''In Search of North Africa.'' *New York Review of Books* (April 22): 20–24.

Hermassi, Elbaki. 1972. *Leadership and National Development in North Africa*. Berkeley: University of California Press.

———. 1991. ''The Islamicist Movement and November 7.'' In I. William Zartman, ed., *Tunisia: The Political Economy of Reform*. Boulder, CO: Lynne Rienner.

Hermassi, Elbaki, and Dirk Vandewalle. 1993. ''The Second State of State Building.'' In I. William Zartman and William Mark Habeeb, eds., *Polity and Society in Contemporary North Africa*. Boulder, CO: Westview Press.

Hopkins, Michael. 1989. *Tunisia to 1993: Steering for Stability*. Economist Intelligence Unit Special Report, no. 1132. London: Economist Intelligence Unit.

Hopkins, Nicholas. 1981. ''Tunisia: An Open and Shut Case.'' *Social Problems* 28, no. 4:385–393.

Hudson, Michael. 1977. *Arab Politics*. New Haven: Yale University Press.

Ibn Khaldun. 1967. *The Muqaddimah: An Introduction to History*. Trans. Franz Rosenthal; ed. N. J. Dawood. Princeton: Princeton University Press.

Kamelgarn, Daniel. 1978. ''Tunisie: Développement d'un capitalisme dépendant.'' *Peuples Méditerranéens* 4:113–145.

———. 1980. ''Strategies de self-reliance et system économique mondial: L'éxperience tunisienne des années 1960.'' *Peuples Méditerranéens* 13:107–126.

Larif-Beatrix, Asma. 1987. ''L'évolution de l'état tunisien.'' *Maghreb-Machrek* 116:35–44.

Larson, Barbara. 1984. ''The Status of Women in a Tunisian Village: Limits to Autonomy, Influence, and Power.'' *Signs: Journal of Women in Culture and Society* 9, no. 3:417–433.

———. 1991. ''Rural Development in Central Tunisia: Constraints and Coping Strategies.'' In I. William Zartman, ed., *Tunisia: The Political Economy of Reform*. Boulder, CO: Lynne Rienner.

Leveau, Rémy. 1989. ''La Tunisie du président Ben Ali: Equilibre interne et environnement Arabe.'' *Maghreb-Machrek* 124:4–17.

Magnuson, Douglas K. 1991. ''Islamic Reform in Contemporary Tunisia: Unity and

Diversity.'' In I. William Zartman, ed., *Tunisia: The Political Economy of Reform*. Boulder, CO: Lynne Rienner.

Manaï, Ahmed. 1995. *Supplice tunisien: Le jardin secret du général Ben Ali*. Paris: La Découverte.

Marsden, Arthur. 1971. *British Diplomacy and Tunis, 1875–1902: A Case Study in Mediterranean Policy*. New York: Africana Publishing.

Marshall, Susan, and Randall Stokes. 1981. ''Tradition and the Veil: Female Status in Tunisia and Algeria.'' *Journal of Modern African Studies* 19, no. 4:625–646.

Maschino, Maurice T., and Fadela Mrabet. 1975. ''La Tunisie: Vingt ans après.'' *Le Monde Diplomatique* (December): 16–19.

Memmi, Albert. 1967. *The Colonizer and the Colonized*. Boston: Beacon Press.

Micaud, Charles A., Leon Carl Brown, and Clement Henry Moore. 1964. *Tunisia: The Politics of Modernization*. New York: Praeger.

Moore, Clement Henry. 1965. *Tunisia since Independence: The Dynamics of One-Party Government*. Berkeley: University of California Press.

———. 1970. *Politics in North Africa: Algeria, Morocco, and Tunisia*. Boston: Little, Brown.

———. 1977. ''Clientalist Ideology and Political Change: Fictitious Networks in Egypt and Tunisia.'' In Ernest Gellner and John Waterbury, eds., *Patrons and Clients in Mediterranean Societies*. London: Duckworth.

Munson, Henry. 1986. ''The Social Base of Islamic Militancy in Morocco.'' *Middle East Journal* 40:267–293.

Nellis, John. 1983. ''A Comparative Assessment of the Development Performances of Algeria and Tunisia.'' *Middle East Journal* 37:370–393.

Nerfin, Marc. 1974. *Entretiens avec Ahmed Ben Salah*. Paris: Maspero.

Parker, Richard. 1984. *North Africa: Regional Tensions and Concerns*. New York: Praeger.

Perkins, Kenneth J. 1986. *Tunisia: Crossroads of the Islamic and European Worlds*. Boulder, CO: Westview Press.

Perrault, Gilles. 1991. *Notre ami le roi*. Paris: Gallimard.

Pomfret, Richard. 1986. *Mediterranean Policy of the European Community: A Study of Discrimination in Trade*. New York: St. Martin's Press.

Poncet, Jean. 1975. ''Les structures actuelles de l'agriculture tunisienne.'' *Annuaire de l'Afrique du Nord* 14:45–56.

Richards, Alan, and John Waterbury. 1990. *A Political Economy of the Middle East: State, Class, and Economic Development*. Boulder, CO: Westview Press.

Rudebeck, Lars. 1970. ''Development Pressure and Political Limits: A Tunisian Example.'' *Journal of Modern African Studies* 8, no. 2:173–198.

Seddon, David. 1986. ''Politics and the Price of Bread in Tunisia.'' In Alan Richards, ed., *Food, States, and Peasants*. Boulder, CO: Westview Press.

Simmons, John L. 1970 and 1971. ''Agricultural Cooperatives and Tunisian Development.'' Parts 1, 2. *Middle East Journal* 24, no. 4:455–465; 25, no. 1:45–75.

Simon, Gildas. 1979. *L'éspace des travailleurs tunisiens en France: Structures et fonctionnement d'un champ migratoire international*. Marseilles: Edisud.

Slim, Habib. 1980. ''Comité permanent consultative du Maghreb entre le présent et l'avenir.'' *Revue tunisienne de droit*, 241–252.

Spencer, Claire. 1993. *The Maghreb in the 1990s: Political and Economic Developments in Algeria, Morocco, and Tunisia.* London: International Institute for Strategic Studies.

Stone, Russell A. 1982. "Tunisia: A Single Party System Holds Change in Abeyance." In I. William Zartman, ed., *Political Elites in Arab North Africa.* New York: Longman.

Tessler, Mark. 1990. "Tunisia's New Beginning." *Current History* 89 (April): 169–172, 182–184.

Tessler, Mark, John Entelis, and Gregory White. 1995. "The Republic of Tunisia." In David E. Long and Bernard Reich, eds., *Government and Politics of the Middle East and North Africa.* Boulder, CO: Westview Press. 423–445.

Tessler, Mark, and Patricia Freeman. 1981. "Regime Orientation and Participant Citizenship in Developing Countries: Hypotheses and a Test with Longitudinal Data from Tunisia." *Western Political Quarterly* 23, no. 4:479–498.

Valensi, Lucette. 1977. *Tunisian Peasants in the Eighteenth and Nineteenth Centuries.* Trans. Beth Archer. New York: Cambridge University Press.

Vandewalle, Dirk. 1988. "From the New State to the New Era: Toward a Second Republic in Tunisia." *Middle East Journal* 42:602–620.

Waltz, Susan. 1986. "Islamicist Appeal in Tunisia." *Middle East Journal* 40, no. 4:651–670.

———. 1991a. "Clientelism and Reform in Ben Ali's Tunisia." In I. William Zartman, ed., *Tunisia: The Political Economy of Reform.* Boulder, CO: Lynne Rienner.

———. 1991b. "Making Waves: The Political Impact of Human Rights Groups in North Africa." *Journal of Modern African Studies* 29:481–504.

Ware, L. B. 1988. "Ben Ali's Constitutional Coup in Tunisia." *Middle East Journal* 42, no. 3:621–640.

White, Gregory, and Jeffrey Cason. 1998. "The State as Naive Entrepreneur: Political Economy of Export Promotion in Brazil and Tunisia." *Policy Studies Journal.*

Young, Crawford. 1994. *The African Colonial State in Comparative Perspective.* New Haven: Yale University Press.

Zartman, I. William, ed. 1991. *Tunisia: The Political Economy of Reform.* Boulder, CO: Lynne Rienner.

Zartman, I. William, and William Mark Habeeb, eds. 1993. *Polity and Society in Contemporary North Africa.* Boulder, CO: Westview Press.

Zghal, Abdelkader. 1991. "The New Strategy of the Movement of the Islamic Way." In I. William Zartman, ed., *Tunisia: The Political Economy of Reform.* Boulder, CO: Lynne Rienner.

Zussman, Mira. 1986. "Pendulum Swings in Land Laws and Rural Development Policies in Tunisia: History and Consequences." In Laurence O. Michalak and Jeswald W. Salacuse, eds., *Social Legislation in the Contemporary Middle East.* Berkeley: University of California Press.

TURKEY

George S. Harris

Political scientists have viewed Turkey from two somewhat different angles over the past half-century. On the one hand, they have called Turkey a "bridge," first between the West and the Middle East and more recently between the West and Central Asia. On the other hand, Turkey has been seen as a "model" of a Muslim state committed to democratize, of a less developed society seeking to develop and modernize, and of a polity with a praetorian background attempting to find balance between the civilians and the military establishment. It is these various bridge or model perspectives that have provided the underlying context within which political science research on Turkey has evolved in the decades since World War II.

Until after World War II, linguistic and other difficulties retarded world scholarship on Turkey. From the mid-1960s to the 1980s, the reluctance of Turkish authorities to accord research permits and to allow survey research, particularly regarding political and ethnic attitudes, complicated efforts by foreign investigators to amass data for political science studies. Moreover, only in the last several decades have Turkish scholars explored their own society in depth rather than deferring to Western experts. As a result, Turkey has been the subject of somewhat less original work than might have been expected, given its role as the only Muslim member of NATO and the uniqueness of its democratic evolution. There remains considerable debate in the literature over how to evaluate many basic aspects of Turkish political culture.

Although the number of studies of Turkish politics is now growing rapidly, fueled in part by interest in the military interventions that marked the transitions from the First to the Second Republic in 1960 and then to the Third Republic in 1980, relatively few investigators have attempted overall country studies of Turkey. Those that have, for example, Frank Tachau, *Turkey: The Politics of Authority, Democracy, and Development* (1984), and Edwin J. Cohn, *Turkish Economic, Social, and Political Change* (1970), are not entirely convincing in their efforts to link various aspects of Turkish political and economic culture. Even such collections as *Politics in the Third Turkish Republic* (1994), edited by Metin Heper and Ahmet Evin, and *Turkey: Political, Social and Economic Challenges in the 1990s* (1995), edited by Cigdem Balim et al., cover only specialized segments of the problem. Thus as political scientists have concentrated in the main on discrete elements of political life, it is appropriate to consider political literature on Turkey by individual topic.

THE POLITICAL SYSTEM

Bernard Lewis, *The Emergence of Modern Turkey* (1961), represented the culmination of the more or less historically centered approach that characterized scholarship on the Turkish polity until the 1960s. Daniel Lerner, *The Passing of Traditional Society* (1958), which addressed the impact of communications on the modernization process, began the serious political science study of Turkey. His successors attempted to test notions derived from comparative political literature against Turkish reality. They based much of their work on the hypotheses of such theoreticians as Samuel P. Huntington, whose *Political Order in Changing Societies* (1969) enunciated the concept of "ruralizing elections," a paradigm in which a counterelite's challenge through the polls led the formerly dominant ruling group to use force to try to regain its central position. Many scholars embraced this paradigm to explain the military takeovers that periodically sidetracked Turkey's democratic development.

Serif Mardin propounded another insight that commanded wide acceptance. His "Center-Periphery Relations: A Key to Turkish Politics?" (1973), adapted from Edward Shils, "Centre and Periphery" (1961), concluded that Turkey's political life over the centuries had consistently taken the form of a struggle by political outsiders against the establishment and its reformist policies. He demonstrated that this dynamic challenge from the traditional practice of the periphery characterized both Ottoman and modern Turkish politics.

Such emphasis on the fate of Turkish reform efforts led Ergun Ozbudun and Frank Tachau, in their "Social Change and Electoral Behavior in Turkey: Toward a 'Critical Realignment'?" (1975), to postulate that economic development in Turkey was producing an environment that encouraged class-based voting. Ozbudun, *Social Change and Political Participation in Turkey* (1976), suggested that the reformist Republican Peoples party should benefit from the growth of an urban, industrial working class. Even after the vote for left-leaning parties declined in the 1980s, however, Ozbudun merely qualified, but did not abandon, his realignment hypothesis in his "Postauthoritarian Democracies: Turkey" (1987). Also despite these contrary indications, Feroz Ahmad, *The Making of Modern Turkey* (1993), and others have continued to hold open the possibility that voting in Turkey may be increasingly along functionalist lines. Nonetheless, as the 1995 elections showed, evidence to the contrary continues to mount.

Ustun Erguder's "Post-1980 Parties and Politics in Turkey" (1988) drew on Mogens N. Pedersen, "The Dynamics of European Party Systems" (1979), to carry the electoral analysis further. Erguder called attention to the great volatility in tenure in parliament characteristic of the Turkish political system in the multiparty competitive era. He and others judged that the resultant weakness of legislative institutionalization was a major source of the periodic bouts of political turbulence that afflicted the Turkish polity.

Another line of analysis considered severe economic crisis responsible for generating the political violence that beset the Turkish polity in the 1970s and helped to trigger the 1980 military intervention. Ergun Ozbudun in the volume he coedited with Aydin Ulusan, *The Political Economy of Income Distribution in Turkey* (1980), even suggested that growing disparity in wealth in Turkey might be incompatible with participatory democracy. Others have not gone that far, particularly as the urban violence of the 1970s has not recurred, despite far more extreme inequity in income between the rich and poor following the 1980 liberalization reforms. In fact, Sabri Sayari, ''Politics and Economic Policymaking in Turkey, 1980–1988'' (1992a), evinced optimism that violence would not again overwhelm the regime, though on the so far somewhat unrealistic grounds that the export-driven market economy would help reduce inflation and ease many of the earlier economic strains.

Beyond economic distribution problems, the relationship of the state to civil society has also been seen as a key to Turkey's troubles by scholars in the past few decades. Influenced by J. P. Nettl, ''The State as a Conceptual Variable'' (1968), Metin Heper singled out extreme centralization of state power in Turkey as the most important cause of its political instability. In *The State Tradition in Turkey* (1985), he contended that polarization between the ruling center and those new groups that aspired to take power led to arbitrariness by the first, producing irresponsibility by the second. Binnaz Toprak in ''Civil Society in Turkey'' (1996) takes issue with this analysis, seeing a strong state as necessary to the evolution of civil society and questioning whether decentralized democracy would guarantee greater freedom and social peace.

Henri J. Barkey, *The State and the Industrialization Crisis in Turkey* (1990), on the other hand, regarded the state as weak and manipulated by pressure groups. He argued that the 1980 military intervention came about as a result of political indecisiveness in economic policy formulation and implementation rather than from the inherent propensity some scholars have attributed to import-substitution systems to descend into economic disorder and thereby invite military intervention. His emphasis on economic indecision is suspect, however, as it was a political government that introduced the current export-led system, while the soldiers who came afterward wavered in holding to the new economic regime. More attention to this problem will be needed to bring political scientists into accord on the role of the state in the perturbations in Turkey's course toward a stable democratic order.

Another approach to explain political turbulence and instability in Turkey has been through inspecting government legitimacy. M. Turker Alkan, ''Turkey: Rise and Decline of Political Legitimacy in a Revolutionary Regime'' (1980), investigated the proposition that industrialization and democratization made

Kemalism lose appeal, but was, he felt, bringing into being a new basis of legitimacy for the government. In view of the coalition difficulties and pressing ethnic challenges Turkey now faces, additional work on the issue of political legitimacy seems desirable.

Rather than approach the Turkish political system from the angle of comparative politics, in my *Turkey: Coping with Crisis* (1985b) I followed the prescription of S. N. Eisenstadt, ''The Kemalist Regime and Modernization: Some Comparative and Analytical Remarks'' (1984), to study trends from Turkey's specific past as the way to understand its democratic behavior. On this basis, it was possible to look behind party splits to identify continuity in the underlying voting constituencies; through all the vicissitudes of the political scene in Turkey, right-of-center parties taken together continually attracted some 60 percent of the vote. This Turkish-centered empirical approach questioned the interpretations of mobilization theory that linked voter-participation rates to economic development in Turkey.

THE TURKISH POLITICAL ELITE AND POLITICAL PARTIES

The Turkish political elite and political parties have been a major subject for political study since Frederick W. Frey's magisterial *The Turkish Political Elite* (1965), which for the first time made a careful, objective analysis of the changing characteristics of parliamentarians and their leaders. He used this study of the elite to elucidate major attributes of the larger political system. Carrying his work further, his ''Patterns of Elite Politics in Turkey'' (1975) argued that continued elitism and inadequate elite-mass linkages threatened the smooth evolution of democracy in Turkey.

Dankwart A. Rustow, ''Ataturk as Founder of a State'' (1968), zeroed in on elite leadership, analyzing the personality of Mustafa Kemal Ataturk to account for Turkey's success in modernizing. Yet Rustow as well recognized the need for the Kemalist elite to broaden if the Ataturk reform movement were to move to completion. This step was not easy. Following the path Frey sketched out, many political scientists, looking at the trouble Turkish democracy has encountered, have attributed much of the difficulty to bitter intraelite struggle. Sabri Sayari's ''The Turkish Party System in Transition'' (1978) linked this struggle to the fragmentation of Turkish political parties. Regarding these tendencies toward fragmentation as a major cause of the country's instability, the Turkish political scientists recruited to help draft the constitution of the Third Republic attempted to elaborate an electoral system that would counteract the trend toward party splintering, but without completely abandoning proportional representation. In my 1985 work cited earlier, I argued, on the other hand, that given the personal rivalries between leaders and the divergence of interests among the many ethnic and social groups composing Turkish society, the emergence of splinter parties was the natural result of proportional representation, however much it might be modified for the Turkish context.

The need to understand these factional rebellions generated considerable political science research. Ilter Turan's chapter in Kim et al.'s *The Legislative Connection: The Representatives and the Represented in Kenya, Korea, and Turkey* (1984) concluded that rapid social and economic change rendered parties merely temporary alignments of forces. In Turan's "The Recruitment of Cabinet Ministers as a Political Process" (1986), he analyzed the leverage of the ruling-party leadership over its deputies, and in subsequent work he noted the destabilizing effects of forming political parties battening on ethnicity and religious differences.

Recognition of the volatility and fragmentation of the elite also pointed Jacob Landau toward the small parties of the extreme left and extreme right in his *Radical Politics in Modern Turkey* (1974). Landau paid great attention to leadership as a major ingredient of electoral success. At the same time, he examined in detail the critical elite-mass link that Frey had earlier spelled out as of increasing importance to party fortunes. Heper and Landau presented a collection of essays in *Political Parties and Democracy in Turkey* (1991) addressing the widening range of significant political bodies on the Turkish scene.

Political scientists have also focused on the bureaucracy as the heart of the reformist elite. Joseph S. Szyliowicz, "Elite Recruitment in Turkey" (1971), analyzed the talent supplied by Ankara University's political science faculty, which he identified as the principal source of recruits for the government. I questioned some of his conclusions, however, in my "Bureaucratic Reform: Atatürk and the Turkish Foreign Office" (1981) and identified other salient formative experiences for aspiring bureaucrats.

Several researchers have seen in the fate of the bureaucracy a key to the health of the larger polity. Leslie L. Roos, Jr., and Noralou P. Roos, *Managers of Modernization: Organizations and Elites in Turkey (1950–1969)* (1971), sought to apply the Huntington thesis that ruralizing elections, after provoking military interventions, would help integrate the rural masses into the political system. They pointed to the reassuring possibility that in Turkey the expansion of the economic pie then under way might give members of the civil/military elite who were losing status a satisfactory outlet for their desire for power. Metin Heper, "The Recalcitrance of the Turkish Public Bureaucracy to 'Bourgeois Politics' " (1976), however, noted the resistance of the bureaucratic elite to accepting a deteriorating position. Ilter Turan in "Stages of Political Development in the Turkish Republic" (1988), on the other hand, demonstrated that the "best and the brightest" were deserting the declining bureaucracy for more lucrative employment, much as the Rooses had foreseen.

IDEOLOGY

A number of scholars have examined the role of ideology in shaping Turkish politics. Kemal Karpat in *Turkey's Politics* (1959) blazed the way by analyzing the Kadro movement, a singular attempt of Kemalist intellectuals to formulate an ideology for the reformist, statist movement Ataturk sponsored in the 1930s.

Paul Dumont, "The Origins of Kemalist Ideology" (1984), and Walter F. Weiker, *Political Tutelage and Democracy in Turkey* (1973), discuss at some length the evolution of the operational code propounded by the Kemalists. Although there was always some question whether these eclectic principles actually determined government policies in Turkey, their revival in the pages of *Yon* after the 1960 military intervention was dissected by Kemal H. Karpat, "Ideology in Turkey after the Revolution of 1960" (1973).

With the opening of the Turkish political scene to socialist parties after the 1960 military takeover, a Marxist party came on the scene. That development and its influence in pushing the mainline Republican Peoples party to take more ideological positions were given considerable attention by Feroz Ahmad, *The Turkish Experiment in Democracy, 1950–1975* (1977). Igor P. Lipovsky, *The Socialist Movement in Turkey, 1960–1980* (1992), highlighted the lack of unity on the left and the failure of socialists to form a mass political organization, though he still somewhat unrealistically judged the "material preconditions" for socialist ideology to be growing in Turkey.

Despite the obvious interest of the generals in 1980 in limiting the scope for legitimate political activity to exclude parties of the extreme left and right, it is clear that ideology drives some current political organizations. Analysis of these more recent developments indicated to Ergun Ozbudun, "Development of Democratic Government in Turkey" (1988a), that a trend toward ideological polarization was generating rising Turkish political violence. The more open toleration of Communist movements in the 1990s and the lifting of articles in the penal code restricting religious or class-based political activity have broadened the political spectrum. Especially after the Welfare party served for a year in power at the head of a coalition in 1996–1997, it is only a question of time before scholars reinspect Ozbudun's conclusions regarding the parties of the extremes.

ISLAM

The creation of a separate Turkish national state contradicted the universalist claims of Islam to unite all believers in the community of the faithful. Niyazi Berkes opened the modern study of religion in Turkey by assessing the dethroning of Islam in his authoritative *The Development of Secularism in Turkey* (1964). Berkes regarded the historical evolution of changes in ideas and values rather than the physical changes associated with economic development as the main agents in the secularization of society.

It was with the emergence of the religiously oriented National Salvation party in the early 1970s that Islam's political role began to receive sustained scholarly attention. Nur Yalman, "Some Observations on Secularism in Islam" (1973), asserted that the Kemalist effort to transform society engendered fanaticism as people cut off from their traditional moorings sought a new identity. Feroz Ahmad, in *The Turkish Experiment in Democracy, 1950–1975* (1977), detailed moves by the parties to exploit Islam for political gain, alleging that government interest in using religion as a weapon against the left was a major factor promoting "reactionary fanaticism." In my "Islam and the State in Modern Turkey" (1979), I called the process of legitimization of the exploitation of religious issues by political parties inexorable, but found it more benign. Binnaz Toprak, *Islam and Political Development in Turkey* (1981), drew attention to the centrifugal force of Islam in Turkey. Metin Heper, on the other hand, in "Islam, Polity and Society in Turkey" (1981) stressed that Turkish democratic development had provided alternatives to religious protest. His conclusion that Islam and secular trends do not ebb and flow in a cyclical pattern in Turkey as in Middle Eastern countries was reached before the upsurge of sectarian violence in Turkey toward the mid-1990s, the strong showing of the Welfare party in the municipal elections of 1994, and that party's plurality in the 1995 general elections.

The firm stand by the generals against allowing Islam a political role obscured for a time after 1980 the course of the political system toward coming to terms with religious issues. Thus Mehmet Yasar Geyikdagi's *Political Parties in Turkey: The Role of Islam* (1984) expected that the prohibitions imposed in the new constitution would prevent the exploitation of religion in politics. Similarly, Nicholas S. Ludington, *Turkish Islam and the Secular State* (1984), dealt with Islam largely as a private, individual affair.

Others have long regarded religion as a key variable. Serif Mardin, "Culture and Religion" (1989a), examined the process of transforming Islam into an ideology. He was followed by Feride Acar's "Islam in Turkey" (1993), which focused on the religious "activist minority," clarifying the rationale behind the selection of the dress issue as a main point of attack. She also identified the fragmented nature of the Islamist movement in Turkey and the differentiation in the Islamist reaction to developments elsewhere in the Muslim world. But her conclusion that the Gulf War of 1991 may have created a less favorable climate for Islamist appeal in Turkey was challenged by Nilufer Gole. Gole's "Authoritarian Secularism and Islamist Politics: The Case of Turkey" (1996) identified the Welfare party as potentially representing "a new way to political legitimacy" by capitalizing on rising expectations of an upwardly mobile population. But she noted that "in moving to the center, it departs from affirming Islamist authenticity," and she expected it to forge alliances with the reformist elites, thereby deepening democracy.

In studying the Islamic dimension of politics, research on individual religious groups has come into vogue. Serif Mardin's study *Religion and Social Change in Modern Turkey: The Case of Bediuzzaman Said Nursi* (1989b) explained the role of the Nurcular, a religious fringe group, in supporting conservative parties rather than seeking to upset the system. Mardin also investigated the important Nakshibandi dervish sect, with its links to such major politicians as Prime Minister and later President Turgut Ozal. Such ties no doubt led Ozay Mehmet, *Islamic Identity and Development* (1990), to conclude that in Turkey it would be possible to advocate nationalism without abandoning Islam. Indeed, by the time Richard Tapper edited the collection *Islam in Modern Turkey* (1991), the place of religion in political life was a major subject of debate in academic circles, although his work was one of the first to rely on fieldwork to differentiate the manifestations of Islam in various parts of Turkey.

THE MILITARY

A striking feature of modern Turkish political life has been the intervention of the military in the political arena at various times during the past half-century. But Dankwart A. Rustow's article "The Army and the Founding of the Turkish Republic" (1959), coming as it did before the first modern public military excursion into politics, stressed merely the nation-building role of the armed forces. It was only the 1960 takeover that pointed political researchers to recognize the continuing political weight of the officer corps. Frederick W. Frey led the way with his "Arms and the Man in Turkish Politics" (1960), which analyzed the complex military tradition in Turkey. Whereas Walter F. Weiker, *The Turkish Revolution, 1960–1961* (1963), saw advantages of "regimes that are not multiparty" in promoting economic takeoff, I argued in "The Role of the Military in Turkish Politics" (1965) that the complexities of Turkey's polity would frustrate any attempt by the armed forces to reestablish lasting dominance in society. In weighing the chances for success of a civilian/military elite coalition, Ergun Ozbudun's *The Role of the Military in Recent Turkish Politics* (1966) dwelt on the likelihood that the military would act in self-defense if threatened by revanchist policies.

The 1971 "coup by memorandum" that brought down the Justice party government of Suleyman Demirel drew further attention to praetorian politics. Roger P. Nye, "Civil-Military Confrontation in Turkey" (1977), stressed the military dimension of the presidency, although his analysis ignored the deep divisions in the armed forces over their political role that others have identified. But it was the 1980 generals' coup that set the seal for much of the current understanding of the military in Turkey's politics. Kemal H. Karpat, "Turkish Democracy at Impasse: Ideology, Party Politics, and the Third Military Intervention" (1981), labeled the takeover by the generals in Turkey as a "definite turning point," reflecting a failure of civilian leadership. He was not alone in seeing this third major excursion into political life in 30 years as making the military the dominant factor in Turkish politics. Many of the contributors to Metin Heper and Ahmet Evin, *State, Democracy and Military: Turkey in the 1980s* (1988), also took this tack. In that same volume, however, I argued for seeing the military in Turkey henceforth not as the decision makers to whom others would defer, but as participants whose guardian role extended primarily to the security area.

Election of a civilian as president in 1989 and of a civilian successor when he died in 1993 made it clear that the civil/military equation had changed. William M. Hale assessed these developments against prevalent political science theories in *Turkish Politics and the Military* (1995). He concluded that despite the worsening of the challenge of Kurdish dissent and rampant inflation, the likelihood of "another military intervention seemed further away than at any time in the country's post-war history," because the armed forces had the unity and distinctiveness to be able "voluntarily" to disengage to a "moderator" or "guardian" role. The complex role played by the military's leaders in the fall of the Welfare party coalition in 1997 and in the formation of the secular-oriented coalition headed by Mesut Yilmaz tests the limits of Hale's conclusion.

CLASSES AND INTEREST GROUPS

Ataturk and the Turkish nationalist reformers of the 1920s and 1930s sought to deny the existence of social classes in republican Turkey because they considered them to be divisive. Ironically, it has since often been held that Turkey's success in implanting democracy depended integrally on Kemalist efforts to have Turkey develop in a secular, industrialized path, a course that ineluctably led to the differentiation of the middle class from the working class. It was this evolution that laid the basis for the emergence of a vigorous civil society.

The role of the Kemalist reform movement in creating institutions representing a broad range of social elements has been only partially studied. Robert Bianchi in *Interest Groups and Political Development in Turkey* (1984) tested theories of state-directed as opposed to pluralistic corporatism. His finding that these different types may coexist in the same society at the same time shed new light on political party competition in Turkey. His conclusions were challenged by Metin Heper in *Strong State and Economic Interest Groups* (1992), who claimed that in Turkey the state virtually "smothered civil society." Rejecting the notion that Turkey's system could be considered "hybrid" in terms of corporatism, Heper paid more attention to autocratic behavior by Prime Minister Ozal and his clique of decision makers than to the underlying changes of the 1980s that fostered civil society. These sharp disagreements in interpretation call for a far more thorough study of this subject.

Interest groups with a clear political role have attracted special attention. Nermin Abadan-Unat focused on workers and youth in particular with "Turkish Workers in West Germany" (1969) and "Values and Political Behavior of Turkish Youth" (1965). Her study *Turkish Workers in Europe, 1960–1975* (1976) analyzed their motives for going abroad and their possible impact on returning home after exposure to new ideas. Joseph S. Szyliowicz, *A Political Analysis of Student Activism: The Turkish Case* (1972), presented a longitudinal, comparative study of the dynamics of student activism that had contributed to the military intervention of 1971. But scholarly attention to student movements has waned after their political role was curtailed by the post-1980 constitutional regime.

As the universities in Turkey became polarized between sympathizers of the right and left, Marxist analysis became fashionable by the late 1960s. Writers such as Dogu Ergil, "Class Conflict and Turkish Transformation, 1950–1975" (1975a) and "Secularization as Class Conflict: The Turkish Example" (1975b), interpreted the modernization process as a struggle of capitalism against feudalism. In the succeeding era, Mehmet N. Uca's *Workers' Participation and Self-Management in Turkey* (1983) and Berch Berberoglu's *Turkey in Crisis: From State Capitalism to Neo-colonialism* (1982) carried on this Marxist analysis with greater shrillness. Caglar Keyder, *State and Class in Turkey: A Study in Capitalist Development* (1987), presented the most thoughtful analysis along these lines. This point of view has been less self-assured and assertive in Turkish universities after the collapse of the Soviet Union. Yet much grist for social science study exists in these polemical treatments of the Turkish scene.

The peasantry also needs closer scrutiny. A detailed peasant survey was conducted by MIT researchers in the mid-1960s. They enlisted hundreds of indigenous interviewers to poll thousands of selected respondents. This unpublished corpus in the MIT library represents baseline data that could inform future work. Otherwise, coverage of the peasantry comes from discrete village studies by scholars such as John F. Kolars, *Tradition, Season, and Change in a Turkish Village* (1963), Joseph S. Szyliowicz, *Political Change in Rural Turkey: Erdemli* (1966), and Paul J. Magnarella, *The Peasant Venture: Tradition, Migration, and Change among Georgian Peasants in Turkey* (1979). These works analyzed the impact of burgeoning communications in undermining traditional leadership roles and generally weakening the villages as discrete communities.

THE KURDS

Only at the end of the 1980s did the government and scholarly community in Turkey come freely to acknowledge that the country had a major Kurdish problem. Before that time, a polite fiction among Turkish officials and many political scientists held that there was an "eastern" problem, but it was termed one of underdevelopment and not ethnic identity. Researchers outside Turkey were not so constrained. But until recent years my "Ethnic Conflict and the Kurds" (1977) was one of relatively few analytical treatments of this subject. It sought to explain why Kurds, including those in Turkey, had not been successful in achieving autonomy or establishing their own state. I updated this story in "Whither the Kurds?" (1997).

Robert Olson, *The Emergence of Kurdish Nationalism and the Sheikh Said Rebellion, 1889–1925* (1989), was one of the first to test the new openness. He presented findings from British archives on the early phases of the Kurdish issue in republican Turkey. His study, however, did not entirely lay to rest the question of whether Kurdish nationalism animated the Sheikh Said rebellion or whether it was essentially a tribal revolt tinged with religious reaction. Michael M. Gunter, *The Kurds in Turkey* (1991), and Ismet G. Imset, *The PKK* (1992), concentrated on the Kurdish Workers party (PKK) and its violent struggle to assert autonomy, but paid relatively little attention to legal political activity by Kurds in Turkey. Mehrdad R. Izady, *The Kurds: A Concise Handbook* (1992), presents much sociological information not available elsewhere, but many of his political judgments are impressionistic and require further study. David McDowall, *A Modern History of the Kurds* (1996), foresees Kurds gaining greater autonomy in Turkey than in other countries. He expected that Kurds in western Turkey would be more destabilizing to the regime than those in the southeast. These conclusions remain open to considerable question, particularly in view of the minimal violence in Turkey's urban areas and the near independence Kurds have enjoyed in northern Iraq in the 1990s. *The Kurdish Nationalist Movement in the 1990s: Its Impact on Turkey and the Middle East* (1996), edited by Robert Olson, addresses the PKK's challenge primarily as a human crisis rather than in analytic fashion. Despite this work, substantial further research is needed to make clear what Kurds in Turkey want and what tactics they will use in their quest. These are questions whose solution has become increasingly important to the political health of Turkey.

LEGAL INSTITUTIONS

The study of legal institutions has lagged behind some other areas of investigation. Tugrul Ansay and Don Wallace, Jr., *Introduction to Turkish Law* (1987), have edited a primer for the nonspecialist that provides a useful guide to the field. Yet there is relatively little literature addressing the role of the legal system in Turkey's polity. An exception is June Starr's *Law as Metaphor: From Islamic Courts to the Palace of Justice* (1992). She used a detailed inspection of one provincial city to draw conclusions applicable to the larger Turkish scene. Setting secular and religious law as polar opposites, she measured the success of the state's legal system and suggested tentative answers to the question of why Islamic groups in Turkey, as opposed to Egypt, have been completely unable to make progress in reinstating religious law.

Legal analysis in English has yet fully to catch up with the replacement of the constitution following the 1980 military takeover. Studies by Joseph S. Szyliowicz, ''The 1961 Turkish Constitution: An Analysis'' (1963), and Rona Aybay, ''Some Contemporary Constitutional Problems in Turkey'' (1977), illuminated aspects of the highly decentralized order instituted in 1961. Ergun Ozbudun, ''The Status of the President of the Republic under the Turkish Constitution of 1982'' (1988c), gave a snapshot of the dynamic reinterpretation process going on to adapt the latest fundamental law to current exigencies. But constitutional practice has gone beyond these studies, and the important relationship of president and prime minister requires further elucidation.

Starting with A.T.J. Matthews, *Emergent Turkish Administrators* (1955), public administration has received attention. Albert Gorvine and Laurence Barber, Jr., *Organization and Functions of Turkish Ministries* (1956), provided a guide to the operation of the Turkish government as it emerged from the one-party era. That was followed by the comparative work of Lynton K. Caldwell, "Turkish Administration and the Politics of Expediency" (1957), who expected that the effectiveness of the Turkish administration would improve slowly in a multiparty environment.

The restoration of civilian rule after the 1960 military takeover posed new challenges for the bureaucracy, which became politicized in ways unexpected by earlier researchers. Clement H. Dodd, "Administrative Reform in Turkey" (1965), described an early stage of the process. Metin Heper, "The Recalcitrance of the Turkish Bureaucracy to 'Bourgeois Politics' " (1976), located the Turkish administration's central position in the "induced" rather than "organic" change paradigm he saw at work in Turkey. Richard Hofferbert and Ustun Erguder, "The Penetrability of Policy Systems in a Developing Context" (1985), postulated that bureaucracies that precede the rise of civil society, as in Turkey, are more apt to play the role of guardians than of servants, a conclusion that invites reinspection.

Vakur Versan, "Local Government in Turkey" (1966), provided a baseline for understanding municipal organs that gained in importance as power began slowly to devolve from central institutions. Melih Ersoy, "Relations between Central and Local Governments in Turkey" (1992), judged that the new efforts at decentralization ushered in by right-of-center governments after 1980 were largely canceled out by the central authority's power to intervene in emergencies. Political party control of locally elected bodies was analyzed by Ersin Kalaycioglu, "Decentralization of Government" (1994), and the countermove against this tendency that began in the mid-1970s was examined in Andrew Finkel, "Municipal Politics and the State in Contemporary Turkey" (1990). Yet the auguries are mixed, and Levent Koker in "Local Politics and Democracy in Turkey: An Appraisal" (1995) found it difficult to divine whether authoritarianism or greater democratic decentralization would take place. Clearly, therefore, more needs to be done to bring the study of public administration up to date.

WOMEN AND HUMAN RIGHTS

Turkey has had the advantage of having some social scientists who early took an interest in the women's movement. Nermin Abadan-Unat, a leading figure in Turkey's political science establishment since the 1960s, led the way with her *Social Change and Turkish Women* (1963). She sharpened and deepened its theses in the volume she edited on *Women in Turkish Society* (1981), ascribing to changes in economic requirements the prime reason for alterations in the role and status of women. Indeed, Abadan-Unat saw Turkey as a case study for crisis-induced change. Others like Cigdem Kagitcibasi, "Women and Development in Turkey" (1982), have followed her lead in this emerging field of study, demonstrating on the basis of extensive survey data how highly resistant to change family roles are, despite a favorable legal and political climate.

The fact that few women went into politics in Turkey, while far larger numbers entered the bureaucracy or became professionals, has intrigued a number of researchers. Deniz Kandiyoti, ''Sex Roles and Social Change: A Comparative Appraisal of Turkey's Women'' (1977), used survey data to buttress her finding that the patriarchal nature of Turkish society was the greatest obstacle to Turkish women's success in politics. Yesim Arat, *The Patriarchal Paradox: Women Politicians in Turkey* (1989), also did not foresee that despite women holding but 8 of the then 450 seats in parliament, one would be elected prime minister just a few years later in 1993. The collection of *Women in Modern Turkish Society: A Reader* (1995), edited by Sirin Tekeli, foreshadows Western-educated Turkish women's concern over the rise of Islamic practices, but does not account for the rise of Tansu Ciller. This development is sure to spur additional research as political scientists seek to assess a development that none expected.

Ergun Ozbudun's ''Human Rights and the Rule of Law'' (1988b) has emphasized the legalistic aspects of the problem of civil rights, celebrating the signature of U.N. conventions as an important step to protect human rights in Turkey. Amnesty International and many others stress the continuing challenge to live up to these promises. In fact, there is much polemical literature that could contribute to analysis of the human rights problem facing Turkey, especially in coping with Kurdish dissidence in eastern Turkey, where guerrillas and the state are engaged in almost continuous warfare. The Kurdish angle is treated in Gunter's study and Olson's collective work, both cited earlier.

I sketched out a more general view of the difficulties of human rights in Turkey in *Turkey: Coping with Crisis* (1985b), attempting to put in historical perspective some of the accomplishments and failures Turkey has recorded in its quest for modernization in this area. Mehmet Semih Gemalmaz, *The Institutionalization Process of the Turkish Type of Democracy: A Politico-juridical Analysis of Human Rights* (1989), followed by attributing continuing human rights violations to the new legal and political structures erected after the 1980 military takeover.

FOREIGN POLICY

It might have been expected that Turkey's membership in NATO starting in 1952 would have occasioned intense study of that country's foreign policy, but until I published *Troubled Alliance* (1972), almost no serious work had been done to explain why Turkey established its major alliance system with the United States and NATO. My analysis focused on the difficulties of maintaining an alliance between two states of greatly differing size and power. Its findings were validated in Bruce R. Kuniholm, *The Origins of the Cold War in the Near East* (1980), who shed more light on how the partnership began. Subsequently the value of Turkey's tie to the United States was assessed in Dankwart A. Rustow, *Turkey: America's Forgotten Ally* (1987), but he based his work on an expectation of an ongoing superpower rivalry with the Soviet Union.

Ferenc A. Valli, *Bridge across the Bosporus* (1971), attempted a broad study, including an investigation of foreign affairs decision making. Yet by covering the subject topically rather than chronologically, he blurred some of the inter-connections between relationships. A. Haluk Ulman and Richard Dekmejian, "Changing Patterns in Turkish Foreign Policy, 1959–1967" (1967), emphasized the start of Turkey's questioning of its alliance structure. *Turkey's Foreign Policy in Transition, 1950–1974* (1975), edited by Kemal H. Karpat, was one of the first to inspect the multidimensional foreign policy that has come to char-acterize Turkey's relations with the world. Most recently, Graham E. Fuller and Ian O. Lesser, *Turkey's New Geopolitics: From the Balkans to Western China* (1993), sought to assess early possibilities for Turkey in the post-Soviet world.

The emerging relationship with Europe has also engaged researchers. Ilter Turan, "Turkey and the European Community" (1989), sketched out four sce-narios running the gamut from admission to the community to exclusion from it, all reflecting Cold War considerations. Duygu Sezer, "Turkish Foreign Policy in the Year 2000" (1989), addressed domestic as well as external factors. Her insight that Turkey was more likely to shift policy in reaction to outside stimuli than out of domestic imperatives gave her work particular value, even though she clearly did not expect the world to change as fast as it did. Canan Balkir and Allan M. Williams, *Turkey and Europe* (1993), pointed to the difficulties facing the relationship with Europe but also saw new opportunities in Eastern Europe and the Commonwealth of Independent States. Sabri Sayari, "Turkey: The Changing European Security Environment and the Gulf Crisis" (1992b), attributed to Ozal the main role in designing Turkey's response to the end of the Cold War. Sayari expected the bureaucracy to regain the initiative in the foreign policy process after Ozal was elected president; the verdict is still to come on that surmise. Despite these more recent treatments, many of the im-portant links between domestic and foreign policy remain largely unresearched.

A major focus of work on Turkey's foreign relations has been the study of connections with the Soviet Union and its successor states. One of the earliest was my attempt to explain why relations with the USSR were improving in "Cross-Alliance Politics: Turkey and the Soviet Union" (1974). Turkkaya Ataov saw opportunities in the post-USSR scene in his "Turkey, the CIS, and Eastern Europe" (1993). Graham Fuller, *Turkey Faces East* (1992), argued strongly that Turkey had begun to see itself as the center of the newly emerging Turkic world, though in fact the Turkish Western orientation remains intact. In "The Russian Federation and Turkey" (1995), I laid out the military, psycho-logical, and economic issues that currently bedevil Turkish-Russian relations. But the flow of events attendant on the breakup of the Soviet Union has yet to settle into a stable channel, and the relationship of Turkey to the Commonwealth of Independent States requires much further study.

The Cyprus dispute has had an outsize impact on Turkey's international po-sition. An objective view of the diplomacy of this issue is rare; however, Tozun Bahcheli, *Greek-Turkish Relations since 1955* (1990), demonstrates considerable detachment in treating the panoply of contentious matters. A useful memoir by Parker T. Hart, *Two NATO Allies at the Threshold of War* (1990), which is less shrill than its title, provides an insider view of the 1967 crisis over Cyprus. Suha Bolukbasi, *The Superpowers and the Third World: Turkish-American Relations and Cyprus* (1990), incorporates U.S. archive material to analyze the limits of influence of the larger power on the smaller. Pierre Oberling, *The Road to Bellapais* (1982), studied refugee resettlement to predict the subsequent unilateral Turkish declaration of independence for northern Cyprus.

Over the past two decades Turkey has paid increasing attention to deepening ties to the Middle East. The Turks have wanted to emphasize commercial relationships, but political ties have inevitably been given prominence by the difficulties of escaping all involvement in the conflicts on Turkey's borders. The contributors to *The Middle East in Turkish-American Relations* (1985a), which I edited, considered how Turkey's role in the Middle East had become an integral part of the country's domestic development strategy as well as an important political asset for Turkish foreign policymakers. On the other hand, the disabilities that hamper Turkey from active leadership in the Middle East were well set out in Philip Robins, *Turkey and the Middle East* (1991), including analysis of water and commercial issues. The Gulf War with Iraq posed new problems that challenged Turkey's traditional stance of noninvolvement in Middle Eastern affairs. While Andrew Mango, *Turkey: The Challenge of a New Role* (1995), makes a start at investigating this mix of opportunity and difficulty, more work needs to be done to put Turkey's international possibilities in perspective.

Much more authoritative treatment of Turkey's foreign affairs would have been possible had the Turkish government not jealously guarded its archival material. As a result, scholarly treatment of the Turkish foreign policy process has thus far generally been more descriptive than analytical. The study of Turkey's foreign relations, therefore, remains a matter worth more attention than it has received.

FUTURE POLITICAL RESEARCH

It is a commonplace that when studying emergent multiparty polities, political researchers focus more on the politics of elections and the political impact of economic and social development than on such topics as the institutions that form the backbone of civil society. So it is in the case of Turkey. There the growth of voluntary associations, including charitable, business, social, and religious organizations, has still not come in for sustained inspection. Yet these bodies play increasingly important political functions. The data for such study may be difficult to assemble, but a deeper look at these institutions needs to be undertaken.

As was pointed out earlier, the peasantry, which still comprises a significant portion of the population, has not been studied in detail since the mid-1960s. A longitudinal study of peasant attitudes over time would have much to contribute to an understanding of where Turkish politics is headed and what changes might be expected.

Another area that is only now beginning to attract attention is that of Turkey's political economy. The dramatic move since 1980 to junk the Kemalist import-substitution regime in favor of an export-led economic system is probably the single most important long-term change in recent years. Yet perhaps because it lies at the intersection of concerns of economists and political scientists, a convincing explanation has not been given for how and why the political climate came to shift to allow a minority government depending on outside parliamentary support to take the basic economic decisions in January 1980 that scrapped fifty years of statist policies in favor of market forces. The impact of continuing high inflation on political attitudes is also worth additional study. Attention to the issue of corruption, though difficult to elucidate, would contribute much to an understanding of Turkey's current political dynamics.

Surprisingly, the question of leadership has been relatively neglected. Party chiefs in Turkey tend to remain on the scene for quite lengthy periods. Ismet Inonu was prime minister first in 1923 and last in 1965. Bulent Ecevit, Suleyman Demirel, Alparslan Turkes, and Necmettin Erbakan emerged in the 1960s and, with the exception of Turkes, who died in April 1977, are all still major players. Brief biographies of these and others are in Bernard Reich, *Political Leaders of the Contemporary Middle East and North Africa* (1990), but only Kemal Ataturk has been the subject of full-dress treatment. With a new generation of leaders emerging, including for the first time a woman who served several years as prime minister and who might perhaps return for another period, greater effort should be devoted to this natural topic for political researchers.

Ethnic politics is a major factor influencing the future of the Turkish polity. The softening of the official denial that Kurds have a separate identity should make it possible to dig more deeply into this subject. Work thus far has been largely descriptive or polemical. It begs for a more conceptual approach.

Finally, the disappearance of the Soviet Union as a commanding issue in Turkey's foreign and security policy is only beginning to be assessed. A judicious investigation of Turkish foreign policy in the age of new ethnically based national states remains an urgent requirement. It should integrate domestic and economic factors as well as international imperatives to make clear the limits of Turkey's freedom of action on the world stage. Also needed is further study of the Turkish role in the Organization of Islamic Conference and Turkish interest and capabilities in the Balkans.

To return to the observations made at the outset, the production of political science literature on Turkey has been increasing, particularly in the past decade, but original work of general interest to political scientists at large remains sparse. Much more must be done before a consensus on major propositions concerning Turkey is achieved.

REFERENCES

Abadan-Unat, Nermin. 1963. *Social Change and Turkish Women*. Ankara: Ankara Universitesi Basimevi.

———. 1965. "Values and Political Behavior of Turkish Youth." *Turkish Yearbook of International Relations, 1963* 4:81–102.

———. 1969. "Turkish Workers in West Germany: A Case Study." *Siyasal Bilgiler Fakultesi Dergisi* 24:21–49.

———. 1976. *Turkish Workers in Europe, 1960–1975*. Leiden: E. J. Brill.

———, ed. 1981. *Women in Turkish Society*. Leiden: E. J. Brill.

Acar, F. 1993. "Islam in Turkey." In Canan Balkir and Allan M. Williams, eds., Turkey and Europe. London: Pinter.

Ahmad, Feroz. 1977. *The Turkish Experiment in Democracy, 1950–1975*. London: Royal Institute of International Affairs.

———. 1993. *The Making of Modern Turkey*. London: Routledge.

Alkan, M. Turker. 1980. "Turkey: Rise and Decline of Political Legitimacy in a Revolutionary Regime." *Journal of South Asian and Middle Eastern Studies* 4, no. 2:37–48.

Ansay, Tugrul, and Don Wallace, Jr., eds. 1987. *Introduction to Turkish Law*. Dobbs Ferry, NY: Oceana Publications.

Arat, Yesim. 1989. *The Patriarchal Paradox: Women Politicians in Turkey*. Rutherford, NJ: Fairleigh Dickinson University Press.

Ataov, T. 1993. "Turkey, the CIS, and Eastern Europe." In Canan Balkir and Allan M. Williams, eds., *Turkey and Europe*. London: Pinter.

Aybay, R. 1977. "Some Contemporary Constitutional Problems in Turkey." *British Society for Middle Eastern Studies Bulletin* 4, no. 1:21–27.

Bahcheli, Tozun. 1990. *Greek-Turkish Relations since 1955*. Boulder, CO: Westview Press.

Balim, Cigdem, et al. 1995. *Turkey: Political, Social and Economic Challenges in the 1990s*. Leiden: E. J. Brill.

Balkir, Canan, and Allan M. Williams, eds. 1993. *Turkey and Europe*. London: Pinter.

Barkey, Henri J. 1990. *The State and the Industrialization Crisis in Turkey*. Boulder, CO: Westview Press.

Berberoglu, Berch. 1982. *Turkey in Crisis: From State Capitalism to Neo-colonialism*. London: Zed Press.

Berkes, Niyazi. 1964. *The Development of Secularism in Turkey*. Montreal: McGill University Press.

Bianchi, Robert. 1984. *Interest Groups and Political Development in Turkey*. Princeton: Princeton University Press.

Bolukbasi, Suha. 1990. *The Superpowers and the Third World: Turkish-American Relations and Cyprus*. Lanham, MD: University Press.

Caldwell, Lynton K. 1957. "Turkish Administration and the Politics of Expediency." In William J. Siffin, ed., *Toward the Comparative Study of Public Administration*. Bloomington: Indiana University Press.

Cohn, Edwin J. 1970. *Turkish Economic, Social, and Political Change*. New York: Praeger.

Dodd, Clement H. 1965. "Administrative Reform in Turkey." *Public Administration* 43: 71–83.

Dumont, Paul. 1984. "The Origins of Kemalist Ideology." In Jacob M. Landau, ed., *Ataturk and the Modernization of Turkey*. Boulder, CO: Westview Press.

Eisenstadt, S. N. 1984. "The Kemalist Regime and Modernization: Some Comparative and Analytical Remarks." In Jacob M. Landau, ed., *Ataturk and the Modernization of Turkey*. Boulder, CO: Westview Press.

Ergil, Dogu. 1975a. "Class Conflict and Turkish Transformation, 1950–1975." *Studia Islamica*, 41:137–161.

———. 1975b. "Secularization as Class Conflict: The Turkish Example." *Asian Affairs* 62:69–80.

Erguder, Ustun. 1988. "Post-1980 Parties and Politics in Turkey." In Turkish Political Science Association, *Perspectives on Democracy in Turkey*. Ankara: Sevinc Matbaasi.

Ersoy, Melih. 1992. "Relations between Central and Local Governments in Turkey: An Historical Perspective." *Public Administration and Development* 12:325–341.

Finkel, Andrew. "Municipal Politics and the State in Contemporary Turkey." 1990. In Andrew Finkel and Nukhet Sirman, eds., *Turkish State, Turkish Society*. New York: Routledge. 202–211.

Frey, Frederick W. 1960. "Arms and the Man in Turkish Politics." *Land Reborn* 11, no. 2:3–14.

———. 1965. *The Turkish Political Elite*. Cambridge, MA: M.I.T. Press.

———. 1975. "Patterns of Elite Politics in Turkey." In George Lenczowski, ed., *Political Elites in the Middle East*. Washington, DC: American Enterprise Institute for Public Policy Research.

Fuller, Graham E. 1992. *Turkey Faces East: New Orientations toward the Middle East and the Old Soviet Union*. Santa Monica, CA: Rand Corporation.

Fuller, Graham E., and Ian O. Lesser. 1993. *Turkey's New Geopolitics: From the Balkans to Western China*. Boulder, CO: Westview Press.

Gemalmaz, Mehmet Semih. 1989. *The Institutionalization Process of the Turkish Type of Democracy: A Politico-juridical Analysis of Human Rights*. Istanbul: Amac Yayincilik.

Geyikdagi, Mehmet Yasar. 1984. *Political Parties in Turkey: The Role of Islam*. New York: Praeger.

Gole, Nilufer. 1996. "Authoritarian Secularism and Islamist Politics: The Case of Turkey." In Augustus Richard Norton, ed., *Civil Society in the Middle East*, vol. 2. Leiden: E. J. Brill. 2:17–43.

Gorvine, Albert, and Laurence Barber, Jr. 1956. *Organization and Functions of Turkish Ministries*. Ankara: Ajans-Turk Matbaasi.

Gunter, Michael M. 1991. *The Kurds in Turkey: A Political Dilemma*. Boulder, CO: Westview Press.

Hale, William M. 1995. *Turkish Politics and the Military*. London: Routledge.

Harris, George S. 1965. "The Role of the Military in Turkish Politics." *Middle East Journal* 19, nos. 2 and 3:54–66, 169–176.

———. 1972. *Troubled Alliance: Turkish-American Problems in Historical Perspective, 1945–1971*. Washington, DC: American Enterprise Institute for Public Policy Research.

———. 1974. "Cross-Alliance Politics: Turkey and the Soviet Union." *Turkish Yearbook of International Relations, 1972* 12:1–32.

———. 1977. "Ethnic Conflict and the Kurds." *Annals of the American Academy of Political and Social Science* 433:112–124.

———. 1979. "Islam and the State in Modern Turkey." *Middle East Review* 11, no. 4: 21–26, 31.

———. 1981. "Bureaucratic Reform: Ataturk and the Turkish Foreign Office." *Journal of the American Institute for the Study of Middle Eastern Civilization* 1, nos. 3–4: 39–51.

———, ed. 1985a. *The Middle East in Turkish-American Relations*. Washington, DC: Heritage Foundation.

———. 1985b. *Turkey: Coping with Crisis*. Boulder, CO: Westview Press.

———. 1995. "The Russian Federation and Turkey." In Alvin Z. Rubinstein and Oles M. Smolansky, eds., *Regional Power Rivalries in the New Eurasia: Russia, Turkey, and Iran*. Armonk, NY: M. E. Sharpe.

———. 1997. "Whither the Kurds?" In Winston A. Van Horne, ed., *Global Convulsions: Race, Ethnicity, and Nationalism at the End of the Twentieth Century*. Albany: State University of New York Press. 205–223.

Hart, Parker T. 1990. *Two NATO Allies at the Threshold of War*. Durham, NC: Duke University Press.

Heper, Metin. 1976. "The Recalcitrance of the Turkish Public Bureaucracy to 'Bourgeois Politics': A Multi-Factor Political Stratification Analysis." *Middle East Journal* 30, no. 4:485–500.

———. 1981. "Islam, Polity and Society in Turkey: A Middle Eastern Perspective." *Middle East Journal* 35, no. 3:345–363.

———. 1985. *The State Tradition in Turkey*. North Humberside: Eothern Press.

———. 1992. *Strong State and Economic Interest Groups: The Post-1980 Turkish Experience*. New York: Walter de Gruyter.

Heper, Metin, and Ahmet Evin, eds. 1988. *State, Democracy and Military: Turkey in the 1980s*. New York: Walter de Gruyter.

———. 1994. *Politics in the Third Turkish Republic*. Boulder, CO: Westview Press.

Heper, Metin, and Jacob M. Landau, eds. 1991. *Political Parties and Democracy in Turkey*. London: I. B. Tauris.

Hofferbert, Richard I., and Ustun Erguder. 1985. "The Penetrability of Policy Systems in a Developing Context." *Journal of Public Policy* 5:87–105.

Huntington, Samuel P. 1969. *Political Order in Changing Societies*. New Haven: Yale University Press.

Imset, Ismet G. 1992. *The PKK: A Report on Separatist Violence in Turkey (1973–1992)*. Ankara: Turkish Daily News.

Izady, Mehrdad R. 1992. *The Kurds: A Concise Handbook*. Washington, DC: Crane Russak.

Kagitcibasi, Cigdem. 1982. "Women and Development in Turkey." *International Journal of Turkish Studies* 2, no. 2:59–70.

Kalaycioglu, Ersin. 1994. "Decentralization of Government." In Metin Heper and Ahmet Evin, eds., *Politics in the Third Turkish Republic*. Boulder, CO: Westview Press.

Kandiyoti, D. 1977. "Sex Roles and Social Change: A Comparative Appraisal of Turkey's Women." *Journal of Women in Culture and Society* 3, no. 1:57–73.

Karpat, Kemal H. 1959. *Turkey's Politics: The Transition to a Multi-Party System.* Princeton: Princeton University Press.

———. 1973. "Ideology in Turkey after the Revolution of 1960." In Kemal H. Karpat, ed., *Social Change and Politics in Turkey: A Structural-historical Analysis.* Leiden: E. J. Brill.

———, ed. 1975. *Turkey's Foreign Policy in Transition, 1950–1974.* Leiden: E. J. Brill.

———. 1981. "Turkish Democracy at Impasse: Ideology, Party Politics, and the Third Military Intervention." *International Journal of Turkish Studies* 2, no. 1:1–43.

Keyder, Caglar. 1987. *State and Class in Turkey: A Study in Capitalist Development.* London: Verso.

Kim, Chong Lim, et al. 1984. *The Legislative Connection: The Representatives and the Represented in Kenya, Korea, and Turkey.* Durham, NC: Duke University Press.

Koker, Levent. 1995. "Local Politics and Democracy in Turkey: An Appraisal." In Henry Teune, ed., *Local Governance around the World.* Thousand Oaks, CA: Sage Periodicals.

Kolars, John F. 1963. *Tradition, Season, and Change in a Turkish Village.* Chicago: University of Chicago Press.

Kuniholm, Bruce R. 1980. *The Origins of the Cold War in the Near East: Great Power Conflict and Diplomacy in Iran, Turkey, and Greece.* Princeton: Princeton University Press.

Landau, Jacob M. 1974. *Radical Politics in Modern Turkey.* Leiden: E. J. Brill.

———, ed. 1984. *Ataturk and the Modernization of Turkey.* Boulder, CO: Westview Press.

Lerner, Daniel. 1958. *The Passing of Traditional Society: Modernizing the Middle East.* Glencoe, IL: Free Press.

Lewis, Bernard. 1961. *The Emergence of Modern Turkey.* London: Oxford University Press.

Lipovsky, Igor P. 1992. *The Socialist Movement in Turkey, 1960–1980.* Leiden: E. J. Brill.

Ludington, Nicholas S. 1984. *Turkish Islam and the Secular State.* Washington, DC: American Institute for Islamic Affairs.

Magnarella, Paul J. 1979. *The Peasant Venture: Tradition, Migration, and Change among Georgian Peasants in Turkey.* Cambridge, MA: Schenkman.

Mango, Andrew. 1995. *Turkey: The Challenge of a New Role.* Wesport, CT: Praeger.

Mardin, Serif. 1973. "Center-Periphery Relations: A Key to Turkish Politics?" *Daedalus* 102, no. 1:169–190.

———. 1989a. "Culture and Religion." In Turkish Political Science Association, *Turkey in the Year 2000.* Ankara: Sevinc Matbaasi.

———. 1989b. *Religion and Social Change in Modern Turkey: The Case of Bediuzzaman Said Nursi.* Albany: State University of New York Press.

Matthews, A.T.J. 1955. *Emergent Turkish Administrators: A Study of the Vocational and Social Attitudes of Junior and Potential Administrators.* Ankara: Turk Tarih Kurumu Basimevi.

McDowall, David. 1996. *A Modern History of the Kurds.* New York: I. B. Tauris.

Mehmet, Ozay. 1990. *Islamic Identity and Development: Studies of the Islamic Periphery.* London: Routledge.

Nas, Tevfik F., and Mehmet Odekon, eds. 1992. *Economics and Politics of Turkish Liberalization.* Bethlehem, PA: Lehigh University Press.

Nettl, J. P. 1968. "The State As a Conceptual Variable." *World Politics* 21:559–592.

Nye, Roger P. 1977. "Civil-Military Confrontation in Turkey: The 1973 Presidential Election." *International Journal of Middle Eastern Studies* 8, no. 2:209–228.

Oberling, Pierre. 1982. *The Road to Bellapais: The Turkish Cypriot Exodus to Northern Cyprus*. New York: Columbia University Press.

Olson, Robert. 1989. *The Emergence of Kurdish Nationalism and the Sheikh Said Rebellion, 1880–1925*. Austin: University of Texas Press.

———, ed. 1996. *The Kurdish Nationalist Movement in the 1990s: Its Impact on Turkey and the Middle East*. Lexington: University Press of Kentucky.

Ozbudun, Ergun. 1966. *The Role of the Military in Recent Turkish Politics*. Cambridge, MA: Harvard University Press.

———. 1976. *Social Change and Political Participation in Turkey*. Leiden: E. J. Brill.

———. 1987. "Postauthoritarian Democracies: Turkey." In Myron Weiner and Ergun Ozbudun, eds., *Competitive Elections in Developing Countries*. Durham, NC: Duke University Press.

———. 1988a. "Development of Democratic Government in Turkey." In Turkish Political Science Association, *Perspectives on Democracy in Turkey*. Ankara: Sevinc Matbaasi.

———. 1988b. "Human Rights and the Rule of Law." In Turkish Political Science Association, *Perspectives on Democracy in Turkey*. Ankara: Sevinc Matbaasi.

———. 1988c. "The Status of the President of the Republic under the Turkish Constitution of 1982." In Turkish Political Science Association, Perspectives on *Democracy in Turkey*. Ankara: Sevinc Matbaasi.

Ozbudun, Ergun, and Frank Tachau. 1975. "Social Change and Electoral Behavior in Turkey: Toward a 'Critical Realignment'?" *International Journal of Middle East Studies* 6, no. 4:460–480.

Ozbudun, Ergun, and Aydin Ulusan. 1980. *The Political Economy of Income Distribution in Turkey*. New York: Holmes and Meier.

Pedersen, Mogens N. 1979. "The Dynamics of European Party Systems: Changing Patterns of Electoral Volatility." *European Journal of Political Research* 7:1–26.

Reich, Bernard, ed. 1990. *Political Leaders of the Contemporary Middle East and North Africa: A Biographical Dictionary*. Westport, CT: Greenwood Press.

Robins, Philip. 1991. *Turkey and the Middle East*. New York: Council on Foreign Relations Press.

Roos, Leslie L., and Noralou P. Roos. 1971. *Managers of Modernization: Organizations and Elites in Turkey (1950–1969)*. Cambridge, MA: Harvard University Press.

Rustow, Dankwart A. 1959. "The Army and the Founding of the Turkish Republic." *World Politics* 11, no. 4:513–552.

———. 1968. "Ataturk as Founder of a State." *Daedalus* 93:793–828.

———. 1987. *Turkey: America's Forgotten Ally*. New York: Council on Foreign Relations Press.

Sayari, Sabri. 1978. "The Turkish Party System in Transition." *Government and Opposition* 13, no. 1:39–57.

———. 1992a. "Politics and Economic Policy-making in Turkey, 1980–1988." In Tevfik F. Nas and Mehmet Odekon, eds., *Economics and Politics of Turkish Liberalization*. Bethlehem, PA: Lehigh University Press.

———. 1992b. "Turkey: The Changing European Security Environment and the Gulf Crisis." *Middle East Journal* 46, no. 1 (Winter): 9–21.

Sezer, Duygu Bazoglu. 1989. "Turkish Foreign Policy in the Year 2000." In Turkish
    Political Science Association, *Turkey in the Year 2000*. Ankara: Sevinc Matbaasi.
Shils, Edward. 1961. "Centre and Periphery." In *The Logic of Personal Knowledge:
    Essays Presented to Michael Polanyi on His Seventieth Birthday, 11 March 1961*.
    Glencoe, IL: Free Press.
Starr, June. 1992. *Law as Metaphor: From Islamic Courts to the Palace of Justice*.
    Albany: State University of New York Press.
Szyliowicz, Joseph S. 1963. "The 1961 Turkish Constitution: An Analysis." *Islamic
    Studies* 2:363–381.
———. 1966. *Political Change in Rural Turkey: Erdemli*. The Hague: Mouton.
———. 1971. "Elite Recruitment in Turkey: The Role of the Mulkiye." *World Politics*
    23, no. 3:371–398.
———. 1972. *A Political Analysis of Student Activism: The Turkish Case*. Beverly Hills,
    CA: Sage Publications.
Tachau, Frank. 1984. *Turkey: The Politics of Authority, Democracy, and Development*.
    New York: Holmes and Meier.
Tapper, Richard, ed. 1991. *Islam in Modern Turkey: Religion, Politics, and Literature
    in a Secular State*. New York: I. B. Tauris.
Tekeli, Sirin, ed. 1995. *Women in Modern Turkish Society: A Reader*. London: Zed
    Books.
Toprak, Binnaz. 1981. *Islam and Political Development in Turkey*. Leiden: E. J. Brill.
———. 1996. "Civil Society in Turkey." In Augustus Richard Norton, ed., *Civil Society
    in the Middle East*, vol. 2. Leiden: E. J. Brill.
Turan, Ilter. 1986. "The Recruitment of Cabinet Ministers as a Political Process: Turkey,
    1946–1979." *International Journal of Middle East Studies* 18, no. 4:455–472.
———. 1988. "Stages of Political Development in the Turkish Republic." In Turkish
    Political Science Association, *Perspectives on Democracy in Turkey*. Ankara:
    Sevinc Matbaasi.
———. 1989. "Turkey and the European Community." In Turkish Political Science
    Association, *Turkey in the Year 2000*. Ankara: Sevinc Matbaasi.
Uca, Mehmet N. 1983. *Workers' Participation and Self-Management in Turkey: An Eval-
    uation of Attempts and Experiences*. The Hague: Institute of Social Studies.
Ulman, A. Haluk, and R. H. Dekmejian. 1967. "Changing Patterns in Turkish Foreign
    Policy, 1959–1967." *Orbis* 11, no. 3:772–785.
Valli, Ferenc A. 1971. *Bridge across the Bosporus: The Foreign Policy of Turkey*. Bal-
    timore: Johns Hopkins University Press.
Versan, Vakur. 1966. "Local Government in Turkey." *Journal of Administration Over-
    seas* 5:251–257.
Weiker, Walter F. 1964. *The Turkish Revolution, 1960–1961*. Washington, DC: Brook-
    ings Institution.
———. 1973. *Political Tutelage and Democracy in Turkey: The Free Party and Its
    Aftermath*. Leiden: E. J. Brill.
Yalcin-Heckmann, Lale. 1991. *Tribe and Kinship among the Kurds*. Frankfurt: Peter
    Lang.
Yalman, Nur. 1973. "Some Observations on Secularism in Islam." *Daedalus* 102, no.
    1:139–168.

THE WEST BANK AND GAZA STRIP SINCE 1967

Ann Mosely Lesch

Political science research on the West Bank and Gaza Strip focuses not only on the policies and practices of the Israeli government, which has ruled these territories since June 1967, but also on the efforts by Palestinians to create their own political structures and achieve independence. Research on Israeli policies is often informed by legal and human rights perspectives, and studies on Palestinian politics draw on economic and sociological analyses. Researchers tend to draw policy implications from their findings in an effort to influence the policies of external powers (notably the United States) as well as Israel and the Palestine Liberation Organization (PLO). Nonetheless, most analyses have strong scholarly underpinnings rather than being stridently partisan. Moreover, Palestinian analysts are producing a rapidly growing corpus of scholarly literature that complements studies by foreign analysts and Israelis.

LEGAL AND HUMAN RIGHTS ISSUES

The legal basis for Israeli rule over the West Bank and Gaza remains highly contentious. For example, an influential article by former Israeli ambassador to the United Nations Yehuda Blum, "The Missing Reversioner" (1968), argues that Israel's right to sovereignty over the territories overrides the claims of either Jordan or the indigenous Palestinians. The Israeli jurist Meir Shamgar, in his edited volume *Military Government in the Territories Administered by Israel, 1967–1980* (1982), provides a more cautious appraisal of the legal bases for Israeli rule under international law. Shamgar's volume also describes the indigenous institutions retained by the Israeli military government (as of 1980) and the respective jurisdictions of Israeli military courts, the high court, and indigenous courts.

International legal scholars critique Israeli claims to sovereignty over the territories and its nonapplication of the Geneva Convention on the Protection of Civilian Persons in Time of War (1949). The strongest refutation of Blum is made by Sally and William T. Mallison in *The Palestine Problem in Interna-*

tional Law and World Order (1986). Additional critiques of Israeli policies, from a legal perspective, are provided by law professors Ilan Peleg in *Human Rights in the West Bank and Gaza* (1995), Allan Gerson in *Israel, The West Bank, and International Law* (1978), and David H. Ott in *Palestine in Perspective* (1980). Peleg analyzes the massive violations of human rights that, in his view, require fundamental political change. Gerson and Ott conclude that Israel's legal status is that of belligerent occupant until a settlement is negotiated. Gerson, in particular, argues that Israel, as the trustee administering the area, must give priority to the needs of the local population. Israel's manipulation of the legal system to seize land for settlements is critiqued by Ian Lustick in "Israel and the West Bank after Elon Moreh" (1981) and Eyal Benvenisti in *Legal Dualism* (1989).

The principal Palestinian analyses are produced by al-Haq (Law in the Service of Man), the human rights organization formed on the West Bank in the late 1970s by the lawyers Raja Shehadeh and Jonathan Kuttab as an affiliate of the International Commission of Jurists. Al-Haq has documented the transformation of the territories wrought by Israeli military orders and the imposition of civilian administration in 1981–1982. Such orders recast the land-tenure, tax, and agricultural systems and enabled Israel to annex increasing amounts of land for Israeli settlements as well as to accord the settlements extraterritorial legal status. Al-Haq has also detailed the mounting violations of civil rights. Its publications include Shehadeh and Kuttab, *The West Bank and the Rule of Law* (1980); Kuttab and Shehadeh, *Civilian Administration in the Occupied West Bank* (1982); and Shehadeh, *Occupier's Law* (1985). Succinct summaries of al- Haq's arguments are available in the chapters by Emma Playfair and Shehadeh in Naseer H. Aruri, editor, *Occupation* (1989).

The difficulties besetting Palestinian lawyers are examined in *Palestinian Lawyers and Israeli Rule* by George Emile Bisharat (1989). He analyzes the decline in the legal profession under occupation that can be ascribed in part to the military courts, which undermine both the concept of the rule of law and the authority of the local court system. Bisharat argues that the decline is also due to such internal problems as a lengthy strike by half the Palestinian lawyers and the residents' preference for informal mediators to resolve disputes.

B'Tselem, the Israeli Information Center for Human Rights in the Occupied Territories established in 1989, publishes annual reports that cover deaths, injuries, house demolitions, deportations, detentions, curfews, curtailment of freedom of expression, and closures of educational institutions. B'Tselem also studies selected issues, notably *The Interrogation of Palestinians during the Intifada* (1991a), *Activity of the Undercover Units in the Occupied Territories* (1992a), and *Collective Punishment in the West Bank and the Gaza Strip* (1992b). B'Tselem provides essential baseline data for policy analysts and human rights activists. The information in these reports differs starkly from the apologetic tract by former military governor Shlomo Gazit, whose *The Carrot and the Stick* (1995) argues that Israeli policies during his tenure relied on the ''carrot'' rather than the ''stick.''

Researchers have also published specialized studies on such issues as censorship, deportations, and settlements. Virgil Falloon provides an overview of Israeli restrictions on the import, distribution, publication, and possession of printed materials for *Index on Censorship* (reprinted by al-Haq as *Excessive Secrecy*, 1985). The Committee to Protect Journalists, based in New York, critiques Israel's use of licenses, censorship, and extrajudicial sanctions (including deporting journalists and editors) to control the Palestinian press in *Journalism under Occupation* (1988). The Israeli analyst Dov Shinar documents restrictions on Palestinian newspapers in Shinar and Danny Rubinstein, *Palestinian Press in the West Bank* (1987). Shinar maintains that Palestinians circumvent efforts to silence them through their poetry, fiction, art, theater, and festivals (Shinar, *Palestinian Voices*, 1986). Palestinians thereby communicate political messages and deepen their sense of nationhood. I compiled a record of the deportation of Palestinians from the occupied territories in ''Israeli Deportation of Palestinians'' (1979), updated in ''The Exiles'' (1993). Al-Haq and B'Tselem also analyze the generally fruitless efforts to use the high court to prevent deportation in Joost Hiltermann, *Israel's Deportation Policy in the Occupied West Bank and Gaza* (1986) and B'Tselem's annual reports (1989, 1991b).

The legal, political, and economic ramifications of Israeli settlements have been assessed by numerous scholars. I provided the initial data on settlements in a series of articles (1977–1978, 1983). Subsequently, William W. Harris focused on the Jordan Valley in *Taking Root* (1980), and Ibrahim Matar provided fresh analyses ''Israeli Settlements and Palestinian Rights'' (1989) and *Jewish Settlements, Palestinian Rights, and Peace* (1996). The World Zionist Organization published the Israeli *Master Plan for the Development of Settlement 1979–83, in Judea and Samaria*, authored by Matityahu Drobles (1978). That plan anticipated the placement of settlements among Palestinian towns and villages in order to absorb the land into Israel. Official perspectives are provided in ''Geographical Review: Settlement Pattern and Economic Changes in the Gaza Strip, 1947–1977'' by Elisha Efrat (1977), a geographer with the Ministry of Interior, and by Moshe Drori, a former legal advisor to the military government. Efrat underlines the security role played by settlements in the Gaza Strip (1977) and the West Bank (1981), claiming that they do not impinge on Arab-populated areas. He outlines six scenarios that would enable settlers to remain in the territories despite Palestinian self-rule. Drori (1981) argues that settlements do not violate international law and seeks to formalize the de facto extension of Israeli law over the settlers and settlements.

The relationship of settlements to Palestinian towns is analyzed critically in monographs published by the West Bank Data Base Project, the research center established by Meron Benvenisti, a former deputy mayor of Jerusalem. Those include Aaron Dehter, *How Expensive Are West Bank Settlements?* (1987); David Grossman, *Jewish and Arab Settlements in the Tulkarm Sub-district* (1986);

and Michael Romann, *Jewish Kiryat Arba versus Arab Hebron* (1985). The attitudes and behavior of Israeli settlers have been subject to official and scholarly inquiries. The first official examination of settler violence against Palestinians came in *The Karp Report* (1984); that inquiry indicated that when settlers take the law into their own hands and kill or injure Palestinians or damage Palestinian property, the settlers often refuse to cooperate with police investigations, and the military officials collude in closing or delaying these investigations.

Academic analyses of the ideology of religious-nationalist settlers include Ian Lustick, *For the Land and the Lord* (1988), Dan Leon, editor, *Settlers against Palestinians* (1996), and David Newman, editor, *The Impact of Gush Emunim* (1985). Newman includes critiques by such Israeli scholars as Ehud Sprinzak, who views Gush Emunim's politico-messianic ideology as the tip of the iceberg of a broad religious subculture in Israel; Yosseph Shilhav, who maintains that the Gush's argument that the land contains immanent holiness verges on paganism; and Gershon Shafir, who notes that the placement of religious-oriented settlements amid Palestinian towns and villages demonstrates the Gush's denial of Palestinian national rights and its insistence on exclusive Jewish sovereignty.

PALESTINIAN POLITICS FROM 1967 TO 1987

Numerous books and articles examine the interaction of Israeli policies and Palestinian politics during the first two decades of Israeli rule. My *Political Perceptions of the Palestinians on the West Bank and Gaza Strip* (1980) provides a succinct overview of the shift from a Jordanian-oriented political elite to an organized nationalist movement, signaled by the formation of the Palestine National Front in 1973–1974 and the municipal council elections in 1976. The study also examines Palestinian politicians' hostile reactions to the autonomy plan offered at Camp David, since they aspired to end the occupation and create an independent state alongside Israel. Jan Metzger, Martin Orth, and Christian Sterzing, *This Land Is Our Land* (1983), also cover the 1970s; they conclude pessimistically that sporadic protests by Palestinians exhaust the Palestinians but do not undermine Israeli control. Indeed, retaliatory deportations, arrests, and land confiscation worsen the conditions of the occupied population.

That pessimism was borne out in the crackdown on the nationalists in 1981–1982, which Palestinians tried to counter by creating diffuse grass-roots structures that could mobilize the public over immediate economic and social concerns. *The Bitter Year* (1983) focuses on these dramatic changes in 1982, including the Israeli invasion of Lebanon. Israel's efforts to repress Palestinian political life and accelerate land confiscation are examined by John P. Richardson, *The West Bank* (1984); Don Peretz, *The West Bank* (1986); and Geoffrey Aronson, *Creating Facts* (1990).

Emile Sahliyeh, a former professor on the West Bank, analyzes indigenous Palestinian elites in *In Search of Leadership* (1988). He provides a thoughtful assessment of the contrasting approaches and actions of the traditional pro-Jordanian elite, pro-PLO urban professionals, the Communist party, student radicals, and Islamist activists. Sahliyeh suggests that a pragmatic leadership can emerge but warns that Israel's failure to accommodate that elite will encourage radical alternatives, notably the Islamist movement.

Moshe Maoz, an Israeli historian who served in the military government, examines the role of mayors on the West Bank in *Palestinian Leadership on the West Bank* (1984). He criticizes the Likud government for dismissing mayors in 1982 and accelerating de facto annexation. Maoz views the elected mayors as authentic leaders whose removal created a zero-sum struggle between the government and Palestinian residents. Maoz also censures Israeli efforts to create alternative leaders, an issue detailed by the leading Palestinian sociologist Salim Tamari in "Israel's Search for a Native Pillar: The Village Leagues" (1989a). The removal of mayors and creation of village leagues was orchestrated by Menachem Milson, civil administrator for the West Bank in the early 1980s. Milson justified his approach in "How to Make Peace with the Palestinians" (1981), arguing that the leagues would attract support from the rural population that resented the political dominance by the cities. (Milson later maintained that his policy would have succeeded had the government not simultaneously expropriated most of the grazing and agricultural land in the southern West Bank, thereby alienating the leagues' potential constituents.)

In line with Milson's approach, some authors advocate federal or communal outcomes that dilute Palestinian nationalism. Daniel Elazar, *Judea, Samaria, and Gaza* (1981), argues that Israeli security and political needs preclude establishing a Palestinian state; Israel and Jordan should share sovereignty over the West Bank, with the Palestinians gaining limited self-rule. Similarly, Shmuel Sandler and Hillel Frisch (1984) view the conflict over the West Bank as largely communal rather than interstate in *Israel, the Palestinians, and the West Bank*. They acknowledge, however, that Israel must share some power with the Arabs on the West Bank in order to gain and retain their support.

In contrast, former West Bank military governor Aryeh Shalev argues in *The West Bank: Line of Defense* (1985) that security should be the sole rationale for the Israeli presence in the occupied territories; Israel should seek a long-term political settlement and work toward the eventual withdrawal of most Israeli forces. Shalev's analysis, originally published by the Jaffee Center for Strategic Studies (Tel Aviv University), represents an early effort by military strategists to articulate security criteria to counter the accelerating annexationist trend.

Jerusalem presents a particularly difficult issue for Israeli analysts, given the city's centrality to Jewish identity and the swift annexation of East Jerusalem after the June War of 1967. Former deputy mayor Meron Benvenisti describes Jerusalem as *The Torn City* (1976) and proposes a borough system that will permit the Palestinians a modicum of self-rule. However, his later *Intimate Enemies* (1995) views the Israeli-Palestinian dispute as virtually intractable and as unlikely to lead to an equitable distribution of power and benefits. The establishment of Jewish settlement-suburbs encircling the city is detailed by Saul B. Cohen in "Geographic Basis for the Integration of Jerusalem" (1977) and Arthur Kutcher in *The New Jerusalem* (1973). Despite the apparent geographic integration of Jerusalem, Israeli geographer Michael Romann and anthropologist Alex Weingrod believe that the Arabs and Jews are still *Living Together Separately* (1991). Their neighborhoods are juxtaposed, but their social, cultural, educational, and business lives remain separate. The authors conclude pessimistically that the official Israeli doctrine of coexistence cannot change the reality of Israeli control and cannot undo each community's desire to minimize contacts with the other. In contrast to the rich social analysis in Romann and Weingrod's study, Daphne Tsimhoni's *Christian Communities in Jerusalem and the West Bank since 1948* (1993) focuses on church institutions without seeing the Palestinian Christians as an integral part of the Palestinian national movement and sharing political aspirations with their Muslim neighbors.

Israeli analysts started to express serious doubts about the occupation during the 1980s when it appeared likely to continue without any political resolution. However, the early study of the takeover of the West Bank in 1967 by Shabtai Teveth reflects a sense of unease in the title: *The Cursed Blessing* (1970). The Israeli Druze Rafik Halabi, who worked in the Jerusalem municipality and became the first Arab journalist with Israeli Television, addresses the complexity of being both Arab and Israeli in *The West Bank Story* (1982), which criticizes Israeli policies that provoked unrest in Jerusalem in the late 1960s, promoted Israeli settlement in Palestinian towns, and undermined the elected mayors. Similarly, the Israeli novelist Amos Oz expresses his concern at Israel's shift toward the right in vivid interviews in *In the Land of Israel* (1983) with settlers and ultranationalists who voice militant claims to all the land and contempt toward the Arab residents.

Israeli author David Grossman provides a complementary set of interviews with Palestinians in *The Yellow Wind* (1988). In an effort to surmount his own fear of Arabs, who live next door but seem remote and unreal, Grossman interviews bitter refugees, struggling university students, activist lawyers, and dishwashers in Israeli restaurants. He attends a military trial in Nablus and talks to a former prisoner who says that jail taught him to be Palestinian and to hate the occupation. Grossman, whose book caused an uproar in Israel, stresses the cost of occupation for both the occupier and the occupied. Grossman had already expressed dismay at the callous behavior of military officers toward the occupied population in his novel *The Smile of the Lamb* (1990; published in Hebrew, 1983).

His critique does not approach the depth of anger expressed by Felicia Langer, an outspoken Communist lawyer. Her two-part diary, *With My Own Eyes* (1975) and *These Are My Brothers* (1979), depicts her passionate struggle with the military courts and prison system. Grace Halsell, an American journalist, covers issues similar to those of Oz and Grossman in her *Journey to Jerusalem* (1981). She provides fresh portraits of her encounters with a variety of Israelis and with

Palestinians living in refugee camps, studying at universities, and working in Israel.

Several Palestinians have written sharply defined and self-critical portraits of life under occupation. Sahar Khalifeh's novel *Wild Thorns* (1985; published in Arabic in 1976) stresses the class and generational conflicts among Palestinians. She criticizes the parlor nationalism of the elite, who mouth slogans without acting, but she also questions whether violence is an effective means to resist Israeli rule. Raymonda H. Tawil confronts dual oppression as a Palestinian and a woman in *My Home, My Prison* (1979), written while she was confined by house arrest for criticizing Israeli policies as well as for helping Israeli and foreign journalists meet Palestinians. Raja Shehadeh confides to his diary his difficulty finding *The Third Way* (1982), which he defines as a form of clear-headed steadfastness that will avoid both hatred and submission. He details his problems functioning as a lawyer, the barriers to forming friendships with Is-raelis across the dehumanizing political divide, and his fears when soldiers threaten his mother and settlers smash the windows of Palestinians' parked cars.

SOCIAL ISSUES

Palestinian society has undergone dramatic changes since 1967 that are closely intertwined with the altered political realities. Israel has constricted the expansion of schools and medical facilities, but Palestinians struggle to over-come these obstacles and improve their daily lives. In areas such as labor and women's movements Palestinians have built locally and factionally based struc-tures that support mass action and social change.

Overviews of two decades of social change are provided by Sarah Graham-Brown (1989) and Lisa Taraki (1989b). In the late 1970s and early 1980s, Emile Nakhleh authored and edited the first Palestinian commentaries in English on social and municipal services as well as on educational institutions: *The West Bank and Gaza* (1979) and *A Palestinian Agenda for the West Bank and Gaza* (1980). A decade later, educators were more pessimistic, given the deterioration of government schools, restrictions on private schools and universities, and mil-itary orders that curtail academic freedom (Aruri, *Occupation*, 1989). Antony T. Sullivan, for example, details the problems facing higher education in *Pal-estinian Universities under Occupation* (1988).

Few studies exist in English on the health situation in the territories. The internationally funded *West Bank Health Care Assessment* (1986) offers a factual presentation of the conditions in hospitals and clinics as the basis for identifying opportunities to improve facilities and train health personnel. The Union of Palestinian Medical Relief Committees critiques current conditions, notes Pal-estinian efforts to overcome obstacles, and outlines priorities (Aruri, *Occupa-tion*, 1989). The union stresses the importance of locally based primary health care, particularly in underserved rural areas. A pioneering effort to improve health conditions is assessed by Rita Giacaman in *Life and Health in Three*

Palestinian Villages (1988). She emphasizes the impact of occupation on rural health caused by the lack of government health services and even piped water. Giacaman also addresses internal problems related to economic status and gender that limit villagers' ability to improve their health conditions. Giacaman stresses the need to involve village women in the production of health for themselves and their families. Although focused on the micro level, her study provides important insight into the dynamics of health and social change in the West Bank.

Labor movements are examined by Joost R. Hiltermann in *Behind the Intifada* (1991). His sophisticated field research explores Palestinian efforts to unionize workers. These efforts are hampered by a perceived need to subordinate labor issues to the national struggle, by the limited industrialization in the territories, and by restrictions on organizing laborers who work inside Israel. Given the competition among Palestinian political groups, the labor movement remains divided and relatively weak.

Hiltermann's study also encompasses the working women's committees established in the 1980s. Although committees are formed by political factions, Hiltermann perceives the women's movement as less fractured than the labor movement. Female activists engage in practical activities, including literacy classes, day care, and clinics, but Hiltermann questions whether the committees enable women to transform their social roles. In contrast, Kitty Warnock's *Land before Honour* (1990) argues that increasing education, job opportunities, and political activism have changed attitudes toward and among women. The vivid *Portraits of Palestinian Women* offered by Orayb A. Najjar (1992) tends to confirm Warnock's perspective. She interviews poor women in villages and towns who confront settlers and soldiers, as well as leaders of women's committees, educators, lawyers, doctors, artists, and journalists who struggle to improve and transform their society. Ebba Augustin's *Palestinian Women* (1993) draws together these themes in essays and poems by women who have sought to resist occupation while also feeling the constraints placed upon them by their society.

ECONOMIC ISSUES

Economic analyses depend largely on Israeli statistics. Palestinian researchers are generally prevented from conducting surveys and gathering statistics, which increases their dependence on Israeli data. Official reports produced in English by the research department of the Bank of Israel include those by Arie Bregman, *Economic Growth in the Administered Areas, 1968–1973* (1975) and *The Economy of the Administered Territories, 1974–75* (1976), and Dan Zakai, *Economic Developments in Judea-Samaria and the Gaza District, 1982–84* (1986). Bregman (1975) notes cautiously that although the territories' economy appeared to grow rapidly in the first decade of Israeli rule, that growth was not caused by increased investment in the territories' agriculture and industry. Rather, the growth reflected enhanced employment by workers traveling to Israel for day labor.

Similar conclusions are drawn by the European economist Brian Van Arkadie, whose *Benefits and Burdens* (1977) is more skeptical than Vivian Bull about the real growth in the indigenous economy. Van Arkadie also emphasizes the economic benefits that accrue to Israel from having a new, closed market for its goods and a source of cheap labor. Bull's *The West Bank: Is It Viable?* (1975) is the weakest work factually and analytically, relying relatively uncritically on Israeli sources and therefore overstating the economic gains made by Palestinians under Israeli occupation. The Jordanian economist Fawzi A. Gharaibeh brings the picture up to 1982 in *The Economies of the West Bank and Gaza Strip* (1985), using Jordanian as well as Israeli data. He notes that employment in Israel is leveling off and land alienation is increasing, which will impact negatively on the territories' economic prospects. Former West Bank economist George T. Abed's *The Palestinian Economy* (1988) underlines further the territories' dependence on Israel and the constraints to growth due to the lack of natural resources and credit facilities as well as the underdeveloped infrastructure. The authors in Abed's edited volume outline creative strategies for development despite the prolonged occupation.

Van Arkadie, Bull, and Gharaibeh analyze the difficulty of disengaging the Palestinian economy from Israel and the options available to Palestinians. They support the formation of a semi-independent Palestinian region both for political reasons and to enable it to control its own development. Bull stresses the difficulty such an entity would have being economically viable. In contrast, Elias H. Tuma and Haim Darin-Drabkin argue in *The Economic Case for Palestine* (1978) that the territories can form the basis of a vibrant economy and even absorb substantial numbers of returning refugees. The credibility of their projections is enhanced by Darin-Drabkin's prominent role in Israeli government programs to absorb Jewish immigrants into Israel in the early 1950s.

In the mid-1980s, detailed annual reports were published by Benvenisti's West Bank Data Base Project (Benvenisti 1984, 1986a, 1987) that emphasize the multifaceted dimensions of the effort to absorb the territories into Israel. The reports are virtually the only source in English for statistics on landownership, trade, employment, taxes, water, and other vital issues. Unfortunately, the project closed in the late 1980s, reducing access to essential data.

Several sectoral studies of varying quality have been written by the West Bank Data Base Project, Palestinian research centers, and the United Nations. These include urban planner Bakr Abu Kishk's *The Industrial and Economic Trends in the West Bank and Gaza Strip* (1981, updated in Abed 1988). Economics professor Hisham Awartani provides *A Survey of Industries in the West Bank and Gaza Strip* (1979), and Israeli economist Simcha Bahiri analyzes the low level of *Industrialization in the West Bank and Gaza* (1987). P. G. Sadler, U. Kazi, and E. Jabr's *Survey of the Manufacturing Industry in the West Bank and Gaza Strip* (1984) articulates a strategy for industrialization, emphasizing

export-oriented industries that can absorb existing and returning Palestinian labor. These studies are relatively sketchy and are now out of date.

Awartani writes extensively on the problems facing agriculture in the West
Bank (*West Bank Agriculture*, 1978, and in Nakhleh, *A Palestinian Agenda*,
1980, and Abed, *The Palestinian Economy*, 1988). David Kahan examines *Ag-
riculture and Water Resources in the West Bank and Gaza, 1967–1987* (1987).
Microstudies of the Jordan Valley have been written by Salim Tamari and Rita
Giacaman in *Zbeidat* (1980) and Alex Pollock (1988).

Water is a crucial resource. Palestinians' access to wells, underground aqui-
fers, and the Jordan River is controlled by Israel. Miriam Lowi provides a comprehensive history in *Water and Power: The Politics of a Scarce Resource in
the Jordan River Basin* (1993). Although Israeli officials view water data as
confidential, a few studies are available by Israeli water engineers and researchers, notably Jehoshua Schwarz (1981) and Hillel Shuval (1992). Palestinian researchers are analyzing the water shortage and pollution problems facing the
West Bank and Gaza; Baskin's *Water* (1992) provides a forum for critiques by
Nader al-Khatib (1992) and Isam R. Shawwa (1992). Anna Bellisari underlines
the acute health problems caused by impure water supplies and water shortages
in her carefully documented ''Public Health and the Water Crisis in the Occupied Palestinian Territories'' (1994). Sherif S. Elmusa offers creative solutions
in ''Dividing the Common Palestinian-Israeli Waters'' (1993) and in his seminal
Negotiating Water (1996). An important set of research papers on water is available in the *Proceedings of the First Israeli/Palestinian International Academic
Conference on Water*, convened jointly by Israeli and Palestinian researchers
and officials in Zurich in December 1993 (Isaac and Shuval 1994). Shuval argues that equity should be the basis for apportioning water resources between
Israel and the territories. Spin-off analyses by water experts who participated in
these meetings include Karen Assaf, Nader al-Khatib, Elisha Kally, and Hillel
Shuval's *A Proposal for the Development of a Regional Water Master Plan*
(1993), Robin Twite and Jad Isaac's *Our Shared Environment* (1994), and the
special issue on water by *Palestine-Israel Journal* (1994). Moreover, the
Palestinian-run Center for Engineering and Planning produced the detailed study
*Water Conservation in Palestine: An Integrated Approach towards Palestinian
Water Resources Management* (1994).

A few studies are available on monetary and taxation systems. A. S. Mansour
addresses the issue of ''Monetary Dualism'' (1982), and Laurence Harris (1988)
discusses the lack of banking institutions. B'Tselem analyzes *The System of
Taxation in the West Bank and the Gaza Strip as an Instrument for the Enforcement of Authority during the Intifada* (1990).

The issues of labor and the employment of Palestinian workers in Israel have
received less attention. Ghassan Harb (1980) outlines the problem, and Kubursi
(1988) and Abu Kishk (1988) discuss the limited job options on the West Bank
and the deskilling of the labor force. Tamari assesses the social and political
implications of Palestinians' work inside Israel in ''Building Other People's

Homes'' (1981), in which he comments with irony that the occupied laborers construct the homes of the occupier. A comprehensive analysis is presented by Israeli sociologists Moshe Semyonov and Noah Lewin-Epstein in *Hewers of Wood and Drawers of Water* (1987). Using Israeli labor-force surveys from 1969 to 1982, they demonstrate the ethnic-based occupational segregation and income differentials and the unaltered subordinate position of Palestinians in Israel's occupational structure.

THE GAZA STRIP

The Gaza Strip is often addressed as a separate entity, with special characteristics and problems. Gerald Butt's *Life at the Crossroads* (1995) offers a sweeping panorama of Gaza's history from ancient times through Israeli rule. My series of essays outlines the history, political forces, and socioeconomic patterns in Gaza since Israel's occupation (''Gaza,'' 1989). The political scientist Ziad Abu-Amr has analyzed systematically the class structure and political elite in Gaza (1989) as well as the dynamics of the Islamic movement there (''Hamas,'' 1993). Joan Mandell's critique of conditions in ''Gaza: Israel's Soweto'' (1985) is complemented by eyewitness accounts presented by Paul Cossali and Clive Robson in *Stateless in Gaza* (1986). Dick Doughty and Mohammed El Aydi's *Gaza* (1995) provides a searing visual portrait of the tenacity of Palestinians in the face of overwhelming pressures.

Sara Roy's extensive analyses of Gaza's political economy culminate in *The Gaza Strip: The Political Economy of De-development* (1995b), which details Israel's systematic dismembering of the Strip's economy. Her first monograph, called *The Gaza Strip Survey*, undertaken for the West Bank Data Base Project (1986), contains statistics on employment, agriculture, industry, trade, education, health, and land issues, based on Israeli, Arab, and U.N. sources. In ''The Gaza Strip: Critical Effects of the Occupation'' (1989), she provides a systematic overview of conditions in Gaza through the mid-1980s. She also analyzes the deterioration of the economy during the intifada (''shaking off'' or uprising) that began in Gaza in December 1987, stressing the socioeconomic and psychological costs for Palestinians (''The Political Economy of Despair,'' 1991, and ''Gaza: New Dynamics of Civic Disintegration,'' 1993).

The causes and initial months of the intifada in Gaza are addressed by Anita Vitullo and Melissa Baumann in *Intifada* (1989), edited by Zachary Lockman and Joel Beinin, and in personal accounts by Rhona Davies and Peter R. Johnson in *The Uzi and the Stone* (1991). I also discuss the organizational and attitudinal changes in the late 1980s that made the intifada sustainable in ''Prelude to the Uprising in the Gaza Strip'' (1990). Davies and Johnson's account is particularly interesting, since they worked in a teacher-training program and lived with a Palestinian family. They experienced directly the byzantine complexity of Gaza society and the surrealistic quality of life under occupation, with its frequent curfews, strikes, and shootings. The journalist Gloria Emerson offers a less nuanced account, based on her visits during 1989, in *Gaza, a Year in the Intifada* (1991). She interviews leading lawyers, doctors, and women's activists and provides a sense of the unremitting violence as well as the severe controls imposed by the Israeli military.

THE INTIFADA

The intifada that began in December 1987 evolved substantially over subsequent years. Many analysts focus on the mass protests and growing violence, but others detail the profound attitudinal and organizational changes undergone by the Palestinian communities. Some emphasize the setback experienced by the Palestinians during the Gulf crisis (1990–1991), while others explore the implications of Israeli-Palestinian negotiations for the future of the territories.

Ian Lustick's "Writing the Intifada" (1993) is a valuable review article that outlines four kinds of analytical approaches to the uprising. One approach views the intifada as an explosion triggered by pent-up despair and humiliation (Zeev Schiff and Ehud Yaari, *Intifada*, 1990). A second, related approach emphasizes that Israel failed to meet even the minimal political and material needs of the Palestinians, especially after 1977. By hastening to absorb the territories into Israel, the government antagonized the entire population. The intifada can therefore be seen as an attempt to change Israel's cost-benefit analysis: if the cost of the occupation is increased, Israelis may seek separation (Beshara Doumani, "Family and Politics in Salfit," 1989; F. Robert Hunter, *The Palestinian Uprising*, 1993; Raja Shehadeh, "Israel and the Palestinians," 1991). Peretz discusses in *Intifada* (1990) how the uprising disoriented Israelis: it undermined the credibility of the army, spawned new protest and human rights organizations in Israel, and thereby both compelled the government to negotiate and contributed to the collapse of the National Unity government in 1990.

According to Lustick, a third set of writers focuses on the uprising as one stage in the ongoing national struggle. Some argue that the PLO played an important partnership role in fostering the uprising (Hanna Siniora, 1988; Daud Kuttab, 1988; Helga Baumgarten, 1990), whereas others maintain that the uprising was partly due to the failures of the PLO since the early 1980s (Peretz, *Intifada*, 1990). One could also place in this category Souad Dajani's *Eyes without Country* (1994), which represents an ambitious attempt to relate the intifada to strategies of nonviolent civilian resistance and liberation. A fourth group of writers emphasizes the grass-roots organizations that provided the initial leadership for the intifada as well as the network of local activists who seek to separate Palestinian society from Israeli control (David McDowall, *Palestine and Israel*, 1989; Tamari, 1990b, 1991; and others mentioned in the following discussion of labor and women's movements during the uprising).

Most authors blend these four approaches. McDowall, a former U.N. official in the territories, views the intifada as not merely an emotional reaction to oppression and miserable conditions but as the culmination of years of institution building in the wake of the weakening of the PLO in 1982. Hunter, who relies heavily on interviews with Palestinian intellectuals, tends to overemphasize mass demonstrations as the essence of the intifada and to underestimate the underlying structural changes. Nonetheless, he comprehends the dynamic interaction between Palestinian mobilization and Israeli countermeasures and the difficulty the intifada has in altering Israel's cost-benefit calculus. Veteran Israeli reporters Schiff and Yaari, who utilize Israeli intelligence reports, stress the responsibility of heavy-handed Israeli policies for provoking the uprising. However, they underestimate the importance of prior institutional developments at the grass-roots level, which sustained the intifada beyond its initial burst of energy. Schiff and Yaari also believe that the uprising represents a distancing from the PLO, rather than a movement integrally related to the broad national struggle. Lustick himself creates a model of collective action that moves beyond the four approaches in order to explain the intifada's mix of spontaneity, organization, and calculation.

Given the rapid evolution of the intifada, edited volumes and special editions of scholarly journals capture the best snapshots of its spirit and structures. Moreover, virtually every issue of the *Journal of Palestine Studies* contains articles or documents on the intifada. *Middle East Report* published four special issues on the uprising (1990, 1992, 1993, 1994). Four edited volumes are devoted to the intifada (Brynen, *Echoes of the Intifada*, 1991; Michael C. Hudson, *The Palestinians*, 1990; Lockman and Beinin, *Intifada*, 1989, which includes most of the initial *Middle East Report* articles; and Nassar and Heacock, *Intifada*, 1990). What is striking in these publications is the increasingly strong voices of Palestinians who articulate and analyze their own political life and aspirations.

Azmy Bishara assesses the initial reaction of Israel to the uprising (1989a), the impact of the Gulf crisis on Palestinian diplomacy (1992), the importance of Jerusalem (1993), and the prospects for self-rule (1994). Ziad Abu-Amr ("The Politics of the Intifada," 1990) examines the interaction between external and internal leadership, arguing that the intifada enabled the PLO to extricate itself from an internal crisis and to shift toward a strategy based on popular mobilization and international diplomacy. Salim Tamari analyzes the Palestinians' transition from a strategy designed to achieve liberation to a strategy to achieve territorial statehood (1989b, 1991) and proposes ways in which internal and external political forces can work together to achieve statehood (1992).

Tamari illuminates the complex impact of the intifada on Palestinian society in an article that assesses the difficulty of constructing civil society during the "limited rebellion" (1990c) and others that describe the role of urban merchants in the uprising (1990b). Tamari argues that merchants supported strongly the strikes in the opening months, but subsequently experienced tension with not only youthful strike enforcers but also manufacturers, who were encouraged to keep their factories open, and peddlers, who sometimes continued to sell when shops were closed. Tamari (1989b) provides a sophisticated analysis of the strengths and weaknesses of the Palestinian strategy to decouple the territories from their total reliance economically on Israel. Tamari (1990a) also documents Israeli efforts to disrupt the uprising by compelling Palestinians to collaborate and by issuing phony communiqués that purport to come from the Palestinian leadership.

The degree to which all sectors of Palestinian society are involved in the intifada can be seen in analyses of elites, villages, and refugee camps. Ali Jarbawi (1990) discusses elite support for the intifada and the strengthening of local PLO groups. His study is complemented by Jad Isaac's firsthand "A Socioeconomic Study of Administrative Detainees at Ansar III" (1989) and by the survey on nationalist trends conducted by Mohammed Shadid and Rick Seltzer and published in the *Journal of South Asian and Middle Eastern Studies* (1988). Hanan Mikhail Ashrawi in "The Politics of Cultural Revival" (1990) explores "the politics of cultural revival" through the revitalization of popular culture in art, songs, dance, and graffiti that enhance national legitimization and self-affirmation. Beshara Doumani's "Family and Politics in Salfit" (1989) examines the importance of the family in maintaining cohesiveness and militancy in Salfit village, and Husain Jameel Bargouti underlines the newly activist role played by villagers in the intifada in "Jeep versus Bare Feet" (1990).

Analyses of the impact of the intifada on women are offered by Rita Giacaman and Penny Johnson ("Palestinian Women," 1989) and Islah Abdul Jawwad (1990a, 1990b). In "Women, the Hijab and the Intifada," (1990) Rema Hammami focuses on the reverses suffered by women as a result of the enhanced power of the Islamist movement. These authors conclude that women broke certain barriers but that most activities remain extensions of women's traditional roles.

Three Palestinian analyses of the Islamist movement attempt to gauge that complex phenomenon. Ahmad Rashad's *Hamas* (1993) stresses the Islamists' efforts to prove their revolutionary credentials and overcome the stigma of the Muslim Brotherhood's de facto collaboration with Israel. Ziad Abu-Amr's *Islamic Fundamentalism in the West Bank and Gaza* (1994), based heavily on interviews with Islamist leaders in the late 1980s, emphasizes the struggle between Islamists and the PLO to define the identity of Palestinian society, its leadership, and its direction. Hisham Ahmad's *Hamas* (1994) reproduces the Hamas charter, but lacks the complexity and insights of Rashad's and Abu-Amr's analyses. Previously, aside from Abu-Amr's own writings on Gaza (cited earlier), the only significant essays on Hamas were by Lisa Taraki ("The Islamic Resistance Movement in the Palestinian Uprising," 1989a) and Jean-François Legrain ("Islamic Movement and the *Intifada*," 1990). These analysts criticized sharply the Islamists' attitudes and their actions against pro-PLO and Communist political groups.

In addition to articles by Palestinians, foreign scholars pen sensitive analyses of the situation on the ground. Hiltermann assesses the role of the labor movement and the working class in the intifada ("Mass Mobilization and the Uprising," 1990a; "Sustaining Movement, Creating Space," 1990b; "Work and

Action,'' 1990c). Glenn Robinson examines efforts by medical and agricultural committees to meet urgent needs and to politicize the rural areas in "The Role of the Professional Middle Class in the Mobilization of Palestinian Society" (1993). Glenn Bowman describes the middle-class tax rebellion in the largely Christian town of Beit Sahour in "Religion and Political Identity in Beit Sahour" (1990). Ellen Cantarow portrays Beita village, where the death of an Israeli girl triggered the demolition of village houses and deportation of six residents in 1988 ("Beita," 1989). Sharry Lapp's "Aftermath" (1992) profiles Tulkarm refugee camp in the wake of the Gulf crisis. Paul Steinberg and A. M. Oliver interpret political images conveyed by *The Graffiti of the Intifada* (1990), and Shaul Mishal and Reuben Aharoni explicate the underground communiqués in *Speaking Stones* (1994). Legal scholar Adrien K. Wing assesses the extent to which the uprising has created embryonic executive and judicial institutions that can regulate economic relations and even conduct trials of collaborators in "Legal Decision-making during the Palestinian *Intifada*" (1993). She concludes that as escalating violence tears at the social fabric, a centralized leadership and publicly enforced constitution are essential; over time, informal mechanisms cannot substitute for organized self-government and a functioning judiciary system.

Helen Winternitz's *A Season of Stones: Living in a Palestinian Village* (1991) depicts her life in Nahalin village near Bethlehem during 1988–1989. As she picks olives, cooks, and chats with friends, she experiences the mounting involvement of villagers in the intifada. Land confiscation, arrests, an attack by Israeli border guards, and tension among Palestinian political groups profoundly alter village lives and bind villagers to the national movement. Her microcosmic view is complemented by impressionist accounts by Andrew Rigby (*Living the Intifada*, 1991), Janet Gunn (*Second Life*, 1995), and Patrick White (*Let Us Be Free*, 1989). Rigby provides a dense account of the impact of Israeli policies on, for example, health, education, and the media during the intifada. Gunn's introspective memoir focuses on the struggles of a Palestinian teenager who was mortally wounded during the uprising. White, a professor at Bethlehem University, details the impact of the university's closure on students and faculty.

During the Gulf crisis, Palestinians endured weeks of curfews, extensive job loss, and psychological trauma. Raja Shehadeh expresses his anger and dismay on the pages of his diary, *The Sealed Room* (1992). In the wake of the crisis, the PLO suffered diplomatic isolation for its support for Iraq. Palestinians struggled to renew the intifada and to find a means to enter diplomatic negotiations. Important self-critiques are offered by the Palestinian Academic Society for the Study of International Affairs (1991). *Middle East Report* published articles and interviews with Palestinians from the territories that explore the Palestinian role in the post–Gulf War Middle East (1992), the importance of Jerusalem (1993), and the obstacles facing the Palestinians after the Israeli-Palestinian declaration of principles in 1993 (1994). Contributors include the intellectuals Salim Tamari (1994; also in *Journal of Palestine Studies*, 1991), Azmy Bishara (1992, 1994),

Ali Jarbawi and Roger Heacock (1992), and Bernard Sabella (1993). *Middle East Report* also interviews such key negotiators as Sami Kilani (1992), Suad Amiry (1993), Hanan Ashrawi (1994), and economic advisor Samir Hleileh (1994).

ISRAELI POLICIES DURING THE INTIFADA

Human rights organizations have examined Israeli actions during the uprising. The studies by B'Tselem have already been mentioned. Human Rights Watch/ Middle East published four major research monographs: *The Israeli Army and the Intifada* (1990), *Prison Conditions in Israel and the Occupied Territories* (1991), *A License to Kill* (1993), and *Torture and Ill-Treatment* (1994). These document the extent to which soldiers use lethal force in non–life-threatening situations, conditions in prisons and detention centers, and the infrequency of official investigations into deaths of Palestinians caused by soldiers. Complementary documentation is published in a three-volume study by Anne Nixon of Save the Children Fund on the injuries and deaths of children, entitled *The Status of Palestinian Children during the Uprising* (1990). Physicians for Human Rights analyzes the health emergency in the territories during 1990–1992 in *Human Rights on Hold* (1993).

Important essays explore the impact of the intifada on Israeli politics and attitudes, in addition to Peretz (*Intifada*, 1990), noted earlier. Mark Tessler examines the degree to which it provokes debate and reassessment inside Israel (*Journal of South Asian and Middle Eastern Studies*, 1988; Brynen, *Echoes of the Intifada*, 1991). Edy Kaufman, a founder of B'Tselem, analyzes "The Intifada and the Peace Camp in Israel" (1988). A former military intelligence director, Yehoshafat Harkabi, (1990, 1992) reflects on Israeli perspectives toward the intifada and on the apparent failure of Israeli moderates to effect policy changes. Lockman and Beinin (*Intifada*, 1989) include commentaries on Israeli views by Lockman (1989), Beinin (1989), Bishara (1989b), and Reuven Kaminer (1989). Yossi Melman and Dan Raviv, in a study largely devoted to Israeli-Jordanian relations (*Beyond the Uprising*, 1989), conclude that the failure by both these governments to acknowledge Palestinian claims to self-government prolongs the conflict. Similarly, Aryeh Shalev argues that Israel cannot restore the status quo ante and must negotiate an accord for Palestinian independence alongside Israel (*The Intifada*, 1991).

ATTEMPTS AT DIALOGUE AND RECONCILIATION

Surprisingly, there are virtually no published records of informal Israeli-Palestinian dialogues. Israeli and Palestinian intellectuals held a pioneering three-session meeting in 1978 in Jerusalem under the auspices of *New Outlook*, a dovish Israeli publication. That painful and illuminating dialogue was published by Simha Flapan in *When Enemies Dare to Talk* (1979). Recent dialogues on substantive issues, such as water, economic policy, and Jerusalem, have been conducted on a confidential basis. Only the ongoing Israeli-Palestinian dialogue in Beit Sahour is documented briefly in Fernea and Hocking (*Israelis and Palestinians*, 1992). Jay Rothman outlines a systematic approach to conducting conflict-management workshops on sensitive political issues in *From Confrontation to Cooperation* (1992). He, Randi Jo Land, and Robin Twite use Jerusalem as a case study in conflict resolution in *The Jerusalem Peace Initiative: Project on Managing Political Disputes* (1994).

Until the mid-1990s, other publications consisted entirely of side-by-side interviews with Israelis and Palestinians rather than dialogues between them. Insights can be extracted from three such collections. Carol J. Birkland's *Unified in Hope* (1987) includes interviews with Gaza activists Mary Khass and Zuheir Rayyes, lawyer Raja Shehadeh, Bethlehem mayor Elias Freij, and Quaker educator Jean Zaru. Haim and Rivca Gordon (1991) interview such political leaders as Faisal Husseini, Hanan Mikhail-Ashrawi, Zahira Kamal, and Haidar Abd al-Shafi in *Israel/Palestine: The Quest for Dialogue*. John and Janet Wallach (1990) juxtapose profiles of three Israeli settlers and ten Palestinians in *Still Small Voices*. Several of the latter overlap with the Gordons' interviews, but the Wallachs also include thoughtful commentaries on an Islamist preacher as well as a father and son who fought, respectively, the British and Israeli occupations. Since 1994, however, the pioneering *Palestine-Israel Journal*, which has Palestinian and Israeli coeditors, always combines analyses by specialists from both national groups. Its topically focused issues include in-depth examinations of religion and politics, refugees, Jerusalem, education, and women's involvement in the conflict. Moreover, the studies by the Israel/Palestine Center for Research and Information (IPCRI) are based on joint research by Israelis and Palestinians (see, for example, Karen Assaf, Nader al-Khatib, Elisha Kally, and Hillel Shuval, *A Proposal for the Development of a Regional Water Master Plan*, 1993, and Gershon Baskin, editor, *New Thinking on the Future of Jerusalem*, 1994b.

FUTURISTIC SCENARIOS

I noted earlier a few books that explore possible political scenarios, including Elazar's proposal for autonomy (*Judea, Samaria, and Gaza*, 1981), Shalev's security projections for the West Bank in the event of Palestinian self-rule (*The West Bank*, 1985, and *The Intifada*, 1991), and Tuma and Darin-Drabkin's assessment of the economic possibilities of a Palestinian state (*The Economic Case for Palestine*, 1978). The most systematic case made by an Israeli analyst in support of a Palestinian state was penned a decade ago by Mark A. Heller for the Jaffee Center for Strategic Studies (1983). He argues that a peace treaty must be negotiated with the PLO, that force-level restrictions must be placed on the Palestinian state, and that a five-to-ten-year transition will be required before independence. Heller maintains that under these circumstances, a Palestinian state is preferable to the alternatives of annexation, the status quo, federation, and a partial or complete return of the West Bank to Jordan. Later, Heller joined Palestinian philosopher Sari Nusseibeh to explore the implications of a two-state solution. Their joint *No Trumpets, No Drums* (1991) ranges across the issues of security, borders, refugees, settlements, water, and Jerusalem.

Outside analysts also try to conceptualize a peace accord. Harvey Sicherman details a decade of discussion in *Palestinian Self-Government (Autonomy)* (1991), and Jerome M. Segal presents an imaginative plan in *Creating a Palestinian State*, urging both peoples to move from mutual destruction to mutual recognition (1989). I served as the primary author for a study, *Transition to Palestinian Self-Government* (1992), sponsored by the American Academy of Arts and Sciences, that details changes needed in administration as well as social, economic, and security policies in order to promote the transition. The American Academy also sponsored the creative analysis of options for Jerusalem by Israeli political scientist and political activist Naomi Chazan, *Negotiating the Non-negotiable* (1991), and an in-depth examination of final-status security arrangements by leading Israeli and Palestinian specialists, *Israeli-Palestinian Security* (1995), authored by study-group leaders Jeffrey Boutwell and Everett Mendelsohn.

Jerusalem has continued to be a focus for analysis and debate. Ian S. Lustick's articles on Israeli policy toward Jerusalem ("Reinventing Jerusalem," 1993–1994, and "Has Israel Annexed East Jerusalem?" 1997) join Chazan's monograph in addressing the prospect for reimagining Jerusalem's status and sovereignty in ways that share the city between the two nations. Gershon Baskin's *Jerusalem of Peace* (1994a) and *New Thinking on the Future of Jerusalem* (1994b) also try to look beyond conventional solutions to that complex problem. A special issue of the *Palestine-Israel Journal* on Jerusalem (1995) gives voice to Palestinians and Israelis who express their concern for and sense of belonging to the city. The Center for Policy Analysis on Palestine's monograph *Jerusalem* (1993) addresses those concerns and also critiques U.S. policy toward Jerusalem.

Only since self-government has become a serious prospect have detailed studies of the economy been concluded, notably the six-volume assessment by the World Bank, *Developing the Occupied Territories* (1993), and the joint Israeli-Palestinian analysis, *Securing Peace in the Middle East* (Stanley Fischer, Leonard J. Hausman, Anna D. Karasik, and Thomas Schelling, 1994; see also the interview with Fischer, "Economic Transition in the Occupied Territories," 1994). *Securing Peace* details labor, fiscal, monetary, agricultural, industrial, and other issues, but may place too much weight on economic relations as the driving force in securing regional peace.

Samir Hazboun, Tariq Mitwasi, Wajih el-Sheikh, and Simcha Bahiri attempt an early critique of the Israeli-Palestinian accords of 1993–1994 in *The Economic Impact of the Israeli-PLO Declaration of Principles* (1994). Sara Roy, George Abed, and Rex Brynen write critical assessments of foreign aid as well as the economic impact of the accords (Roy, "Separation or Integration," 1994; Roy, "Gaza: Alienation or Accommodation?" 1995a; Abed, "Developing the

Palestinian Economy,'' 1994; Brynen, ''Buying Peace? A Critical Assessment of International Aid to the West Bank and Gaza,'' 1996). Roy, in particular, stresses the disastrous drop in living standards in Gaza after the Strip achieved self-rule and the growing tensions between the public and the Palestinian Authority that was formed in 1994.

This chapter covers the period of Israeli rule over the West Bank and Gaza Strip and therefore does not assess the practices of the emerging political system since the Oslo accords of 1993 and 1995. Nonetheless, a few important studies should be highlighted. These include Graham Usher's *Palestine in Crisis* (1995), which analyzes the first Oslo accord, the debut of the Palestinian authority, and the mounting Islamist challenge. Raja Shehadeh's ''Questions of Jurisdiction: A Legal Analysis of the Gaza-Jericho Agreement'' (1994) exposes the flaws in the accord. Glenn E. Robinson's *Building a Palestinian State: The Incomplete Revolution* (1997) offers a candid analysis of the disjunctions between the grassroots structures that were created on the West Bank and Gaza and the centralizing institutions of the PLO, imposed by the Palestinian Authority. Usher's ''The Politics of Internal Security'' (1996) provides a frank appraisal of the authority's intelligence services and the violations of human rights that were quickly apparent. That concern is also the focus of *International Human Rights Enforcement* (1996) by the Centre for International Human Rights Enforcement, in which Palestinian, Israeli, and international human rights specialists address the problems facing the emerging Palestinian political system.

The elections for the presidency and the legislative council in January 1996 are assessed by Lamis Andoni in ''The Palestinian Elections'' (1996) and Khalil Shikaki in ''The Palestinian Elections'' (1996). The elections and the authority are also critiqued in monographs by the Center for Policy Analysis on Palestine, notably *Palestinian Self-Government: An Early Assessment* (1994a), *Palestinian Elections* (1995a), *The Palestinian National Authority* (1995b), and *Palestinian Elections and the Future of Palestine* (1996). *Palestine-Israel Journal* also critiques the accords in its special issue on Oslo (1995), as does *Middle East Report* in three special issues (1994, 1995, 1996).

FUTURE RESEARCH

The Israeli-Palestinian accords in 1993–1995 began to disengage Israel from the territories and to enable the Palestinians to create their own self-governing institutions. While this process can still be set back, a major watershed in the Israeli-Palestinian relationship has been crossed. This is an appropriate moment to pause to outline and assess the quality and range of writings on the West Bank and Gaza Strip during the period of Israeli rule.

Given the reality of occupation, a significant portion of the writings focus on the political and human rights situation in the territories. They stress the impact of a wide range of Israeli policies on the Palestinians and examine the behavior of Palestinian elites and nationalist groups in attempting to counter the effects of the occupation. These studies serve immediate educational and policy purposes by making governments and publics aware of the situation on the ground and the depth of Palestinian nationalism. Although they have a political purpose, the studies are increasingly scholarly in their approach and judicious in their assessments. Moreover, the futuristic monographs serve important policy-making purposes, particularly as they bring together Israeli and Palestinian scholars and practitioners in the conceptualizing of alternative futures. Although none of the studies engage in the rigorous theory building that engages many political scientists, they will provide essential documentation for future historians and political scientists when they assess the period of Israeli rule and seek to comprehend the political forces at work in the Palestinian community.

Investigations of underlying social forces, social change, and the various sectors of the society and economy are not as comprehensive and systematic as the political writings. This has been due, in part, to the difficulty of conducting field research and gaining access to economic data. It has also been due to the small number of Palestinian sociologists and economists available to conduct such research. Substantial gaps remain in the sociological literature on urban, rural, and refugee life. The examination of key economic sectors, such as agriculture, trade, and industry, remains fragmentary. This is beginning to change as Palestinians gain control over their economy, begin to generate economic data, and are able to undertake systematic sociological studies. As Palestinians struggle to construct their civil society and to build their economy, such studies will be vital for them and will be illuminating for outside observers.

REFERENCES

Abed, George T., ed. 1988. *The Palestinian Economy: Studies in Development under Prolonged Occupation*. London: Routledge.
———. 1994. "Developing the Palestinian Economy." *Journal of Palestine Studies* 23, no. 4:41–51.
Abu-Amr, Ziad. 1989. "Class Structure and the Political Elite in the Gaza Strip: 1948–1988." In Naseer H. Aruri, ed., *Occupation: Israel over Palestine*. 2d ed. Belmont, MA: Association of Arab-American University Graduates.
———. 1990. "The Politics of the Intifada." In Michael C. Hudson, ed., *The Palestinians: New Directions*. Washington, DC: Center for Contemporary Arab Studies, Georgetown University.
———. 1993. "Hamas: A Historical and Political Background." *Journal of Palestine Studies* 22, no. 4:5–19.
———. 1994. *Islamic Fundamentalism in the West Bank and Gaza: Muslim Brotherhood and Islamic Jihad*. Bloomington: Indiana University Press.
Abu Kishk, Bakr. 1981. *The Industrial and Economic Trends in the West Bank and Gaza Strip*. Vienna: ECWA/UNIDO.
———. 1988. "Industrial Development and Policies in the West Bank." In George T. Abed, ed., *The Palestinian Economy: Studies in Development under Prolonged Occupation*. New York: Routledge.

Ahmad, Hisham H. 1994. *Hamas: From Religious Salvation to Political Transformation*. Jerusalem: PASSIA.

Amiry, Suad. 1993. "Representing Jerusalem." *Middle East Report* No. 182 (May–June).

Andoni, Lamis. 1996. "The Palestinian Elections: Moving toward Democracy or One-Party Rule?" *Journal of Palestine Studies* 25, no. 3:5–16.

Aronson, Geoffrey. 1990. *Creating Facts: Israel, Palestinians, and the West Bank*. Rev. ed. Washington, DC: Kegan Paul International and Institute for Palestine Studies.

Aruri, Naseer H., ed. 1989. *Occupation: Israel over Palestine*. 2d ed. Belmont, MA: Association of Arab-American University Graduates.

Ashrawi, Hanan Mikhail. 1990. "The Politics of Cultural Revival." In Michael C. Hudson, ed., *The Palestinians: New Directions*. Washington, DC: Center for Contemporary Arab Studies, Georgetown University.

———. 1994. "The Accord Incorporated Key Concessions We Couldn't Get [in Washington]." *Middle East Report* no. 186 (January–February).

Assaf, Karen, Nader al-Khatib, Elisha Kally, and Hillel Shuval. 1993. *A Proposal for the Development of a Regional Water Master Plan*. Jerusalem: Israel/Palestine Center for Research and Information.

Augustin, Ebba, ed. 1993. *Palestinian Women: Identity and Experience*. London: Zed Books.

Awartani, Hisham. 1978. *West Bank Agriculture: A New Outlook*. Nablus: al-Najah University Research Bulletin, no. 1.

———. 1979. *A Survey of Industries in the West Bank and Gaza Strip*. Bir Zeit: Bir Zeit University.

———. 1980. "Agriculture." In Emile A. Nakhleh, ed., *A Palestinian Agenda for the West Bank and Gaza*. Washington, DC: American Enterprise Institute for Public Policy Research.

———. 1988. "Agricultural Development and Policies in the West Bank and Gaza." In George T. Abed, ed., *The Palestinian Economy: Studies in Development under Prolonged Occupation*. New York: Routledge.

Azar, George Baramki, with introduction by Ann M. Lesch. 1991. *Palestine: A Photographic Journey*. Berkeley: University of California Press.

Bahiri, Simcha. 1984. *Peaceful Separation or Enforced Unity: Economic Consequences for Israel and the West Bank/Gaza Area*. Tel Aviv: International Center for Peace in the Middle East.

———. 1987. *Industrialization in the West Bank and Gaza*. Jerusalem: West Bank Data Base Project.

———. 1989. *Construction and Housing in the West Bank and Gaza*. Jerusalem: West Bank Data Base Project.

Bargouti, Husain Jameel. 1990. "Jeep versus Bare Feet: The Villages in the Intifada." In Jamal R. Nassar and Roger Heacock, eds., *Intifada: Palestine at the Crossroads*. New York: Praeger.

Baskin, Gershon, ed. 1992. *Water: Conflict or Cooperation*. Jerusalem: Israel/Palestine Center for Research and Information.

———. 1994a. *Jerusalem of Peace: Sovereignty and Territory in Jerusalem's Future*. Jerusalem: Israel/Palestine Center for Research and Information.

———, ed. 1994b. *New Thinking on the Future of Jerusalem: A Model for the Future of Jerusalem: Scattered Sovereignty*. Jerusalem: Israel/Palestine Center for Research and Information.

Baumann, Melissa. 1989. "Gaza Diary." In Zachary Lockman and Joel Beinin, eds., *Intifada: The Palestinian Uprising against Israeli Occupation*. Boston: South End Press.

Baumgarten, Helga. 1990. " 'Discontented People' and 'Outside Agitators': The PLO in the Palestinian Uprising." In Jamal R. Nassar and Roger Heacock, eds., *Intifada: Palestine at the Crossroads*. New York: Praeger.

Beinin, Joel. 1989. "From Land Day to Peace Day . . . and Beyond." In Zachary Lockman and Joel Beinin, eds., *Intifada: The Palestinian Uprising against Israeli Occupation*. Boston: South End Press.

Bellisari, Anna. 1994. "Public Health and the Water Crisis in the Occupied Palestinian Territories." *Journal of Palestine Studies*, 23, no. 2:52–63.

Benvenisti, Eyal. 1989. *Legal Dualism: The Absorption of the Occupied Territories into Israel*. Jerusalem: Jerusalem Post and West Bank Data Base Project.

Benvenisti, Meron. 1976. *Jerusalem: The Torn City*. Minneapolis: University of Minneapolis Press.

———. 1984. *The West Bank Data Project: A Survey of Israel's Policies*. Washington, DC: American Enterprise Institute for Public Policy Research.

———. 1986a. *1986 Report: Demographic, Economic, Legal, Social, and Political Developments in the West Bank*. Jerusalem: West Bank Data Base Project.

———. 1986b. *The West Bank Handbook: A Political Lexicon*. Boulder, CO: Westview Press.

———. 1987. *1987 Report: Demographic, Economic, Legal, Social, and Political Developments in the West Bank*. Jerusalem: West Bank Data Base Project.

———. 1995. *Intimate Enemies: Jews and Arabs in a Shared Land*. Berkeley: University of California Press.

Birkland, Carol J. 1987. *Unified in Hope: Arabs and Jews Talk about Peace*. New York: Friendship Press.

Bishara, Azmy. 1989a. "Israel Faces the Uprising: A Preliminary Assessment." *Middle East Report*, no. 157:6–14.

———. 1989b. "The Uprising's Impact on Israel." In Zachary Lockman and Joel Beinin, eds., *Intifada: The Palestinian Uprising against Israeli Occupation*. Boston: South End Press.

———. 1992. "Palestine in the New Order." *Middle East Report* no. 175 (March/April).

———. 1993 "Jerusalem Voices." *Middle East Report* no. 182 (May–June).

———. 1994. "Peres Gave Arafat a Stick Which He Grasped Because He Was Drowning." *Middle East Report* no. 186 (January–February).

Bisharat, George Emile. 1989. *Palestinian Lawyers and Israeli Rule: Law and Disorder in the West Bank*. Austin: University of Texas Press.

The Bitter Year: Arabs under Israeli Occupation in 1982. 1983. Washington, DC: American-Arab Anti-Discrimination Committee.

Blum, Yehuda. 1968. "The Missing Reversioner: Reflections on the Status of Judea and Samaria." *Israel Law Review* 3:279–301.

Boutwell, Jeffrey, and Everett Mendelsohn. 1995. *Israeli-Palestinian Security: Issues in the Permanent Status Negotiations*. Cambridge, MA: American Academy of Arts and Sciences.

Bowman, Glenn. 1990. "Religion and Political Identity in Beit Sahour." *Middle East Report* nos. 164/165 (May).

Bregman, Arie. 1975. *Economic Growth in the Administered Areas, 1968–1973*. Jerusalem: Bank of Israel.

————. 1976. *The Economy of the Administered Territories, 1974–75.* Jerusalem: Bank of Israel.

Brynen, Rex, ed. 1991. *Echoes of the Intifada: Regional Repercussions of the Palestinian-Israeli Conflict.* Boulder, CO: Westview Press.

————. 1996. "Buying Peace? A Critical Assessment of International Aid to the West Bank and Gaza." *Journal of Palestine Studies* 25, no. 3:79–92.

B'Tselem. 1989. *Annual Report 1989: Violations of Human Rights in the Occupied Territories.* Jerusalem: B'Tselem.

————. 1990. *The System of Taxation in the West Bank and the Gaza Strip as an Instrument for the Enforcement of Authority during the Intifada.* Jerusalem: B'Tselem.

————. 1991a. *The Interrogation of Palestinians during the Intifada: Ill-Treatment, "Moderate Physical Pressure," or Torture?* Jerusalem: B'Tselem.

————. 1991b. *Violations of Human Rights in the Occupied Territories, 1990/1991.* Jerusalem: B'Tselem.

————. 1992a. *Activity of the Undercover Units in the Occupied Territories.* Jerusalem: B'Tselem.

————. 1992b. *Collective Punishment in the West Bank and the Gaza Strip.* Jerusalem: B'Tselem.

Bull, Vivian. 1975. *The West Bank: Is It Viable?* Lexington, MA: Lexington Books.

Butt, Gerald. 1995. *Life at the Crossroads: A History of Gaza.* Nicosia, Cyprus: Rimal Publications.

Cantarow, Ellen. 1989. "Beita." In Zachary Lockman and Joel Beinin, eds., *Intifada: The Palestinian Uprising against Israeli Occupation.* Boston: South End Press.

Center for Engineering and Planning. 1994. *Water Conservation in Palestine: An Integrated Approach towards Palestinian Water Resources Management.* Ramallah, Palestine: Center for Engineering and Planning.

Center for Policy Analysis on Palestine. 1993. *Jerusalem.* Washington, DC: Center for Policy Analysis on Palestine.

————. 1994a. *Palestinian Self-Government: An Early Assessment.* Washington, DC: Center for Policy Analysis on Palestine.

————. 1994b. *Palestinian Statehood.* Washington, DC: The Center for Policy Analysis on Palestine.

————. 1995a. *Palestinian Elections.* Washington, DC: Center for Policy Analysis on Palestine.

————. 1995b. *The Palestinian National Authority: A Critical Appraisal.* Washington, DC: Center for Policy Analysis on Palestine.

————. 1996. *Palestinian Elections and the Future of Palestine.* Washington, DC: Center for Policy Analysis of Palestine.

Centre for International Human Rights Enforcement. 1996. *International Human Rights Enforcement: The Case of the Occupied Palestinian Territories in the Transitional Period.* Jerusalem: Centre for International Human Rights Enforcement.

Chazan, Naomi. 1991. *Negotiating the Non-negotiable: Jerusalem in the Framework of an Israeli-Palestinian Settlement.* Cambridge, MA: American Academy of Arts and Sciences.

Cohen, Saul Bernard. 1977. "Geographical Basis for the Integration of Jerusalem." *Orbis* 20, no. 2:287–313.

Committee to Protect Journalists. 1988. *Journalism under Occupation: Israel's Regula-*

tion of the Palestiniun Press. New York: Committee to Protect Journalists and Article 19.

Cossali, Paul, and Clive Robson. 1986. *Stateless in Gaza.* London: Zed Books.

Dajani, Souad R. 1994. *Eyes without Country: Searching for a Palestinian Strategy of Liberation.* Philadelphia: Temple University Press.

Dakkak, Ibrahim. 1985. "Development and Control in the West Bank." *Arab Studies Quarterly* 7, nos. 2–3:74–87.

Davies, Rhona, and Peter R. Johnson. 1991. *The Uzi and the Stone.* Calgary: Detselig Enterprises.

Dehter, Aaron. 1987. *How Expensive Are West Bank Settlements? A Comparative Analysis of the Financing of Social Services.* Jerusalem: West Bank Data Base Project.

Doughty, Dick, and Mohammed El Aydi. 1995. *Gaza: Legacy of Occupation: A Photographer's Journey.* West Hartford, CT: Kumarian Press.

Doumani, Beshara. 1989. "Family and Politics in Salfit." In Zachary Lockman and Joel Beinin, eds., *Intifada: The Palestinian Uprising against Israeli Occupation.* Boston: South End Press.

Drobles, Matityahu. 1978. *Master Plan for the Development of Settlement in Judea and Samaria, 1979–83.* Jerusalem: World Zionist Organization, Department for Rural Settlement.

Drori, Moshe. 1982. "The Israeli Settlements in Judea and Samaria: Legal Aspects." In Daniel J. Elazar, ed., *Judea, Samaria, and Gaza: Views on the Present and Future.* Washington, DC: American Enterprise Institute for Public Policy Research.

Drury, Richard T., and Robert C. Winn, with Michael O'Connor. 1992. *Plowshares and Swords: The Economics of Occupation in the West Bank.* Boston: Beacon Press.

Efrat, Elisha. 1977. "Geographical Review: Settlement Pattern and Economic Changes in the Gaza Strip, 1947–1977." *Middle East Journal* 31, no. 3:349–356.

———. 1981. "Spacial Patterns of Jewish and Arab Settlements in Judea and Samaria." In Daniel J. Elazar, ed., *Judea, Samaria, and Gaza: Views on the Present and Future.* Washington, DC: American Enterprise Institute for Public Policy Research.

Elazar, Daniel, ed. 1981. *Judea, Samaria, and Gaza: Views on the Present and Future.* Washington, DC: American Enterprise Institute for Public Policy Research.

Elmusa, Sherif S. 1993. "Dividing the Common Palestinian-Israeli Waters." *Journal of Palestine Studies* 22, no. 3:57–77.

———. 1996. *Negotiating Water: Israel and the Palestinians.* Washington, DC: Institute for Palestine Studies.

Emerson, Gloria. 1991. *Gaza, a Year in the Intifada: A Personal Account from an Occupied Land.* New York: Atlantic Monthly Press.

Falloon, Virgil. 1985. *Excessive Secrecy, Lack of Guidelines: A Report on Military Censorship in the West Bank.* Ramallah: Law in the Service of Man.

Fasheh, Munir. 1982. "Political Islam in the West Bank." *Middle East Report,* no. 103: 15–16.

Fernea, Elizabeth Warnock, and Mary Evelyn Hocking, eds., 1992. *Israelis and Palestinians: The Struggle for Peace.* Austin: University of Texas Press.

Fischer, Stanley. 1994. "Economic Transition in the Occupied Territories." *Journal of Palestine Studies* 23, no. 4:52–61.

Fischer, Stanley, Leonard J. Hausman, Anna D. Karasik, and Thomas Schelling. 1994.

Securing Peace in the Middle East: Project on Economic Transition. Cambridge, MA: MIT Press.

Flapan, Simha, ed. 1979. *When Enemies Dare to Talk: An Israeli-Palestinian Debate*. London: Croom Helm.

Gazit, Shlomo. 1995. *The Carrot and the Stick: Israel's Policy in Judea and Samaria*. Washington, DC: B'nai B'rith Books.

Gerson, Allan. 1978. *Israel, The West Bank, and International Law*. London: Frank Cass.

Gharaibeh, Fawzi A. 1985. *The Economies of the West Bank and Gaza Strip*. Boulder, CO: Westview Press.

Giacaman, Rita. 1988. *Life and Health in Three Palestinian Villages*. London: Ithaca Press.

Giacaman, Rita, and Penny Johnson. 1989. "Palestinian Women: Building Barricades and Breaking Barriers." In Zachary Lockman and Joel Beinin, eds., *Intifada: The Palestinian Uprising against Israeli Occupation*. Boston: South End Press.

Gordon, Haim, and Rivca Gordon, eds. 1991. *Israel/Palestine: The Quest for Dialogue*. Maryknoll, NY: Orbis Books.

Graham-Brown, Sarah. 1989. "Impact on the Social Structure of Palestinian Society." In Naseer H. Aruri, ed., *Occupation: Israel over Palestine*. 2d ed. Belmont, MA: Association of Arab-American University Graduates.

Grossman, David. 1986. *Jewish and Arab Settlements in the Tulkarm Sub-district*. Jerusalem: West Bank Data Base Project.

———. 1988. *The Yellow Wind*. New York: Farrar, Straus and Giroux.

———. 1990. *The Smile of the Lamb*. New York: Pocket Books (published in Hebrew, 1983).

Grossman, David, and Amiram Derman. 1989. *The Impact of Regional Road Construction on Land Use in the West Bank*. Jerusalem: West Bank Data Base Project.

Gunn, Janet Varner. 1995. *Second Life: A West Bank Memoir*. Minneapolis: University of Minnesota Press.

Halabi, Rafik. 1982. *The West Bank Story*. New York: Harcourt Brace Jovanovich.

Halsell, Grace. 1981. *Journey to Jerusalem*. New York: Macmillan.

Hammami, Rema. 1990. "Women, the Hijab and the Intifada." *Middle East Report*. nos. 164/165 (May).

Harb, Ghassan. 1980. "Land and Manpower." In Emile A. Nakhleh, ed., *A Palestinian Agenda for the West Bank and Gaza*. Washington, DC: American Enterprise Institute for Public Policy Research.

Harkabi, Yehoshafat. 1990. "Reflections on Recent Changes in the Conflict." In Michael C. Hudson, ed., *The Palestinians: New Directions*. Washington, DC: Center for Contemporary Arab Studies, Georgetown University.

———. 1992. "Arab-Israeli Conflict at the Threshold of Negotiations." In Elizabeth Warnock Fernea and Mary Evelyn Hocking, eds., *The Struggle for Peace: Israelis and Palestinians*. Austin: University of Texas Press.

Harris, Laurence. 1988. "Money and Finance with Undeveloped Banking in the Occupied Territories." In George T. Abed. ed., *The Palestinian Economy: Studies in Development under Prolonged Occupation*. New York: Routledge.

Harris, William Wilson. 1980. *Taking Root: Israeli Settlement in the West Bank, the Golan, and Gaza-Sinai, 1967–1980*. New York: Wiley.

Hazboun, Samir, Tariq Mitwasi, Wajih el-Sheikh, and Simcha Bahiri. 1994. *The Eco-

nomic Impact of the Israeli-PLO Declaration of Principles. Jerusalem: Israel/ Palestine Center for Research and Information.

Heller, Mark A. 1983. *A Palestinian State: The Implications for Israel.* Cambridge, MA: Harvard University Press.

Heller, Mark A., and Sari Nusseibeh. 1991. *No Trumpets, No Drums: A Two-State Settlement of the Israeli-Palestinian Conflict.* New York: Hill and Wang.

Hiltermann, Joost R. 1986. *Israel's Deportation Policy in the Occupied West Bank and Gaza.* Ramallah: Al-Haq.

———. 1990a. "Mass Mobilization and the Uprising: The Labor Movement." In Michael C. Hudson, ed., *The Palestinians: New Directions.* Washington, DC: Center for Contemporary Arab Studies, Georgetown University.

———. 1990b. "Sustaining Movement, Creating Space: Trade Unions and Women's Committees." *Middle East Report* nos. 164/165 (May).

———. 1990c. "Work and Action: The Role of the Working Class in the Uprising." In Jamal R. Nassar and Roger Heacock, eds., *Intifada: Palestine at the Crossroads.* New York: Praeger.

———. 1991. *Behind the Intifada: Labor and Women's Movements in the Occupied Territories.* Princeton: Princeton University Press.

Hleileh, Samir. 1994. "The Economic Protocols Are the Price We Had to Pay." *Middle East Report* no. 186 (January–February).

Hudson, Michael C., ed. 1990. *The Palestinians: New Directions.* Washington, DC: Center for Contemporary Arab Studies, Georgetown University.

Human Rights Watch/Middle East. 1990. *The Israeli Army and the Intifada: Policies That Contribute to the Killings.* New York: Human Rights Watch.

———. 1991. *Prison Conditions in Israel and the Occupied Territories.* New York: Human Rights Watch.

———. 1993. *A License to Kill: Israeli Undercover Operations against "Wanted" and Masked Palestinians.* New York: Human Rights Watch.

———. 1994. *Torture and Ill-Treatment: Israel's Interrogation of Palestinians from the Occupied Territories.* New York: Human Rights Watch.

Hunter, F. Robert. 1993. *The Palestinian Uprising: A War by Other Means.* Berkeley: University of California Press.

Isaac, Jad. 1989. "A Socio-economic Study of Administrative Detainees at Ansar III." *Journal of Palestine Studies* 18:102–109.

Isaac, Jad, and Hillel Shuval, eds. 1994. *Proceedings of the First Israeli/Palestinian International Academic Conference on Water.* Amsterdam: Elsevier.

Jarbawi, Ali. 1990. "Palestinian Elites in the Occupied Territories: Stability and Change through the *Intifada.*" In Jamal R. Nassar and Roger Heacock, eds., *Intifada: Palestine at the Crossroads.* New York: Praeger.

Jarbawi, Ali, and Roger Heacock. 1992. "Winds of War, Winds of Peace: The Palestinian Strategy Debate." *Middle East Report* no. 175 (March/April).

Jawwad, Islah Abdul. 1990a. "The Evolution of the Political Role of the Palestinian Women's Movement in the Uprising." In Michael C. Hudson, ed., *The Palestinians: New Directions.* Washington, DC: Center for Contemporary Arab Studies, Georgetown University.

———. 1990b. "From Salons to the Popular Committees: Palestinian Women, 1919–89." In Jamal R. Nassar and Roger Heacock, ed., *Intifada: Palestine at the Crossroads.* New York: Praeger.

Journal of Palestine Studies. 1988. Special issue, "The Palestinian Uprising," 17, no. 3.

Journal of South Asian and Middle Eastern Studies. 1988. Special issue: "Uprising for Palestine," 11, no. 4.

Kahan, David. 1987. *Agriculture and Water Resources in the West Bank and Gaza, 1967–1987.* Jerusalem: West Bank Data Base Project.

Kaminer, Reuven. 1989. "The Protest Movement in Israel." In Zachary Lockman and Joel Beinin, eds., *Intifada: The Palestinian Uprising against Israeli Occupation.* Boston: South End Press.

Karp, Yehudit, et al. 1984. *The Karp Report: An Israeli Government Inquiry into Settler Violence against Palestinians on the West Bank.* Washington, DC: Institute for Palestine Studies.

Kaufman, Edy. 1988. "The Intifadah and the Peace Camp in Israel: A Critical Introspection." *Journal of Palestine Studies* 17:66–80.

Khalidi, Walid. 1988. "Toward Peace in the Holy Land." *Foreign Affairs* 66:771–789.

Khalifeh, Sahar. 1985. *Wild Thorns.* London: Saqi.

al-Khatib, Nader. 1992. "Palestinian Water Rights." In Gershon Baskin, ed., *Water: Conflict or Cooperation.* Jerusalem: Israel/Palestine Center for Research and Information.

Khouja, N. W., and P. G. Sadler. 1981. *Review of the Economic Conditions of the Palestinian People in the Occupied Arab Territories.* Vienna: UNCTAD.

Kilani, Sami. 1992. "Why We Negotiate." *Middle East Report* no. 175 (March/April).

Krogh, Peter F., and Mary C. McDavid, eds. 1989. *Palestinians under Occupation: Prospects for the Future.* Washington, DC: Center for Contemporary Arab Studies, Georgetown University.

Kubursi, Atif A. 1988. "Jobs, Education and Development: The Case of the West Bank." In George T. Abed, ed., *The Palestinian Economy: Studies in Development under Prolonged Occupation.* New York: Routledge.

Kutcher, Arthur. 1973. *The New Jerusalem: Planning and Politics.* London: Thames and Hudson.

Kuttab, Daoud. 1988. "A Profile of the Stonethrowers." *Journal of Palestine Studies* 17, no. 3.

Kuttab, Jonathan, and Raja Shehadeh. 1982. *Civilian Administration in the Occupied West Bank: Analysis of Israel Military Order No. 947.* Ramallah: Law in the Service of Man.

Langer, Felicia. 1975. *With My Own Eyes: Israel and the Occupied Territories, 1967–1973.* London: Ithaca Press.

———. 1979. *These Are My Brothers: Israel and the Occupied Territories, Part II.* London: Ithaca Press.

Lapp, Sharry. 1992. "Aftermath: A Profile of Tulkarm Camp." *Middle East Report* no. 175 (March/April).

Legrain, Jean-François. 1990. "The Islamic Movement and the *Intifada.*" In Jamal R. Nassar and Roger Heacock, eds., *Intifada: Palestine at the Crossroads.* New York: Praeger.

Leon, Dan, ed. 1996. *Settlers against Palestinians.* Special Report. Jerusalem: *Palestine-Israel Journal.*

Lesch, Ann M. 1977–1978. "Israeli Settlements in the Occupied Territories, 1967–1977." *Journal of Palestine Studies* 7, no. 1:26–47; updated, 8, no. 1:100–119.

————. 1979. "Israeli Deportation of Palestinians from the West Bank and the Gaza Strip, 1967–1978." Parts 1, 2. *Journal of Palestine Studies* 8, no. 2:101–131; 8, no. 3:81–112.

————. 1980. *Political Perceptions of the Palestinians on the West Bank and Gaza Strip*. Washington, DC: Middle East Institute.

————. 1983. "Israeli Settlements on the West Bank: Mortgaging the Future." *Journal of South Asian and Middle Eastern Studies* 7, no. 1:3–23.

————. 1989. "Gaza: History and Politics" and "Gaza: Life under Occupation." In *Israel, Egypt, and the Palestinians: From Camp David to Intifada*, with Mark Tessler. Bloomington: Indiana University Press.

————. 1990. "Prelude to the Uprising in the Gaza Strip." *Journal of Palestine Studies* 20, no. 1:1–23.

————. 1992. *Transition to Palestinian Self-Government: Practical Steps toward Israeli-Palestinian Peace*. Cambridge, MA: American Academy of Arts and Sciences.

————. 1993. "The Exiles." *The Link* 26, no. 5. New York: Americans for Middle East Understanding.

Lockman, Zachary. 1989. "Original Sin." In Zachary Lockman and Joel Beinin, eds., *Intifada: The Palestinian Uprising against Israeli Occupation*. Boston: South End Press.

Lockman, Zachary, and Joel Beinin, eds. 1989. *Intifada: The Palestinian Uprising against Israeli Occupation*. Boston: South End Press; *Middle East Report*.

Lowi, Miriam R. 1993. *Water and Power: The Politics of a Scarce Resource in the Jordan River Basin*. Cambridge: Cambridge University Press.

Lustick, Ian. 1981. "Israel and the West Bank after Elon Moreh: The Mechanics of de Facto Annexation." *Middle East Journal* 35, no. 4:557–577.

————. 1988. *For the Land and the Lord: Jewish Fundamentalism in Israel*. New York: Council on Foreign Relations.

————. 1993. "Writing the Intifada: Collective Action in the Occupied Territories." *World Politics* 45:560–594.

————. 1993–1994. "Reinventing Jerusalem." *Foreign Policy* 93:41–59.

————. 1997. "Has Israel Annexed East Jerusalem?" *Middle East Policy* 1:34–45.

Mallison, W. Thomas and Sally Mallison. 1986. *The Palestine Problem in International Law and World Order*. New York: Longman.

Mandell, Joan. 1985. "Gaza: Israel's Soweto." *Middle East Report*, no. 136–137:7–19.

Mansour, A. S. 1982. "Monetary Dualism: The Case of the West Bank under Occupation." *Journal of Palestine Studies* 11, no. 3:103–116.

Maoz, Moshe. 1984. *Palestinian Leadership on the West Bank: The Changing Role of the Mayors under Jordan and Israel*. London: Frank Cass.

Matar, Ibrahim. 1989. "Israeli Settlements and Palestinian Rights." In Naseer H. Aruri, ed., *Occupation: Israel over Palestine*. 2d ed. Belmont, MA: Association of Arab-American University Graduates.

————. 1996. *Jewish Settlements, Palestinian Rights, and Peace: Palestinian Elections and the Future of Palestine*. Washington, DC: Center for Policy Analysis on Palestine.

McDowall, David. 1989. *Palestine and Israel: The Uprising and Beyond*. Berkeley: University of California Press.

Melman, Yossi, and Dan Raviv. 1989. *Behind the Uprising: Israelis, Jordanians, and Palestinians*. New York: Greenwood Press.

Metzger, Jan, Martin Orth, and Christian Sterzing. 1983. *This Land Is Our Land: The West Bank under Israeli Occupation*. London: Zed Books.

Middle East Report. 1990. No. 164–165, "Intifada Year Three."

———. 1992. No. 175, "Palestine and Israel in the New World Order."

———. 1993. No. 182, "Jerusalem and the Peace Agenda."

———. 1994. No. 186, "After Oslo: The Shape of Palestine to Come."

———. 1995. Nos. 194/195, "Odds against Peace: Palestine, Israel, and the Crisis of Transition."

———. 1996. No. 201, "Israel and Palestine: Two States, Bantustans or Binationalism?"

Milson, Menachem. 1981. "How to Make Peace with the Palestinians." *Commentary* 71, no. 7:25–35.

Mishal, Shaul, and Reuben Aharoni. 1994. *Speaking Stones: Communiques from the Intifada Underground*. Syracuse: Syracuse University Press.

Najjar, Orayb Aref. 1992. *Portraits of Palestinian Women*. Salt Lake City: University of Utah Press.

Nakhleh, Emile A. 1979. *The West Bank and Gaza: Toward the Making of a Palestinian State*. Washington, DC: American Enterprise Institute for Public Policy Research.

———, ed. 1980. *A Palestinian Agenda for the West Bank and Gaza*. Washington, DC: American Enterprise Institute for Public Policy Research.

Nassar, Jamal R., and Roger Heacock, eds. 1990. *Intifada: Palestine at the Crossroads*. New York: Praeger.

Newman, David, ed. 1985. *The Impact of Gush Emunim: Politics and Settlement in the West Bank*. New York: St. Martin's Press.

Nixon, Anne. 1990. *The Status of Palestinian Children during the Uprising in the Occupied Territories*. 3 vols. Stockholm, Sweden: Save the Children Fund.

Ott, David H. 1980. *Palestine in Perspective: Politics, Human Rights, and the West Bank*. London: Quartet Books.

Oz, Amos. 1983. *In the Land of Israel*. New York: Harcourt Brace Jovanovich.

Palestine-Israel Journal. Jerusalem:1994–   .

Palestinian Academic Society for the Study of International Affairs. 1991. *Palestinian Assessments of the Gulf War and Its Aftermath*. Jerusalem: PASSIA.

Peleg, Ilan. 1995. *Human Rights in the West Bank and Gaza: Legacy and Politics*. Syracuse: Syracuse University Press.

Peretz, Don. 1986. *The West Bank: History, Politics, Society, and Economy*. Boulder, CO: Westview Press.

———. 1990. *Intifada: The Palestinian Uprising*. Boulder, CO: Westview Press.

Physicians for Human Rights. 1993. *Human Rights on Hold: A Report on Emergency Measures and Access to Health Care in the Occupied Territories, 1990–1992*. Boston: Physicians for Human Rights.

Playfair, Emma. 1989. "The Legal Aspects of the Occupation: Theory and Practice." In Naseer H. Aruri, ed., *Occupation: Israel over Palestine*. 2d ed. Belmont, MA: Association of Arab-American University Graduates.

Pollock, Alex. 1988. "Society and Change in the Northern Jordan Valley." In George T. Abed, ed., *The Palestinian Economy: Studies in Development under Prolonged Occupation*. New York: Routledge.

Rashad, Ahmad. 1993. *Hamas: Palestinian Politics with an Islamic Hue*. Springfield, VA: United Association for Studies and Research.

Richardson, John P. 1984. *The West Bank: A Portrait*. Washington, DC: Middle East
    Institute.
Rigby, Andrew. 1991. *Living the Intifada*. London: Zed Books.
Robinson, Glenn E. 1993. "The Role of the Professional Middle Class in the Mobili-
    zation of Palestinian Society: The Medical and Agricultural Committees." *Inter-
    national Journal of Middle East Studies* 25, no. 2:301–326.
———. 1997. *Building a Palestinian State: The Incomplete Revolution*. Bloomington:
    Indiana University Press.
Romann, Michael. 1985. *Jewish Kiryat Arba versus Arab Hebron*. Jerusalem: West Bank
    Data Base Project.
Romann, Michael, and Alex Weingrod. 1991. *Living Together Separately: Arabs and
    Jews in Contemporary Jerusalem*. Princeton: Princeton University Press.
Rothman, Jay. 1992. *From Confrontation to Cooperation: Resolving Ethnic and Regional
    Conflict*. Newbury Park, CA: Sage Publications.
Rothman, Jay, Randi Jo Land, and Robin Twite. 1994. *The Jerusalem Peace Initiative:
    Project on Managing Political Disputes*. Jerusalem: Leonard Davis Institute, He-
    brew University of Jerusalem.
Roy, Sara. 1986. *The Gaza Strip Survey*. Jerusalem: West Bank Data Base Project and
    the Jerusalem Post.
———. 1989. "The Gaza Strip: Critical Effects of the Occupation." In Naseer H. Aruri,
    ed., *Occupation: Israel over Palestine*. 2d ed. Belmont, MA: Association of Arab-
    American University Graduates.
———. 1991. "The Political Economy of Despair: Changing Political and Economic
    Realities in the Gaza Strip." *Journal of Palestine Studies* 20:58–69.
———. 1993. "Gaza: New Dynamics of Civic Disintegration." *Journal of Palestine
    Studies* 22, no. 4:20–31.
———. 1994. "Separation or Integration: Closure and the Economic Future of the Gaza
    Strip Revisited." *Middle East Journal* 48, no. 1:11–30.
———. 1995a. "Gaza: Alienation or Accommodation?" *Journal of Palestine Studies*
    24, no. 4:73–82.
———. 1995b. *The Gaza Strip: The Political Economy of De-development*. Washington,
    DC: Institute for Palestine Studies.
Sabella, Bernard. 1993. "Russian Jewish Immigration and the Future of the Israeli-
    Palestinian Conflict." *Middle East Report* no. 182 (May–June).
Sadler, P. G., U. Kazi, and E. Jabr. 1984. *Survey of the Manufacturing Industry in the
    West Bank and Gaza Strip*. Vienna: United Nations Industrial Development Or-
    ganization.
Sahliyeh, Emile. 1988. *In Search of Leadership: West Bank Politics since 1967*. Wash-
    ington, DC: Brookings Institution.
Said, Edward W. 1995. "Projecting Jerusalem." *Journal of Palestine Studies* 25, no. 1:5–
    14.
Sandler, Shmuel, and Hillel Frisch. 1984. *Israel, the Palestinians, and the West Bank:
    A Study in Intercommunal Conflict*. Lexington, MA: Lexington Books.
Sayigh, Yezid. 1995. "Redefining the Basics: Sovereignty and Security of the Palestinian
    State." *Journal of Palestine Studies* 24, no. 4:5–19.
Schiff, Zeev, and Ehud Yaari. 1990. *Intifada: The Palestinian Uprising, Israel's Third
    Front*. New York: Simon and Schuster.
Schwarz, Jehoshua. 1981. "Water Resources in Judea, Samaria, and the Gaza Strip." In

Daniel J. Elazar, ed., *Judea, Samaria, and Gaza: Views on the Present and Future*. Washington, DC: American Enterprise Institute for Public Policy Research.

Segal, Jerome M. 1989. *Creating a Palestinian State: A Strategy of Peace*. Chicago: Lawrence Hill.

Sellick, Patricia. 1994. ''The Old City of Hebron: Can It Be Saved?'' *Journal of Palestine Studies* 23, no. 4:69–82.

Semyonov, Moshe, and Noah Lewin-Epstein. 1987. *Hewers of Wood and Drawers of Water: Noncitizen Arabs in the Israeli Labor Market*. Ithaca: Industrial and Labor Relations Press, Cornell University.

Shadid, Mohammed, and Rick Seltzer. 1988. ''Trends in Palestinian Nationalism: Moderate, Radical, and Religious Alternatives.'' *Journal of South Asian and Middle Eastern Studies* 11, no. 4.

Shalev, Aryeh. 1985. *The West Bank: Line of Defense*. New York: Praeger.

———. 1991. *The Intifada: Causes and Effects*. Boulder, CO: Westview Press.

Shamgar, Meir, ed. 1982. *Military Government in the Territories Administered by Israel, 1967–1980* Vol. 1, *The Legal Aspects*. Jerusalem: Hebrew University.

Shawwa, Isam R. 1992. ''The Water Situation in the Gaza Strip.'' In Gershon Baskin, ed., *Water: Conflict or Cooperation*. Jerusalem: Israel/Palestine Center for Research and Information.

Shehadeh, Raja. 1982. *The Third Way: A Journal of Life in the West Bank*. London: Quartet Books.

———. 1985. *Occupier's Law: Israel and the West Bank*. Washington, DC: Institute for Palestine Studies.

———. 1989. ''The Changing Juridical Status of Palestinian Areas under Occupation.'' In Naseer H. Aruri, ed., *Occupation: Israel over Palestine*. 2d ed. Belmont, MA: Association of Arab-American University Graduates.

———. 1991. ''Israel and the Palestinians: Human Rights in the Occupied Territories.'' In Rex Brynen, ed., *Echoes of the Intifada: Regional Repercussions of the Palestinian-Israeli Conflict* Boulder, CO: Westview Press.

———. 1992. *The Sealed Room*. London: Quartet Books.

———. 1994. ''Questions of Jurisdiction: A Legal Analysis of the Gaza-Jericho Agreement.'' *Journal of Palestine Studies* 23, no. 4:18–25.

Shehadeh, Raja, and Jonathan Kuttab. 1980. *The West Bank and the Rule of Law*. New York: International Commission of Jurists and Law in the Service of Man.

Shikaki, Khalil. 1996. ''The Palestinian Elections: An Assessment.'' *Journal of Palestine Studies*, 25, no. 3:17–22.

Shinar, Dov. 1986. *Palestinian Voices: Communication and Nation Building in the West Bank*. Boulder, CO: Lynne Rienner.

Shinar, Dov, and Danny Rubinstein. 1987. *Palestinian Press in the West Bank: The Political Dimension*. Jerusalem: West Bank Data Base Project.

Shuval, Hillel. 1992. ''Approaches to Finding an Equitable Solution to the Water Resources Problems Shared by Israel and the Palestinians over the Use of the Mountain Aquifer.'' In Gershon Baskin, ed., *Water: Conflict or Cooperation*. Jerusalem: Israel/Palestine Center for Research and Information.

Sicherman, Harvey. 1991. *Palestinian Self-Government (Autonomy): Its Past and Its Future*. Washington, DC: Washington Institute for Near East Policy.

Siniora, Hanna. 1988. ''An Analysis of the Current Revolt.'' *Journal of Palestine Studies* 17, no. 3.

Steinberg, Paul, and A. M. Oliver. 1990. *The Graffiti of the Intifada.* Jerusalem: PASSIA.

Sullivan, Antony Thrall. 1988. *Palestinian Universities under Occupation.* Cairo Papers in the Social Sciences. Cairo: American University in Cairo Press.

Sullivan, Denis J. 1996. "NGOs in Palestine: Agents of Development and Foundation of Civil Society." *Journal of Palestine Studies* 25, no. 3:93–100.

Szulc, Tad. 1992. "Who Are the Palestinians?" *National Geographic* 181, no. 6:85–113.

Tamari, Salim. 1981. "Building Other People's Homes: The Palestinian Peasant's Household and Work in Israel." *Journal of Palestine Studies* 11, no. 1:31–66.

———. 1989a. "Israel's Search for a Native Pillar: The Village Leagues." In Naseer H. Aruri, ed., *Occupation: Israel over Palestine.* 2d ed. Belmont, MA: Association of Arab-American University Graduates.

———. 1989b. "What the Uprising Means." In Zachary Lockman and Joel Beinin, eds., *Intifada: The Palestinian Uprising against Israeli Occupation.* Boston: South End Press.

———. 1990a. "Eyeless in Judea: Israel's Strategy of Collaborators and Forgeries." *Middle East Report* nos. 164/165 (May).

———. 1990b. "The Revolt of the Petite Bourgeoisie: Urban Merchants and the Palestinian Uprising." In Jamal R. Nassar and Roger Heacock, eds., *Intifada: Palestine at the Crossroads.* New York: Praeger.

———. 1990c. "The Uprising's Dilemma: Limited Rebellion and Civil Society." *Middle East Report* nos. 164/165 (May).

———. 1991. "The Palestinian Movement in Transition: Historical Reversals and the Uprising." *Journal of Palestine Studies* 20, no. 2:57–70.

———. 1992. "The Future in the Present: Issue of Palestinian Statehood." In Elizabeth Warnock Fernea and Mary Evelyn Hocking, eds., *The Struggle for Peace: Israelis and Palestinians.* Austin: University of Texas Press.

———. 1994. "The Critics Are Afraid of the Challenge of Opposing Their Own Bourgeoisie." *Middle East Report* no. 186 (January–February).

Tamari, Salim, and Rita Giacaman. 1980. *Zbeidat: The Social Impact of Drip Irrigation on a Palestinian Peasant Community in the Jordan Valley.* Bir Zeit: Bir Zeit University.

Taraki, Lisa. 1989a. "The Islamic Resistance Movement in the Palestinian Uprising." In Zachary Lockman and Joel Beinin, eds., *Intifada: The Palestinian Uprising against Israeli Occupation.* Boston: South End Press.

———. 1989b. "Mass Organizations in the West Bank." In Naseer H. Aruri, ed., *Occupation: Israel over Palestine.* 2d ed. Belmont, MA: Association of Arab-American University Graduates.

Tawil, Raymonda Hawa. 1979. *My Home, My Prison.* New York: Holt, Rinehart and Winston.

Tessler, Mark A. 1988. "Thinking about Territorial Compromise." *Journal of South Asian and Middle Eastern Studies* 11, no. 4.

Teveth, Shabtai. 1970. *The Cursed Blessing: The Story of Israel's Occupation of the West Bank.* New York: Random House.

Tsimhoni, Daphne. 1993. *Christian Communities in Jerusalem and the West Bank since 1948.* Westport, CT: Praeger.

Tuma, Elias H., and Haim Darin-Drabkin. 1978. *The Economic Case for Palestine.* London: Croom Helm.

Twite, Robin, and Jad Isaac, eds. 1994. *Our Shared Environment: Israelis and Palestinians Thinking Together about the Environment of the Region in Which They Live*. Jerusalem: Israel/Palestine Center for Research and Information.

Union of Palestinian Medical Relief Committees. 1989. ''Health and Health Services under the Occupation.'' In Naseer H. Aruri, ed., *Occupation: Israel over Palestine*. 2d ed. Belmont, MA: Association of Arab-American University Graduates.

Usher, Graham. 1995. *Palestine in Crisis: The Struggle for Peace and Political Independence after Oslo*. East Haven, CT: Pluto Press in association with the Transnational Institute and *Middle East Report*.

———. 1996. ''The Politics of Internal Security: The PA's New Intelligence Services.'' *Journal of Palestine Studies* 25, no. 2:21–34.

Van Arkadie, Brian. 1977. *Benefits and Burdens: A Report on the West Bank and Gaza Strip Economies since 1967*. New York: Carnegie Endowment for International Peace.

Vitullo, Anita. 1989. ''Uprising in Gaza.'' In Zachary Lockman and Joel Beinin, eds., *Intifada: The Palestinian Uprising against Israeli Occupation*. Boston: South End Press.

Wallach, John, and Janet Wallach. 1990. *Still Small Voices*. New York: Citadel Press.

Warnock, Kitty. 1990. *Land before Honour: Palestinian Women in the Occupied Territories*. New York: Monthly Review Press.

West Bank Health Care Assessment. 1986. 3 vols. Washington, DC: American Public Health Association.

White, Patrick. 1989. *Let Us Be Free: A Narrative before and during the Intifada*. Princeton: Kingston Press.

Wing, Adrien Katherine. 1993. ''Legal Decision-making during the Palestinian *Intifada*: Embryonic Self-Rule.'' *Yale Journal of International Law* 18, no. 1:95–153.

Winternitz, Helen. 1991. *A Season of Stones: Living in a Palestinian Village*. New York: Atlantic Monthly Press.

World Bank. 1993. *Developing the Occupied Territories: An Investment in Peace*. 6 vols. Washington, DC: World Bank.

Zakai, Dan. 1986. *Economic Developments in Judea-Samaria and the Gaza District, 1982–1984*. Jerusalem: Bank of Israel.

YEMEN

Manfred W. Wenner

Political science research on Yemen is a late phenomenon in both Middle East studies and in comparative political science. In fact, it is a phenomenon of the 1960s and later, and the reasons are not hard to find. First, until 1970, access to Yemen was essentially impossible, thus putting an important damper on either the willingness or ability of scholars in Arab politics to undertake any systematic (primary) research. Second, the majority of scholars in and of the Arab Middle East were less than interested in a country that had no oil and that had played no significant role in either inter-Arab or regional politics. Third, Yemen had not been a part of any colonial system and therefore had not developed a set of officials, administrators, and scholars ipso facto interested in its social, economic, and political systems (such as happened with the Mediterranean Arab states).

Members of the first group of contemporary scholars (Ingrams 1966; Wenner 1967) were at pains to provide information on various historical, social, demographic, economic, and other factors in order to try to explicate the political system, then still much under the influence of the imamic heritage. The revolution of 1962 and the subsequent civil war (to 1970) made physical access, accurate information (including valid quantitative data), and the development of institutions with any kind of continuity impossible. The motive for including Yemen in any systematic survey or analysis of Arab politics was not particularly strong, and such inclusion had to wait until the 1970s. In fact, most of the textbooks on Middle East politics that were used in the 1950s, 1960s, and even early 1970s had very limited discussion or analysis of Yemen (Lenczowski 1952; al-Marayati 1972; an early exception was Ismael 1970).

The end of the civil war made it possible for a veritable army of scholars to enter the country; the new government positively encouraged research in all disciplines and even promoted analyses of various political topics and subjects considered inviolable in other Arab states. The number of political scientists interested in Yemen, however, remained extraordinarily low: comparative politics did not get the kinds of quantitative and qualitative studies that were appearing on, say, Egypt or Syria.

In view of the political history of Yemen between 1918 and the mid-1990s, the first part of this survey will be chronological in orientation, with the obvious dividing line of the 1962 revolution, because it both changed the political system and inaugurated the era of modern political research. There is, however, another important divide, that of May 1990, when the two states that had ''Yemen'' in their official name (the Yemen Arab Republic and the People's Democratic Republic of Yemen) merged. The merger brought together two states with dramatically different political histories over the last 150 years. Indeed, coverage of their political development was commonly undertaken by two different sets of scholars, with very different research priorities and concerns.

THE IMAMIC PERIOD (TO 1962)

Few works appeared during the period up to 1962 that contemporary political scientists would consider a significant contribution to our understanding of Arab political systems, much less to comparative politics as a theoretically oriented social science. There were some anecdotal accounts and general surveys of the governmental system that the two imams of this period (Yahya, 1918–1948, and Ahmad, 1948–1962) headed (see, for example, Heyworth-Dunne 1952). There were also the occasional chapters and parts of works devoted to other priorities that provided insights and more detailed accounts of certain aspects of the system (Scott 1942). Overwhelmingly, however, the literature on Yemen consisted of the accounts of travelers, adventurers, and the occasional diplomat or scholar. It was not until World War II that a full-scale effort to cover all aspects of the country, including areas that political scientists would consider important (e.g., the social structure, the demographics, the economic system, and the land-tenure system), was even attempted. This was the compilation undertaken by the Naval Intelligence Division of the British Admiralty (Great Britain 1946); its purpose, however, was to inform British military and intelligence personnel as thoroughly as possible concerning all aspects of the country that might be relevant to the war effort, rather than contribute to the field of comparative politics. Declassified at the end of the war, it rapidly became a classic because of its thoroughness, and it remains a highly sought-after work to the present day, in part, at least, because it provides scholars with some baseline data for comparisons with the present day.

There was, in fact, very little coverage of either North Yemen (the old Mutawakkilite Kingdom) or of South Yemen (either as Aden and its protectorates or as South Arabia) in the various textbooks and surveys of the politics of the Middle East that were used in political science courses in the 1950s or early 1960s (e.g., Lenczowski 1952, 1956). It was not until after the revolution of 1962 that the first country studies began to appear; these sought, for the first time, to deal with the old regime as well as its replacement in some systematic fashion (see the section "Government and Institutions").

THE REPUBLICAN PERIOD

In the 1970s and 1980s, a veritable spate of books appeared; these covered nearly all aspects of the country, literally from anthropology to zoology. Some undertook serious treatment of domestic and foreign policy issues and the politics of the new republican government (North Yemen, as it became known). At the same time, however, coverage of South Yemen was quite limited. Due to its adoption of the Marxist-Leninist ideology shortly after independence (and its associated and deliberate decision to cut itself off from nearly all forms of contact with the Western world, including scholars), most of the literature and analyses were within the rubric of Communist political systems. In the meantime, North Yemen was increasingly marginalized as the coverage in American texts and articles tended to emphasize the politics of the oil exporters and the Arab states of the Mediterranean basin.

RELIGION AND POLITICS

Since Zaydi Islam played such an important role in the birth and development of Yemen, no matter its boundaries or relative importance during the last thousand years, most analysts of the politics of Yemen have provided at least a brief review and analysis of its role in the state, that is, its connection to the politics and policies of various leaders (imams). The first systematic studies of Zaydi Islam were undertaken in the early twentieth century by Rudolf Strothmann (1912), and these remain an important source to the present time (despite the official abolishment of the imamate at the time of the revolution of 1962). Although his works are available only in German, a number of later scholars have drawn on them, and much of their content has made its way into other works that are important to an understanding of Zaydism, its impact on Yemeni culture, and its continuing (indirect but nevertheless significant) influence on some important aspects of contemporary politics (Madelung 1971; Serjeant 1969). Recent developments, such as the increasing influence of Islamist political organizations in the political system, have been effectively traced and analyzed by Cigar (1990) for South Yemen, and by Dresch and Haykel (1995) for the North.

THE SOCIAL STRUCTURE AND ITS IMPACT ON POLITICS

One of the important reasons for the attention to Zaydi theory and practice is that even though not all residents of Yemen were or are Zaydis (there are also Shafiis, Ismailis, and Jews), it is Zaydism that over the centuries has been the strongest influence on the social organization of the society at large. Unfortunately, there are very few studies that attempt an analysis of the relationship between the two in any rigorous manner; on the other hand, there are a few studies that effectively describe elements of the social structure and how it has been shaped by the policies and practices of the Zaydi elite (Stookey 1974; Gerholm 1977; Chelhod 1984). This remains one of the most fertile fields for additional research, especially the question of whether the republican governments and their policies have had an impact on the contemporary social system; if so, which policies have been effective and to what extent, and where and how were they applied? The area of greatest interest to many political scientists is the role of the (northern Zaydi) tribes, whose organization, distribution, priorities, and actions are generally considered to have been, and continue to be, the most important component of the political life of the state (Meissner 1987; Swagman 1988; Dresch 1989).

THE ECONOMY AND POLITICS

Because Yemen has one of the least developed economies on earth (at least according to the standard criteria), we have no verifiable or valid baseline data from the imamic period other than what is found in Heyworth-Dunne 1952, and modern data collection does not begin until 1970, it is extremely difficult to describe, much less analyze, in any rigorous fashion the usual links between economics and politics. Political economists have long either speculated on or investigated the link between landownership patterns, occupation, class or caste membership, region of residence, age, and other factors and specific political orientations or behavior. In fact, the republican government undertook the gathering and publication of a great variety of data in the 1970s and early 1980s (Yemen, *Statistical Yearbooks*); however, public access to the data became increasingly restricted after 1986, and as a result, sophisticated analyses became almost impossible. On the other hand, certain characteristics of the economy that had a significant impact on Yemeni emigration patterns, the attempts to promote economic development, and demographic change were the subject of some studies that clearly understood their political impact (Cohen and Lewis 1979; El Mallakh 1986; Friedlander 1988; Meyer 1986; Carapico and Tutwiler 1981).

In economic terms, the most important event since the 1962 revolution was the discovery of significant high-quality oil and gas deposits in the eastern regions of North Yemen and in the northwestern areas of South Yemen (Burrowes 1989; Cranfield 1987; Melamid 1991). Unfortunately, although the discovery of oil and natural gas played an important role in the ability of the regime to survive two major economic setbacks—the dramatic decline in remittances after the expulsion of hundreds of thousands of Yemenis from Saudi Arabia (Hartmann 1995; Stevenson 1993) and the punitive measures imposed by the United States for Yemen's support of Iraq in the Gulf War of 1990–1991 (Parodi

1994)—the income derived from these deposits has not been enough to solve Yemen's many economic and political problems.

Two studies (World Bank 1979a and 1979b) attempted to analyze nearly all aspects of the economies of both North and South Yemen in their entirety; neither of these has been the basis of any systematic analysis of the relationship between economic characteristics and political developments. Furthermore, it took until 1992 for the first comparative study of the two economies to appear (al-Hagari 1992). In other words, modern political economy as a discipline in conjunction with comparative politics has yet to systematically treat the Yemeni case.

GOVERNMENT AND INSTITUTIONS

Since government and politics under the Imams Yahya and Ahmad were personalized rule (although it had the passive support of a majority of the population and the active support of the *sayyid* class), there was very little need or desire to undertake extensive analysis of the political system or the institutional framework (such as it was). With the birth of the republic in 1962, the governmental system became more complex: governmental ministries with actual responsibilities were founded (under the imams such ''ministries'' were sinecures for relatives, offspring, or important allies and had no independent authority, budget, or responsibilities). As the number and variety of such governmental institutions (and responsibilities) grew, many of these bodies became politicized in typical Yemeni fashion; that is, they were colonized by different tribes, confederations, and other nongovernmental social organizations.

The imamic system has been described and analyzed by a number of scholars (Ingrams 1966; Wenner 1967); nearly all, in addition, cover the rise and development of the opposition movements that were to eventually result in the overthrow of the imamate in 1962 (Douglas 1987). In the 1970s and early 1980s, works that more clearly made use of some comparative political science concepts and had access to more recent research began to provide a more sophisticated picture of the political systems of the two Yemens (Peterson 1982; Stookey 1978, 1982; Zabarah 1982). Nevertheless, there were still works that retained the rather more traditional approach to the treatment of the two states (Bidwell 1983; Peretz 1983; Long and Reich 1980).

As the government in the North became more firmly established and expanded its operations and territorial control, the system became more complex and institutionalized. The nearly continual state of political flux from 1970 to the 1990s was covered by a number of scholars (Burrowes 1987; Wenner 1991); all were considerably more analytical than their predecessors, yet their treatment and analysis still were only rarely suffused with the concepts and tools of contemporary comparative politics. Burrowes was a notable exception.

Meanwhile, the descriptions of political ''development'' in the South were, after the first historical and chronological accounts of ''the road to independence,'' more concerned with how South Yemen fit into the Soviet Union's foreign affairs worldview than with analyzing the country's domestic politics. The emphasis was on the Marxist elite, its members, their policies, and how they exercised control, and, in general, on what South Yemen added to our knowledge of Soviet policy (Ismael and Ismael 1986; Page 1985). Although some useful works on South Yemen appeared in the 1980s (Lackner 1985; Ismael and Ismael 1986), the South clearly did not get the same attention as the North: it took until the 1990s before we had a full-scale treatment of the Marxist regime in South Yemen (Halliday 1990). Most illuminating here was the fact that only two writers (Halliday 1986; Wenner 1970a, 1988a) continued to suggest that some of the traditional tribal and social patterns could still be discerned below the Marxist veneer. Furthermore, comparative studies of the two Yemen states within the same rubric were rather rare: Peterson 1984; Serjeant 1979; and Stookey 1984 were exceptions.

The definitive description and analysis of the process whereby the two states decided to merge in 1990 remains to be written; however, there are a few articles that have attempted to cover the major economic and political factors, domestic and foreign, that influenced the two Yemens to try to resolve their differences. The most complete of these is by Kostiner (1996). The civil war of 1994 and some of the political, religious, economic, and ethnic issues that surfaced or resurfaced at that time will make the task even more difficult. Some useful accounts and surveys are Braun 1992; Burrowes 1991; Carapico 1993a, 1993b; and al-Suwaidi 1995.

THE MILITARY AND POLITICS

In one fashion or another, the military has played an important political role in both Yemens; in the North, it is appropriate to categorize the state as a military autocracy, after a brief period as a multiparty system. In the South, although the military played a key role in the process of obtaining independence from Great Britain and then in subduing the protectorates and the multiplicity of armed factions operating there, it eventually fell under the civilian control of the Yemen Socialist party (YSP), a party on the Soviet/Communist model. On the other hand, it became clear in the paroxysm of January 1986 that whoever controlled the military had the upper hand, even in nominally civilian affairs (Halliday 1988; Wenner 1988a, 1988b).

Although it was not universally acknowledged, it later became clear that in both the North and the South, the military tended to reflect the tribal and ethnic configurations of the respective societies. Specific studies of the role of the military in the development of the political system do not exist. On the other hand, nearly all contemporary scholars of Yemen do at least discuss some aspects of the military, since the government is military in its origins, orientation, and operations, and many characteristics of the social and tribal system continue to have their impact upon the military (Beeri 1969; Haddad 1973; Nyrop 1986, especially 193–212 and 306–324; see also the works under ''Political Development and Leadership'').

POLITICAL DEVELOPMENT AND LEADERSHIP

Many analysts, in the academic world as well as in the U.S. government's research and analysis bureaus, believe firmly that the only way to understand the politics and policies of countries such as Yemen is through a detailed knowledge of the characteristics of its leaders and their rivals and opponents. The basic assumption is that the social and political institutions are so weak that their impact on policy making is marginal, at least in comparison with the personal power, charisma, influence, and support of the incumbent leader. In the case of Yemen, this method of analysis was both appropriate and essential to an understanding of policy and politics under the imams Yahya (1918–1948) and Ahmad (1948–1962).

On the other hand, the revolution of 1962 would and could not have taken place had it not been for the collective efforts of a large number of people in various organizations, political parties, and other social institutions. In other words, it was both important and relevant to be aware of the many currents of opposition that existed during the reign of the imams, even if their direct impact on specific policies was relatively small. One scholar (Douglas 1987) has provided the most detailed description and analysis of the various strains of military, religious, social, and economic opposition that developed within the constraints of one of the most closed and authoritarian societies ever recorded.

One important result of the civil war of 1962–1970 was the development of alternative loci of political influence and power. Among these one would have to include the military, various civilian groupings (based upon domestic interests), political organizations of assorted ideological orientations, and, last but not least, the representatives of foreign powers with an interest in Yemeni domestic and foreign policy goals (e.g., Saudi Arabia). In fact, the political system created after the end of the civil war was quite unstable for nearly a decade (two presidents were assassinated in office); there also existed a major domestic opposition movement with extensive foreign support (the National Democratic Front). Nevertheless, the system was sufficiently organized and effective to recruit and staff a very diverse and large set of institutions and agencies to carry out the functions and responsibilities associated with a modern government (Peterson 1984). Furthermore, there arose a uniquely Yemeni institution in the rural areas: the local development associations, organized to mobilize local and governmental resources to deal with the problems of development (schools, clinics, road building, and so on). These were the focus of a number of studies of some interest to political scientists interested in local politics (Carapico 1984; Cohen, Hebert, Lewis, and Swanson 1981; Tutwiler 1984; and others).

Ironically, in view of the orientation of analysts both within and without the governments of the Western world, there are no biographies of either Imam

Yahya or Imam Ahmad, nor of any of the major political leaders who so radically altered the political system (e.g., Abdullah al-Sallal or Ibrahim al-Hamdi,
not to mention Ali Abdullah Salih himself; however, on the latter's important
role in the North's development, see Burrowes 1985). Descriptions and analyses
of their policies and influence may be found in a number of the works that
appeared in the 1980s and 1990s (Peterson 1982; Burrowes 1987; Wenner
1991); without question, the most complete and important study of the period
since unification, that is, on the process of "liberalization and democratization,"
is the one by Glosemeyer (1995).

FOREIGN RELATIONS

Treatment of Yemeni foreign relations must be divided into two distinct periods: before and after the unification agreement of 1990. Prior to that date, the
two Yemens were separate and distinct political entities, with their own priorities, orientations, and goals in the regional and international arenas.

North Yemen's foreign relations were overwhelmingly concerned with two
states: Saudi Arabia and South Yemen. This is not to suggest that other states
were inconsequential; they did matter. It is, however, to make the point that
relations with Egypt, the USSR, or even the United States took second place.
Nevertheless, despite the fact that Yemen's relationship with Saudi Arabia had
sometimes been a conflictual one (they fought a war in 1934 over their boundary), it did not attract the attention of scholars of inter-Arab relations, and despite
the fact that Saudi Arabia, once it had become a major oil exporter and the
dominant force in the Arabian Peninsula, consistently sought to influence the
policies of its neighbors, and most especially Yemen, the techniques employed
and their consequences did not make it into the general literature of inter-Arab
relations (e.g., Kerr 1971). Even the eight-year civil war, in which Saudi Arabia
was only one of many participants (including Egypt, the USSR, Iran, Jordan,
and even the United States and Great Britain), did not warrant much attention
as part of any larger analysis of inter-Arab relations or security issues (but see
Wenner 1993a, 1993b). In fact, two of the major works on the subject were the
work of journalists (Schmidt 1968; O'Ballance 1971).

South Yemen's foreign relations were similarly dominated by two or three
states; in the period immediately after independence these included Great Britain, North Yemen, and Saudi Arabia. Soon thereafter, as a result of its political
move into the group of Marxist-Leninist states, the role of the Soviet Union and
its major Eastern European allies became increasingly important, and Great Britain disappeared from the list of relevant powers (Halliday 1984a; Katz 1986;
and Page 1985, among others).

After unification, the new state's major foreign policy concern was Saudi
Arabia, which saw the independent republican government as a significant threat
to the stability and political orientation of the Arabian Peninsula. It is at this
time that we get the first full-length study of the relationship between North

Yemen and its chief foreign policy concern, Saudi Arabia (Gause 1990). For-
tuitously, at the same time, we get the first thorough analysis of the foreign
policy concerns of the South (Halliday 1990). Later, when Yemen played a role
in the Iran-Iraq conflict and then in the Gulf War, its relations with the United
States, which sought to punish the country for its stand in the United Nations,
assumed greater significance since U.S. influence in a variety of international
agencies—the IMF, for one—had an impact on the economy and political developments in the mid-1990s. We do not, however, have systematic studies of
most of these developments; the first efforts to cover some of these issues were
Parodi (1994) and Almadhagi (1996).

THE UNITY AGREEMENT OF 1990 AND CONFLICT
BETWEEN THE YEMENS

Arguably, the agreement to unite North and South Yemen in May 1990 is
the most important political event in the history of both Yemens since World
War II. That it took place at all, in view of the two previous wars between them
(in 1972 and 1979), is of considerable importance in understanding some of the
economic and political features of Yemeni politics. The fact that it led to major
changes in the political landscape, and even eventually to the civil war of 1994
(which in some ways was simply a resurfacing of the kinds of disagreements
and frictions that had characterized the wars of the 1970s), provides some in-
dication of its impact. It is probably too early to expect a full account, much
less one that places the conflict and its antecedents effectively within the complex political rubric that has developed. Nevertheless, there are a number of
reports that are worth considering in the effort to understand politics in the Arab
world in general, and in Yemen in particular (Burrowes 1992; Carapico 1994;
Dunbar 1992; Dunn 1994; Gause 1987; Halliday 1984a, 1984b, 1995). The most
complete political account of the 1994 war is in al-Suwaidi (1995); for those
interested in the specific military details of the war, see Warburton (1995).

PARTIES, INTEREST GROUPS, AND ELECTIONS

Unquestionably the greatest impact of the unity agreement was on the nature
and characteristics of the newly formed joint political system. Since neither of
the two Yemens wished to appear to be imposing its economic, social, or political system on the other, the two states agreed to establish a democratic political system, including a free press, a practically unlimited right to political
organizing, and all of the other appurtenances and institutions of a parliamentary
democracy, including free elections, which were to have been held after a thirty-
month transition period.

Shortly after the agreement, more than forty political parties made their appearance; more than eighty-five journals, magazines, and other periodicals of
various political leanings began to publish; and a number of pieces of legislation

to legalize and regularize these momentous changes were passed. Although more than a dozen of the original list of parties disappeared rather quickly (as a result of their being melded into other, larger groupings, or out of lassitude on the part of their founders), about fifteen entered candidates throughout the country (i.e., in every constituency) and participated actively in the new environment. The press was fiercely independent and also contributed to the electric atmosphere generated by these momentous changes.

Although the elections were postponed past the thirty-month deadline originally set in 1990, they did in fact take place in April 1993. The outcome may be viewed as the logical precursor to the events of the summer of 1994: the Yemeni Socialist party (the party formerly dominant in South Yemen) did not do as well as expected; on the other hand, the General People's Congress (GPC) (the party formerly dominant in North Yemen) also failed to do as well as expected. A new political force appeared to hold the balance of power in the new state: a combination of tribal and Islamic forces, seen by many progressives and reformers as a regression to the ''bad old days'' of the imamate and tribalism.

Few descriptions and analyses yet exist of the consequences of the unity agreement (see, however, Carapico 1993a, 1993b; Detalle 1993; Glosemeyer 1993; Wenner 1994). As might be expected, however, the civil war of 1994 significantly affected the balance of political forces within the country as well as making it more difficult, at least for a while, for scholars to undertake research. The war also had its impact on the domestic policy priorities of the government, now completely dominated by the GPC and its Islamic/tribal allies, and made it possible for the government to erode many of the rights that had resulted from the unity agreement. Meantime, while the oil industry continued to expand and become increasingly important to the economy and the programs of the government, the government sought to bring an ever-larger number and variety of groups, programs, and activities under its influence and control. Analyses of these developments await future scholars, who will probably use the ongoing accounts of the *Yemen Times* as a source.

THE FUTURE OF POLITICAL RESEARCH IN YEMEN

In general, it seems fair to contend that contemporary Yemen and the characteristics of its social, economic, and political systems have not been of significant interest to most scholars of the Islamic world or the Arab Middle East. Indeed, a glance at most of the survey works on the Middle East that have appeared in the last two decades typically omit Yemen or give it short shrift.

Contemporary social science disciplines, not to mention Middle East studies, could in fact benefit from greater attention to many aspects of Yemen. Certain features of its economy (e.g., the sizeable emigrant population and the impact of its emigration and return and its remittances on the domestic economy) challenge some of the conclusions and theories based upon other case studies (Cohen and Lewis 1979; Swanson 1979). In the field of comparative politics, the development of the political system between 1970 and 1990 and then from 1990 to 1994 provides an interesting "check" on some theories of democratization that have been propounded. Further, some theories of ethnic-group mobilization and political involvement could benefit from detailed knowledge of the relationship between Zaydis and Shafiis in Yemen.

Perhaps most glaringly, Yemen for long made available an incredible variety of data on various aspects of the economy, not to mention its social and political characteristics, none of it employed by quantitative scholars in their analyses of the Arab states. In fact, North Yemen was for years so thorough in its reporting of governmental expenditures that it regularly included the amount of the government's subsidies (read bribes) to some of the tribal elements in the northern areas.

Conversely, of course, it is necessary to report that South Yemen during its Marxist-Leninist period very clearly either manipulated data for political purposes or refused to allow many types of information to be made public. It was, in fact, not until the World Bank undertook a major study at the government's request (1979a) that some hard data on various aspects of the state and its economy and social characteristics were made public.

On at least two occasions when events in Yemen provided a relevant comparison to similar events elsewhere, they were essentially ignored by the media, comparative political scientists, and most Middle East specialists. The first was the process of unification of two disparate economic and political systems. Even though it occurred at roughly the same time as the unification of Germany, and its characteristics provided a relevant second instance of Communist/capitalist political integration, little systematic comparative analysis of the two has yet appeared (but see Braun 1992). (Ironically, however, it has been extensively studied by Korean political scientists for its potential lessons to their own situation.)

The second occasion was the full-blown experiment in establishing a parliamentary democratic system in an Arab state. To the dismay of many, the Yemeni experiment with a democratic political system was dismissed by American sources at the same time as it was feared and opposed by other states in the Arabian Peninsula because of its destabilization potential for these regimes (Parodi et al. 1994). Then, unfortunately, the 1994 civil war produced a substantial reluctance on the part of the government to continue to allow the political openness in the media and the freewheeling organizational activity that had characterized the period immediately after unity. A number of explicitly political studies that would have contributed to our knowledge of economic, social, and political interrelationships in an Arab state experimenting with political democracy became impossible to carry out (for example, the author had hoped to obtain the results of the 1993 elections at the electoral-district level in order to make comparisons with census data for the same districts, based upon age, gender, religious affiliation, occupation, and other characteristics; it was not to be). For the moment, contemporary studies of the political system and its correlates have been relatively few in number and still tend to be ignored by other scholars in Middle East studies, not to mention comparative politics in general.

The unification agreement, of course, created a brand-new political system with dramatically altered territorial boundaries, new institutions, more and different participants and political traditions, additional ethnoreligious groups, a significantly different economy, and a host of new problems. These changes should provide fertile ground for description and analysis by the next generation of scholars of comparative politics with an interest in the Arab Middle East as a source of case studies. For example, we could use a study of the postunification parliament: how it is organized (e.g., its committee structure), its modus operandi, its effect on public policy (if any), and other aspects.

In a related vein, although we have a compilation of Yemen's many political parties from the 1940s to the early 1990s (Wenner 1994), we do not have a full-scale study of their bases of support (in demographic, spatial, economic, general demographic, and other terms), nor do we have any studies of their leadership, their recruitment patterns, internal organization, ideologies, or funding practices. Certainly, none of these possibilities have been undertaken with any comparative perspective to other Arab states, much less to cases in other parts of the developing world.

In the mid-1990s, therefore, it is possible to argue that Yemen continues to be peripheral to most studies of the Middle East and the Arab world. Perhaps one can forgive contemporary scholars of Yemen for feeling a bit frustrated with the lack of interest in, and even seemingly deliberate lack of concern for, the contribution to our knowledge of political development in the Arab world that greater knowledge of Yemen could provide.

REFERENCES

Beeri, Eliezer. 1969. *Army Officers in Arab Politics and Society*. New York: Praeger.
Bidwell, Robin. 1983. *The Two Yemens*. London: Longman.
Braun, Ursula. 1992. ''Yemen: Another Case of Unification.'' *Aussenpolitik* 43, no. 2: 174–184.
Burrowes, Robert. 1985. ''The Yemen Arab Republic and the Ali Abdullah Salih Regime, 1978–1984.'' *Middle East Journal* 39, no. 3:287–316.
———. 1987. *The Yemen Arab Republic: The Politics of Development, 1962–1986*. Boulder, CO: Westview Press.
———. 1988. ''State-Building and Political Construction in the Yemen Arab Republic.'' In Peter Chelkowski and Robert Pranger, eds., *Ideology and Power in the Middle East*. Durham, NC: Duke University Press.
———. 1989. ''Oil Strike and Leadership Struggle in South Yemen.'' *Middle East Journal* 43, no. 3 (Summer): 437–454.
———. 1991. ''Prelude to Unification: The Yemen Arab Republic, 1962–1990.'' *International Journal of Middle East Studies* 23 (November): 483–506.

————. 1992. "The Yemen Arab Republic's Legacy and Yemeni Unification." *Arab Studies Quarterly* (Fall): 41–68.

Carapico, Sheila. 1984. "The Political Economy of Self-Help: Development Cooperatives in the Yemen Arab Republic." Ph.D. dissertation, State University of New York at Binghamton.

————. 1993a. "Elections and Mass Politics in Yemen." *Middle East Report*, no. 185 (November/December): 2–7.

————. 1993b. "Yemen Unity: The Economic Dimension." *Middle East Report*, no. 184 (September/October): 9–14.

————. 1994. "From Ballot Box to Battlefield: The War of the Two Alis." *Middle East Report*, no. 190 (September/October): 24–27.

Chelhod, Joseph. 1984. "L'Ordre Social." In J. Chelhod, ed., *L'Arabie du Sud*. Vol. 3. Paris: Maisonneuve et Larose.

Cigar, Norman. 1990. "Islam and the State in South Yemen: The Uneasy Coexistence." *Middle Eastern Studies* 26, no. 2:185–203.

Cohen, John, Mary Hebert, David Lewis, and Jon Swanson. 1981. "Development from Below: Local Development Associations in the Yemen Arab Republic." *World Development* 9 (November/December): 1039–1061.

Cohen, John, and David Lewis. 1979. "Capital Surplus, Labor Short Economies: Yemen as a Challenge to Rural Development Strategies." *American Journal of Agricultural Economics* (Fall): 523–528.

Cranfield, John. 1987. "North Yemen: New Middle East Exporter." *Petroleum Economist* (July): 257–258.

Detalle, Renaud. 1993. "The Yemeni Elections Up Close." *Middle East Report*, no. 185 (November/December): 8–12.

Douglas, J. Leigh. 1987. The Free Yemeni Movement, 1935–1962. Beirut: American University of Beirut.

Dresch, Paul. 1989. *Tribes, Government, and History in Yemen*. Oxford: Oxford University Press.

Dresch, Paul, and Bernard Haykel. 1995. "Stereotypes and Political Styles: Islamists and Tribesfolk in Yemen." *International Journal of Middle East Studies* 27, no. 4 (November): 405– 431.

Dunbar, Charles. 1992. "The Unification of Yemen: Process, Politics, and Prospects." *Middle East Journal* 46, no. 3 (Summer): 456–476.

Dunn, Michael. 1994. "The Wrong Place, the Wrong Time: Why Yemeni Unity Failed." *Middle East Policy* 3, no. 2 (Spring): 148–156.

Friedlander, Jonathan, ed. 1988. *Sojourners and Settlers: The Yemeni Immigrant Experience*. Salt Lake City: University of Utah Press.

Gause, F. Gregory. 1987. "The Idea of Yemeni Unity." *Journal of Arab Affairs* (Spring): 55–87.

————. 1990. *Saudi-Yemeni Relations*. New York: Columbia University Press.

Gerholm, Tomas. 1977. *Market, Mosque, and Mafraj: Social Inequality in a Yemeni Town*. Stockholm: Department of Social Anthropology, University of Stockholm.

Glosemeyer, Iris. 1993. "The First Yemeni Parliamentary Elections in 1993: Practicing Democracy." *Orient* (September): 439–451.

————. 1995. *Liberalisierung und Demokratisierung in der Republik Jemen, 1990–1994*. Hamburg: Deutsches Orient-Institut.

Great Britain. Admiralty. Naval Intelligence Division. 1946. *Western Arabia and the Red Sea*. London: Naval Intelligence Division (HMSO).

Haddad, George. 1973. *Revolutions and Military Rule in the Middle East* (Part 2 includes Yemen). New York: Robert Speller.

al-Hagari, Ali Saleh. 1992. ''A Comparative Study of the Economies of the Yemen Arab Republic and the People's Democratic Republic of Yemen (1970–1988).'' Ph.D. dissertation, University of Nebraska.

Halliday, Fred. 1984a. ''Soviet Relations with South Yemen.'' In B. R. Pridham, ed., *Contemporary Yemen: Politics and Historical Background*. London: Croom Helm.

———. 1984b. ''The Yemens: Conflict and Coexistence.'' *World Today* 40 (August/September): 355–362.

———. 1986. ''Shootout in Yemen.'' *The Nation* 242 (March): 262.

———. 1988. ''Catastrophe in South Yemen: A Preliminary Assessment.'' *Middle East Report*, no. 151 (March/April): 37–39.

———. 1990. *Revolution and Foreign Policy: The Case of South Yemen, 1967–1987*. Cambridge: Cambridge University Press.

———. 1995. ''The Third Inter-Yemeni War and Its Consequences.'' *Asian Affairs* 26 (Summer): 131–140.

Hartmann, Rainer. 1995. ''Yemeni Exodus from Saudi Arabia: The Gulf Conflict and the Ceasing of the Workers' Emigration.'' *Journal of South Asian and Middle Eastern Studies* (Winter): 2–28.

Heyworth-Dunne, Gamal-Eddine [James]. 1952. *Al-Yemen*. Cairo: Renaissance Bookshop.

Hudson, Michael C. 1995. ''Bipolarity, Rational Calculation, and War in Yemen.'' *Arab Studies Journal* 3 (Spring): 9–19.

Ingrams, Harold. 1966. *The Yemen: Imams, Rulers, and Revolutions*. London: John Murray.

Ismael, Tareq, ed. 1970. *Governments and Politics of the Contemporary Middle East*. Homewood, IL: Dorsey Press.

Ismael, T., and Jacqueline Ismael. 1986. *The People's Democratic Republic of Yemen: Politics, Economics and Society: The Politics of Socialist Transformation*. Boulder, CO: Lynne Rienner.

Katz, Mark. 1986. *Russia and Arabia: Soviet Foreign Policy toward the Arabian Peninsula*. Baltimore: Johns Hopkins University Press.

———. 1992. ''Yemeni Unity and Saudi Security.'' *Middle East Policy* 1:117–135.

Kerr, Malcolm. 1971. *The Arab Cold War: Gamal 'Abd al-Nasir and His Rivals, 1958–1970*. 3d ed. Oxford: Oxford University Press.

Kostiner, Joseph. 1984. *The Struggle for South Yemen*. New York: St. Martin's Press.

———. 1996. *Yemen: The Tortuous Quest for Unity, 1990–94*. London: Royal Institute of International Affairs.

Lackner, Helen. 1985. *PDR Yemen: Outpost of Socialist Development in Arabia*. London: Ithaca Press.

Lenczowski, George. 1952, 1956. *The Middle East in World Affairs*. 1st and 2d eds. Ithaca: Cornell University Press.

Long, David, and Bernard Reich, eds. 1980. *The Government and Politics of the Middle East and North Africa*. Boulder, CO: Westview Press.

Madelung, Wilferd. 1971. "Imama." In *Encyclopaedia of Islam*. 2d ed. Leiden: E. J. Brill. 3:1192–1198.

Almadhagi, Ahmed Noman Kassim. 1996. *Yemen and the United States: A Study of a Small Power and Super-State Relationship, 1962–1994*. London: I. B. Tauris.

El Mallakh, Ragaei. 1986. *The Economic Development of the Yemen Arab Republic*. London: Croom Helm.

al-Marayati, Abid A. 1972. *The Middle East: Its Governments and Politics*. Belmont, CA: Duxbury Press.

Meissner, Jeffrey R. 1987. "Tribes at the Core: Legitimacy, Structure, and Power in Zaydi Yemen." Ph.D. dissertation, Columbia University.

Melamid, Alexander. 1991. *Oil and the Economic Geography of the Middle East and North Africa*. Princeton: Darwin Press.

Meyer, Günter. 1986. *Arbeitsemigration, Binnenwanderung, und Wirtschaftsentwicklung in der Arabischen Republik Jemen*. Wiesbaden: Ludwig Reichert.

Nyrop, Richard F., ed. 1986. *The Yemens*. Washington, DC: U.S. Government Printing Office.

O'Ballance, Edgar. 1971. *The War in the Yemen*. Hamden, CT: Archon Books.

Page, Stephen. 1985. *The Soviet Union and the Yemens: Influence in Asymmetrical Relationships*. New York: Praeger.

Parodi, Carlos, et al. 1994. "The Silent Demise of Democracy: The Role of the Clinton Administration in the 1994 Yemeni Civil War." *Arab Studies Quarterly* (Fall): 65–76.

Peretz, Don. 1983. *The Middle East Today*. New York: Praeger.

Peterson, John E. 1982. *Yemen: The Search for a Modern State*. Baltimore: Johns Hopkins University Press.

———. 1984. "Nation Building and Political Development in the Two Yemens." In B. R. Pridham, ed., *Contemporary Yemen: Politics and Historical Background*. London: Croom Helm.

Pridham, Brian, ed. 1984. *Contemporary Yemen: Politics and Historical Background*. London: Croom Helm.

———, ed. 1985. *Economy, Society, and Culture in Contemporary Yemen*. London: Croom Helm.

Schmidt, Dana Adams. 1968. *Yemen: The Unknown War*. London: Bodley Head.

Scott, Hugh. 1942. *In the High Yemen*. London: John Murray.

Serjeant, R. B. 1969. "The Zaydis." In A. J. Arberry, ed. *Religion in the Middle East*. Vol. 2. London: Cambridge University Press.

———. 1979. "Perilous Politics in Two Yemeni States." *Geographical Magazine* 51 (November): 769–774.

———. 1982. "The Interplay between Tribal Affinities and Religious (Zaydi) Authority in Yemen." In *State and Society in the Arab World*, special issue of *al-Abhath* [Lebanon] edited by Fuad Khuri, no. 30:11–50.

Stevenson, Thomas. 1993. "Yemeni Workers Come Home: Reabsorbing One Million Migrants." *Middle East Report*, no. 181 (March/April): 15–24.

Stookey, Robert W. 1974. "Social Structure and Politics in the Yemen Arab Republic." *Middle East Journal* 28 (Summer): 248–260; (Autumn): 409–418.

———. 1978. *Yemen: The Politics of the Yemen Arab Republic*. Boulder, CO: Westview Press.

————. 1982. *South Yemen: A Marxist Republic in Arabia*. Boulder, CO: Westview Press.

————. 1984. *The Arabian Peninsula: Zone of Ferment*. Stanford, CA: Hoover Institution Press.

Strothmann, Rudolf. 1912. *Das Staatsrecht der Zaiditen*. Strassburg: Karl J. Truebner.

al-Suwaidi, Jamal S., ed. 1995. *The Yemeni War of 1994: Causes and Consequences*. London: Saqi Books.

Swagman, Charles F. 1988. "Tribe and Politics: An Example from Highland Yemen." *Journal of Anthropological Research* 44 (Autumn): 251–261.

Swanson, Jon. 1979. "Some Consequences of Emigration for Rural Economic Development in the Yemen Arab Republic." *Middle East Journal* (Winter): 34–43.

Tutwiler, Richard. 1984. "Ta'wun Mahwit: A Case Study of a Local Development Association in Highland Yemen." In Louis Cantori and Iliya Harik, eds., *Local Politics and Development in the Middle East*. Boulder, CO: Westview Press.

Carapico, Sheila, and Richard Tutwiler. 1981. *Yemeni Agriculture and Economic Change*. Milwaukee: American Institute for Yemeni Studies.

Warburton, David. 1995. "The Conventional War in Yemen." *Arab Studies Journal* 3 (Spring): 20–44.

Wenner, Manfred. 1967. *Modern Yemen, 1918–1966*. Baltimore: Johns Hopkins University Press.

————. 1970a. "The People's Republic of South Yemen." In Tareq Ismael, ed., *Governments and Politics of the Contemporary Middle East*. Homewood, IL: Dorsey Press.

————. 1970b. "Yemen." In Tareq Ismael, ed., *Governments and Politics of the Contemporary Middle East*. Homewood, IL: Dorsey Press.

————. 1984. "South Yemen since Independence: An Arab Political Maverick." In Brian Pridham, ed., *Contemporary Yemen: Politics and Historical Background*. London: Croom Helm.

————. 1988a. "Ideology vs. Pragmatism in South Yemen, 1968–1986." In Peter Chelkowski and Robert Pranger, eds., *Ideology and Power in the Middle East: Studies in Honor of George Lenczowski*. Durham, NC: Duke University Press.

————. 1988b. "The 1986 Civil War in Yemen: A Preliminary Assessment." In Brian Pridham, ed., *The Arab Gulf and the Arab World*. London: Croom Helm.

————. 1988c. "The Political Consequences of Yemeni Migration." In Jonathan Friedlander, ed. *Sojourners and Settlers: The Yemeni Immigrant Experience*. Salt Lake City: University of Utah Press.

————. 1991. *The Yemen Arab Republic: Development and Change in an Ancient Land*. Boulder, CO: Westview Press.

————. 1993a. "The Civil War in Yemen, 1962–1970." In Roy Licklider, ed., *Stopping the Killing: How Civil Wars End*. New York: New York University Press.

————. 1993b. "National Integration and National Security: The Case of Yemen." In Bahgat Korany, Paul Noble, and Rex Brynen, eds., *The Many Faces of National Security in the Arab World*. London: Macmillan.

————. 1994. "[Political Parties of] Yemen." In Frank Tachau, ed., *Political Parties of the Middle East and North Africa*. Westport, CT: Greenwood Press.

World Bank. 1979a. *People's Democratic Republic of Yemen: A Review of Economic and Social Development*. Washington, DC: World Bank.

———. 1979b. *Yemen Arab Republic: Development of a Traditional Economy*. Wash-
    ington, DC: World Bank.
Yemen, Government of. 1986. *Statistical Yearbook 1986*. Sanaa: Central Planning Office.
Zabarah, Mohammed. 1982. *Yemen: Traditionalism vs. Modernity*. New York: Praeger.

MIDDLE EAST INTERNATIONAL RELATIONS

Bahgat Korany

On the surface, scholars of Middle East international relations should be happy. Their region is so newsworthy that there is no dearth of literature about it. During the 1960s and the 1970s Middle East visibility in the American elite press was even slightly greater than the Vietnamese issue. But the region's newsworthiness has resulted in a voluminous literature, a liability rather than an asset when attempting to distill a pattern of international relations for the region. The existing literature covers diplomatic history and informed journalism, as well as systematic academic analyses. Because issues central to Middle East international relations (for example, the Arab-Israeli conflict, Islamic fundamentalism or Islamism, petroleum, the status of women) involve so many passions for and against, many publications tend to be polemical, sensational, and based on instant research and hidden agendas. To borrow from communications and cybernetics terminology, the reviewer is at a loss to distinguish between distracting "noise" and functional "substance."

Given the plethora of material, this chapter focuses on books rather than articles, and especially those that conceptually contribute to the state of the field. By definition they are not short-lived and are usually quoted inside and outside the Middle East. In this present examination of the existing literature during the past several decades, the chapter organizes the material according to three conceptual categories that are the building blocks of present international relations conceptualization: (1) Studies that concentrate on the structure, or the macro aspect, of regional international relations. The dominant approach adopted by most analysts is that of international subsystem applied to the region. (2) Studies that concentrate on the actor/agent level: foreign policy analysis. Although the literature is dominated by the single-case-study approach, its findings are increasingly generalizable. In addition, the literature is becoming comparative, with solid bridges to the general field of comparative foreign policy analysis. (3) This third category identifies studies that aim to concentrate on patterns of interaction among states and other groups, essentially within the region. Are these patterns mainly conflictual or cooperative, privileging high (e.g., military-diplomatic) or low (e.g., economic-cultural) politics? Finally, we look at the future and suggest some areas of Middle Eastern international relations research that are needed, both empirically and conceptually.

DELINEATING THE AREAS OF ANALYSIS

To some, there are two ambiguities in Middle East international relations. International relations theory—that is, the way we decode the international system (Korany et al. 1987)—is in flux. Its basis, international reality, has been evolving faster than our concepts and methods, our decoding tools. Empires, as the "evil empire" showed, could surprisingly crumble within a short time. During the 1991 Gulf War, Syria and Israel, supposed to be deadly enemies, were part of the same coalition against Iraq. In both the Middle East and at the global level, political and conceptual geographies are in disarray, and their boundaries are in need of redrawing (Lebow and Risse-Kappen 1995; Macmillan and Linklater 1995; Rosenau 1990).

Similarly, the Middle East is an ambiguous term. Its delimitation changes depending on the analyst's perspective. But the term has been sanctioned by usage, even by people of the region. Do we not have the London-based Saudi newspaper *El-Sharq El-Awsat?* Moreover, local books and periodicals as well as departments in many ministries of foreign affairs in the region use the label. As used here, the Middle East denotes the members of the Arab League, the two Muslim countries of Iran and Turkey, and a Jewish state, Israel.

Though the Middle East is an ancient region, indeed the cradle of various civilizations and a locus for the birth of three monotheistic religions, the study of its international relations (as a subdiscipline of political science) is still struggling to distinguish itself from journalism and diplomatic history. International relations analysis is consequently marginalized. An indicator of this state of affairs is the little space devoted to international relations studies in study reviews of the region.

REVIEWING THE REVIEWS

In his fifty-page pioneering chapter, I. W. Zartman (1976) devotes less than 10 percent to international relations per se. Indeed, he does not hold this subdiscipline in high esteem at all.

Endemic conflict in the area throughout the century has made it a natural subject of study, but at the same time has burned much of the scholarly detachment out of many of its students. As a discipline or sub-discipline, international relations is a residual grab bag even less developed than political science, and it has found no other discipline to turn to as a source of theory on relations between or among large groups. (Zartman 1976, 299)

We will indeed see how these plagues continue to depress current studies on different aspects of Middle East international relations. At this level, then, very little change in the literature seems to have taken place in the last twenty years.

This is also the view of Lisa Anderson (1990), who came to the subject through a survey of political science. Concentrating on the United States, where the major part of conceptualization about the Middle East is taking place, she still deplores the academic state not only of international relations but also of the political science of the Middle East as a whole. "The American study of politics in the Middle East leaves a great deal to be desired. Although there are notable exceptions to the general rule, much of what passes for political science in Middle Eastern studies is a theoretical description: modern diplomatic history, journalism, the regional counterpart of Kremlinology sometimes known as 'mullah-watching' " (Anderson 1990, 52). The result is that Middle East political studies is a "field intellectually aimless and politically malleable"; it is liable to confuse description with analysis and conviction with rigor (Anderson 1990, 53). As for international relations, Anderson devotes even less specific space than Zartman to this subfield, which is touched upon in her final part on agendas of research and in some of the references to Brown (1984), Ismael (1986), and Korany and Dessouki (1991). Since the international relations of the Middle East are still part of the underdeveloped study of underdeveloped countries (Korany 1983, 1986), and given Anderson's view of the state of Middle East political science, the reader can easily surmise how harsh her evaluation of the region's international relations studies would be. Increasingly, however, the analysis of the Middle Eastern state—a major focus for students of international relations—is rigorously tackled, indeed in the works of Anderson herself. Here lies a means not only to establish a strong bridge between political science and its international relations subfield, but also to pave the way for theory building in Middle Eastern studies in general.

This is perhaps why, differently from Zartman and Anderson, the book by Sullivan and Ismael (1991) deals directly with aspects of international relations. Thus out of eleven chapters, three are devoted to one or another dimension of international relations as a defined academic discipline. Consequently, Korany evaluates the state of the art in foreign policy analysis (181–205), and Halley reviews U.S. periodical literature on strategic studies for the decade of the 1980s (1991, 206–221). Halley's chapter is then complemented by Kamel Abu Jaber (1991), who, on the eve of his nomination as Jordan's foreign minister, summarily evaluates strategic studies and especially draws attention to some regional specificities in concept and method. Thus a subfield of Middle East international relations increasingly exists. Rather than ignoring it, we must periodically evaluate it to help it become integrated with other studies in Middle East theory building.

THE STRUCTURAL-SYSTEMIC APPROACH TO THE REGION

The structural-systemic approach came to occupy a central place in international relations debates from the late 1950s onwards. The trigger was the publication of one of the pioneering books purporting to establish a scientific approach to the international system. Morton Kaplan, a professor at the University of Chicago, was inspired by cybernetics and game theory to analyze *System and Process in International Politics* (1957). It was one of his colleagues in the same department of political science, Leonard Binder, who contested this approach's overconcentration on the global aspect to the neglect of regional specificities. Binder (1958) used his area of specialization, the Middle East, as a rebuttal to Kaplan. Thus to avoid the liability of overgeneralization and overhomogenization inherent in international systems analysis, while saving some of the concept's advantages of rigor and integrative synthesis, Binder and some regional specialists tried to have their cake and eat it too. They arrived at a compromise, an intermediary level of analysis between the state (or actor level) and system (or structure level). Hence was born the concept of an international subsystem to concentrate on, and compare, various regions. The first systematic study in this respect was by two Middle East specialists, Louis Cantori and Steven Spiegel (1970). Though the analysis of the Middle East figured prominently in the various readings, the emphasis was on conceptualization and comparison of different regions: from Africa to Latin America and passing by Europe. It is still relevant, but needs to be supplemented by a similar but more recent volume such as Wriggins (1992).

Almost a quarter of a century apart, these two volumes, in addition to a score of articles cited in the bibliographies of the material surveyed here, show the popularity and perseverance of the international subsystem approach as a means of conceptualization and comparison of regional dynamics across the globe. The Wriggins volume, differently from Cantori and Spiegel's, limits itself to three other regions of the Third World in addition to the Gulf (South Asia, Southeast Asia, and the Horn of Africa). Thus Gause's analysis of the Gulf, though detailed and thorough, does not embrace the region as a whole and has nothing to say about the Maghreb. Indeed, the reader has to be resigned to the absence of this subregion in general studies of the Middle East, whether by Brecher (1969), Hudson (1976) or Noble (1991). Despite differences in emphasis among these established authorities, they all manage to combine masterfully international relations concepts (in this case systems analysis) and data from the region.

The application of the international subsystem approach appealed also to historians, who still constitute the majority of analysts among scholars of Middle East international relations. The most prominent example is the volume by L. Carl Brown (1984). A historian and area specialist (he was then the director of the Program in Near Eastern Studies at Princeton University), he adopts a mode of systems analysis through the study of the balance of power across time.

Historical analysis is not included per se, but mainly to develop Brown's overall explanatory theory of international politics of and in the Middle East. The basis of the theory is the presence of a specific Middle East diplomatic culture, a culture determined by the two-century-old Eastern Question that created the existing "old rules" that shape the present "dangerous game" (Brown's subtitle). Brown identifies seven rules of this historical puzzle—the Eastern Question—to develop the thesis that local powers promote their political objectives by bringing great powers into the region and by exploiting their differences, a concretization of the age-old maxim of small states—"divide that ye may not be ruled." As a result, "the Middle East is the most penetrated international relations subsystem in to-day's world" (4).

Indeed, in the last two decades the field has been littered with books devoted to this aspect of penetration, whether by the old colonial powers or by the Soviet Union or the United States in the age of the Cold War and global bipolarity. Limiting our examples to the most conceptually relevant, we find that some analysts focused on a specific event, while others continued the well-established tradition of historical study. Thus Telhami (1990), inspired by Waltz's structural *Theory of International Politics* (1979), attempted to reveal the path to the 1978 Camp David Accords by concentrating on the influence of power and leadership in bargaining patterns. More in continuity with Brown and subsystem analysis is Gerges's analysis (1994) of superpowers' relations with the Middle East. From the 1956 Suez crisis to the 1967 Arab-Israeli war, and considering Egypt's intervention in Yemen (1962–1967), "the concept of an international or regional sub-system is applied to the scrutiny of historical sources" (16). The important finding is that Middle East great-power relations function in both directions where the pattern of conflict and cooperation within each set affects their interaction. An aspect of research cumulativeness is thus emerging in this area of Middle East international relations studies.

To synthesize, then, international relations research on the structural-systemic aspect of the region has manifested the following patterns: First, the historical approach has been dominant. This dominance could be logical, for we cannot understand the present Middle East without understanding, for instance, the problems of the Ottoman Empire and its successor states. But to do this, we surely do not need to equate international relations with history in general or, even less, uniquely with diplomatic history. For in this dominant historical school of Middle East international relations we have very little reference to economic or social forces and their possible role "in the making of history" (Cox 1987).

Second, the dominant emphasis has been on the role of the great powers and their penetration of the region. For those historically minded analysts interested in international relations conceptualization, the most frequently used concept was the Middle East as an international subsystem.

Third, most analysts using the concept at present are political scientists more interested in international relations conceptualization than in history. They share with historians, however, this emphasis on the linkage between the global system and its Middle Eastern subsystem. This linkage appeals equally to some scholars (Ismael 1986) who have mastered both an intimate knowledge of the region and familiarity with Western social science concepts. This combined knowledge is increasingly the characteristic of some prominent scholars who live in the region itself and who publish primarily in its major native language (Dessouki and Matter 1977 and 1983). In this pioneering application of international subsystem analysis published in Arabic, the authors succeeded also in integrating institutional analysis through the study of the Arab League. As seen in this example, even local analysts differ about the delimitation of their subsystem frontiers: Arab or Middle Eastern? The subsystem concept directly or indirectly seems to accommodate this ambiguity, whether the analysis deals with the Baghdad Pact (later CENTO) or the search for Arab unity (Kerr 1971). Whether the ''Arab nation'' will be one state or not, regional organizations, as a halfway stage between state and collective action, for example, the Arab League or the Gulf Cooperation Council (GCC), are a compromise solution similar to the one between the macro and micro levels, between the regional structure and its components.

THE ACTOR LEVEL

In two surveys of more than two hundred periodicals for the periods 1975–1981 and 1982–1988, it was found that at least until the end of the second period, the field of Middle East international relations was still unclear about the ''what'' of foreign policy (for details, see Korany and Dessouki 1991, chapter 1). Does this output mean a specific action or behavior or, alternatively, a strategy and general orientation, or both? The field also frequently deviated into focusing on current affairs. With very few exceptions, the analysis of foreign policy in the 1970s and 1980s was more chronological than analytical, and decision-making analysis was virtually absent.

One notable exception to this poor state of the field was Michael Brecher's three volumes that studied Israel's foreign policy system and its decisions (Brecher 1972, 1975; Brecher and Geist 1980). Their importance lies in the amount and quality of data offered; the elaboration of an explicit detailed framework for foreign policy analysis; the framework's systematic application; and the application of foreign policy theory to the region. As in standard foreign policy analysis, this framework starts with the inputs or determinants (that is, the independent variables). These are divided, following Sprout and Sprout (1965), into the elite's operational environment or ''the reality up there'' and the psychological environment (their images or perception of this ''reality''). As for foreign policy outputs, they are the country's acts or decisions. The conversion of foreign policy inputs into outputs is the foreign policy process, which is divided into policy formulation and policy implementation. This foreign policy process is the focus of the 1974 and 1980 volumes, in which seven of Israel's foreign policy decisions ranging across a quarter of a century are analyzed in detail. In all three volumes, Brecher follows faithfully the suggested framework, bases his analysis on extensive long-term interviews, and ends his study by long concluding chapters explicating the findings and integrating them into efforts of foreign policy theory building.

The Brecher volumes are specimens of the behavioralist or scientific revolution in political science at its best. But Brecher's example has not been duplicated for other countries of the region. One possible reason is that such a work occupies a big portion of a lifetime where money and years of research have to be available in abundance. Brecher managed to have both. But even Brecher himself, who hoped to push forward the comparative dimension and repeat the application of the model in the analysis of India's foreign policy, shied away from the effort. Brecher's example raises the crucial question of the most functional trade-off point between a research project's feasibility (in terms of available time and financial resources) and its "scientific definitiveness" (in terms of concepts and data collection).

Whatever the answer to this question, Brecher's work inspired quite a few young researchers in the region, in North America, and in Europe. A notable example is Adeed Dawisha's studies of Egyptian foreign policy (1976), his analysis of Egypt's intervention in Yemen (1975), and his examination of Syria's 1976 decision to intervene in Lebanon (1980). In all of these studies, Dawisha emphasizes parts of Brecher's model (especially the elite's psychological environment) and conducts interviews. Given the research climate in many countries of the region, Dawisha sometimes had difficulty in applying fully the framework and its methodology and thus could not secure all the data he needed (e.g., the 1980 study of Syria's intervention in Lebanon). These difficulties forced him as well as others to elaborate some adaptation to Brecher's ambitious approach. Such adaptations made the framework more workable and advanced the analysis of foreign policy decision making (Abu Diyya 1990; Khalidi 1986; Zahran 1987, 1993). Studies on the countries of the Maghreb followed (Deeb 1991; Grimaud 1984; Ihraï 1986) to make Middle East foreign policy theory building as comprehensive as realistically possible at this stage in time. Despite their methodological-conceptual sophistication and informative aspect, these analyses are still single-case studies. Though their findings are generalizable (Stein 1991), the basis of generalizability needs to be complemented by comparative multicase studies.

Either because of temperament or of the field's needs, other researchers tried their hand at comparative analysis. Two studies published within a seven-year interval are taken as examples because they explicitly purport to integrate conceptualization into the analysis of Middle East foreign policies. McLaurin, Mughisuddin, and Wagner's (1977) seven-chapter book deals with four cases: Egypt, Iraq, Israel, and Syria. The emphasis is on domestic sources of foreign policy. To allow "maximum comparability," the authors focused on three dimensions: people, processes, and policies. One of this book's strong points is its attempt to link the structure and process of the political systems of the four countries to their foreign policies, but it remains stronger on events than on the linkage itself. It is, however, an early example of the necessity for applying comparative foreign policy analysis to the Middle East.

Rather than limiting itself to domestic sources, the second attempt drew attention to the political economy dimension, to integrate global dynamics into the analysis of Third World countries' foreign policies (Korany and Dessouki 1991). In addition to elaborating the analytical framework, the two senior authors wrote, individually or jointly, seven of the book's thirteen chapters. The six remaining chapters were written by authors from Canada, the United States, and the Middle East. Since comparative foreign policy is essentially a collaborative enterprise, the objective was to have researchers other than those who had elaborated the framework apply and adapt it. The framework was based on the three building blocks of foreign policy theory building: the "why" (or foreign policy sources), the "what" (or foreign policy output), and the "how" (the decision-making process) (Korany 1983). In addition to dealing with some nagging problems in theory and method (e.g., definition of the foreign policy output; comparability), the book attempted to widen the population of foreign policy cases by bringing in the Maghreb (Algeria) and nonstate actors (the Palestine Liberation Organization [PLO]).

The most notable element in Middle East foreign policy analysis is the revitalizing of this field by a number of younger-generation scholars who build on earlier approaches. As a recent book on Jordan's inter-Arab relations purports to do (Brand 1994), the objective is to bridge the gap between "low politics" and "high politics," or between political economy and security studies (Korany, Noble, and Brynen 1993). In this case, the analysis focuses on the "political economy of alliance-making and thus broadens" the concept of security to include challenges to the domestic economy (Brand 1994). At the Arab-Israeli interaction level, Barnett (1982) has pioneered a similar effort. I will return to the relationship between high and low politics, for we have to deal now with what Barnett's book suggests: the interaction or central-issues dimension of Middle East international relations.

PRIVILEGED INTERACTION PATTERNS OR CENTRAL ISSUES

Despite literature on negotiations and the linkage of domestic and external politics (Zartman 1989; Quandt 1988), the analysis of Middle East interaction patterns is conflict-ridden and crisis dominated. This is logical given the series of crises that have plagued the region since the early postwar period: for example, the refusal of Soviet troops to leave Iran in 1946. Crises continued with the overthrow of Mossadeq in Iran in 1953, the establishment of the state of Israel in 1948, the successive Arab-Israeli wars, the Gulf wars, and the myriad of border disputes from the Algerian-Moroccan "guerre du sable" in 1963 to the border disputes in the Gulf region in the 1990s. We should not forget that nominally, at least, the longest war in the post-1945 era, the Iran-Iraq War, was a dispute over the Shatt al-Arab (Kaikobad 1988), and the second Gulf War was about "lines in the sand" (Finnie 1992). The result is that the study of international relations of the region has been reduced to its conflictual dimension, dominated by a focus on high (militarized) politics through the prism of a balance-of-power approach.

Even wide-ranging multivolume studies have approached the analysis of the region's interactions through emphasis on war making (Cordesman and Wagner 1990; Cordesman 1984, 1993), with increasing interest in the different aspects of nuclearization (Pry 1984; Catudel 1991; Aronson and Brosh 1992; Hersh 1991; Karsh 1993; Evron 1994; Feldman 1982). Looking at the region mainly through the prism of the Arab-Israeli conflict is in major part responsible for this quasi-exclusive concentration on high politics. Surveying 410 publications about Middle East international relations between 1960 and 1990, I found that about 83 percent concerned the Arab-Israeli conflict, emphasizing its "coercive" dimension. Among 13 books reviewed in the British periodical *International Affairs* in the two-year period 1975–1977, 10 focused directly on the Arab-Israeli conflict, 2 were connected to it (that is, relations between Jordan and the Palestinians; the Arabs' New Frontier), and 1 was about Lebanon's civil war. Even when the involvement of powers other than the great ones in the region is approached, it is mainly this dimension that is looked at (Ward 1992). Similarly, issues of global order are also perceived through it (Mallison and Mallison 1986). Despite their well-researched but different contributions, the *Journal of Palestine Studies* and *Jerusalem Journal of International Relations* both reflect and accentuate this tendency.

The problem is not that this protracted conflict does not deserve attention, but rather that it has become an obsession and polemical in outlook. At first glance, it would seem as if there are no other regional dynamics worth studying. Some publications, to their credit, reacted by making available a systematic documentary record (Moore 1974, 1991; Lukacs 1991; Tessler 1994). Others emphasized new approaches in conflict resolution and third-party intervention (Touval 1982).

Whether dealing with the Arab-Israeli conflict or not, the language of high politics predominates. Conflict shapes the region. Either deliberately or by miscalculation (Parker 1993), this literature seems to thrive on the presence of "death lobbies" (Timmerman 1991) and demonization. Consequently, international relations in the Middle East seem to be limited to "the battlefield" (Arnett 1994) amid "fire and embers" (Hiro 1993) and combatants who are "forever enemies" (Kemp 1994) in this "generals' war" (Gordon and Trainor 1995). It is the quasi-exclusive predominance of an ever-present geopolitical struggle for power (Campredon and Schweitzer 1986; Reich 1986; Segev 1988; Kuniholm 1988; Chubin 1994; Fuller and Lesser 1993) where countries are pawns whose souls are to be taken (Kostiner 1984) or constitute a "flank" (Helms 1984) in the ever-unattainable search for strategic stability (Farid 1984); Kienle 1990). Even major regional powers are entangled or "embattled allies" (Safran 1978) and at best "peaceful belligerents" (Sella and Yishai 1986).

The predominance of traditional high politics is such that even the treatment of emerging low-politics issues is colored by the former's language and prism (Hurewitz 1976; Licklider 1988; Creighton 1992; Farid 1981; Rostow 1982; Mohaddessin 1993; Bani-Sadr 1991). Yet there is a growing trend toward the serious analysis of low-politics issues and aspects of cooperation (Pennisi 1981; Kerr and Yassin 1982; al-Moussa 1988). The impact of such studies goes beyond their relatively small number, for these low-politics studies put in doubt the prevalent perception of a one-dimensional (conflictual) Middle East international relations. For example, they can occasion in the future the type of epistemological and conceptual debates existing in Latin American studies.

So we are now exposed to the idea that some countries of the region, even though they are among the smallest, purport to play a major role in international political economy and do indeed influence the flow and volume of development assistance (Demir 1976; Hunter 1984). In international interaction with the global system, powers other than the traditional ones are present (Sharif 1986; Ilgen and Pempel 1987). Even in analyzing relations of traditional dominant powers, aspects other than the military-coercive ones happen to be systematically tackled (Brenchley 1989; Owen 1981). The "new Middle East" (Peres 1993) is already engendering its own literature, a process that is bound to continue (Fischer, Hausman, Karasik, and Schelling 1994).

THE WAY AHEAD

The lopsidedness and even the underdevelopment of Middle East international relations can have positive effects for the emerging generation of newer scholars. They have *l'embarras du choix*, a golden opportunity to make their contributions felt at an early period in their career. Some areas of research are immediate candidates.

Different aspects of low politics and cooperative behavior are increasingly present in the region. Relevant research problems should reflect this change and attenuate the obsession with traditional high politics and the almost exclusively balance-of-power rationale. The issue of water comes immediately to mind (Kliot 1994; Naff and Matson 1984; Starr and Stoll 1988; Waterbury 1979). Conflict patterns will not disappear overnight, and hydraulic politics will have its share of them. But the whole regional dynamics should not be equated with the analysis of conflict. Consequently, the gamut of Middle East international relations will be seen in a much more balanced way, that is, revealing a mixture of conflict and cooperation as in the wider international relations field, thus profiting from its more advanced level in theory building. For instance, there is the research puzzle of why Arab unity and the building of regional organizations have not proved successful. Yet in the wider field of international relations, areas of research on international integration, international organizations, and international regimes are rich in concepts and methods that could possibly contribute to our knowledge and understanding.

While accepting the critique against the excesses of orientalism (Edward Said 1978), the study of Middle East international relations seems to have gone to the other extreme by neglecting cultural factors (Cohen 1990 is a notable exception). Compared to the research done in other subfields of Middle East analysis on the role of political Islam (Ayubi 1992) and Islamic fundamentalism in general (Haddad et al. 1991), international relations specialists are only in the preliminary stage (Dawisha 1983; Piscatori 1986). We have a very shy attempt to raise the issues of whether there is an Islamic theory of international relations or not (AbuSulayman 1987; Malik 1979; Karaosmanoglu 1984). Others are in the process of tackling the interstate organizational aspect among Moslem countries (al-Ahsan 1988 and especially Selim 1991). But there is still very little drawing on recent efforts in international relations theory building. We have not yet started tackling, with explicit conceptual international relations questions in mind, the analysis of the Islamic doctrine, the Prophet's practice, the behavior of the early Islamic state and its treaty-making patterns, and the presence of transnational Islamic interactions, old and new. Even in the relatively advanced field of foreign policy analysis, the study of decision making for the majority of the countries of the region is still a barren field. Even when we consider traditional high-politics issues from the Arab-Israeli war of 1948 to the Gulf crisis of 1990, detailed decision-making analyses are available for the United States and Britain but almost nonexistent for Turkey, Iran, and Iraq. Conceptually, the field is so advanced, empirically, many members of the decision-making elite are writing their memoirs, and a prosperous expatriate press publishes reports to fill data gaps. Therefore there is no reason why the analysis of foreign policy decision making should not advance in the very near future.

At a more general level, our analytical tools have to emphasize much more the linkage between international relations and comparative politics (Brynen 1992), epistemologically, conceptually, and methodologically. Aspects like the domestication of foreign policy (for example, international pursuit of Moslem opposition groups) and the internationalization of domestic politics (for example, foreign intervention in civil wars) have to be treated in a more than anecdotal way. For instance, there is a huge upsurge in the study of democratization to the point where this phenomenon is becoming an instant research industry (Korany 1994). There are now serious attempts to tackle the issue directly (Brynen, Korany, and Noble 1995; Salame 1994; Norton 1995–1996; Schwedler 1995). But most of these attempts still take state frontiers too literally and hence confine their analyses to domestic aspects only. Obviously, the change in the characteristics of political regimes is bound to have its impact on foreign policy, as general foreign policy scholars tell us (Hagan 1993). Moreover, if the opening up of political regimes becomes a widespread characteristic in the region, not only foreign policy but also the structure of regional politics itself is bound to feel the change. Attempts to raise the question are just starting (Gause 1995; Hudson 1995). We must hope that these and other research innovations will continue.

REFERENCES

Abu Diyya, Saad. 1991. *Decision-making Process in Jordan's Foreign Policy* (in Arabic). Beirut: Center for Arab Unity Studies.

Abu Jaber, Kamel. 1991. "Strategic Studies and the Middle East: A View from the Inside." In Earl L. Sullivan and J. Ismael, eds., *The Contemporary Study of the Arab World*. Edmonton: University of Alberta Press. 221–235.

AbuSulayman, Abdulhamid. 1987. *The Islamic Theory of International Relations*. Herndon, VA: International Institute of Islamic Thought.

Al-Ahsan, Abdullah. 1988. *The Organization of the Islamic Conference: An Introduction to an Islamic Institution*. Herndon, VA: International Institute of Islamic Thought.

Anderson, Lisa. 1990. "Policy-making and Theory-building: American Political Science and the Islamic Middle East." In Hisham Sharabi, ed., *Theory, Politics, and the Arab World*. New York: Routledge. 58–80.

Arnett, Peter. 1994. *Live from the Battlefield: From Vietnam to Baghdad*. New York: Simon and Schuster.

Aronson, S., with O. Brosh. 1992. *The Politics and Strategy of Nuclear Weapons in the Middle East: Opacity, Theory, and Reality, 1960–1991: An Israeli Perspective*. Albany: State University of New York Press.

Ayubi, N. 1992. *Political Islam*. London: Routledge.

Bani-Sadr, A. 1991. *My Turn to Speak: Iran, the Revolution and Secret Deals with the U.S.* Washington, DC: Brassey's.

Barnett, Michael. 1992. *Confronting the Costs of War: Military Power, State, and Society in Egypt and Israel*. Princeton: Princeton University Press.

Binder, Leonard. 1958. "The Middle East as a Subordinate International System." *World Politics* 10, no. 3.

Brand, Laurie. 1994. *Jordan's Inter-Arab Relations: The Political Economy of Alliance Making*. New York: Columbia University Press.

Brecher, Michael. 1969. "The Middle East Subordinate System and Its Impact on Israel's Foreign Policy." *International Studies Quarterly* 16, no. 2.

———. 1972. *The Foreign Policy System of Israel*. London: Oxford University Press.

———. 1975. *Decisions in Israel's Foreign Policy*. London: Oxford University Press.

Brecher, Michael, and Benjamin Geist. 1980. *Decisions in Crisis: Israel, 1967 and 1973*. Berkeley: University of California Press.

Brenchley, Frank. 1989. *Britain and the Middle East: An Economic History, 1945–1987*. London: Lester Crook Academic.

Brown, L. Carl. 1984. *International Politics and the Middle East: Old Rules, Dangerous Game*. Princeton: Princeton University Press.

Brynen, Rex. 1992. "Between Parsimony and Parochialism: International Relations Theory, Comparative Politics, and the Study of Middle East Foreign Policy." Paper presented at the 89th Annual Convention of the APSA. Washington, DC, September.

Brynen, Rex, B. Korany, and Paul Noble, eds. 1995. *Political Liberalization and Democratization in the Arab World*. Vol. 1, Boulder, CO: Lynne Rienner.

Campredon, J.-P., and J.-J. Schweitzer, eds. 1986. *France, Océan Indien, Mer Rouge*. Paris: Fondation pour les études de défense nationale.

Cantori, Louis J., and Steven L. Spiegel. 1970. *The International Politics of Regions: A Comparative Approach*. Englewood Cliffs, NJ: Prentice-Hall.

Catudel, Honore Marc, Jr. 1991. *Israel's Nuclear Weaponry: A New Arms Race in the Middle East*. London: Grey Seal.

Chubin, Shahram. 1994. *Iran's National Security Policy: Capabilities, Intentions and Impact*. Washington, DC: Carnegie Endowment for International Peace.

Cohen, Raymond. 1990. *Culture and Conflict in Egyptian-Israeli Relations: A Dialogue of the Deaf*. Bloomington: Indiana University Press.

Cordesman, Anthony. 1984. *The Gulf and the Search for Strategic Stability*. Boulder, CO: Westview Press.

———. 1993. *After the Storm: The Changing Military Balance in the Middle East*. Boulder, CO: Westview Press.

Cordesman, Anthony, and A. Wagner. 1990. *The Lessons of Modern War*. Boulder, CO: Westview Press.

Cox, Robert. 1987. *Production, Power, and World Order: Social Forces in the Making of History*. New York: Columbia University Press.

Creighton, John. 1992. *Oil on Troubled Waters: Gulf Wars, 1980–91*. London: Echoes.

Dawisha, Adeed. 1975. "Intervention in Yemen: An Analysis of Egyptian Perception and Policies." *Middle East Journal* 29 (Winter): 47–63.

———. 1976. *Egypt in the Arab World: The Elements of Foreign Policy*. London: Macmillan.

———. 1979. "Internal Values and External Threats: The Making of Saudi Foreign Policy." *Orbis* 23 (Spring): 129–143.

———. 1980. *Syria and the Lebanese Crisis*. New York: St. Martin's Press.

———, ed. 1983. *Islam in Foreign Policy*. Cambridge: Cambridge University Press.

Deeb, Mary-Jane. 1991. *Libya's Foreign Policy in North Africa*. Boulder, CO: Westview Press.

Demir, Soliman. 1976. *The Kuwait Fund and the Political Economy of Arab Regional Development*. New York: Praeger.

Dessouki, Ali E. Hillal, Ahmad Yusuf Ahmad, and Bahgat Korany. 1991. *The Foreign Policy of Arab States: The Challenge of Change*. 2d ed. Boulder, CO: Westview Press.

Evron, Yair. 1994. *Israel's Nuclear Dilemma*. Ithaca: Cornell University Press.

Farid, Abdel Majid, ed. 1981. *Oil and Security in the Arabian Gulf*. New York: St. Martin's Press.

———, ed. 1984. *The Red Sea: Prospects for Stability*. New York: St. Martin's Press.

Feldman, Shai. 1982. *Israeli Nuclear Deterrence: A Strategy for the 1980s*. New York: Columbia University Press.

Finnie, D. H. 1992. *Shifting Lines in the Sand: Kuwait's Elusive Frontier with Iraq*. Cambridge, MA: Harvard University Press.

Fischer, S., L. Hausman, A. Karasik, and T. Schelling. 1994. *Securing Peace in the Middle East: Project on Economic Transition*. Cambridge, MA: MIT Press.

Fuller, Graham E., and I. Lesser. 1993. *Turkey's New Geopolitics: From the Balkans to Western China*. Boulder, CO: Westview Press.

Gause, F. Gregory, III. 1992. "Gulf Regional Politics: Revolution, War, and Rivalry." In W. Howard Wriggins, ed., *Dynamics of Regional Politics*. New York: Columbia University Press.

―――. 1995. "Regional Influences on Experiments in Political Liberalization in the Arab World." In Rex Brynen, B. Korany, and Paul Noble, eds., *Political Liberalization and Democratization in the Arab World*, vol. 1, *Theoretical Perspectives*. Boulder, CO: Lynne Rienner.

Gerges, Fawaz. 1994. *The Superpowers and the Middle East*. Boulder, CO: Westview Press.

Gordon, Michael R., and Bernard E. Trainor. 1995. *The Generals' War*. Boston: Little, Brown.

Grimaud, Nicole. 1984. *La politique extérieure de l'Algérie (1962–1978)*. Paris: Karthala.

Haddad, Yvonne, et al. 1991. *The Contemporary Islamic Revival: A Critical Survey and Bibliography*. New York: Greenwood Press.

Hagan, Joe. 1993. *Political Opposition and Foreign Policy in Comparative Perspective*. Boulder, CO: Lynne Rienner.

Halley, P. Edward. 1991. "Strategic Studies and the Middle East: Periodical Literature in the U.S., 1980–1990." In Earl Sullivan and J. Ismael, eds., *The Contemporary Study of the Arab World*. Edmonton: University of Alberta Press.

Helms, Christine Moss. 1984. *Iraq: Eastern Flank of the Arab World*. Washington, DC: Brookings Institution.

Hersh, S. 1991. *The Samson Option: Israel, America, and the Bomb*. London: Faber.

Hiro, Dilip. 1993. *Lebanon: Fire and Embers: A History of the Lebanese Civil War*. New York: St. Martin's Press.

Hudson, Michael. 1976. "The Middle East." In J. Rosenau et al., eds. *World Politics*. New York: Free Press.

―――. 1995. "Democracy and Foreign Policy in the Arab World." In D. Garnham and M. Tessler, eds., *Democracy, War, and Peace in the Middle East*. Bloomington: Indiana University Press.

Hunter, Shireen. 1984. *OPEC and the Third World: The Politics of Aid*. Bloomington: Indiana University Press.

Hurewitz, J. C, ed. 1976. *Oil, the Arab-Israeli Dispute, and the Industrial World: Horizons of Crisis*. Boulder, CO: Westview Press.

Ihraï, Said. 1986. *Pouvoir et influence. Etat, partis, et politique étrangère au Maroc*. Rabat: Edino.

Ilgen, T., and J. J. Pempel. 1987. *Trading Technology: Europe, Japan, and the Middle East*. New York: Praeger.

Ismael, Tareq. 1986. *International Relations of the Contemporary Middle East*. Syracuse: Syracuse University Press.

Kaikobad, K. H. 1988. *The Shatt al-Arab Boundary Question: A Legal Reappraisal*. Oxford: Clarendon Press.

Kaplan, Morton. 1957. *System and Process in International Politics*. New York: Wiley.

Karaosmanoglu, Ali. 1984. "Islam and Its Implications for the International System." In M. Heper and R. Israeli, eds., *Islam and Politics in the Modern Middle East*. London: Croom Helm.

Karsh, Efraim, et al. 1993. *Non-Conventional-Weapons Proliferation in the Middle East*. Oxford: Clarendon Press.

Kemp, Geoffrey. 1994. *Forever Enemies? American Policy and the Islamic Republic of Iran*. Washington, DC: Carnegie Endowment for International Peace.

Kerr, Malcolm. 1971. *The Arab Cold War: Gamal 'Abd al-Nasir and His Rivals, 1958–1970*. 3d ed. Oxford: Oxford University Press.

Kerr, Malcolm, and Yassin, Al-Sayid, eds. 1982. *Rich and Poor States in the Middle East: Egypt and the New Arab Order*. Boulder, CO: Westview Press.

Khalidi, Rachid. 1986. *Under Siege: PLO Decisionmaking during the 1982 War*. New York: Columbia University Press.

Kienle, Eberhard. 1990. *Ba'th v. Ba'th: The Conflict between Syria and Iraq, 1968–1989*. London: I. B. Tauris.

Kliot, N. 1994. *Water Resources and Conflict in the Middle East*. London: Routledge.

Korany, Bahgat. 1978. "Dependance financière et comportement international." *Revue Française de Science Politique* 23 (December): 1067–1093.

———. 1983. "The Take-off of Third World Studies? The Case of Foreign Policy." *World Politics* 33 (April): 465–487.

———. 1986. *How Foreign Policy Decisions Are Made in the Third World: A Comparative Analysis*. Boulder, CO: Westview Press.

Korany, Bahgat, and Ali E. H. Dessouki, eds. 1991. *The Foreign Policy of Arab States: The Challenge of Change*. 2d ed. Boulder, CO: Westview Press.

Korany, Bahgat, et al. 1987. *Analyse des relations internationales: Approches, concepts, et données*. Montreal and Quebec: G. Morin et Centre Québécois des Relations Internationales.

———. 1994. "Arab Democratization: A Poor Cousin?" *Political Science and Politics* 27 (September): 511–514.

Korany, Bahgat, Paul Noble, and Rex Brynen, eds. 1993. *The Many Faces of National Security in the Arab World*. London: Macmillan; New York: St. Martin's Press.

Kostiner, Joseph. 1984. *The Struggle for South Yemen*. New York: St. Martin's Press.

Kuniholm, Bruce. 1988. *The Geopolitics of U.S.-Turkish Relations: Implications for the Future*. Washington, DC: Wilson Center.

Lebow, Richard N., and Th. Risse-Kappen, eds. 1995. *International Relations Theory and the End of the Cold War*. New York: Columbia University Press.

Licklider, Roy. 1988. *Political Power and the Arab Oil Weapon*. Berkeley: University of California Press.

Lukacs, Y., ed. 1991. *The Israeli-Palestinian Conflict: A Documentary Record, 1967–1990*. Cambridge: Cambridge University Press.

Macmillan, John, and A. Linklater, eds. 1995. *Boundaries in Question: New Directions in International Relations*. London: Pinter; New York: St. Martin's Press.

Malik, Hafeez. 1979. "Islamic Theory of International Relations." *Journal of South Asian and Middle Eastern Studies* 11, no. 3 (Spring): 84–92.

Mallison, W. Thomas, and Sally Mallison. 1986. *The Palestine Problem in International Law and World Order*. Harlow, Essex: Longman.

McLaurin, R. D., M. Mughisuddin, and Abraham R. Wagner. 1977. *Foreign Policymaking in the Middle East*. New York: Praeger.

Mohaddessin, M. 1993. *Islamic Fundamentalism: The New Global Threat*. Washington, DC: Seven Locks Press.

Moore, John N., ed. 1974. *The Arab-Israeli Conflict*. Princeton: Princeton University Press.

————, ed. 1991. *The Arab-Israeli Conflict*. Vol. 4, *The Difficult Search for Peace*. Princeton: Princeton University Press.

al-Moussa, A. 1988. *The Gulf Cooperation Council: An Experiment in Regional Organization*. Geneva: Institut Universitaire des Hautes Etudes Internationales.

Naff, Thomas, and R. C. Matson, eds. 1984. *Water in the Middle East: Conflict or Cooperation?* Boulder, CO: Westview Press.

Noble, Paul. 1991. ''The Arab System: Pressure, Constraints and Opportunities.'' In Bahgat Korany and Ali E. H. Dessouki, eds., *The Foreign Policies of Arab States: The Challenge of Change*. 2d ed. Boulder, CO: Westview Press.

Norton, Augustus R., ed. 1995–1996. *Civil Society in the Middle East*. 2 vols. Leiden: E. J. Brill.

Owen, Roger. 1981. *The Middle East in the World Economy, 1800–1914*. London: Methuen.

Parker, R. B. 1993. *The Politics of Miscalculation in the Middle East*. Bloomington: Indiana University Press.

Pennisi, G. 1981. *Development, Manpower, and Migration in the Red Sea Region: The Case for Cooperation*. Hamburg: Deutsches Orient-Institut.

Peres, Shimon, with Arye Noar. 1993. *The New Middle East*. New York: Henry Holt.

Piscatori, James. 1986. *Islam in a World of Nation-States*. Cambridge: Cambridge University Press.

Pry, Peter. 1984. *Israel's Nuclear Arsenal*. Boulder, CO: Westview Press.

Quandt, William, ed. 1988. *The Middle East: Ten Years after Camp David*. Washington, DC: Brookings Institution.

Reich, Bernard, ed. 1986. *The Powers in the Middle East: The Ultimate Strategic Arena*. New York: Praeger.

Richards, Alan, and John Waterbury. 1990. *A Political Economy of the Middle East*. Boulder, CO: Westview Press.

Rosenau, James. 1990. *Turbulence in World Politics: A Theory of Change and Continuity*. Princeton: Princeton University Press.

Rostow, Dankwart. 1982. *Oil and Turmoil: America Faces OPEC and the Middle East*. New York: Norton.

Safran, Nadav. 1978. *Israel: The Embattled Ally*. Cambridge, MA: Harvard University Press.

Said, Edward. 1978. *Orientalism*. New York: Pantheon Books.

Said, Mohamed E. 1992. *The Future of the Arab System after the Gulf Crisis* (in Arabic). Kuwait: Alam El Maarifa.

Salame, Ghassan. 1994. *Democratie sans democrates*. Paris: Fayard.

Schwedler, Jillian, ed. 1995. *Toward Civil Society in the Middle East: A Primer*. Boulder, CO: Lynne Rienner.

Segev, Samuel. 1988. *The Iranian Triangle: The Untold Story of Israel's Role in the Iran-Contra Affair*. New York: Free Press.

Selim, Mohamed. 1991. *Relations among Islamic States* (in Arabic). Riyadh: King Saud University Press.

Sella, A., and Y. Yishai. 1986. *Israel, the Peaceful Belligerent, 1967–1979*. London: Macmillan for St. Antony's College, Oxford University.

Sharabi, Hisham, ed. 1990. *Theory, Politics, and the Arab World: Critical Responses*. New York: Routledge.

Sharif, Walid I., ed. 1986. *The Arab Gulf States and Japan: Prospects for Co-operation.* London: Croom Helm.

Sprout, Harold Hance, and Margaret Tuttle Sprout. 1965. *The Ecological Perspective on Human Affairs, with Special Reference to International Politics.* Princeton: Princeton University Press.

Starr, J. R., and D. C. Stoll, eds. 1988. *The Politics of Scarcity: Water in the Middle East.* Boulder, CO: Westview Press.

Stein, Janice. 1991. "Inadvertent War and Miscalculated Escalation: The Arab-Israeli War of 1967." In Alexander George, ed., *Avoiding War: Problems of Crisis Management.* Boulder, CO: Westview Press.

Sullivan, Earl, and J. Ismael, eds. 1991. *The Contemporary Study of the Arab World.* Edmonton: University of Alberta Press.

Telhami, Shibley. 1990. *Power and Leadership in International Bargaining: The Path to the Camp David Accords.* New York: Columbia University Press.

Tessler, Mark. 1994. *A History of the Israeli-Palestinian Conflict.* Bloomington: Indiana University Press.

Timmerman, Kenneth. R. 1991. *The Death Lobby: How the West Armed Iraq.* Boston: Houghton Mifflin.

Touval, Saadia. 1982. *The Peace Brokers: Mediators in the Arab Israeli Conflict, 1948– 1979.* Princeton: Princeton University Press.

Walt, Stephen. 1987. *The Origins of Alliances.* Ithaca: Cornell University Press.

Waltz, Kenneth. 1979. *Theory of International Politics.* Reading, MA: Addison-Wesley.

Ward, R. E. 1992. *India's Pro-Arab Policy: A Study in Continuity.* New York: Praeger.

Waterbury, John. 1979. *Hydropolitics of the Nile Valley.* Syracuse: Syracuse University Press.

Wriggins, W. Howard, ed. 1992. *Dynamics of Regional Politics.* New York: Columbia University Press.

Zahran, Gamal. 1987. *Egypt's Foreign Policy* (in Arabic). Cairo: Madboli Press.

———. 1993. *Who Governs Egypt? A Study in Political Decision-Making in Egypt and the Third World* (in Arabic). al-Qahirah: J. A. Zahran.

Zartman, I. William. 1976. "Political Science." In Leonard Binder, ed., *The Study of the Middle East: Research and Scholarship in the Humanities and the Social Sciences.* New York: J. Wiley and Sons.

———. 1989. *Ripe for Resolution: Conflict and Intervention in Africa.* New York: Oxford University Press.

THE POLITICAL ECONOMY OF THE MIDDLE EAST

Jenab Tutunji

The literature on the political economy of the Middle East is expanding. Interest in the field has begun to grow rather rapidly in the past few years, but the available books on the subject remain few in number. Of these, only about a dozen books are either concerned with the political economy of the Middle East as a whole or offer a comparative study of several states (the subject of this chapter) from the perspective of political economy, as opposed to books on specific countries in the area.

Political economy is taken to mean not merely a treatment of economics alongside the politics of the region, but a discipline that relates economics to politics through a theoretical model that explicitly or implicitly posits a relationship between economics, society, and the state. Of course, the first question that comes to mind is: is there a political economy of the Middle East, as the title implies? In other words, is there a paradigm that can be applied to all of the countries of the area? Is it possible to make observations of sufficient generality to be applicable to Turkey, Iran, Israel, Egypt, Saudi Arabia, Iraq, and Lebanon, just to take a third of the countries concerned? Fears that an effort to find a common model is too ambitious are well founded. For one thing, the proper way to proceed would be a series of case studies on a country-by-country basis that could then serve as the basis for induction to higher levels of generality. Although some very good books have appeared, none of them offers us a model that can apply to all countries of the area. Perhaps one should be more modest and seek two or three different models, for instance, one for the oil-producing monarchies, another for the republics that operate on the basis of state capitalism, and yet another for states such as Lebanon that have a private enterprise system. The literature on the political economy of the region can be divided into three categories according to the underlying theoretical concern with the role of the state and of public policy in the allocation of resources within society and the political consequences thereof; the role of class and class analysis in determining politics of specific countries; and the integration of the Middle East region into the existing world order or world system.

THE ROLE OF THE STATE

Halpern (1963) is one of the very few classics on the political economy and social history of the Middle East and North Africa. It was written very early in the import-substitution phase and therefore lacks the benefit of the perspective enjoyed by later works. However, readers may want to refer to it for the insights it contains. Trimberger (1978) is another classic. It should be of interest to those who wish to assess the consequences of the fact that the Turkish and Egyptian statist experiments were the results of revolutions from above.

In the first category, the principal bibliographic entry of most general concern is *A Political Economy of the Middle East*, by Richards and Waterbury, which has gone through two editions between 1990 and 1996. The first edition carries the subtitle *State, Class, and Economic Development*, while the second does not, because the significance of class has come into question, although the role of the state in economic development continues to occupy a central place. There is a great deal in common between the two editions, the principal difference being that in the first the underlying theoretical framework presupposes a dialectical relationship between three variables: economic growth patterns, state structures and policies, and class. As such, one can categorize the underlying, although by no means obtrusive, approach as neomarxist class analysis filtered through a neoinstitutionalist approach. Still, theories used by Waterbury are not always well integrated into the text, with clear implications drawn, and there is a tendency to adopt theories that are fashionable at the time.

However, by the end of the first edition, Richards and Waterbury are found questioning whether class is not simply a dependent variable after all. The state in the Middle East is not only autonomous, it actually creates classes. First, they attributed the rise of private property to the need of the Ottoman state for revenues, which made the state indirectly responsible for creating a landowning class and, by implication, a class of peasants—the two basic classes of a traditional agrarian economy. The old landowning classes and rather newly emergent bourgeoisie during the colonial period fled from the scene in Turkey, Egypt, Algeria, Tunisia, Syria, Iraq, and Iran at various periods, retreating before waves of nationalization and the emergence of state capitalism and a "state bourgeoisie," proving the weakness of social classes and the quasi-omnipotence of the state. The development policies followed by the state bourgeoisie in socialist and capitalist states alike, which primarily took the form of import-substitution industrialization followed by "deepening" (or the provision of intermediate or primary goods to feed the import-substitution sector) and subsequent moves toward privatization as the drawbacks of state capitalism became apparent, resulted in capitalist development. The extension of the market and other social programs by the state led to the emergence and growth of white-collar professionals, small-scale traders and manufacturers, and the new middle class. At the end, the authors conclude that the urban and rural entrepreneurs and the sizeable middle class are creations of the state.

It is interesting to trace the course of Waterbury's evolving approach to the study of the bureaucratic authoritarian state and state socialism or state capitalism. The application of the theories of O'Donnell to the Middle East was undertaken by Waterbury in *The Egypt of Nasser and Sadat* (1983), an excellent, richly detailed, and rigorous study. Here Waterbury elaborates the paradigm of state-led import-substitution industrialization, the adoption of market socialism under Gamal Abdel Nasser, and the subsequent transition to state capitalism, which was completed under Anwar Sadat. Following the ''easy phase'' of import-substitution industrialization, the process of deepening necessitates the forging of an alliance of state technocrats, military leaders, local investors, and foreign capital, according to O'Donnell (1973, 1979), leading to bureaucratic authoritarianism. Waterbury (1990) thought this was taking shape in Egypt in the late 1970s (172). Yet Richards and Waterbury (1990) admit that the only state to approximate O'Donnell's model was Turkey after the coup of 1980, based not on deepening but export-led growth (359). Inflation, import controls, and a need for foreign finance are followed by devaluation, balance-of-payments problems, and export promotion. The state feels the need to extend its control farther over the economy, leading to state capitalism and the emergence of a state capitalist class.

The interesting thing is that Waterbury applies class analysis here not in the traditional sense of class conflict, but primarily to the state bourgeoisie and the petty bourgeoisie or emerging middle class. This is a very problematic approach in that none of these are straightforward classes in the traditional Marxist sense. To posit that the upper crust of the bureaucracy and public enterprise managers (state bourgeoisie) constitute a class lands one in a great deal of difficulty. To begin with, the members of this class do not own, although they control, the means of production. Other difficulties abound. Waterbury's most rigorously theoretical treatment of this question is perhaps to be found in ''Twilight of the State Bourgeoisie'' (1991), where he points out that the state bourgeoisie does not possess consciousness of itself as a class, nor is it able to perpetuate itself. It is deficient as a class in these two respects in addition to the fact that it does not own the enterprises it controls, in contrast to the grand bourgeoisie in other societies. When all is said and done, the state bourgeoisie is best understood as a functional stratum rather than a class proper.

The other controversial point raised by Waterbury is that this putative state bourgeoisie class is autonomous, that is, it is not controlled by other classes or interest groups in society. Waterbury stresses this point in knocking down various versions of the argument that the state bourgeoisie is subordinate to or a proxy for the would-be dominant petite bourgeoisie. I believe that Waterbury's rebuttal is quite sound here; however, the assertion of autonomy for the state makes the paradigm inapplicable to Lebanon or, more significantly, Saudi Arabia or the Gulf states. In a rare moment of candor on this point, Richards and Waterbury (1990) acknowledge, ''Until 1976 Lebanon's business elite . . . in effect controlled the state apparatus. It was in pre-1976 Lebanon that Marx's famous dictum that the state is the executive board of the dominant class came closest to realization in the Middle East'' (408). In Saudi Arabia and Kuwait, where state revenues for a long while were indistinguishable from the privy purse of the ruling family, and where even now the royal family is inseparable from the state bureaucracy, it is absurd to maintain that the decision makers in the state enjoy autonomy from the extensive royal family. Richards and Waterbury make no such claim. Still, it is reasonable for them to argue that in the Arabian Peninsula as well as Turkey, Egypt, Algeria, Tunisia, Libya, Sudan, Syria, Iraq, and Iran—which contain the majority of the population of the area— the state is a major and irreplaceable actor. Furthermore, Richards and Waterbury (1990 and 1996) do not maintain that, once created, the grand or petty bourgeoisie (notably in Turkey) or even rural-class actors are unable to influence state policy. The public and private sectors may be said to enjoy a symbiotic relationship, and to constrain each other's autonomy.

In *Exposed to Innumerable Delusions*, Waterbury (1993) offers a very informative comparative study of the public sector in four countries, two of them from outside the Middle East: Turkey, Egypt, Mexico, and India. All four states share a central commonality: a large state-owned industrial base. All of them also contend with the problems facing economic restructuring and privatization. Waterbury is not persuaded by explanations in terms of either class or political culture. Here his theoretical starting point is property regimes (i.e., sets of principles, rules, and decision-making procedures concerning property rights around which actors' expectations converge) and state enforcement of such. ''In the four countries, the state established mixed property regimes in which the state was proprietor of a vast range of strategic and productive assets'' (20). He differentiates between principals (cabinet-level and other top officials who play the role of owners of public enterprises in lieu of the public) and agents (the managers of these enterprises). He adopts a choice theoretic approach to the study of the state bureaucracy and assumes rent-seeking, revenue-maximizing behavior. He relies on concepts such as agency costs and the logic of principal-actor relationships, with the state owners cast in the role of principals and managers of public-sector enterprises as the agents. Cabinet ministers and top-level planners cannot exercise effective control over the bureaucrats administering state enterprises, which renders state capitalism ineffective. ''The legal designation of property has had a profound impact on the functioning of the statist experiments. Public ownership of economic assets gave rise to an institutional culture that, over time, transformed the nature of state intervention from one of benevolent public-spiritedness to one of narrow pursuit of agency interests at the expense of society and in the absence of a sense of national purpose'' (262).

Waterbury still characterizes the state in the four countries as autonomous. Its role starts out as benevolent, but later becomes malevolent. Economic crises force the state to move either from market socialism to state capitalism or from state capitalism to privatization. Ironically, managers of state enterprises fail to muster an efficient defense against restructuring reformers because they fall prey to the free-rider problem, which gets in the way of collective action. Similarly,

workers cannot protect their cozy positions and submissively surrender privileges bestowed on them from above. Waterbury finds that when incumbents
remain in office and are able to restructure their power basis, this is to be
explained neither through rational choice nor class analysis, but is due to the
severity of the economic crisis. Interestingly, Waterbury suggests that the private
sector in such countries itself needs to be privatized, that is, weaned away from
dependence on the public sector for subsidies, contracts, protection, and other
assistance. Waterbury gives precedence to domestic over international causes for
the restructuring, as opposed to Samir Amin (1997), for example. Perthes (1995),
writing on *The Political Economy of Syria under Asad*, speaks of Syria's new
commercial bourgeoisie, dubbed the "new class," descended from the petty
bourgeoisie and dependent on the state. "All principal activities of the new class
have in some way or the other been related to the state, utilizing its authoritarian
nature. What has constituted the source of complaints of other entrepreneurs—
namely, government control over foreign exchange, imports, exports, and prices;
state tutelage over the economy in general; the anarchy of import regulations—
has allowed new-class businessmen to make profits that could hardly be made
in free-market systems. By virtue of their connections and influence, they have
been able to secure for themselves special exemptions, monopolies and quasi-
monopolies" (112). Of course, there is a symbiotic relationship between the
state bourgeoisie and the new class. In an article in 1992 entitled "The Heart
of the Matter? Public Enterprise and the Adjustment Process," Waterbury had
already expounded the ideas that he was later to develop in greater detail in
Exposed to Innumerable Delusions.

Clement Henry, who reviewed *Exposed to Innumerable Delusions* for the
International Journal of Middle East Studies (1996), lauds Waterbury for providing us with a treasure trove of information. However, Henry questions
whether the formal property relationship on which so much of Waterbury's
argument rests really renders insignificant class, cultural, institutional, and sectoral variables. He also criticizes Waterbury for not analyzing the differences
between the four countries so as to extract a "significant variation" that could
be informative for a comparative study. Henry contends that economic motives
alone, without resorting to ideology and political will, cannot explain the "cas-
cading reform." Henry accuses Waterbury of reflecting the "new institutional-
ism" fashionable among academics in the United States. Henry concludes that
"although Waterbury insists in his discussion of culture that 'the Virgin of
Guadalupe provides no answer to my riddles' . . . maybe she did after all" (425).
I believe that Waterbury is right in maintaining that differences in culture among
the four countries pale in significance when compared to the institutional culture
of public ownership. However, I believe that Waterbury is too eager to focus
on domestic causes for the restructuring and to underplay the significance of
external economic factors. The political economy of privatization is also dealt
with in an article by Bienen and Waterbury (1989), in which they point out that
privatization is not a linear or irreversible process.

The second edition of Richards and Waterbury (1996) takes account of the evolution in Waterbury's thought and Richards's increasing willingness to recommend the deregulation of national markets and political liberalization. This book is indeed a treasure trove of information on the Middle East, dealing with economic growth and structural change, the impact of population growth, human capital, labor migration and the future of the oil economies, water and food security, the emergence of the public sector, the contradictions of state-led growth, political regimes, "solidarism" and its enemies, and the military and the state. There is a valuable new section on Islamists in opposition and in power. It should be required reading for state planners, economy and finance ministers, and development specialists throughout the Middle East. Unfortunately, the theoretical sections of interest to the political scientist are few and limited, and vast tracts of the text consist either of economic analysis or background information on countries of the area that is all too familiar to the area specialist, but invaluable to the student approaching the Middle East for the first time.

The economic analysis is excellent and enlightening (reflecting the authors' combined fifty years of experience with the region). For instance, an important cause of the failure of import-substitution industrialization is shown to lie in the decline of rural demand caused by government policies that discriminate against agricultural production. A good case is made for the fact that in the import-substitution phase, the state plays an essential role because of the weakness of the local capitalists and entrepreneurs. In Gramscian terms, one can argue, as Robert Cox (1987) does, that the absence of bourgeois hegemony forces the state to step in to fill the gap—hence what he terms the neomercantilist developmentalist state. (This notion is too complicated to delve into here, but readers who are interested are encouraged to refer to Cox's excellent analysis.) The virtues of market deregulation, industrial restructuring, and export-led growth are well argued.

In the second edition, Richards and Waterbury make a point of rejecting both Marxist and liberal approaches that adopt an "instrumentalist" view of the state (34). The authors' perspective is that the state is better viewed as having the power to create interests and social actors (35). The autonomy of the state is highlighted, and it is argued that development policies give rise to social and economic processes that create new social actors, including classes. "The Middle East state is best seen as the instrument of the upper echelons of its own personnel" (35). The "more autonomous" states, Turkey, Iran, Egypt, Algeria, and Syria, and Iraq after 1958, are seen as "being engaged in far-reaching class engineering" (43). State enterprises, not least among which are the military industries, function as a major catalyst for the creation of an emergent entrepreneurial class. "Crucial struggles . . . have occurred not so much between the state and forces in civil society . . . as within the ranks of the state elites themselves" (35). Class, as an analytic tool, cedes its primacy to other forms of group-interest representation, but is not altogether eliminated. Corporatism, or the collaboration of labor and capital, as well as various social groups, under the aegis of the state, is described as a characteristic of the Middle Eastern state where social divisions are abhorred, although the meaning of corporatism is rather stretched. It is argued, however, that the important area of change to watch is the transition from solidarism to democratic pluralism, whose success hangs in the balance. The economic record of states in the Middle East is mixed, but their political record is much worse.

There are many grounds for criticism as well. Although Middle East specialists owe Richards and Waterbury a debt for the development of such a significant paradigm, there is a tendency by the authors to overgeneralize. One is also not sure whether the neoinstitutional approach was chosen by the authors because it reflects the logic of relations between state and society or because it merely reflects a specific historical conjuncture. One cannot escape the feeling that corporatism is stretched so far that it obscures class issues. Israel's distinctive political economy does not receive sufficient attention. The political economy of oil also fails to receive its due, apart from a discussion of the nature of rentier states. International political economy is largely ignored in this respect as well as others. These comments apply to both editions.

Import-substitution policies had fit in nicely with the social purpose of socialist and reformist states in the Middle East, whose aims had been redistributive, combining economic growth with the amelioration of severe economic injustice, all in the name of social solidarity. These states had not pursued economic efficiency as their primary objective. Yet as weak and uncompetitive industries developed, the state sector proved inefficient and unwieldy, and many states were burdened with a debt problem, a population explosion, and coping with international recession, the need arose to privatize and liberalize their economies, under prodding from the IMF and the Paris Club in most cases. Following heady growth in the 1960s and 1970s, it was time to pay the piper in the 1980s, with stabilization and structural adjustment plans for most countries of the area. Three other books published in the early 1990s address the issue of economic change. *The Politics of Economic Reform in the Middle East*, edited by Barkey (1992), offers economic analysis of stabilization and structural adjustment in seven countries (Algeria, Egypt, Tunisia, Jordan, Syria, Israel, and Turkey) and attempts to provide the reader with a better understanding of the political economy of the countries concerned and the complex relationship between state and society. In the concluding article, Patrick Clawson defends the rationale for stabilization and adjustment programs for economic reasons. He also notes that "the general lesson of the Middle East in the 1980s has been that economic stabilization leads to more democracy." This generalization is based on political developments in Jordan, Tunisia, Egypt and Algeria (where Clawson's optimism is not well founded). His argument is that authoritarian rulers have greater incentive to monopolize power during periods of prosperity, but are far more eager to share responsibility during periods of economic contraction or recession. Clawson adds that if the only consideration were the promotion of democracy, then the best prescription would be to tighten the economic screws on Middle Eastern and other Third World regimes so as to induce them to hand over power to the elected politicians (230). This approach suffers from a propensity to attribute democratization to economic constraints while ignoring the political ones.

The second book, *Privatization and Liberalization in the Middle East*, edited by Iliya Harik and Denis J. Sullivan (1992), offers four case studies of Egypt (which take up a third of the book) and chapters on Turkey, Syria and Iraq, Iraq and Saudi Arabia, Jordan, Algeria, and Tunisia. In the introduction, Harik offers an all-too-rare and therefore valuable discussion of property rights and state intervention in the economy. He argues that "when property rights are viewed as claims to usage rather than title deeds, then . . . no single actor possesses all the property rights to an object." Public claims constitute diverse restrictions on private property rights (6). It is necessary, therefore, to transcend the public/private dichotomy and think of ownership claims as representing a sort of continuum (8). Harik goes on to discuss the vast role that the state plays even in a free-market economy. He points out that liberalization is not a response to pressures from business or political groups in society, but an attempt by Middle Eastern states to shore up their quickly eroding credibility and legitimacy. Harik remarks that economic liberalization is due to the failure of state economic enterprises, while political liberalization is a defensive measure by the states that could not deal with the problem at the economic level. When economic remedies are insufficient, states tend to resort to political as well as economic liberalization (20–21). Harik acknowledges but plays down political motives for democratization (and incidentally fails to sense the direction in which liberalization in Algeria is proceeding). In her chapter on Jordan, Laurie Brand attributes the political liberalization in Jordan to the action of a rentier state experiencing economic retrenchment (combined with fear of the contagious effect of the intifada). Brand, who otherwise knows Jordan very well, attempts to strengthen her argument by playing down the fact that Jordan was experimenting with a return to democracy (which had existed in the 1950s) by creating the National Consultative Council in the 1970s—which had far greater freedom to criticize the government than she admits—at the heyday of Jordan's economic prosperity, when GNP was growing at a real 8 percent annually, unemployment was running at about 2 percent, and aid was flowing in very generous quantities. Burden sharing was indeed the government's motive, but it was the political dimension and problems with the Middle East peace and the occupied West Bank (preceding the intifada) that loomed large at the time, not economic difficulties. She is right in that economic retrenchment did in fact facilitate political liberalization later on.

Finally, there is *Economic and Political Liberation in the Middle East*, edited by Tim Niblock and Emma Murphy (1993), the fruit of the labors of the Research Unit for the International Study of Economic Liberalization and Its Social and Political Effects at the University of Exeter. Half the book is dedicated to theoretical issues, from the role of the state in relation to the expanding role of

the market to the very enlightening chapter on the origins of liberal institutions
in the ancient Middle East (by Patricia Springborg, who takes us back to the
Muqaddimah of Ibn Khaldun, and who argues that the inability of full-scale
capitalism to emerge in the Middle East may have been due to the failure to
develop the appropriate type of business organization, such as the joint-stock
company). David Pool, in a separate chapter, argues that the timing, form, and
nature of political liberalization are primarily influenced by economic liberalization and strategies for regime survival. In contrast to more simplistic explanations to the effect that when beset by economic problems, states tend to want
to share the burden of decision making so as to spread responsibility as widely
as possible, Pool offers a pointed reminder that whereas a certain measure of
political liberalization may in fact smooth the path of unpopular economic reforms, the social impact and political repercussions of cuts in subsidies and
governmental spending on welfare are an incentive for governments to retain
authoritarian controls. There is "dialectical tension between the two processes,
economic liberalization is marked by progress and regress and political liberalization is authoritarian, cautious and controlled'' (49). He further argues that
the relationship between state and class will determine the outcome of this dialectical and symbiotic relationship between the two processes.

   Tim Niblock examines the international and domestic factors in the economic
liberalization process in Arab countries. He notes that economic development
policies of the state have given rise to a bourgeoisie that is weak and dependent
on the state, and that is therefore not ready to displace the public sector. He
also explains economic restructuring in the Arab countries primarily in terms of
"the articulation of these economies with the international economy" (83). He
points out that "the core relationship around which economic policy is formulated comes to be that between the governing institutions and the international
financial institutions," rather than between the state and the local bourgeoisie
(84). It is difficult for stable democracies to emerge when the government is
unable to provide an adequate safety net to those adversely affected by economic
restructuring, or to direct investment to areas of the country where it is most
needed. There is need for state machinery capable of collecting taxes, effecting
social reform, and running welfare programs. Other theoretic topics discussed
in the book include austerity protests in response to economic liberalization, the
achievements and prospects of privatization programs, and the relationship between economic liberalization and foreign investment in the Middle East. In
addition, there are case studies of Egypt, Tunisia, Syria (by Raymond Hinn-
busch), Iran, Israel, Oman, and Yemen and of economic liberalization and the
suq in Syria. Not only is the theoretic content better integrated and more elaborate than the other two books, the authors also avoid making dangerous (and
outrageously erroneous) predictions about the prospects for democracy in Algeria.

   Roger Owen's *State, Power, and Politics in the Making of the Modern Middle
East* (1992) deals in a lucid and admirably concise manner with a wide range

of subjects, from the historical analysis of the emergence of modern states in the Middle East and the growth of state power and single-party regimes to nationalism and the politics of religion and the military in state and society. Special emphasis is placed on single-party regimes and steps toward democratization. A central section on the politics of economic restructuring is political economy proper and thus falls directly within our purview.

Owen displays a heightened sensitivity to the power of words and the ideological baggage stored in concepts. When ideas (whether of the state, civil society, or religious fundamentalism) are transposed—along with their associated organizational practices—from their original European context to a Middle Eastern one, this poses the danger of misleading rather than guiding analysis. The boundaries between state and civil society are blurred. In Middle Eastern scholarship, he warns, "the idea of the supposed coherence of the state as a single actor with a systematic programme of social transformation is impossible to sustain." The dichotomies of state versus society, legal versus illegal, or scientific planning versus private self-interest are abstractions that are untrue of reality. The tacit understanding that the state is "a coherent entity with a single intent" that attempts "to penetrate and transform a second entity called 'society'" (50) leads to the paradox of a strong state with weak powers. Civil society, if the concept is adopted with all the requisite provisos, neither is passive nor acts through the expected channels. In the cases of noted efforts to push the boundary between state and society in one direction or the other, as in programs of privatization or political liberalization, the action has most probably been the result of temporary political alliances rather than the pressure of powerful interest groups. The material and cultural conditions out of which liberal ideology grew in the West are lacking in the Middle East. The scholar's task is not so much to test the ability of the state, seen as the Leviathan, to mold society, as it is "to interpret a significant moment, when the veil of omnipotence created around itself by the authoritarian regime slips to reveal the bundle of competing, and often contradictory, interests that have always lain just beneath" (52). One can say that Owen's starting point is the concrete, existing state, warts and all, rather than an abstract model.

On the issue of economic liberalization, Owen deals separately with North Africa, the Baathist regimes in Syria and Iraq, and Turkey, Iran, and Israel. In Egypt, Tunisia, and Algeria, "single-party directed, state-dominated, development strategies" came under attack from foreign creditors and from an alliance of outside forces, such as the Agency for International Development (AID), and local landowning interests. In Syria and Iraq, oil revenues kept foreign creditors at bay (for a while, at least) while the regimes pursued privatization policies for their own political as well as economic motives. By contrast, Turkey, Israel, and Iran had, to various degrees, completed the stage of import-substitution industrialization by the beginning of the 1980s and were ready to dismantle controls and seek export-led growth in keeping with supply-side adjustment policies.

In contrast to the tone of general approval one encounters in Richards and Waterbury on the topic of economic liberalization, Owen is more critical. He points out that liberalization in Egypt, Tunisia, and Algeria, as elsewhere in the world, has exacerbated inequalities of income and the problem of unemployment while it has encouraged corruption. Cuts in subsidies have led to inflation, currency depreciation, and a flourishing of black markets. The IMF-like prescriptions are not a panacea. The weakness of the private sector, its dependence on the public sector for subsidies and cheap imports and on foreign firms for capital and technology, highlights the limits of what can be expected of it. Furthermore, the benefits of privatization will be limited to those firms in the public sector that are efficient enough to attract foreign buyers or foreign partners for joint ventures. The remaining firms continue to provide safe jobs and subsidized goods, serving as a burden on the public welfare system in Egypt, for example.

Owen notes four common features of structural adjustment in North Africa as a whole: first, the mechanisms employed to stimulate an inefficient public sector and the moves toward deregulation and decentralization have not really set managers of public enterprise free, nor have they unleashed the creative talents of entrepreneurs. The move to cut red tape, however, has concentrated power over licensing of private-sector activities in the hands of a few (instead of many) bureaucrats. Second, economic reforms have not been accompanied by the necessary political reforms. The third characteristic of reform in North Africa is the exacerbation of economic problems by the fall in oil prices and growing indebtedness, generally involving governments in the effort to fend off foreign pressures. Finally, structural reform coupled with increasing indebtedness has led to governmental efforts to leash working-class opposition, while workers have been fighting to preserve job security and wages and to prevent unemployment from rising.

The two Baathist regimes provide a contrast. In the case of Syria, a symbiotic and transparent relationship between state and society is being forged during economic restructuring or *infitah*, with the Alawite-dominated regime winning the support of Damascene Sunni merchants; and an alliance of public-sector managers, Baathist officials, and trade unionists joining forces to propagate the direction of the economy by the state, but with the regime making it possible for its clients in the private sector to ignore the barriers between them and the public sector. Iraq emerges as perhaps the most extreme case of the minimal relaxation of political controls in the move to encourage the private sector.

Alnasrawi (1994) provides an excellent assessment of development policies in Iraq in relation to regime changes since 1950 and offers an indictment of "the destruction of development." He examines sanctions, reparations, debt, and the prospects of reconstruction. According to Owen, Turkey's restructuring occurred when the country had completed its ISI stage, and it benefitted from the oil boom and the outbreak of the Iran-Iraq War. Ironically, Turkey's competitiveness was enhanced by the military intervention, which suppressed labor unions and kept wages low. Owen notes that the conspicuous success of Ozal's policies was as much due to these factors as to sound economics. *The Political Economy of Turkey*, edited by Arkanli and Rodrik (1990), contains articles on Turkey's trade liberalization in the 1980s, fiscal aspects of adjustment, growth in manufactured exports, external balance, the private sector's response to liberalization, policy dilemmas in macroeconomic management, changes in income distribution among and within classes under structural adjustment in Turkey, and the political economy of Turkey's external debt. *The Political and Socio-economic Transformation of Turkey*, edited by Eralp, Tünay, and Yeşilada (1993), delves into the Turkish New Right's attempt at hegemony, the ideology and social bases of political parties after 1980, the development of manufacturing, and labor-market policies, as well as aspects of international political economy. *Strong State and Economic Interest Groups*, edited by Heper (1991), takes up the relationship between the state and interest groups, including labor, agriculture, commercial groups, exporters, the manufacturing industry, and big business, and examines the micropolitics of banks in relation to the macropolitics of deregulation. Quataert (1994) is a collection of four papers on labor recruitment by Suraiya Faroqhi, Ottoman industry in the eighteenth century by Mehmet Genc, manufacturing in the nineteenth century by Quataert, and manufacturing from 1900 to 1950 by Caglar Keyder, with an introduction and afterword by Quataert. The papers were presented at a conference at the State University of New York at Binghamton in November 1990. The book, as Quataert aptly puts it, ''marks the continuing maturation of Ottoman and Turkish studies.''

We have already mentioned Waterbury's *The Egypt of Nasser and Sadat*. In addition, *Tunisia: The Political Economy of Reform*, edited by Zartman (1991), examines the broad areas of political reform, economic restructuring, and social resistance, including articles on state enterprises and privatization policy and private-sector development through public-sector restructuring. Gurney (1996) examines the political economy of oil in a study of Libya.

Owen (1992) points out that Israel began the process of economic restructuring by attempting to wean Israeli industry from dependence on government subsidies, improve competitiveness, and encourage the growth of exports following the recession of 1966–1967. The June 1967 war boosted defense industries and led to increased foreign aid and business expansion. A number of publicly owned companies were privatized, and the industries operated by the Histadrut were made more responsive to the profit motive. Shalev (1992) argues that after 1973, the defense industry proved highly vulnerable to shifts in defense spending and fluctuations in orders from abroad, and growth slowed. In the 1980s, under the government of national unity, subsidies to industry were cut further, there was a showdown over the decision not to go ahead with the Lavi fighter, and privatization experienced further difficulties, partly due to the state's desire to maintain control over strategic industries. Plessner (1994) argues that Israel's economic culture has its roots in Zionism, and that the exigencies of the creation of Israel constituted an imperative to set economic considerations aside. The economic and political culture that evolved in this process was perpetuated by waves of immigration and wars, leading to a state-dominated economy. One should therefore not approach Israel's economy from the ideological perspective of statism versus liberalism, as in the West; these categories need to be understood in the context of Israel's history. Plessner examines the main features of Israel's economy, including its legal and institutional framework, but technical analysis is handled in appendixes, so that the text is readable by non-economists. Plessner explains and evaluates the government's post-1973 economic stabilization measures.

Tuma (1987) in *Economic and Political Change in the Middle East* deals with Middle East development problems, the sociopolitical context, demographics, infrastructure, agriculture, industrialization, and trade, but his theoretical framework dates back to the early 1970s, when what we now call political economy was just getting off the ground.

The Psychological Approach?

Galal Amin (1974) offers a study of nine Arab countries that is rather dated now. There is no solid theoretical framework for analysis, and it was written too early, perhaps, to benefit from the rapid progress in the field of political economy. The book nevertheless contains many insights and gems of satire that can be a source of delight. Amin argued that Arab countries had come to resemble one another despite their manifest differences. As examples of this growing similarity, traditional landlords had been divested of their extensive holdings, but the tenants of agricultural land were still the objects of discrimination, and there was a growing reliance on food imports; the public sector was growing everywhere; government and public waste was increasing, but the rate of savings was not; governments failed to recognize that runaway population growth had to be controlled not by distributing birth-control devices but by providing security against deprivation in old age. Whole populations are enlisted in an impossible game to catch up with per capita income in the West from which only a few benefit. Meanwhile, land-based elites were being replaced by army officers, and foreign domination was being replaced by that of a native class. The greatest common denominator among the Arab countries was the putative desire to achieve rapid economic development, whereas the motive driving governments was the desire to remain in power. The coincidence of the two motives results in modernizing states that borrow superficial aspects of European civilization, such as the premature adoption of comprehensive planning, the adoption of capital-intensive technologies, and the creation of an ineffective common market. The upshot is that Arab leaders pursue modernization because they believe that it is the politically correct thing to do. In such states poverty is hidden behind a facade of modernity while cultural differentiation is being lost and the environment deteriorates.

In the same vein as Amin's *The Modernization of Poverty*, Chatelus and Schemeil (1984), who appear to rely on personal reflections, come to the conclusion that psychological inferiority serves as an incentive for Middle Eastern states to build strong administrative institutions in order to be validated as serious actors in regional or world affairs. Still, the economies they oversee are based not on production but circulation (trade and rent), their societies are clientelist, and their polities are built on the city-state model; that is, they are not centralized and coordinated units with full-fledged bureaucracies. They exhibit a preference for corporate forms of organization. They practice "economic pluralism," which allows for societal intervention in the development rather than in the political process. The social objectives of justice, security, and liberty are pursued through economic rather than political processes. Industrialization in a "circulation economy" is rarely efficient; it is pursued largely for the sake of prestige and cannot serve as the basis for a productive economy. "Restricted to its core functions, state is just gas and power, water, sewage, and industry. Paraphrasing Lenin when he stated socialism meant electricity plus the Soviets, could we not premise that Arabism today is industry plus allegiance?" (263).

The Economists Have Their Say

El-Naggar has edited three IMF publications on the issues of *Adjustment Policies and Development Strategies in the Arab World* (1987), *Privatization and Structural Adjustment in the Arab World* (1989), and *The Uruguay Round and the Arab Countries* (1996). The first is based on the papers and proceedings of a seminar held in Abu Dhabi, the United Arab Emirates, in 1987 and focuses on Egypt, Jordan, and Morocco. The second also is a compilation of papers from a seminar held in Abu Dhabi the following year, including presentations on topics of broad interest and others focusing on Egypt, Tunisia, Jordan, and regional joint ventures in the Gulf Cooperation Council states, while the third groups papers from a seminar held in Kuwait in 1995 sponsored by the Arab Fund for Economic and Social Development, the Arab Monetary Fund, the IMF, and the World Bank. We list them here because of their direct relevance to the issues that have occupied the attention of political economists writing on the contemporary Arab world.

THE ROLE OF CLASS

Workers and Working Classes in the Middle East, edited by Zachary Lockman (1994), can be described as an attempt to bring the concept of class back into the equation. The book is a collection of papers by authors such as Lockman, Donald Quataert, Ellis Goldberg, and Edmund Burke III originally presented at a workshop sponsored and funded by Harvard University's Center for Middle Eastern Studies in 1990. They cover workers in Turkey, Egypt, Iran, and the Ottoman Empire. In introducing the volume, Lockman warns that the region's diversity may not allow for more than superficial generalizations. Furthermore, he inquires whether "the working class" is a coherent historical agent and legitimate object of inquiry, to which he responds with a "properly nuanced and contingent 'yes' " (xxviii). He observes, "It can be said that all the essays in this volume are in a sense revisionist, because whether through explicit theoretical contention or through pathbreaking empirical work they contribute to the ongoing effort to critique and rethink the premises of Middle Eastern working-class history" (xxi). One should not think of workers' consciousness being formed in the workplace alone, but in the entirety of "overlapping social matrices" by political struggles and ethnic affiliation. Prodded by remarks by one of the discussants, Dipesh Chakrabarty, Lockman remarks that the language in which workers express their grievances is not simply proletarian but is "inflected by many discourses (nationalism, religion, craft, local origins, etc.)." This is totally consistent with my own study of Lebanon, where working-class ideology is heavily influenced by the symbolic universe of the different ethnic communities to which the members of that class belong.

The volume edited by Goldberg (1996) rounds out the picture by examining Syria, Israel, and North Africa as well as the countries in the book edited by Lockman. Goldberg's emphasis is on the social history of labor. The essays in this volume challenge the notion that the transition to a capitalist economy took place under colonialism with a forced and sudden imposition of markets. Artisanal and industrial production coexisted under the Ottoman Empire, a point Quataert makes in his essay in this volume as well as in *Manufacturing in the Ottoman Empire and Turkey, 1500–1950* (1994). The question to ask is when industrially produced goods drove artisans from a particular market. Goldberg points out that the historical trajectory of the Middle East toward capitalism did not merely copy the example of Europe. Labor in Middle Eastern countries sought strength through the right to form unions and through support for state-owned enterprises. Marxist intellectuals and political parties influenced the tide of events, and the growth of industrialization brought leftists to positions of leadership in labor unions. The expansion of state-owned enterprises led to corporatism, which stripped unions of their power.

Kazemi and Waterbury (1991), a collection of articles that deal with peasant protest and rebellion in the Middle East and North Africa, fills an important lacuna in the field. In a short introduction, Waterbury identifies two crucial causal variables for peasant unrest: "penetration of markets into partially subsistence agriculture, and the growing extractive reach of the state" (4), which seems to reflect the opinion of many contributors to the volume. He speaks of four phases or periods of peasant unrest: nineteenth-century attempts to restore a preferred status quo ante; protest in a more mature rural market economy, directed largely against colonial powers; and a third phase after World War II, consisting mostly of everyday forms of nonviolent protest, primarily directed against the state, interspersed with incidents of violent revolution in rural areas. Waterbury speculates that the fourth phase would involve the state giving up its role as the defender of rural egalitarianism as the market comes to be viewed as the best way to secure increased production and higher incomes.

Edmund Burke III discusses changing patterns of peasant protest in the Middle East between 1750 and 1950, while Donald Quataert takes up rural unrest in the Ottoman Empire from 1830 to 1914. Linda Schatkowski Schilcher offers a very informative treatment of violence in rural Syria in the last two decades of the nineteenth century, relating it to state centralization, rural integration, and the world market. Axel Havemann analyzes the impact of peasant resistance on nineteenth-century Mount Lebanon; Farhad Kazemi deals with peasant uprisings in twentieth-century Iran, Iraq, and Turkey; Sevket Pamuk explains resistance by agricultural producers in Turkey during World War II; and Kenneth Stein analyzes rural change and peasant destitution as contributing causes to the Arab revolt in Palestine (1936–1939). Writing on Egypt, Reinhard Schulze, Nathan Brown, and Timothy Mitchell discuss the peasant rebellion of 1919, social banditry and peasant attitudes, and the representation of rural violence in the writings on political development in the Nasserist era, respectively. Nicholas Hopkins compares clan and class in two villages, one in Libya and the other in Egypt; Ahmad Ashraf comments on state and agrarian relations in Iran, 1960–1990; and Fereydoun Safizadeh takes up the topic of peasant protest in Iranian Azerbaijan.

Lockman (1996) challenges the ''dual-society'' paradigm, according to which the Jewish and Arab communities in Palestine were self-contained, monolithic entities. Using a ''relational paradigm'' he explores the ''complex matrix of economic, political, social, and cultural interactions'' (8) among the two communities, and among Arab and Jewish workers, trade unions, labor movements, and labor-oriented political parties'' from 1906 to 1948. He deals with such topics as Labor Zionism and the Arab working class during the period 1920–1929; an in-depth study of the interaction of class, nationalist, and cultural politics in the struggle for Arab-Jewish unity, and cooperation and conflict among railway workers during the period 1919–1939; Arab workers and the Histadrut, 1929–1936; the Arab revolt and Labor Zionism, 1936–1939; and workers, labor movements, and the left during World War II. Though focusing on class, Lockman cautions that class ''is best understood . . . as a relation which is itself constituted by many other social relations and practices'' (13).

Ben-Porat (1986), in contrast, focuses solely on the formation of the Jewish working class up to 1948. He argues that the Jewish working class was able to realize its class interest by establishing a socialist state; however, the maintenance of the social and political dominance gained by the agents of that class in the Yishuv necessitated the embrace of nationalistic rather than class interests, which impeded the process of further class formation. Roy (1995), as her title implies, traces the undermining of the formal economy of the Gaza Strip under Israeli occupation and the growing importance of the informal economy under conditions of scarcity resulting from deliberate neglect and political dependence. The study is based on extensive and comprehensive data collected by the author.

Moaddel (1993) offers a fresh causal analysis of the Iranian revolution based on revolutionary discourse and political mobilization. He emphasizes that the interaction of class, politics, and ideology determines the content of revolution; however, ideology enjoys primacy. He maintains that it "mediates class relations as well as the relations between the state and civil society" (15). Moaddel treats ideology "as an autonomous category, with a dynamic of its own, not reducible to its psychological function nor to the dynamics of political or class interests" (265). The 1979 revolution is best understood through "revolutionary Islamic discourse." Moaddel makes a valuable contribution, but his defense of the autonomy of ideology is not convincing.

Haj (1997) offers a sophisticated discussion of the formation of capital, modernization, nationalism, revolution, social conflict, and oil and social change in Iraq. Batatu's (1978) book is a very well respected classic and a gold mine of information for the researcher into Iraq's land-owning and commercial families under the monarchy as well as revolutionary movements in Iraq.

THE STATE IN THE INTERNATIONAL ECONOMY

The third approach is concerned with theories of the relationship between core and periphery in a capitalist world system dominated by the advanced industrialized countries (the core). Those writing in this vein often embrace theories of imperialism or take their point of departure from *dependencia* theories that may be Marxist or structuralist, and that were developed primarily by a group of Latin American thinkers, such as Raul Prebisch and Guillermo O'Donnell. In the Middle East, the chief scholarly advocate of this approach is Samir Amin, who cooriginated or elaborated on theories of unequal development and the development of underdevelopment. He is a prolific writer, and we have not attempted to list all his publications. He argues that Core and Periphery (or North and South) are integrated into a single world system through the relations of exchange and a hierarchical (and highly unequal) system of global production.

In *Accumulation on a World Scale* (1974), he points out that underdevelopment in the Periphery is characterized by uneven productivity across sectors of the economy; the virtual absence of positive spillover effects, the absence of integration and linkage between inputs and outputs or the "disarticulation of the economic system" within the peripheral country, and articulation with industrial economies in the Center; and dependence of nations of the Periphery on the outside for production equipment and semifinished goods, entailing domination from the outside. Within this system, development means the uneven development of the "modern" sector, which is comprised of a few large-scale enterprises, often foreign, which only exacerbates differentials or the gap between it and the traditional sector. Due to political domination by the Center, transfer of value flows in an uneven pattern from the Periphery to the Center, or from South to North. In *Unequal Development* (1976), Amin argues that the principle of comparative advantage does not apply in trade between the Core and Periphery. Exploitation in the Periphery is more severe than it is in the Core, he maintains.

The principal application of this perspective to the modern Arab world as a whole is Samir Amin's *The Arab Economy Today* (1982), in which he argues that among nations of the Third World, the Arab world is the region that is most fully integrated into the world system. He says that formal ownership of assets in the Arab world by multinationals is no longer the issue; rather, it is the imposition of monopoly prices by the multinationals for industrial plant and strategic inputs, the sale of plants solely on a turnkey basis, and the refusal to sell technological inputs that would allow the Arab countries to assume control of the production process. Amin concludes with the recommendations for a decoupling from the world system or, as he puts it, "a selective disconnection and corresponding reduction of the Arab productive system's integration into a world system dominated by multinational monopolies," regional economic co-operation, the development of a skilled labor force, a quest for appropriate technologies, and "a drastic re-orientation of priorities in favour of agriculture" (80). Amin never has a satisfactory explanation of how disengaging from the world system of exchange and production is supposed to allow the South to catch up with the North. He does point out, however, that by decoupling he means not autarchy, but giving national development precedence over integration into the world economy. Amin's ideas and dependency theory in general were very influential among the Group of 77 at the United Nations, with Arab intellectuals and leftist political parties, and with the leaders of the Lebanese National Movement in 1975–1976. Amin's most influential works appeared in the 1960s and 1970s.

Norman Girvan's book *Corporate Imperialism: Conflict and Expropriation* (1976), while not exclusively about the Middle East, is nevertheless an excellent study of mineral-exporting economies and therefore of the relationship between the oil companies and the oil-producing states of the Middle East up to the early 1970s. Solidly in the dependency tradition, it emphasizes, among other things, the dependence of the mineral-exporting countries on multinationals for badly needed foreign exchange and government revenues. Perhaps it is most useful in understanding the logic of corporate strategy and power relations within multinational corporations (MNCs), which are not often compatible with the best interests of the host country. It analyzes the external diseconomies of the mineral industry in relation to agriculture and the manufacturing sector and its effect on agricultural labor, the structure of wage rates, and consumer demand, as well as its failure to generate backward and forward linkages. Written in the following decade, Stephen Krasner's *Structural Conflict: The Third World against Global Liberalism* (1985), among other things, traces the evolving relationship between oil companies and countries of the Persian Gulf, the breakup of vertical integration, and the replacement of the oil-exploration and extraction concession with service contracts, production-sharing agreements, and technical assistance deals. The same evolutionary process is traced in passing by Charles Lipson in *Standing Guard: Protecting Foreign Capital in the Nineteenth and Twentieth Centuries* (1985). Krasner's book, however, reflects the changing perspectives on the causes of underdevelopment; instead of blaming the structure of the world capitalist economy, it blames the governments of the countries of the South for employing inappropriate development policies. The problem is thus laid at the door of the developing countries themselves. Yergin (1991) is not properly a work on political economy according to our definition, but it provides very useful information on the history of oil and the OPEC countries.

The world-system paradigm was dominant in the 1960s and the 1970s, when government policies hewed to the line of import substitution industrialization; that paradigm was beginning to become outmoded in the early 1980s with the triumph of neoconservatism in the West, the collapse of the Soviet Union, and the growing Third World debt problem and the discrediting of import-substitution industrialization. Progressive denationalization followed. Privatization and export-led growth emerged as the enlightened trend in the 1980s and 1990s, and many countries of the region hastened to begin the process of dismantling visible and invisible protective trade barriers that went hand in hand with ISI in order to gain unhindered access to foreign markets. Amin's earlier recommendations became passé. Governments have begun to enact legislation for the protection of intellectual property rights and industrial copyrights and to embrace the principles of nondiscrimination and reciprocity expressed in the idea of "most favored nation" underlying the multilateral approach to free trade, which has been extended to trade in services as well as goods since the Uruguay Round of the General Agreement on Tariffs and Trade (GATT) negotiations that led to the creation of the World Trade Organization (WTO). Middle Eastern countries, reversing a trend that had succeeded in eliminating foreign ownership outside the oil sector by the 1950s (and that had extended to the oil sector by the 1970s), hastened to find a niche for themselves among the "emerging markets" and to open the door to foreign direct and portfolio investment (more than $20 trillion are said to be available to global fund managers today). To do this, they have to accede to international agreements such as GATT and join the WTO. At this writing, ten countries of the region have already become members (Bahrain, Djibouti, Egypt, Israel, Kuwait, Morocco, Qatar, Tunisia, Turkey, and the United Arab Emirates), and five others (Algeria, Jordan, Saudi Arabia, Sudan, and the Sultanate of Oman) have submitted applications to join the WTO and have observer status. These developments open the door for theoreticians to examine the implications of Middle Eastern countries becoming part of the "world system of production" and the effect of this process on the nature and role of states in the area. Robert Cox's work *Production, Power, and World Order* seems particularly relevant to this question, although it is not primarily concerned with the Middle East.

In his latest book, *Capitalism in the Age of Globalization* (1997), Amin argues that the classical form of the polarization of the world into Core and Periphery is now obsolete and has given way to a different polarization to suit the interests of the globalization of capital, in which the Center enjoys five monopolies: a technological monopoly; financial control of worldwide financial markets; monopolistic access to the planet's natural resources; media and communications monopolies; and monopolies over weapons of mass destruction. "What results is a new hierarchy, more unequal than ever before, in the distribution of income on a world scale, subordinating the industries of the peripheries and reducing them to the role of subcontracting. This is the new foundation of polarization, presaging its future forms" (5). The International Monetary Fund, the World Bank, and what he terms GATT–World Trade Organization are helping to facilitate this globalization of capital and the process of privatization. They are helping to weaken organized labor throughout the world. Managing the world through the market will lead to unhampered exploitation of defenseless workers. The attempts to dismantle and weaken the nation-state, according to Amin, will spell disaster for labor in various parts of the world, because workers will no longer have anything to protect them against predatory capital. Structural adjustment programs administered by the Bretton Woods institutions will lead to the "recompradorization of the peripheries." Certain parts of the world are fairly well placed to cope with this change, notably East and Southeast Asia and perhaps sections of Latin America. However, the Arab world and Africa will fare worst.

Amin is clearly going against the conventional wisdom. To do him justice, one must take him in context. He argues that the expansion of world trade is the consequence, not the cause, of economic growth and that "relative prices are not determined by the market, but by the social conditions, beyond supply and demand, in which production operates" (26–27). Also to be fair, one ought to note that the International Labor Organization, which seeks to help labor throughout the world to organize, is at odds with the IMF and the International Bank for Reconstruction and Development (IBRD), which think that this will hamper growth.

REFERENCES

Political Economy References

Amin, Galal A. 1974. *The Modernization of Poverty: A Study in the Political Economy of Growth in Nine Arab Countries, 1945–1970*. Leiden: E. J. Brill.
Amin, Samir. 1974. *Accumulation on a World Scale: A Critique of the Theory of Underdevelopment*. Trans. Brian Pierce. 2 vols. New York: Monthly Review Press.
———. 1976. *Unequal Development: An Essay on the Social Formations of Peripheral Capitalism*. Trans. Brian Pierce. New York: Monthly Review Press.
———. 1982. *The Arab Economy Today*. Trans. Michael Pallis. London: Zed Books.
———. 1997. *Capitalism in the Age of Globalization: The Management of Contemporary Society*. London: Zed Books.
Barkey, Henri J. 1992. *The Politics of Economic Reform in the Middle East*. New York: St. Martin's Press.
Bienen, Henry, and John Waterbury. 1989. "The Political Economy of Privatization in Developing Countries." *World Development* 17, no. 5 (May): 617–632.
Chatelus, Michel, and Yves Schemeil. 1984. "Towards a New Political Economy of

State Industrialization in the Arab Middle East." *International Journal of Middle East Studies* 16, no. 2 (May): 251–265.

Cox, Robert W. 1987. *Production, Power, and World Order: Social Forces in the Making of History*. New York: Columbia University Press.

Girvan, Norman. 1976. *Corporate Imperialism: Conflict and Expropriation: Transnational Corporations and Economic Nationalism in the Third World*. White Plains, NY: M. E. Sharpe.

Goldberg, Ellis J., ed. 1996. *The Social History of Labor in the Middle East*. Boulder, CO: Westview Press.

Halpern, Manfred. 1963. *The Politics of Social Change in the Middle East and North Africa*. Princeton: Princeton University Press.

Harik, Iliya, and Denis J. Sullivan, eds. 1992. *Privatization and Liberalization in the Middle East*. Bloomington: Indiana University Press.

Henry, Clement M. 1996. Book review of "John Waterbury, *Exposed to Innumerable Delusions: Public Enterprise and State Power in Egypt, India, Mexico and Turkey*." *International Journal of Middle East Studies* 28, no. 3 (August): 423–426.

Kazemi, Farhad, and John Waterbury, eds. 1991. *Peasants and Politics in the Modern Middle East*. Miami: Florida International University Press.

Krasner, Stephen D. 1985. *Structural Conflict: The Third World against Global Liberalism*. Berkeley: University of California Press.

Lipson, Charles. 1985. *Standing Guard: Protecting Foreign Capital in the Nineteenth and Twentieth Centuries*. Berkeley: University of California Press.

Lockman, Zachary, ed. 1994. *Workers and Working Classes in the Middle East: Struggles, Histories, Historiographies*. Albany: State University of New York Press.

El-Naggar, Said, ed. *Adjustment Policies and Development Strategies in the Arab World*. Washington, DC: International Monetary Fund.

———, ed. 1989. *Privatization and Structural Adjustment in the Arab Countries*. Washington, DC: International Monetary Fund.

———, ed. 1996. *The Uruguay Round and the Arab Countries*. Washington, DC: International Monetary Fund.

Niblock, Tim, and Emma Murphy, eds. 1993. *Economic and Political Liberalization in the Middle East*. London: British Academic Press.

O'Donnell, Guillermo A. 1973. *Modernization and Bureaucratic-Authoritarianism*. 2d ed with postscript. Berkeley: Institute of International Studies, University of California at Berkeley.

———. 1979. "Tensions in the Bureaucratic Authoritarian State and the Question of Democracy." In David Collier, ed., *The New Authoritarianism in Latin America*. Princeton: Princeton University Press.

Owen, Roger. 1992. *State, Power, and Politics in the Making of the Modern Middle East*. London: Routledge.

Quataert, Donald, ed. 1994. *Manufacturing in the Ottoman Empire and Turkey, 1500–1950*. Albany: State University of New York Press.

Richards, Alan, and John Waterbury. 1990. *A Political Economy of the Middle East: State, Class, and Economic Development*. Boulder, CO: Westview Press.

———. 1996. *A Political Economy of the Middle East*. 2d ed. Boulder, CO: Westview Press.

Trimberger, Ellen K. 1978. *Revolution from Above: Military Bureaucrats and Development in Japan, Turkey, Egypt, and Peru.* New Brunswick, NJ: Transaction Books.

Tuma, Elias H. 1987. *Economic and Political Change in the Middle East.* Palo Alto, CA: Pacific Books.

Waterbury, John. 1991. "Twilight of the State Bourgeoisie?" *International Journal of Middle East Studies* 23, no. 1 (February): 1–17.

———. 1992. "The Heart of the Matter? Public Enterprise and the Adjustment Process." In Stephen Haggard and Robert Kaufman, eds., *The Politics of Economic Adjustment.* Princeton: Princeton University Press.

———. 1993. *Exposed to Innumerable Delusions: Public Enterprise and State Power in Egypt, India, Mexico, and Turkey.* New York: Cambridge University Press.

Yergin, Daniel. 1991. *The Prize: The Epic Quest for Oil, Money, and Power.* New York: Simon and Schuster.

Country References

Alnasrawi, Abbas. 1994. *The Economy of Iraq: Oil, Wars, Destruction of Development, and Prospects, 1950–2010.* Westport, CT: Greenwood Press.

Arkanli, Tosun, and Dani Rodrik, eds., 1990. *The Political Economy of Turkey: Debt, Adjustment, and Sustainability.* New York: St. Martin's Press.

Batatu, Hanna. 1978. *The Old Social Classes and the Revolutionary Movements of Iraq: A Study of Iraq's Old Landed and Commercial Classes and of Its Communists, Ba'thists, and Free Officers.* Princeton: Princeton University Press.

Ben-Porat, Amir. 1986. *Between Class and Nation: The Formation of the Jewish Working Class in the Period before Israel's Statehood.* Westport, CT: Greenwood Press.

Eralp, Atila, Muharrem Tünay, and Birol Yeşilada, eds. 1993. *The Political and Socioeconomic Transformation of Turkey.* Westport, CT: Praeger.

Gurney, Judith. 1996. *Libya, the Political Economy of Oil.* Oxford: Oxford University Press.

Haj, Samira. 1997. *The Making of Iraq, 1900–1963: Capital, Power, and Ideology.* Albany: State University of New York Press.

Heper, Metin, ed. 1991. *Strong State and Economic Interest Groups: The Post-1980 Turkish Experience.* Berlin: Walter de Gruyter.

Lockman, Zachary. 1996. *Comrades and Enemies: Arab and Jewish Workers in Palestine, 1906–1948.* Berkeley: University of California Press.

Moaddel, Mansoor. 1993. *Class, Politics, and Ideology in the Iranian Revolution.* New York: Columbia University Press.

Perthes, Volker. 1995. *The Political Economy of Syria under Asad.* London: I. B. Tauris.

Plessner, Yakir. 1994. *The Political Economy of Israel: From Ideology to Stagnation.* Albany: State University of New York Press.

Roy, Sara. 1995. *The Gaza Strip: The Political Economy of De-development.* Washington, DC: Institute for Palestine Studies.

Shalev, Michael. 1992. *Labour and the Political Economy in Israel.* London: Oxford University Press.

Waterbury, John. 1983. *The Egypt of Nasser and Sadat: The Political Economy of Two Regimes.* Princeton: Princeton University Press.

Zartman, I. William, ed. 1991. *Tunisia: The Political Economy of Reform.* Boulder, CO: Lynne Rienner.

APPENDIX: REFERENCE WORKS FOR MIDDLE EAST POLITICS, ECONOMICS, AND SOCIETY

Sanford R. Silverburg

The literature on the Middle East is enormous and growing continuously. Research on any aspect of this region may begin with a variety of goals and perspectives, for example, empirical and scientific, ideological and normative with a persuasive argument, rational, or faith based. Study can be approached with disciplinary interests as well, from anthropology and archaeology to Zionism and zoology. The information sources provided here are for assistance in conducting research in areas concerning politics and related subject matter in economics and sociology. Attention is paid to the rapid development of electronic sources of information on the Internet, although it must be noted that while useful, they should not be understood to be a full substitute for hard copy. For a general survey of the literature on the Middle East and North Africa, the researcher might want to consult Sanford R. Silverburg, *Middle East Bibliography* (Metuchen, NJ: Scarecrow Press, 1992). Because of the transitive nature of so many of the institutional research organizations in the region, interested scholars should check to see what support exists at the time of interest or intraregional travel. One institutional source is: Council of American Overseas Research Centers (CAORC), 1100 Jefferson Drive, S.W., IC-3123, Washington, DC 20560.

CURRENT DEVELOPMENTS

American-Mideast Educational and Training Services. *The Middle East and North Africa.* Washington, DC: AMIDEAST, 1991.

Arab Political Documents. Beirut: Political Studies and Public Administration Department of the American University of Beirut, 1963. Annual.

Arab Report and Record (ARR). London: Arab Report and Record, 1966–1978.

Cahiers de l'Orient contemporain. Paris: G. P. Maisonneuve, 1948– .

Current World Affairs. Great Falls, VA: George Daoust.

Daily Report: Middle East and Africa. Springfield, VA: National Technical Information Service (for the Foreign Broadcast Information Service), 1980–1987.

Drysdale, Alasdair. *The Middle East and North Africa: A Political Geography.* New York: Oxford University Press, 1985.

Fenton, Thomas P., and Mary J. Heffron, comps. and eds. *Middle East: A Directory of Resources.* Maryknoll, NY: Orbis Books, 1988.

Hurewitz, J. C. *Diplomacy in the Near and Middle East: A Documentary Record.* 2 vols. Princeton: Van Nostrand, [1956].

———. *The Middle East and North Africa in World Politics: A Documentary Record.* 2d ed., rev. and enl. New Haven: Yale University Press, 1975.

Jawed, Mohammed Nasir, ed. *Year Book of the Muslim World: A Handy Encyclopedia.* New Delhi: Medialine, 1996.

Keesing's Contemporary Archives. London: Longman, 1931–1934, 1943–1986.

Mansoor, Menahem. *Political and Diplomatic History of the Arab World, 1900–1967.* 8 vols. Englewood, CO: Information Handling Services, [1978].

MEED Arab Report. London: Middle East Economic Digest, 1979.

The Middle East: Abstracts and Index. Pittsburgh: Northumberland Press, 1978– .

Middle East. London: Europa Publications, [1st ed.], 1948–1963; *Middle East and North Africa*, [11th ed.], 1964– . Annual.

Middle East Annual Review. Saffron Walden, England: Middle East Review, 1974–1980.

Middle East Contemporary Survey. New York: Holmes and Meier, 1976–77. Annual.

Middle East File. Medford, NJ: Learned Information, 1982–1988.

Middle East Journal. Washington, DC: Middle East Institute, 1947– .

Middle East Monitor. Washington, DC: Middle East Institute, 1971– .

Middle East Monitor. London: Business Monitor International, 1991– .

Middle East Record. Tel Aviv: Israel Oriental Society, Reuven Shiloah Research Center, 1969–70.

Oriente moderno. Rome: Istituto per l'oriente, 1921– .

The Political Risk Yearbook: Middle East and North Africa. New York: Frost and Sullivan, 1987.

Record of the Arab World. [Beirut]: Research and Publishing House, 1969– .

Sluglett, Peter, and Marion Farouk-Sluglett. *The Times Guide to the Middle East: The Arab World and Its Neighbours.* 3d ed. London: Times Books, 1996.

Summary of World Broadcasts: Part 4, Middle East, Africa, and Latin America. Caversham Park, Reading: Monitoring Service of the British Broadcasting Corp, 1983– .

Travaux et jours. Beirut: Centre culturel universitaire, 1961– .

SURVEY INFORMATION

Arab Countries' World Wide Web Sites. URL: http://www.liii.com/~hajeri/arab.html

Behn, W. H. *Index Islamicus, 1665–1905: A Bibliography of Articles on Islamic Subjects in Periodicals and Other Collective Publications.* Millersville, PA: Ad yok Publications, 1989.

———. *Index Islamicus: Supplement, 1665–1980.* Part 1, *A Bibliography of Articles on Islamic Subjects in Periodicals and Other Collective Publications.* Bio-bibliographic supplement to Index Islamicus, vol. 2, Bibliographical supplement, part 1. Millersville, PA: Ad yok Publications, 1995.

Bibliographie de l'Occident Musulman (BOM). Trimestral publication. Casablanca: Foundation du Roi Abdul Aziz al Saoud pour les Etudes Islamiques et les Sciences Humaines, 1989– . Beginning with nos. 1/2 (Winter–Spring 1996), the title is *Études Maghrébines: Revue de recherche et de bibliographié maghrébines.*

The Cambridge Encyclopedia of the Middle East and North Africa. Cambridge: Cambridge University Press, 1988.

Current Contents of Periodicals on the Middle East. Tel Aviv: Moshe Dayan Center for Middle Eastern and African Studies, Documentation Center, Tel Aviv University, 1980– .

DOMES: Digest of Middle East Studies. Milwaukee: School of Library and Information Science at the University of Wisconsin–Milwaukee, 1992– .

E. J. Brill's First Encyclopaedia of Islam, 1913–1936. Leiden: E. J. Brill, 1987.

The Encyclopaedia of Islam. Leiden: E. J. Brill, 1960–[1954-<1995- >].

Fairbanks-Bodman, Ellen, ed. *The World of Islam, Images and Echoes: A Critical Guide to Films and Recordings.* New York: American Council of Learned Societies, 1980.

Fenton, Thomas P., and Mary J. Heffron, comps. and eds. *Middle East: A Directory of Resources.* Maryknoll, NY: Orbis Books, 1988.

Friday Grabhorn, Ann, and Robert Staab, eds. *A Resource Guide for Middle Eastern Studies.* 2d Rev. ed. Salt Lake City, UT: Middle East Outreach Council, 1988.

Georgetown University. Center for Contemporary Arab Studies. http://sfswww. georgetown.edu/sfs/programs/ccas/ccas/html

Harvard Middle East Studies. http://fas-www.harvard.edu/~mideast/

Index Islamicus. London: Mansell, 1983–date. (Issued in two parts, 1976–1980, [1981– 1985]). East Grinstead, West Sussex, England: Bowker-Saur, 1994– .

Institut du Monde Arabe (Paris). URL: http://www.imarabe.com/ email: ima@imarabe. com

Internet Resources on the Arab World. http://www.liii.com/~hajeri/organ.html

Jones, Charles E. "ABZU: Guide to Resources for the Study of the Ancient Near East Available on the Internet." A project and publication of The Research Archives of the Oriental Institute, Chicago. URL: http://www-oi.uchicago.edu/OI/DEPT/ RA/ABZU/ABZU.HTML

Levin, Michael Graubart. *The Guide to the Jewish Internet.* San Francisco: No Starch Press, 1996. Software included.

McClintock, Marsha Hamilton. *The Middle East and North Africa on Film: An Annotated Filmography.* New York: Garland, 1982.

Middle East Resource Center. http://gpg.com/MERC/merc.html

The Muslim World Book Review, accompanied by supplement of *Index of Islamic Literature.* Leicester: Islamic Foundation and International Institute of Islamic Thought, 1980– .

Netherlands Institute for the Near East. http://www.leidenuniv.nl/nino/nino.html

Pearson, J. D., with Julia F. Ashton. *Index Islamicus, 1906–1955: A Catalog of Articles on Islamic Subjects in Periodicals and Other Collective Publications.* London: Mansell, [1972].

Periodica Islamica. Kuala Lumpur: Berita Publishing, 1991– .

Roberts, Joseph W. "The Middle East–North Africa Internet Resource Guide." *Periodica Islamica* 5, no. 3 (1995): 109–126, and on the World Wide Web as http: // www.cc.utah.edu/~jwr9311/MENA.html.

Romm, Diane. *The Jewish Guide to the Internet.* Northvale, NJ: Jason Aronson, 1996. This reference source is updated with address changes, keyed to the page on which the source appears in the book: http://www.uscj.org/metny/bellmobj/ jnet.htm

Selim, George Dimitri, comp. *American Doctoral Dissertations on the Arab World, 1883–1968.* Washington, DC: Library of Congress, 1970.

———, comp. *American Doctoral Dissertations on the Arab World, 1883–1974.* 2d ed. Washington, DC: Library of Congress, 1976.

———, comp. *American Doctoral Dissertations on the Arab World: Supplement.* Washington, DC: Library of Congress, 1983.

Shimoni, Yaacov. *Political Dictionary of the Arab World.* New York: Macmillan, 1987.

Sluglett, Peter, comp. *Theses on Islam, the Middle East, and North-West Africa, 1880–1978, Accepted by Universities in the United Kingdom and Ireland.* London: Mansell, 1983.

Universidad de Granada. Estudios Arabes Contemporaneos. Estudios Arabes Contemporaneos: Adquisiciones de la Biblioteca. [Granada]: Universidad de Granada.

University of Arizona. Middle East Collection. URL: http://dizzy.library.arizona.edu/users/midhatta/mdes.htm

University of California at Berkeley. Center for Middle Eastern Studies. http://violet.berkeley.edu/~cmes

Wakim, Edward. *Contemporary Political Leaders of the Middle East.* New York: Facts on File, 1996.

Western Books: The Middle East from the Rise of Islam. Woodbridge, CT: Research Publications of Primary Source Media, 1995– . 12 units of 1,000 microfiche, approximately 3,600 titles.

Ziring, Lawrence. *The Middle East: A Political Dictionary.* Santa Barbara, CA: ABC-CLIO, 1992.

GENERAL REFERENCE WORKS

Gassner, Ingrid Jaradat, et al., comps. *Palestine/Israel Directory: A Guide to Independent Palestinian and Israeli Initiatives for Human Rights, Women Rights, Social and Economic Justice, Peace and Cooperation; Palestinian and Israeli Authorities and Official Institutions.* 4th and rev. ed. Jerusalem: Alternative Information Center, April 1996.

Ljunggren, Florence, and Charles L. Geddes. *An International Directory of Institutes and Societies Interested in the Middle East.* Amsterdam: Djambatan, 1962.

Netton, Ian Richard, ed. and comp. *Middle East Materials in United Kingdom and Irish Libraries: A Directory.* London: Library Association in association with the Centre for Arab Gulf Studies, University of Exeter, 1983.

Non-governmental Organizational Guide. Istanbul: Turkish Economic and Social History, 1996.

STATISTICS

Bleaney, C. H. *Official Publications on the Middle East: A Selective Guide to the Statistical Sources.* Middle East Libraries Committee Research Guides, 1. Durham, England: University of Durham, Centre for Middle Eastern and Islamic Studies, 1985.

Gibbons, Virginia H. "A Bibliography of Middle Eastern Statistical Documents (1945+)." *Middle East Studies Association Bulletin* 8, no. 2 (May 31, 1974):

20–34.

The Statesman's Year-Book. New York: St. Martin's Press, 1864–date.

BIBLIOGRAPHIES AND INDEXES

Four series of books are devoted, in part, to individual states in the region, each of which maintains a relatively extensive and reasonably up-to-date bibliography, in book form, to which a researcher should turn for appropriate attention. The series are Foreign Area Studies/Area Handbook Program sponsored by the U.S. Department of the Army and now produced by the Federal Research Division of the Library of Congress, the Historical Dictionaries from Scarecrow Press, the Nations of the Contemporary Middle East Series of Westview Press, and the World Bibliographic Series from ABC-CLIO. Additionally, there are a few other nationally oriented sources that follow:

Saudi Arabia

Philipp, Hans-Jürgen, comp. *Saudi-Arabien Bibliographie zu Gesellschaft, Politik, Wirtschaft: Literatur seit dem 18. Jahrhundert in westeuropäischen Sprachen mit Standortnachweisen.* Munich: Saur, 1984.

Turkey

Özer, Soyasal. "A Historical Glance at the Development of the Current Turkish National Bibliography and Other Major Bibliographical Sources in Turkey." *Middle East Studies Association Bulletin* 11, no. 3 (October 1, 1977): 1–30.

Yemen

Stevenson, Thomas B., comp. *Studies on Yemen, 1975–1990: A Bibliography of European-Language Sources for Social Scientists.* Westbury, NY: American Institute for Yemeni Studies, 1994.

MAJOR RESEARCH CENTERS AND INSTITUTES IN THE MIDDLE EAST

The Middle East Studies Association Bulletin, from time to time, has published Foreign Research Reports outlining archival and other institutional repositories that ought to benefit the serious researcher.

Bahrain

Bahrain Institute of Banking and Finance
P.O. Box 20525
Bahrain
Tel.: 728008
Telex: 9822
FAX: 729928

Historical Documents Center
  P.O. Box 28882
  Manama, Bahrain

Ministry of Information
  P.O. Box 253
  Manama, Bahrain
  Tel.: 243311

Egypt

Arab Lawyers Union
  13 Ittehad El-Mouhamen El-Arab Street
  Garden City
  Cairo, Egypt
  Tel.: 20-2-355-7132
  FAX: 20-2-355-2486

Center for Political and Strategic Studies (CPSS)
  Al Ahram Foundation
  Al Galaa Street
  Cairo, Egypt
  Tel.: 5747037
  FAX: 5747023

Coordinating Committee of Arab Peace Organizations
  16 Mohamed Shafik Street
  Madinet, Al-Muhandisin 12411
  Giza
  Cairo, Egypt
  Tel.: 20-2-355-5502
  FAX: 20-2-355-0871

Ibn Khaldun Center for Development Studies
  Lot 688, Street 12
  P.O. Box 13 Mokkatam
  Cairo, Egypt
  Tel.: 506-1617
  FAX: 506-1030

Institut Dominican d'Études Orientales du Caire
  1 Masna al-Tarabich Street
  P.O. Box 18 Abbassiah
  Cairo 11381
  Egypt

Institute for Diplomatic Studies
  Ministry for Foreign Affairs
  Tahrir Square
  Cairo, Egypt
  Tel.: 30957

The Institute of Arab Research and Studies
  Arab League Educational, Cultural, and Scientific Organization
  Cairo, Egypt

Israel Academic Center in Cairo
  92 El-Nil Street
  Apartment 33
  Dokki, Giza
  Cairo, Egypt
  Tel.: 20-2-349-6232
  FAX: 20-2-348-8995

National Center for Middle East Studies
  1 Kasr El-Nil Street
  2d Floor
  Cairo, Egypt
  Tel.: 770041/770042/771125
  FAX: 770063

The Population Council
  Office for West Asia and North Africa
  P.O. Box 115
  Dokki
  Cairo, Egypt
  Tel.: 20-2-729-023
  FAX: 20-2-729-384

Iran

Institute for Development and Economic Research
  Faculty of Economics
  University of Tehran
  P.O. Box 14155-6445
  Tehran, Iran
  Tel.: 634001

The Institute for Political and International Studies (IPIS)
  P.O. Box 19395-1793
  Tehran, Iran
  Tel.: 98-21-457-1010
  FAX: 98-21-270-964

Iranian Documentation Center (IRANDOC)
  P.O. Box 13185-1371
  1188 Enqelab Avenue
  Tehran, Iran
  Tel.: 662548

Iraq

Center for Arab Gulf Studies
  University of Basrah
  Basrah, Iraq

Union of Arab Historians
  P.O. Box 4085
  Baghdad, Iraq

Israel

Arab Association for Human Rights
  P.O. Box 215
  Mary's Well Street 34/604
  Nazareth 16101
  Israel
  Tel.: 972-6-561-923; 570-903
  FAX: 972-6-564-934

Begin-Sadat Center for Strategic Studies (BESA)
  Department of Political Studies
  Bar-Ilan University
  Ramat Gan 52900
  Israel
  Tel.: 972-3-535-9198; 8959
  FAX: 972-3-535-9195
  email: besa@popeye.cc.biu.ac.il
  URL: http://www.biu.ac.il/Besa/
  and
  5485 Pare Street
  Montreal, Quebec, Canada H4P 1P7
  Tel.: 514-735-1155
  FAX: 514-735-3361

The Center for Study and Documentation of Israeli Society
  Faculty of Social Science
  The Hebrew University of Jerusalem
  Jerusalem 91905
  Israel

David Horowitz Research Institute for Developing Countries (DHI)
  Tel-Aviv University
  Ramat-Aviv
  Tel-Aviv 69978
  Israel
  Tel.: 419679

Harry Sacher Institute for Legislative Research and Comparative Law
  Faculty of Law
  The Hebrew University of Jerusalem
  Jerusalem 91905
  Israel
  Tel.: 972-2-882535

The Harry S. Truman Research Institute for the Advancement of Peace
  Davis Building
  The Hebrew University of Jerusalem
  Jerusalem 91905
  Israel
  Tel.: 972-2-882300/1
  FAX: 972-2-828076; 332545
  email: mstruman@pluto.mscc.huji.ac.il

The Institute for Advanced Strategic and Political Studies
  4 Chopin Street
  Jerusalem, Israel
  Tel.: 972-2-5638171
  FAX: 02-5638176
  URL: http://www.iasps.org.il/
  and
  1020 Sixteenth St., N.W.
  Suite 310
  Washington, DC 20036
  Tel.: 202-833-8716
  FAX: 202-862-4981

Institute for Research in International and Comparative Law
  Faculty of Law
  Bar-Ilan University
  Ramat-Gan 52100
  Israel
  Tel.: 718414

Institute of Asian and African Studies
  The Faculty of the Humanities
  The Hebrew University of Jerusalem
  Jerusalem 91905
  Israel

International Center for Peace in the Middle East
  13 Kalisher Street
  P.O. Box 29335
  Tel Aviv 61292
  Israel
  Tel.: 972-3-660-337
  FAX: 972-3-660-340

Israel Council for Israel-Palestinian Peace (ICIPP)
  P.O. Box 956
  Tel Aviv 61006

Israel
  Tel.: 972-3-556-5804
  FAX: 972-3-556-5804

Israel Foreign Ministry
  gopher://israel-info.gov.il
  URL: http://www.israel.mfa.gov.il

Israel Government Press Office
  Beit Agron
  Hillel Street 37
  Jerusalem, Israel
  Tel.: 972-2-233-385

Israel/Palestine Center for Research and Information (IPCRI)
  1 Nablus Road
  P.O. Box 51358
  Jerusalem, Israel
  Tel.: 972-2-285-210
  FAX: 972-2-289-094

Israeli Institute of International Affairs
  P.O. Box 17027
  Tel Aviv 61170
  Israel
  Tel.: 414256

The Jaffee Center for Strategic Studies
  Gilman Building
  Tel-Aviv University
  Ramat-Aviv
  Tel-Aviv 69978
  Israel
  Tel.: 972-3-6409926
  FAX: 972-3-6422404
  email: jcssjb@post.tau.ac.il
  URL: http://www.tau.ac.il/jcss

Jerusalem Center for Public Affairs
  13 Tel-Hai Street
  Jerusalem, Israel
  FAX: 011-972-2-561-9112
  email: elazar@rms.huji.ac.il

Jerusalem Institute for Western Defense
  URL: gopher.jer1.co.il

The Jewish-Arab Center
  Haifa University
  23rd Floor
  Mt. Carmel, Haifa, Israel
  Tel.: 972-4-240-156; 240-271
  FAX: 972-4-348-908; 972-4-24031

The Leonard Davis Institute for International Relations
  The Hebrew University of Jerusalem
  Jerusalem 91905
  Israel
  Tel.: 972-2-820914
  FAX: 972-2-322545

Levi Eshkol Institute for Economic, Social, and Political Research
  Social Sciences Building
  The Hebrew University of Jerusalem
  Jerusalem 91905
  Israel

Marjorie Mayrock Center for Soviet and East European Research
  Social Sciences Building
  The Hebrew University of Jerusalem
  Jerusalem 91905
  Israel
  Tel.: 972-2-883180

The Maurice Falk Institute for Economic Research in Israel
  P. Naphtali Building
  The Hebrew University of Jerusalem
  Jerusalem 91905
  Israel
  Tel.: 972-2-883130
  FAX: 972-2-5816071
  email: msfalkin@pluto.mscc.huji.ac.il

Menachem Begin Institute for the Study of Underground and Resistance Movements
  Bar-Ilan University
  Ramat Gan 52100
  Israel
  Tel.: 347500

The Moshe Dayan Center for Middle East and African Studies
  Shiloah Institute
  Gilman Building
  Tel-Aviv University
  Ramat-Aviv 69978
  Israel
  Tel.: 420111
  FAX: 972-3-96409646
  email: dayancen@ccsg.tau.ac.il

Peace Now (Shalom Achshav)
    6 Lloyd George Street
    P.O. Box 8159
    Jerusalem 91081
    Israel
    Tel.: 972-2-660-648
    FAX: 972-2-690-134; 617-254

Pinchas Lavon Labor History Research Center
    Faculty of Social Sciences
    The Hebrew University of Jerusalem
    Jerusalem 91905
    Israel
    Tel.: 972-2-883009

Shaine Center for Research in the Social Sciences
    Social Sciences Building
    The Hebrew University of Jerusalem
    Jerusalem 91905
    Israel

The Shalem Center of Jerusalem
    5 Eliash Street
    Jerusalem, Israel
    Tel.: 02-6254185
    FAX: 02-6256720
    email: shalem@jer1.co.il

Tami Steinmetz Center for Peace Research
    Tel Aviv University
    Ramat Aviv 69978
    Israel
    Tel.: 972-3-640-9646
    FAX: 972-3-641-5802

Van Leer Jerusalem Institute
    43 Jabotinsky Street
    Albert Einstein Square
    West Jerusalem
    P.O. Box 4070
    Jerusalem 91040
    Israel
    Tel.: 972-2-667141
    email: 100320.1742@compuserve.com

Jordan

Arab Organization of Administrative Sciences (AOAS)
    P.O. Box 17159
    Amman, Jordan
    Tel.: 814118

Arab Thought Forum
  P.O. Box 925418
  Amman, Jordan
  Tel.: 962-6-678-707; 708
  FAX: 962-6-675-325

Center for Research on Arms Control and Security (CRACS)
  P.O. Box 141939
  Amman, Jordan
  FAX: 962-6-818062
  email: Hostmaster@jo.rdg.ac.uk

National Information Center
  P.O. Box 259 al-Jubaiha
  Amman 11941
  Jordan
  Tel.: 962-6-837184
  FAX: 962-6-837168
  email: info@nic.gov.jo

Al-Urdun Al-Jadid Research Center
  P.O. Box 940631
  Amman 11194
  Jordan
  Tel.: 962-6-81007
  FAX: 962-6-99351
  email: ujrc@go.com.jo

Kuwait

Arab Planning Institute
  P.O. Box 5834
  13059 Safat
  Kuwait
  Tel.: 843130
  Telex: 22996

Gulf Arab States Educational Research Center
  P.O. Box 25566
  Safat, Kuwait
  Tel.: 835203
  Telex: 44118

Gulf National Forum
  P.O. Box 8672
  Sulmiya, Kuwait
  Tel.: 965-245-6191
  FAX: 965-245-6193

Lebanon

Center for Contemporary Studies and Research on the Middle East
  (Centre d'Études et de Recherches sur le Moyen-Orient Contemporaine, CERMOC)
  Rue de Damas
  P.O. Box 2691
  Beirut, Lebanon
  Tel.: 387-514

Centre for Arab Unity Studies
  ''Sadat Tower'' Building, 9th Floor
  Lyon Street
  P.O. Box 113-6001
  Beirut, Lebanon
  Tel.: 961-869-164; 801-582
  FAX: 961-865-548

Institute of Money and Banking
  American University of Beirut
  Beirut, Lebanon
  Tel.: 961-3500-000, ext. 28452
  FAX: 873-1450-231

Institute for Palestine Studies
  P.O. Box 11-7164
  Beirut, Lebanon
  Tel.: 319-627

Institute for Women's Studies in the Arab World
  Beirut University College
  P.O. Box 13-5053
  Beirut, Lebanon

The Lebanese Association of Women Researchers (Al-Bahithat)
  P.O. Box 13-5375
  Beirut, Lebanon

Lebanese Center for Documentation and Research
  ''Bayat al-Mustaqbal''
  P.O. Box 70-285
  Antelias, Beirut, Lebanon
  Tel.: 414-640
  Telex: 22555

Oman

Ministry of Information
  P.O. Box 600
  Muscat, Oman
  Tel.: 600591
  Telex: 3625 INFORM MB

Palestinians/Palestinian Authority

The Alternative Information Center
  6 Coresh Street
  P.O. Box 31417
  Jerusalem, Israel
  Tel.: 2-241159; 2-747854
  FAX: 2-253151
  email: aicmail@trendline.co.il
  URL: http://www.aic.org/

Applied Research Institute–Jerusalem (ARIJ)
  P.O. Box 860
  Caritas Street
  Bethlehem
  Tel.: 972-2-741889
  email: ji@arij.pl.org
  URL: http://www.arij.org/

Arab Studies Society-Jerusalem
  10 Abu Obida Street
  Orient House
  P.O. Box 20479
  East Jerusalem, Israel
  Tel.: 972-2-272383
  FAX: 972-2-286820
  email: arabs@planet.edu
  URL: http://www.arabstudies.org/

The Arab Thought Forum
  Al-Multaqa
  9 Ali Ibn Taleb Street
  East Jerusalem
  P.O. Box 19012
  Jerusalem, Israel
  Tel.: 972-2-289126; 972-2-894774
  FAX: 972-2-894338
  URL: http://www.planet.edu/~multaqa.htm

Center for Palestine Research and Studies (CPRS)
  P.O. Box 132
  Nablus, Palestine
  Tel.: 972-9-380383
  FAX: 972-9-380384
  email: cprs@cprs_palestine.org
  URL: http://www.cprs_palestine.org

Israel/Palestine Center for Research and Information (IPCRI)
  P.O. Box 51358
  Jerusalem 91513
  Israel
  Tel.: 972-2-274382
  FAX: 972-2-274383
  email: peace@netvision.net.il
  URL: http://www.pirsonet.co.il/IPCRI/

Jerusalem Media and Communications Centre (JMCC)
  P.O. Box 25047
  18 Nashashibi Street
  Sheikh Jarrah
  East Jerusalem 97300
  Israel
  Tel.: 972-2-819777
  FAX: 972-2-829534
  email: jmcc@baraka.org

Palestine Academic Society for the Study of International Affairs (PASSIA)
  18 Hatem Al-Ta'i Street, Wadi al-Joz
  P.O. Box 19545
  Jerusalem, Al-Quds Ash-Sharif, Israel
  Tel.: 972-2-6264426
  FAX: 972-2-6282819
  email: PASSIA@palnet.com
  URL: http://www.passia.org

Palestine Human Rights Information Center
  12 Al-Masoudi Street
  P.O. Box 20479
  Jerusalem, Israel
  Tel.: 972-2-287077
  FAX: 972-2-297070
  email: phric@baraka.org

The Palestinian Association for Cultural Exchange (PACE)
  P.O. Box 841
  Ramallah, West Bank
  Tel.: 972-2-9986854
  FAX: 972-2-9986854
  email: PACE@PLANET.edu
  URL: http://www.planet.edu/~pace

Palestinian Center for Public Opinion (PCPO)
  P.O. Box 15
  Beit Sahour, Israel
  Tel.: 972-2-6472034
  FAX: 972-2-6472034
  Mobile Phone: 972-50-281721

Palestinian Center for the Study of Non-Violence
    P.O. Box 20999
    Jerusalem 91202
    Israel
    Tel.: 972-2-273-275
    FAX: 972-2-273-275

The Palestinian Energy and Environment Research Center
    URL: http://www.planet.edu/~pec/

The People-to-People Program
    c/o fafo
    P.O. Box 21751
    Jerusalem, Israel
    Tel.: 972-2-5822358
    FAX: 972-2-5822856
    email: ask@people-to-people.org
    URL: http://www.people-to-people.org/

Shaml (Palestinian Diaspora and Refugee Center)
    P.O. Box 38152
    Jerusalem 97800
    Israel
    Tel.: 972-2-9957537
    FAX: 972-2-9956538
    email: shaml@netvision.net.il

Women's Affairs Technical Committee (WATC)
    Radio Street
    Zeituna Building
    East Jerusalem, Jerusalem, Israel
    Tel.: 2-9986497; 50-377363
    email: watcorg@palnet.com
    URL: http://www.pal-watc.org/body.htm

Qatar

Documentation and Humanities Research Center (DHRC)
    University of Qatar
    P.O. Box 2713
    Doha, Qatar
    Tel.: 867630
    FAX: 871332

Saudi Arabia

Arab Urban Development Institute
    P.O. Box 6892
    Riyadh 11452
    Saudi Arabia
    Tel.: 966-1-411-8100; 441-9876
    FAX: 966-1-411-8235

Centre for Research in Islamic Economics
King Abdulaziz University
P.O. Box 16711
Jeddah, Saudi Arabia

King Faisal Center for Research and Islamic Studies (KFCRIS)
P.O. Box 51049
Riyadh-11543
Saudi Arabia

Syria

Center for Historical Documents
Damascus, Syria

L'Institut Français d'Archaelogie du Proche Orient (IFAPO)
Damascus, Syria

L'Institut Français des Études Arabes à Damas (IFEAD)
P.O. Box 344
Damascus, Syria
Tel.: 963-11-333-6249
FAX: 963-11-332-7887

Turkey

American Research Institute in Turkey
Citlembik Sokak 18/2
Serencebey, Besiktas, Istanbul, Turkey
Tel.: 463188

DEIK Foreign Economic Relations Board
Odakule Is Merkezi Istiklal
Cad. 286 Beyoglu
Istanbul, Turkey
Tel.: 90-1434180
FAX: 90-1434184

The Economic and Social History Foundation
email: tarihvakfi@tarihvakfi.org.tr
URL: http://www.tarihvakfi.org.tr

Foreign Policy Institute
Hacettepe University
06531 Beytepe
Ankara, Turkey
Tel.: 90-235-3582; 235-2500
FAX: 90-235-2934

Foundation for Middle Eastern and Balkan Research
  Kasap Veli Sokak 10
  81060 Istanbul
  Turkey
  Tel.: 90-216-333-41-58
  FAX: 90-216-310-82-42

Foundation for Strategic Research
  3. Sokak 26/3
  06520 Ankara
  Turkey
  Tel.: 90-312-285-71-72
  Fax: 90-312-285-71-73

Hydropolitics and Strategic Research and Development Centre
  Hacettepe University
  06532 Ankara
  Turkey
  Tel.: 90-312-235-25-00, ext. 1640
  FAX: 90-312-235-29-34

Institute of Economics and Social Sciences
  Bilkent Universitesi Rektorlugu
  Ankara, Turkey
  Tel.: 90-266-4040
  FAX: 90-266-4306

Institute of International Economic Relations
  Feuzi Cakmak
  Caddesi 49
  Bornova-Izmir, Turkey
  Tel.: 18-01-10

Institute of Population Studies
  Hacettepe University
  Ankara, Turkey
  Tel.: 10-79-06

Research Center for Islamic History, Art, and Culture (IRCICA)
  Yıdız Sarayı
  Seyir Köşkü
  P.O. Box 24
  80692 Beşiktaş
  Istanbul, Turkey

SISAV—The Political and Social Studies Foundation
  Abdi Ipekci Cadessi, Arzu Apt. 5/3
  80200 Nisantasi
  Istanbul, Turkey
  Tel.: 90-146-4218; 5739
  FAX: 90-141-4921

Turkish Foundation of Economic and Social History
  Zindankapi Degirmen Sokak 15
  34460 Istanbul
  Turkey
  Tel.: 90-212-513-52-35
  FAX: 90-212-513-21-77

United Arab Emirates

Center for Documentation and Research
  P.O. Box 2380
  Abu Dhabi, United Arab Emirates
  Tel.: 345371

The Emirates Center for Strategic Studies and Research
  URL: http://www.ecssr.ac.ae/

Strategic Studies and Information Technology
  P.O. Box 4567
  Abu Dhabi, United Arab Emirates
  FAX: 9712-762122

NAME INDEX

SUBJECT INDEX

ABOUT THE EDITOR
AND CONTRIBUTORS

AMATZIA BARAM is associate professor and chairman of the Department of Middle East History at the University of Haifa. Among his numerous works on Iraq are *Culture, History and Ideology in the Formation of Ba'thist Iraq, 1968–1989* (1991) and an edited work, *Iraq's Road to War* (1993). He has also been a senior associate member at St. Antony's College, Oxford, and twice a fellow at the Woodrow Wilson International Center for Scholars in Washington, D.C., and a senior fellow at the United States Institute of Peace.

MARIUS DEEB is a professor of Middle East studies at the School of Advanced International Studies of Johns Hopkins University and teaches also at George Washington University. He has written widely about Middle East policy and coauthored *Libya Since the Revolution: Aspects of Social and Political Development*. His publications include *Party Politics in Egypt: The Wafd and Its Rivals 1919–1939* (1979), *The Lebanese Civil War* (1980), and *Militant Islamic Movements in Lebanon* (1986).

MARY-JANE DEEB holds a Ph.D. from the School of Advanced International Studies, Johns Hopkins University, and serves as editor of the *Middle East Journal*. She is the author of *Libya's Foreign Policy in North Africa*.

BECKY DIAMOND served as a research assistant at the Washington Institute for Near East Policy from 1992 to 1994. She received her master's degree in Middle Eastern studies from New York University and is currently a news producer in New York.

MICHAEL EPPEL (Ph.D., Tel Aviv University) is a lecturer at the University of Haifa and at Oranim College of Education. He has written *The Palestine Conflict in the History of Modern Iraq* as well as numerous articles on Middle Eastern history and politics.

GEORGE S. HARRIS served as director of the Office of Analysis for the Near East and South Asia in the Bureau of Intelligence and Research of the Department of State. Among his publications are *The Origins of Communism in Turkey*; *Troubled Alliance: Turkish-American Problems in Historical Perspective, 1945–1971*; and *Turkey: Coping with Crisis*.

GERSHON R. KIEVAL (Ph.D., Johns Hopkins University) is a senior analyst at the U.S. Central Intelligence Agency and former adjunct professor of political science and international affairs at George Washington University. He is the author of a number of works on Israel and Israeli national security policy, including *Party Politics in Israel and the Occupied Territories* (Greenwood, 1983), and coauthor and coeditor of *Israeli National Security Policy* (Greenwood, 1988) and of *Israel Faces the Future* (Praeger, 1986) and coauthor, with Bernard Reich, of *Israel: Land of Tradition and Conflict*.

BAHGAT KORANY is professor in the Department of Political Science at Université de Montréal, Director of the Inter-University Consortium of Arab Studies, and Fellow of the Royal Society of Canada. He has published widely on various aspects of the international relations of the Middle East and North Africa; some of these works have been translated in Arabic, Italian, Spanish, and Chinese.

ANN MOSELY LESCH is professor of political science at Villanova University and a former associate director of the Center for Arab and Islamic Studies. She worked for the American Friends Service Committee in Jerusalem (1974–1977), the Ford Foundation in New York and Cairo (1977–1984), and Universities Field Staff International in Cairo (1984–1987). She wrote *Arab Politics in Palestine, 1917–1939* (1979), *Political Perceptions of the Palestinians on the West Bank and the Gaza Strip* (1980), *Israel, Egypt, and the Palestinians*, with Mark Tessler (1989), and *Transition to Palestinian Self-Government* (1992). She has published numerous articles on Palestinian issues, most recently "Contrasting Reactions to the Persian Gulf Crisis: Egypt, Syria, Jordan, and the Palestinians," *Middle East Journal* 45, no. 1 (Winter 1991), and "Palestinians in Kuwait," *Journal of Palestine Studies* 20, no. 4 (Summer 1991). She was president of the Middle East Studies Association (1994–1995) and serves on the board of Middle East Watch.

DAVID E. LONG is a consultant on the Middle East. He is retired from the U.S. Foreign Service and is the author of a number of works on the politics of Saudi Arabia, including *The United States and Saudi Arabia: Ambivalent Allies; Saudi Arabia*; and *The Hajj Today: A Survey of the Contemporary Makkah Pilgrimage*. His most recent work is *The Kingdom of Saudi Arabia* (1997).

MOHSEN M. MILANI is professor of comparative politics at the University of South Florida in Tampa. He has also been a research fellow at Harvard and St. Antony's College at Oxford University. He has written extensively about Iran and the Persian Gulf. Among his recent publications are *The Making of Iran's Islamic Revolution* (1994).

MALCOLM C. PECK has been a program officer at Meridian International Center in Washington, D.C., since 1984. Before that, he was director of programs at the Middle East Institute and served as the Arabian Peninsula affairs analyst at the Department of State. In addition to articles and book chapters on the Gulf and the Arabian Peninsula, he is the author of *The United Arab Emirates: A Venture in Unity* (1986) and *Historical Dictionary of the Gulf Arab States* (1997).

PAMELA DAY PELLETREAU has lived for more than 15 years in the Arab world, most recently in Egypt where she taught at the American University in Cairo and worked with the U.S. Agency for International Development. In Egypt and Tunisia she helped develop USAID's democracy and governance programming. She has written on the political economy of Algeria and Tunisia.

BERNARD REICH is professor of political science and international affairs at George Washington University in Washington, D.C. He is the author of numerous books and articles on various aspects of Middle East politics and international relations. Among them is *The Government and Politics of the Middle East and North Africa*, 3d edition, coedited and coauthored with David E. Long.

ROBERT B. SATLOFF is the executive director of the Washington Institute for Near East Policy. He is the author of *From Abdullah to Hussein: Jordan in Transition* (1994) and *Troubles on the East Bank: Challenges to the Domestic Stability of Jordan* (Praeger, 1986).

SANFORD R. SILVERBURG is professor of political science and chairman of the department at Catawba College in Salisbury, North Carolina. He is the author of numerous articles and chapters on various aspects of Middle East politics, served as bibliographic editor of *An Historical Encyclopedia of the Arab-Israeli Conflict*, and has produced a series of bibliographical works on the region, including *Middle East Bibliography*.

ROBERT SPRINGBORG is professor of politics at Macquarie University in New South Wales, Australia. He is the author of a number of works on Egyptian politics and coauthor, with James A. Bill, of *Politics in the Middle East*.

JENAB TUTUNJI was managing editor of the *Jordan Times* from 1976 to 1980 and later was assistant editor of the *Journal of Palestine Studies*. He is an adjunct faculty member in political science at George Washington University and has published widely on various aspects of Middle East politics.

MANFRED W. WENNER is professor of political science at Northern Illinois University and a prolific author on the politics of Yemen.

GREGORY WHITE is assistant professor of government at Smith College in Northampton, Massachusetts. The author of several articles and book chapters on Maghrebi and sub-Saharan Africa political economy, he is completing a book comparing Morocco and Tunisia's relationship with Europe. He gratefully acknowledges the research assistance of Marilyn Rackley and Jennifer Zaslow.

ISBN 0-313-27372-3

90000>

EAN

9 780313 273728

HARDCOVER BAR CODE